Interdependent Systems
Structure and Estimation

Interdependent Systems

Systems

Structure and Estimation

by
Ernest J. MOSBAEK
Research Economist, Jack Faucett Associates, Silver Spring, Md.

and

Herman O. WOLD
Professor of Statistics, University of Uppsala

with contributions by
Ejnar Lyttkens, Anders Ågren and Lennart Bodin
University of Uppsala

1970

NORTH-HOLLAND PUBLISHING COMPANY
AMSTERDAM – LONDON

AMERICAN ELSEVIER PUBLISHING COMPANY, INC.
NEW YORK

Library of Congress Catalog Card Number 77 – 108278

ISBN North-Holland   0 7204 3042 9

ISBN American Elsevier 0 444 10051 2

PUBLISHERS:

NORTH-HOLLAND PUBLISHING COMPANY – AMSTERDAM
NORTH-HOLLAND PUBLISHING COMPANY, LTD. – LONDON

SOLE DISTRIBUTORS FOR THE U.S.A. AND CANADA:

AMERICAN ELSEVIER PUBLISHING COMPANY, INC.
52 VANDERBILT AVENUE
NEW YORK, N.Y. 10017

PRINTED IN THE NETHERLANDS

Preface

Our basic purpose in initiating the research that led to this monograph was to compare the new fix-point method with other familiar methods for estimating the parameters of simultaneous equations models. Early results in our project revealed the need to expand the scope of research to include review and analysis of two fundamental topics in econometrics. First, the important but confusing issues in the dichotomy between estimation and operative use of parameters of a model had to be cleared up in order that desirable properties of a method of estimation could be more clearly defined [1]. Second, the mathematical properties of a fairly wide range of designs for models had to be studied in order that observed differences among methods of estimation could be related to fundamental properties of models. Two specific outcomes of this second topic are the reformulated interdependent (REID) model and the general interdependent (GEID) model. The results of this and other Monte Carlo studies reveal that the relative performance among methods of estimation depends heavily on the size and type of model being estimated.

Although this is not a handbook, the research upon which it is based and the presentation of results have been designed to provide the applied

---

[1] Note marks of this type refer to the Notes given at the end of the volume.

econometrician with a convenient reference as well as a fundamental understanding of the properties of four basic methods of estimation. On the one hand, he can quickly determine the major problems he must anticipate in estimation of a specified model with a given sample size. On the other hand, he can refer to these results to help determine the range of parameter values from which a particular set of empirical estimates he has obtained could have arisen.

The reader is warned that there is no unequivocal "best" method of estimation. For any specified criterion the relative performance among methods varies with the type of model being estimated. For any specified model the relative performance among methods varies depending on which of many types of criterion is used. The results of this monograph reveal the importance of both the criterion to be used and the type of model being estimated in selecting the "best" method of estimation.

Progress is being made in deriving exact distributions of estimates for various methods of estimation. An exact distribution for estimates of a specific parameter in any particular model has, of course, more information than any finite set of Monte Carlo runs on the same model. However, it is likely that Monte Carlo results such as are presented in this monograph will be the major source of information on any reasonable range of models for an indefinite period of time.

The 46 models covered in this investigation are small, with a maximum of 7 equations, and thus do not approach the large complex models that are reported by various groups of economists, such as the Brookings model [2]. It is our philosophy that the economist should understand the basic properties of a model before attempting to estimate the parameters and especially before attempting to use an estimated model to answer policy questions or test hypotheses. There are a few general comments concerning difficulties in gaining the suggested understanding. First, if all of the residuals are small the understanding can be acquired quite easily and in a straightforward manner regardless of the size of the model. Likewise, estimation poses no severe problems. Second, if residuals are large and the model is large (say 100 equations) we are in a situation considerably beyond the frontier of knowledge. Although there are conflicting opinions on this among econometricians we predict that this view will be generally accepted within the next few years. The results presented in this monograph are short of the large residual-large model situation because all our models are small, but they are beyond the very simple situation because residuals in most models are quite large.

The Monte Carlo sample data as well as some of the less interesting parameters of models are not presented in this volume. The space requirements for publication would be enormous. However, all computer programs were written so that sample data as well as estimates can easily be regenerated. With modern computer equipment it is easier and cheaper to build programs so that data can be regenerated as opposed to storing or printing large volumes of little used data.

The project on which this monograph is based was initiated in early 1965 as a joint project between Battelle Memorial Institute and the University of Uppsala, Uppsala, Sweden. Initial funding was provided by Dr. B. D. Thomas as a Battelle Memorial Basic Research project. This funding carried through 1965 and 1966. In 1966 further funds were made available for work in Uppsala as a result of a grant from the Tercentenary Fund of the National Bank of Sweden. Much of the computing was performed at the Computational Laboratory at the University of Uppsala.

There is no sharp demarcation between the research leading up to this monograph and independent research in Uppsala. We are indebted to Professor E. Lyttkens, Dr. A. Ågren, and Dr. L. Bodin, all of the University Institute of Statistics at Uppsala, for their assistance in the preparation of this monograph. The chapters for which they are listed as authors are based on results from their independent research.

Washington, D.C. and Uppsala   *Ernest J. Mosbaek*
March 1969   *Herman O. Wold*

Contents

List of Tables

Chapter 11.7

List of Charts

CHAPTER 1

Introduction

1.1. Focus and Emphasis of Monograph

This monograph includes a report on Monte Carlo investigations of four methods of estimation on four causal chain systems, and 42 interdependent systems. The models and sample data were designed to represent situations likely to be encountered in applied econometrics. The models range in size from two to seven relations and, therefore, cannot be said to be representative of large models, let alone such a giant as the Brookings SSRC model (Duesenberry *et al.*, 1965).

The main incentive for the Monte Carlo investigation was development of a new method, Fix-point (Wold, 1965c, 1966c). This method appeared to hold promise in avoiding the problem of overfitting in the first stage of Two-stage Least Squares and promise for more flexibility in being able to estimate models that have non-linear relationships among current endogenous variables. Besides Fix-point (FP) the Monte Carlo investigation included Ordinary Least Squares (OLS), Two-stage Least Squares (TSLS) and unrestricted estimates of the reduced form coefficients (URF). During the course of the research being reported the FP method was supplemented by related techniques; Fractional Fix-point (FFP), Recursive Fix-point (RFP), and non-iterative FP estimation. The non-iterative solution has been worked out for Summers' two-relation model and some few other simple models. Results for FFP and RFP are reported for only a small number of samples on five different models.

The availability of the FP method permits a generalization in interdependent models by removing certain restrictions on independence between residuals and predetermined variables. Consequently, eight of the 46 models include features that will be unfamiliar in terms of previous investigations of alternative methods of estimation. These models are labeled general interdependent (GEID) systems. The design and analysis of GEID models led to several new insights into specification and estimation of interdependent systems. These insights helped guide development of the overall set of 46 models and the presentation of Monte Carlo results.

Besides the empirical Monte Carlo work the monograph presents several topics in a purely theoretical dimension. This is in the form of a discussion and presentation of new concepts for coping with problems that have been more or less serious stumbling blocks in applied work. Sections 1.2.1−1.2.11 bring into relief a number of points that are essential for understanding both the aims and conclusions of the research being reported in this monograph. Whereas Section 1.2 takes up specific points and presents new concepts in a verbal exposition, some of these features are subject to a more technical discussion in Chapters 1.3 and 1.4. Speaking broadly, the emphasis of this introductory chapter is on general topics in econometric model building, and how the Monte Carlo results presented in Chapters 2−9 relate to the familiar problems in applied work. The reader that has a working knowledge of model building in general and multirelational models in particular should check the points in Section 1.2, take a look at Chart 1.4.1, and can then skip to Chapter 2.

1.2. Special Features Reconsidered [1]

1.2.1. A Difference in Kind between Uni- and Multirelational Models

In the unirelational model

$$y = \alpha + \beta x + \epsilon \tag{1}$$

the systematic part

$$E(y \mid x) = \alpha + \beta x \tag{2}$$

will be referred to as the "kernel" of the model. The kernel cannot be directly observed by the model builder because it is covered up by the random component ϵ. Although a larger residual makes for greater cover, the problems associated with larger residuals are a matter of degree rather than kind. This is illustrated by the OLS estimate of β, which, assuming ϵ is independent of x, is

$$b = \frac{\sum_i (x - \bar{x}) y}{\sum_i (x - \bar{x})^2} \tag{3}$$

where, under the wellknown classical conditions, the standard deviation of the estimate is given by the large sample formula

$$\text{S.D.}(b) = \frac{s(\epsilon)}{s(x)} \frac{1}{\sqrt{N-2}} \tag{4}$$

showing that b is a consistent estimate of β for any size of $s(\epsilon)$. The classical assumptions require the residuals ϵ to be mutually independent; however, the OLS estimate (3) remains consistent under much more general assumptions. In particular, (3) provides consistent estimates when the residuals are autocorrelated, whereas formula (4) then in general breaks down (see 3.3.5).

The same general concepts apply to interdependent models but they must be handled more carefully. To illustrate we refer to Summers' model [2] specified as

$$y_1 = \beta_1 y_2 + \gamma_1 z_1 + \gamma_2 z_2 + \delta_1 \tag{5}$$

$$y_2 = \beta_2 y_1 + \gamma_3 z_3 + \gamma_4 z_4 + \delta_2 \tag{6}$$

with reduced form

$$y_1 = \omega_{11}z_1 + \omega_{12}z_2 + \omega_{13}z_3 + \omega_{14}z_4 + \epsilon_1 , \qquad (7)$$

$$y_2 = \omega_{21}z_1 + \omega_{22}z_2 + \omega_{23}z_3 + \omega_{24}z_4 + \epsilon_2 . \qquad (8)$$

The coefficients ω_{ik} and the residuals ϵ_i are algebraic expressions in the coefficients and residuals specified in the structural form,

$$\omega_{ik} = ([I-\beta]^{-1}\Gamma)_{ik} , \qquad (9)$$

$$\epsilon_i = ([I-\beta]^{-1}\delta)_i . \qquad (10)$$

Dropping the residuals in relations (7) and (8) leaves only the systematic part or what we can again refer to as the "kernel" of the model. The kernel in both forms of the model is blurred by two different residuals, δ_1 and δ_2 or ϵ_1 and ϵ_2.

As $\sigma(\epsilon_1)$ and $\sigma(\epsilon_2)$ increase, making the kernel smaller, there is a threshold beyond which the problems in penetrating the ϵ layer shown in Chart 1 become more and more serious. These problems differ in kind from the problems that arise as the residual layer becomes larger in a unirelational model. This is because interdependent systems, although formally linear, involve nonlinear features in their predictor specifications and, as a consequence, nonlinear features in the estimation of parameters.

For small $\sigma(\epsilon)$ the non-linearity is negligible, and serious problems do not arise. The parametric representation is unique. As $\sigma(\epsilon)$ increases, multiplicities may arise in the parameter representation. These multiplicites and other difficulties make hard nuts to crack. Chart 1b refers to an interesting aspect of the situation. On the whole the difficulties increase as the residuals become larger. The problems are linked to the interdependence, however. For example, if the beta coefficients are zero there is no interdependence, and no problems arise. This special case is represented by the horizontal axis of Chart 1b. Hence the difficult part of the kernel divides into two "hard nuts", one above the axis (beta coefficients positive) and the other below the axis (beta coefficients negative). The problems that arise are in several respects analogous to the stochastic process of moving summation. This will be discussed further in Section 3.8.

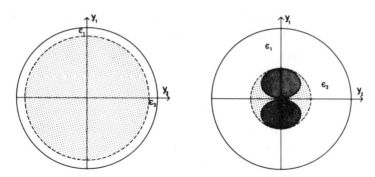

Chart 1.2.1. Relative size of kernel and residual layer

As is well known, and emphasized in the theory of ID systems from the beginning, OLS is inconsistent when applied to the relations in the structural form. This statement is subject to the qualification that the large-sample bias is small or negligible if the residual layer shown in Chart 1 is small. From the "proximity theorem" of regression analysis, it follows readily as a corollary that if the residuals are small relative to the current endogenous variables, say, with a standard deviation making a proportion $\leqslant \Delta$, the large sample bias in OLS estimates will be of order of magnitude $c \cdot \Delta^2$ (see 3.3.3).

1.2.2. Small vs Large Systems

Throughout this monograph the research reported is limited to small models with 2, 3, up to 7 relations in the structural form. A main reason for this restriction is that the model design is complex even for small interdependent systems, and poses quite intricate problems. Summers' model is one of the simplest overidentified interdependent models and yet it involves 16 relevant second order moments $E(y_i^2)$, $E(z_i z_k)$, $E(y_i z_k)$ and 6 parameters β_i, γ_i.

If it were not for the interdependent nature of most economic models each equation in a set could be considered a small model and the overall set would be merely n small models. It is worthwhile noting that the feature of interdependence can be properly viewed as a matter of degree depending on the size of the β coefficients. In the special case where all β's are zero the structural form coincides with the reduced form and the system is nothing more than a set of ordinary regressions (vector regression). Hence, it can be said that the interdependence is weaker the smaller the β coefficients.

Speaking generally, we have found that the transition from vector regression to ID systems creates no problem in the statistical treatment even in large models in either of the following cases: (1) the residuals δ_i or ϵ_i are small and (2) the parameters β_i are small. In the first case OLS will provide almost consistent parameter estimates, granted that the parameters β_i, γ_i are not too large. In the second case the interdependence is weak and the FP, FFP, and RFP methods work without trouble.

The monograph establishes the two special cases and explores the situation in 38 small size models where the residuals ϵ_i and coefficients β_i are not small. The results from analyses of these 38 models are presented in detail in Chapters 4–10. It turns out that FP and the related FFP and RFP methods often work to satisfaction. However, in some models difficulties arise in the form of slow or even no convergence in the successive iterations and difficulties arise in the form of plural solutions for the parameter representation. The problems to a large extent are inherent in the models investigated and are not due to the estimation techniques under analysis.

The importance of the problems associated with nonlinearities and plural solutions were realized early in the research effort and it was decided to investigate only small models. Further research is needed to determine the properties of FP and related techniques in large models. [3]

1.2.3. Intended Use of Estimated Models

There are five phases in the construction of a cognitive model when only non-experimental data are available for estimating parameters. In general terminology they are:

1. Specification of intended use.
2. Specification of hypotheses in development of model.
3. Estimation of unknown parameters of the model.
4. Testing hypotheses.
5. Resulting use of the estimated model.

Phases 2—4 are well known from R.A.Fisher (1935). Fisher was mainly dealing with experimental data, in which case the first and last phases in the above list are obvious, and usually not spelled out.

In econometrics, and more generally in all non-experimental model building, it is essential to specifically identify the first and, as a consequence, the last point above. This will become evident in the discussion of the problem areas that are in focus in this monograph.

Typically the intended use of econometric models includes the following three categories:

O_1. Intended use of the structural form as specified.

O_2. Intended use of the reduced form.

O_3. Interchange between instrument and target variables (among current endogenous variables) for evaluating policy considerations.

It is a question whether the first and third uses are permissible. Within these two types of intended uses the model builder meets with veritable stumbling blocks. These stumbling blocks are at the crossroads of two lines of evolution in model building, namely,

  (i) unirelational to multirelational models,

  (ii) exact to stochastic relations.

The problems at issue are of general scope not only in econometrics, but in the whole area of non-experimental model building. The early recognition and relatively greater concern for these problems in econometric model building shows that econometrics has been pioneering in the development of non-experimental techniques.

At the 1965 International Congress of the Econometric Society the authors presented a new view on the use of estimated coefficients in the structural form [4]. In this case they used one of the two coefficients which make the system interdependent, but they used it outside the framework of an interdependent system. This illustration highlights the important dichotomy between estimation and operative use of interdependent models.

The need to add and emphasize intended and resulting use in the phases of construction of a model can be easily visualized if we reflect for a moment on the prime incentive for models. The model builder cannot employ the *ceteris paribus* phase of replications that is applicable in experimental work. We build models in economics with the hope of developing forecasts and economic policies which often change the conditions that existed in the past and, therefore, change the conditions that led to the data which are used in developing the model.

Intended and resulting use are differentiated for two reasons. First, the number of possible uses of an estimated model can be much greater than those visualized when the model is being developed. Second, in some cases it might not be possible to use the model in the manner intended because of lack of information about the qualities of the estimated model.

The current outlook on the three modes of intended uses shows several partings of the ways. The position of the authors on these matters is presented in Sections 1.2.4–1.2.6.

1.2.4. Apparent vs Genuine Scatter

Continuing with Summers' model (5)–(6) we first consider the exact version with structural relations

$$y_1 = \beta_1 y_2 + \gamma_1 z_1 + \gamma_2 z_2 , \tag{11}$$

$$y_2 = \beta_2 y_1 + \gamma_3 z_3 + \gamma_4 z_4 , \tag{12}$$

and reduced form relations

$$y_1 = \omega_{11} z_1 + \omega_{12} z_2 + \omega_{13} z_3 + \omega_{14} z_4 , \tag{13}$$

$$y_2 = \omega_{21} z_1 + \omega_{22} z_2 + \omega_{23} z_3 + \omega_{24} z_4 , \tag{14}$$

where ω_{ij} are as given in (9). We consider the relations in the light of the three modes of intended use (see 1.2.3, O_1-O_3). Formally, the requisite inference from the exact model involves no problem but we shall spell it out in detail and paraphrase so as to facilitate the subsequent treatment of stochastic relationships.

The various modes of operative inference from the exact relations (11)–(12) are illustrated with the help of Chart 2.

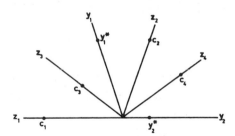

Chart 1.2.2. Forecasting by Summers' model.

Mode O_1: *Autonomous relations — no joint inference from the set of structural relations*

In this type of inference, structural relation (11) tells us how y_1 will change for specified changes in y_2 (to y_2^*), z_1, z_2 and structural relation (12) tells us how y_2 will change for specified changes in y_1 (to y_1^*), z_3, z_4. Since there is no joint inference in this mode the reduced form equations do not enter the picture. There is no need to consider an interchange between y_1 and y_2 (i.e., an interchange between target and instrument variables) in either of the relations because the effect of either variable on the other is given explicitly in one of the two relations as originally specified.

Mode O_2: *The structural relations used jointly*

With specified values for all of the predetermined variables z_1, z_2, z_3, z_4 but with unspecified values for y_1 and y_2 the structural relations must be used jointly in determining y_1 and/or y_2. Using the structural form to solve for y_1 and y_2 gives the reduced form (13)–(14).

Inference under Mode O_1 is a straightforward extension of inference from an exact behavioral relation in a unirelational model. Inference under mode O_2 can be classified as inference from both the structural and reduced form versions of the model; implicit inference from the structural form and explicit inference from the reduced form.

Inference under Mode O_2 from exact relations is completely compatible with inference under Mode O_1. If we specify the values c_1, c_2, c_3, c_4 for all of the predetermined variables (see Chart 2) the values for y_1 and y_2 from inference in Mode O_2 will be y_1^*, y_2^*. This is compatible with inference from Mode O_1 in that

$$\text{the values } z_1 = c_1, z_2 = c_2, y_1 = y_1^* \to y_2 = y_2^* , \qquad (15)$$

$$\text{the values } z_3 = c_3, z_4 = c_4, y_2 = y_2^* \to y_1 = y_1^* . \qquad (16)$$

Turning to stochastic models, we see that it is not a straightforward matter to make inferences under both Mode O_1 and Mode O_2. The question of two modes of inference in stochastic interdependent models has been the source of much debate. The main part of Section 1.4 is devoted to a review of the situation.

Mode O_3: *Interchange Between Instrument and Target Variables*

We now turn to the third type of inference, namely, inference from a structural relation after an interchange of variables. For example, suppose that structural relation (11) is appropriate for a specific policy consideration where y_1 is a target variable and y_2 is an instrument variable. An interchange between y_1 and y_2 would transform (11) so that

$$y_2 = \frac{1}{\beta_1} y_1 - \frac{\gamma_1}{\beta_1} z_1 - \frac{\gamma_2}{\beta_1} z_2 \qquad (17)$$

and y_2 would be the target variable and y_1, z_1, z_2 would be instrument variables. We must, however, look closely at any interchange among variables.

An interchange of variables is not permissible in stochastic relations. It is also questionable as to whether an interchange is permissible in exact economic relations. An analogy with the non-reversible heat and energy laws in physics would suggest that, in general, exact relations are not reversible (see 1.4.7).

The policy maker might well change his target variable from, say, price of a specific commodity to quantity of this commodity but he might not be able to carry out his evaluation with one-and-the-same mathematical relation as shown in (11) and (17). More research is needed to determine if interchange of variables does, indeed, present a stumbling block even in the case of exact (theoretical) relations in economics.

Stochastic Relations

In the transition from the exact model (11)–(12) to the stochastic model (5)–(6) the distinction between apparent and genuine scatter marks two fundamentally different specifications of the structural relations. This difference in specification (apparent vs genuine scatter) affects the type of inference that can be made from the model.

A typical case of apparent scatter arises when the relations (11)–(12) are subject to observational errors ϵ_1 and ϵ_2. Conceptually, the observational errors do not interfere with the intended use of the model. Hence with regard to the three modes O_1-O_3 of intended uses (see 1.2.3) this is, in point of principle, the same as in the case of the exact model.

A typical case of genuine scatter arises when the errors ϵ_1 and ϵ_2 are due to factors that have been ignored in the model. This type of residuals cannot be ignored when making inferences from the model. It is necessary to draw inferences in terms of predictors, that is, conditional expectations. The types of inferences that can be made from an exact model do not in general carry over to predictors.

It is important to note that conceptually and observationally the hypothesis of genuine scatter is very tenable in econometrics and other behavioral sciences. Each relation in an econometric model could contain many more variables than it is feasible to include in the specification and, therefore, the relations are seldom, if ever, exact.

In the current econometric literature, relations are usually specified in terms of "errors in relations". Unfortunately, this term blurs the fundamental distinction between apparent and genuine scatter. At the same time the term blurs the fact that the first two intended uses O_1-O_2 referred to in Section 1.2.3 do carry over to stochastic relations if the relations can be recast in terms of predictors. However, the inability to carry over the intended use of structural relations expressed in terms of observed variables has created a dilemma in current econometrics. This dilemma is a focal point as we turn to the treatment of the situation of genuine scatter in terms of predictors.

1.2.5. Predictor Specifications [5]

Under the intended use of both the structural and reduced form of the model it would be desirable to specify each as predictors; in symbols,

$$E(y_1|y_2, z_1, z_2) \; (=) \; \beta_1 y_2 + \gamma_1 z_1 + \gamma_2 z_2 \,, \tag{18}$$

$$E(y_2|y_1, z_3, z_4) \; (=) \; \beta_2 y_1 + \gamma_3 z_3 + \gamma_4 z_4 \,, \tag{19}$$

$$E(y_1|z_1, z_2, z_3, z_4) = \omega_{11} z_1 + \omega_{12} z_2 + \omega_{13} z_3 + \omega_{14} z_4 \,, \tag{20}$$

$$E(y_2|z_1, z_2, z_3, z_4) = \omega_{21} z_1 + \omega_{22} z_2 + \omega_{23} z_3 + \omega_{24} z_4 \,, \tag{21}$$

where the parentheses (=) indicate that the equations in general cannot be satisfied. The fact that both sets of predictors (18)–(19) and (20)–(21) do not hold is a dilemma and it cannot be cleared up if we specify residuals in the structural form as "errors in relations".

One approach out of the dilemma is to specify residuals as apparent scatter and then drop the residuals and treat the relations as exact. This, however, is too unrealistic in applied econometrics. In most cases we know that there are determining variables that have been left out of the relations and that the residuals might well be quite large.

Another way out of the dilemma is the REID (reformulated interdependent system) specification. This is the approach followed in this monograph.

The REID approach allows predictor specification in both the structural and reduced form and requires no change in the numerical values of the parameters β_i, γ_i. The reduced form is specified as in (20)–(21) and the structural form is specified in terms of the expected values (η_i^*) for the current endogenous variables that appear on the right-hand side of the equation, giving

$$E(y_1|\eta_2^*, z_1, z_2) = \beta_1 \eta_2^* + \gamma_1 z_1 + \gamma_2 z_2 \,, \tag{22}$$

$$E(y_2|\eta_1^*, z_3, z_4) = \beta_2 \eta_1^* + \gamma_3 z_3 + \gamma_4 z_4 \,, \tag{23}$$

where the expected values η_1^* and η_2^* are obtained from the reduced form. In this specification the residuals in the structural form turn out to be the same as in the reduced form.

The point of the REID specification is to make the structural form amenable to operative use in line with the intended use of the structural form (see 1.2.3, Mode O_1). Without this specification the structural

form would not make a predictor, for (18)–(19) in general are not satisfied, and so this intended use cannot be carried through consistently.

This last point gives a clearcut answer to the question. "What is the
causal interpretation, if any, of the structural form of the model?" The
answer is that the right-hand variables y_q, z_p do allow interpretation as
a causal influence on the effect variable but do so subject to the qualification that it is expected values y_q^* rather than the observed values y_q
that enter on the right-hand side of each relation.

It should be noted that there is a distinction between stochastic and
psychological expectation. A constructive device to handle this dualism
is due to J.F.Muth (1962). His approach is to assume that psychological
expectations are rational and, therefore, in the first approximation they
are equal to the stochastic expectations. The REID specification allows
a corresponding interpretation. [6] Typically, Muth's argument refers to
relations of type (18)–(21), his hypothesis being that each left-hand
member makes an expectation both in the stochastic and the psychological sense. Furthermore, Muth's hypothesis can be adapted so as to
cover the expectations that occur in the right-hand members of (22)–
(23).

Interdependent models have always been recognized as having a predictive interpretation in terms of each relation in the reduced form.
With the REID specification, furthermore, each behavioral relation in
the structural form may be put to operative use as an *autonomous* relation. This makes for a distinct consolidation of the approach of interdependent models since the behavioral interpretation of each relation is
kept at the forefront and the basic cognitive element is well specified.
Nonetheless, the structural relations are pushed to the side in much of
the current applied work in econometrics. This, undoubtedly, is because
of the inconsistency in the predictor inference when a structural relation
is expressed in terms of observed values for current endogenous variables.
The REID specification should eliminate this bothersome problem and
allow for easier interpretation of problems in both operative use and
estimation of interdependent models.

1.2.6. Classic ID vs GEID Specification

There are many aspiration levels in the general evolution from exact to stochastic interdependent models. Those that should be distinguished for the subject matter of this monograph are outlined as follows:

1. Exact model: exact variables and exact relations in the specification of the theoretical model and no observational error in the variables that are used to develop estimates of parameters.
2. Apparent scatter: exact variables and exact relations in the specification of the theoretical model but observational errors in the variables that are to be used to develop estimates of parameters.
3. Genuine scatter: the relations in the theoretical structure are not specified to be exact but the REID specification allows a predictor interpretation of the structural form that is in accordance with the reduced form.
4. Generalized assumptions concerning residuals ϵ_i: the residuals in the model using observed variables are not specified to be uncorrelated with every predetermined variable.

In this section we discuss the fourth aspiration level. Since there are less assumptions concerning correlation between residuals and predetermined variables it is called "general interdependent systems", briefly GEID systems. It incorporates and extends the concept of the REID specification.

The classical specification of interdependent systems will be referred to as Classic ID systems, or sometimes briefly, CLID systems. Each of the residuals in the structural form of Classic ID systems is assumed to be uncorrelated with every predetermined variable in the entire model (for ease in illustration we are assuming that the structural form contains no equations that are already in the reduced form). This in turn means that each residual in the reduced form version of the model is also uncorrelated with every predetermined variable.

In the GEID specification the residual in the ith relation (ϵ_i) of the structural form is assumed to be uncorrelated with the variables y_q^*, z_p that occur in the same ith relation. In the case of moderate and large models the GEID specification assumes many fewer zero correlations than the REID specification. For example, in a model with 10 relations each having 2 predetermined variables that do not appear elsewhere in the system and 2 endogenous variables, there are 30 required zero correlations in the GEID specification but 200 in the classic and the REID specification. The GEID specification is similar to the situation in ordinary regression inasmuch as the number of assumptions of zero correlations is the same as the number of coefficients to be estimated.

In a just identified model the assumptions in the GEID specification are equivalent to the assumptions in the REID specification. However, in overidentified systems which are the ones of greater interest in econometrics, the number of zero correlations in the GEID specification is always less.

In Classic ID and REID specifications there are more zero correlations than there are coefficients to be estimated. Hence, in general it is not possible for the data under analysis to satisfy all of the assumptions of the model or the estimation process. For example, in TSLS the estimated residuals δ_i are not uncorrelated with every predetermined variable. It appears that assumptions in the classic specification are made because of the estimation process but that the residuals d_i from the estimation techniques being used do not satisfy all of the assumptions with respect to δ_i. For example, in TSLS the assumptions are required and satisfied in the first stage but are not satisfied when moving to the second stage.

We have asked, What is the rationale of the classic assumptions? Since there seems to be no answer other than for purposes of employing relatively easy estimation techniques we have emphasized the GEID approach. It is a weak feature if an assumption is made for no other reason than estimation. Specifications should start with hypotheses but not necessarily with the conditions required for a certain procedure in estimation.

We now ask if it is always possible to express a GEID model in terms of predictors. This is possible but it is better discussed after introducing the concept in the next section.

1.2.7. Linear vs Non-Linear Models

The classical specification of interdependent models can be said to pose a linear problem in estimation in that it is essentially the coefficients β_i and γ_i that have to be estimated. In the GEID specification, on the other hand, the expectations η_j^* must also be estimated from the sample data. Consequently, such terms as $\beta_1\eta_2^*$ and $\beta_2\eta_1^*$ in (22)–(23) make the model non-linear. Recognition of the non-linear feature brings to light several advantages as well as disadvantages.

The advantages in recognizing and using the terms $\beta_1\eta_2^*$ and $\beta_2\eta_1^*$ as well as $\beta_1\gamma_2$ and $\beta_2\gamma_1$ in Summers' model are

1. each structural relation can be interpreted as an autonomous relation when the expressions η_q^* are used;
2. each structural relation can be specified in terms of predictors when η_q^* are used;
3. the structural relations can be interpreted in terms of genuine scatter, with an option to express them in terms of endogenous variables as observed (y_q) or as expected (η_q^*).

These advantages hold for both the REID and GEID specifications.

The price paid for the above advantages is that the non-linear nature in the GEID specification sometimes involves more than one parameter specification and sometimes gives rise to difficulties in the estimation of parameters. These pluralities and difficulties are one of the main points of focus in this monograph.

With recognition that such terms as $\beta_1\eta_2^*$ incorporate a non-linear feature, other non-linear features such as y_i^2 and $\log y_i$ do not add any new types of problems for the estimation process. In particular, the iterative procedure in FP allows one to estimate the parameters β_i and γ_i when expressions such as y_q^2 occur in the structural form. In FP it is not necessary to estimate the reduced form directly and, therefore, the need to have explicit expressions for each current endogenous variable in terms of only predetermined variables does not exist. This aspect is only pointed out in passing since the investigation reported in this monograph did not focus on the general topic of non-linear ties among variables.

The predictor specification is possible in GEID models under very general conditions even though the model is non-linear for estimation purposes and the residuals are not uncorrelated with all of the predetermined variables. That is, both the structural and reduced form models can be expressed in terms of predictors; see (20)–(21) and (22)–(23). Furthermore, even though the structural form contains non-linear expressions for current endogenous variables (y_i) it can be expressed in terms of predictors. It is, of course, sometimes quite difficult to derive mathematical expressions for the reduced form in these cases.

1.2.8. Asymmetric vs Symmetric Specification

The asymmetric REID or GEID specification covers the special case when all structural relations are behavioral relations. As applied to Summers' model (5)–(6) the specification reads

$$y_1 = \beta_1 \eta_2^* + \gamma_1 z_1 + \gamma_2 z_2 + \epsilon_1 , \tag{24a}$$

$$y_2 = \beta_2 \eta_1^* + \gamma_3 z_3 + \gamma_4 z_4 + \epsilon_2 , \tag{24b}$$

with

$$\eta_1^* = E(y_1 | \eta_2^*, z_1, z_2) = \beta_1 \eta_2^* + \gamma_1 z_1 + \gamma_2 z_2 , \tag{25a}$$

$$\eta_2^* = E(y_2 | \eta_1^*, z_3, z_4) = \beta_2 \eta_1^* + \gamma_3 z_3 + \gamma_4 z_4 . \tag{25b}$$

As to the case of models with more than two relations, all of which are behavioral, each of the current endogenous variables will appear as a dependent variable, and $\beta_{ii} = 0$ in the ith relation, so that a variable y_i on the left of the equality does not also appear on the right.

Symmetric specifications cover cases where the structural form contains identities, equilibrium relations and perhaps other types of relations in addition to behavioral relations. This topic will be dealt with in detail in Chapters 3.2 and 11 but some of the main implications will be sighted here.

The REID specification is invariant to asymmetric vs symmetric specification. That is, if the variables are interchanged, which in Summers' model (5)–(6) would give

$$y_2 = \frac{1}{\beta_1} \eta_1^* - \frac{\gamma_1}{\beta_1} z_1 - \frac{\gamma_2}{\beta_1} z_2 + \epsilon_2 , \tag{26}$$

$$y_1 = \frac{1}{\beta_2} \eta_2^* - \frac{\gamma_3}{\beta_2} z_3 - \frac{\gamma_4}{\beta_2} z_4 + \epsilon_1 , \tag{27}$$

the corresponding expectations of type (25) still hold in the formal sense. Before discussing invariance from the standpoint of the subject matter of economics we will look at the same feature for GEID models.

The GEID specification in general is not invariant, even in the formal sense, to an interchange among endogenous variables. That is, for expressions like (26)–(27) to provide conditional expectations the coefficients will not be given by $1/\beta_1$, $-\gamma_1/\beta_1$, $-\gamma_2/\beta_1$, $1/\beta_2$, etc. In the GEID specification, moreover, the systematic parts η_i^* in general will not be invariant relative to a formal interchange of two current endogenous variables. Hence, such a formal interchange of variables is generally not permissible.

The above discussion was in reference to invariance with respect to conditions on correlations between residuals and predetermined variables, and the ensuing invariance conditions of the expectations η_i^*. There is a question whether the seeming invariance in the REID specification is realistic. The question is whether, in fact, the economic phenomena under analysis are invariant to an interchange of instruments (determining variables) and targets (dependent variables).

Results from experiments on physical phenomena have indicated that invariance in general will not exist. For example, the relation between pressure and heat using the heat pump is not the inverse of the relation between heat and pressure using a heat machine. That is, the parameters of the model have to be modified when instruments and targets (heat and pressure in this case) are interchanged. This is precisely what is required in the GEID specification.

The question about interchange of variables pertains only to estimation of structural equations and operative use of each structural equation as an autonomous relation. The interchange of endogenous variables in the structural equations does not, of course, affect the mathematical solution of the reduced form for any *given* set of values for coefficients in the structural equations.

1.2.9. Estimation

FP was developed for estimation of (a) linear REID models, (b) linear GEID models, and (c) REID and GEID models which contain non-linear expressions in current endogenous variables (e.g. $\log y_i$ and y_i^2). Features (a) and (b) are explained in detail in Chapter 3. There are, as is well known, a large number of other methods (limited information maximum likelihood – LIML, full information maximum likelihood – FIML, two-stages least-squares – TSLS, instrumental variables, etc.) which provide consistent estimates of parameters under the classical assumptions in the REID specification. The multiplicity of consistent estimates of parameters exists because there are more assumptions than parameters to be estimated. In comparing the performance of the FP estimation with other techniques, we focus in this monograph on the TSLS method. In the REID specification TSLS can be expected to have an advantage over FP in linear models, because it exploits the specific information that each residual ϵ_i is uncorrelated with every predetermined variable. On the other hand FP has the advantage over TSLS that it fits the data to the structural relations by an iterative procedure, and therefore can squeeze the data for more information than the TSLS approach. It can be expected that the relative importance of the two tendencies will be different in different models; this is a typical research problem in the present monograph.

Most discussion of alternative methods of estimation has centered on consistency of estimates. Although the focus of this monograph is on small sample properties of estimates it is well to briefly review the topic of consistency.

We can consider a predictor relation

$$y = \sum_{i=1}^{h} \beta_i x_i + \epsilon \tag{28}$$

$$E(y|x_1, ..., x_h) = \sum_{i=1}^{h} \beta_i x_i \tag{29}$$

either as a unirelational model or as part of a multirelational model. If the predictor relation (29) holds, the method of OLS will give consistent estimates of β_i under very general conditions of stochastic regularity. It will suffice that the variables $x_1, ..., x_h$ are not linearly interdependent, and that the product moments in the sample will tend to the corresponding moments in the population (see Section 1.3.5).

Under the classical assumptions for interdependent systems the reduced form is a set of predictor relations. The method of TSLS provides consistent estimates of coefficients in the structural relations since the variables η_i^* estimated from the first stage and inserted into the structural relations form another set of predictor relations. As mentioned earlier, there are several methods that provide consistent estimates for parameters interdependent models under the classical assumptions.

In the GEID specification OLS as well as the familiar methods for estimating interdependent models (TSLS, LIML, FIML) are inconsistent. One of the possible procedures for using FP is to start with TSLS estimates. In this situation the successive iterations in the FP procedure eliminate the large-sample bias of the TSLS estimates.

1.2.10. Predictive Testing

Prediction is use of the estimated model to predict values of endogenous variables in observation periods that lie outside the sample period; predictive testing is to subject the model to trial by comparing in due course the predicted values with fresh observations. For most interdependent models, the prediction will depend on all of the estimated parameters of the model. Predictive testing raises two issues of special interest. First, it is in contrast to R.A.Fisher's view for experimental work, namely, that not only the estimation but also the testing should be based exclusively on the sample data under analysis (the principle of the self-contained experiment) [7]. Second, predictive testing is one possible scheme for meeting the need for an overall assessment of estimation accuracy. The quality of estimates for different parameters of a model can differ greatly and, consequently, there is need for an index of the quality of the overall set of estimates.

In experimental work, Fisher's principle of the self-contained experiment is quite acceptable since experiments can be reproduced and the number of sample observations can be increased at the discretion of the researcher. In non-experimental model building, especially in the case of interdependent models, testing on the basis of sample data should be supplemented by predictive testing. There are several reasons for this. First, sample data are often few in number and further testing should be carried out at most every opportunity. Second, in the case of interdependent models it is possible for several different specifications of a model to give a fairly good fit to sample data unless the sample is very large. Third, the structure of the economic mechanism being modeled can change through time.

To avoid semantic problems in defining change in structure it is, perhaps, better to say that data in the sample period do not always permit the model builder to identify the structure that will characterize the prediction period.

Whenever an estimated model is in operative use the forecasts generated by the model provide further tests of the model. Since there is always some question about the accuracy of the model, especially those built from non-experimental data, the model is always subject to revision in light of the tests provided in the operative use. [8]

Predictive testing for an overall assessment of the estimation accuracy is systematically used in the evaluation provided in this monograph. Each of the 46 models contained several parameters to be estimated in each Monte Carlo run (sample). Each Monte Carlo run involved the generation of $N+P$ observations in a time series. The first N observations are called the sample period and the last P observations are called the prediction period. The comparison of actual endogenous variables in the prediction period with the forecasts of the same variables using the estimated model developed from the corresponding sample data constitutes the predictive testing. This comparison provides a measure of the accuracy of each of the different methods of estimation.

The accuracy of predictions is measured as

$$R^2 = 1 - \frac{V(y_i - \text{pred } y_i)}{V(y_i)}, \tag{30}$$

where pred y_i is the predicted value of the ith endogenous variable and $V(y_i - \text{pred } y_i)$ and $V(y_i)$ are variances estimated from data for the prediction period. There are many possible measures but this one is easily interpreted and corresponds to the familiar R^2 statistic that is computed in most least squares estimation techniques. There is further the point that R^2 as a criterion of prediction accuracy allows a clearcut interpretation from the point of view of information theory; we shall come back to this in 1.4.8.

1.2.11. Other Features Not Considered

The features selected for special discussion in 1.2.1 through 1.2.10 are either those for which our results shed new light or those which must be understood in order to properly interpret our results. It is important to point out that there are many other important aspects of model building such as those mentioned below which are not discussed in detail in this monograph.

Only a small amount of discussion is devoted to aspiration levels even though this is of paramount significance in applied works. Specific aspects in selection of aspiration levels include: Goal of prediction or explanation; choice between instrument and target variables; and acceptance or rejection of the *ceteris paribus* clause.

Once a tentative aspiration level is specified there are many aspects in sample data and model design other than the choice between interdependent and non-interdependent systems that must be considered. For example, model size was only touched upon in earlier sections but it is one of the most difficult choice variables in model building. [9]

Before the model can be completely specified it is necessary to consider many aspects of different measures of variables. Choices here include: Observation period such as annual or quarterly data; seasonally or non-seasonally adjusted data; constant or current dollars; and choice between absolute measures such as total income and per capita measures such as income per capita.

The choice of sample data for estimating unknown parameters in the model is another important aspect in model building. Specific considerations include the following: Length of sample period; advisability of deleting certain observations (such as war years) from the sample period; and the choice between using all available observations as sample data and saving some observations for use only in testing the quality of the estimated model.

Topics like those mentioned in the above paragraphs were left out of focus so that more attention could be placed on our central theme, namely, structure and estimation of interdependent systems.

1.3. Apparent vs Genuine Scatter — A Fundamental Feature in Model Building

In Chapter 1.2 we have given a brief review of some ten aspects of model building that are in focus in this monograph. In 1.3–1.4 we shall follow up with a more technical treatment of some of these aspects. The argument in these introductory sections is expository; background references will be given for further details.

In the present short section we shall give seven illustrations, selected so as to show that apparent vs genuine scatter is a fundamental dichotomy that cuts through the dichotomy known as "errors in variables" vs "errors in relations". [1]

1.3.1. "Errors in Variables"

Illustration 1A: Apparent scatter. We want to measure an agricultural field that has the form of a square, and in particular we are interested in the length L of the sides of the field, and the area S of the field. To reduce measurement errors, repeated measurements are made, and it is required that the assessment of L and S should honor the relation

$$S = L^2 . \tag{1}$$

We consider two situations.

(i) N measurements are made of the total boundaries of the field, say

$$4x_1, ..., 4x_N . \tag{2}$$

The following simple estimation formulas will under general conditions provide consistent estimates of L and S,

$$\text{est } L = \bar{x} = N^{-1}(x_1 + \cdots + x_N) , \tag{3a}$$

$$\text{est } S = (\bar{x})^2 . \tag{3b}$$

(ii) N measurements are made of the area of the field, say

$$y_1, ..., y_N . \tag{4}$$

The following estimates will under general conditions be consistent,

$$\text{est } L = \sqrt{\bar{y}} , \tag{5a}$$

$$\text{est } S = \bar{y} = N^{-1}(y_1 + \cdots + y_N) . \tag{5b}$$

Illustration 1B: Genuine scatter. Measurements are given on N agricultural fields which have different sizes, and all of which have square form. We are interested in the average area of the fields, say $E(S)$, and in the average length of the sides of the fields, say $E(L)$. We are here referring to averages in the sense of expected values $E(.)$.

Again we consider two situations.

(i) The total boundaries of each field has been measured; for the measurements we use the same notation as in (2).

The following formulas will under general conditions provide consistent estimates of $E(L)$ and $E(S)$

$$\text{est } E(L) = \bar{x} , \tag{6a}$$

$$\text{est } E(S) = (\bar{x})^2 + s^2 , \tag{6b}$$

where s^2 is the observed variance of the side length,

$$V = s^2 = N^{-1} \sum_i (x_i - \bar{x})^2 . \tag{7}$$

(ii) The area of each field has been measured; for the measurements we use the same notation as in (4).

The following estimates will under general conditions be consistent

$$\text{est } E(L) = N^{-1} \sum_i \sqrt{y_i} , \tag{8a}$$

$$\text{est } E(S) = \bar{y} . \tag{8b}$$

Comment. The difference between the formulas in Illustrations 1A and 1B will be noted. The salient point is, of course, that formula (1) remains valid for the measurements of each square in Illustration 1B, but it does not carry over to the averages; in fact,

$$E^2(L) \neq E(S) .$$ (9)

Hence, if the estimate (3b) is consistent, then (6b) is not consistent, and *vice versa*, and similarly for formulas (5a) and (8a).

Illustration 1A involves apparent scatter; 1B genuine scatter. The fundamental difference between these situations shows up in the estimation formulas. Further we note that both situations 1A and 1B are in the nature of "errors in variables", confirming what we have stated, namely that this dichotomy is cut across by the more fundamental dichotomy of apparent vs genuine scatter.

1.3.2. "Errors in Variables" vs "Errors in Relations"; Descriptive Relations

Illustration 2A: Apparent scatter. The orbit of a comet or sputnik is observed over an interval so short that the orbit is assumed to be linear in the celestial coordinates ξ, η; say

$$\eta = \alpha + \beta\xi .$$ (10)

Say that N observations are available,

$$x_i, y_i , \qquad i = 1, ..., N ,$$ (11)

and that the observations are subject to observational errors δ_1, δ_2, giving

$$x_i = \xi_i + \delta_{1i} ,$$ (12a)

$$i = 1, ..., N .$$

$$y_i = \eta_i + \delta_{2i} ,$$ (12b)

As is well known, a relation of type (10) cannot be consistently estimated from the data (11) unless we have some specific information on the relative size of the observational errors, for example on their standard deviations. [2] [The model (10)–(12) and the ensuing considerations were a standard argument in the problem of "the choice of regression" in the 1920s and 1930s. A typical conclusion is that "the regression of y and x should be used if there are errors only in y". For an early reference, see Gini (1921).] It turns out that relation (10) in general cannot be consistently estimated by ordinary least squares regression, neither by the regression of y on x, nor by the regression of x on y.

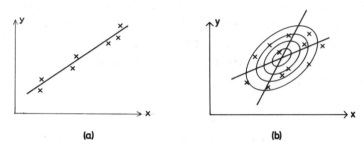

(a)   (b)

Chart 1.3.1. "Errors in relations": (a) apparent scatter; (b) genuine scatter.

Illustration 2B: Genuine scatter. Anthropological measurements of a tribe in New Guinea are available for the length x and width y of the sculls of N male adults. For the measurements we use the same notation as in (11). We assume that the data are a random sample from a bivariate normal distribution. This assumption constitutes our theoretical model. The ensuing theoretical regressions are linear, say for the regression of y on x

$$y = \alpha_1 + \beta_1 x + \epsilon_1 , \tag{13a}$$

$$E(y|x) = \alpha_1 + \beta_1 x . \tag{13b}$$

and for the regression of x on y

$$x = \alpha_2 + \beta_2 y + \epsilon_2 , \tag{14a}$$

$$E(x|y) = \alpha_2 + \beta_2 y . \tag{14b}$$

Thus if the length of a scull is known to be x, its expected width is $\alpha_1 + \beta_1 x$, and if the width of the scull is known to be y, its expected length is $\alpha_2 + \beta_2 y$. The residuals ϵ_1, ϵ_2 are the deviations from the expected values.

Forming the regression of y on x and the regression of x on y on the basis of the observed sample, say

$$y = a_1 + b_1 x + e_1 , \qquad (15a)$$

$$x = a_2 + b_2 y + e_2 , \qquad (15b)$$

these empirical regressions will under general conditions of stochastic regularity (see Section 1.3.5) make consistent estimates for the theoretical regressions (13a) and (14a), respectively.

1.3.3. "Errors in Variables" vs "Errors in Relations"; Explanatory Experiments

Illustration 3A. We consider Boyle's law for ideal gases,

$$PV = c , \qquad (16)$$

where V is the volume of the gas container, and P the pressure of the gas. Using logarithmic variables,

$$\xi = \log P , \qquad \eta = \log V , \qquad (17a\text{--}b)$$

we obtain Boyle's law in the linear form

$$\xi + \eta = \log C . \qquad (18)$$

We assume that the measurements of ξ, η are subject to observational errors δ_1, δ_2. Say that N measurements are available

$$x_i = \xi_i + \delta_{1i} , \qquad y_i = \eta_i + \delta_{2i} , \qquad i = 1, ..., N . \qquad (19a\text{--}b)$$

As to estimation, the situation is much the same as in Illustration 2A. The unit coefficients in relation (18) cannot be consistently estimated from the data unless we have some specific information on the relative size of the observational errors. Specifically, the relation cannot in general be consistently estimated by ordinary least squares regression.

Illustration 3B. We consider a stimulus-response experiment on the banana fly, with dose of X-radiation per time unit as stimulus variable x, and mutation frequency per time unit as response variable y, giving the relation

$$y = f(x) + \epsilon , \qquad\qquad (20\,a)$$

$$E(y \mid x) = f(x) . \qquad\qquad (20b)$$

For small doses of X-radiation the relationship is nearly linear, say

$$y = \alpha + \beta x + \epsilon , \qquad\qquad (21\,a)$$

$$E(y \mid x) = \alpha + \beta x . \qquad\qquad (21b)$$

Under general conditions of stochastic regularity (see 1.3.5) the least squares regression of y on x gives a consistent estimate of relation (21a).

Comment. Illustrations 3A and 3B are clearcut cases of apparent scatter and genuine scatter, respectively. In Illustration 3A the variables P, V are connected by an exact relationship (16), and the measurement of the relation is blurred by observational errors. In Illustration 3B the observed variables x, y are subject to an expectational relationship (21b), and the observed scatter is due to genuine variation in y, a variability due to variables that are not explicitly taken into account in the model, but are covered by the residual ϵ.

Conceptually, the transition from an exact relationship (18) subject to apparent scatter (19) to an expectational relationship (21) subject to genuine scatter is a generalisation that radically changes the nature of the model. It is not a coincidence that the exact relations (1), (10) and (16) belong under geometry and physics; outside these areas exact relations subject to apparent scatter are rare. Biological variation and individual variability are typical sources of genuine scatter; relation (21) is a case in point. Hence for model building in biological and social sciences to be realistic the relationships must as a rule be specified in terms of genuine scatter.

The radical difference between relations with apparent and genuine scatter shows up in the fact that they require different estimation techniques; to repeat, ordinary least squares is consistent when dealing with genuine scatter, but not so in the case of apparent scatter.

1.3.4. "Errors in Relations"; Non-Experimental Explanation

Illustration 4. We consider a demand relation with constant price elasticity λ,

$$d = c\, p^{-\lambda} \tag{22}$$

or in logarithmic variables

$$y = \alpha + \beta x \tag{23}$$

with

$$x = \log p\,, \quad y = \log d\,, \quad \alpha = \log c\,, \quad \beta = -\lambda\,. \tag{24}$$

To assess the price elasticity from empirical data we stochasticize the model as follows:

$$x = \alpha + \beta x + \epsilon\,, \tag{25a}$$

$$E(y\,|\,x) = \alpha + \beta x\,. \tag{25b}$$

Formally, this is the same model as (21a). Again, under general conditions of stochastic regularity, the least squares regression of y on x gives a consistent estimate of relation (25a), and thereby of the price elasticity $\lambda = -\beta$.

Comments. (1) Reference is made to "the problem of choice of regression", first posed by the Danish economist E.P.Mackeprang (1906) with regard to the statistical assessment of a demand relation [3]. Should the relation be estimated by the regression of demand on price, y on x, or by the regression of x on y? Dealing with the demand for sugar in

England, annual data 1826–1850, Mackeprang calculated the two regressions, and left open the problem of which regression should be chosen. In Illustration 4 the answer to the problem is given by the regression of demand on price. The conceptual basis for this solution to the problem is the intended use of the demand relation model under analysis, in this case the demand relation (22). To specify, we distinguish between two aspiration levels of the intended use:

a. *Non-causal prediction.* It has been observed in the past that the variables are interrelated, and it is assumed that the same type of interrelation will remain in the future. Then if we are interested in forecasting y in terms of x, we use the regression of y on x, and if we want to forecast x in terms of y, we use the regression of x on y.

This situation is similar to Illustration 2B, and is a case of bivariate description.

b. *Cause-effect prediction.* In this case, model (22) is specified as causal in the sense that a change in price p will bring about a change in demand in accordance with the relation (22), and the intended use of the relation (22) is in conformity with this causal specification.

With regard to such cause-effect specification and its stochastic version (25), model (22) is similar to the stimulus-response model (21). The difference is that (21) is experimental, whereas (25) is nonexperimental. An experiment can be randomised, and we can then estimate (21) by simple regression of y on x. In non-experimental data we must as a rule use not only x but also other explanatory variables to avoid specification errors, and the relation will then have to be estimated by multiple regression of y on x and the other explanatory variables.

(ii) *Cause-effect reversibility?* It is a meaningful question to ask how price p is influenced by a change in demand d. According to economic theory, the answer is given by the *price mechanism,* a relationship for price p that involves not only demand but also supply. Hence the answer is *not* given by the reversion of (22), that is, *not* by

$$p = c^{1/\lambda} d^{-1/\lambda} . \tag{26}$$

To put it otherwise, it is an inadmissible shortcut to treat (22) as causally reversible, and accept (26) as a cause-effect relation.

The inadmissible shortcut sometimes occurs in the disguise of "errors in relations". That is, in the statistical treatment the demand relation is dealt with as exact and subject to observational error, and the exact relationship is dealt with as reversible in the sense of (26), a typical result being that the ratio $1/\lambda$ is interpreted as the "price flexibility". In such cases "errors in relations" is an ambiguous term that blurs the distinction between apparent and genuine scatter. More precisely, it blurs the fact that relations are dealt with as involving apparent scatter, whereas in actual fact this approach is not realistic, and should be replaced by the approach of genuine scatter. At bottom, the source of the ambiguity is that the reversion from (22) to (26) is an operative procedure that is formally admissible in exact relations, but it does not carry over to expectational relations (25). Otherwise expressed, the reversion is not admissible in models that involve genuine scatter.

The ambiguity of the approach of "errors in relations" will come in still more glaring light in Chapter 1.4 when coming to multirelational models.

1.3.5. Predictor Specification and the Consistency of Ordinary Least Squares (OLS) Regression

The following simple theorem is of key relevance for the rationale of the iterative least squares procedures that are studied in this report.

Theorem. We consider a theoretical regression,

$$y = \beta_0 + \beta_1 x_1' + \cdots + \beta_h x_h + \epsilon , \tag{27}$$

and its least squares estimate as given by the regression of y on $x_1,...,x_h$,

$$y = b_0 + b_1 x_1 + \cdots + b_h x_h + e , \tag{28}$$

calculated from a sample of N observations. For the regression (28) to be consistent,

$$\operatorname*{prob\ lim}_{N \to \infty} b_i = \beta_i , \qquad i = 1, ..., h , \tag{29}$$

the following conditions are sufficient:

A. The regression is a predictor, that is

$$E(y \mid x_1, ..., x_h) = \beta_0 + \beta_1 x_1 + \cdots + \beta_h x_h . \tag{30}$$

B. In the limit, as the sample size N increases indefinitely, the product moments

$$\frac{1}{N} \sum x_i y , \quad \frac{1}{N} \sum x_i x_k \quad (i, k = 1, ..., h) \tag{31}$$

as calculated from the sample data tend to the corresponding theoretical moments

$$E(x_i y) , \quad E(x_i x_k) \quad (i, k = 1, ..., h) . \tag{32}$$

C. None of the variables $x_1, ..., x_h$ can be expressed in terms of the other variables as a linear relation with vanishing residual.

For the simple proof of the theorem, see Wold [10]. The point of the theorem is that the consistency requires no assumptions about the correlation properties of the residual ϵ.

Comments. (i) The key feature of the above theorem is Assumption A, showing that the predictor specification (30) is essentially sufficient for establishing the consistency of OLS regression. Further assumptions are needed if we want more information than consistency, for example, the standard errors of the empirical regression coefficients b_i. On the classical assumption that the residuals ϵ_t in the population are mutually uncorrelated and normally distributed, the variances and covariances of the estimates b_i are given by the large-sample formula

$$\sigma^2(b) = [X X']^{-1} \sigma^2(\epsilon) . \tag{33}$$

Reference is made to large-sample standard errors covering the case when the regression (27) is based on stationary time series data. For the case when the variables $x_1, ..., x_h$ are exogenous relative to y, see Wold-Juréen [1] and for the case when one or more x_i are lagged values of y, see Lyttkens [2].

(ii) Estimation accuracy being the general problem area of this report, our attention will to a large extent focus on consistency and small-sample accuracy. In the comparison between two or more consistent estimation methods, standard errors and small-sample bias come to the foreground. To some extent there is also a trade-off, inasmuch as consistency and small standard errors are advantages that can be more or less illusory if the small-sample bias is sizable.

(iii) Reference is made to two systems for concise writing of statistical formulas, namely

(a) Vector notation.

(b) Dropping the index that specifies the items of a sample; in time-series analysis this index is t, the observation period.

To combine the advantages of devices (a) and (b) we shall follow the system of vector notation used by C.F.Christ (1966). Thus for a matrix of observations on the variables $x_1, ..., x_h$ we write

$$X = \| x_{it} \| = \begin{bmatrix} x_{11} \cdots x_{1N} \\ \cdots \cdots \\ x_{h1} \cdots x_{hN} \end{bmatrix}, \tag{34}$$

where the variables are arranged by rows and the time periods by columns, not the other way round as in the customary usage. Note that the device (34) is in conformity with the arrangement of variables and time periods in Tinbergen's arrow scheme. [4]

For vector variables we shall use capital letters. This allows us to use device (b) without confusion between vector observations X_t and component variables x_i, giving

$$X_t = \begin{bmatrix} x_{1t} \\ \vdots \\ x_{ht} \end{bmatrix}; \qquad x_i = [x_{i1}, ..., x_{iN}] . \tag{35a-b}$$

That is, X_t is the column vector of variables x_t ($i = 1, ..., h$) as observed at time point t, and x_i is the row vector of the variable x_i as observed at the time points under consideration ($t = 1, ..., N$).

In this volume we need vector and matrix notation mainly for purposes of convenience in writing. Extensive matrix operations are not in the picture. Hence our need for the transpose symbol " ′ " is infrequent, and sometimes it is tacitly dropped if the interpretation is clear from the context.

Again to avoid transpose signs, coefficient matrices are defined so as to factorize with the relevant vector variables. For example, system (1.2.5−6) is written

$$Y = \beta Y + \Gamma Z + \delta \tag{36}$$

with

$$\beta = \begin{bmatrix} 0 & \beta_1 \\ \beta_2 & 0 \end{bmatrix}, \quad \Gamma = \begin{bmatrix} \gamma_1 & \gamma_2 & 0 & 0 \\ 0 & 0 & \gamma_3 & \gamma_4 \end{bmatrix}, \tag{37a–b}$$

$$\delta = \begin{bmatrix} \delta_1 \\ \delta_2 \end{bmatrix}. \tag{37c}$$

Note that we write vector residuals by small letters; this is because capital letters for δ or ϵ would cause confusion with other symbols.

For further illustration how these notations work, we rewrite the multiple regression (27) as referring to an arbitrary time period t, and drop the constant term β_0,

$$y_t = \beta X_t + \epsilon_t. \tag{38a}$$

Here β is the row vector of parameters,

$$\beta = [\beta_1, ..., \beta_h]. \tag{38b}$$

Using vector notations for the sample sets of observations, the product moments (31) become

$$\frac{1}{N} x_i y', \qquad \frac{1}{N} x_i x_k'. \tag{39a–b}$$

The familiar OLS estimates of the regression coefficients take the form

$$b = y X' [X X']^{-1} . \tag{40}$$

1.4. Some General Features of Multirelational Model Building

Many threads of evolution in science run together in ID systems, the type of multirelational model in focus in this monograph. To provide a background for the problem taken up in our report, we shall in this introductory section briefly review the formal and operative properties of ID systems as compared with Causal Chains (CC) and Vector Regression (VR) systems. The VR systems in this context mainly serve to emphasise the similarities and differences between ID and CC systems. [1]

As to *terminology* and *notation* of multirelational models we follow current econometric usage. Thus our models involve *endogenous* and *exogenous* variables; exogenous variables and lagged endogenous variables are called *predetermined* variables. The observations of the variables take the form of time-series, with observations equidistant in time, and the theoretical models are in the nature of stochastic processes.

Endogenous variables are those which it is the purpose of the system to explain. Their observed values are denoted

$$y_{it} \quad (i = 1, ..., n \; ; \; t = 1, ..., N) , \tag{1}$$

where n is the number of endogenous variables, and the observations extend over N time units. As random variables the endogenous variables are denoted $y_1, ..., y_n$, or in vector notation

$$Y = \begin{bmatrix} y_1 \\ \vdots \\ y_n \end{bmatrix} ; \qquad Y_t = \begin{bmatrix} y_{1t} \\ \vdots \\ y_{nt} \end{bmatrix} \tag{2a--b}$$

where Y_t denotes the vector of component variables y_i as observed at time t.

Exogenous variables are auxiliary explanatory variables, say r in number, and their observed values are denoted

$$x_{jt} \qquad (j = 1, ..., r ; \quad t = 1, ..., N) . \tag{3}$$

Predetermined variables are either exogenous or lagged endogenous variables, say m in number. Their observed values are denoted

$$z_{kt} \qquad (k = 1, ..., m ; \quad t = 1, ..., N) , \tag{4}$$

where either

$$z_{kt} = x_{jt} \qquad (t = 1, ..., N) \quad \text{for some } j = 1, ..., r , \tag{5a}$$

or

$$z_{kt} = y_{i,t-s} \qquad (t = 1, ..., N) \quad \text{for some } i = 1, ..., n , \tag{5b}$$
$$s = 1, 2, ..., s_o$$

and s_o is the largest lag that occurs in the model.

For exogenous variables and predetermined variables, vector notation is used in the same way as for endogenous variables. For example, Z_t is the column vector of predetermined variables $z_1, ..., z_m$ as observed at time t.

1.4.1. Vector regression (VR) systems

The main part of this monograph deals with ID systems where *all relations are behavioral*. This special case is fundamental from the point of view of the operative properties of the model. In this introductory section the operative properties of purely behavioral systems will be discussed with regard to VR, CC and ID systems. The differences and similarities between these three types of model are clearcut and fundamental.

We shall first consider the case when all relations are exact (deterministic; residual-free) and then turn to stochastic models specified in terms of predictors.

A. *Exact VR systems* take the form

$$Y = \Gamma Z, \tag{6}$$

where

$$\Gamma = \| \gamma_{ik} \| ; \quad i = 1, ..., n ; \quad k = 1, ..., m \tag{7a}$$

is a *position matrix*; that is, $\gamma_{ik} = 0$ except possibly for a set of specified entries, called *positions*; in symbols

$$\gamma_{ik} = 0 \text{ for } k \neq p_i(1), ..., p_i(a_i) ; \quad i = 1, ..., n , \tag{7b}$$

where $p_i(1), ..., p_i(a_i)$ are the positions in the ith row of the matrix Γ. If all elements γ_{ik} arc positions, all $a_i = m$, and Γ is called a *full* matrix.

For example, the VR system

$$y_{1t} = \gamma_{11} z_{1t} + \gamma_{12} z_{2t} , \tag{8a}$$

$$y_{2t} = \gamma_{23} z_{3t} + \gamma_{24} z_{4t} \tag{8b}$$

takes the vector form (6) with

$$\Gamma = \begin{bmatrix} \gamma_{11} & \gamma_{12} & 0 & 0 \\ 0 & 0 & \gamma_{23} & \gamma_{24} \end{bmatrix}. \tag{9}$$

showing that the positions of Γ are

$$p_1(1) = 1 ; \quad p_1(2) = 2 ,$$
$$\tag{10}$$
$$p_2(1) = 3 ; \quad p_2(2) = 4$$

with two positions in each row, $a_1 = a_2 = 2$.

As to the *intended use* of VR systems (6) we consider two general modes of operative procedures, say O_1 and O_2.

Intended use O_1: Direct prediction on the basis of any one of the behavioral relations. This means that the relations are *autonomous* in the sense that they can be applied separately. The prediction requires prior information (or ancillary prediction) of any exogenous variables x_{jt} among the predetermined variables z_{kt} in the right-hand members.

An example: Assuming that the predetermined variables z_1 and z_2 are known for some specified time t in the past, the present, or the future, relation (8a) is intended to predict the corresponding value of y_{1t}, in symbols

$$\text{pred } y_{1t} = \gamma_{11} z_{1t} + \gamma_{12} z_{2t} \tag{11}$$

and similarly for the prediction of y_{2t} by means of (8b).

Intended use O_2: Prediction by the *chain principle*; that is, by iterative substitution of predetermined variables z_{kt} in terms of predicted values y_{it}. If the system involves one or more exogenous variables x_{jt}, the procedure requires some ancillary prediction of these variables. [2]

An example: We consider the system (8) with predetermined variables specified as follows,

$$z_{1t} = y_{2,t-1} \ ; \quad z_{2t} = y_{1,t-2} \ ;$$
$$\tag{12}$$
$$z_{3t} = y_{1,t-1} \ ; \quad z_{4t} = y_{2,t-2}$$

giving

$$y_{1t} = \gamma_{11} y_{2,t-1} + \gamma_{12} y_{1,t-2} \ , \tag{13a}$$

$$y_{2t} = \gamma_{23} y_{1,t-1} + \gamma_{24} y_{2,t-2} \ . \tag{13b}$$

Assuming that the variables y_i, z_k have been observed up to and including the time point $t-1$, we want to make forecasts of y_{it}, $y_{i,t+1}$, ... We write pred y_{it} for the predicted value of y_{it} at time t, and introduce the notations

$$\text{pred } y_{it} = \begin{array}{l} \eta_{it}^* \text{ as a theoretical concept} \\ y_{it}^* \text{ as an empirical concept} \end{array}$$

Direct prediction gives:

$$\text{pred } y_{1t} = \eta_{1t}^* = \gamma_{11} y_{2,t-1} + \gamma_{12} y_{1,t-2} \,, \tag{14a}$$

$$\text{pred } y_{2t} = \eta_{2t}^* = \gamma_{23} y_{1,t-1} + \gamma_{24} y_{2,t-2} \,. \tag{14b}$$

To predict $y_{i,t+1}, y_{i,t+2}, \dots$ we use the chain principle, which gives

$$\text{pred } y_{1,t+1} = \eta_{1,t+1}^* = \gamma_{11} \eta_{2t}^* + \gamma_{12} y_{1,t-1} \,, \tag{15a}$$

$$\text{pred } y_{2,t+1} = \eta_{2,t+1}^* = \gamma_{23} \eta_{1t}^* + \gamma_{24} y_{2,t-1} \,, \tag{15b}$$

and the iterative substitutions lead to similar formulas for $y_{i,t+2}, y_{i,t+3}, \dots$.

B. *Stochastic VR systems.* There is here a parting of the ways between specification in terms of apparent scatter vs genuine scatter.

In the approach of *apparent scatter* it is assumed that the variables are subject to observational errors, and that the relations between the error-free variables are exact. As in the case of unirelational models (1.3.10) and (1.3.18) it is necessary to have some information on the relative size of the various errors in order to obtain consistent estimates of the parameters of the model. The operative procedures O_1 and O_2 carry over from the case of exact systems to stochastic models with apparent scatter, provided the stochastic model is consistently estimated, and provided we can apply the procedures to the variables as assessed without observational errors. We shall not enter here upon the problems that arise if we want to take this last snag into account when using models with apparent scatter for prediction.

In the approach of *genuine scatter* the relations of VR systems are specified in terms of *predictors,* namely

$$Y = \Gamma Z + \epsilon \,, \tag{16a}$$

$$E(Y|Z) = \Gamma Z \,, \tag{16b}$$

where ϵ is the column vector of residuals $\epsilon_1, \dots, \epsilon_n$, and the interpretation of the residuals is the same as in the unirelational models (1.3.21) or (1.3.25). The specification (16b) is a brief notation; to spell out,

$$E(y_i | z_{p_i(1)}, ..., z_{p_i(a_i)}) = \gamma_{i,p_i(1)} z_{p_i(1)} + ... + \gamma_{i,p_i(a_i)} z_{p_i(a_i)} \quad (17)$$

with $i = 1, ..., n$. That is, the left-hand members in (17) make the vector $E(Y|Z)$ with components $E(y_i|Z)$, where for each i the conditional vector Z involves only those variables $z_{p_i(a_i)}$ that are picked up by the positions $p_i(a_i)$ in the ith row of matrix Γ.

For example, the stochastic version (16) of system (13) is

$$y_{1t} = \gamma_{11} y_{2,t-1} + \gamma_{12} y_{1,t-2} + \epsilon_{1t}, \quad (18a)$$

$$y_{2t} = \gamma_{23} y_{1,t-1} + \gamma_{24} y_{2,t-2} + \epsilon_{2t} \quad (18b)$$

with

$$E(y_{1t} | y_{2,t-1}, y_{1,t-2}) = \gamma_{11} y_{2,t-1} + \gamma_{12} y_{1,t-2}, \quad (19a)$$

$$E(y_{2t} | y_{1,t-1}, y_{2,t-2}) = \gamma_{23} y_{1,t-1} + \gamma_{24} y_{2,t-2}. \quad (19b)$$

The two modes O_1, O_2 of intended use of the model carry over from the case of exact models (6). The ensuing predictions are formally the same; see, for example (11) and (14)–(15). The specification of an exact or stochastic model reflects the differences in the aspiration level (intended accuracy) in the resulting predictions. Formula (11) is exact, whereas (16b) and (19) give expectational predictions. When using systems (16) and (18) in practice, the parameters $\Gamma = \| \gamma_{ik} \|$ will have to be replaced by estimates, say

$$G = \| g_{ik} \| . \quad (20)$$

If the parameter estimates are consistent in the large-sample sense, the resulting predictions (16b) and (19) will under general conditions of stochastic regularity be consistent.

Comments. (i) In exact VR systems (6) the formulas (14)–(15) for prediction by the chain principle follow as an immediate implication from the formulas (13) for direct prediction. In stochastic VR systems

(16) a corresponding transition from (13) to (14)–(15) is valid thanks to the fact that the chain principle works by linear substitution of future non-observed y_i-values by predicted η_i^*-values. The salient point is that expectational relations under general conditions remain expectational after such substitutions. [3]

(ii) As to this last point, the requisite "general conditions" set certain restrictions for the consistency of the substitutive predictions. Speaking broadly, it will suffice that the time-series under analysis are generated by a stationary normal process. For later reference, the point we wish to emphasize in this context is that the two operative procedures O_1, O_2 may or may not be compatible in stochastic models, and that they are compatible under general conditions in VR systems (16) specified in terms of genuine scatter.

1.4.2. Causal Chain (CC) Systems [4]

Terminology and notations carry over from VR systems as shown in (21). In CC and ID systems we must distinguish between the systems in *structural form* and in *reduced form*. When all relations of the system are behavioral, these constitute the structural form. The reduced form is obtained by solving the structural form for the current endogenous variables y_{it}.

Again we shall first consider the special case of exact systems.

A. *Exact CC systems.* When all relations are behavioral, the structural form of CC systems allows the representation

$$Y = \beta Y + \Gamma Z , \tag{21}$$

where

$$\beta = \| \beta_{ij} \| \tag{22a}$$

is an $n \times n$ position matrix that is *subdiagonal*, that is, all non-zero elements lie below the main diagonal, giving

$$\beta_{ij} = 0 \quad \text{for} \quad j \geqslant i ; \quad i, j = 1, ..., n , \tag{22b}$$

say with positions

$$j = q_i(1), ..., q_i(b_i) ; \qquad i = 2, ..., n , \tag{23a}$$

where (22b) implies

$$q_i(b_i) < i ; \qquad i = 2, ..., n . \tag{23b}$$

Solving (21) for the current endogenous variables y_i, we obtain the CC system in reduced form, say

$$Y = \Omega Z \tag{24a}$$

with

$$\Omega = [I - \beta]^{-1} \Gamma , \tag{24b}$$

where

$$\Omega = \| \omega_{ij} \| ; \qquad i = 1, ..., n ; \;\; j = 1, ..., m \tag{24c}$$

is always well-defined since $[I - \beta]$ is an $n \times n$ matrix with mere units in the diagonal and mere zeros above the diagonal.

For example,

$$y_{1t} = \qquad\qquad \gamma_{11} y_{2,t-1} + \gamma_{12} y_{1,t-2} , \tag{25a}$$

$$y_{2t} = \beta_{21} y_{1t} + \gamma_{23} y_{1,t-1} + \gamma_{24} y_{2,t-2} \tag{25b}$$

is the structural form of a CC system which in vector form (21) is specified by (9), (12) and

$$\beta = \begin{bmatrix} 0 & 0 \\ \beta_{21} & 0 \end{bmatrix} . \tag{26a}$$

Matrix β is here the simplest possible, with just one position, namely

$$i = 2 ; \quad k = q_2(1) = 1 . \tag{26b}$$

The reduced form is

$$y_{1t} = \gamma_{11}y_{2,t-1} + \gamma_{12}y_{1,t-2} \, , \tag{27a}$$

$$y_{2t} = \beta_{21}\gamma_{11}y_{2,t-1} + \beta_{21}\gamma_{12}y_{1,t-2}$$
$$+ \gamma_{23}y_{1,t-1} + \gamma_{24}y_{2,t-2} \, , \tag{27b}$$

showing that the coefficients ω_{ik} in this case are given by

$$\omega_{11} = \gamma_{11} \quad ; \quad \omega_{12} = \gamma_{12} \quad ;$$
$$\omega_{13} = 0 \quad ; \quad \omega_{14} = 0 \quad ; \tag{28a}$$

$$\omega_{21} = \beta_{21}\gamma_{11} \, ; \quad \omega_{22} = \beta_{21}\gamma_{12}$$
$$\omega_{23} = \gamma_{23} \quad ; \quad \omega_{24} = \gamma_{24} \tag{28b}$$

Comment. Since matrix β of CC systems (21) is subdiagonal in the sense of (22), the operation that carries from the structural form (21) to the reduced form (24) is a procedure that involves nothing else than a sequence of iterative substitutions of current endogenous variables y_{it} in terms of predetermined variables z_{kt}.

Turning to the intended use of CC systems, the operative procedures O_1 and O_2 always carry over from exact VR systems.

Intended use O_1: To prepare for later partings of the ways, we shall consider three conceptually distinct procedures under O_1.

> *Intended use O_1*: Direct prediction on the basis of any one of the behavioral relations; that is, the relations of the structural form are *autonomous* in the same sense as in VR systems.
> *Intended use O_1'*: Direct prediction on the basis of the behavioral relations, using them simultaneously.
> *Intended use O_1''*: Prediction of all endogenous variables simultaneously, for given values of all predetermined variables.

Procedure O_1'' is nothing else than prediction from the reduced form. Hence this intended use is covered by procedure O_2, and need not be taken up under O_1.

Procedure O'_1, owing to the interdependence of the predictions, is subject to the qualification that the variables y_{it} $(i = 2, ..., n)$ that enter as ancillary information in the right-hand members of the structural form (21) must coincide with the predictions generated by the consecutive substitutions (or by the reduced form). Subject to this qualification, procedure O'_1 is numerically equivalent to procedure O''_1. There is a conceptual difficulty in procedure O'_1, however, namely with regard to the simultaneous use of the structural relations. For example, if we use the second equation for prediction, then the right-hand variables are known and y_{2t} is unknown, which implies that it is not meaningful to assume y_{2t} to be known in order to predict y_{3t} (or y_{it} for $i > 3$) on the basis of the third (ith) relation of the structural form. Hence O'_1 in general is not meaningful as a mode of joint prediction; in CC systems joint prediction of the endogenous variables is covered by procedure O_2 (which, as we have seen, covers O''_1). In this last argument there is an exception, inasmuch as the first structural relation has no current endogenous variable in the right-hand member, and so the first equation can be combined with any other structural relation for joint prediction in the sense of procedure O'_1. This exception is of little relevance, however, and will be disregarded in what follows.

To sum up, we have clarified the intended use O_1, and shall take it in the autonomous sense indicated above, and disregard the modes O'_1 and O''_2.

Intended use O_2: Prediction by the chain principle. In this procedure, typically, all endogenous variables are predicted by the reduced form.

In the operative use of CC systems, both procedures O_1 and O_2 are in play. As regards procedure O_2 the typical intended use is to predict future endogenous variables y_i in terms of current or past predetermined variables z_k. This situation is much the same as in exact VR systems. We can use either the structural form or the reduced form, but the reduced form is specifically derived for the purpose, and the resulting forecasts will be exactly the same. In VR systems, to repeat, the two forms coincide.

An example: Calculating the forecasts of y_{it} and $y_{i, t+1}$ that correspond to (14) and (15), pred y_{1t} and pred y_{2t} will be given by (27) and further we obtain

$$\text{pred}\, y_{1,t+1} = \gamma_{11}\eta^*_{2t} + \gamma_{12}y_{1,t-1} = \tag{29a}$$

$$= \beta_{21}\gamma^2_{11}y_{2,t-1} + (\gamma_{12} + \gamma_{11}\gamma_{23})y_{1,t-1}$$

$$+ \beta_{21}\gamma_{11}\gamma_{12}y_{1,t-2} + \gamma_{11}\gamma_{24}y_{2,t-2} \tag{29b}$$

and a straightforward but lengthier formula for pred $y_{2,t+1}$.

Comments. (i) Summarizing from the point of view of structural vs reduced form, procedure O_1 operates on exact CC systems in structural form (21), whereas procedure O_2 operates on the reduced form (24), or, which gives exactly the same results, by iterative application of the structural form.

Conceptually, O_1 is a more general procedure than O_2. In fact, prediction by way of O_2 can always be interpreted as a set of predictions by way of O_1, but the converse is not necessarily true. For example, an autonomous prediction of y_{1t} is not conceptually combined with a prediction of y_{2t}. The situation is illustrated by Chart 1a (upper left): The predictions by procedure O_2 are a subclass of the predictions by procedure O_1.

(ii) Letting the position matrices β, Γ be given by (7) and (22), we form

$$\Pi = \| \pi_{ik} \|, \quad (i = 1, ..., n\; ;\; k = 1, ..., m) \tag{30}$$

as the $n \times m$ position matrix which has the same positions as matrix Ω as given by (24b).

Definitions. We shall say that matrix Ω is *compatible with* Π, in symbols

$$\Omega \approx \Pi \tag{31}$$

if for any numerically specified matrix Π there is at least one set of matrices β, Γ such that $\Omega = [I - \beta]^{-1}\Gamma = \Pi$, and that Ω is *over-identified* relative to Π if there is some Π for which no such set β, Γ exists.

In most cases Ω is over-identified relative to Π, and this is always so if Π has more positions than the total number of positions in β and Γ.

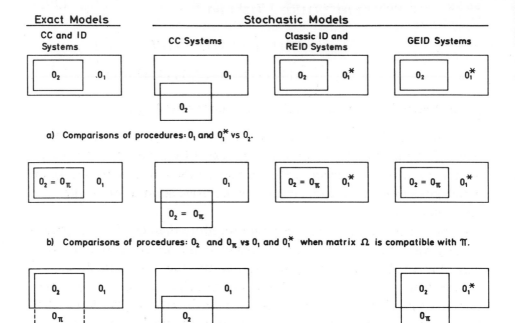

a) Comparisons of procedures: 0_1 and 0_1^* vs 0_2.

b) Comparisons of procedures: 0_2 and 0_π vs 0_1 and 0_1^* when matrix Ω is compatible with π.

c) Comparisons of procedures: 0_2 and 0_π vs 0_1 and 0_1^* when matrix Ω is overidentified relative to π.

Chart 1.4.1. Relative scope of the operative procedures O_1, O_1^*, O_2 and O_π in CC and ID systems.

With matrix Π thus defined we form

$$Y = \Pi Z . \tag{32}$$

Systems (24a) and (32) express the endogenous variables y_i as linear functions of the predetermined variables z_k. Formally, system (32) is more general than (24a), except in the case when $\Omega \approx \Pi$.

In (24a) and (32) we meet for the first time a dualism which is of fundamental relevance for the theory of interdependent systems and related multirelational models. We shall now proceed to a discussion of the operative aspects of system (32).

Intended use O_π: Prediction by the chain principle, using system (32) and subsequent models obtained by analogous generalisations from Ω to Π-matrices. It is typical for this operative use that all endogenous variables are predicted simultaneously.

The situation is illustrated in Chart 1b—c (first column). In the special case $\Omega \approx \Pi$, Charts 1a and 1b are the same, inasmuch as the operative procedure O_π has the same scope as procedure O_2. If, on the other hand, Ω is over-identified relative to Π, procedure O_π has potential applications that are not covered by O_2. These other applications, however, are not compatible with procedures O_1 and O_2, and they may therefore be regarded as fictitious. In Chart 1c they are, accordingly, marked by broken lines.

Illustration 1. In system (25) there is a total of 5 positions in matrices β and Γ, whereas the corresponding matrix Π in (32) has 6 positions. Hence Ω is over-identified relative to Π, and system (25) belongs under Chart 1c. To put it otherwise: If we allow the five parameters in β, Γ to vary freely, the resulting parameters Ω will cover only a subspace of the entire domain of variation of the unrestricted matrix Π.

Illustration 2. Let (25*) denote the system (25) as modified by deleting the two terms $\gamma_{12}z_{1,t-2}$ and $\gamma_{24}z_{2,t-2}$. Matrix Ω of system (25*) is readily recognized as being compatible with the corresponding matrix Π, and system (25*) belongs under Chart 1b.

B. Stochastic CC systems. The distinction between apparent and genuine scatter is the same as for VR systems. Again the prediction formulas for exact models carry over, conceptually, to the approach of *apparent scatter.* And as before, the approach of apparent scatter is unrealistic in econometric model building.

In the approach of *genuine scatter,* the operative procedures O_1 and O_2 require a predictor specification of the CC system in structural form (21) and reduced form (24), respectively.

In the approach of genuine scatter and predictors, the structural form of CC systems is specified as follows,

$$Y = \beta Y + \Gamma Z + \delta , \qquad (33a)$$

$$E(Y \mid Y, Z) = \beta Y + \Gamma Z . \qquad (33b)$$

In analogy to (16b) and (17), the brief formulation of the predictor specification (33b) is to be spelled out in terms of the positional elements of matrices β and Γ.

The corresponding predictor specification of the reduced form is as follows,

$$Y = \Omega Z + \epsilon , \tag{34a}$$

$$E(y_i \mid [\Omega Z]_i) = [\Omega Z]_i ; \quad i = 1, ..., n , \tag{34b}$$

with

$$\Omega = [I - \beta]^{-1} \Gamma , \tag{35a}$$

$$\epsilon = [I - \beta]^{-1} \delta . \tag{35b}$$

The similarities and differences between the predictors (33b) and (34b) will be noted. Both are conditional expectations in the sense of probability theory. As spelled out for the ith variable y_i, both predictors involve conditional variables that are a set of free variables, in (33b) the explanatory variables y_{p_i}, z_{q_i} in the ith relation of the structural form, in (34b) the predetermined variables z_{r_i} that occur in the ith relation of the reduced form, letting

$$r_i = r_i(1), r_i(2), ..., r_i(c_i) \tag{36}$$

denote the positions in the ith row of matrix $\Omega = [I - \beta]^{-1} \Gamma$. In (33a−b) the coefficients β, Γ may be either
  I. numerically specified, or
  II. conceptually unknown, and subject to some suitable numerical estimation procedure.
In (34a−b) the coefficients Ω are assumed to be numerically specified, namely by way of predetermined values for β, Γ. Hence the notation system marks that (33b) is more general than (34b), inasmuch as (33b) allows both specifications I and II, whereas (34b) only allows specification I.

Illustration. The following CC system links up with the exact VR system (8), and except for the specification (12) of the predetermined variables it links up with the stochastic VR system (18) and the exact CC system (25). The structural form is

$$y_1 = \qquad \gamma_{11}z_1 + \gamma_{12}z_2 + \delta_1 , \qquad (37a)$$

$$y_2 = \beta_{21}y_1 + \gamma_{23}z_3 + \gamma_{24}z_4 + \delta_2 , \qquad (37b)$$

with the predictor specification

$$E(y_1|z_1, z_2) = \qquad \gamma_{11}z_1 + \gamma_{12}z_2 , \qquad (38a)$$

$$E(y_2|y_1, z_3, z_4) = \beta_{21}y_1 + \gamma_{23}z_3 + \gamma_{24}z_4 . \qquad (38b)$$

The reduced form of the system is

$$y_1 = \gamma_{11}z_1 + \gamma_{12}z_2 + \epsilon_1 , \qquad (39a)$$

$$y_2 = \beta_{21}\gamma_{11}z_1 + \beta_{21}\gamma_{12}z_2 + \gamma_{23}z_3 + \gamma_{24}z_4 + \epsilon_2 , \qquad (39b)$$

where

$$\epsilon_1 = \delta_1 , \qquad (40a)$$

$$\epsilon_2 = \beta_{21}\delta_1 + \delta_2 . \qquad (40b)$$

The predictor specification of the reduced form is given by

$$E(y_1|z_1, z_2) = \gamma_{11}z_1 + \gamma_{12}z_2 , \qquad (41a)$$

$$E(y_2|\beta_{21}\gamma_{11}z_1 + \beta_{21}\gamma_{12}z_2 + \gamma_{23}z_3 + \gamma_{24}z_4)$$

$$= \beta_{21}\gamma_{11}z_1 + \beta_{21}\gamma_{12}z_2 + \gamma_{23}z_3 + \gamma_{24}z_4 , \qquad (41b)$$

where specification (41a) is of type (33b) and specification (41b) is of type (34b).

To illustrate the operative use of the above formulas, we shall now spell out some of the ensuing predictions.

The operative procedure O_1 as applied to the structural form (37)–(38) gives

$$\text{pred } y_{1t} = \gamma_{11} z_{1t} + \gamma_{12} z_{2t} , \tag{42a}$$

$$\text{pred } y_{2t} = \beta_{21} y_{1t} + \gamma_{23} z_{3t} + \gamma_{24} z_{4t} . \tag{42b}$$

In formula (42a) the variables z_{1t}, z_{2t} are assumed to be known, whereas in formula (42b) the known variables are y_{1t}, z_{3t}, z_{4t}.

The operative procedure O_2 as applied to the reduced form (39)–(41) gives for y_{1t} the same prediction (42a) as procedure O_1, and for y_{2t} it gives

$$\text{pred } y_{2t} = \beta_{21} \gamma_{11} z_{1t} + \beta_{21} \gamma_{12} z_{2t} + \gamma_{23} z_{3t} + \gamma_{24} z_{4t} . \tag{43}$$

Predictors and least squares. [5] Comparing specifications I and II, we shall comment upon three aspects of the situation.

(i) As applied to the ith relation of the structural form (33a), specification I implies

$$E(\delta_i) = 0 \tag{44}$$

whereas specification II implies, as a corollary to the theorem in 1.3.5,

$$E(\delta_i) = 0 ; \quad r(y_{q_i}, \delta_i) = r(z_{p_i}, \delta_i) = 0 . \tag{45}$$

As applied to the ith relation of the reduced form (34a), specification I implies

$$E(\epsilon_i) = 0 . \tag{46}$$

(ii) Under very general conditions of stochastic regularity the predictor specification II of the structural form (33a–b) implies — as a corollary to (45) — that consistent estimates of the coefficients β, Γ are given by least squares regression of y_i on the set y_{q_i}, z_{p_i}.

In multiple regression (1.3.27) the number of parameters to be estimated is the same as the number of zero correlations assumed for the residuals. By (45), this parity extends to the structural form of CC systems.

(iii) From an operative point of view, specification II is more general than I, conceptually, inasmuch as in specification II the coefficients β, Γ may be regarded as known or unknown when posing the prediction problem, whereas in specification I these same coefficients must be regarded as known.

For direct comparison with (34) from this last point of view we consider the following model specification,

$$Y = \Pi Z + v , \tag{47a}$$

$$E(y_i | z_{r_i}) = [\Pi Z]_i . \tag{47b}$$

The predictor (47b) is seen to allow both specifications I–II; hence in the sense of comment (iii) the predictor (47b) is more general than (34b).

With reference to Chart 1 for illustration, we shall now discuss the operative aspects of the CC system (33)–(34).

Procedure O_1 works on the structural form (33a–b), and allows us to predict any endogenous variable y_i for given values of $y_1, ..., y_{i-1}$ and the predetermined variables z_k; more precisely stated, for those variables y_{q_i} and z_{p_i} that occur in the right-hand member of the ith structural relation. The prediction error constitutes the corresponding residual δ_i, and the prediction is unbiased in the sense that δ_i under the specified conditions has expectation zero.

Procedure O_2 works on the reduced form (34a–b), assuming the parameters β, Γ to be known, and allows us to predict any endogenous variable y_i for given values of the predetermined variables z_k; more precisely stated, for those variables z_{r_i} that occur in the ith relation of the reduced form. The prediction error is the corresponding residual ϵ_i, and the prediction is unbiased in the sense that ϵ_i under the specified conditions has expectation zero.

As applied to stochastic CC systems we see that the procedures O_1 and O_2 answer different problems, inasmuch as the conditional variables for prediction mode O_1 are y_{q_i}, z_{p_i} and for prediction mode O_2 are z_{r_i}. Furthermore, procedure O_2 assumes the parameters β, Γ to be known. The difference is reflected in the fact that the residuals δ_i and ϵ_i in general are different. The situation is illustrated in Chart 1a (2nd column). Procedures O_1 and O_2 have different operation domains, except for the first relation; according to the recursive design of CC systems this relation is the same in the structural form and the reduced form. The overlapping area covers the first relation.

For procedure O_π the situation resembles that in exact CC systems. In the special case $\Omega \approx \Pi$ procedures O_π and O_2 are equivalent (see Chart 1b). Otherwise, procedure O_π has potential applications that are not covered by O_2. In exact CC systems these applications involve a conceptual clash with the basic procedures O_1 and O_2 and are therefore of a fictitious nature. In stochastic systems, however, this clash is screened off by the random variation that is embodied in the residuals, and there may be cases where procedure O_π is relevant. Chart 1c marks the difference by letting the broken contour in column 1 have a full-drawn counterpart in column 2.

An example: As applied to system (37)–(38), specification (47a–b) and procedure O_π give

$$\text{pred } y_{2t} = \pi_{21} z_{1t} + \pi_{22} z_{2t} + \pi_{23} z_{3t} + \pi_{24} z_{4t} , \tag{48}$$

where the coefficients π_{2k} may or may not be the same as in (41b).

The predictive specification (34a–b) of the reduced form of a CC system allows an equivalent formulation, as follows,

$$Y = \Omega Z + \epsilon , \tag{49a}$$

$$\mathrm{E}(y_{it} \mid \eta^*_{q_i(1),t}, \, ..., \, \eta^*_{q_i(b_i),t}, \, z_{p_i(1),t}, \, ..., \, z_{p_i(a_i),t})$$

$$= \eta^*_{it} = [\Omega Z_t]_i = \big[[\mathrm{I} - \beta]^{-1} \Gamma Z_t\big]_i ; \quad i = 1,...,n. \tag{49b}$$

The left-hand expectations in (49b) are specified in accordance with the calculation of the reduced form by recursive substitutions in the structural form. In fact, the left-hand indexes $q_i(1), ..., q_i(b_i), p_i(1), ..., p_i(a_i)$ mark the positions in the ith row of matrices β, Γ, and η^*_{qt} denotes the forecast for y_{qt} in terms of predetermined variables z_{k_t}, that results from recursive substitutions in the q first relations of the structural form. The left-hand member of (49b), as indicated by the second member, is nothing else than the expectation η^*_{it} as resulting from the structural form after $i-1$ substitutions in accordance with the chain principle. Hence if we substitute η_{it}^* for y_{it} all through the structural form, and omit the residuals, we can solve for $\eta_{1t}^*, ..., \eta_{nt}^*$; this gives the two last equalities in (49b).

To form the conditional variables η_{it}^* in (49b), the parameters β, Γ must be known. Hence formula (49b), like (34b), is subject to specification I as defined in connection with (36).

Illustration. As applied to system (37)–(38), formula (49b) gives

$$E(y_{2t} \mid \eta_{1t}^*, z_{3t}, z_{4t}) = \beta_{21}\eta_{1t}^* + \gamma_{23}z_{3t} + \gamma_{24}z_{4t} \tag{50}$$

and

$$\text{pred } y_{2t} = \beta_{21}\eta_{1t}^* + \gamma_{23}z_{3t} + \gamma_{24}z_{4t} , \tag{51a}$$

with

$$\eta_{1t}^* = \gamma_{11}z_{1t} + \gamma_{12}z_{2t} . \tag{51b}$$

Note that (51a) is numerically the same as (43), as seen from (50). Further note that the prediction errors are the same in (34a–b) and (49a–b), namely ϵ_i, but are not the same in (34a–b) and (33a–b). The point of this remark is that the predictor specification (49) of the reduced form is to be interpreted as resulting from the chain principle as applied to the expected values $\eta_1^*, ..., \eta_{n-1}^*$, not to the observed values $y_1, ..., y_{n-1}$ occurring in the structural form (33a–b). The situation has the important implication that the structural residuals δ_i of CC systems in general will have smaller variance than the residuals ϵ_i of the reduced form. This feature of the structural form is known as the minimum-delay property of CC systems; see Robinson-Wold (1963). To paraphrase, the prediction of y_i by (33b) exploits the information embodied in the residuals $\delta_1, ..., \delta_{i-1}$, whereas this information is not exploited in the prediction by (34b).

Comments

(i) The differences in purpose and scope between the operative procedures O_1 and O_2 can hardly be exaggerated. Procedure O_1 is an application of causal analysis that exploits the information on the endogenous variables that is inherent in their intercorrelations within one and the same time period, whereas procedure O_2 aims at the best possible prediction from one time period to the next. Hence the structural form of CC systems in general has residuals δ_i with smaller variance than the residuals ϵ_i of the reduced form. Even the specification (47a–b) that underlies the operative procedure O_π cannot give smaller residuals than the structural form, provided the model design exploits all the available information.

(ii) Reference is made to two general theorems on the possibility of representing time-series or stochastic processes in accordance with predictor specifications of VR systems (16) and CC systems (33).[6] It will suffice for our purpose to consider processes and corresponding time-series that are stationary and normal.

a. A stationary normal process allows, to any prescribed accuracy, a representation in the form of VR systems (16).

b. A stationary normal process allows, to any prescribed accuracy, a representation in the form of CC systems with structural form (33) and reduced form (34) or (49).

(iii) For one and the same stochastic process or set of time series y_{it}, z_{kt} the two representations a and b referred to in Comment (ii) will have characteristic similarities and differences. We note the following points:

a. To the prescribed accuracy, there will be zero intercorrelation between any two residuals ϵ_{it}, ϵ_{ju} $(t \neq u)$ in the VR system (16); between any two residuals ϵ_{it}, ϵ_{ju} $(t \neq u)$ in the reduced form (34) or (49) of CC systems; and between two residuals $(\delta_{it}, \delta_{ju})$ $(t \neq u$ or $t = u)$ in the structural form (33) of CC systems.

b. Accordingly, any residual ϵ_{it} in the VR system (16) will have the same variance as the corresponding residual ϵ_{it} in the reduced form (34) or (49) of the CC system, whereas the corresponding residual δ_{it} in the structural form (33) of the CC system in general will have smaller variance.

c. At first sight it might seem a paradoxical feature of CC systems that it is possible to specify both the structural form (33a) and the reduced form (34a) in terms of predictors (33b) and (34b). This feature might seem so much the more remarkable in view of Comment (ii), point b, which is to the effect that all parameters of the structural form (33a) are needed to establish the predictor relations (33b), so that there should remain no degrees of freedom to satisfy relations (34b). The situation is explained by two facts: First, the passage from the structural form (33a) to the reduced form (34a) is a matter of linear substitutions; second, predictors under general conditions will remain predictors if the conditional variables are substituted by predictors; see Wold [9]. We note that the requisite general conditions include the zero intercorrelations of any two simultaneous residuals δ_{it}, δ_{jt}, in accordance with point b of the present comment.

d. The predictor specifications (33b) and (49b) are the same, except that the current endogenous variables y_{qt} that enter as conditions in the left-hand expectations in (33b) are in (49b) replaced by their expectations η_{qt}^*. Again, this might seem paradoxical at first sight, and again the answer lies in the general representation theorem referred to in Comment (ii) b, the salient point being the zero intercorrelation between any two simultaneous residuals δ_{it}, δ_{jt}.

Remembering that predictor relations can be consistently estimated by ordinary least squares (OLS) regression (see Section 1.3.5), it follows that OLS should give equivalent results if applied (a) to the relations of the structural form (33a), and (b) to the relations of the structural form after replacing the right-hand current variables y_{qt} by their systematic parts η_{qt}^* as obtained in the estimation (a). In point of principle, the equivalence provides a criterion that the CC system is correctly specified from the point of view of the general representation theorem referred to in Comment (ii) b.

(iv) Seemingly, point b of Comment (iii) contradicts the implication of point a of Comment (i), page 45, that specification (49b) is more general than (34b). Part of the answer to this remark lies in the dualism of full vs position matrices Γ as defined in (7b). If we try to represent an arbitrary process (Y_t, Z_t) by a VR system (16) or a CC system (33), matrix Γ in general will be a full matrix both in (16) and (33); hence β becomes redundant in the CC system (33), and these relations become a VR system (16), with the result that the reduced forms (34b) and (49b) coincide with the same VR system.

In practice, the model builder tries to make his model as simple as possible, and therefore he designs his VR and CC systems by the use of matrices Γ, β with as few positions as possible. Hence such models should not be seen as fullfledged representations in the sense of Comment (ii), points a and b, but rather as approximations and shortcuts relative to such ideal representations. As a consequence, we cannot expect that the VR and CC systems used in practice will possess the general properties stated in Comment (iii), points a and b; these features should rather be regarded as ideal conditions that are fulfilled more or less approximately. Within the margin of such approximations, specification (49b) is more general than the corresponding specification (34b).

1.4.3. Interdependent (ID) Systems [7]

Formally and conceptually, VR, CC and ID systems mark three levels of increasing generality in the basic assumptions. Terminology and notations for discussion of ID systems carry over from VR and CC systems. Again we shall first consider the special case of exact systems.

A. *Exact ID systems.* When all relations are behavioral the structural form of ID systems may be written as in (21), to repeat

$$Y = \beta Y + \Gamma Z . \tag{52}$$

Here Γ is a position matrix of the same type as in (6) and (16), and β a position matrix with mere zeros in the main diagonal,

$$\beta_{ii} = 0 ; \quad i = 1, ..., n , \tag{53}$$

say with positions (23), and subject to no other conditions than (53) and the requirement that the matrix $[I - \beta]$ should have a well defined inverse $[I - \beta]^{-1}$.

Solving (52) for the current endogenous variables we obtain the ID system in reduced form, which we write as for CC systems (24), to repeat

$$Y = \Omega Z , \tag{54a}$$

where the matrix

$$\Omega = \| \omega_{ik} \| = [I - \beta]^{-1} \Gamma \tag{54b}$$

is well defined, as assumed.

Illustration. Linking up with illustrations (13) and (25) of VR and CC systems, we consider the ID system with structural form

$$y_{1t} = \beta_{12}y_{2t} + \gamma_{11}y_{2,t-1} + \gamma_{12}y_{1,t-2} \,, \tag{55a}$$

$$y_{2t} = \beta_{21}y_{1t} + \gamma_{23}y_{1,t-1} + \gamma_{24}y_{2,t-2} \,. \tag{55b}$$

In vector form (52) the ID system (55) is specified by (9), (12) and

$$\beta = \begin{bmatrix} 0 & \beta_{12} \\ \beta_{21} & 0 \end{bmatrix}. \tag{56}$$

This matrix has two positions, namely

$$i = 1 \,; \quad k = q_1(1) = 2 \,, \tag{57a}$$

$$i = 2 \,; \quad k = q_2(1) = 1 \,. \tag{57b}$$

Writing Δ for the determinant of $[I - \beta]$, the condition that the inverse $[I - \beta]^{-1}$ shall exist gives

$$\Delta = 1 - \beta_{12}\beta_{21} \neq 0 \,. \tag{58}$$

The reduced form of system (55) is

$$y_{1t} = \frac{1}{\Delta} (\gamma_{11}y_{2,t-1} + \gamma_{12}y_{1,t-2} + \beta_{12}\gamma_{23}y_{1,t-1}$$

$$+ \beta_{12}\gamma_{24}y_{2,t-2}) \,, \tag{59a}$$

$$y_{2t} = \frac{1}{\Delta} (\beta_{21}\gamma_{11}y_{2,t-1} + \beta_{21}\gamma_{12}y_{1,t-2} + \gamma_{23}y_{1,t-1}$$

$$+ \gamma_{24}y_{2,t-2}) \,, \tag{59b}$$

$$\omega_{11} = \frac{\gamma_{11}}{\Delta} \; ; \qquad \omega_{12} = \frac{\gamma_{12}}{\Delta} \; ;$$

$$\omega_{13} = \frac{\beta_{12}\gamma_{23}}{\Delta} \; ; \qquad \omega_{14} = \frac{\beta_{12}\gamma_{24}}{\Delta} \; ;$$
(60a)

$$\omega_{21} = \frac{\beta_{21}\gamma_{11}}{\Delta} \; ; \qquad \omega_{22} = \frac{\beta_{21}\gamma_{12}}{\Delta} \; ;$$

$$\omega_{23} = \frac{\gamma_{23}}{\Delta} \; ; \qquad \omega_{24} = \frac{\gamma_{24}}{\Delta} \; ;$$
(60b)

Proceeding to the operative use of exact ID systems, the situation is much the same as in CC systems. The main difference is that the passage from structural form (52) to reduced form (54) cannot be performed by iterative substitutions, but this does not matter until we come to systems specified in terms of predictors and genuine scatter.

Intended use O_1: Exact ID systems allow direct prediction on the basis of any relation of the structural form (52); that is, with the structural relation used autonomously.

With reference to the discourse on the procedure O_1' in exact CC systems, more specifically, the exceptional case when the first structural equation is used pairwise in combination with another structural relation, it will be noted that this exceptional case does not carry over to exact ID systems, inasmuch as matrix β is no longer subdiagonal.

An example: Considering the exact ID system (55) with general notation (12) for the predetermined variables, we assume that for some specified time t we know the endogenous variable y_2 and the predetermined variables z_1, z_2. The structural form (55) is intended to predict y_{1t}, giving

$$\operatorname{pred} y_{1t} = \beta_{12} y_{2t} + \gamma_{11} z_{1t} + \gamma_{12} z_{2t}$$
(61)

and similarly for y_{2t}.

Intended use O_2: In applying the chain principle to exact ID systems the situation is essentially the same as in exact CC systems. The main difference is that in forecasting the endogenous variables y_i for the periods $t, t+1, \ldots$ we must now start in the reduced form, not in the structural form, since the operation that leads from the structural form to the reduced form is no longer a chain of substitutions.

An example: Again we write $\eta_{it}^*, \eta_{i,t+1}^*, \ldots$ for the forecasts based on the predetermined variables z_j up to time t, and again the calculations proceed as in CC systems; see (29a–b). The initial forecasts η_{it}^* are given by the reduced form (52) as it stands, giving for y_{1t}

$$\text{pred } y_{1t} = \eta_{1t}^* = \omega_{11} z_{1t} + \omega_{12} z_{2t} + \omega_{13} z_{3t} + \omega_{14} z_{4t} \quad (62)$$

and similarly for pred y_{2t}. The forecasts $\eta_{i,t+1}^*, \eta_{i,t+2}^*, \ldots$ are obtained by iterative substitutions. This gives

$$\eta_{1,t+1}^* = \frac{1}{\Delta} (\gamma_{11} \eta_{2t}^* + \gamma_{12} y_{1,t-1} + \beta_{12} \gamma_{23} \eta_{1t}^*$$

$$+ \beta_{12} \gamma_{24} y_{2,t-1}) \quad (63)$$

and similarly for $\eta_{2,t+1}^*$. As in (29b) we can express the right-hand member of (63) in terms of predetermined variables z_k up to time $t-1$.

B. *Stochastic ID systems.* With regard to the parting of the ways between apparent and genuine scatter the considerations carry over from CC systems. Again the prediction formulas for exact models remain valid, conceptually, in the approach of *apparent scatter.* And again the approach of apparent scatter is unrealistic in econometric model building.

Turning to the approach of *genuine scatter* as applied to ID systems, we shall as before limit the treatment to models where all relations of the structural form are behavioral. Then in accordance with the corresponding case of exact ID systems (52), the stochastic ID system in structural form is

$$Y = \beta Y + \Gamma Z + \delta \quad (64)$$

and in reduced form

$$Y = \Omega Z + \epsilon \quad (65)$$

with

$$\Omega = [I - \beta]^{-1}\Gamma ; \quad \epsilon = [I - \beta]^{-1}\delta , \qquad (66a-b)$$

which are the same formulas as in (35), subject to the shift from (22) to (53) in the definition of matrix β.

As applied to ID systems, the operative procedures O_1 and O_2 again require a predictor specification both of the structural form (64) and the reduced form (65). We are now coming to the crucial parting of the ways relative to CC systems, inasmuch as ID systems in general do not allow us to cast both forms (64) and (65) in a predictor specification. [8] In the theory and application of ID systems the emphasis is on the reduced form rather than the structural form, or, to put it otherwise, on the operative procedure O_2 rather than O_1. Accordingly, leaving the structural form to the side for the moment, we specify the reduced form (65) in terms of predictors; that is,

$$E(y_{it} | z_{1t}, ..., z_{mt}) = \left[[I - \beta]^{-1}\Gamma Z_t\right]_i = \qquad (67a)$$

$$= [\Omega Z_t]_i \qquad (67b)$$

or briefly

$$E(Y|Z) = [I - \beta]^{-1}\Gamma Z = \qquad (68a)$$

$$= \Omega Z . \qquad (68b)$$

The specification (64)–(68) is in line with the current literature on ID systems; hence such systems will be referred to as "*Classic* ID systems", or sometimes for brevity "CLID systems". The classic specification (67) allows us to carry over procedure O_2 from exact ID systems. Procedure O_1, however, does not carry over, inasmuch as the predictor specification (67) of the reduced form in general cannot be combined with a predictor specification of type (33b) for the structural form (64).

Illustration: We consider the stochastic version of the exact ID system (55). Subject to general specification (12) of the predetermined variables, this is known as Summers' model; see 1.2.1. The structural form is

$$y_{1t} = \beta_{12}y_{2t} + \gamma_{11}y_{2,t-1} + \gamma_{12}y_{1,t-2} + \delta_{1t} \,, \tag{69a}$$

$$y_{2t} = \beta_{21}y_{1t} + \gamma_{23}y_{1,t-1} + \gamma_{24}y_{2,t-2} + \delta_{2t} \tag{69b}$$

and the reduced form

$$y_{1t} = \omega_{11}y_{2,t-1} + \omega_{12}y_{1,t-2} + \omega_{13}y_{1,t-1}$$
$$+ \,\omega_{14}y_{2,t-2} + \epsilon_{1t} \,, \tag{70a}$$

$$y_{2t} = \omega_{21}y_{2,t-1} + \omega_{22}y_{1,t-2} + \omega_{23}y_{1,t-1}$$
$$+ \,\omega_{24}y_{2,t-2} + \epsilon_{2t} \,, \tag{70b}$$

where

$$\epsilon_{1t} = \frac{1}{\Delta} \left(\delta_{1t} + \beta_{12}\delta_{2t} \right), \tag{71a}$$

$$\epsilon_{2t} = \frac{1}{\Delta} \left(\delta_{2t} + \beta_{21}\delta_{1t} \right), \tag{71b}$$

and the coefficients ω_{ik} again are given by (60). The predictor specification (67) for the reduced form gives

$$E(y_{1t}|y_{1,t-1}, y_{2,t-1}, y_{1,t-2}, y_{2,t-2})$$
$$= \omega_{11}y_{2,t-1} + \omega_{12}y_{1,t-2} + \omega_{13}y_{1,t-1} + \omega_{14}y_{2,t-2} \tag{72}$$

and similarly for y_{2t}. The structural form (69a) does not allow predictor specification of type (38) for general values of variables y_i, z_k and coefficients β, Γ; that is,

$$E(y_{1t}|y_{2t}, z_{1t}, z_{2t}) \neq \beta_{12}y_{2t} + \gamma_{11}z_{1t} + \gamma_{12}z_{2t} \tag{73}$$

and similarly for $E(y_{2t}|y_{1t}, z_{3t}, z_{4t})$.

With reference to the two modes I–II for predictive specification of CC systems in reduced form (33b) and (34b), respectively, we see that specification (67) is of type II. This marks a difference relative to CC systems, for the operative use of the reduced form of CC systems is based on the predictor specification (34b), which is of type I. The difference arises because ID systems in structural form (64) in general do not allow a predictor specification that can be taken as a basis for the parameter estimation needed to give the reduced form (65) a predictor specification of type I or II. At the same time (67b) marks a parting of the ways in the design of ID systems, for we shall later come to a predictor specification of type I of the reduced form (65).

As to notations it is seen from the left-hand member of (67a) that matrix Ω in (67)–(68) corresponds to matrix Π in the predictor specification (47a–b) for CC systems in reduced form. In the reduced forms of CC and Classic ID systems it is the specification (34b) and (67b) that are in operative use, and it is to mark the operative aspect that we have used the same matrix symbol Ω in both of these forms.

To conclude: The intended use O_2 of ID systems (64), prediction by the chain principle on the basis of the reduced form, carries over from exact to stochastic ID systems by way of predictions in terms of the conditional expectations (67b), but the intended use O_1 does not carry over.

The subsequent illustrations will be based on system (69)–(70), simplified by writing z_{kt} for the predetermined variables, and often dropping the subscripts "t". As an example, the exact prediction formulas (62) and (63) carry over to the stochastic ID system (69a–b) in the sense of expectational predictions. To specify,

$$\text{pred } y_{it} = E(y_{it} \mid z_{1t}, z_{2t}, z_{3t}, z_{4t})$$

$$= \omega_{i1} z_{1t} + \omega_{i2} z_{2t} + \omega_{i3} z_{3t} + \omega_{i4} z_{4t} \qquad (74)$$

with $i = 1$ or 2. Similarly, assuming that intervening residuals and variables in consecutive time points are independent, the predictions $\eta^*_{i, t+1}$, $\eta^*_{i, t+2}$, ... calculated by the chain principle carry over.

Comment. The rejection of procedure O_1 marks a weak point in the Classic ID approach. The structural form contains the behavioral relations of the model, and therefore it is awkward if these relations cannot be used autonomously for predictive purposes. [9] Procedure O_1 can be rescued by adopting the approach of apparent scatter, but this again is awkward inasmuch as the assumption of apparent scatter is not realistic in econometric model building. In the mainstream of the literature on ID systems this dilemma is blurred, the typical approach being first to deal with exact systems and then proceed to stochastic systems specified in terms of "errors in equations", which is an approach in the nature of apparent scatter rather than genuine scatter.

At bottom, the crucial feature is that the passage from structural form to reduced form (the solving of the system for the current endogenous variables) is a procedure that is trivial in exact systems, but does not carry over to ID systems if we want to specify both the structural and the reduced form in terms of predictors.

A way out of the dilemma is offered by the approach that is in focus in this monograph. The approach involves a reformulation of the structural form, the salient point being that the current endogenous variables y_{qt} that occur in the right-hand members are replaced by their systematic parts, say η_{qt}^*, as given by the structural and/or reduced form. The ensuing model is called a *reformulated interdependent* (REID) *system.* [10] The reformulation makes no changes in the positions $q_i(\ .\ )$, $p_i(\ .\ )$ of the matrices β, Γ, nor in the numerical values of their elements β_{iq}, γ_{ip}. We note that the reformulation, conceptually, is in line with the two-stage least squares (TSLS) method for the estimation of classic ID systems as introduced by H.Theil (1958).

REID systems open up a possibility to work with a less stringent predictor specification than (67), and thereby with fewer assumptions of zero intercorrelation between residuals and explanatory variables. The ensuing extension is called *general interdependent* (GEID) *systems.* Speaking broadly, the generalisation from REID to GEID systems will affect the numerical values of the positional elements β_{iq}, γ_{ip} of matrices β, Γ. The transition from REID to GEID systems is similar to the dualism between modes II and I for the predictor specification of CC systems in reduced form, (49b) and (34b), respectively.

The following exposition of REID and GEID systems is on the brief side, since the arguments in essence are the same as in our treatment of CC systems.

We can begin directly with stochastic REID and GEID systems, for in the case of exact systems both coincide with ordinary ID systems (52). And both are specified in terms of genuine scatter, not apparent scatter.

1.4.4. Reformulated Interdependent (REID) Systems [11]

By definition, REID systems are stochastic, and are specified in terms of genuine scatter. Hence there are no residual-free REID systems; or, to put it otherwise, exact REID systems coincide with exact ID systems.

As before, limiting ourselves to Classic ID systems (64) where all relations are behavioral, and letting H^* denote the column vector with components $\eta_1^*, ..., \eta_n^*$, the corresponding REID system in structural form is

$$Y = \beta H^* + \Gamma Z + \epsilon , \tag{75}$$

and in reduced form

$$Y = [I - \beta]^{-1} \Gamma Z + \epsilon \tag{76a}$$

$$= \Omega Z + \epsilon , \tag{76b}$$

with predictor specifications for both forms, namely for the structural form

$$H^* = E(Y | H^*, Z) = \beta H^* + \Gamma Z , \tag{77a-b}$$

and for the reduced form

$$H^* = E(Y | Z) = \left[[I - \beta]^{-1} \Gamma Z\right]_i , \quad i = 1, ..., n , \tag{78a}$$

$$= \Omega Z , \tag{78b}$$

where the expectational relation (77b) is to be interpreted and spelled out in the same way as in (33b), and the expectations (78a–b) are of the same type as in (34b), for each $i = 1, ..., n$ involving a joint specification of all predetermined variables $z_{1t}, ..., z_{mt}$.

Comments. (i) Conceptually, the variables η_i^* are first defined by (78b). Using the matrix relation (66a) we see that (78b) implies

$$H^* = \beta H^* + \Gamma Z \tag{79}$$

which in conjunction with (76b) gives (78a). Since

$$E(y_i | \eta_i^*) = \eta_i^* = [\beta H^* + \Gamma Z]_i \; ; \quad i = 1, ..., n \; , \tag{80}$$

we infer that the relation (78a) implies (77b).

   (ii) It is a key feature of REID and GEID systems that the residuals are the same in the structural form and the reduced form. In fact, re-writing (75) in the classic form (64) the ensuing residuals δ will be given by

$$\delta = \epsilon - \beta(Y - H^*) = [I - \beta]\epsilon \; . \tag{81}$$

Hence if we cast the classic system in reduced form, the residuals will transform into

$$(I - \beta)^{-1}\delta = \epsilon \tag{82}$$

in accordance with (66b).

   Illustration. Considering the Classic ID system (69), with general nota-tion (12) for the predetermined variables, the corresponding REID sys-tem has the structural form

$$y_{1t} = \beta_{12}\eta_{2t}^* + \gamma_{11}z_{1t} + \gamma_{12}z_{2t} + \epsilon_{1t} \; , \tag{83a}$$

$$y_{2t} = \beta_{21}\eta_{1t}^* + \gamma_{23}z_{3t} + \gamma_{24}z_{4t} + \epsilon_{2t} \; , \tag{83b}$$

where

$$\eta_{1t}^* = E(y_{1t} | z_{1t}, z_{2t}, z_{3t}, z_{4t}) \tag{84a}$$

$$= \omega_{11}z_{1t} + \omega_{12}z_{2t} + \omega_{3t}z_{3t} + \omega_{4t}z_{4t} \; , \tag{84b}$$

and similarly for η_{2t}^*. The REID system (83) has the same reduced form (70) as the Classic ID system (69), and the residuals are the same in the structural form (83) as in the reduced form (70).

   The REID system in structural form (83) is subject to the predictor specification

$$E(y_{1t} \mid \eta_{2t}^*, z_{1t}, z_{2t}) = \beta_{12}\eta_{2t}^* + \gamma_{11}z_{1t} + \gamma_{12}z_{2t} \qquad (85)$$

and similarly for y_{2t}. The reduced form of the REID system has the same predictor specification (72) as the corresponding Classic ID system.

We shall write O_1^* for the intended use O_1 of the structural form of an ID system when O_1 is qualified in accordance with (77). To spell out in detail:

Intended use O_1^* of REID systems: direct prediction on the basis of any relation of the structural form (75), carries over from exact ID systems (52). In this procedure the following two features are the same as in CC systems (33) specified in terms of genuine scatter:

(1) The structural relations are used autonomously.

(2) In the cause-effect specification of a behavioral relation the effect variable is a current endogenous variable y_{it}, and a number of predetermined variables z_{pt} enter as causal variables.

In the cause-effect specification of a behavioral relation there is the following difference relative to CC systems:

(3) The expected values η_{qt}^* of a number of current endogenous variables may enter as causal variables, not their observed values y_{qt}.

An example: Assuming that we know the predetermined variables z_1, z_2 and the expected value η_2^* of the endogenous variable y_2 for some specified time t, relation (83a) is intended to predict y_{1t}, giving

$$\mathrm{pred}\, y_{1t} = \beta_{12}\eta_{2t}^* + \gamma_{11}z_{1t} + \gamma_{12}z_{2t} . \qquad (86)$$

For the prediction of y_{2t} the situation is analogous, the prediction being given by (42b), except that in the right-hand member we must substitute the known value of η_{1t}^* for y_{1t}.

The intended use O_2 of REID systems, prediction by the chain principle on the basis of the reduced form, carries over from exact ID systems (52) and is formally the same procedure as for stochastic ID systems (64). With reference to modes I–II of predictive specification, there is the following difference relative to CC systems: the specification of the reduced form is of type I for CC systems (34b) and of type II for REID systems (78).

For illustration it will suffice to refer to formula (74), which carries over from the corresponding Classic ID system, as do — under the appropriate assumptions of interdependence between consecutive observations — the predictions $\eta_{i,t+1}^*, \eta_{i,t+2}^*, \ldots$ calculated iteratively by the chain principle.

For a graphic illustration of the scope of procedures O_1^* and O_2, reference is made to Chart 1, third column. In stochastic ID systems there is no room for procedure O_1, unbiased prediction based on the structural relations in classic form (64). It is replaced by procedure O_1^*, unbiased prediction based on the structural relations in REID form (75). The situation is much the same as for exact ID systems (Chart 1a, first column). The autonomous use of O_1^* makes this procedure of more general scope than procedure O_2. As compared with stochastic CC systems (Chart 1a, second column) there is the difference that procedure O_2 does not bring us outside the scope of procedure O_1^*, for both are based on the information embodied in the set of predetermined variables z_k; indeed, each variable η_i^* is a linear function of the variables z_k.

To repeat an earlier comment, matrix Ω in (67a—b) corresponds to matrix Π of stochastic CC systems when their reduced form is specified by (47b). Hence for REID systems procedure O_π is the same as O_2, and the situation is as shown in Chart 1b, third column, whereas the situation in the second column of Chart 1c has no parallel at the same level of the third column.

1.4.5. General Interdependent (GEID) Systems [11]

GEID systems are formally the same as REID systems (75), the difference lying in the predictor specification of the reduced form. With reference to the procedures O_2, O_π for the operative use of CC systems in reduced form, formulas (34b) and (49b) respectively, the substitutive procedure O_π has no counterpart in Classic ID systems and REID systems. By (67b) and (78b), Classic ID systems and REID systems are specified so as to imply (34b). As a basis for procedure O_2 in Classic ID systems, the left-hand specification (34b) is more restrictive than necessary. The ensuing possibility of generalisation in the left-hand members of the predictor specification is exploited by GEID systems.

As stated, REID systems (75) and the corresponding GEID systems are formally the same in structural form, namely

$$Y = \beta H^* + \Gamma Z + \epsilon , \tag{87a}$$

$$E(Y|H^*, Z) = \beta H^* + \Gamma Z . \tag{87b}$$

This GEID system in reduced form reads

$$Y = [I - \beta]^{-1}\Gamma Z + \epsilon \tag{88a}$$

$$= \Omega Z + \epsilon , \tag{88b}$$

subject to the predictor specification

$$E(Y|[[I - \beta]^{-1}\Gamma Z]_i) = E(Y|[\Omega Z]_i) = \tag{89a}$$

$$= [[I - \beta]^{-1}\Gamma Z]_i = [\Omega Z]_i ; \quad i = 1, ..., n . \tag{89b}$$

Whereas (88) and the two versions of the right-hand member of (89) are formally the same as in the reduced form (76), (78a–b) of REID systems, the left-hand member in (89a) involves a generalization relative to (78). The salient point is that specification (78) allows us to estimate the coefficients ω_{ik} by OLS as applied to each relation of the reduced form separately, whereas (88)–(89) are primarily concerned with the parameters β_{iq}, γ_{ip} of the structural form. Inasmuch as the parameters β_{iq}, γ_{ip} are fewer in number than the coefficients ω_{ik} the GEID approach will be less restrictive than the REID specification (78).

Illustration. The REID system (83) carries over as illustration of GEID systems, with no other change than in the left-hand member of the predictor specification of the reduced form, the corresponding specification of the GEID system being

$$\eta_{1t}^* = E(y_{1t}|[[I - \beta]^{-1}\Gamma Z_t]_1) \tag{90a}$$

$$= \omega_{11}z_{1t} + \omega_{12}z_{2t} + \omega_{13}z_{3t} + \omega_{14}z_{4t} \tag{90b}$$

and similarly for y_{2t}.

The intended uses O_1^* and O_2 of GEID systems carry over from REID systems, with no other formal or conceptual change than the shift from (78) to (89) on the left-hand side in the predictor that constitutes the systematic part of the reduced form. Again with reference to the two modes I–II of predictive specification, the shift in the reduced form is from specification mode II to specification mode I.

An example: For given z_1, z_2, z_3, z_4 the reduced form of GEID system (87) gives predictions for y_1 and y_2 which are given by the same formula (74) as for Classic ID systems and REID systems. Spelling out for REID systems, the predictor again takes the form

$$\text{pred}\, y_{it} = \eta_{it}^* = \text{E}(y_{it}\,|z_{1t}, z_{2t}, z_{3t}, z_{4t}) \tag{91a}$$

$$= \omega_{i1}z_{1t} + \omega_{i2}z_{2t} + \omega_{i3}z_{3t} + \omega_{i4}z_{4t} \tag{91b}$$

whereas the corresponding formula for GEID systems is

$$\text{pred}\, y_{it} = \eta_{it}^* = \text{E}(y_{it}\,|\,[[I - \beta]^{-1}\Gamma Z_t]_i) \tag{92a}$$

$$= \omega_{i1}z_{1t} + \omega_{i2}z_{2t} + \omega_{i3}z_{3t} + \omega_{i4}z_{4t} \tag{92b}$$

with $i = 1, 2$ all through.

Comments. (i) The generalisation of Classic ID systems through REID to GEID systems brings changes on several scores, and in particular so with regard to the causal aspects and estimation problems.

According to the theory of OLS estimation, the Classic ID systems and REID specification (74) of the structural form implies that each residual δ_i or ϵ_i ($i = 1, ..., n$) will be uncorrelated with all of the predetermined variables z_k ($k = 1, ..., m$). This makes just as many zero intercorrelations as there are coefficients ω_{ik} in the reduced form. In overidentified systems, however, and this is by far the majority of cases, there are more coefficients ω_{ik} than parameters β_{iq}, γ_{ip}. Hence Classic ID and REID systems are in the awkward situation that the parameters β_{iq}, γ_{ip} at disposal are less in number than the zero intercorrelation conditions which are to be fulfilled in the system.

On the other hand, the specification (87b) of GEID systems implies that each residual ϵ_i will be uncorrelated with those variables η_{iq}^*, z_{ip} that occur in the right-hand member of the ith relation. Hence the parameters β_{iq}, γ_{ip} at disposal are just as numerous as the zero intercorrelations assumed in the model. In this respect GEID systems are similar to the ordinary type of unirelational regression models.

(ii) Chart 1, 4th column illustrates the situation from the point of view of the shift from mode II to mode I in the predictive specification of the reduced forms (78b) and (89a–b), and at the same time with regard to the structure of matrix Ω. In REID systems the matrix Ω is in the nature of the matrix Π in the specification (47a–b), but in GEID systems Ω is in the nature of the specification (34b) that is the basis of the operative use O_2 of CC systems in reduced form. Hence in Chart 1 the situation for GEID system is analogous to REID systems at level (b), and analogous to CC systems (apart from the shift from O_1 to O_1^*) at level (c).

(iii) If for each observed y_{it} the corresponding expectation η_{it}^* were known, the specifications (77b) and (87b) would imply that the parameters β_{iq}, γ_{ip} of REID and GEID systems could be consistently estimated by applying OLS to the individual relations of the structural form. There is the snag however that η_{it}^* is to be assessed as part of the estimation procedure. Under the REID specification, the TSLS estimation procedure of H.Theil (1958) gives consistent estimates. The GEID specification however does not meet the assumptions of the TSLS method, and, therefore, this method in general cannot be expected to provide consistent estimates when applied to GEID models. The fix-point (FP) estimation method (Wold [15–16]) provides consistent estimates of REID systems, and, under fairly general conditions, of GEID systems; see Chapters 3.1 and 3.6.

Illustration. Again with reference to our various versions of Summers' model (69a–b), we see that there are six parameters β_{iq}, γ_{ip}, whereas each of the Classic ID and REID specifications (67) and (78a) implies eight assumptions of zero intercorrelations between residuals (δ_{it} or ϵ_{it}) and predetermined variables z_{kt}. The available parameters thus in general will not suffice to construct the model in accordance with its basic assumptions, an awkward situation for the model builder.

In the corresponding GEID system there are the same six parameters, whereas the specification (87b) only implies six zero intercorrelations between residuals ϵ_i and right-hand variables η_{qt}^* and z_{pt}. The parity between the number of parameters and zero intercorrelations has been bought at a price, however. The estimation problem has become nonlinear, inasmuch as it involves the simultaneous estimation of the expectations η_{qt}^* and their coefficients β_{iq}. As we shall see in later chapters, this may make the estimation quite complicated even in systems as simple as Summers' model.

(iv) The GEID specification sheds light on an important feature of CC systems, namely that their residuals in the structural form (δ_i) in general have smaller variance than the reduced form residuals (ϵ_i). The GEID specification (87)–(89) can be applied to a CC system (33a); this involves a loss of information inasmuch as the observed variables y_i in the right-hand member of (33a) are replaced by their expected values η_i^*; the loss of information makes the residuals of the structural form larger, and at the same time the parameters β, Γ will change; in the resulting GEID version of the CC system the structural and reduced forms will have the same residuals ϵ_i.

1.4.6. Graphic Illustration of the REID-GEID Version of Summers' Model [12]

The transition from Classic ID to REID and GEID systems brings in relief the nonlinear aspects of interdependent systems. Being of key relevance for an understanding of the models, we shall now subject the nonlinear features to a graphic illustration, with special regard to GEID systems. The situation is rather complex even in simple models, and we shall therefore limit the exposition to Summers' two-relation model. Reference is made to Summers' model in classic form (69), in REID form (75) and in GEID form (87).

We shall consider Summers' model in two versions:

Chart 2: This is the REID case when $\gamma_{12} = \gamma_{24} = 0$. In this case the system is "just identified" in the sense of the classic theory of ID systems.

Chart 3: The general GEID case of arbitrary γ-parameters. This is the case of "overidentified" systems in the classic theory.

Chart 2 refers to the REID system with structural form

$$y_1 = \beta_{12}\eta_2^* + \gamma_{11}z_1 + \epsilon_1 , \qquad (93a)$$

$$y_2 = \beta_{21}\eta_1^* + \gamma_{23}z_3 + \epsilon_2 , \qquad (93b)$$

which has two relations and is just identified. With O as origin, the coordinate axes z_1, z_3 are drawn in the plane P of the paper. The axes y_1, y_2 are in two other dimensions; hence the graph is four-dimensional. All four variables y_1, y_2, z_1, z_3 are normalized so as to have zero mean and unit standard deviation. Hence the vectors Oy_1, Oy_2, Oz_1, Oz_3 are taken to be of unit length. Since Oz_1 and Oz_3 are in the plane of the paper, it follows that the lengths of these two vectors are in true proportions in the graph, whereas the lengths of Oy_1 and Oy_2 are distorted by the perspective.

The reduced form of system (93a–b) is

$$y_1 = \omega_{11}z_1 + \omega_{13}z_3 + \epsilon_1 , \qquad (94a)$$

$$y_2 = \omega_{21}z_1 + \omega_{23}z_3 + \epsilon_2 . \qquad (94b)$$

We note the fundamental formulas

$$y_1 = \eta_1^* + \epsilon_1 , \qquad (95a)$$

$$y_2 = \eta_2^* + \epsilon_2 , \qquad (95b)$$

$$\eta_1^* = \beta_{12}\eta_2^* + \gamma_{11}z_3 , \qquad (96a)$$

$$\eta_2^* = \beta_{21}\eta_1^* + \gamma_{22}z_3 . \qquad (96b)$$

The relations (93)–(96) allow simple graphic interpretation. The following comments serve to elucidate the situation portrayed in Chart 2.

(i) The full-drawn lines refer to observed variables: y_1, y_2, z_1, z_3. The broken lines refer to constructed variables: $\eta_1^*, \eta_2^*, \epsilon_1, \epsilon_2$.

(ii) The variables η_1^*, η_2^* are linear combinations of z_1, z_3 and thus lie in the plane P of the paper.

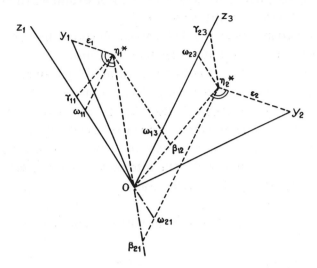

Chart 1.4.2. Graphic illustration of the REID specification for a just identified two-equation interdependent model.

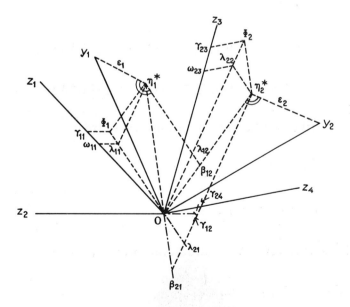

Chart 1.4.3. Graphic illustration of the GEID specification for an overidentified two-equation interdependent model.

(iii) The graph marks 90° angles by $\sphericalangle$. For example, the vector $\epsilon_1 = y_1 - \eta_1^*$ is orthogonal to the vector $O\eta_1^*$.

(iv) In accordance with (ii)–(iii) the graph shows that η_1^* and η_2^* in general have standard deviations smaller than unit.

(v) The two relations (96a–b) are illustrated by broken lines that emerge from η_1^* and η_2^* respectively. The parameters β, γ come out as line segments from the origin O, along the corresponding coordinate axes. We see that all parameters are positive, except β_{21}.

(vi) Similarly, each of the two relations (94a–b) is illustrated (a) by another broken line, and (b) by the intersection between a broken line and the corresponding non-parallel z-axis.

Chart 3 refers to the GEID system with structural form

$$y_1 = \beta_{12}\eta_2^* + \gamma_{11}z_1 + \gamma_{12}z_2 + \epsilon_1 , \tag{97a}$$

$$y_2 = \beta_{21}\eta_1^* + \gamma_{23}z_3 + \gamma_{24}z_4 + \epsilon_2 , \tag{97b}$$

and in reduced form

$$y_1 = \omega_{11}z_1 + \omega_{12}z_2 + \omega_{13}z_3 + \omega_{14}z_4 + \epsilon_1 , \tag{98a}$$

$$y_2 = \omega_{21}z_1 + \omega_{22}z_2 + \omega_{23}z_3 + \omega_{24}z_4 + \epsilon_2 . \tag{98b}$$

Following Lyttkens' system of notations, we write

$$\Phi_1 = \gamma_{11}z_1 + \gamma_{12}z_2 , \tag{99a}$$

$$\Phi_2 = \gamma_{23}z_3 + \gamma_{24}z_4 , \tag{99b}$$

which allows us to rewrite the structural form as follows,

$$y_1 = \beta_{12}\eta_2^* + \Phi_1 + \epsilon_1 , \tag{100a}$$

$$y_2 = \beta_{21}\eta_1^* + \Phi_2 + \epsilon_2 , \tag{100b}$$

and the reduced form as follows,

$$y_1 = \lambda_{11}\Phi_1 + \lambda_{12}\Phi_2 + \epsilon_1 , \tag{101a}$$

$$y_2 = \lambda_{21}\Phi_1 + \lambda_{22}\Phi_2 + \epsilon_2 . \tag{101b}$$

Chart 3 is drawn so as to have Φ_1 and Φ_2 in the plane P of the paper. In general none of the variables y_i, z_k will be in the plane P. Hence the graph involves a total of 8 dimensions. The following comments elucidate the illustration in Chart 3.

(i) The variables Φ_1, Φ_2 are constructed, and therefore drawn as broken lines. In general they are not of unit length.

In several respect, as noted in the following points (ii)–(v), Φ_1 and Φ_2 in Chart 3 correspond to z_1 and z_3 in Chart 2.

(ii) For one thing, η_1^* and η_2^* are linear in Φ_1 and Φ_2 and therefore lie in the plane P of the paper.

(iii) As in Chart 2, the residual vectors ϵ_1, ϵ_2 make 90° angles with the plane P.

(iv) The coefficients $\lambda_{11}, \lambda_{12}, \lambda_{21}, \lambda_{22}$ in Chart 3 correspond to the coefficients $\omega_{11}, \omega_{13}, \omega_{21}, \omega_{23}$ in Chart 2.

(v) The interpretation of β_{12}, β_{21} is the same in the two graphs.

(vi) Turning to the differences between the two graphs, let P_{12} denote the plane spanned by the two vectors Oz_1 and Oz_2 in Chart 3. Knowing from (99a–b) that Φ_1 is linear in z_1 and z_2, the vector $O\Phi_1$ lies in P_{12}, and makes the intersection between P_{12} and the plane P of the paper. This gives a graphic interpretation of λ_{11} and λ_{12}. Note that the lines that measure γ_{12} and γ_{12} do not lie in P; hence the magnitudes of γ_{11} and γ_{12} as given by the graph in general will be distorted by the perspective. Similarly, Φ_2 is linear in z_3 and z_4, which gives a graphic interpretation of λ_{23} and λ_{24}. As to the lines that mark the intersects γ_{12} and γ_{24}, the first is shown in the graph, but not the second, to avoid overburdening the graph.

If we draw a vector $O\epsilon_1$ from the origin O parallel to the residual vector ϵ_1, we may note in Chart 3 that the vector $O\epsilon_1$ is orthogonal to the vectors Oz_1, Oz_2. Furthermore, the vector $O\epsilon_1$ is orthogonal to the vectors $O\Phi_1$ and $O\Phi_2$. The situation is similar for ϵ_2.

Making use of the relations

$$\omega_{11} = \lambda_{11}\gamma_{11} \; ; \quad \omega_{21} = \lambda_{21}\gamma_{11} \, ,$$

$$\omega_{12} = \lambda_{11}\gamma_{12} \; ; \quad \omega_{22} = \lambda_{21}\gamma_{12} \, ,$$

$$\omega_{13} = \lambda_{12}\gamma_{23} \; ; \quad \omega_{23} = \lambda_{22}\gamma_{23} \, ,$$

$$\omega_{14} = \lambda_{12}\gamma_{24} \; ; \quad \omega_{24} = \lambda_{22}\gamma_{24} \, ,$$

$$(102)$$

which are implied by (98) and (101), Chart 3 provides a graphic inter-pretation of the coefficients ω_{ik} of the reduced form (98). In order not to overburden the graph, Chart 3 gives only the illustration of ω_{11} and ω_{23}.

Let us now compare the models (93) and (97) in the light of the graphs. The emphasis is on the orthogonality properties of the residuals, "orthogonality" being the geometric equivalence to "zero intercorrela-tion". In (93) and (97) the models are written in GEID (or REID) form, with residuals denoted by ϵ_1, ϵ_2. We shall also consider the same models as written in the classic form (69), with residuals denoted by δ_1, δ_2.

In Chart 2 the model is just identified. Hence the REID and GEID specifications coincide. Each residual ϵ_1, ϵ_2 is orthogonal to (uncorre-lated with) both z_1 and z_3. The classic residuals δ_1, δ_2 are linear expres-sions in ϵ_1, ϵ_2 and will therefore likewise be orthogonal to z_1 and z_3.

In Chart 3 the model is overidentified. Each ϵ_1, ϵ_2 (and therefore also each of the classic residuals δ_1, δ_2) will be orthogonal to both Φ_1 and Φ_2. Note that this property in general does not carry over to systems with three or more relations.

In Classic ID and REID systems each ϵ_1, ϵ_2 (and therefore each of the classic residuals δ_1, δ_2) will be orthogonal to all z_1, z_2, z_3, z_4.

Turning to the GEID specification, each of the classic residuals δ_1, δ_2 in general will be correlated with some or all of z_1, z_2, z_3, z_4. The GEID residual ϵ_1 will be orthogonal to z_1 and z_2 but in general not to z_3 and z_4. The ensuing non-zero correlations $r(\epsilon_i, z_k)$ will be called *GEID cor-relations*. It will be noted that the zero correlation between ϵ_1 and Φ_2 leaves only one degree of freedom for the GEID correlations between the nonzero correlations between ϵ_1 and the two variables z_3 and z_4.

Thus, if the correlation $r(\epsilon_1, z_3)$ is known, $r(\epsilon_1, z_4)$ can be deduced. For ϵ_2 and Φ_1 the situation is the same with regard to the GEID correlations between ϵ_2 and z_1 and z_2.

Let us examine the GEID correlations more closely. The GEID specification determines the coefficients γ_{ip} (apart from multiple solutions) and thereby determines Φ_1 and Φ_2, which fixes the plane P of the paper. The residual vector ϵ_1 is orthogonal to z_1 and z_2, and thereby orthogonal to Φ_1. Further, the vector ϵ_1 is orthogonal to Φ_2. Hence only one degree of freedom is left for the GEID correlations between ϵ_1 and the two variables z_3 and z_4. To put it otherwise, once the plane P of the paper is fixed, the angles between the vector ϵ_1 and the two vectors z_3 and z_4 will be determined. These angles are nothing else than the correlation coefficients between ϵ_1 and each of z_3 and z_4; the two angles (correlation coefficients) are however restricted by the linear relation that expresses that Φ_2 lies in the plane P_{34} spanned by z_3 and z_4.

Again the situation is similar for ϵ_2 and Φ_1.

Comments. (i) The graphic representation in Charts 2–3 has been phrased so as to refer to the populations. It allows immediate extension to the models as estimated from a sample by the FP method, inasmuch as the FP method carries over all relations (93)–(102) to the sample.

(ii) The graphic interpretation readily extends to models with three relations. The Lyttkens vectors Φ_1, Φ_2, Φ_3 will then span an ordinary three-dimensional space, and η_1^*, η_2^*, η_3^* will be vectors in this space.

1.4.7. Causal aspects of multirelational models

Causal analysis is a main purpose of model building, and this is so both for unirelational models and models that take the form of a multirelational system. This is in particular true in econometrics, as is clear from the systematic use of macroeconomic models for purposes of economic policy in terms of instruments and targets. Clearly, instruments and targets are terms with a causal meaning, instrument being a conceptual synonym for causal variable, and target a synonym for intended effect. First and foremost, reference is made to Tinbergen (1956).

The present monograph focusses on the rationale of interdependent systems with regard to probability structure and estimation techniques.

Hence the causal properties of a model are a side issue in the monograph. It will serve our purpose however to give in this introductory section a brief review of the causal aspects of multirelational models. There are several incentives for such a review. Most of these pertain to causal aspects that are of key relevance for considering operative uses of estimated models like those studied in this monograph. Our review will focus on concepts and problem areas that have been subject to persistent and partly confused debate, such as the notion of autonomous relation, the distinction between predictive and causal relations, and the notion of causal reversibility. The review is mainly expository, and draws to a large extent from earlier work of the two authors. [13]

Linking up with the exposition in section 1.3.1, let us consider two variables x, y that are related as follows,

$$y = \alpha + \beta x + \epsilon , \tag{103a}$$

$$E(y \mid x) = \alpha + \beta x . \tag{103b}$$

This is a very simple unirelational model. The model is predictive, in the sense that if x is known, the right-hand member of (103b), called predictor, gives the *expected* value of y.

The predictive relation (103) may or may not be a cause-effect relation, in symbols

$$x \Longrightarrow y , \tag{104}$$

with x as causal variable and y as effect variable. The notion of a cause-effect relationship is here taken in the sense of the following definition.

The definition proceeds in two steps: Cause-effect relations in controlled experiments, and in nonexperimental situations.

As to the experimental category of cause-effect relations (104), the typical case is a stimulus-response experiment designed to assess the relationship between stimulus x and response y. Hence in experimental situations the terms stimulus and response are synonyms for cause and effect. Formula (103) covers the special case when the causal relation is linear. The following notation serves to specify relation (103) as causal,

$$y|_{cp} = \alpha + \beta x + \epsilon \,, \tag{105a}$$

$$E(y|_{cp}x) = \alpha + \beta x \,, \tag{105b}$$

where "cp" refers to the *ceteris paribus* clause of controlled experiments, namely that the experiment is performed under constant conditions except for the controlled variation of the causal variable x.

As to nonexperimental situations, the predictive model (103) may or may not include the hypothesis that *if* x could be directed in the sense of a stimulus-response experiment, *then* y would present a corresponding variation, as specified by (103). If model (103) includes this hypothesis, we shall write it as in (104) and (105), and adopt the same causal terminology, saying that (103) is a *causal* or *cause-effect* relation with x for *causal* variable and y for *effect* variable.

The above definition of cause-effect relations is quite general inasmuch as it covers both experimental and nonexperimental situation. To sum up: Cause-effect relationships are stimulus-response relations in genuine or fictitious experiments.

Clearly, this definition allows immediate extension to the case of nonlinear relations, say

$$y|_{cp} = f(x) + \epsilon \,, \tag{106a}$$

$$E(y|_{cp}x) = f(x) \,, \tag{106b}$$

and to the case when there are several causal variables x and several effect variables, say

$$y_i|_{cp} = f_i(x_1, ..., x_h) + \epsilon_i \,; \quad i = 1, ..., n \,, \tag{107a}$$

$$E(y_i|_{cp}x_1, ..., x_h) = f_i(x_1, ..., x_h) \,. \tag{107b}$$

An exact relationship between two variables, say

$$y = f(x) \,, \text{ in the linear case } y = \alpha + \beta x \,, \tag{108a-b}$$

is formally reversible under general conditions of analytical regularity, giving

$$x = f^{-1}(y) \text{ , in the linear case } x = -\frac{\alpha}{\beta} + \frac{1}{\beta} y \text{ ,} \qquad (109a-b)$$

where $f^{-1}(\, . \,)$ is the inverse of the function $f(\, . \,)$.

An exact causal relationship

$$y|_{cp} = f(x) \qquad (110)$$

with formal inverse (109a) may or may not be causally reversible; that is, we may or may not have

$$x|_{cp} = f^{-1}(y) \text{ .} \qquad (111)$$

To quote a classic example from physics, Boyle-Gay Lussac's law of ideal gases $PV = cT$ makes a causal relationship with V and absolute temperature T for causal variables and pressure P for effect variable, in the notation (110)

$$P|_{cp} = c\,\frac{T}{V} \text{ .} \qquad (112)$$

This relation is causally reversible with respect to pressure P and volume V, giving

$$V|_{cp} = c\,\frac{T}{P} \text{ ,} \qquad (113)$$

but none of (112) or (113) causally reversible with respect to absolute temperature T; that is, the relation

$$T = \frac{1}{c}PV \qquad (114)$$

is predictive but not causal.

Another instructive illustration is given by Carnot's laws for the transformation of energies by a process that involves a circular raise and lowering of absolute temperature T. The *heat machine* transforms heat H into work W, subject to an (ideal) exchange relation which in point of principle is a causal relation, namely

$$W|_{cp} = c_1 H, \quad \text{with } c_1 = \frac{T_1 - T_2}{T_1}. \tag{115}$$

The heat pump is the reverse process that transforms work into heat, subject to the exchange relation

$$H|_{cp} = c_2 W, \quad \text{with } c_2 = \frac{T_2}{T_1 - T_2}. \tag{116}$$

Although Carnot's process itself is reversible, involving an interchange of causes and effects ($H \Rightarrow W; W \Rightarrow H$), and although the ensuing relations (115) and (116) ideally are exact, these relations are not causally reversible, inasmuch as $c_1 \neq 1/c_2$.

The above review may be summed up as follows:

(i) A cause-effect relation (105) is more informative than the corresponding predictive relation (103). The additional information serves as a basis for operative use of the causal relation, namely to direct the causal variable x and thereby bring about desired changes in the effect variable y.

(ii) It may or may not be realistic to specify a predictive relation (103) as causal. The causal specification (105) is hypothetical, and it is a matter for hypothesis testing to explore whether or not the causal specification is realistic, just as for any other hypothesis. Different procedures are available for the testing of causal hypotheses in experimental and non-experimental situations, and there are deepgoing differences between the procedures in these situations.

(iii) In unirelational models (115)–(116) there is no formal difference in the appearance between predictive and causal relations. Hence in such models the testing of a causal hypothesis is entirely a matter of realism in the application at issue.

We are now in a position to examine the causal aspects of VR, CC and ID systems. Our exposition in section 1.3.3 focusses on the predictive specification of these models; we shall now review the possibilities of a causal specification.

The previous comments (i)–(ii) carry over without essential change to multirelational models, but this is not true with respect to (iii). In the following we shall to a large extent be concerned with formal properties of the models that complicate their causal specification.

VR systems (16)

(iv) Such a system is nothing else than a set of unirelational predictive relations. The VR systems are therefore covered by the simple model (103), if we interpret y and x as vector variables, as in (107). Hence the previous comment (iii) carries over without qualification to VR systems.

(v) The notion of autonomous relation carries over from predictive to causal relations. Hence any relation in a VR system that is causal can be applied separately for cause-effect inference.

CC systems (33)

(vi) CC systems are designed for causal specification of the relations in the structural form. This statement is in perfect agreement with the fact that comment (iii) carries over without qualification to CC systems in structural form.

(vii) Remembering that the structural relations of CC systems are autonomous in the predictive sense, any causal relation in the structural form can be applied separately for cause-effect inference.

(viii) Turning to the reduced form, we shall again use the two-relational system (37) for illustration. Since the first equation of a CC system is always the same in both structural and reduced form, it will suffice to consider the second equation.

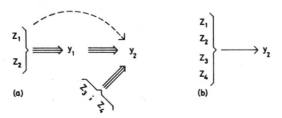

Chart 1.4.4. Interrelations in a CC system: (a) in the structural form;
(b) in the reduced form.

To repeat from (vi) and (vii), the structural relations for y_1 and y_2 are designed for the possibility of being specified not only as predictors but also as cause-effect relationships. Chart 4 illustrates the situation.

The reduced-form relation illustrated in Chart 4b is designed for predictor specification, but not for cause-effect specification, or at least not cause-effect specification in the same direct sense. Let us elaborate this last point.

(ix) In a CC system, the structural relations can be conceived of as referring to a chain of fictitious stimulus-response experiments. In system (37) the first of these experiments has y_1 for effect (response) variable, while the second experiment has y_1, z_3, z_4 for causal (stimulus) variables and y_2 for effect variable. If we try to interpret the reduced form in this way there is the crucial difference that in the second experiment y_1 as causal variable is replaced by z_1 and z_2. Hence the dependence of y_2 upon z_1, z_2 is indirect, passing through the endogenous variable y_1. We can say that the reduced form relation for y_2 is essentially descriptive, non-causal, and is subject to a *ceteris paribus* clause with regard to the behaviour of y_1. To paraphrase, using an attenuated causal terminology, we can say that y_2 is exposed to an *indirect* causal influence from the variables z_1, z_2, and again we have to impose the *ceteris paribus* clause that there must be no structural change in the variability of y_1.

(x) The difference between the direct and indirect causal relations of the structural form and reduced form, respectively, is reflected in the quantitative fact that from the second equation onwards the residuals will have smaller standard deviation in the structural form than in the reduced form.

ID systems

(xi) It is a much debated question which operative use, if any, can be made of the individual relations in the structural form of an ID system. [14] In any case, they are not designed for autonomous prediction, let alone for autonomous cause-effect inference.

In section 1.3.3 we have dismissed the ordinary ID system (64) on the argument that their structural relations cannot be specified as predictive in the sense of conditional expectations. Coming now to the causal aspects of ID systems, we note an analogous and much-discussed feature that is an apparent contradiction to a cause-effect interpretation of the model. This feature occurs already in the simple two-relational exact model (55): How is it that the first structural equation (55a) has y_{2t} for cause and y_{1t} for effect, whereas the second equation has y_{1t} for cause and y_{2t} for effect? In any case, it is clear that this situation cannot be portrayed by a chain of fictitious stimulus-response experiments, as was the case for CC systems in point (ix). To quote a related difficulty: The structural form of an ordinary ID system (52) is not realizable in the sense of computer simulation. [15] For example, the simulation of system (55) would have y_{2t} for input and y_{1t} as output in the first equation, whereas the second equation would have y_{1t} for input and y_{2t} for output, and these requirements are not technically realizable on a computer.

(xii) The reduced form of ID systems is designed for forecasting by the chain principle. [16] The classic theory of ID systems is specified in terms of apparent scatter, and as to causal specification it is customary to say that the current endogenous variables are subject to a joint causal dependence upon the predetermined variables.

In the present monograph we have adopted the approach of genuine scatter. The question about predictive vs causal specification of the reduced form will then be much the same as for CC systems. Again we can say that the reduced form relations are essentially descriptive, non-causal, subject to a *ceteris paribus* clause with regard to the variability of the endogenous variables. And again we can paraphrase in an attenuated causal terminology, saying that the predetermined variables z_k exert an indirect causal influence upon an endogenous variable y_i, namely via the other endogenous variables y_q, and subject to a *ceteris paribus* clause with regard to their variability as specified by the structural relations.

REID and GEID systems

(xiii) Considering the behavioral relation that constitutes the ith relation in the structural form of a REID system (75) or GEID system (87), the difficulty referred to in point (xi) is cut through by the reformulation that replaces the explanatory endogenous variables y_q by their expected values η_q^*. The reformulation makes the structural relations of REID and GEID systems predictive (autonomously predictive). How about a causal specification of these same relations? Keeping in mind that the expected values η_q^* take the form of linear combinations of the predetermined variables, it is safe to say that the structural relations of REID and GEID systems are largely descriptive, in a sense related to the reduced form of CC and CLID systems. And if they are to be specified as cause-effect relations, it is safe to say that this will be in an attenuated sense, related to that of the reduced form relations, and subject to a

corresponding *ceteris paribus* clause, inasmuch as the expectations η_q^*
are linear expressions in the predetermined variables.

The cause-effect interpretation of the structural relations can however
be pushed a bit further. Conceptually, the ith structural relation involves
the observed values of the right-hand endogenous variables y_q as causal
factors. Now if these variables are replaced by their expected values or
systematic parts η_q^*, this need not shift the active causation from y_q to
the predetermined variables that combine to form η_q^*. Instead, and perhaps more adequately, the situation can be interpreted by saying that it
is not an entire y_q variable that is assumed to exert active causal influence upon y_i, only its expected value or systematic part. In any case,
the *ceteris paribus* clause remains the same, namely that there must be
no structural change in the variability of the endogenous variable.

(xiv) Irrespective of whether the model builder uses the REID or
GEID approach, he finds himself at a parting of the ways when it comes
to the final formulation and operative use of the model:

a. The model can be formulated and used as a REID or GEID system.
   Comment (xiii) is concerned with this alternative.

b. The model can be reformulated into an ordinary ID system (52) by
   resubstituting the endogenous variables y_q for their expectations η_q^*
   in the right-hand members of the structural form. In this alternative
   the REID or GEID specification serves as an intermediate step for the
   purpose of the parameter estimation. Once the estimation is carried
   through, the system is recast in the ordinary form (52) for operative
   use.

(xv) Now what can be said in the final analysis about the merits and disadvantages of the alternatives (xiv) a and b?

As to the reduced form, it is clear from the previous comments that
the two alternatives are exactly equivalent.

The difference between the two courses lies in the potential use of
the structural form. In point (xi) we have dismissed the structural form
of ordinary ID systems (64) on two arguments: (1) their relations cannot be specified as predictive in the sense of conditional expectations;
(2) a cause-effect specification of the structural relations leads to an
apparent causal contradiction. As to REID and GEID systems their
structural relations can be specified as predictive, but this advantage is
bought at a price, as we have seen in point (xiii), inasmuch as the struc-

tural relations are not amenable to a direct cause-effect specification; there is the possibility of an indirect cause-effect specification, but the operative use of this specification is obviously very limited.

The great advantage that lies in the operative use of cause-effect relations brings the second alternative in point (xiv) to the foreground, and leads us to reconsider the dismissal of ordinary ID systems in section 1.3.3 and point (xi). In this report we shall only raise the question, and shall not endeavour a definitive answer. A tentative comment is that it is relatively easy to renounce the predictive specification of the structural form. After all, the model is subject to small-sample bias anyway, and in practice the small-sample bias may be more important than the inescapable large-sample inconsistency of this second alternative. The apparent causal contradiction is more difficult to swallow, especially since our aim is a cause-effect specification. In the operative use of the model, however, the apparent contradiction inherent in the cause-effect specification of this type of model must be taken with a grain of salt, and for several reasons. For one thing, by and large there is a general lack of precision in macroeconomic model building in the present stage of development. Of specific relevance in this connection is the aggregate treatment of lags and leads in the cause-effect relationships; thus the apparent contradiction will relax or disappear if we think of one or both sets of cause and effect variables as not being simultaneous, but subject to lags or leads that are neglected in the model construction.

1.4.8. Information aspects of forecasting models and least squares regression

Reference is made to the foundations of information theory as set forth by André Kolmogorov (1957) on the basis of the notions of entropy and relative entropy. We quote his fundamental formula

$$\mathcal{I}(\xi, \eta) = H(\eta) - EH(\eta | \xi) , \qquad (117)$$

where ξ, η are two sets of random variables with a joint probability distribution; $\mathcal{I}(\xi, \eta)$ is the information about η which is contained in ξ; $H(\eta)$ is the entropy or average uncertainty of η. In the case of a discrete probability distribution $H(\eta)$ is given by the classic formula

$$H(\eta) = - \sum_i p_i \log p_i ; \tag{118}$$

$EH(\eta|\xi)$ is the conditional entropy or average uncertainty of η when ξ is known.

In the case of a discrete probability distribution, Kolmogorov's information formula (117) gives, in obvious symbols,

$$\mathcal{I}(\xi, \eta) = \sum_{i,j} p_{ij} \log \frac{p_{ij}}{P(\xi=x_i)P(\eta=y_j)} \tag{119a}$$

and in the continuous case

$$\mathcal{I}(\xi, \eta) = \int\limits_x \int\limits_y P(dx, dy) \log \frac{P_{\xi\eta}(dx, dy)}{P_{\xi}(dx)P_{\eta}(dy)} . \tag{119b}$$

As is clear from (119), Kolmogorov's information concept is symmetric in the variables ξ, η; in symbols,

$$\mathcal{I}(\xi, \eta) = \mathcal{I}(\eta, \xi) . \tag{120}$$

Further we quote the explicit formula for $\mathcal{I}(\xi, \eta)$ as given by Gelfand-Yaglom (1957) for the case when the probability distribution of all variables ξ, η is jointly normal,

$$\mathcal{I}(\xi, \eta) = \tfrac{1}{2} \log \frac{D(\xi)\, D(\eta)}{D(\xi, \eta)}, \tag{121}$$

where $D(\xi)$ denotes the dispersion determinant (also called variance-covariance determinant) of the set ξ, and similarly for the set η and the combined set ξ, η.

Information theory throws new light on the problem area of this monograph. Our limited purpose being to report a series of Monte Carlo experiments, it would carry us too far to develop our approach in the direction of information theory. Some brief comments may however be in order.

Comments. (i) Let us consider a multiple regression with theoretical specification

$$y = \beta_0 + \beta_1 x_1 + \ldots + \beta_h x_h + \epsilon ,\qquad(122)$$

and let the sets ξ, η of random variables be defined by

$$\xi = (x_0, x_1, \ldots, x_h) ; \quad \eta = y \qquad(123a-b)$$

with x_0 = const = 1. We apply Gelfand-Yaglom's formula (121) and obtain

$$\mathcal{G}(\xi, \eta) = -\log \frac{\sigma(\epsilon)}{\sigma(y)} ,\qquad(124)$$

where $\sigma(\epsilon), \sigma(y)$ are the standard deviations of the variables ϵ, y.

Formula (124) brings in relief the close relationship between information theory on the one hand and prediction theory and least squares regression on the other. By the regression (122) the explanatory variables $x_1, \ldots, x_h$ provide information about the left-hand variable y; the more information, the smaller is the standard deviation of the residual; the information is a one-to-one functional transform of the residual standard deviation; the residual standard deviation may therefore serve as a measure of the information that the variables $x_1, \ldots, x_h$ contain about y, or to spell out the relationship,

$$\sigma(\epsilon) = \sigma(y) \exp [-\mathcal{G}(\xi, \eta)] .\qquad(125)$$

(ii) With reference to 6.1 and our use of prediction error variances $s^2(e)$ as a criterion to assess the overall accuracy in the statistical estimation of the parameters of a model, it will be noted that formula (124) lends support to this type of criterion. The formula refers to linear relations between normally distributed variables, and there, via a functional transform (124)–(125) that is steadily decreasing (respectively, increasing), the residual variance measures the information that is contained in the relation when its parameters are numerically specified, and the prediction error variance is a statistical estimate of this same residual variance.

(iii) As a simple example of information aspects of prediction over several time periods we consider Yule's autoregressive process, say y_t as given by the dual representation

$$y_t + \beta_1 y_{t-1} + \beta_2 y_{t-2} = \epsilon_t , \tag{126a}$$

$$y_t = \epsilon_t + \alpha_1 \epsilon_{t-1} + \alpha_2 \epsilon_{t-2} + \ldots \tag{126b}$$

and assuming the process to be stationary and normal with zero mean.[17] Given the past development $y_t, y_{t-1}, y_{t-2}, \ldots$ the formulas for predicting $y_{t+1}, y_{t+2}, \ldots$ are, as is well known,

$$\operatorname{pred} y_{t+1} = \eta^*_{t+1} = \beta_1 y_t \quad + \beta_2 y_{t-1} \quad , \tag{127a}$$

$$\operatorname{pred} y_{t+2} = \eta^*_{t+2} = \beta_1 \eta^*_{t+1} \quad + \beta_2 y_t \quad , \tag{127b}$$

$$\operatorname{pred} y_{t+k} = \eta^*_{t+k} = \beta_1 \eta^*_{t+k-1} + \beta_2 \eta^*_{t+k-2} \; ; \; k = 3, 4, \ldots \tag{127c}$$

and the variance of the prediction error, say σ^2_k, is given by

$$\sigma^2_k = \sigma^2(y_{t+k} - \eta^*_{t+k}) = (1 + \alpha^2_1 + \cdots + \alpha^2_{k-1}) \, \sigma^2(\epsilon) \; ; \tag{128}$$

$$k = 1, 2, \ldots .$$

Now let for any fixed $k \geqslant 1$ the sets ξ, η of random variables be defined by

$$\xi = y_t, y_{t-1}, y_{t-2}, \ldots ; \quad \eta = y_{t+k} \; ; \tag{129}$$

then, as readily follows from (121), the information that the present and past observations $y_t, y_{t-1}, \ldots$ contain about the variable y_{t+k} to be predicted is given by

$$\mathcal{G}(\xi, \eta) = -\log \frac{\sigma_k}{\sigma(y)} \tag{130a}$$

$$= -\log \frac{\sigma(\epsilon)}{\sigma(y)} (1 + \alpha^2_1 + \cdots + \alpha^2_{k-1}) . \tag{130b}$$

We see that the information $\mathcal{I}(\xi, \eta)$ is positive, and decreases as the span k of the forecast (127c) increases. In the limit (130) gives

$$\lim_{k \to \infty} \mathcal{I}(\xi, \eta) = 0 , \tag{131}$$

in accord with the fact that for Yule's process the present and past gives only a trivial forecast about the remote future, namely

$$\lim_{k \to \infty} \operatorname{pred} y_{t+k} = 0 \tag{132}$$

or in words: As $k \to \infty$ the forecast (127c) reduces to the mean of the process.

(iv) How about the ordering of the structural relations of a multi-relational model from the point of view of information theory? We adduce two remarks towards a partial reply.

a. *Given a VR, CC, ID, REID or GEID system where all structural relations are behavioral, and such that the joint distribution of all current endogenous variables y_i or predetermined variables z_k of the system is jointly normal. Then the information that the predetermined variables contain about the current endogenous variables is invariant with respect to the ordering of the structural relations.*

In fact, letting the variables ξ, η be defined by

$$\xi = z_t, z_{t-1}, z_{t-2}, \dots ; \qquad \eta = y_t \tag{133a}$$

with

$$y_t = (y_{1t}, \dots, y_{nt}) , \qquad z_t = (z_{1t}, \dots, z_{mt}) , \tag{133b}$$

the statement follows as an immediate corollary to (121), for this formula gives the information as a function of the variance and covariances of the variables y_{it}, $z_{k,t-s}$ and these variances and covariances are invariant with respect to the ordering of the structural form.

b. *We refer to multirelational models of the same type as in point a. In CC systems, but not in REID or GEID systems, the information contained in the structural form is dependent upon the ordering of the relations.*

First, we note that in the REID and GEID systems, but not in the CC systems, each relation in the structural form has the same residual as the corresponding relation in the reduced form. In this sense, the information that is contained about the current endogenous variables in the structural form is the same as the information that the predetermined variables contain about the same current endogenous variables. Second, according to point (a) this last information is independent of the ordering of the structural relations.

As to CC systems, we know from 1.4.2(iii)a that in point of principle it will not impede the generality of the argument if we assume that current residuals are mutually independent. In such case the total information contained in the structural form is obtained by summing the information over the various structural relations. This sum total of information in general will depend upon the ordering of the structural relations, as can readily be shown by considering simple numerical examples. [18]

It is a question how this briefing stands to the recent developments of information theory in econometrics. If we understand correctly, most authors have worked with (118), not with (117), and expression (118) is used as a measure of information. As a result, there is some confusion, first of all with regard to the sign, a typical feature being that what in current theory is called "the principle of minimum information" in the theory (117)–(126) would have to be called "the principle of minimum uncertainty".

CHAPTER 2

Framework for Analysis of
Monte Carlo Results

In applied econometrics we frequently have too little knowledge about (a) the real world being modeled, (b) the mathematical properties of the model that is constructed, and (c) the properties of estimates from the particular method of estimation that was employed. Our knowledge in each of these categories must improve if econometrics is to make more significant contributions to understanding economic phenomena and evaluating economic policy. This monograph and the research behind it are oriented to the last two of the above three problem areas.

The research was originally oriented towards a comparison of the fix-point method with other methods of estimation. We expected that the properties of every method of estimation are heavily dependent on the structure of the model being studied. [1] Consequently, our project was planned so as to provide insight into the properties of estimates for many different types of models and a wide range of values in such parameters as size of beta coefficients, size of residual variances and size of correlation among variables. With the exception of Cragg (1967) [2], earlier Monte Carlo studies focus on one or some few model designs; see, for example, Basmann (1958), Nagar (1960), Summers (1965), and Wagner (1958).

An outline of all the models considered in this research project is given in Chapter 2.3. The experimental results are summarized under the appropriate subject areas in Chapters 4—9 and 13. The complete set of

92

results for the 46 models is presented in Chapter 10.2. An *Addendum* at the end of Chapter 2, page 108, discusses the possibility of extending the results from time-series models to cross-section models.

2.1. Monte Carlo Investigations as a Research Tool

It is important for readers to be aware of the authors' understanding of the role of Monte Carlo work in a discipline such as economics. The conclusions presented in this volume will have more meaning to the reader if he is aware of the general expectation under which the research project was designed.

The best context for describing Monte Carlo work is the spectrum of types of data, namely, experimental, non-experimental, and intermediate or what might be called hybrid. Speaking generally, experiments provide reproducible knowledge about the real world. In analysis of non-experimental data the researcher explores regularities in the real world. Both in the analysis of experimental and nonexperimental data the approach involves model building. [1] Model building, in turn, involves the matching of theory and empirical observations (experimental or non-experimental). Monte Carlo studies provide a means to study the random aspects in the matching of theory and observation.

Experiments are not necessary for scientific research, but they certainly facilitate analysis of causal relationships among variables. Monte Carlo studies are not a substitute for experiments because the results do not allow the investigator to infer cause and effect relationships. Economics as a typical non-experimental science does not differ from the experimental sciences in its objectives, but it does differ in the extent to which it is possible to use the convenience of experiments in obtaining understanding of predictive or causal relationships among variables; see Mosbaek-Wold (1965).

Monte Carlo work can help overcome some of the handicaps resulting from not being able to conduct controlled experiments in economics. First, it can be used to obtain reproducible knowledge about the accuracy of parameter estimates. That is, the results obtained from non-experimental data can be used in a Monte Carlo setting to determine to what extent the same estimation method applied to Monte Carlo data will reproduce the estimates obtained from the non-experimental data. Second, although a Monte Carlo experiment cannot tell us whether in actual fact there is a cause-effect relationship between two variables x and y, it can help the researcher in establishing confidence intervals in causal prediction. On the assumption that x is cause and y is effect, subject to random disturbance, a Monte Carlo experiment can help us to obtain a confidence interval for a prediction of how a given change in x will affect y. In this sense, Monte Carlo experiments improve the analyst's skills in using non-experimental data and reduce the importance of the convenience provided by experiments.

The best test of an empirical model is, of course, to use it to predict or explain phenomena outside the sample period. When data are not too scarce it is tempting to exclude some of the data from being used in the parameter estimation, using them instead for a quasi-predictive test, but this practice has its obvious disadvantages. [2] Data are so scarce in economics that it is highly desirable to include all relevant observations in the sample. And as a touchstone in predictive testing, neglected data is not as good as fresh observations.

If the model builder uses all available observations in the sample he must be willing to wait several periods or resort to the opportunity provided by Monte Carlo experiments for a partial testing of his model. The Monte Carlo test of a real world model proceeds in a stepwise fashion. First, the model builder makes a tentative hypothesis that the model estimated from real world data is valid and that each estimate of a parameter of the model can be interpreted as coming from a population with specific stochastic properties (mean equal to the observed mean; variance equal to the estimated variance; autocorrelation properties in accordance with observations; and so on). Second, he can use the estimated model to generate Monte Carlo samples to be used for obtaining several new sets of estimates of parameters. Third, he can determine if the estimates obtained by using the Monte Carlo data trace out the distribution he assumed in testing the hypothesis. If the distribution in the Monte Carlo results does not agree with the assumptions used in formulating the hypothesis about the validity of the model the credibility of that hypothesis is reduced. As in all scientific work, agreement between new information and an *a priori* hypothesis is only approximate, and cannot validate the hypothesis in an absolute sense but it can provide greater support for the credibility of the hypothesis.

The use of Monte Carlo experiments under the concept of reproducible knowledge is demonstrated in the case of one model, namely,
the model for food constructed by Girshick-Haavelmo (1947). The
results in this set of Monte Carlo experiments (see Model 4a, Table
10.2.24) provide what appears to be a vivid illustration of rejecting the
hypothesis that the original set of estimates has the properties specified
by the authors.

Monte Carlo work is not a complete substitute for mathematical
analysis of the properties of estimates from a specified method of estimation. It is, however, an efficient substitute. It is likely to be a long
time before mathematical expressions for the exact distributions for
small samples are available for more than a small class of models. In the
meantime Monte Carlo work can be used to detect the really significant
differences in methods of estimation. The possible minor differences
that would require a prohibitive Monte Carlo expense or explicit mathematical analysis are not likely to be of crucial importance in the current
state-of-the-art in econometrics.

2.2. Generating Monte Carlo Data

Observations on current and lagged endogenous variables are generated
by the model once the exogenous and residual variables are specified.
There are, however, several alternatives in choosing a method to generate
observations of these latter variables. The method used in this project is
illustrated with the aid of the following model:

$$y_{1t} = \beta_1 y_{2t} + \gamma_1 y_{1,t-1} + \gamma_2 x_{1t} + \alpha_1 + \delta_{1t} \tag{1}$$

$$= \frac{\gamma_1}{1-\beta_1\beta_2} y_{1,t-1} + \frac{\gamma_2}{1-\beta_1\beta_2} x_{1t} + \frac{\beta_1\gamma_3}{1-\beta_1\beta_2} x_{2t} + \frac{\alpha_1+\beta_1\alpha_2}{1-\beta_1\beta_2} + \epsilon_{1t} ,$$

$$y_{2t} = \beta_2 y_{1t} + \gamma_3 x_{2t} + \alpha_2 + \delta_{2t} \tag{2}$$

$$= \frac{\gamma_1\beta_2}{1-\beta_1\beta_2} y_{1,t-1} + \frac{\beta_2\gamma_2}{1-\beta_1\beta_2} x_{1t} + \frac{\gamma_3}{1-\beta_1\beta_2} x_{2t} + \frac{\beta_2\alpha_1+\alpha_2}{1-\beta_1\beta_2} + \epsilon_{2t} .$$

The observations that are exogenous to the model are the initial observation on $y_{1,t-1}$, the vectors of observations on x_{1t} and x_{2t} for all values of t and the vectors of observations on δ_{1t} and δ_{2t} for all values of t.

For each sample for each model a vector of $T = M + 1 + N + P$ observations ($t = -M, -M+1, ..., N+P$) was generated for every endogenous, exogenous, and residual variable. Observations $t = -M, -M+1, ..., -1$ were discarded in order to obtain an initial observation ($t-1=0$) on $y_{1,t-1}$ that was, for all practical purposes, in accordance with the model specification, and independent from sample to sample. The value of M was 20 in the models presented in Chapter 10.2.

Observations $t = 1, ..., N$ were used as sample data. Observations $t = N+1, ..., N+P$ were designed as a prediction period. Predictions of endogenous variables in the prediction period were made by using the estimated parameters from the sample period, the actual observations on exogenous variables, and the actual observation for $y_{1,N}$. The objective was to simulate the situations in applied econometrics where a specified *segment* of a continuous series of observations is used as sample data and the estimated model is then used to predict the endogenous variables in the time periods immediately following the sample period. [1] In these experiments the exogenous variables are known whereas in applied econometrics the exogenous variables are assumed to be more easily predicted than endogenous variables but are not known unless a firm policy governing them has been established.

The models were constructed with the constant term equal to zero in all equations (i.e. in (1)–(2) $\alpha_1 = \alpha_2 = 0$). This causes no loss in generality and there is a convenience in specifying and computing the Monte Carlo data. Since the mean of all exogenous variables is zero and all models were constructed so as to be non-explosive the equilibrium value for all endogenous variables is zero. Therefore, the specification of the initial values ($t = -M$) for all lagged endogenous variables was zero. As pointed out above, the first M observations in each set of data were discarded so that any data on endogenous variables before the sample period ($t = 0, -1, ...$) were random variables, and not necessarily zero.

The set of observations on x_1 and x_2 and/or the set of observations on δ_1 and δ_2 can be specified *a priori* or they can both be generated so as to be independent from sample to sample. If both sets are specified *a priori* there would, of course, be no variation in estimates of parameters

from sample to sample. To impose an *a priori* specification on only one
of the two sets is sometimes desirable for one of two reasons. First, we
might want to reduce the source of variation from sample to sample in
the Monte Carlo work. Second, we might want to investigate the distribution of estimates of parameters in a situation of a given set of observations on one or the other of the two sets of variables. For example,
with a given set of observations on the exogenous (residual) variables
and the estimated variance-covariance matrix for residuals (exogenous
variables) we might wish to know the frequency with which each of the
estimated parameters would fall within, say, 10% of the estimate that
was obtained when estimating the parameters from available real world
data (assuming no specification error).

   With the exception of the Girshick-Haavelmo model (4a in Chart 2.3.1)
data for both the exogenous and residual variables in all models were
generated independently from sample to sample. The specified distribution for all exogenous and residual variables was the normal distribution
with mean zero. All lagged correlations among exogenous and residual
variables were specified to be zero but the correlations between these
variables in the same time period were frequently specified to be non-
zero.

   Data for the 100 samples for each exogenous and residual variable in
each model specification was generated by (a) selecting a random number
for initiating the random number generating sub-routine, (b) generating
a rectangular distribution, (c) transforming the rectangular distribution
into the standard normal distribution with zero mean and unit variance,
and (d) transforming the standard normal to the normal distribution with
specified variances and covariances among the variables. The rectangular
distribution was generated from subroutine RANF which is available
through the library for Control Data Corporation computers. The transformation to the standard normal distribution was

$$x = \sqrt{0.75}\left(\sum_{i=1}^{16} c_i - 8\right), \tag{3}$$

where c_i is the rectangular distribution with values between zero and
unity.

   The data for the samples were not saved because of the great amount of storage that would be required. However, the initial random number for each sample for each model has been saved. This means that the data for any sample can be easily re-generated and printed and the parameters for that sample can be re-estimated with only a few seconds of computer time.

2.3. Six Groups of Models

The relative performance of different methods of estimation varies with the type of model being estimated. The six groups of models shown in Chart 1 were designed in part to reflect on the main issues in applied econometrics and in part to investigate more fully the hypotheses developed from the pilot Monte Carlo runs. It was not feasible to investigate an indefinite range of models so each of the six groups has been designed to investigate the effect of a particular phenomenon. The overall set of results should enable one to make a good estimate of the relative performance of the different methods of estimation for most any type of model within the scope of the present study. Specific characteristics such as sample size, number of equations, and size of residuals have been analyzed in such a way that most results can be projected to situations beyond the scope actually investigated in this project.

The six series of models also give insight into the intrinsic properties of familiar types of econometric models. In order to gain better understanding of models and to facilitate analysis of Monte Carlo results most of the models have been designed so the theoretical variance of both endogenous and exogenous variables is unity (see Appendix II for details). Under this condition the variances of the residuals are determined by the specified R^2 statistic in the reduced form equation for each variable (on the REID and GEID specifications the R^2 statistic is the same for the reduced form and structural form; see Appendix I,D for definitions).

The size of beta coefficients in the structural model has a large effect on the relative performance among the different methods of estimation. For this reason, both the first and third series of models were designed around the size of beta coefficients.

Beta coefficients were specified to be plus or minus one in all but two of the models in groups 2, 5, and 6. If all beta coefficients in a model are (a) less than one, (b) equal to one, or (c) greater than one it is easy to obtain unit variance for endogenous variables without introducing inter-dependencies among exogenous variables. The absolute value of one was chosen for beta coefficients in many of the 46 models because small beta values would produce small differences among methods of estimation and large beta values would introduce severe problems in multicollinearity.

Except for models specifically designed to study the effect of sample size and size of residuals, the Monte Carlo samples had 40 observations and the models were designed with R^2 equal to 0.5 or 0.8 in each re-duced form equation. 40 observations is a fairly typical sample size for macro models estimated from quarterly data. R^2's of 0.8 are typical of results in applied research. An R^2 of 0.5 was sometimes used in order to increase the differences among methods of estimation.

Each of the models in the first series is relatively simple for one of two reasons. Either there are only two equations and therefore only two beta coefficients to be estimated, or the β coefficients are fairly small and problems of estimation are minimal. Much of the difficulty in econo-metrics arises from the feature of simultaneous determination of endogenous variables. This feature is, however, a matter of degree. If the beta coefficients are small the endogenous variables can be quite accu-rately determined from only the exogenous variables in each equation. The Monte Carlo results confirm what is intuitively obvious, namely, that the complexity of the model and the possible problems in estima-tion increase rapidly as the number of beta coefficients increases unless all beta coefficients are small. The first two sets within the first group of models show the relative effect of increasing the complexity by increas-ing the number of equations vs increasing the size of beta coefficients. The third set of four Causal Chain Models in the first group are included to illustrate the differences between causal chains and interdependent systems with respect to problems of estimation.

The second group is oriented around the two dimensions of model size, namely, the number of equations and number of variables per equation. Each dimension has been investigated separately in order to keep the number of models within manageable limits.

The third group is an investigation of the effects of more than two current endogenous variables per equation and an investigation of the

1. SIMPLEST MODELS
($R^2 = 0.8; N = 40$)

Interdependent systems

Size of β (2 eqs.)	No. of equations ($\beta = \pm 0.5$; 1 loop)
a. 0.5, −0.5	g. 2 (= 1a)
b. 1 , −1	h. 5
c. 3 , −3	i. 7
d. 0.5, −0.9	
e. 0.5, −3	
f. 1.1, −3	

Causal chain systems

Normalized	Not normalized
m	p
n	q

2. MODEL SIZE
($R^2 = 0.8; N = 40$)

No. of eqs. (1 loop; $\beta = \pm 1$)	No. of exogenous variables per eq. (2 eqs.; $\beta = \pm 1$)
a. 2 (= 1b)	e. 2 (= 1b)
b. 3	f. 4
c. 5	g. 7
d. 7	

3. THREE-EQUATION MODELS
($R^2 = 0.5; N = 40$)

Size of β (1 loop)	Size of β (full β matrix)
a. ± 0.5	d. ± 0.5
b. ± 1	e. ± 1
c. ± 2	f. ± 1

4. FAMILIAR MODELS

a. Girshick-Haavelmo Model
b. Simple Keynesian model, A
c. Simple Keynesian model, B

5. GENERAL INTEREST ITEMS

Intercorrelated exogenous variables
($R^2 = 0.8; N = 40$)

a. $r(x_1, x_3) = r(x_2, x_4) = 0.7$
b. $r(x_1, x_3) = r(x_2, x_4) = -0.7$

Lagged endogenous variables
($R^2 = 0.9; N = 40$)

Three models: c, d, and e

Varying sample size ($R^2 = 0.8$)

f.	$N = 10$	i.	$N = 10$
g.	= 40 (= 1b)	j.	= 40 (= 1d)
h.	= 80		

Varying size residuals ($N = 40$)

m.	$R^2 = 0.2$	r.	$R^2 = 0.2$
n.	= 0.5	s.	= 0.8 (= 1d)
p.	= 0.8 (= 1b)		
q.	= 0.95		

6. GEID CORRELATIONS
($R^2 = 0.8, 0.5; N = 40$)

No. of eqs. (Small corr.)	Size of correlation (2-eq. model)
a. 2	e. 0.00 (= 5n)
b. 3	f. 0.01
c. 5	g. 0.05
	h. 0.10
	i. 0.20
	j. 0.40

Chart 2.3.1. Six groups of models for which Monte Carlo results are available. Detailed specification of each of the 46 models is given in Part A of the corresponding table in Chapter 10.2.

effects of increasing the size of beta coefficients. The three-equation size was selected because pilot Monte Carlo runs showed that they revealed the essential properties of larger models whereas two-equation models do not. Three-equation models are much easier to analyze and are, of course, much cheaper in computer time than larger models in Monte Carlo investigations.

The fourth group provides examples of familiar models in economics. Although the theme of the entire project was to discover the essential properties of almost all types of small models, it seemed wise to concentrate some of the research effort on models actually used in economics. In this group the endogenous variables do not have unit variance. The first model uses the empirical estimates of parameters obtained by Girshick and Haavelmo (1947) and also uses the same set of observations on the *exogenous* variables. The Monte Carlo results on this model are a test of the validity of the model in the manner described in Chapter 2.1. The other two models in this group are simple Keynesian-type models. The parameters were chosen to correspond closely to several sets of empirical results and at the same time generate a realistic Capital-Output ratio.

The fifth group concentrates on four factors that are relevant in all empirical work in economics. The same simple β matrix was used in the design of most all of the models in group 5 in order to simplify the analysis of results. In Models 5a and 5b, a rather high degree of multicollinearity among the predetermined variables has been introduced explicitly. Multicollinearity among exogenous variables also appears in Model 1e but this was necessitated by other design features and was not introduced for the explicit purpose of studying multicollinearity. Very little theoretical work has been done on determining the effects of lagged endogenous variables so Models 5c–5e are oriented around this feature. The remaining models in group 5 concentrate on the two very familiar features of sample size and size of residuals.

The last group of models – number 6 – introduces a feature for which only FP of the four methods studied will give consistent estimates of coefficients in the structural and reduced form equations. This feature is a correlation, called a GEID correlation, between the residual in one equation and the predetermined variables in other equations; see 1.2.6 and 1.4.5. Models 6a–6c are designed to study the effect of increasing

size of model measured in terms of number of equations. The GEID correlations in these 3 models are relatively small since all are 0.2 or less in
absolute value. Models 6e–6j were designed to investigate the effect of
increasing size of GEID correlations. A small two-equation model is used
as the basic model in the Series 6e–6j in order to simplify the analysis.

The six groups of models were designed to provide insight into the
properties of methods of estimation and into the intrinsic properties of
models of the type often used in econometrics. The models were grouped
in a way that the authors believe will provide a good reference for empirical work in econometric model building. Hopefully, future model
builders will frequently find that features in the model they have specified and the sample data they are using will have been investigated in
these six groups of models.

Some explanation must be given for our exclusion of very large models. The explanation is very simple; our philosophy has been to go from
the simple to the complex, beginning with small models, and leaving the
large models to the side as being too difficult in this round.[1] As stated in
the introduction, the complexity of a model depends to a large extent
on the size of model and size of residual terms (ϵ). This research project
included only minor effort on analysis of the simplest situation – small
models and small residuals – and no effort on the most complex situation – large models and large residuals. The 300 plus equations in the
Brookings-SSRC Model surely has no close resemblance to any model
included in the six groups described above. It is possible to gain some
appreciation for the complexity of large models by extrapolating from
the results presented here, but the extrapolation cannot carry as far as
a 300-equation model.

The results presented in this study suggest that the interdependent
nature per se does not necessarily cause great difficulty even in large
models. Since the number of explanatory variables in the Brookings-SSRC
Model is so large, the residuals are probably very small and the proximity
theorem would imply that OLS would work quite well for estimation.
The difficulty arises from the severe problem of multicollinearity and
the enormous complexity of a set of several hundred causal relationships.
It is possible for the model builder(s) himself to get lost in the maze of
relationships he specifies and calls a model; see Mosbaek (1968).

All models designed for this project have been kept small to permit the

insight that is necessary for meaningful scientific pursuits. This special
design is reflected in the conclusions presented in Chapter 13 – Any Verdict Yet? Some recent work by the Uppsala group indicates that the FP
method might have more advantages over TSLS in large models. [2] If this
is true, the results presented in this monograph give a somewhat biased
view of the relative advantages of FP and TSLS.

2.4. Four Methods of Estimation in Focus

There are a large number of variations in the basic methods for estimating interdependent models. Only four were selected for this study.
First, the authors felt that it was better to limit the number of different
methods so that available resources could be devoted to obtaining a more
definitive verdict on the methods selected for analysis. Second, it seemed
that four of the available methods would fairly well represent the spectrum of methods that are likely to be available for some time. [1]

Fix-point (FP) was included because it was a new method recently developed by one of the authors and it had many promising features. [2]
Two-stage least squares (TSLS) was included because it has given relatively good results in previous experiments and it is the simplest among
the available set of consistent estimates for interdependent models under
classic specification (see 1.2.6). Ordinary least squares as applied to the
structural form (OLS) was included because of its frequent use in applied econometrics, its good performance indicated by the proximity
theorem (see Chapter 3.3), and its robustness in handling non-linear relationships among current endogenous variables. Unrestricted least squares
(URF), that is estimates of OLS as applied to the reduced form, is included and referred to as a fourth method because it is an alternative for
developing a forecasting model even though it does not provide estimates
of the parameters in the structural equations. The advantage of URF is
that it is a shortcut across some types of identification and multicollinearity problems.

These four methods really represent four philosophies in estimation,
and the Monte Carlo results give additional information for a verdict on
these philosophies. The philosophy in full information methods is best
defined in terms of degree to which the estimation process honors the

a priori information that is contained in structural relations that are numerically unspecified. (Such information is often referred to as "restrictions", a term that does not rhyme well with such a positive feature as prior information.) Fix-point is in the direction of full information since all equations are estimated simultaneously. [3] That is, estimates of parameters in each equation affect the estimates in all structural equations not already in reduced form. The FP method imputes more information from the model specification than OLS and TSLS, but less information than the method of full information maximum likelihood (FIML). The information that is contained in numerically unspecified structural relations cannot be honored without estimating the entire set of parameters simultaneously, and the performance of FIML in this respect leaves much to be desired, especially when dealing with small samples. It belongs to the research program of this monograph to explore the performance of FP in this respect. It can be expected that some of the difficulties of FIML will carry over to FP in small samples; on the other hand, in comparable systems FIML sets up a larger number of parameters to be estimated, a feature that implies a relative advantage for FP in small samples.

Unrestricted estimates of the reduced form are in the philosophy of disregarding the *a priori* information (restrictions). The method also disregards the need to test specific hypotheses concerning specifications of structural relations. The Monte Carlo results presented in the monograph show the reductions in forecasting power when valid *a priori* information is not honored. The other major limitation of unrestricted reduced form estimates, namely, the loss of opportunities in not using structural parameters in policy considerations cannot be studied in a Monte Carlo setting (see 1.4.7 and Mosbaek-Wold [1]).

TSLS is within the philosophy that while the method should yield consistent estimates, it is appropriate to disregard some of the information in the model specification in order to estimate each structural equation separately. In actual fact, TSLS is consistent in the classic specification of interdependent models but not in the GEID specification. Both TSLS and FP are consistent under the classic specification; each method has an advantage over the other, and which tendency is the strongest varies from model to model. The classic specification imputes more information about the model than the GEID specification, and

TSLS (but not FP) is designed to take advantage of this larger amount of information, while FP squeezes more for the information that it can utilize. Both advantages increase with the size of the equation system, so it is a question whether one tendency or the other will dominate when coming to large systems. Determining the advantage of FP relative to TSLS is a typical problem for the research reported in this volume.

Unless the proximity theorem is known to apply, OLS is selected for estimating interdependent models only under the philosophy that bias is a small price to pay for a simple method with minimum variance in the estimates. This philosophy carries over to nonlinear models, inasmuch as the minimum variance property is the same in linear and nonlinear models. In linear interdependent systems the smaller variance of OLS relative to multi-stage methods results from the hypothesis specification about the residuals in the structural form, a specification which also, of course, causes bias in the parameter estimates. Multi-stage methods in contrast to OLS require linear approximations of nonlinearities among the current endogenous variables and, consequently, add another component to the residual. In general, when variances of residuals in reduced form equations are large relative to the variance of the endogenous variables OLS estimates have a significantly smaller variance and larger bias than TSLS, FP and all other consistent estimators.

It is likely that new methods for the formal part of estimation (i.e., the mathematical routines) will continue to be proposed for many years. Except for very special circumstances it is not likely, however, that any of the new methods will give results that differ greatly from one or more of the four methods discussed in this monograph. The qualification with respect to *special* circumstances must be emphasized, since, given *any* specified method it is possible to construct or hypothesize a set of circumstances in which this method will be superior to other methods. Unfortunately, a superior method for only special circumstances is of little value because the econometrician usually has no way of judging *a priori* if the special circumstances exist. Incidentally, this is especially true for new methods designed around the Bayesian principle.

In the Uppsala team, A.Ågren is developing the fractional fix-point method and L.Bodin is developing the recursive fix-point method. A report on extensive investigation of these variants will appear in forthcoming publications. [4] Although it is too early to draw firm conclusions it appears that variants of the FP method hold promise for reducing the severity of bias and convergence problems that appear in some of the FP results reported in this volume.

2.5. Criterion in Judging Alternative Methods of Estimation

There are three basic sets of choices in selecting a criterion. One choice involves the type of model to be estimated. A second choice involves the selection of one or more estimated parameters of the model upon which the test is to be focused. The third choice involves selection of one or more properties of the estimated parameters upon which the test is to be based. For example, we might select the property of mean square error in the estimates of the coefficient of consumption on income in a specific macro model.

Econometric models can be used for a very wide range of purposes and, therefore, it is not possible to design a single best test in Monte Carlo or other basic research investigations. In applied econometrics the best test is, of course, dictated by the particular decisions that will be based on the estimated model. In this investigation the authors have designed a wide range of models and have presented the results in a way that will permit easy evaluation of the different methods in specific situations that an econometrician might encounter in applied work. With respect to which parameter(s) of the model to use in a test the authors decided to present results on three basic sets of parameters, namely, structural coefficients, reduced form coefficients, and R^2 statistics. R^2 serves as a test of the predictive power of the model, its power of predicting the endogenous variables outside the sample period. Hence, R^2 provides a test of the entire set of estimated coefficients in a model and is, therefore, a specific choice within the second and third sets of criteria referred to above.

For each model the summary tables in Chapter 10.2 give four statistics on each coefficient in the structural and reduced form equations:

1. Average of the estimates from 100 samples.
2. Observed standard deviation of estimates around the mean.
3. Observed standard deviation of the estimates around the true coefficient.

4. Average of 100 estimates of the standard deviation from the large sample formula.

Graphs of the cumulative distribution for several parameter estimates in the different models are included throughout the text to provide better insight into the differences among the four methods.

The mean absolute error is a good summary of the estimates of a particular parameter in a specified model for a given sample size. This value can be estimated from the third statistic in the above list — observed standard deviation of the estimate around the true value. Since bias in TSLS and FP is a function of sample size, the qualities of bias and variance around the mean must be evaluated separately if these methods are to be judged for different sample sizes. Consequently, the first and second items in the above list are presented in addition to the observed standard deviation of the estimates around the true value.

Unless there is specific interest in individual parameters in the structural or reduced form equations the predictive power test (R^2) is a good summary of the entire set of estimates for a model. In most models the prediction of each endogenous variable depends on all of the estimated structural coefficients. The R^2 test should be computed from observations not included in the sample period; otherwise overfitting can cause a severe bias in the evaluation process. To illustrate the problem of overfitting summary tables present R^2 statistics for observations both within and outside the sample period (see description of sample and forecasting periods in Chapter 2.2).

Our measure and use of predictive power as a criterion is in line with recent developments in information theory and measures of information; see 1.4.8. Some writers in this field have proposed that the most meaningful measure is one that characterizes randomness or what the authors of this monograph visualize as "degree of chaos". It seems to us that a much more fruitful concept is the one proposed by André Kolmogorov (1957). For the present context the implication is that information content can be measured by the familiar R^2 statistic. Unless a particular parameter is known to be of special interest we propose that the predictive power (R^2 as measured outside the sample period) is the best summary statistic on the quality of the estimates from a specified method of estimation. Instead of presenting various tests for significant differences among estimates of specific parameters from different methods of estimation we have provided measures of predictive power for each method of estimation on each model.

The results from the Monte Carlo experiments on the 46 models investigated are presented in many forms since no specific test is satisfactory for making a general verdict on the best method of estimation. The results will be of maximum benefit in applied work if they can be used as a handy reference for answers to specific questions that come up in applied work. Part of the value of this monograph will be in demonstrating that different criteria lead to different choices in selecting a preferred method of estimation.

2.6. Time-series vs cross-section data

The Monte Carlo data generated and used for analysis in the research reported in this monograph resembles time-series data but the authors feel that the conclusions presented are appropriate for model building using both time-series and cross-section data. A few comments on this aspect are in order.

A time-series model regards the magnitudes of certain variables in all of a certain set of time intervals (years, months, etc.) as described or explained by a set of equations; a cross-section model regards certain behavior of all of a certain set of individuals (consumers, producers, etc.) as described or explained by a set of equations. A model in either case can contain one or more of the commonly recognized types of equations, namely, behavioral relations, technological relations, identities and equilibrium relations. Consequently, the models do not differ in basic principle and ID models can be an appropriate approach in both cases. In the operative use of estimated models for prediction outside the set of sample observations there is an additional data requirement in the case of cross-section models. Since prediction by the chain principle starting with observations on lagged variables in the sample data is not appropriate, new observations on lagged variables must be obtained for each prediction.

The severity of specific problems such as multicollinearity and independence of observations might well be somewhat less in cross-section data but the basic nature of the associated problems are the same. Most empirical work has shown that predictive power (i.e., the R^2 statistic as measured from sample data in regression analysis) of econometric models is less in the case of cross-section data than in time-series data but this again is a difference in degree rather than a difference in kind. The models presented in this monograph were designed to represent a wide range in the familiar characteristics of models such as degree of multicollinearity, size of residuals, number of equations, etc. and this is one of the reasons why the authors suggest that the conclusions are appropriate to model building using both time-series and cross-section data.

Methods of Estimation

3.1. Scope and Evolution of the Present Study

In Chapter 1 the background and scope of this monograph have been described in broad outline. In Chapter 2 we have presented the 46 models selected for generating the Monte Carlo experiments that have been analysed in our investigation. We are now in a position to present our estimation techniques in detail, and at the same time explain the gradual evolution in posing of problems and in ways of handling them during the four years of research.

In 1964 the fix-point (FP) method was launched as a new approach towards the estimation of interdependent (ID) systems; see Wold [15,18]. By that time the techniques available for the estimation of ID systems had run into difficulties in the treatment of medium size and large ID systems, an obvious obstacle being that all of these techniques make their approach via the reduced form of the model, and since all the predetermined variables generally pile up in each relation of the reduced form the estimation runs out of degrees of freedom when it comes to systems with many relations. A first key feature of the FP method is that it stays in the structural form, where there are no more coefficients than parameters to be estimated, and only some few parameters in each relation. The FP method works by an iterative procedure, and once the structural form has been estimated, the reduced form with its coefficients is obtained by algebraic solution of the structural form. A second distinguishing feature of the FP method is that it is designed for systems specified in terms of predictors and genuine scatter. For one thing, in the "classical" design of ID systems this leads to a formal respecification, REID systems, where the parameters are numerically the same as in Classic ID systems. Second, it leads to a generalization of REID systems, GEID systems, a key feature of which is that they honor the "parity principle" of involving the same number of assumptions (zero correlations between residuals and explanatory variables) as there are parameters to cope with these same assumptions.

Under the auspicies of Battelle Memorial Institute our investigation started in January 1965, while the initiating paper (Wold [15]) was still in press. Our investigation was planned as a comparative study, with special attention paid to the related two-stage least squares (TSLS) method of H.Theil (1958).

Since the FP method was new and the problem area very large, we followed the principle of exploring simple cases before turning to complex ones; and planning our study to be of restricted scope, we limited ourselves to systems with the following two special features:

(i) All relations of the structural form are behavioral.

(ii) The systems are small, from two or three up to seven structural relations.

When the FP method was under construction in 1963 and 1964 it looked very promising; the iterative procedure worked smoothly in some 20 sample models where it was tried. Now in an early stage of the present study we found — as reported by Wold [18] — that there must be something wrong somewhere, for contrary to the general theorem in the initiating paper (Wold [15]) we found cases where the FP iterations failed to converge. In the alleged proof based on the principle of contraction a grave error was soon discovered, inasmuch as the requisite normalization to unit variance of the proxies $y_i^{(s)}$ had been forgotten. Fresh research was triggered along several lines, as reported by E.Lyttkens (1967), A.Ågren (1967) and L.Bodin (1968); manyfaceted research is still in progress. We are greatly indebted to Lyttkens, Ågren and Bodin for their contributions to Chapters 3, 9 and 11 of this volume, and for

allowing us to draw freely from their results in our analysis as reported
in other chapters.

Reference is made to two main lines of analysis in Lyttkens' work.
First, the FP approach leads to a system of normal equations – formed
by product moments of the variables y_i, z_k – which in general cannot
be solved for the parameter estimates by a finite procedure. Lyttkens
shows that in certain simple models the iterative procedure of the FP
method can be replaced by a finite algebraic solution. In Summers' two-
relation model with six parameters the finite method involves the solving
of an algebraic equation of fifth order. The solution may or may not be
unique, and Lyttkens shows that there are cases when one and the same
set of product moments of y_i, z_k can be reproduced by five different sets
of parameter estimates. Lyttkens' results on this line have been very
valuable in throwing light on several problems encountered in the course
of our investigations. Lyttkens gives a brief report of these results in
Chapters 3.8–3.10 and 9.3.

Second, the present study is in the main limited to the case (i) where
the structural form contains nothing else than behavioral relations. In
Chapter 3.2 the desirability of removing this restriction is commented
upon from the general points of view of causal analysis and econometric
method. Lyttkens has extended the approach of predictors and genuine
scatter from case (i) to more general models, in particular models that
involve identities and equilibrium relations. In Chapter 11, Lyttkens
gives a brief report of his results along this line, including iterative methods for the parameter estimation. In special cases the parameters can be
obtained by finite calculations; this category is shown to include the
well-known model by Girshick-Haavelmo (1947) with five behavioral
relations and one relation of instantaneous equilibrium.

By the use of standard devices in numerical analysis the FP method
can be modified and generalized in various respects. Two approaches
have proved particularly useful in dealing with problems encountered in
our investigation. The device known as "relaxation" has been adapted to
the FP method by A.Ågren (1967); in Chapter 3.6 he presents his device
under the name of *Fractional Fix-point* (FFP) *Estimation.* Using consecutive instead of simultaneous computation of proxies for the expectations η_{it}^* of current endogenous variables, L.Bodin (1968a,c) has elabor-
ated the FFP method; the device is presented in Chapter 3.7 under the
name of *Recursive FFP* (RFP) estimation.

Whenever the FP, FFP or RFP procedures converge, the resulting estimates coincide, and are consistent in the large-sample sense. This is so since the estimates are functions of the product moments of the variables y_i, z_k; indeed, whenever these sample moments converge toward the corresponding theoretical moments as the sample increases indefinitely, the parameter estimates will converge in probability to the corresponding theoretical parameters.

In planning this study the sampling properties of the FP estimates were scheduled to be explored by Monte Carlo techniques. General expressions for standard errors for FP estimates of REID and GEID models were not available. However, E.Lyttkens has recently obtained large-sample formulas for the standard errors, and asymptotic expressions for the small-sample bias. Lyttkens reports some typical formulas along this line in Chapter 3.9. We repeat that these results fall outside the scope of our study as originally planned, and the results were obtained so recently that examples of their applied use could not be incorporated in our report.

3.2. Reference to More General ID Systems
by E. Lyttkens and H. Wold

The reformulation that carries from Classic ID to REID systems (see 1.4.4) and the generalization from REID to GEID systems (see 1.4.5) have repercussions on the patterns for the design of interdependent systems. This aspect of model construction will now be briefly discussed, with special regard to the dualism

$$\text{asymmetric vs symmetric design of the structural form.} \qquad (1)$$

As before, the operative aspects of the model will be in focus, and in particular so the operative use of the model in

$$\text{structural form vs reduced form} \qquad (2)$$

and the specification of the relations of the model in the terms of

$$\text{apparent scatter vs genuine scatter.} \qquad (3)$$

In the literature on Classic ID systems the structural form is usually written as

$$\beta Y_t = \Gamma Z_t + \delta_t . \tag{4}$$

This will be referred to as the *symmetric* design, or symmetric form, as distinct from (1.4.64) or (1.4.75), to repeat,

$$Y_t = \beta Y_t + \Gamma Z_t + \delta_t \tag{5a}$$

$$= \beta H_t^* + \Gamma Z_t + \epsilon_t , \tag{5b}$$

which is called the *asymmetric* design or the asymmetric form.

In Classic ID systems the y- and z-variables are moved freely across the equality sign of the structural form. This indicates that the stochastic specification of the model is to be interpreted in terms of apparent scatter (see 1.3). For another thing, the classic theory assumes all residuals to be uncorrelated with all predetermined variables (see 1.4.5), in symbols

$$r(\delta_i, z_k) = 0 , \qquad i = 1, ..., n ; k = 1, ..., m \tag{6}$$

and this implies that the y-variables can be moved freely across the equality sign (this statement refers to the theoretical specification of the structural form, and for the empirical relations it holds true in the large-sample sense). REID and GEID systems are specified in terms of genuine scatter. In REID systems the residuals are assumed to satisfy the classical assumptions (6). In GEID systems the assumptions are more general (again, see 1.4.5, Comment (i)), namely

$$r(\epsilon_i, \eta_q^*) = r(\epsilon_i, z_p) = 0 ; \qquad i = 1, ..., n , \tag{7}$$

where η_q^*, z_p are the variables that occur in the right-hand member of the ith relation in the structural form (5b). As a consequence, GEID systems cast in asymmetric form (5) do not in general allow a free move of the variables into the symmetric form (4). Hence we are led to ask whether the asymmetric design (5) sets restrictions for the potential scope of the model in operative use, and to what extent the scope can be broadened by designs of the symmetric type (4). To take up this question for a brief discussion we shall consider the designs from the point of view of the various types of structural relations used in the construction of econometric models. We follow the standard listing into four categories:

(a) behavioral relations,
(b) identities,
(c) technological or institutional relations,
(d) equilibrium relations.

With reference to Chart 1 for illustration, the situation may be summed up as follows.

Chart 3.2.1. Asymmetric vs symmetric specification of ID systems: joint use of structural form and reduced form vs reduced-form orientation.

A. The REID and GEID specifications of ID systems in terms of genuine scatter and predictors bring the dualism (1) to the foreground.
B. Equilibrium relations call for a generalization of the asymmetric design (5) of the structural form.
C. As the structural form gets a more symmetric design, the operative

use of the structural form must be moved to the background, and the model becomes what we will call "reduced-form oriented".

The three conclusions are rather immediate, and they will be developed in some more detail in the following comments.

(i) If a model involving apparent scatter is stripped of its residuals, its relationships become exact; for example, (4) gives

$$\beta Y_t = \Gamma Z_t . \qquad (8)$$

When a model specified in terms of genuine scatter and predictors is stripped of its residuals, the relations become conditional expectations; for example, (5b) gives

$$E(Y_t | H_t^*, Z_t) = \beta H_t^* + \Gamma Z_t , \qquad (9)$$

whereas (5a) in general does not allow a corresponding interpretation.

In the following comments the argument is at two levels. One is to explore the limitations inherent in the asymmetric specification (5) from the point of view of potential applications of ID systems; at the other level are the problems of probability analysis that arise when the approach of genuine scatter is extended from asymmetric to symmetric model designs. A problem area of key importance at the second level refers to the parity between the number of free coefficient parameters in the model and the number of zero correlation assumptions (6)–(7) imposed on its residuals. Classic ID systems and REID systems do not satisfy this "parity principle", and a main feature in the extension from REID to GEID systems is that the parity principle is honored.

The present monograph is in the main limited to the study of asymmetric ID systems (5). As should be clear from Chapters 1 and 2, this fact has no other rationale than the authors' research policy of "simple things first", and it must not be construed to imply that the authors believe that symmetric ID systems are not needed. The present comments on asymmetric vs symmetric designs are of a broad, non-technical nature. In Chapter 11 one of the authors (E.L.) gives a brief report on his research on symmetric ID systems as specified in terms of predictors for the reduced form, with special regard to the parity principle.

(ii) To repeat, the present monograph is mainly concerned with models where all structural relations are behavioral, category (a) in the list above. As is well known this case can be taken to cover also the categories (b) and (c). As to (b), each identity can be used to eliminate one endogenous variable from the structural system and thereby the entire model. This is evidently so in ID systems. In CC systems this device is subject to the qualification that the identity and the ensuing elimination must not break the chain pattern of the causal specification. As to (c), the statement covers all cases where the technological relations take the form of functional relationships or corresponding predictors, say relations (1.4.103a–b) or (1.4.107a–b).

(iii) With respect to the fourth category of relations, reference is made to the fundamental distinction between (α) long-range equilibria; that is, equilibrium relations as limiting relationships in a dynamic system, and (β) relations of instantaneous equilibrium. For a simple example, let us consider the model

$$d_t = D(z_{1t}, z_{2t}, ..., z_{mt}) + \epsilon_{1t} , \tag{10a}$$

$$s_t = S(z_{1t}, z_{2t}, ..., z_{mt}) + \epsilon_{2t} , \tag{10b}$$

$$d_t = s_t = q_t , \tag{10c}$$

where d_t denotes demand; s_t denotes supply; d_t is assumed to depend upon some or all of the variables $z_{1t}, ..., z_{mt}$, and similarly for s_t; relation (10c) is the hypothesis of instantaneous equilibrium, assuming that demand and supply are exactly the same in each observation period t; the common value of d_t and s_t is denoted q_t, "the quantity bought and sold".

As a source of interdependence in a multirelational model, the hypothesis of instantaneous equilibrium is radically different from interdependence in the sense of Chapter 1.4, Comments (xiii)–(xv).

The fundamental difference between the notions of equilibrium modes (α) and (β) can hardly be exaggerated. Typically, relations of instantaneous equilibrium are imposed as hypotheses or assumptions in the model construction, whereas long-range equilibrium relations are implications from the model. Thus for the relation of instantaneous equilibrium (10c) the corresponding equilibrium relation mode (α) would read

$$\lim_{t \to \infty} d_t = \lim_{t \to \infty} s_t \tag{11}$$

or it might take an even more relaxed form, say that demand and supply
tend to be equal on the average,

$$\lim_{k \to \infty} \frac{1}{k} (d_{t+1} + \cdots + d_{t+k}) = \lim_{k \to \infty} \frac{1}{k} (s_{t+1} + \cdots + s_{t+k}) . \qquad (12)$$

Conceptually and observationally, demand and supply are different
notions, and the difference cannot be glossed over by phrasings such as
"quantity bought and sold". This is also the case in other applications of
instantaneous equilibrium, for example savings and investment. Hence
the assumption of instantaneous equilibrium is in the nature of a shortcut, a deliberate simplification, which has to be judged with regard to
its degree of realism and its possible consequences in the estimation and
operative use of the model.

   This last point is of crucial relevance. To ignore the conceptual difference between demand and supply can be accepted even if the approximation is rather crude, provided the shortcut is neutral and does not involve a loss of important information. In this respect the hypothesis of
instantaneous equilibrium is a dangerous shortcut because the information that lies in the actual deviation from the instantaneous equilibrium
might well be a main point of interest. [1] For example, it is typical for
the price mechanism in dynamic demand-supply models that the deviation
$d_t - s_t$ between demand and supply serves as the main driving force of
the mechanism. Models that are dynamic in this sense do not involve the
assumption of instantaneous equilibrium; on the other hand, an equilibrium of type (11) or (12) may or may not enter as a theorem derived
from the model.

   Whether or not to include an assumption of instantaneous equilibrium
is a matter of aspiration levels of the model construction. A full-fledged
dynamic model that keeps apart demand and supply gives more information, but on the other hand it requires more detailed data and a more
elaborate model than a corresponding model of instantaneous equilibrium. Hence it may be perfectly all right from the point of view of research strategy to use the shortcut of instantaneous equilibrium for variables that are of secondary interest in the applications of the model, and
to reserve the full-fledged dynamic approach for variables that are of
primary relevance.

(iv) We shall briefly refer to two types of approach for the generalization of the asymmetric design (5) to situations where the model builder wants to supplement the behavioral relations with other types of relations.

To illustrate the first approach we consider a two-relation model of Summers' type, and include an instantaneous equilibrium relation of type (10c), which we write

$$y_{1t} = d_t = s_t . \tag{13}$$

The structural form may then be written

$$JY_t = \beta Y_t + \Gamma Z_t + \delta_t , \tag{14}$$

where

$$J = \begin{bmatrix} 1 & 0 \\ 1 & 0 \end{bmatrix}; \qquad \beta = \begin{bmatrix} 0 & \beta_{12} \\ 0 & \beta_{22} \end{bmatrix}, \tag{15}$$

while other notations in (14) are the same as in (1.4.64). The corresponding reduced form is

$$Y_t = [J - \beta]^{-1} \Gamma Z_t + \epsilon_t , \tag{16}$$

with

$$\epsilon_t = [J - \beta]^{-1} \delta_t . \tag{17}$$

The reformulation that carries from (5a) to (5b) extends to (14), and throws the structural relations into the form

$$JY_t = \beta H_t^* + \Gamma Z_t + \epsilon_t , \tag{18}$$

where the residual is the same in both relations, and the same as in the first relation of the reduced form (16).

The approach (13)–(18) extends to asymmetric models (5) where all structural relations are behavioral, and one or more assumptions of instantaneous equilibrium are imposed on the current endogenous variables y_i. Subject to the modifications that follow from the change from I

to J in the left-hand member, much of the theory of REID and GEID models in Chapter 1.4 extends to models of type (14). For each relation of instantaneous equilibrium there is one endogenous variable y_i that occurs twice in the left-hand member of the structural form, and some other variable y_q that does not occur in the left-hand member. The operative procedure O_1^* as applied to the structural form gives two predictions y_i^* for y_i; these predictions are exactly the same, and are subject to the same prediction error ϵ_i, and the result is the same if the prediction is obtained by applying procedure O_2 to the reduced form. As to the variable y_q, the procedure O_1^* and the structural form (14) give no prediction; procedure O_2 applies, and gives a prediction of y_q on the basis of the reduced form.

From the point of view of information theory we see that the approach (14) is not very attractive, inasmuch as the structural form provides a two-fold forecast for some endogenous variables, and no forecast for other ones. We shall leave it at this; may it just be mentioned that the FP method and related estimation techniques can be extended to the approach (14).

(v) The second type of approach is to give up altogether inference from the structural form; to write it in accordance with the symmetric design (4); and to base all predictions and other applications of the model on the reduced form. Again, this approach is not attractive from the point of view of information theory, inasmuch as information embodied in the structural form is not utilized.

(vi) To sum up, the symmetric form (4) of structural ID system is formally more general than the asymmetric form (5), but we have seen that the formal generalization is bought at a high price, namely the loss of operative inference from the structural form in the sense of cause-effect interpretation of behavioral relations. Thus whereas asymmetric ID systems allow operative inference both from the structural form and the reduced form (procedures O_1^* and O_2 in Chapter 1.4), symmetric ID systems are oriented toward operative use of the reduced form (the same as procedure O_2). The shift in the orientation of the operative use is depicted in Chart 1.

The present monograph focusses on interdependent systems where all relations are behavioral; that is, the inner circle of Chart 1. Out of the 46 models in Chart 2.3.1 that are the main object of our study, 43 have the asymmetric design of behavioral relations. Of these 43 models, 35 are ID systems of the classic type; that is, their residuals satisfy correlation assumptions (6) that make the models ambivalent with regard to asymmetric vs symmetric specification. Only 8 of the 35 models, namely Models 6a—c and 6f—j, are GEID models, and thereby strictly asymmetric in the sense that they do not possess the ambivalence referred to. The three remaining models, namely Models 4a—c, are designed for Monte Carlo simulation of symmetric models familiar from the econometric literature. The three models are overidentified, which implies that we cannot expect that the classical correlation assumptions (6) will be satisfied when the models are applied to empirical data. The Monte Carlo data for these models, however, have been generated in accordance with the classical assumptions (6).

3.3. **Ordinary Least Squares (OLS) Estimation**
by E. Lyttkens and H. Wold

Chapters 3.3 to 3.8 present the various estimation methods that have been used in the present study. For each method we indicate the formal procedure, and comment briefly on the sampling properties of the estimates, especially their consistency. In the main expository, the presentation emphasises the predictor specification of the models under estimation.

Linking up with the treatment of OLS regression in 1.3.5, we consider the predictor model (1.3.27), now in vector form with right-hand variables $z_0, z_1, ..., z_h$,

$$y = \beta Z + \epsilon , \tag{1a}$$

$$E(y|Z) = \beta Z , \tag{1b}$$

where

$$y = [y_1, ..., y_N] \tag{2}$$

is the row vector of observations $y_1, ..., y_N$;

$$\beta = [\beta_0, \beta_1, ..., \beta_h] \tag{3}$$

is the row vector of parameters $\beta_0, \beta_1, ..., \beta_h$;

$$Z = \| z_{it} \| ; \quad i = 0, 1, ..., h ; \quad t = 1, ..., N \qquad (4)$$

is the $(h + 1) \times N$ matrix of observations z_{it}, with

$$z_{01} = ... = z_{0N} = 1 . \qquad (5)$$

The coefficients b_i of the observed regression (1.3.28) are the OLS estimates. In vector notation, they are given by (1.3.40); to repeat

$$b = yZ'[ZZ']^{-1} . \qquad (6)$$

3.3.1. Applications of OLS to Multirelational Models [1]

As simple corollaries to the theorem in 1.3.5 we note the following two theorems.

Theorem 1. On the conditions specified in Theorem 1.3.5, OLS estimation is consistent if applied to the relations of a VR regression system (1.4.16) or to the structural relations (1.4.33) of a CC system.

Theorem 2. OLS estimation in general is inconsistent if applied to the structural relations of an ID system (1.4.64).

Proof. Theorem 2 is an immediate consequence of Theorem 1.3.5 and what we know from (1.4.73), namely that the structural relations of linear ID systems (1.4.64) in general do not constitute predictors.

Comment. Theorem 2 is in line with the fact that the approach of ID systems was initiated by a wholesale dismissal of OLS regression as applied to multirelational models. [2] Theorem 1 shows that this dismissal was exaggerated, inasmuch as the argument behind the dismissal applies to ID systems but not to CC systems.

3.3.2. Unrestricted Reduced Form (URF) Regression

The following theorems are immediate implications of the arguments in play in 3.3.1.

Theorem 3. On the assumptions of Classic ID systems (1.4.64) and REID systems (1.4.75), URF regression is consistent if applied to the systems in reduced form, (1.4.65) and (1.4.76b).

Theorem 4. URF regression in general is inconsistent if applied to the reduced form of a GEID system (1.4.88b).

3.3.3. Proximity theorem for ID Systems

The following theorem brings a considerable qualification of Theorem 2.

Theorem 5. Given an ID system (1.4.64) such that each residual ϵ_i of the corresponding system (1.4.75) or (1.4.87a) has a standard deviation not surpassing Δ,

$$\sigma(\epsilon_i) \leqslant \Delta \; ; \quad i = 1, ..., n , \tag{7}$$

and writing b_{iq}^*, g_{ip}^* for the limiting OLS estimates of β_{iq}, γ_{ip} in large samples,

$$b_{iq}^* = \lim_{T \to \infty} b_{iq} \; ; \qquad g_{ip}^* = \lim_{T \to \infty} g_{ip} . \tag{8}$$

the inconsistency of the OLS estimates is of an order of magnitude that does not surpass Δ^2,

$$\mathrm{E}(|b_{iq}^* - \beta_{iq}|) \leqslant c_1 \Delta^2 \; ; \;\; \mathrm{E}(|g_{ip}^* - \gamma_{ip}|) \leqslant c_2 \Delta^2 , \tag{9a--b}$$

where c_1, c_2 are constants that can be evaluated in terms of the product moments of the variables y_i, z_k.

Proof. First stated by Wold [23], Theorem 5 is a simple corollary of the proximity theorem of ordinary regression analysis[3]. Considering the ith structural relation, (1.4.87b) implies that the assumptions of the proximity theorem are automatically satisfied with regard to the intercorrelation between ϵ_i and z_p. This is true also as regards the intercorrelation between ϵ_i and y_q, for relation (1.4.87b) implies

$$E[y_q \epsilon_i] = E[(y_q^* + \epsilon_q)\epsilon_i] = E(\epsilon_q \, \epsilon_i) \, , \qquad (10)$$

which gives

$$|r(y_q, \epsilon_i)| \leqslant \sigma(\epsilon_q)/\sigma(y_q) \leqslant \text{const } \Delta \, . \qquad (11)$$

3.3.4. Overfitting

Theorem 5 is a source of comfort in applied work with ID systems, inasmuch as OLS estimation is very simple to handle. The back side of the coin is that small residuals of OLS regression sometimes are illusory because of "overfitting". The pitfall of overfitting is of old standing, whereas the term is recent; see Wold [14]. For any set of sample data, the residuals in the expression will automatically become small and eventually vanish if explanatory variables are introduced in larger number than the available observations. There is further the point that the overfitting is aggrevated by the autocorrelations which as a rule occur in time series data, and which often make the residual variances elusively small even when corrections for degrees of freedom are applied by the standard formula. Hence in practice the model builder must balance between the advantages of working with many explanatory variables and small residuals, and the ensuing dangers of overfitting. To strike a sound balance is very much a matter of having a sound subject-matter theory as a basis when designing the model and specifying the explanatory variables of the structural relations. To check the balance, purely statistical tests on the parameter estimates are of limited scope, for such tests require a working knowledge about the distributional properties of the residuals, and such knowledge is seldom if ever available in time series analysis. This is one reason for subjecting the estimated model to predictive testing; that is, generating forecasts from the model, and comparing the forecasts with fresh observations.

3.3.5. Standard Errors of OLS and URF Estimates

While Theorems 1 and 3–4 provide sufficient conditions for consistency of OLS and URF estimates, more restrictive assumptions are needed to establish standard errors and confidence intervals of the estimates. We quote the classical formula for variances and covariances of the OLS regression coefficients (6):

$$E[(b-\beta)'\,(b-\beta)] = [ZZ']^{-1}\sigma^2(\epsilon)\,. \tag{12}$$

For the validity of formula (12) the assumption of mutually uncorrelated residuals is essential.

In econometric forecasting models, the data are usually time series. When the time series are stationary, Theorem 1.3.5 implies that the OLS estimates (6) are consistent even if the residuals are autocorrelated. As to the requisite modification of (12), reference is made to Wold (1950) or Wold-Juréen (1952) for the case when no lagged variable y occurs among the variables Z, and to Lyttkens (1964a) for the case when one or more lagged variables y may occur among the variables Z.

3.4. Two-Stage Least Squares (TSLS) Estimation
by E. Lyttkens and H. Wold

The TSLS method, due to Theil (1954, 1958), is designed for the estimation of Classic ID systems. A great step forward in the statistical treatment of ID systems, TSLS has been widely used. Reference is made to Basmann [1–3, 5–6] for his analysis of the TSLS method from the point of view of generalized linear estimation.

As shown by Theil (1958) the TSLS method is consistent as applied to Classic ID systems (1.4.64). The consistency carries over to REID systems (1.4.75) as an immediate corollary. When it comes to GEID systems (1.4.87) the TSLS method in general is inconsistent.

The TSLS procedure as applied to a Classic ID system (1.4.64) or a REID system (1.4.75) is as follows. Let Y^* denote the systematic part of Y as given by URF estimation; that is

$$Y^* = WZ, \tag{1}$$

where W is an auxiliary estimate of matrix Ω in (1.4.65). This is the first stage of the TSLS procedure. In the second stage Y^* is carried into the structural form (1.4.64), replacing Y in the right-hand member, and OLS is applied to the structural form as modified by this substitution. In symbols, the second stage of the TSLS procedure is, thus, to apply OLS to obtain the parameter estimates B, G in the system

$$Y = BY^* + GZ + e. \tag{2}$$

As briefly mentioned by Theil (1958), the TSLS procedure allows a formal rearrangement, here to be called the TSLS* method, which leads to the same numerical parameter estimates in all cases where each reduced form relation contains all predetermined variables. The TSLS* procedure is as TSLS in the first stage, and differs in the second stage by substituting Y^* in both members of (1.4.64). The second stage of TSLS* thus applies OLS to obtain the estimates B, G in the system

$$Y^* = BY^* + GZ + v. \tag{3}$$

In Classic ID systems and REID systems, the residuals v will vanish asymptotically in large samples. Irrespective of the sample size, however, the parameter estimates B, G will be identical in (2) and (3) in most cases. In fact, as is readily seen, the two procedures will give precisely the same normal equations for the parameter estimates.

Conceptually, the TSLS method is closely related to REID systems, and more so than the TSLS* method. This is the main reason why the TSLS version rather than the TSLS* version has been used in the applications of two-stage least squares reported in this monograph.

Comments. (i) The consistency of TSLS as applied to Classic ID systems or REID systems follows by the same general argument as in 1.3.5. The theoretical parameters β, Γ are solutions to the theoretical normal equation system in the second stage, and thereby are rational functions of the theoretical product moments of the variables y_i, z_k. Hence the parameter estimates B, G will have the corresponding theoretical parameters β, Γ for probability limits, provided the product moments in the sample tend to the corresponding theoretical moments as the sample increases indefinitely. [1]

(ii) The assumptions in Classic ID systems are essential for the consistency of the first stage of the TSLS procedure; see Comment (iii) in 1.4.5. In fact, if each current residual δ_{it} were not uncorrelated with all of the predetermined variables z_{kt}, the first stage estimates w_{ij} of the coefficients in the reduced form would not be consistent estimates of the corresponding theoretical parameters ω_{ij}.

(iii) In (2)–(3) we have described the TSLS and TSLS* procedures as applied to Classic ID systems (1.4.64) where all structural relations are behavioral. As is well known, both versions extend to Classic ID systems of more general design, and in particular to models that include relations of instantaneous equilibrium; see 3.2. For each instantaneous equilibrium one of the current endogenous variables y_{it} will occur to the left in two behavioral relations of the structural form. The assumptions of Classic ID systems remain essential for TSLS estimation to be consistent, namely that each current residual is uncorrelated with all of the predetermined variables.

3.4.1. Standard Errors of TSLS Estimates

We quote the large-sample formula of the variances and covariances of TSLS estimates as given by Basmann (1957),

$$E[(a_i - \alpha_i)'\,(a_i - \alpha_i)] = [V_i V_i']^{-1}\, s^2(d_i)\,, \qquad (4)$$

where

$$\alpha_i = [\beta_{iq}, \gamma_{ip}] \qquad (5)$$

is the row vector of coefficients β_{iq}, γ_{ip} of the variables η_{iq}^*, z_{ip} that occur in the right-hand member of the ith structural relation;

$$a_i = [b_{iq}, g_{ip}] \qquad (6)$$

are the TSLS estimates of the coefficients a_i; we write

$$V_i = \begin{bmatrix} y^*_{iq} \\ z_{ip} \end{bmatrix} \tag{7}$$

for the column vector of observed values of variables; and $s^2(d_i)$ is the observed residual variance of the ith structural relation. Theil (1958) gives a large-sample formula which is numerically equivalent to (4), there being only the formal difference that Theil gives the product moments $[V_i V'_i]$ in terms of product sums $\sum_t y_{qt} z_{pt}$ instead of $\sum_t y^*_{qt} z_{pt}$.

3.5. Fix-Point (FP) Estimation

The fix-point (FP) method due to Wold (1965c, 1966c) is designed for the estimation of Classic ID systems (1.4.64), REID systems (1.4.75) and GEID systems (1.4.87). The FP procedure works on the structural form of the system; once the structural form is estimated the reduced form is obtained by the algebraic transform (1.4.76). The FP method is designed for models where the structural form is specified in terms of predictors, as in (1.4.75) or (1.4.87). For application to a Classic ID system (1.4.64), the system must first be reformulated as in (1.4.75).

The FP procedure performs a simultaneous estimation of the parameters β, Γ and the expectations η^*_i. The procedure is iterative, in accordance with the fact that the structural forms (1.4.75) and (1.4.87) are nonlinear in β, Γ and η^*_i. Starting by an initial proxy $Y^{(0)}$ for H^*_t, the FP procedure calculates consecutive proxies for β, Γ and H^*_t, denoted by

$$B^{(s)}, G^{(s)}, Y^{(s)}_t ; \quad s = 1, 2, \dots ; \quad t = 1, \dots, N . \tag{1}$$

The limiting elements, denoted

$$B = \lim_{s \to \infty} B^{(s)}, \quad G = \lim_{s \to \infty} G^{(s)}, \quad Y^*_t = \lim_{s \to \infty} Y^{(s)}_t \quad (2a-c)$$

constitute the FP estimates of β, Γ and H_t^*.

We shall describe the FP procedure by specifying the start and the passage from the $(s-1)$st to the sth proxies.

The start. The initial proxy $Y_t^{(0)}$ is largely arbitrary. The typical device is to start by a linear combination of the predetermined variables z_{kt} $(k = 1, ..., m)$, say

$$y_{it}^{(0)} = 0, \qquad (i = 1, ..., n ; \quad t = 1, ..., N) \tag{3a}$$

briefly called "zero start", [1] or the first stage of the TSLS method,

$$y_{it}^{(0)} = \sum_{k=1}^{m} w_{ik} z_{kt}, \qquad (i = 1, ..., n ; \quad t = 1, ..., N), \tag{3b}$$

where matrix $W = \| w_{ik} \|$ is the URF estimate of matrix Ω in (1.4.76b) or (1.4.88b).

Sometimes, and in particular so in FFP and RFP estimation — the generalized FP procedures to be described in Chapters 3.6 and 3.7 — it may be appropriate to start with

$$y_{it}^{(0)} = y_{it}, \qquad (i = 1, ..., n ; \quad t = 1, ..., N). \tag{3c}$$

The step from the $(s-1)$st to the sth iteration. The proxy $Y_t^{(s-1)}$ as obtained in the $(s-1)$st step is substituted to the right in the structural form (1.4.75) or (1.4.87). Applying OLS regression to the structural form thus modified, the resulting regression coefficients constitute the proxies $B^{(s)}$, $G^{(s)}$; in symbols,

$$Y_t = B^{(s)} Y_t^{(s-1)} + G^{(s)} Z_t + e_t^{(s)}, \tag{4}$$

the ensuing residuals being denoted $e^{(s)}$. The proxy $Y_t^{(s)}$ is given by the systematic parts of the regression relations (4); in symbols

$$Y_t^{(s)} = B^{(s)} Y_t^{(s-1)} + G^{(s)} Z_t \tag{5}$$

The FP procedure stops if the proxies $B^{(s)}$, $G^{(s)}$, $Y_t^{(s)}$ remain the same in the $(s+1)$st step; in accordance with (2a–c) these proxies then constitute the FP estimates B, G, Y_t^*.

Comment. The main purpose of the present monograph is to explore the performance of the FP method as compared with other methods for the estimation of ID systems, especially TSLS. The results are reported in Chapters 4 to 10, and summarized in Chapters 12 and 13. In the course of our investigation the FP method was supplemented by three related techniques described in Chapter 3.6 to 3.8, namely the iterative FFP and RFP procedures and the non-iterative algebraic treatment of special cases.

3.6. Fractional Fix-Point (FFP) Estimation [1]
by A.Ågren

3.6.1. The Method

The fractional fix-point (FFP) method is designed for the estimation of the same type of models as the FP method. In fact, the FFP method is very similar to the FP method. The difference lies in the calculation of the new proxies for H^* in each iteration. In the description of FFP given below we shall use exactly the same notations as in the previous section.

Assuming that we have completed the step '$s-1$' and have obtained estimates $B^{(s-1)}$, $G^{(s-1)}$ and $Y^{(s-1)}$, the calculations for step 's' are as follows:

(i) Apply OLS regression on the structural form (1.4.87a) where we use the proxies $Y^{(s-1)}$ instead of H*. This gives us $B^{(s)}$ and $G^{(s)}$.

(ii) $Y^{(s)}$ is obtained from

$$Y^{(s)} = \alpha \mathsf{Y}^{(s)} + (1-\alpha)\, Y^{(s-1)}, \tag{1}$$

where

$$\mathsf{Y}^{(s)} = B^{(s)}\, Y^{(s-1)} + G^{(s)} Z. \tag{2}$$

Hence, substituting for $\mathsf{Y}^{(s)}$,

$$Y^{(s)} = [\alpha B^{(s)} + (1-\alpha)\, \mathrm{I}]\, Y^{(s-1)} + \alpha\, G^{(s)} Z, \tag{3}$$

with I as the identity matrix. The iteration procedure is continued until successive estimates of either β and Γ or of H* deviate from each other by a value that is less than a prescribed convergence criterion. α is a constant in the interval $(0,2)$. It will be shown below that the choice of α is of great importance to the convergence properties of the iteration procedure. In the special case $\alpha = 1$ we have the FP method, and FP can therefore be considered as a special case of the FFP method.

If the matrices β and Γ were known from the beginning we see that the FP method is nothing else than the Jacobi method for solving a system of linear equations, and the FFP method is the Jacobi method combined with a relaxation factor α. In this case the OLS regression in (i) would be skipped, and only (ii) above would be performed in step 's'. In estimating econometric models β and Γ are not known and have to be estimated in each step. Consequently the iteration matrix is changed in each step and the convergence properties of a model are not easy to evaluate before the iterations have started. However, we can state that the FFP method is the Jacobi method combined with a relaxation factor where the iteration matrix is adjusted in each step of the iterations.

A reasonable approach to the convergence problem is the following: If the procedure will converge we must reach a point in the iteration process when $B^{(s)}$ and $G^{(s)}$ are very close to the final values. From that point we can regard them as constant and only do part (ii) above. For constant β and Γ we can state the following theorem. [2]

Theorem. Let $\beta = (n \times n)$, $\Gamma = (n \times m)$ and $Z = (n \times N)$ be known constant matrices, where $(I - \beta)$ is assumed to be non-singular. Let $U^{(0)} = (n \times N)$ be an arbitrary matrix and apply the iteration procedure

$$U^{(s+1)} = \alpha U^{(s+1)} + (1 - \alpha) U^{(s)}, \tag{4}$$

where

$$U^{(s+1)} = \beta U^{(s)} + \Gamma Z. \tag{5}$$

Then

$$\lim_{s \to \infty} U^{(s)} = U \quad \text{and} \quad U = \beta U + \Gamma Z \tag{6a--b}$$

for any $U^{(0)}$ if and only if all the eigenvalues of the following matrix K

lie inside the unit circle in the complex plane,

$$K = K(\alpha) = \alpha\beta + (1-\alpha)I$$

The existence of an α such that this is the case is assured if and only if the real parts of the eigenvalues of β are all less than 1.

For the proof reference is made to Ågren [1].

Comment. From what has been said above about $B^{(\Sigma)}$ and $G^{(s)}$ changing in each step of the iterative process, it is evident that we cannot expect this theorem which is based on a constant β and Γ to be strictly valid in all situations. But empirical investigations have shown that it explains a great deal about the convergence properties of FFP and, since FP is a special case of FFP, of FP.

Illustration. It is revealing to analyze what the theorem tells us about convergence in the simple Summers' model. We write Summers' model in the following way

$$y_1 = \beta_{12}\eta_2^* + \gamma_{11}z_1 + \gamma_{12}z_2 + \epsilon_1 , \qquad (7a)$$

$$y_2 = \beta_{21}\eta_1^* + \gamma_{23}z_3 + \gamma_{24}z_4 + \epsilon_2 \qquad (7b)$$

and we assume that the coefficients β_{ik} and γ_{ik} are obtained by the direct solution described by E.Lyttkens in Chapter 3.8. The matrix β in the theorem is in this case

$$\beta = \begin{bmatrix} 0 & \beta_{12} \\ \beta_{21} & 0 \end{bmatrix} \qquad (8)$$

and the eigenvalues of β are easily found to be

$$\lambda_i = \pm\sqrt{\beta_{12}\beta_{21}} ; \quad i = 1, 2 . \qquad (9)$$

Now the theorem states that it is possible to find an α such that all the eigenvalues of $K(\alpha) = \alpha\beta + (1-\alpha)I$ lie inside the unit circle if and only if the real parts of the eigenvalues of β are all less than one. Hence we must have

$$-\infty < \beta_{12}\beta_{21} < 1 . \tag{10}$$

If this condition is not satisfied it is not possible to choose α such that the iterations will converge.

As regards the value of α which shall be used in the FFP method we can expect that the iteration procedure converges faster, the smaller the spectral radius of the iteration matrix $K(\alpha)$. We define α_{opt} as the value of α which minimizes the spectral radius of $K(\alpha)$. By some simple calculations we obtain

$$\alpha_{opt} = \frac{1}{1 + |\beta_{12}\beta_{21}|} \qquad \text{when} \qquad -\infty < \beta_{12}\beta_{21} < 0 \tag{11}$$

and

$$\alpha_{opt} = 1 \qquad \text{when} \qquad 0 < \beta_{12}\beta_{21} < 1 . \tag{12}$$

The upper limit of those α which make the spectral radius of $K(\alpha)$ less than 1 shall be called α_{max}. We have

$$\alpha_{max} = \frac{2}{1 + |\beta_{12}\beta_{21}|} \qquad \text{when} \qquad -\infty < \beta_{12}\beta_{21} < 0 \tag{13}$$

and

$$\alpha_{max} = \frac{2}{1 + \sqrt{\beta_{12}\beta_{21}}} \qquad \text{when} \qquad 0 < \beta_{12}\beta_{21} < 1 . \tag{14}$$

Provided that the FP estimates for β_{ik} and γ_{ik} are valid for assessing convergence we now have a formula for determining the necessary conditions for convergence in a Summers' model, namely, $\alpha < \alpha_{max}$ and condition (10) above. We can also use formulas (11)–(12) to determine the α which will minimize the number of iterations.

We shall now apply and test our theorem on the Monte Carlo results for the 46 models presented in this volume. Illustrations will be taken from those few models in which convergence of FP was a problem.

3.6.2. Empirical Illustrations

Example 1. Convergence for FP and FFP. With reference to Ågren [1] for further details we shall give results from FFP estimates of Models 1c, 1e and 1f, Chart 2.3.1. They are Summers' type models with beta matrices

$$\begin{bmatrix} 0 & 3 \\ -3 & 0 \end{bmatrix}, \quad \begin{bmatrix} 0 & 0.5 \\ -3 & 0 \end{bmatrix} \quad \text{and} \quad \begin{bmatrix} 0 & 1.1 \\ -3 & 0 \end{bmatrix}$$

respectively. The data in the 100 samples is the same as used in the FP estimation of which the results are reported in Tables 10.2.3, 10.2.5 and 10.2.6. Table 3.6.1 shows the number of samples in which FP and FFP converged within 200 iterations; the minimum and maximum number of iterations among the samples for which there was convergence in each model; the average and standard deviation of the number of iterations, always honoring the limit 200; and the value of α which was used.

Table 3.6.1
Illustrations of convergence for FP and FFP

Model	Method	No. of convergent samples	No. of iterations				α
			Min	Max	Average	S.D.	
1c	FP	40	6	16	123.8	93.8	1
	FFP	95	43	78	62.1	32.3	0.2
1e	FP	40	11	88	134.3	81.6	1
	FFP	95	19	75	40.5	37.6	0.4
1f	FP	78	5	30	51.9	79.1	1
	FFP	98	26	144	43.3	28.6	0.3

Comments. (i) The values of α_{max} for the specified beta matrices are 0.2, 0.8 and 0.47, respectively, but for the generated samples of each model we have variation in b_{12} and b_{21} which leads to variation in a_{max}, i.e. the estimate of α_{max}. This explains why we have some samples which did not give convergence even though we used an α-value below 0.8 and 0.47 for Models 1e and 1f.

(ii) In the calculation of the average number of iterations those samples which did not give convergence are also included.

(iii) The poor results of the FP method for these three models can be improved by using the FFP method. A report on further applications of the FFP method is in preparation.

(iv) We see that the FP method gives convergence for quite a few samples even though the α_{max} is considerably less than one. This surprising result is due to "apparent convergence", a phenomenon which has been investigated by Bodin (see 3.7.4). If the convergence criterion had been sufficiently small, all samples where the observed a_{max} was less than one would have led to divergence.

Example 2. Convergence as influenced by the size of residuals. In this example we shall again use Summers' model to illustrate how the size of the residuals influences the convergence properties of the FP method (i.e., the FFP method with $\alpha = 1$).

We shall consider two different situations, namely when the value of α_{max} for the specified model is (a) less than one and (b) greater than one. In case (a) we expect divergence and in case (b) we expect convergence with the FP method. If in a Monte Carlo study under situation (a) the

Table 3.6.2
Four designs for Summers' model

Model	R^2	α_{max}	β_{12}	β_{21}	γ_{ik}	$\sigma^2(\delta_i)$
1	0.80	0.75	1.291	−1.291	1.0328	0.5333
2	0.20	0.75	1.291	−1.291	0.5164	2.1333
3	0.80	1.25	0.7746	−0.7746	0.8000	0.3200
4	0.20	1.25	0.7746	−0.7746	0.4000	1.2800

Table 3.6.3
Results of a Monte Carlo study on a_{max}

Model	α_{max}	$\bar{a}_{max}$	S.D.	M
1	0.75	0.778	0.125	5
2	0.75	1.10	0.424	39
3	1.25	1.27	0.121	97
4	1.25	1.41	0.378	85

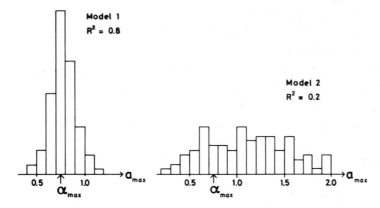

Chart 3.6.1. Distribution of a_{max} in 100 samples from Models 1 and 2 in Table 2.

value of R^2 is close to 1, sampling variation will be small and few of the generated samples will have an $a_{max} > 1$. That is, few samples will converge. On the other hand, if R^2 is small a larger number of samples can have $a_{max} > 1$ and, therefore, there will be more samples that converge. Under situation (a), for a given model, FP will thus converge for a larger number of samples as R^2 is decreased.

Under situation (b) we see that FP will converge for a higher percentage of samples as R^2 is increased. This is because the FP solution for the β matrix approaches the specified values (and values for which there will be convergence) as R^2 increases.

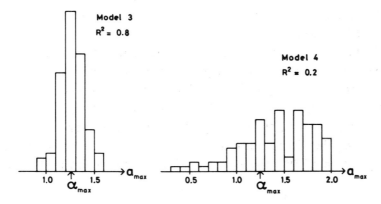

Chart 3.6.2. Distribution of a_{max} in 100 samples from Models 3 and 4 in Table 2.

In order to test the two statements about the effect of size of R^2 on number of converging samples in situations (a) and (b) four models were designed as is shown in Table 2.

For each model 100 samples were generated. The critical value a_{max} was calculated for each sample based on the estimates of β_{12} and β_{21}, using Lyttkens' direct method for calculating b_{12} and b_{21} (see Chapter 3.8). Table 3 shows the mean value of a_{max} ($\bar{a}_{max}$), its standard deviation (S.D.) and the number of samples (M) with an a_{max} greater than unity. Finally, Charts 1 and 2 show the distribution of the a_{max} values for the four different designs.

Models 1 and 2 belong to situation (a) since $\alpha_{max} = 0.75 < 1$. When R^2 is decreased from 0.80 to 0.20 the number of samples with a_{max} greater than one increases from 5 to 39 (see Table 3.6.3). Models 3 and 4 belong to situation (b) since $\alpha_{max} = 1.25 > 1$. When R^2 is increased from 0.20 to 0.80 the number of samples with a_{max} greater than one increases from 85 to 97 (see Table 3). These results are in agreement with the argument based on $(11)-(14)$.

3.7. Recursive Fix-Point (RFP) Estimation [1]
by L.Bodin

Two additional modifications of the FP procedure will be presented, called R_1FP and RFP. Both modifications are designed for the estimation of the same type of models for which FP is intended.

The differences between the FP method and the two modifications presented here are:

(i) The need for computer storage will be smaller than in FP.

(ii) The calculations of the new proxies for the component variables η_i^* are done in a recursive (sequential) way in R_1FP and RFP.

(iii) In RFP the new proxies for H* are used in the least squares regression in the same iteration step 's' in which they were computed.

Following the same notations as in the previous chapters, we define a decomposition of $B^{(s)}$, the estimate of the β-matrix in the sth step:

$$B^{(s)} = E^{(s)} + F^{(s)} , \tag{1}$$

where $E^{(s)}$ contains only zeros above the main diagonal and $F^{(s)}$ contains only zeros below the main diagonal. $E^{(s)}$ and $F^{(s)}$ are said to be *lower* and *upper* triangular matrices.

3.7.1. Recursive FP Estimation; Single Sequence (R₁FP)

This procedure has been presented as *Modified Fractional Fix-Point (MFP) Estimation* (see Bodin [1]), now renamed and denoted R_1FP.

The start is the same as in FP and FFP estimation.

The step from the $(s-1)$st to the sth iteration is as follows:

In step '$s-1$' the proxies $B^{(s-1)}$, $G^{(s-1)}$, $Y_t^{(s-1)}$ are obtained.

(i) Since H* is not known, $Y^{(s-1)}$ is used to the right instead of H* to form the OLS regression of the structural form (1.4.75) or (1.4.87). This will give $B^{(s)}$ and $G^{(s)}$. Hence the regression is equivalent to FP and FFP:

$$Y = B^{(s)} Y^{(s-1)} + G^{(s)} Z + e^{(s)} . \tag{2}$$

(ii) $Y^{(s)}$ is then obtained from the equation

$$Y^{(s)} = [I - \alpha E^{(s)}]^{-1} [(1-\alpha)I + \alpha F^{(s)}] Y^{(s-1)}$$

$$+ \alpha [I - \alpha E^{(s)}]^{-1} G^{(s)} Z , \tag{3}$$

where I is the identity matrix, and α is a constant, $0 < \alpha < 2$.

The characteristic feature of this calculation of $Y^{(s)}$ is that the first calculated components of $Y^{(s)}$, that is, $y_j^{(s)}$ where $1 \leqslant j < i$, are used in the calculation of $y_i^{(s)}$ together with $y_k^{(s-1)}$ where $i \leqslant k \leqslant n$.

If $E^{(s)}$ and $F^{(s)}$ were constant and $\alpha = 1$, the procedure R_1FP would be equivalent to the Gauss-Seidel method for the iterative solution of a system of linear equations. For constant $E^{(s)}$ and $F^{(s)}$ and $\alpha \neq 1$, the procedure is equivalent to the successive (over-)relaxation method (see Varga [1]). In the estimation of econometric models the iteration matrix is not constant throughout the iterations; consequently, the R_1FP procedure is not strictly comparable to either the Gauss-Seidel or the over-relaxation method.

The convergence problem for R_1FP could be attacked by the same approach as in Chapter 3.6. In practice, however, it turns out that the determination of the spectral radius of the iteration matrix of R_1FP is much more troublesome than for FFP.

3.7.2. Recursive FP Estimation, Double Sequence (RFP)

The start is equivalent to that in the FP method.

The step from the $(s-1)$st to the sth iteration is as follows:
(i) OLS regression is performed in the first relation of the structural form with the use of components $y_q^{(s-1)}$ to the right instead of the components $\eta_q^{(s-1)}$.
(ii) $y_1^{(s)}$ is calculated according to (3).
(iii) OLS regression is performed in the second relation of the structural form but with the use of $y_1^{(s)}$ and requisite components $y_q^{(s-1)}$ to the right.

Then all other relations are estimated according to the same principle, which can be formulated into the OLS regression

$$Y = E^{(s)} Y^{(s)} + F^{(s)} Y^{(s-1)} + G^{(s)} Z + e^{(s)} \tag{4}$$

followed by the calculation of $Y^{(s)}$ from (3).

The characteristic feature of RFP is that the procedure in step 's' alternates between least squares regression and calculation of new component proxies $y_i^{(s)}$. The design of RFP implies that the information about the component proxies $y_i^{(s)}$ that are available during the iteration step 's' is used without delay.

3.7.3. Comparisons between the Iteration Methods

An immediate consequence of the recursive computation of $Y^{(s)}$ used in R_1FP and RFP is that the order in which the relations are estimated is of great importance. By choosing an appropriate order it is possible to reduce the number of iterations considerably. In some cases it is possible to have either convergence or divergence depending on which ordering of the relations is used (Bodin [4]).

Table 3.7.1
Speed of convergence for different fix-point estimation methods

| | Number of iterations required for convergence | | | |
	Model 1e	Model 3c	Model 2c	Model 2d
FP	62	no conv.	79	63
FFP	28	180	73	63
R_1FP	15	83	40	31
RFP	10	37	12	11

In order to compare the different fix-point methods, several models of the type studied in this monograph and some models with empirical data have been estimated with the FP, FFP, R_1FP and RFP methods. If the methods are ranked according to the results of this estimation as regards region of convergence and number of iterations the ranking will show RFP as the best method, followed by R_1FP, FFP and FP (Bodin [2,4]). Table 1 shows a typical result from this comparison. The number of iterations for four Monte Carlo models, one sample from each, is the smallest for method RFP. For FFP, R_1FP and RFP the number of iterations are given for the best choice of α, and for the best ordering of equations in the case of R_1FP and RFP.

Chart 1 shows similarities and differences between the FP method and its modifications FFP, R_1FP and RFP as regards the computation of the new component proxies $y_i^{(s)}$ and the parameter proxies $B^{(s)}$ and $G^{(s)}$. The arrows indicate that information from a preceding computation in

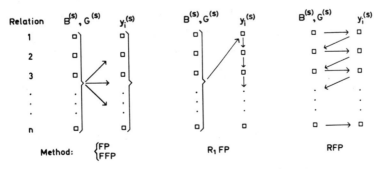

Chart 3.7.1. Computation of $B^{(s)}$, $G^{(s)}$ and $y_i^{(s)}$ for different fix-point estimation methods.

step 's' is used in the actual computation, and the brackets indicate that there is no sequential use of information within a bracket.

3.7.4. Apparent Convergence

As pointed out in Chapter 3.6, it is necessary in the analysis of the convergence properties of the FP method and its modifications FFP, R_1FP and RFP to distinguish between two kinds of convergence, namely, true convergence and apparent convergence.

Suppose that the convergence of the FP method is tested on the estimated parameters of the β and Γ matrices by the following convergence criterion:

$$\left| \frac{a_{ij}^{(s)} - a_{ij}^{(s-1)}}{a_{ij}^{(s)}} \right| < 10^{-k}, \tag{5}$$

where $a_{ij}^{(s)}$ and $a_{ij}^{(s-1)}$ denote the estimated parameters of the β and Γ matrices in steps 's' and 's−1'. For $k = k_0$ we assume for the moment that (5) is satisfied for all i and j when $s = s_0$, giving

$$\left| \frac{a_{ij}^{(s_0)} - a_{ij}^{(s_0-1)}}{a_{ij}^{(s_0)}} \right| < 10^{-k_0} \tag{6}$$

Definitions: (i) True convergence means that (5) is satisfied for *all* $s \geqslant s_0$. When s increases (5) will be satisfied for larger values of k until the accuracy of the computer puts a limit on k.

(ii) Apparent convergence means that (5) is satisfied only for a limited sequence of $s \geqslant s_0$, that is, $s_0, s_0 + 1, s_0 + 2, ..., s_0 + v$. When s increases (5) will not be satisfied for $k = k_0$ and some $s > s_0 + v$, and the iterations will diverge.

Comments: (i) True convergence coincides with the ordinary definition of convergence.

(ii) In actual estimation the accuracy of the computer will limit the range of k in (5). This limit also depends on whether the calculations are performed in single or double precision of the computer.

Illustration. A typical example of true and apparent convergence is given by the following FP estimation of two samples of Model 1f. The samples were estimated with the first-stage estimates of TSLS as starting values. For the first sample 10,000 iterations were done and for the second 5000 iterations. As a test of convergence (5) was used with $k = 6$ but the iterations were allowed to continue even if (5) had been satisfied. In this way the estimates obtained when the convergence criterion (5) with $k = 6$ was satisfied could be compared with those obtained for $s = 10,000$ and 5000, respectively. Earlier investigations had shown that both samples satisfied (5) for $k = 6$. For each sample the fix-point estimates were also calculated by Lyttkens' non-iterative method (see Chapter 3.8).

The results are summarized in the following table.

Table 3.7.2
Illustration of true vs apparent convergence

		Sample 1	Sample 2
Non-iterative solution	β_{12}	1.117541	1.002653
	β_{21}	−1.428967	−0.110643
TSLS	β_{12}	1.149435	1.036816
	β_{21}	−1.394619	−0.091248
FP estimates when the convergence criterion is satisfied [1]	β_{12}	1.117541	1.002653
	β_{21}	−1.428967	−0.110643
FP estimates for the iteration limit [2]	β_{12}	(1.072605)	1.002653
	β_{21}	(−0.887871)	−0.110643

[1] Apparent convergence after 16 iterations for sample 1.
   True convergence after 11 iterations for sample 2.
[2] Divergence in sample 1; the parameter values have no meaning.

The results of the FP estimation of Sample 1 illustrate apparent convergence. The estimate of the parameters of the β and Γ matrices obtained after 16 iterations satisfied the convergence criterion (5) for $k = 6$ but they are not stable and diverge as the iterations continue. The estimates obtained for $s = 10,000$ cannot be interpreted as FP estimates. The spectral radius of the β matrix, with the FP estimates inserted, is larger than unity.

The results of the FP estimation of Sample 2 exemplifies true convergence. This is shown by the fact that the estimates for $s = 11$ are with seven figures the same as those for $s = 5000$. The spectral radius of the β matrix for this sample is smaller than unity.

Comments: (i) The problems of apparent convergence are rather similar to those appearing in connection with semi-convergent series. Another name for "apparent convergence" could be "semi-convergence".

(ii) For a given k in (5), estimates obtained under apparent convergence as a rule show deviations from the non-iterative FP estimates that are of size $c \cdot 10^{-k}$.

(iii) We have never obtained apparent convergence in cases when the spectral radius of the β matrix is smaller than unity. Our interpretation of the final divergence in samples that first show apparent convergence is that rounding errors are accumulated from step to step. This accumulated error will grow and cause divergence if the spectral radius of the β matrix, the iteration matrix, is larger than unity. In the opposite case the accumulated error will decrease and vanish.

(iv) Apparent convergence was rather frequent in this study for the three Models 1c, 1e and 1f, as shown in Table 3.

(v) For further studies of apparent convergence, see Bodin [3, 4].

Table 3.7.3
Frequency of apparent and true convergence in Models 1c, 13 and 1f

Model	Samples with convergence	Samples with apparent convergence	Samples with true convergence
1c	40	40	0
1e	40	25	15
1f	78	63	15

3.8. Algebraic FP (AFP) Estimation of Summers' Model [1]
by E. Lyttkens

Least squares estimates (OLS) as applied to REID and GEID systems leads to a non-linear system of normal equations for the parameter estimates. The FP method is an iterative approach for solving the normal equations. This section deals with a special case, the REID and GEID versions of the simple two-relation model known as Summers' model. It is shown that the solution for normal equations and the ensuing parameter estimates here take algebraic (non-iterative) form (Lyttkens, 1967). The algebraic solution is explored with regard to the existence of plural solutions. Although Summers' model is one of the simplest interdependent systems it turns out that five different parameter sets are obtained, and it is shown by an example that all these solutions may be real. This lack of uniqueness was the first indication of a flaw in the FP theorem in its original version (Wold, 1965c). Concerning the ensuing revision of the theorem, see Ågren–Wold (1969).

We consider Summers' model (1.2.5–6) in estimated form, and in the notations of the respecified version (1.4.83–84),

$$y_{1t} = b_{12}y_{2t}^* + g_{11}z_{1t} + g_{12}z_{2t} + e_{1t}, \tag{1a}$$

$$y_{2t} = b_{21}y_{1t}^* + g_{23}z_{3t} + g_{24}z_{4t} + e_{2t}. \tag{1b}$$

Since z_{1t} and z_{2t} occur explicitly in the first structural equation and z_{3t} and z_{4t} in the second structural equation it is convenient to introduce two auxiliary variables, say y_{1t}^{**} and y_{2t}^{**}, by means of the relations

$$y_{1t}^{**} = w_{11}z_{1t} + w_{12}z_{2t}, \tag{2a}$$

$$y_{2t}^{**} = w_{23}z_{3t} + w_{24}z_{4t}. \tag{2b}$$

Then the respecified structural equations can be written as

$$y_{1t} = b_{12}y_{2t}^{**} + w_{11}z_{1t} + w_{12}z_{2t} + e_{1t}, \tag{3a}$$

$$y_{2t} = b_{21}y_{1t}^{**} + w_{23}z_{3t} + w_{24}z_{4t} + e_{2t}, \tag{3b}$$

where the parameters of the reduced form are related to those of the structural form by means of the formulas

$$g_{11} = w_{11}(1-b_{12}b_{21}), \tag{4a}$$

$$g_{12} = w_{12}(1-b_{12}b_{21}), \tag{4b}$$

$$g_{23} = w_{23}(1-b_{12}b_{21}), \tag{4c}$$

$$g_{24} = w_{24}(1-b_{12}b_{21}). \tag{4d}$$

It can be shown that the conditions $\sum y_{2t}^* e_{1t} = \sum z_{1t} e_{1t} = \sum z_{2t} e_{1t} = 0$ imply $\sum y_{2t}^{**} e_{1t} = 0$, and in the same way we obtain $\sum y_{1t}^{**} e_{2t} = 0$. Therefore we can apply OLS regression to the equations of system (3) instead of those of system (1).

In this way we obtain

$$
w_{11} = \frac{
\begin{vmatrix}
\sum z_{1t} y_{1t} & \sum z_{1t} z_{2t} & \sum z_{1t} y_{2t}^{**} \\
\sum z_{2t} y_{1t} & \sum z_{2t}^2 & \sum z_{2t} y_{2t}^{**} \\
\sum y_{2t}^{**} y_{1t} & \sum z_{2t} y_{2t}^{**} & \sum y_{2t}^{**2}
\end{vmatrix}
}{
\begin{vmatrix}
\sum z_{1t}^2 & \sum z_{1t} z_{2t} & \sum z_{1t} y_{2t}^{**} \\
\sum z_{1t} z_{2t} & \sum z_{2t}^2 & \sum z_{2t} y_{2t}^{**} \\
\sum z_{1t} y_{2t}^{**} & \sum z_{2t} y_{2t}^{**} & \sum y_{2t}^{**2}
\end{vmatrix}
} \tag{5}
$$

Let D be the determinant where the element of the ith row and jth column is $\sum z_{it} z_{jt}$, and F the determinant which is obtained if the first column of D is replaced by $\sum z_{1t} y_{1t}, \sum z_{2t} y_{1t}, \sum z_{3t} y_{1t}$ and $\sum z_{4t} y_{1t}$. The minors obtained by deleting the ith row and jth column of D and F are denoted by D_{ij} and F_{ij}, the factor $(-1)^{i+j}$ for obtaining cofactors not being applied. Then by introducing the expression for y_{2t}^{**} according to (2) into formula (5), we obtain an expression which can be transformed to

$$w_{11} = \frac{F_{44}w_{23}^2 + (F_{34} + F_{43})w_{23}w_{24} + F_{33}w_{24}^2}{D_{44}w_{23}^2 + 2D_{34}w_{23}w_{24} + D_{33}w_{24}^2}. \tag{6}$$

Denoting by H the determinant which is obtained if the second column of D is replaced by $\sum z_{1t}y_{1t}, \sum z_{2t}y_{1t}, \sum z_{3t}y_{1t}$ and $\sum z_{4t}y_{1t}$ we obtain in the same way

$$w_{12} = \frac{H_{44}w_{23}^2 + (H_{34} + H_{43})w_{23}w_{24} + H_{33}w_{24}^2}{D_{44}w_{23}^2 + 2D_{34}w_{23}w_{24} + D_{33}w_{24}^2}. \tag{7}$$

From the formulas (6) and (7) the following homogeneous relation is obtained

$$w_{11}[H_{44}w_{23}^2 + (H_{34} + H_{43})w_{23}w_{24} + H_{33}w_{24}^2] =$$

$$= w_{12}[F_{44}w_{23}^2 + (F_{34} + F_{43})w_{23}w_{24} + F_{33}w_{24}^2]. \tag{8}$$

Turning now to the second equation of (3), we apply the method of least squares in the same way. The determinants which are obtained if the elements of the third or fourth column of D are replaced by $\sum z_{1t}y_{2t}, \sum z_{2t}y_{2t}, \sum z_{3t}y_{2t}$ and $\sum z_{4t}y_{2t}$ are denoted by J and K, respectively. Then we have

$$w_{23} = \frac{J_{22}w_{11}^2 + (J_{12} + J_{21})w_{11}w_{12} + J_{11}w_{12}^2}{D_{22}w_{11}^2 + 2D_{12}w_{11}w_{12} + D_{11}w_{12}^2}, \tag{9}$$

$$w_{24} = \frac{K_{22}w_{11}^2 + (K_{12} + K_{21})w_{11}w_{12} + K_{11}w_{12}^2}{D_{22}w_{11}^2 + 2D_{12}w_{11}w_{12} + D_{11}w_{12}^2}. \tag{10}$$

If these expressions for w_{23} and w_{24} are introduced into (8) the following homogeneous equation of the fifth degree in w_{11} and w_{12} is obtained,

$$(H_{44}w_{11} - F_{44}w_{12}) \{J_{22}w_{11}^2 + (J_{12} + J_{21})w_{11}w_{12} + J_{11}w_{12}^2\}^2 +$$

$$+ \{(H_{34} + H_{43})w_{11} - (F_{34} + F_{43})w_{12}\} \times$$

$$\times \{J_{22}w_{11}^2 + (J_{12} + J_{21})w_{11}w_{12} + J_{11}w_{12}^2\} \times$$

$$\times \{K_{22}w_{11}^2 + (K_{12} + K_{21})w_{11}w_{12} + K_{11}w_{12}^2\} + \tag{11}$$

$$+ (H_{33}w_{11} - F_{33}w_{12}) \{K_{22}w_{11}^2 + (K_{12} + K_{21})w_{11}w_{12} + K_{11}w_{12}^2\}^2 = 0.$$

For each real value of the ratio between w_{12} and w_{11} obtained from this equation we calculate w_{23} and w_{24} from (9) and (10) and thereafter w_{11} and w_{12} from (6) and (7). The coefficients b_{12} and b_{21} are then obtained from the normal equations directly.

Alternatively, b_{12} and b_{21} can be obtained by similar formulas as for the other coefficients. Let L denote the determinant obtained if both the third and fourth columns of D are replaced by $\sum z_{1t}y_{1t}, \sum z_{2t}y_{1t}, \sum z_{3t}y_{1t}, \sum z_{4t}y_{1t}$, and let the minors of this determinant be denoted by L_{ij}. Then with the aid of the same procedure as before we have

$$b_{12} = \frac{L_{44}w_{23} + L_{33}w_{24}}{D_{44}w_{23}^2 + 2D_{34}w_{23}w_{24} + D_{33}w_{24}^2}. \tag{12}$$

Furthermore, let M denote the determinant obtained from D if both the first and second columns of D are replaced by $\sum z_{1t}y_{2t}, \sum z_{2t}y_{2t}, \sum z_{3t}y_{2t}$ and $\sum z_{4t}y_{2t}$, and let the minors be denoted by M_{ij}. Then analogously to the preceding formula we have

$$b_{21} = \frac{M_{22}w_{11} + M_{11}w_{12}}{D_{22}w_{11}^2 + 2D_{12}w_{11}w_{12} + D_{11}w_{12}^2}. \tag{13}$$

Finally, the estimates of the coefficients of the predetermined variables in the original structural form are obtained from formulas (4).

In the special case where $\sum z_{1t}z_{3t} = \sum z_{1t}z_{4t} = \sum z_{2t}z_{3t} = \sum z_{2t}z_{4t} = 0$, the normal equations yield two linear relations between w_{11} and w_{12} and two linear relations between w_{23} and w_{24}. In this case only one set of values of the coefficients is obtained. When more than one real solution for the coefficients is obtained we have the problem of choice between the solutions. A rule pertaining directly to the specifications has not yet been found. It seems appropriate to calculate the total sum of squares of the residuals, $\Sigma\ e_{1t}^2 + \Sigma\ e_{2t}^2$ for each one of the real solutions, and accept the one, which gives the smallest value for the sum. It must be stated, however, that the parameter values thus obtained are in general not those which minimize $\Sigma\ e_{1t}^2 + \Sigma\ e_{2t}^2$, where e_{1t} and e_{2t} are given by equations (3) with the expressions (2) for y_{1t}^{**} and y_{2t}^{**} introduced. The last-mentioned solution minimizes the total sum of squares of the residuals of the reduced form with due regard to the fact that the system is overidentified.

The data in Table 1 illustrate plural FP solutions for Summers' model (1), a case with $N = 10$ observations in the sample, and with three real solutions.

Table 3.8.1

Numerical example of Summers' model with three solutions for the asymmetric GEID specification

y_{1t}	y_{2t}	z_{1t}	z_{2t}	z_{3t}	z_{4t}
−3	−2	1	0	1	0
1	0	0	1	0	−1
−9	9	0	0	0	0
−9	−9	0	0	0	0
0	9	0	0	0	0
0	−9	0	0	0	0
7	−1	0	0	0	1
11	1	0	0	−1	0
1	1	0	−1	0	0
1	1	−1	0	0	0

The following three solutions are obtained, of which the first one was used for constructing the model:

First solution: $\Sigma_t\ e_{1t}^2 = 324,\ \Sigma_t\ e_{2t}^2 = 324$;

$$y_{1t} = 2y_{2t}^* + z_{1t} + z_{2t} + e_{1t}\ , \tag{14a}$$

$$y_{2t} = y_{1t}^* + z_{3t} + z_{4t} + e_{2t}\ ; \tag{14b}$$

Second solution: $\Sigma_t e_{1t}^2 = 276$, $\Sigma_t e_{2t}^2 = 327$;

$$y_{1t} = 4y_{2t}^* + z_{1t} - z_{2t} + e_{1t}, \tag{15a}$$

$$y_{2t} = -1.5 z_{3t} - 0.5 z_{4t} + e_{2t}; \tag{15b}$$

Third solution: $\Sigma_t e_{1t}^2 = 292.8$, $\Sigma_t e_{2t}^2 = 326.4$;

$$y_{1t} = 3y_{2t}^* - 0.2 z_{1t} + 0.6 z_{2t} + e_{1t}, \tag{16a}$$

$$y_{2t} = 0.5 y_{1t}^* + 0.8 z_{3t} + 0.4 z_{4t} + e_{2t}. \tag{16b}$$

When the iterative FP method was applied, this model gave strange results. $Y_t^{(0)} = 0$ was used as starting values, as proposed by Wold [15]. This means that the first approximation $Y_t^{(1)}$ was obtained by putting $b_{12}^{(1)} = b_{21}^{(1)} = 0$. With this start the iterative method gives the results shown in Table 2.

Table 3.8.2
FP estimation of Summers' model using data in Table 1
and the start $Y_t^{(0)} = 0$.

Iteration number	b_{12}	g_{11}	g_{12}	b_{21}	g_{23}	g_{24}
1	0	−2	0	0	−1.5	−0.5
2	4	1	−1	0.5	0	−0.5
3	4.8	5.2	−1.2	0	−1.5	−0.5
4	4	1	−1	0.5	0.8	0.4
5	3	−0.2	0.6	0	−1.5	−0.5
6	4	1	−1	0.5	0.8	0.4
7	3	−0.2	0.6	0	−1.5	−0.5
8	4	1	−1	0.5	0.8	0.4

We see that the iterations soon evolve into a pattern of alternation between two combinations of the solutions in (14)−(16). One combination consists of the first equation of the second solution and the second equation of the third solution; the other consists of the first equation of the third solution and the second equation of the second solution.

The explanation for this is that in a sense the FP method applied to a two-relation model gives rise to two different iteration series, which do not interfere with one another. It is obvious that $y_{1t}^{(s+1)}$ depends on $y_{2t}^{(s)}$ but not on $y_{1t}^{(s)}$. For a given start $Y_t^{(0)}$ we get two iterated series which do not interfere with each other, namely

$$y_{1t}^{(0)}, y_{2t}^{(1)}, y_{1t}^{(2)}, \dots$$

and

$$y_{2t}^{(0)}, y_{1t}^{(1)}, y_{2t}^{(2)}, \dots .$$

Only one of these series is needed for the iterative estimation of the model, but by an unfortunate choice of the starting value it may happen that one series leads to one solution and the other series leads to another solution. The values chosen for $w_{13}^{(0)}$, $w_{14}^{(0)}$, $w_{21}^{(0)}$, and $w_{22}^{(0)}$ do not affect the iterated values $y_{1t}^{(s)}$ and $y_{2t}^{(s)}$ for $s > 0$; they affect the values of the structural coefficients in the first iteration but not those in the following ones. Moreover, if we choose another start than $w_{11}^{(0)} = w_{12}^{(0)} = 0$, the iterated values $y_{2t}^{(1)}, y_{1t}^{(2)}, \dots$ of the first series depend only on the ratio between $w_{11}^{(0)}$ and $w_{12}^{(0)}$. These features point out another way of proceeding after having determined the values of the ratio between w_{11} and w_{12} from the fifth degree equation (11). Choosing one of these values as starting point of the iteration, according to the FP method, the first series gives y_{2t}^* in the first iteration, the coefficients b_{12}, g_{11}, and g_{12} and y_{1t}^* in the second iteration and, at last, the coefficients b_{21}, g_{23}, and g_{24} in the third iteration.

We note that the start $Y_t^{(0)} = 0$ obviously favours the second solution. In fact, (15b) is attained immediately in the first approximation of one of the series, and then (15a) is obtained in the second approximation of the same series. The third solution also happens to be reached quickly, because (16b) is reached exactly in the fourth approximation of the other series, while (16a) is reached in the fifth approximation of this series.

Further we note that if the FP procedure starts by the first step of the TSLS method, the iterations in a few steps lead to the first solution in both series.

As a second numerical example we consider a case where all solutions are real:

Table 3.8.3

Numerical example of data for Summers' model with five solutions.

y_{1t}	y_{2t}	z_{1t}	z_{2t}	z_{3t}	z_{4t}
3	7	1	0	1	0
1	−4	0	1	0	0
−2	1	0	0	0	1
−1	−3	0	0	0	0
2	−1	0	0	0	−1
−4	3	0	0	−1	0
0	4	0	−1	0	0
1	−7	−1	0	0	0

First solution: $\Sigma_t\, e_{1t}^2 = 1.5,\ \Sigma_t\, e_{2t}^2 = 12$;

$$y_{1t} = -2\,y_{2t}^* + 15\,z_{1t} - 7.5\,z_{2t} + e_{1t}\ , \tag{17a}$$

$$y_{2t} = -8\,y_{1t}^* + 30\,z_{3t} - 15\,z_{4t} + e_{2t}\ ; \tag{17b}$$

Second solution: $\Sigma_t\, e_{1t}^2 = 25.5,\ \Sigma_t\, e_{2t}^2 = 108$;

$$y_{1t} = -2\,y_{2t}^* + 9\,z_{1t} + 4.5\,z_{2t} + e_{1t}\ , \tag{18a}$$

$$y_{2t} = 4\,y_{1t}^* + 9\,z_{4t} + e_{2t}\ ; \tag{18b}$$

Third solution: $\Sigma_t\, e_{1t}^2 = 25.5,\ \Sigma_t\, e_{2t}^2 = 108$;

$$y_{1t} = y_{2t}^* + 4.5\,z_{2t} + e_{1t}\ , \tag{19a}$$

$$y_{2t} = -8\,y_{1t}^* + 18\,z_{3t} + 9\,z_{4t} + e_{2t}\ ; \tag{19b}$$

Fourth solution: $\Sigma_t\, e_{1t}^2 = 31.36,\ \Sigma_t\, e_{2t}^2 = 131.43$;

$$y_{1t} = 0.732\,y_{2t}^* - 0.660\,z_{1t} - 0.572\,z_{2t} + e_{1t}\ , \tag{20a}$$

$$y_{2t} = 2.928\,y_{1t}^* - 1.321\,z_{3t} - 1.144\,z_{4t} + e_{2t}\ ; \tag{20b}$$

Fifth solution: $\sum_t e_{1t}^2 = 3.64$, $\sum_t e_{2t}^2 = 20.57$;

$$y_{1t} = -2.732\, y_{2t}^* + 16.660\, z_{1t} - 14.428\, z_{2t} + e_{1t}, \quad (21a)$$

$$y_{2t} = -10.928\, y_{1t}^* + 33.321\, z_{3t} - 28.856\, z_{4t} + e_{2t}. \quad (21b)$$

In this example TSLS gives the third solution. This is constructed so as to fulfill the conditions $\sum z_{it} e_{1t} = \sum z_{it} e_{2t} = 0$ for $i = 1, 2, 3, 4$, which means that its generated reduced form is the same as the unrestricted reduced form. The occurrence of such a solution is of course an exception, but it shows an important thing concerning such a specification: Even if there exists a solution which fulfills the classical condition that the residuals are uncorrelated with all predetermined variables, the GEID specification may also admit other solutions (always with larger residual variances, of course). Similarly, if a solution which is free from residuals exists, the GEID specification may also admit other real solutions, which are not free from residuals. An example of this can easily be constructed from the previous example by replacing the y_{it}-values in Table 3 by values according to the unrestricted form, after removing its residuals. This substitution does not change the second order moments needed for the determining of the coefficients. and therefore only the residuals are changed in the five solutions presented before. In the third solution the residuals vanish entirely, and an example of the required type has thus been constructed.

In practice each of the two equations also contains a constant term. In this case, the procedure presented in this chapter can be applied to the deviations from the empirical mean. Another way of handling the problem is to border the symmetrical determinant D by a fifth row and a fifth column with the elements $\sum z_{1t}, \sum z_{2t}, \sum z_{3t}, \sum z_{4t}, N$. After this change the determinant occurring in formula F is obtained by replacing the first column of D by $\sum z_{1t} y_{1t}, \sum z_{2t} y_{1t}, \sum z_{3t} y_{1t}, \sum z_{3t} y_{1t}, \sum y_{1t}$. The other fourth order determinants used are replaced by fifth order determinants in the same way; and after that change formulas (6)−(13) are valid for the case where constant terms occur in the equations. The constant terms are of course obtained by equating the means of both sides of the structural equations.

3.9. Some Asymptotic Formulas for Standard Errors and Small-Sample Bias of FP Estimates
by E. Lyttkens

A general method for obtaining asymptotic formulas for the standard errors and small sample bias of the FP method will be outlined. The method is applicable to a GEID as well as a REID system. Explicit formulas are, however, worked out only for a two-relation system. It proved to be advantageous to modify the general method a little in this case.

In Wold's pioneering paper (Wold, 1965c, p. 235) it is suggested that the standard errors of the coefficients should be calculated by a formula analogous to that of the TSLS method. In this formula the coefficients of each equation are treated separately. The FP method, however, makes the estimated coefficients from different structural equations much more dependent on each other, and if these effects are taken into account the formulas for the asymptotic variances and covariances become more involved. The results presented in this section are quite recent, and therefore have not been used in the other parts of this volume.

Given the theoretical GEID (or REID) system

$$Y_t = \beta H_t^* + \Gamma Z_t + \epsilon_t \tag{1}$$

and the corresponding estimated system

$$Y_t = B Y_t^* + G Z_t + e_t , \tag{2}$$

the following relation is obtained by subtraction,

$$\epsilon_t - e_t = (B - \beta)Y_t^* + \beta(Y_t^* - H_t^*) + (G - \Gamma)Z_t . \tag{3}$$

Since

$$Y_t^* - H_t^* = \epsilon_t - e_t , \tag{4}$$

we obtain

$$(I - \beta)(\epsilon_t - e_t) = (B - \beta)Y_t^* + (G - \Gamma)Z_t , \tag{5}$$

which gives

$$\epsilon_t - e_t = (I - \beta)^{-1} [(B - \beta) Y_t^* + (G - \Gamma)Z_t] . \tag{6}$$

If η_{kt}^* and z_{lt} occur in the ith equation, the non-correlation assumptions of the FP method as applied to the sample imply $\sum_t y_{kt}^* e_{it} = 0$ and $\sum_t z_{lt} e_{it} = 0$. Hence the two product sums $\sum_t y_{kt}^* e_{it}$ and $\sum_t z_{lt} e_{it}$ can be expressed linearly in the differences between the estimated and true values of all the coefficients of the structural form. Solving for these differences we obtain linear expressions in the product sums of the regressors and theoretical residuals, and it follows that the variances and covariances of the estimated structural coefficients can be expressed in terms of the variances and covariances of these product sums. If we consider the case where the residuals pertaining to different time points are independent, and the predetermined variables are non-stochastic, we have for instance

$$E\left(\sum_{t=1}^N y_{kt}^* \epsilon_{it} \sum_{\tau=1}^N z_{l\tau} \epsilon_{j\tau}\right) = E(\epsilon_i \epsilon_j) \sum_{t=1}^N \eta_{kt}^* z_{lt} , \tag{7}$$

where y_{kt}^* has been replaced by its theoretical counterpart η_{kt}^*. The case of autocorrelated residuals can be handled in the same way as in the case of OLS regression (Lyttkens, 1964a). Thus if we assume that Y_t and Z_t are generated by a stationary multivariate normal process and ϵ_t is independent of ϵ_τ and Z_τ for $\tau < t$, the corresponding formula for the GEID-specification is

$$\frac{1}{N}E\left(\sum_{t=1}^N \eta_{kt}^* \epsilon_{it} \sum_{\tau=1}^N z_{l\tau} \epsilon_{j\tau}\right) = E(\epsilon_{it}\epsilon_{jt}) E(\eta_{kt}^* z_{lt}) +$$

$$+ E(\eta_{kt}^*\epsilon_{jt}) E(z_{lt}\epsilon_{it}) . \tag{8}$$

where a condition for the occurrence of the last term is that y_{kt} does not occur in the jth equation and z_{lt} does not occur in the ith equation.

Here it can be argued that the estimation should be corrected for degrees of freedom by subtracting the number of coefficients in the equation from N. This procedure, however, does not take into account that one of the regressors is estimated. A compromise used in other parts of the paper is to always subtract the average number of coefficients per equation. The same change should then be applied to formula (8).

Concerning the small-sample bias, let us first assume that the pre-determined variables are non-stochastic. The bias is then entirely due to the fact that the empirical values y_{kt}^* have been used as regressors in-stead of the theoretical values η_{kt}^*. In the expressions for the differences between the empirical and theoretical coefficients, as derived in advance of the calculation of the asymptotic variances, we put $y_{it}^* = \eta_{it}^* + \epsilon_{it} - e_{it}$, which allows us to separate the main terms of the bias. For the GEID specification we have also to take account of the deviation between ob-served product moments of the predetermined variables and the theo-retical ones.

3.9.1. A Two-relation GEID Model: Standard Errors

Asymptotic standard errors have recently been derived for GEID sys-tems. For considerations of space the present treatment will be limited to a two-relation model with m_1 predetermined variables in the first equation and $m_2 = m - m_1$ other predetermined variables in the second equation.

To abbreviate the formulas we shall use vector notation. Thus let y_1 and y_2 be the row vectors formed by the endogenous variables as ob-served over the whole sample period, and let Z_1, Z_2 be the matrices of the observed values of the predetermined variables present in the first and second equation, respectively. Then the system takes the form

$$y_1 = \beta_{12} y_2 + \gamma_1 Z_1 + \delta_1 , \tag{9a}$$

$$y_2 = \beta_{21} y_1 + \gamma_2 Z_2 + \delta_2 , \tag{9b}$$

where γ_1 and γ_2 are the row vectors of coefficients of the predetermined variables that occur in the first and second relation, respectively. In the REID or GEID version the system reads

$$y_1 = \beta_{12} \eta_2^* + \gamma_1 Z_1 + \epsilon_1 , \tag{10a}$$

$$y_2 = \beta_{21} \eta_1^* + \gamma_2 Z_2 + \epsilon_2 . \tag{10b}$$

Until further notice (Section 3.9.5) we assume that no variables z_i occur in both relations.

In order to simplify the deductions that follow we introduce

$$\eta_1^{**} = \omega_1 Z_1 , \tag{11a}$$

$$\eta_2^{**} = \omega_2 Z_2 , \tag{11b}$$

where ω_1 is the row vector of the m_1 first reduced form coefficients in the expression for y_1, and ω_2 is the row vector of the $m - m_1$ last coefficients in the expression for y_2. Then

$$y_1 = \beta_{12}\eta_2^{**} + \omega_1 Z_1 + \epsilon_1 , \tag{12a}$$

$$y_2 = \beta_{21}\eta_1^{**} + \omega_2 Z_2 + \epsilon_2 , \tag{12b}$$

which in conjunction with (11) implies

$$\gamma_1 = (1 - \beta_{12}\beta_{21})\omega_1 , \tag{13a}$$

$$\gamma_2 = (1 - \beta_{12}\beta_{21})\omega_2 . \tag{13b}$$

In the estimated version we write the system as

$$y_1 = b_{12}y_2^{**} + w_1 Z_1 + e_1 , \tag{14a}$$

$$y_2 = b_{21}y_1^{**} + w_2 Z_2 + e_2 . \tag{14b}$$

Subtracting from the corresponding theoretical equations we obtain

$$\epsilon_1 - e_1 = (b_{12} - \beta_{12})y_{2t}^{**} + (w_1 - \omega_1)Z_1 + \beta_{12}(w_2 - \omega_2)Z_2 , \tag{15a}$$

$$\epsilon_2 - e_2 = (b_{21} - \beta_{21})y_{1t}^{**} + \beta_{21}(w_1 - \omega_1)Z_1 + (w_2 - \omega_2)Z_2 . \tag{15b}$$

For the column vector of differences between estimated and theoretical coefficients we introduce the notation c',

$$c' = \begin{bmatrix} b_{12} - \beta_{12} \\ w_1' - \omega_1' \\ b_{21} - \beta_{21} \\ w_2' - \omega_2' \end{bmatrix}. \tag{16}$$

In this partition of the vector c' it should be remembered that $w_1' - \omega_1'$ and $w_2' - \omega_2'$ are themselves column vectors.

The conditions $y_2^* e_1' = 0$ and $Z_1 e_1' = 0$ are seen to imply $y_2^{**} e_1' = 0$. Similarly, the conditions $y_1^{**} e_2' = 0$ and $Z_2 e_2' = 0$ give $y_1^{**} e_2' = 0$. Making use of these relations, we have from (15a–b)

$$\begin{bmatrix} y_2^{**} e_1' \\ Z_1 \, e_1' \\ y_1^{**} e_2' \\ Z_2 \, e_2' \end{bmatrix} = Qc' , \tag{17}$$

where Q is the following matrix,

$$Q = \begin{bmatrix} y_2^{**} y_2^{**'} & y_2^* Z_1' & 0 & b_{12} y_2^{**} Z_2' \\ Z_1 y_2^{**'} & Z_1 Z_1' & 0 & b_{12} Z_1 Z_2' \\ 0 & b_{21} y_1^{**} Z_1' & y_1^{**} y_1^{**'} & y_1^{**} Z_2' \\ 0 & b_{21} Z_2 Z_1' & Z_2 y_1^{**'} & Z_2 Z_2' \end{bmatrix}. \tag{18}$$

This matrix is partitioned, since for instance $Z_1 Z_2'$ is a matrix with m_1 rows and m_2 columns. As is customary in similar deductions, the theoretical parameters β have been replaced by estimates b, which does not affect the resulting large-sample approximation.

The following notations will be used for the residual variances and covariances as obtained from the sample,

$$s_{11} = \frac{1}{N} e_1 e_1', \qquad s_{22} = \frac{1}{N} e_2 e_2', \qquad s_{12} = \frac{1}{N} e_1 e_2'. \tag{19}$$

Further we introduce the column vectors u_1 and u_2 by writing

$$u_1 = Z_1 e_2' ; \quad u_2 = Z_2 e_1' , \tag{20a–b}$$

and the matrix U by

$$U = \frac{1}{N} u_1 u_2' . \tag{21}$$

Solving the matrix equation (17) for the vector c' of the differences between estimated and theoretical values of the coefficients we obtain

$$c' = Q^{-1} \begin{bmatrix} y_2^{**} e_1' \\ Z_1 \, e_1' \\ y_1^{**} e_2' \\ Z_2 \, e_2' \end{bmatrix} . \tag{22}$$

The asymptotic covariance matrix of the coefficients β, ω is now obtained as the mean of the matrix $c'c$. Making use of formula (8) and the notations (19) and (21), we obtain

$$E(c'c) \sim Q^{-1} \begin{bmatrix} s_{11} y_2^{**} y_2^{**'} & s_{12} y_2^{**} Z_1' & s_{12} y_2^{**} y_1^{**'} & s_{12} y_2^{**} Z_2' \\ s_{11} Z_1 y_2^{**'} & s_{11} Z_1 Z_1' & s_{12} Z_1 y_1^{**'} & s_{12} Z_1 Z_2' + U \\ s_{12} y_1^{**} y_2^{**'} & s_{12} y_1^{**} Z_1' & s_{22} y_1^{**} y_1^{**'} & s_{22} y_1^{**} Z_2' \\ s_{12} Z_2 y_2^{**'} & s_{12} Z_2 Z_1' + U' & s_{22} Z_2 y_1^{**'} & s_{22} Z_2 Z_2' \end{bmatrix} \; (Q') \tag{23}$$

In the special case of classical specification the matrix U and its transpose U' are left out from this asymptotic expression. With the matrices U and U' retained the asymptotic expression is valid for the normal process that underlies formula (8).

In order to obtain the variances and covariances of all the coefficients of the structural form we consider the first order terms in the Taylor expansion of the row vector (13); that is,

$$g_1 - \gamma_1 \sim (1 - b_{12}b_{21})(w_1 - \omega_1) - b_{21}w_1(b_{12} - \beta_{12}) -$$
$$- b_{12}w_1(b_{21} - \beta_{21}) , \qquad (24a)$$

$$g_2 - \gamma_2 \sim (1 - b_{12}b_{21})(w_2 - \omega_2) - b_{21}w_2(b_{12} - \beta_{12}) -$$
$$- b_{12}w_2(b_{21} - \beta_{21}) . \qquad (24b)$$

Using these formulas in combination with (17) and (23) it is straightforward matrix algebra to calculate the variances and covariances of the structural form coefficients in terms of the variances and covariances already known.

3.9.2. The Two-relation Model: Small-Sample Bias

With non-stochastic predetermined variables, the small-sample bias is entirely due to the fact that we must use estimated values of the regressors, in our case y_{2t}^{**} and y_{1t}^{**}. Let us write the difference between the estimates and the theoretical values of these regressors as

$$y_1^{**} - \eta_1^{**} = v_1 Z_1 ; \quad y_2^{**} - \eta_2^{**} = v_2 Z_2 , \qquad (25a-b)$$

where

$$v_1 = w_1 - \omega_1 ; \qquad v_2 = w_2 - \omega_2 . \qquad (26a-b)$$

Further we denote by Q^{**} the matrix which is obtained from Q if y_1^{**} and y_2^{**} are replaced by their theoretical counterparts η_1^{**} and η_2^{**}. Then the following formula for the small-sample bias is obtained from (22),

$$E(c') = Q^{-1} \begin{bmatrix} E(v_2 Z_2 \epsilon_1') \\ 0 \\ E(v_1 Z_1 \epsilon_2') \\ 0 \end{bmatrix} - Q^{-1}E[(Q - Q^{**})c'] , \qquad (27)$$

where we have replaced the factor $(Q^{**})^{-1}$ by Q^{-1}, which is equivalent in the present approximation. Using again the formula (22) the mean values of type $E(c' \epsilon_1 Z_2')$ can be evaluated. The last m_2 rows of this expression form the square matrix $E(v_2' \epsilon_1 Z_2')$, where the trace gives us the mean value $E(v_2 Z_2 \epsilon_1')$. The mean $E(v_1 Z_1 \epsilon_2')$ is obtained in the same way. For the second term in (27) we note the following expression for $Q - Q^{**}$,

$$Q - Q^{**} \approx \begin{bmatrix} 2w_2 Z_2 Z_2' v_2' & v_2 Z_2 Z_1' & 0 & b_{12} v_2 Z_2 Z_2' \\ Z_1 Z_2' v_2' & 0 & 0 & 0 \\ 0 & b_{21} v_1 Z_1 Z_1' & 2w_1 Z_1 Z_1' v_1' & v_1 Z_1 Z_2' \\ 0 & 0 & Z_2 Z_1' v_1' & 0 \end{bmatrix},$$

(28)

if second order terms are neglected. The mean $E[(Q-Q^{**})c']$ consists of linear expressions of the variances and covariances, which have already been obtained by formula (23). Thus formula (28) enables us to calculate small-sample bias of the order $1/N$.

Considering now the case when the predetermined variables are stochastic, an additional term in the small-sample bias can occur because of the deviations of the product sums of the predetermined variables from their means. Let Q_0 be the matrix which is obtained from Q if the product sums of the predetermined variables are replaced by their expected values. Then the following formula for the small-sample bias is obtained in the same way as before,

$$E(c') \sim Q^{-1} \begin{bmatrix} E(v_2 Z_2 \epsilon_1') \\ 0 \\ E(v_1 Z_1 \epsilon_1') \\ 0 \end{bmatrix} - Q^{-1} E[(Q-Q^{**})c'] - Q^{-1} E[(Q-Q_0)c'] .$$

(29)

To the order $1/N$ the first and second term of the right hand side are the same as in formula (27), with the exception that the variance and covariance of the coefficients needed for evaluating the second term are taken from formula (23) with the terms U and U' due to the GEID specification retained.

In order to evaluate the last term of formula (29) for the small-sample bias we need to know the components of vectors of the type $E[c'(z_i z_j' - N\lambda_{ij})]$, where $\lambda_{ij} = E(z_{it} z_{jt})$, and z_i, z_j are any components of the column vector $Z = (Z_1, Z_2)$. These mean values are obtained by formula (22). At first we shall adopt the conditions underlying formula (8), with the additional condition that not only $E(Z_t \epsilon_{t+k}') = 0$ but also $E(Z_{t+k} \epsilon_k') = 0$ for $k > 0$. On these very restrictive GEID assumptions, the means of the fourth order moments can be treated in the same way as in formula (23), making use of formula (22), one of the residuals being replaced by a predetermined variable. The following expression is obtained,

$$E[c'(z_i z_j' - N\lambda_{ij})] \sim \frac{1}{N} Q^{-1} \begin{bmatrix} y_2^{**} z_i' e_1 z_j' + y_2^{**} z_j' e_1 z_i' \\ Z_1 z_i' e_1 z_j' + Z_1 z_j' e_1 z_i' \\ y_1^{**} z_i' e_2 z_j' + y_1^{**} z_j' e_2 z_i' \\ Z_2 z_i' e_2 z_j' + Z_2 z_j' e_2 z_i' \end{bmatrix}. \tag{30}$$

According to the FP conditions $e_1 z_i'$ or $e_2 z_i'$ vanishes, and so does $e_1 z_j'$ or $e_2 z_j'$.

The assumptions underlying the last-mentioned formula exclude the use of lagged endogenous variables as predetermined variables. In order to see what changes are to be made if the assumption $E(z_{t+k} \epsilon_t') = 0$ for $k > 0$ is abandoned, we will consider the first element of the vector on the right-hand side of formula (30). Again, the mean $E(\eta_2^{**} \epsilon_1' z_i z_j')$ is of the type shown in formula (8), now with one residual replaced by a predetermined variable. But this change admits some lagged terms to survive, and on the same assumptions as those underlying formula (8) we obtain

$$\frac{1}{N} E \left\{ \sum_{t=1}^{N} \eta_{2t}^{**} \epsilon_{1t} \sum_{\tau=1}^{N} z_{i\tau} z_{j\tau} \right\} \sim E(z_{it} \eta_{2t}^{**}) E(z_{jt} \epsilon_{1t}) + E(z_{jt} \eta_{2t}^{**}) E(z_{it} \epsilon_{1t}) +$$

$$+ E(z_{it} \eta_{2,t-1}^{**}) E(z_{jt} \epsilon_{1,t-1}) + E(z_{jt} \eta_{2,t-1}^{**}) E(z_{it} \epsilon_{1,t-1}) +$$

$$+ E(z_{it} \eta_{2,t-2}^{**}) E(z_{jt} \epsilon_{1,t-2}) + E(z_{jt} \eta_{2,t-2}^{**}) E(z_{it} \epsilon_{1,t-2}) + \dots . \tag{31}$$

The appearance of the lagged residuals is quite natural when lagged endogenous variables occur among the predetermined variables. If for instance $z_{1t} = y_{1,t-1}$ occurs in the first equation, we have $E(z_{1t}\epsilon_{1,t-1}) = \sigma^2(\epsilon_1)$. Of course such terms involving lagged residuals may occur in REID as well as in GEID systems.

In order to get the bias of the coefficients of the predetermined variables in the structural form, we have to extend the expansions (23) so as to include terms of the second degree. Therefore it is essential that the expansion is performed in such a way that the partial derivatives are evaluated with the aid of the theoretical coefficients. After having formed the expressions for the mathematical expectations, however, we replace the coefficients by their estimated values in the usual way. Then the following formulas for the small-sample bias of the order $1/N$ are obtained for the row vectors g_1, g_2:

$$E(g_1 - \gamma_1) = (1 - b_{12}b_{21})\, E(w_1 - \omega_1) - b_{21} w_1\, E(b_{12} - \beta_{12}) -$$

$$- b_{12}\, w_1\, E(b_{21} - \beta_{21}) - b_{21}\, E[(b_{12} - \beta_{12})(w_1 - \omega_1)] - \quad (32a)$$

$$- b_{12}\, E[(b_{21} - \beta_{21})(w_1 - \omega_1)] - w_1\, E[(b_{12} - \beta_{12})(b_{21} - \beta_{21})] \,,$$

$$E(g_2 - \gamma_2) = (1 - b_{12}b_{21})\, E(w_2 - \omega_2) - b_{21} w_2\, E(b_{12} - \beta_{12}) -$$

$$- b_{12}\, w_2\, E(b_{21} - \beta_{21}) - b_{21}\, E[(b_{12} - \beta_{12})(w_2 - \omega_2)] - \quad (32b)$$

$$- b_{12}\, E[(b_{21} - \beta_{21})(w_2 - \omega_2)] - w_2\, E[(b_{12} - \beta_{12})(b_{21} - \beta_{21})] \,.$$

3.9.3. Special Case: The Predetermined Variables of one Equation are Uncorrelated with Those of the Other Equation

The special case where the predetermined variables have zero mean and no correlations exist between predetermined variables not belonging to the same equation leads to especially simple expressions for the asymptotic standard errors and the bias. In the final expressions, all product moments with zero expectation are regarded as having vanishing estimated values.

For a comparison we treat Nagar's formulas for the asymptotic variances and small-sample bias of the TSLS estimates (Nagar, 1959) in the same way. On the assumptions adopted it is seen that the standard errors and the leading term in the small-sample bias of b_{12} and b_{21} are the same for the FP method and the TSLS method. The standard errors of the components of w_1 and w_2 are the same as those obtained for the corresponding coefficients of the unrestricted reduced form, with the modification that the residual variance is taken from the respecified structural form [1]. The standard errors and small-sample bias of the structural coefficients of the predetermined variables are obtained in the way indicated in 3.9.2; that is, with the aid of equations (29) and (32a–b).

By introducing the scalar statistics k_1 and k_2 of order $1/N$ as defined by

$$k_1 = (g_1 Z_1 Z_1' g_1')^{-1} \; ; \quad k_2 = (g_2 Z_2 Z_2' g_2')^{-1} , \quad (33a–b)$$

the asymptotic standard errors of b_{12} and b_{21} can be written as

$$d(b_{12}) \sim s(\delta_1) \sqrt{k_1 (1 - b_{12} b_{21})^2} , \quad (34a)$$

$$d(b_{21}) \sim s(\delta_2) \sqrt{k_2 (1 - b_{12} b_{21})^2} , \quad (34b)$$

while the asymptotic standard errors of the structural coefficients of the predetermined variables are obtained as the square roots of the diagonal elements of the following matrices:

$$E[(g_1' - \gamma_1')(g_1 - \gamma_1)] = s^2(\delta_1)[(Z_1 Z_1')^{-1} + b_{21}^2 k_2 g_1' g_1] +$$

$$+ [2b_{12} r(\delta_1, \delta_2) s(\delta_1) s(\delta_2) + b_{12}^2 s^2(\delta_2)] \times$$

$$\times [(Z_1 Z_1')^{-1} - k_1 g_1' g_1] , \quad (35a)$$

$$E[(g_2' - \gamma_2')(g_2 - \gamma_2)] = s^2(\delta_2)[(Z_2 Z_2')^{-1} + b_{12}^2 k_1 g_2' g_2] +$$

$$+ [2b_{21} r(\delta_1 \delta_2) s(\delta_1) s(\delta_2) + b_{21}^2 s^2(\delta_2)] \times$$

$$\times [(Z_2 Z_2')^{-1} - k_2 g_2' g_2] . \quad (35b)$$

The first term on the right hand side in each expression gives the corresponding covariance matrices for the estimates according to the TSLS method, and the second term can be considered a correction of the formula in order to get the corresponding covariance for the estimate according to the FP method.

For the small-sample bias to the order $1/N$ the following formulas are obtained in a similar way (note that g_1, g_2 are row vectors, as before):

$$E(b_{12}-\beta_{12}) = (m_2-2)\, r(\delta_1, \epsilon_2)\, s(\delta_1)\, s(\epsilon_2)\, k_2(1-b_{12}b_{21})^2 \,, \quad (36a)$$

$$E(b_{21}-\beta_{21}) = (m_1-2)\, r(\delta_2, \epsilon_1)\, s(\delta_2)\, s(\epsilon_1)\, k_1(1-b_{12}b_{21})^2 \,, \quad (36b)$$

$$E(g_1 - \gamma_1) \;=\; \frac{1}{N}(1-b_{12}b_{21})\, u_1'\, (Z_1 Z_1')^{-1} -$$

$$- (1-b_{12}b_{21})[(m_2-2)\, r(\delta_1, \epsilon_2)\, s(\delta_1)\, s(\epsilon_2)\, b_{21} k_2 +$$

$$+ (m_1-3)\, r(\delta_2, \epsilon_1)\, s(\delta_2)\, s(\epsilon_1)\, b_{12} k_1]g_1 \,. \quad (36c)$$

$$E(g_2 - \gamma_2) \;=\; \frac{1}{N}(1-b_{12}b_{21})\, u_2'(Z_2 Z_2')^{-1} -$$

$$- (1-b_{12}b_{21})[(m_1-2)\, r(\delta_2, \epsilon_1)\, s(\delta_2)\, s(\epsilon_1)\, b_{12} k_1 +$$

$$+ (m_2-3)\, r(\delta_1, \epsilon_2)\, s(\delta_1)\, s(\epsilon_2)\, b_{21} k_2]g_2 \,. \quad (36d)$$

We note that the bias to the order $1/N$ of the coefficients b_{12} and b_{21} vanish for Summers' model, where $m_1 = m_2 = 2$. In the formulas given in this section, special GEID terms occur only in the formulas for the small-sample bias of the coefficients of the predetermined variables, where the row vectors u_1', u_2' as given by (20) occur. It should be mentioned, however, that GEID terms are obtained in the formulas for the asymptotic covariances between coefficients of the predetermined variables belonging to different equations.

3.9.4. The Existence of the Mean and Variance of the Estimates

At first we shall consider Summers' model where $m_1 = m_2 = 2$, for non-stochastic predetermined variables and normally distributed residuals. Then the denominator in formula (3.8.6) for w_{11} is a positive definite quadratic form in w_{23} and w_{24}. In the numerator the components of the vector Zy_1' occur too, and therefore we shall consider the conditional distribution for given values of this vector. Since also the denominator of (3.8.6) is a homogeneous second degree polynomial in w_{23} and w_{24} it follows that the conditional mean and variance as well as higher moments of w_{11} exist. Since the components of Zy_1' only enter the numerator it follows that the same holds for the overall distribution of w_{11}. The same thing holds for w_{12}, and from the formulas $w_{13} = b_{12}w_{23}$ and $w_{14} = b_{12}w_{24}$ together with formula (3.8.12) for b_{12} it follows that the argument can be extended to w_{13} and w_{14} as well. (Note that w_{13} and w_{14} do not enter the vector w_1 according to its definition.) The formula for b_{12}, however, contains only an expression of the first degree in w_{23} and w_{24} in the numerator, and considering again the conditional distribution for given values of Z_1y_1', we find that the mean but not the variance of b_{12} exists, and this result can be extended to the overall distribution of b_{12}. The corresponding arguments hold for the coefficients of the second equation. With the aid of formula $g_{11} = w_{11} - b_{12}w_{21}$ we find that the mean but not the variance exists for this estimator, and the same holds of course true for the remaining coefficients of the structural form. That the mean exists but not the variance is also found by Basmann (1962) for the TSLS estimators of Summers' model.

A similar analysis for higher values of m_2 shows that already for $m_2 = 3$ the mean and the variance of the FP estimators of the structural coefficients of the first equation exist. On the other hand, for $m_2 = 1$, which means that the first equation is just identified, not even the mean exists.

In most sampling experiments of this volume, the predetermined variables are stochastic, and the generated sample can be considered as N independent observations from a multivariate normal distribution. Then, even if the variances do not exist, the asymptotic covariance matrix of the structural coefficients, as obtained in this section, is meaningful and provides the asymptotic multivariate normal distribution of the estimates (Cramér, 1945/1946, p. 366). Some 20 graphs in Chapters 4–9 show Monte Carlo distributions for estimated parameters, but the corresponding normal approximations have not been assessed.

3.9.5. The Occurrence of Constant Terms and Common Variables

In practice a constant term usually occurs in the equations. In this case the asymptotic standard errors and small-sample bias can be found by taking the product sums of the deviations for the sample mean and otherwise use the same formulas as before. The constant terms themselves are linear functions of the other coefficients; hence their asymptotic standard errors and small-sample bias can be obtained afterwards. Another way of proceeding is to add a row of units to both of the matrices Z_1 and Z_2, and use the formulas of Sections 3.9.1 and 3.9.2.

Similar procedures can also be used when common predetermined variables z_i occur in both equations. Either the analysis is performed with respect to the residuals of the OLS regressions of Z_1 and Z_2 on the common predetermined variables, or the common predetermined variables are included in both matrices.

3.10. Maximum Likelihood Aspects of the FP Estimates of GEID Models
by E. Lyttkens

Letting ζ_i^* denote the column vector of the variables η_q^* and z_p that occur in the ith equation, and writing α_i for the row vector of those elements of the ith row of the combined matrix $[\beta, \Gamma]$ which are not prescribed zeros, we have according to the asymmetric GEID specification

$$y_{it} = \alpha_i \zeta_{it}^* + \epsilon_{it} ,\tag{1}$$

with

$$E(y_{it} | \eta_{qt}^*, z_{pt}) = \alpha_i \zeta_{it}^* .\tag{2}$$

For an overidentified equation, this conditional mean is in general not the same thing as the conditional mean of y_{it} for given values of all predetermined variables z_k. It will be assumed, however, that the regressions are linear, so that

$$Y_t = \Pi Z_t + \delta_t^* ,\tag{3}$$

with

$$E(Y_t | z_{1t}, ..., z_{mt}) = \Pi Z_t .$$ (4)

We shall now rewrite the ith relation of the reduced form (3) in terms of the variables ζ_i^* and a set of auxiliary variables $\psi_{i1}^*, \psi_{i2}^*, ...$, as many as the number of predetermined variables in the system exceeds the number of component variables in ζ_i^*, and such that each ψ_{ik}^* is uncorrelated with all components of ζ_i^*. Then the regression of y_i on all predetermined variables z_k gives the same residual as the regression of y_i on the components of ζ_i^* and the variables ψ_{ik}^*. In this last regression we let the linear form in the variables ψ_{ik}^* be denoted $\kappa_i \psi_i$, where κ_i is an auxiliary coefficient to be disposed of later. This gives

$$y_{it} = \alpha_i \zeta_{it}^* + \kappa_i \psi_{it} + \delta_{it}^*$$ (5)

with

$$E(y_{it} | z_{1t}, ..., z_{mt}) = \alpha_i \zeta_{it}^* + \kappa_i \psi_{it} .$$ (6)

The following formula is then obtained with the aid of (1),

$$E(\epsilon_{it} | z_{1t}, ..., z_{mt}) = \kappa_i \psi_{it} ; \quad i = 1, ..., n .$$ (7)

We shall now impose a number of restrictive conditions. First, we assume the conditional distribution of ϵ_t for a given Z_t to be multivariate normal with the means given by formula (7) and the covariance matrix Φ (say) independent of Z_t. Then the conditional distribution of Y_t for given values of Z_t is multivariate normal with the means given by formula (6) and with covariance matrix Φ. It follows that the vector δ_t^* has a multivariate distribution with zero mean and covariance matrix Φ. Furthermore we assume that δ_t^* and δ_τ^* are uncorrelated if $t \neq \tau$ and that ϵ_t and δ_t are independent of all predetermined variables referring to time points before t, and as regards exogenous variables also after t. It will be noted that this last assumption is rather restrictive.

On the assumptions thus specified, the logarithm of the likelihood function — conditional on the values of lagged endogenous variables dating from before the observation period, if such values occur in the equations — is given by

$$\log L = -\tfrac{1}{2}nN\log 2\pi - \tfrac{1}{2}N\log|\Phi| - \tfrac{1}{2}\sum_{t=1}^{N}\delta_t^*\Phi^{-1}(\delta_t^*)', \quad (8)$$

where the expression for δ_t^* is taken from (3) or alternatively from (5). Because of the auxiliary coefficient vectors $\kappa_1, \kappa_2, ..., \kappa_n$ there are no restrictions for the elements of the matrix Π. Therefore, as in the case of the reduced form of a just identified system, the maximum likelihood method reduces to OLS regression applied to each equation separately. Denoting the maximum likelihood estimates of Π, Φ, and δ_t^* by P, $\hat{\Phi}$, and d_t^* we have

$$\hat{\Phi} = \frac{1}{N}\sum_{t=1}^{N}d_t^*(d_t^*)', \quad (9)$$

and

$$\sum_{t=1}^{N}d_t^*z_t' = 0, \quad (10)$$

with

$$d_t^* = y_t - PZ_t. \quad (11)$$

Let a_i and z_{it}^* denote the estimates of the vectors α_i and ζ_{it}^*, while the estimates of the vectors κ_i and ψ_{it} are denoted by $\hat{\kappa}_i$ and $\hat{\psi}_{it}$. In analogy to the condition $E(\zeta_{it}^*\psi_{it}') = 0$, we prescribe

$$\sum_{t=1}^{N}z_{it}^*\hat{\psi}_{it}' = 0. \quad (12$$

Then the following expression is obtained for the estimated residual of the ith equation,

$$d_{it}^* = y_{it} - a_i z_{it}^* - \hat{\kappa}_i\hat{\psi}_{it}. \quad (13)$$

Equation (10) gives

$$\sum_{t=1}^{N} d_t^* (z_{it}^*)' = 0 \tag{14}$$

since the components of z_{it}^* are linear expressions in the components of Z_t. Introducing expression (13) for d_{it}^* with due regard to the condition (12) we obtain

$$\sum_{t=1}^{N} y_{it} (z_{it}^*)' = a_i \sum_{t=1}^{N} z_{it}^* (z_{it}^*)' , \tag{15}$$

which is the normal equation for the regression coefficients pertaining to the asymmetric GEID specification. Having determined a_i we choose a vector $\hat{\psi}_{it}^*$ that fulfills the condition (10). The auxiliary vector $\hat{\kappa}_i$ then is determined from the relation

$$\sum_{t=1}^{N} y_{it} \hat{\psi}_{it}' = \hat{\kappa}_i \sum_{t=1}^{N} \hat{\psi}_{it} \hat{\psi}_{it}' . \tag{16}$$

Since the value of d_t^* is the same if we use expression (11) or (13) it follows that also the likelihood function is the same for both specifications. Therefore we conclude that if the estimation leads to more than one set of real values of the coefficients a_i or — returning to the original notation — different sets of real values of the estimated matrices B and G, the likelihood as given by formula (8) is the same for all sets of coefficient values, which are obtained. Therefore, the likelihood function cannot discriminate between different sets of coefficient values obtained from the asymmetric GEID specification as applied to the sample.

To summarize, the key difference between ML and FP estimation of the present type of GEID systems is that in the ML approach the GEID correlations (or rather the quantities $\alpha_i \psi_i$) are included in the estimation procedure at the outset, while the FP approach ignores the GEID correlations in the beginning and obtains them in terms of the parameter estimates.

CHAPTER 4

Predictive Power

A Summary Statistic

4.1. Summary of Overall Set of Estimates for a Model

There are many choices in judging the quality of estimates for a particular model. [1] One choice involves the selection of a specific parameter. A second choice involves some characteristic such as bias, standard deviation around the mean, estimated standard deviation around the mean, mean absolute error, and extreme value. [2] The summary tables in Chapter 10 present 55 characteristics of estimates for a small 2-equation system such as Model 1b.

It is very helpful to have a summary statistic on the overall quality of an estimated model. Predictive power is a good candidate as a summary statistic. Specific reference is made to the familiar R^2 as a measure of predictive information (see 1.4.8). Hence, in this work we have chosen R^2 as the measure of predictive power: [3]

$$R_i^2 = 1 - \frac{\sum_t [Y - \text{pred } Y]_t^2}{\sum_t [Y^2]_t}.$$ (1)

There are still choices with respect to the variable on which R_i^2 is to be measured and whether it should be measured inside or outside the sample period.

The tables in Chapter 10 give R_i^2 for each endogenous variable and the mean R^2 for all variables. As explained in Chapter 2.2 only part of the Monte Carlo data in each series of generated data was used in estimating the parameters of the model. The remaining 40 observations form a prediction period which provides an opportunity to obtain an unbiased estimate of the predictive power of the estimated model. The summary tables give R^2 statistics for both the sample period and the prediction period. The latter is certainly a better test, but both are shown to provide insight into how good the R^2 for the sample period is as a predictor of R^2 for the prediction period.

Models 4a–4c and 5c–5e have lagged endogenous variables and, therefore, there are two ways to measure R^2, namely by the way of the predictions given by

$$Y_t = BY_t^* + G_1 X_t + G_2 Y_{t-\alpha} \tag{2}$$

or

$$Y_t = BY_t^* + G_1 X_t + G_2 \text{ pred } Y_{t-\alpha} . \tag{3}$$

In (2) the true values of all lagged endogenous variables ($Y_{t-\alpha}$) are used in developing the prediction for Y_t. In (3) predictions (pred $Y_{t-\alpha}$) of the values of lagged endogenous variables $Y_{t-\alpha}$ are used. Since any differences ($Y_{t-\alpha} - $ pred $Y_{t-\alpha}$) are another source of error, the expected R^2 from (3) is smaller than from (2). In Part E of the tables in Chapter 10.2 R^2 for the sample period is measured by formula (2) but the R^2 in the prediction period is measured by formula (3) with the true values of lagged endogenous variables used in the first observation of the prediction period. Although the prediction period has 40 observations (see Chapter 2.2) the effects from prior periods diminishes rapidly as the lag increases because the models were designed to be stable (i.e., the absolute values of the roots of the characteristic difference equation are less than one).

If an estimated model is to be used for forecasting several periods into the future, R^2 should be measured from (3). Unfortunately, the sample period is usually so short that if lagged endogenous variables occur in the model there are very few independent sets of observations where the set is longer than 1 period. Consequently, the estimate of R^2 from the sample period is usually derived from formula (2). For example, if the sample period were 40 observations and the prediction was to be

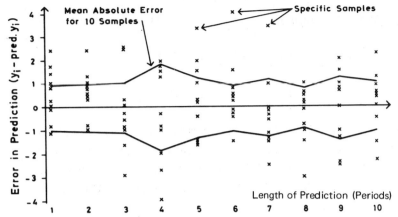

Chart 4.1.1. Length of prediction and magnitude of error in prediction (FP method).

10 observations there would only be 4 independent sets of 10 observations in the sample period that could be used in developing an estimate of R^2 from (3). It is well to note, however, that if we just want a point estimate of R^2, we should use all sets of 10 observations regardless of whether or not they are independent.

The computer program was designed to compute the average absolute error for each successive observation in the prediction period. Although the expected value is a monotonically increasing function of the length of prediction, the example in Chart 1 shows the random nature of the prediction error. The average error over the 100 samples for each of the models in Chapter 10 would, of course, show a more regular pattern than the results of the 10 samples in Chart 1. The model specifications for the results in Chart 1 are given below:

Structural equations:

$$y_{1t} = 0.8\, y_{2t} + 0.48\, y_{2,t-1} + x_{1t} + \delta_{1t} , \tag{4}$$

$$y_{2t} = 0.8\, y_{1t} - 0.48\, y_{1,t-1} + x_{2t} + \delta_{2t} . \tag{5}$$

The general solution of the corresponding characteristic difference equation has the form:

$$y_{it} = A_i (0.8)^t \cos(\tfrac{1}{2}\pi t - \varphi_i) , \qquad i = 1, 2 . \tag{6}$$

Average from 10 samples:

$$V(y_1) = 11.6 ; \qquad V(y_2) = 12.4 , \tag{7}$$

$$R^2(y_1) = 0.84 ; \qquad R^2(y_2) = 0.85 . \tag{8}$$

The model was specially designed to produce a 4 period cycle with a relatively large damping factor (in equation (6) note the values of $\frac{1}{2}\pi$ and 0.8). The estimated model in each sample does not necessarily have a design similar to that of the model used to generate the data.

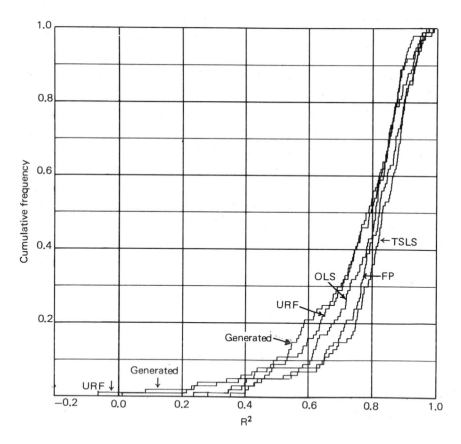

Chart 4.1.2. Cumulative distribution of R^2 for the sample period in Model 5f.

As pointed out by Mosbaek-Wold [1] there are many different uses of part or all of the estimated parameters in an economic model. In applied econometrics the use that is to be made of the estimated model is known and it is immediately clear from the situation which characteristic in quality of estimates is most important. There is no specific characteristic that is always the most important. However, as mentioned earlier, the R^2 for a prediction period can serve as a useful summary statistic in Monte Carlo investigations. In addition, economic forecasting is certainly one important use of econometric models.

In the literature of econometrics the values of R^2 are sometimes cited

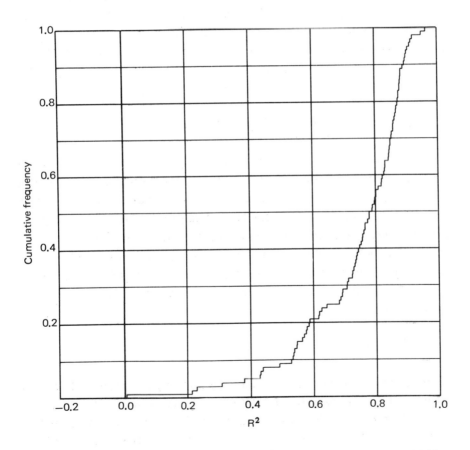

Chart 4.1.3. Cumulative distribution of generated R^2 for the sample period in Model 5f.

as a criterion for judging when a model is well formulated. Monte Carlo results such as those in Charts 2 and 3 show how frequently a correct specification would be rejected for any arbitrary criterion on required size of R^2. Chart 3 shows that in approximately 10% of the samples the generated R^2 in Model 5f (that is, R^2 as calculated from formula (2) for the prediction period in each of 100 samples of the Monte Carlo generated data) was less than 0.5 even though the model was designed with an R^2 of 0.8. Chart 2 shows that all 4 methods gave considerable overfitting in the range of 0.5 to 0.8 but in each case 5—10% of the samples gave results that would have led to rejection of the model with a criterion of 0.5 for minimum acceptable predicted R^2. We do not recommend any form of rule for accepting or rejecting a model based on an R^2 computed for the sample period. The decision on acceptance or rejection of an estimated model should incorporate a great number of considerations. This will not be discussed further in other parts of the monograph because it is not in focus in our problem area.

4.2. Predictions from Reduced Form Equations

Since all of the models investigated in this study are linear in the current endogenous variables, it is easy to transform each set of estimates into the reduced form. These results are given in parts C.1—C.4 of the tables for each model in Chapter 10.2. The predictions of endogenous variables were made from the reduced form equations. The unrestricted estimates, or what is commonly labeled the directly estimated reduced form, is the fourth set and is identified as URF in Part C of the tables.

The estimated reduced form for OLS, TSLS, and FP are the generated coefficients

$$W = [I - B]^{-1}G .\tag{1}$$

We have not endeavored to estimate the large sample standard deviation, but it is, of course, easy to calculate the observed standard deviation among the Monte Carlo results (see Part C.2 in the tables in Chapter 10.2). The predictions from models estimated by OLS, TSLS, and FP could have been made from the structural or reduced form equations, but the latter is easier computationally.

The accuracy of many types of predictions is determined by the quality of estimates of reduced form coefficients. For example, if we were interested in determining the quality of the estimate of the effect of, say, a particular exogenous variable on a specified endogenous variable, we would look at a specific reduced form coefficient since

$$\text{est} \left[\frac{dy_i}{dx_j} \right] = w_{ij} \; . \tag{2}$$

On the other hand, to judge the quality of an estimated model by looking only at specific reduced form coefficients is difficult because the number of coefficients is large and the estimates are usually correlated. The R^2 in a prediction period, however, is a single summary statistic on the quality of the overall set of coefficient estimates.

We wish to emphasize that predictive power measured in terms of accuracy of predicting endogenous variables in a prediction period is centered on only one of the interesting forms of prediction from an estimated model. [1] We do offer the selected measure R^2 as an overall summary of quality of an estimated model when no specific use has been pinpointed.

Specific coefficients of the reduced form as generated from the various types of estimates of structural coefficients will not be discussed in detail in the monograph. They will be discussed to some extent in the chapters on bias and dispersion and are referred to occasionally in explaining examples of low predictive power in the next two sections of this chapter. Bias and dispersion in estimated reduced form coefficients result in part from the familiar problem of overfitting.

4.3. R^2 Computed from Data Within the Sample Period

In applied econometrics data are usually so scarce that all available data are used to estimate parameters of the model. It then becomes necessary to estimate R^2 from the same data that were used in estimating the model.

An R^2 for the sample period and an R^2 for a prediction period were computed for each sample in the Monte Carlo results of our investigation. They provide insight into three phenomena of interest in applied econometrics. First, the relation between the R^2 for prediction and sample periods reveals how good the latter is as a predictor of the former. Second, the relation between the R^2 from an estimated model and the R^2 in the Monte Carlo generated data reveals the degree of overfitting. Third, the adjustment for degrees of freedom that was used provides information as to whether adjustments can be devised whereby an R^2 computed from sample data can be a better estimator of R^2 when the estimated model is used for prediction.

The results in Part E of each table in Chapter 10.2 show two sets of results for the sample period for OLS, TSLS and FP. In Part E.1 the results for URF have been adjusted for degrees of freedom, but the results for OLS, TSLS, and FP have not. In Part E.3 of the tables the results have been corrected for degrees of freedom in the following way:

$$R^2 = 1 - \frac{\sum_t (Y - \text{est } Y)_t^2 / (N - k)}{\sum_t (Y)_t^2 / N} \tag{1}$$

where k is the number of unknown coefficients in the structural equations divided by the number of structural equations to be estimated. Techniques for adjusting for degrees of freedom in each structural equation and in unrestricted reduced form equations are well known. However, there is little information in the literature concerning the proper adjustment for degrees of freedom in computing R^2 for simultaneous equations models.

Table 1 gives information for comparing both the adjusted and unad-

---

Notes to Table 4.3.1

[1] The ratio is based on $(1 - R^2)$, with R^2 computed in accordance with formula (4.1.1) when it refers to the prediction period or the sample period but is unadjusted for degrees of freedom. R^2 is computed in accordance with formula (1) when it refers to the sample period and is adjusted for degrees of freedom.

[2] OLS is the method of ordinary least squares as applied to the structural equations. TSLS and FP are two-stage least squares and fix-point as applied to the REID specification (see Chapters 3.4 and 3.5). URF is direct estimates of the reduced form by the method of least squares. The results are the average R^2 for the model as estimated by each of the respective methods in the 100 Monte Carlo samples.

Table 4.3.1

Ratio of variance of prediction error from estimated model to variance of generated residual [1]

	Sample period		Prediction period	Sample period		Prediction period
	Unadj.	Adjusted		Unadj.	Adjusted	
	A. *Series on sample size*			B. *Series on population* R^2		
	Model 5f: 10 observations			Model 5m: $R^2 = 0.2$		
OLS [2]	0.8828	0.9547	1.8798	1.0448	1.1294	1.1649
TSLS	0.7293	0.7887	1.5022	0.9421	1.0186	1.1080
FP	0.7840	0.8477	1.7382	0.9434	1.0198	1.1009
URF	0.5996	0.9996	1.8026	0.8997	0.9998	1.1187
	Model 5g: 40 observations			Model 5n: $R^2 = 0.5$		
OLS	1.0950	1.1833	1.2264	1.1258	1.2172	1.2676
TSLS	0.9267	1.0019	1.0767	0.9245	0.9994	1.1003
FP	0.9557	1.0324	1.1104	0.9427	1.0192	1.1210
URF	0.8967	0.9962	1.1155	0.8939	0.9933	1.1222
	Model 5h: 80 observations			Model 5q: $R^2 = 0.95$		
OLS	1.1207	1.2117	1.1974	0.9703	1.0495	1.1434
TSLS	0.9616	1.0394	1.0464	0.9248	1.0000	1.0780
FP	0.9737	1.0526	1.0574	0.9527	1.0297	1.1125
URF	0.9523	0.9985	1.0607	0.8970	0.9960	1.1053
	C. *Series on number of variables per equation*			D. *Series on number of structural equations*		
	Model 1b: 4 variables per equation			Model 2b: 3 equations		
OLS	1.0950	1.1833	1.2264	1.0377	1.1221	1.1833
TSLS	0.9267	1.0019	1.0767	0.9303	1.0057	1.0910
FP	0.9557	1.0324	1.1164	0.9769	1.0566	1.1488
URF	0.8967	0.9962	1.1155	0.8582	1.0094	1.1898
	Model 2f: 6 variables per equation			Model 2c: 5 equations		
OLS	1.0341	1.1819	1.2978	0.9925	1.0729	1.1625
TSLS	0.8821	1.0080	1.1252	0.9229	0.9976	1.0796
FP	0.9411	1.0758	1.1935	1.0183	1.1011	1.2367
URF	0.8064	1.0080	1.2138	0.7508	1.0014	1.3120
	Model 2g: 9 variables per equation			Model 2d: 7 equations		
OLS	0.9265	1.1219	1.4648	0.9902	1.0704	1.1384
TSLS	0.8046	0.9744	1.2803	0.9311	1.0064	1.0842
FP	0.8956	1.0846	1.4110	1.0910	1.1796	1.3135
URF	0.6509	1.0014	1.5421	0.6437	0.9906	1.5723

justed R^2 for the sample period with the R^2 for the prediction period. In order to eliminate the effect of variation in the Monte Carlo data the R^2 evaluation is in terms of the variances of residuals. The ratio in Table 1 is based on 1 minus R^2 (the adjusted R^2 for the sample period is computed as shown in formula 1). It is the ratio of the unbiased estimate of variance of residuals from the estimated model to the variance of the true residuals.

The results in Table 1 have been arranged into 4 sets in order to show how overfitting varies with size of sample, size of residuals, number of variables per equation, and number of equations.

Overfitting is somewhat of a misnomer in the case of OLS, TSLS, and FP because it is not obvious that the generated reduced form coefficients will display the same overfitting that occurs in the structural equations. For example, the residual variance ratio given in Table 1 cannot be greater than 1.0 for URF but it can be greater than 1.0 for OLS, TSLS and FP as evidenced by many of the ratios in the table. However, it is meaningful to ask if there is an adjustment that would make the R^2 for the sample period a better estimate of the R^2 for the prediction period even though there is no overfitting by the usual criterion.

With one exception, the correction for the degrees of freedom in the 11 models shown in Table 1 was in the right direction but not sufficient to provide an unbiased estimate of R^2. Except for OLS in Model 5h the mean for 100 samples shows the adjusted R^2 lying between the unadjusted R^2 and the R^2 in the prediction period. This is as it should be since the R^2 computed from the generated data is a prediction of R^2 with no errors in the regression coefficients. The error in a prediction of an observation outside the sample includes the true residual plus the error in the estimated coefficient multiplied by the value of the predetermined variable.

Instead of evaluating the adjustment for overfitting by comparing the adjusted R^2 with the R^2 computed from generated data in the prediction period it is better to compare it with the R^2 from generated data in the sample period. For example, if the adjustment for overfitting were perfect, it is the values in the second column in Table 1 that would be 1.

The intricate problems concerning overfitting and adjustment are clarified if we distinguish between the following two objectives in making an adjustment for degrees of freedom.

A. An adjustment is needed in order to obtain an unbiased estimate of the residual variance in the regression equation because of overfitting. It is not clear if overfitting in the regression equations in the structural form always leads to overfitting in the generated reduced form.

B. Whenever there is overfitting in the generated reduced form, an adjustment is needed in order to make the R^2 calculated from sample data a better predictor of R^2 for observations outside the sample period.

In order to better understand the nature of the adjustment in the second objective it is helpful to recognize three components in errors in predictions.

(i) The true residuals in the observations that are predicted comprise one component.

The errors resulting from incorrect estimates of reduced form coefficients comprise two components, namely:

(ii) The variance of the estimated reduced form coefficients around the expected values.

(iii) The bias in the estimated reduced form coefficients.

Returning to Table 1 we can say that a value of 1 in the second column implies a good adjustment for the first component but not for the two parts of the second. An adjustment for R^2 computed from sample data should compensate for (ii) but it is not designed to handle component (iii). It is interesting that so little has been done in this area even though prediction ranks as an important goal of econometric model building. Unfortunately, it is not possible to go into this matter more deeply in this monograph.

The adjustment to obtain an unbiased estimate of the residual variance in the case of URF is very good. The mean of the 100 samples in each of the 11 models shows that the adjusted value is closer to the true than the unadjusted value. For OLS the adjusted value was further from the true value than the unadjusted value in 10 of the 11 models. It is only in the case of a very small sample size in Model 5f that the adjusted estimate of R^2 for OLS was made closer to the true value in the sample period. For TSLS the adjusted was closer than the unadjusted R^2 in 10 of the 11 models and for FP the adjusted was closer in 7 of the 11 models.

The quality of the adjustment for purposes of an unbiased estimate of residual variance is a function of special features such as sample size, as can be quickly seen from Chart 1. The adjustment for URF is approp-

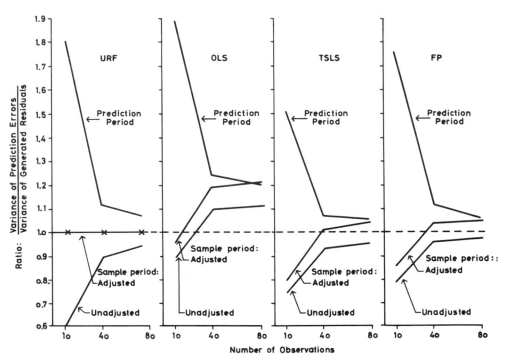

Chart 4.3.1. Ratio of variance of prediction error to variance of generated residual as function of sample size (data from Table 1).

riate for all sample sizes, but the adjustment applied to the other three methods appears to overadjust for all but small sample sizes.

The main reason that the adjustment gives poor results in the case of OLS and FP is that these methods have considerable bias in the estimates of structural coefficients in most REID models. Another factor in FP is the partial lack of convergence which leads to larger errors in the estimates of structural coefficients. This bias in structural coefficients is overfitting in the case of structural equations but not in the case of generated reduced form equations. In many cases for OLS and several cases for FP even the unadjusted estimate of residual variance is larger than the true residual variance. An example is shown in Chart 2 in results for Model 5m where bias in OLS estimates of parameters is quite large. The graph for FP is not shown on Chart 2; however, the distributions of estimates for FP and TSLS in Model 5m are very similar.

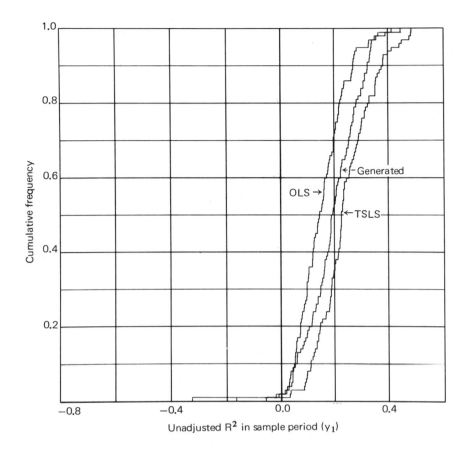

Chart 4.3.2. Positive and negative bias in unadjusted values of R^2 for y_1 in Model 5m.

When bias in estimates of parameters of the model lead to an unadjusted estimate of residual variance that is larger than the true residual variance, two points must be considered. First, the estimate is obviously a biased overestimate of the true residual variance. Second, the error in the use of the model for a prediction period will be larger than what can be explained in terms of the variance of the true residual and standard deviation of estimates of coefficients around the mean — the two items that constitute components (i) and (ii) above. For example, even though the estimated residual variances for sample sizes of 40 and 80 in Chart 1 are greater than the true variance of the residual they are not necessarily

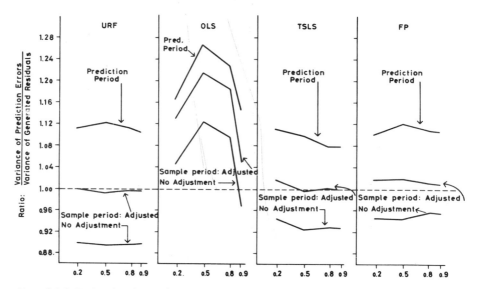

Chart 4.3.3. Ratio of variance of prediction error to variance of generated residual as function of size of residual (data from Table 1).

an overestimate of the prediction error for observations outside the sample. Except for OLS in the case of 80 observations the adjusted R^2 is still larger than the R^2 for observations outside the sample period. In this one exception we know the adjustment was too great because the one component of prediction error not included in the adjustment (i.e., item (iii) above) must, of course, be negative.

Chart 3 shows the relation between R^2 for observations outside the sample and R^2 calculated from sample data in some models where OLS and FP estimates of structural coefficients are strongly biased. Here again the adjustment makes the estimated residual variance greater than the true residual variance, but this is the type of adjustment that is necessary in order to account for prediction error that will result from small-sample bias in estimated coefficients (i.e., component (iii) above).

In summary we can say that these Monte Carlo results confirm the widely accepted hypothesis that overfitting is a serious problem in regression equations. The unadjusted figures in Column 1 of Table 1 give evidence of the degree of overfitting. The quality of R^2 computed from sample data as an estimate of R^2 for predictions outside the sample should be analyzed as follows:

(i) In most models where OLS, TSLS, and FP have large bias in estimates of structural coefficients the unadjusted estimate of the residual variance in reduced form equations is likely to be a biased overestimate (e.g., see results for OLS in Model 5g in Table 1). On the other hand, most overfitting in the regression equations carries into the reduced form equation, and where bias in structural estimates is not serious, the estimated residuals in the reduced form are biased underestimates of the true residual (e.g., see results for FP, Model 5f, Table 1).

(ii) The adjustment for degrees of freedom shown in equation (1) leads to a biased overestimate of the true residual variance because of the bias in estimates of reduced form coefficients (e.g., see results for FP, Model 5g, Table 1).

(iii) It appears that the adjustment for degrees of freedom shown in equation (1) is appropriate for providing an unbiased estimate of R^2 for observations outside the sample. That is, the adjustment appears to be appropriate for components (i) and (ii) above. Component (ii) cannot, of course, be handled until the specific values of the predetermined variables in the prediction period are known. Also, the theory of econometrics has to be expanded to include estimates of the standard deviation of the generated reduced form coefficients.

Unfortunately, the issue of overfitting and unbiased estimates of R^2 cannot be properly dealt with in this short monograph. The Monte Carlo data presented provide valuable raw material that the authors hope will prove useful for further investigations by others and by themselves. At this point we offer only the tentative conclusion that the adjustment for degrees of freedom does not appear to be a desirable way to handle the component of prediction error resulting from bias in estimates of reduced form coefficients. The correction is in the right direction, but the correction should be a function of the numerical values on predetermined variables that are involved in the prediction error components. For a partial understanding of components (ii) and (iii) on page 179, some guidance is provided by the concept of standard deviation of estimates around the true value; see the statistics in Part C.4 of the tables in Chapter 10.2.

In the absence of better theory on predictive power of estimated models the Monte Carlo results in this monograph provide insight for applied work. In Monte Carlo work it is not necessary to untangle the interactions from the three components (i) — (iii) of prediction error. By our having built a prediction period into the Monte Carlo data and having used a little more computer time to make and evaluate predictions outside the sample, the results of this research provide insight into the combined effect of all components of prediction error.

4.4. R^2 Computed from Data Outside the Sample Period

The predictive power of an estimated model measured in terms of the familiar R^2 statistic has two random components. First, the estimates of parameters developed from the sample period are random variables. Second, the residual variables in the prediction period are random variables. Chart 1 is the cumulative distribution of the generated R^2 in the prediction period (40 observations, as always) for Model 1b. That is,

$$R_i^2 \text{ (generated)} = 1 - \frac{\sum_t \epsilon_{it}^2}{\sum_t y_{it}^2}, \tag{1}$$

where ϵ_{it} is the actual residual in the Monte Carlo sample data. We note that one value of R^2 is as low as 0.57 among the 100 Monte Carlo samples on Model 1b although the population R^2 is specified as 0.80.

Part E of the tables for each model in Chapter 10.2 gives the mean of the generated R^2 for both the sample and the prediction periods. The quality of a set of estimates should be judged by comparing the R^2 from the prediction period with the generated R^2 rather than the theoretical R^2 from the design of the model. The results for most models show slight downward bias in the generated R^2. Whereas the distribution of each residual variable ϵ_i is symmetrical, the distribution of R^2 is asymmetrical because of the limited upper tail ($R^2 \leqslant 1$).

The results for the basic Model 1b show a small but significant difference between three sets of estimators. OLS is the worst, TSLS is the best, and FP and URF are in between (see Chart 2). The very similar distributions for FP and URF are not easily seen in Chart 2, but other graphs show the two distributions to be practically identical. The low R^2 for OLS results from the inconsistency in parameter estimates (see

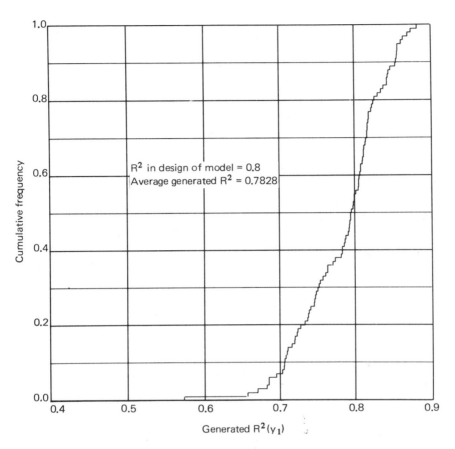

Chart 4.4.1. Cumulative distribution of generated $R^2(y_1)$ in the prediction period for Model 1b.

Part C.1 of Table 10.2.3). The TSLS, FP and URF methods are consistent, which on the whole makes for large and rather equal R^2. When it comes to a closer comparison between these three methods, the size of R^2 is influenced by several features. For one thing, TSLS is designed for classical ID systems, FP for the more general class of GEID systems; in other words, the properties of Classic ID systems are automatically exploited by the TSLS method, and this makes for larger R^2. From another point of view, R^2 for FP and URF are lower than for TSLS because of the greater dispersion in the estimated reduced form coefficients.

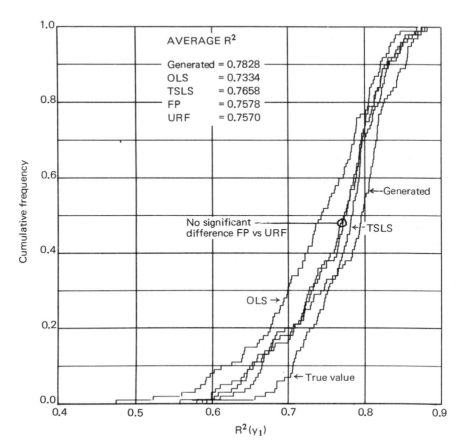

Chart 4.4.2. Cumulative distribution of $R^2(y_1)$ in the prediction period for Model 1b.

The difference between the predictive power of FP and TSLS in Model 1b is shown in Chart 3. There is no noticeable difference in the tails of the distribution, but the distribution for TSLS does appear to be shifted to the right over most of the range of observed values.

The relative predictive power among the four methods will now be compared under the following variations:

A. Changes in the size of beta coefficients: Models 1a–1f
B. Changes in the size of the model: Models 1g–1i
C. Changes in the number of variables per equation: Models 2e–2g
D. Changes in the degree of multicollinearity among exogenous variables: Models 1b, 5a and 5b

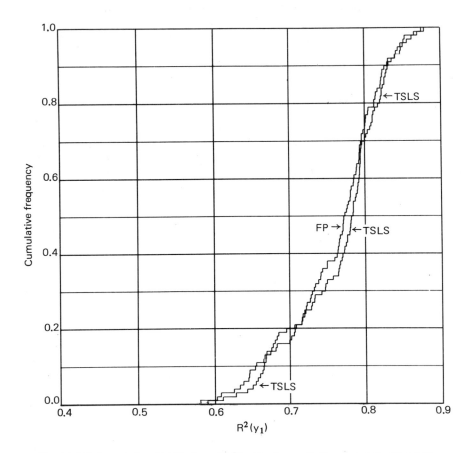

Chart 4.4.3. Cumulative distribution of $R^2(y_1)$ in the prediction period for Model 1b:
FP and TSLS estimation

E. With and without lagged endogenous variables: Models 1b and
   5c—5e
F. Changes in size of residuals: Models 5m—5s
G. Changes in sample size: Models 5f—5j
H. Classical vs GEID specification: Models 1b, 6a—6c, and 6f—6j.
Table 1 shows Monte Carlo results for each type of variation except for
the last two (sample size and classical vs GEID specification). The latter
variation is complex and will be taken up in the special discussion in
Chapter 9. The results from analysis of sample size are given in Table 2.

Table 4.4.1
Relative predictive power for different types of models
(average R^2 for 100 samples).

Model	Feature	Generated	OLS	TSLS	FP	URF
A. *Size of beta coefficients*						
Beta coeffs.						
1a	0.5, −0.5	0.7925	0.7659	0.7728	0.7719	0.7669
1b	1, −1	0.7862	0.7378	0.7698	0.7626	0.7615
1c	3, −3	0.7947	0.5025	0.7755	0.5448	0.7690
1d	0.5, −0.9	0.7905	0.6630	0.7729	0.7699	0.7659
1e	0.5, −3	0.7956	0.6237	0.7761	0.7486	0.7705
1f	1.1, −3	0.7981	−41.9819	0.7693	0.0741	0.7736
B. *Size of model*						
No. eqs. $|\beta_i| = 1$						
2a	2	0.7862	0.7378	0.7698	0.7626	0.7615
2b	3	0.7924	0.7533	0.7735	0.7615	0.7530
2c	5	0.7926	0.7589	0.7761	0.7435	0.7279
2d	7	0.7898	0.7607	0.7721	0.7239	0.6695
No. eqs. $|\beta_i| = 0.5$						
1g	2	0.7925	0.7659	0.7728	0.7719	0.7669
1h	3	0.7889	0.7728	0.7719	0.7682	0.7149
1i	7	0.7877	0.7718	0.7708	0.7671	0.6677
C. *Number of variables per equation*						
Var/eq						
2e	3	0.7862	0.7378	0.7698	0.7626	0.7615
2f	5	0.7891	0.7263	0.7627	0.7483	0.7440
2g	8	0.7956	0.7006	0.7383	0.7116	0.6848
D. *Multicollinearity among exogenous variables*						
$r(x_i, x_j)$						
1b	0	0.7862	0.7378	0.7698	0.7626	0.7615
5a	0.7	0.7908	0.7413	0.7760	0.7687	0.7690
5b	−0.7	0.7979	0.7451	0.7789	0.7746	0.7727
E. *Lagged endogenous variables in the model*						
1b	none	0.7862	0.7378	0.7698	0.7626	0.7615
5c	one eq. [1]	0.8881	0.8560	0.8781	0.8747	0.8743
5d	own lag [1]	0.9163	0.9017	0.9087	0.9060	0.9059
5e	opp. lag [1]	0.9158	0.9009	0.9086	0.9060	0.9058

Table 4.4.1 (continued)

Model	Feature	Generated	OLS	TSLS	FP	URF
F. Changes in size of residuals						
	R^2					
5m	0.2	0.1882	0.0543	0.1005	0.1063	0.0918
5n	0.5	0.4794	0.3401	0.4272	0.4164	0.4158
5p	0.8	0.7862	0.7378	0.7698	0.7626	0.7615
5q	0.9	0.9449	0.9370	0.9406	0.9387	0.9391
G. Changes in sample size						
See Table 2						
H. Classical ID vs GEID specification						
See Chapter 9						

[1] In Model 5c $y_{1,t-1}$ and $y_{2,t-1}$ were used in the same equation; in Model 5e the lagged dependent variable was used in the equation, and in Model 5d the lag of the current endogenous variable appearing on the right was used in the equation. Models 5c and 5d have the same underlying difference in equation with roots equal to 0.8 and −0.8 but this is impossible in Model 5e, so it was designed to have roots equal to 0.8 and zero.

The relative performance among the four methods varies considerably within the dimension of size of beta coefficients, but there appears to be no significant variation within the dimensions of multicollinearity and presence of lagged endogenous variables. Each of the dimensions will be discussed in greater detail below in order to emphasize one of the main observations in our research project, namely, that relative performance among alternative methods of estimation is very sensitive to the type of model being fitted. Therefore, it is important to consider a wide range of models when judging the performance of alternative methods of estimation.

4.4.1. Size of beta coefficients

There is no significant difference in predictive power as measured by R^2 among any of the methods in Model 1a where both beta coefficients are small. This result is in line with the general experience that when beta coefficients are small the problem of estimation is essentially that of vector regression and all methods operating on the structural equations give about the same results.

The predictive power of TSLS and URF does not change significantly as the size of beta coefficients changes. This result would be true for URF regardless of sample size but it would not be true for TSLS if sample size were small. As sample size decreases and approaches the number of predetermined variables in the entire model, TSLS estimates approach OLS estimates, and predictive performance of TSLS would become sensitive to size of beta coefficients.

It is easily seen from Chart 4 and Part A of Table 1 that in models with large betas and models where the absolute value of one or more but not all betas approach unity predictive power of OLS and FP esti-

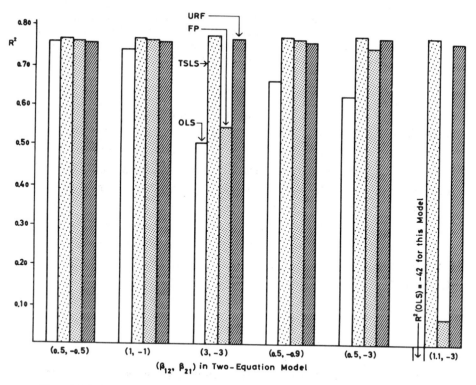

Chart 4.4.4. Predictive power R^2 for models with beta coefficients of different size.

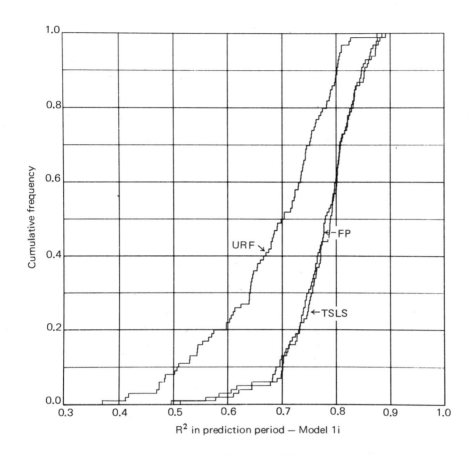

Chart 4.4.5. Relative performance of FP, TSLS, and URF in large model with small betas.

mates are seriously affected. Chart 4 was made to show the correlation between the performance of FP and OLS. The pattern of performance for FP is more similar to OLS than to any of the other three methods but there are some significant differences. FP is superior to OLS in every case. OLS is decidedly inferior to FP in the case of Models 1f and 1c. OLS parameter estimates in Model 1f have large bias as well as wide dispersion.

The relative performance between FP and TSLS for larger models can be seen in Charts 5 and 6. There is no significant difference between FP and TSLS when betas are small (Model 1i: Chart 5), but there is a significant difference when all beta coefficients are not small.

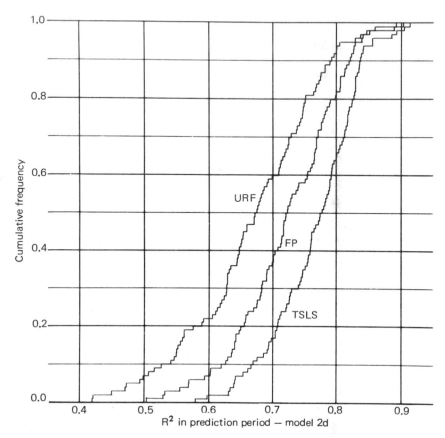

Chart 4.4.6. Relative performance of FP, TSLS, and URF in large model when beta coefficients are not small.

We conclude that the size of beta coefficients is a very important factor in the relative predictive power among methods of estimation. In applied econometrics where sample sizes are frequently 20 observations or less, TSLS is also sensitive to the size of beta coefficients. From the Monte Carlo results in Part A of Table 1 the analyst could conclude that URF is always at least as good as other methods, but this is only because 40 observations is a very large sample compared to the total of four predetermined variables in these 2-equation models. As models become larger the number of degrees of freedom in URF compared to that in methods applicable to structural equations becomes less, and the relative performance of URF decreases as shown in Charts 5 and 6.

4.4.2. Sample Size

The effects from small sample size depend very much on the model being fitted. To measure the relative effect of sample size on predictive power of FP and TSLS we use the ratio φ defined by

$$\varphi = \frac{1 - R^2 \text{ based on FP estimates of the parameters}}{1 - R^2 \text{ based on TSLS estimates of the parameters}}, \qquad (2)$$

where $1 - R^2$ in both cases refers to the prediction period. Chart 7 shows

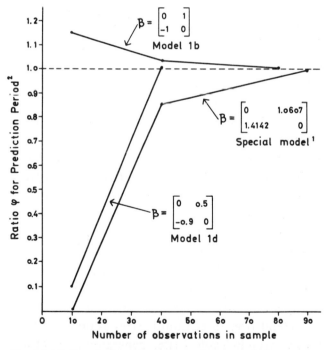

Chart 4.4.7. Sample size and relative performance of FP and TSLS.

[1] This model was designed with a population R^2 of 0.5 whereas the other two models were designed with an R^2 of 0.8.

[2] The value for φ is computed as shown in equation (2).

Table 4.4.2

Predictive power R^2 and sample size for three sets of two-equation models [1].

Model	Sample size	Gener- ated	OLS	TSLS	FP	URF
$\beta_{12} = 1, \beta_{21} = -1$						
5f	10	0.7953	0.6152	0.6925	0.6442	0.6310
5g	40	0.7862	0.7378	0.7698	0.7626	0.7615
5h	80	0.7908	0.7495	0.7811	0.7788	0.7781
$\beta_{12} = 0.5, \beta_{21} = -0.9$						
5i	10	0.7912	−0.3333	−2.1643	0.6798	0.6447
5j	40	0.7905	0.6630	0.7729	0.7699	0.7659
$\beta_{12} = 1.0607, \beta_{21} = 1.4142$						
A	10	0.489	−31.	−204.	0.060	0.118
B	40	0.482	−7000.	0.313	0.407	0.419
C	90	0.411	−9.	0.382	0.383	0.386

[1] Models A, B and C in the third set were designed with a population R^2 of 0.5 whereas the other models in this table were designed with a population R^2 of 0.8. Results for Models A, B and C are not included in Chapter 10.

the ratio φ for three different models. All of the results shown in Chart 7 represent 100 Monte Carlo samples, but the model with beta coefficients of +1.0607 and +1.4142 was designed with a population R^2 of 0.5 as opposed to 0.8 in the other two models. However, we expect that the pattern of change in the relative performance of FP and TSLS would be approximately the same for different R^2 in the design of the model. The model with beta coefficients of 0.5 and −0.9 was estimated from samples of only two different sizes, but results are included because of the small amount of information available on the effect of sample size.

The graphs in Chart 7 were drawn in terms of error in prediction $(1-R^2)$ rather than R^2 because of the large negative values for TSLS for small sample size in two of the models. A firmer conclusion can be drawn on the effect of sample size if the trends in relative performance can be seen to extend over three sample sizes as opposed to only two.

Actual R^2's are given in Table 2 (i.e., generated from Monte Carlo data). There is no significance to the fact that the predictive power of OLS was less with 40 observations than with 10 observations (Models B and C) and predictive power of FP was less with 90 observations than with 40 observations (Models C and B). The R^2 from generated data in the case of 90 observations was 0.411 compared to 0.482 in the case of 40 observations, and the predictive power of FP relative to the R^2 from generated data was actually larger in the case of 90 observations. The large negative value of -7000 for OLS in the case of Model B was dominated by the results of one sample.

It is unfortunate that Model 1b was selected for extensive Monte Carlo runs on sample size. It is probably the only model in Series 1a—1f for which FP does not become superior to OLS and TSLS as sample size becomes small. The differences in the relative performance among methods in Model 1b and relative performance in the other models in Series 1a—1f seem to result from the absolute value of betas being unity which is an important factor on bias. This will be discussed in Chapter 7.

The results discussed in this chapter show the importance of the form of the model in judging relative performance of alternative methods. In spite of the results for the Series 5f—5h we conclude that for most models the performance of FP relative to other methods increases as sample size reduces.

4.4.3. Size of Residuals

In this section we analyze the effects of the size of population R^2 on relative predictive power among alternative methods. Since the variances of all endogenous variables in this series have been normalized to one the value of population R^2 is determined by the size of residuals. The term size of residuals refers primarily to reduced form equations. REID and GEID systems have the same residuals in the structural and reduced forms (see 1.4.5), while in Classic ID systems the structural and reduced form residuals are connected by a relation that involves the matrix β.

The results from varying R^2 are very similar to the results from varying sample size. The results for Model 1b are again quite different from the results for other models as is easily seen in Chart 8. In contrast to results on sample size in Chart 7 the trend for Model 1b is in the same direction as for other models, but the trend is of little interest because it is so small.

The relative performance of FP and URF will change with decrease in

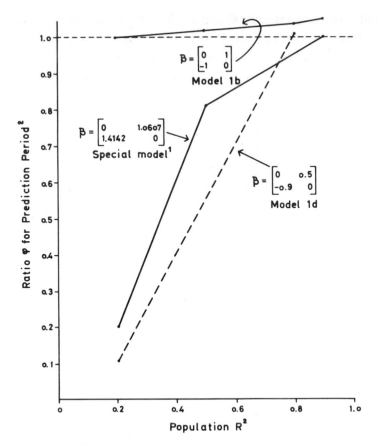

Chart 4.4.8. Size of residuals and relative performance of FP and TSLS.

[1] This model was estimated from samples of 10 observations while the other two models were estimated from samples of 40 observations. Results for this model are not included in Chapter 10.

[2] The value for φ is computed as shown in equation (2).

population R^2 only when degrees of freedom for URF estimates are small. Two-equation models with only two predetermined variables per equation do not show much difference between the degrees of freedom for URF and the degrees of freedom for methods applicable to the structural equations.

Chart 9 shows a slight trend in the relative performance of URF and FP. If the model were larger such as Model 2d the trend in the relative performance of FP and URF as a function of size of residuals would be

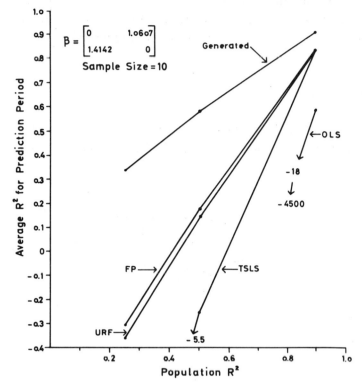

Chart 4.4.9. Size of residuals and predictive power of alternative methods.
(These results are not included in Chapter 10.2.)

more dramatic than the trend shown in Chart 9. The effect of model size
on relative performance of FP and URF can be seen in Chart 10.

The predictive power of FP relative to TSLS as size of residuals increase can be deduced for small sample sizes from our understanding of
bias. When sample size is small TSLS is approximately the same as
OLS because of the overfitting in the first stage of TSLS. The bias of
OLS increases rapidly as size of residual increases and it increases relative
to the bias in FP. Therefore, we can expect the predictive power of FP
relative to TSLS to increase as size of residuals increases whenever bias
in OLS is significant. Model 1b happens to be a model where bias in OLS
is relatively small.

This analysis again points up the importance of the type of model in
judging alternative methods of estimation. We conclude, however, that

in most models predictive power of FP relative to the other three methods increases as size of residuals increases. In many cases the predictive power of FP will be superior to that of TSLS when R^2 is less than 0.5.

4.4.4. Size of Model

Part B of Table 1 shows what we expect, namely that URF is the most affected by increasing the size of model when sample size is fixed. When

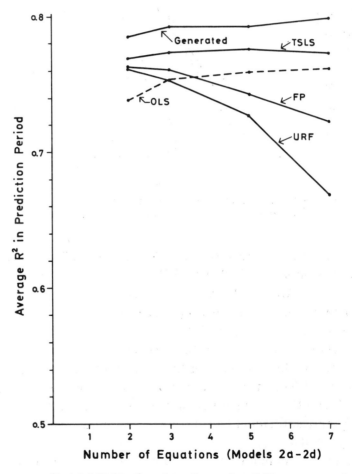

Chart 4.4.10. Number of equations and predictive power.

beta coefficients are small, the predictive power of OLS, TSLS and FP remain nearly constant as size of model is increased. This is easily seen in the second half of Part B in Table 1. The model for this set of results had all beta coefficients equal to ± 0.5. The size of beta coefficients, of course, has no effect on the predictive power of URF estimates.

If beta coefficients are not small, FP changes as the number of parameters to be estimated increases. This is easily seen in Charts 10 and 11. This illustrates a problem with methods that approach so-called full information. The dispersion of estimates increases rapidly as the number of parameters to be estimated increases. OLS and TSLS, in contrast to FP and URF, do not lose degrees of freedom as the number of equations increase because they operate on only one equation at a time.

The performance of OLS actually increases as number of equations increases when beta coefficients are small. This is because the quality of OLS estimates depends on the size of the residuals in the structural equations while all multi-stage methods depend on the size of residuals in the reduced form equations. The size of the reduced form residuals (ϵ_i) is the same in Models 2a–2d because the population R^2 was held constant. In order to keep R^2 constant the variance of the residual in the structural equations (δ_i) were specified as follows: Model 2a = 0.4; Model 2b = 0.267; Model 2c = 0.2; Model 2d = 0.114. It is obvious that bias and dispersion of OLS must be greater with a residual variance of 0.4 in Model 2a than with a residual variance of 0.114 in Model 2d.

This raises an interesting question as to whether OLS becomes a relatively better method in applied econometrics when models become larger. Besides the unknown about the specific nature of the beta matrix in models of real world phenomena, we have an unknown as to whether residual variance in the structural or reduced form equations or neither remain constant as size of model increases. We know from experience that R^2 measured from sample data usually fall between 0.5 and 0.999 in applied work regardless of model size. If this reflects something other than overfitting and spurious correlation, it then suggests that OLS becomes relatively better as model size becomes larger. We suggest that empirical results provide relatively weak clues when it comes to analyzing the size of residuals as a function of model size because of the problem of overfitting

Models larger than 7 equations and 3 explanatory variables per equation were not investigated in this project. However, it seems safe to conclude that the trends noted above continue as models become larger than those investigated in this study. The same pattern would very likely hold for sample sizes other than 40 observations used in obtaining these results. The trends would be more dramatic if sample size were smaller and less dramatic if sample size were larger.

4.4.5. Number of Variables per Equation

Increasing the number of predetermined variables per equation has the same effect as increasing the number of equations on URF, approximately the same effect on FP, and a quite different effect on OLS and TSLS. This statement must be qualified somewhat since the supporting results are limited to situations where sample size was 3–10 times the number of predetermined variables. As sample size decreases and approaches the number of predetermined variables in the model, FP estimates would probably begin to show significant differences between increasing number of equations and increasing number of variables per equation.

Chart 11 shows how predictive power of each of the methods is affected by number of variables in an equation. The generated or actual R^2 for the Monte Carlo data is shown for reference purposes. The differences among the three models in the R^2 from generated data represent only sampling variation. URF is affected the most because of the relative greater loss in degrees of freedom. FP and TSLS are affected more than OLS. In OLS estimates only dispersion increases as degrees of freedom become smaller, whereas both bias and dispersion increase in the case of FP and TSLS.

If the number of variables per equation were increased beyond that shown in Chart 11 or, alternatively, if the sample size were reduced to, say, 20 for the three models, the relative position of TSLS and FP would change. Increasing the number of variables per equation beyond eight is not realistic because in applied econometrics the multicollinearity problems become unmanageable. Since the relevant factor is the number of degrees of freedom, the phenomenon of number of variables per equation can be analyzed further from data in 4.4.2 on varying sample size.

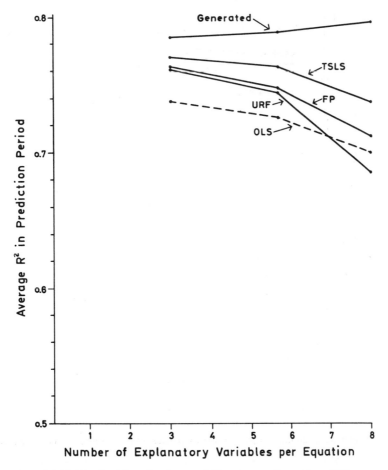

Chart 4.4.11. Number of explanatory variables per equation and predictive power.

A most interesting comparison between FP and TSLS is the difference between the effects from increasing the number of equations and increasing the number of variables per equation. Chart 12 shows three sets of models where the number of predetermined variables is the same in each of the two models within each set. There is little difference in the results for the two sets in the case of FP but a considerable difference in the case of TSLS. The results for FP are typical of what can be expected for so-called full information methods. FP has more degrees of freedom and gives a better performance than URF but a poorer performance than TSLS in both series. FP and so-called full information

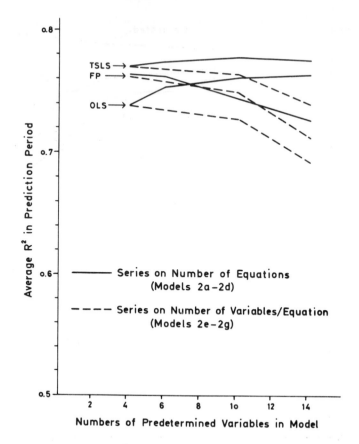

Chart 4.4.12. Increasing number of variables per equation vs increasing number of equations.

methods have less degrees of freedom than TSLS because the latter operates on only one equation at a time. As can be seen from Chart 12 the performance of TSLS is little affected by increasing the number of equations, while FP is affected approximately the same way as in the case of increasing the number of variables per equation.

Both dispersion and bias in FP estimates of parameters are affected by the number of predetermined variables in the entire model. In TSLS, on the other hand, only bias is affected by total number of predetermined variables. Dispersion in TSLS estimates is affected by the number of variables per equation. For all models shown in Chart 12 the bias in TSLS was very small. Consequently, TSLS estimates are little affected by increasing degree of overfitting in the first stage as number of predetermined variables increases in line with the increasing number of equations in the model specification.

There is a difference between the models analyzed in Chart 12 and applied econometric models where lagged endogenous variables frequently constitute a significant portion of the predetermined variables. In multi-period predictions each lagged endogenous variable is a source of prediction error because the value of the lagged variable is itself a predicted variable (see equation 4.1.3 and the accompanying discussion). In applied models the number of lagged variables usually increases as the number of equations increases. The presence of lagged endogenous variables is discussed in the next section.

In general the performance of FP relative to TSLS is likely to be similar to that shown in Chart 12. The predictive power of both will fall as number of variables per equation increases, but the relative predictive power will stay the same unless sample size falls below, say, 2 times the total number of predetermined variables. The predictive power of TSLS relative to FP is a balance between opposite tendencies as number of equations in the model increases (see 1.2.9).

In applied econometrics the multicollinearity among predetermined variables is more severe than for the Monte Carlo data generated for the models discussed in this section. Multicollinearity among all explanatory variables in a structural equation is of greater interest than that between the predetermined variables only. It depends on the structure of the model, however, and no general statements can be made about Monte Carlo vs real world data. Greater multicollinearity would have the following effects in terms of the results in Chart 12:

1. The predictive power for TSLS would reduce more rapidly in the equation size series (hence, the spread between the results for model size and equation size would increase).
2. The predictive power for FP would reduce more rapidly in both the model size and equation size series.
3. The predictive power of TSLS relative to FP would increase for all models in the series on number of equations but would not change among models within the series on number of variables per equation.

These statements are qualified in that they hold only when sample size is considerably larger than the total number of predetermined variables in the model. For most models, FP gains considerably relative to TSLS when sample size becomes very small.

4.4.6. Lagged Endogenous Variables in the Model

Models 5c–5e incorporating lagged endogenous variables were designed with $R^2 = 0.9$, so they are not directly comparable to the basic
system in Model 1b which is used as a reference model for evaluating
the effect of lagged endogenous variables. However, the results for the
three models shown in Chart 13 and in Part E of Table 1 suggest firmly
that the presence of lagged endogenous variables has little or no significant effect on estimates of parameters as far as predictive power is concerned.

Except for OLS in Model 5c there was no significant difference among
the methods with respect to predictive power of the estimated models.
The R^2 for each of the four methods is only slightly less than the R^2 for
the generated Monte Carlo data.

The degree of multicollinearity did not increase significantly over that
in models without lagged endogenous variables (e.g., Model 1b) in spite
of the presence of lagged endogenous variables. In Model 5c where two
lagged endogenous variables appear in the first equation multicollinearity
was somewhat of a problem in the second equation but not in the first
(see eigenvalues in Part D of tables in Chapter 10.2).

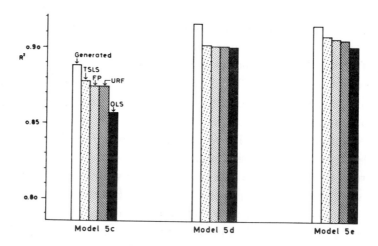

Chart 4.4.13. Predictive power R^2 for three models with lagged endogenous variables.

It is not possible to generalize from the results on three models with lagged endogenous variables. The nature of the underlying difference equation depends on the particular specification of the model (see equations 4.1.4−5 and 4.1.6).

Multicollinearity can be a serious problem depending on the positioning of lagged endogenous variables in the equations and the form of the underlying difference equation. The results from these three models do suggest, however, that the mere presence of lagged endogenous variables has no significant effect on the four methods of estimation analyzed in this study. Lagged variables will lead to problems of estimation only when the model generates data that have very high auto- and serial correlations.

4.4.7. Multicollinearity among exogenous variables

The multicollinearity that is of most concern is that between the variables on the right in the regression equations for each behavioral relationship in the structural equations. In the model below, which we write in estimated form, the variables y_2^*, x_1, and x_2 in the first equation and y_1^*, x_3, and x_4 in the second equation are the variables among which multicollinearity is of major concern;

$$y_{1t} = b_1 y_{2t}^* + g_1 x_{1t} + g_2 x_{2t} + e_{1t} , \qquad (3)$$

$$y_{2t} = b_2 y_{1t}^* + g_3 x_{3t} + g_4 x_{4t} + e_{2t} , \qquad (4)$$

where the estimation procedure gives y_{1t}^* and y_{2t}^* which are estimates of η_{1t}^* and η_{2t}^* and which are linear combinations of $x_1 - x_4$ in TSLS and FP while they are linear combinations of $x_1 - x_4$, ϵ_{1t} and ϵ_{2t} in the case of OLS.

The degree of multicollinearity is determined by two factors, namely, the correlation among exogenous variables and the values of the beta and gamma coefficients. The latter determine the correlation between the η_i^* variables and each of the predetermined variables. Examples of the effects from varying sizes of beta coefficients are best studied in the models in the Series 1a−1f. Multicollinearity from correlations among exogenous variables is studied in this section.

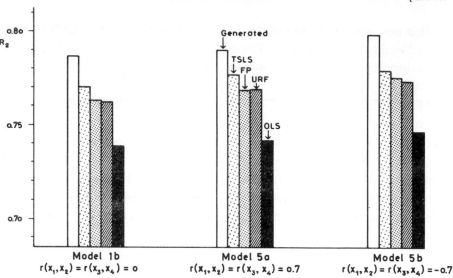

Chart 4.4.14. Predictive power R^2 and correlation among exogenous variables.

In the three models cited in Part D of Table 1, multicollinearity was introduced in the form of correlations between the two exogenous variables in each structural equation. As is easily seen from Chart 14 and the results in Table 1 there is no perceptible difference in the predictive power for any of the methods among Models 1b, 5a, and 5b. Although Chart 14 shows the generated R^2 as varying among Models 1b, 5a and 5b, these models were all designed with $R^2 = 0.8$. In any case, the values of R^2 for each of the four methods show about the same pattern among the three models as do the values of R^2 for the generated data. The correlations among exogenous variables in Models 5a and 5b did increase the multicollinearity as can be seen from the eigenvalues of the product moment matrices shown in Table 3.

There are some differences among Models 1b, 5a, and 5b with respect to estimates of structural and reduced form coefficients, but they did not significantly affect predictive power. The effects of correlations among exogenous variables on estimates of coefficients will be discussed in Chapters 7 and 8.

The eigenvalues of the product moment matrix for (η_2^*, x_1, x_2) in estimating equation one and for (η_1^*, x_3, x_4) in estimating equation two are in the nature of standard measures of multicollinearity. The eigenvalues for the Monte Carlo results in 5 models are presented in Table 3.

Table 4.4.3
Eigenvalues in the product moment matrices of (y_1^*, x_3, x_4) and (x_1, x_2, x_3, x_4). [1]

	λ_0	λ_1	λ_2	λ_3
Model 1b				
OLS	0.0723	0.1196	0.3226	0.5578
TSLS	0.0486	0.0915	0.3396	0.5689
FP	0.0418	0.0920	0.3415	0.5665
URF	0.0894	0.1520	0.2087	0.2788
Model 5a				
OLS	0.0436	0.0915	0.1580	0.7505
TSLS	0.0360	0.0842	0.1360	0.7798
FP	0.0322	0.0848	0.1366	0.7786
URF	0.0278	0.0544	0.0833	0.3423
Model 5b				
OLS	0.0217	0.0489	0.3503	0.6008
TSLS	0.0165	0.0408	0.3295	0.6297
FP	0.0163	0.0413	0.3270	0.6317
URF	0.0295	0.0550	0.0846	0.3386
Model 1c				
OLS	0.0200	0.0492	0.3270	0.6237
TSLS	0.0014	0.0178	0.3456	0.6366
FP	0.0035	0.0562	0.3608	0.5829
URF	0.1064	0.1511	0.2092	0.2780
Model 1f				
OLS	0.0199	0.0372	0.3268	0.6360
TSLS	0.00005	0.0052	0.3455	0.6492
FP	0.0004	0.0066	0.3451	0.6483
URF	0.1064	0.1511	0.2092	0.2780

[1] λ_0 is the smallest eigenvalue in 100 samples. λ_1 is the average of the smallest eigenvalues for each of the 100 samples. λ_2 and λ_3 are the averages of the second and third smallest eigenvalues in each of the 100 samples. The product moment matrix of (y_1^*, x_3, x_4) is used in estimating the coefficients in the second structural equation and the product moment matrix of (x_1, x_2, x_3, x_4) is used in estimating the URF estimates of coefficients in the reduced form equations. For further definition of eigenvalues see Part D of Table 10.1.1.

The differences between Model 1b on the one hand and Models 5a and 5b on the other hand reflect only the correlation among exogenous variables x_3 and x_4 in these models. The differences among Models 1b, 1c, and 1f reflect the results from different values of beta coefficients in the specification of the model. It should be noted in this connection that all variables x, y have been normalized to unit variance, and that this feature is part of the argument behind the comparisons at issue.

It is quickly seen that the effects from varying beta coefficients were considerably greater than that from introducing a correlation of ± 0.7 among exogenous variables. However, this is true primarily for methods which estimate coefficients in the structural equations since correlations among exogenous variables are unaffected by beta coefficients and, therefore, the quality of estimates from the method of URF are in the main unaffected.

The eigenvalues for Models 1b, 5a, and 5b indicate relatively small increase in multicollinearity from a correlation of ± 0.7 among two exogenous variables. In applied econometrics multicollinearity arising from correlation among predetermined variables is often more severe than that in Models 5a and 5b. For one thing, correlations among variables are often larger than 0.7; for another, there are frequently more than two predetermined variables in a structural equation. If the number of predetermined variables in the entire model is large, the smallest eigenvalue in the product moment matrix for obtaining URF estimates can easily be less than any value shown in Table 3.

The authors have computed eigenvalues for several models fitted from real world data and obtained eigenvalues of less than 10^{-5}. This dramatic multicollinearity problem is another incentive for the economist to estimate the structural form of the model.

Eigenvalues for all Monte Carlo results in the 46 different models are given in Part D of the tables in Chapter 10.2. Multicollinearity was not a major point of study in our research, but it is a convenient concept for analyzing some of the results. Since we knew that it is a major problem in econometrics, the computer program was designed to calculate the eigenvalues shown in Table 3 and part D of all the tables in Chapter 10.2.

CHAPTER 5

Convergence

5.1. General Appraisal

Convergence posed a problem in a small portion of the over 200 models developed and estimated in this project. Among the 46 different models for which detailed results are presented in this monograph convergence posed a serious problem in Models 1c, 1f, 3c, 3e, 3f, 4b, and 4c (see appropriate tables in Chapter 10.2 for detailed specifications). Information on convergence for the 46 models in Chapter 10 is given in Table 1. Reference is made to the analysis of convergence problems by A.Ågren and L.Bodin in Chapters 3.6 and 3.7.

Now that we have considerable knowledge about some of the conditions under which convergence is a problem it is, of course, possible to design a set of models where convergence would be a problem in nearly every sample. This can be done via selection of beta coefficients as shown in the next section. However, even in models where the design does not meet the specified conditions for convergence, it is possible to obtain convergence for many sets of sample data. First, as sample size increases in the REID specification FP estimates approach TSLS estimates, and it is possible to get apparent convergence in many samples (see Bodin's analysis in Chapter 3.7). Second, in small samples the Monte Carlo data can lead to a set of FP estimates that are sufficiently

Table 5.1.1
Number of iterations and convergence criterion for 46 models.

Model	Number of iterations			Samples with no convergence [1]	Iteration limit [2]	Criterion [3]	Spectral radius [4]
	Smallest	Average	Largest				
1a	4	6.3	10				0.5
1b	4	8.4	17				1.0
1c	6	9.4	10	75	10	10^{-6}	3.0
1c	3	31	200	12	200	10^{-3}	3.0
1c	6	124	200	60	200	10^{-6}	3.0
1d	4	7.1	13				0.67
1e	11	134	200	10			1.2
1f	5	52	200	22			1.8
1g	4	6.3	10				0.5
1h	13	15	19				0.5
1i	15	17	20				0.5
1m	3	3	3				0
1n	3	3	3				0
1p	3	3	3				0
1q	3	3	3				0
2a	4	8.4	17				1.0
2b	15	25	50				1.0
2c	32	67	200	3			1.0
2d	61	120	200	9			1.0
2e	4	8.4	17				1.0
2f	9	15	35				1.0
2g	14	28	200	1			1.0
3a	9	12	20				0.5
3b	12	30	200	3			1.0
3c	18	142	200	64			2.0
3d	11	51	200	12			0.87
3e	200	200	200	100			2.0
3f	36	187	200	91			1.73
4a	6	117	200	50	200	10^{-6}	2.06
4a	5	5	5		200	10^{-3}	2.06
4b	200	200	200	100			2.12
4c	29	189	200	93			2.0
5a	5	9.1	32				1.0
5b	4	7.9	14				1.0
5c	5	8.2	21				1.0
5d	5	8.2	17				1.0
5e	4	8.0	14				1.0

Table 5.1.1 (continued)

Model	Number of iterations			Samples with no conver-gence [1]	Iteration limit [2]	Criterion [3]	Spectral radius [4]
	Small-est	Aver-age	Larg-est				
5f	6	16	50	7	50		1.0
5g	4	8.4	17				1.0
5h	4	7.4	14				1.0
5i	5	158	200	2			0.67
5j	4	7.1	13				0.67
5m	5	18	200	5			1.0
5n	5	8.4	19				1.0
5p	4	8.4	17				1.0
5q	5	7.9	14				1.0
5r	5	12	200	2			0.67
5s	4	7.1	13				0.67
6a	4	8.4	16				1.0
6b	17	31	200	1			1.0
6c	35	64	104				1.0
6e	5	8.4	19				1.0
6f	5	8.5	25				1.0
6g	4	8.9	27				1.0
6h	5	8.2	15				1.0
6i	6	9.3	20				1.0
6j	5	12.5	200	1			1.0

[1] Empty entries indicate that all samples converged.
[2] The limit was 200 unless specified otherwise.
[3] The criterion was $k = 10^{-6}$ unless specified otherwise.
[4] The spectral radius is the largest absolute value among the roots of the equation $\det[\lambda I - \beta] = 0$. The significance of the spectral radius is discussed in Chapter 5.2.

different from the specified matrix that true convergence is indeed possible.

It is also possible to specify control limits for convergence that exceed the accuracy of the computer and convergence will not be possible. Letting α denote any coefficient in the structural relations, and a_i ($i = 1, 2, ...$) its proxies as computed in the ith iteration, the acceptance criterion used in the study is

$$\frac{a_i - a_{i-1}}{a_i} < k , \tag{1}$$

where k is prescribed; the point at issue then is that it is possible that the error in computing a_i is greater than k.

Our first choice for k in the 46 models discussed in detail was 10^{-6}. This value was used in all cases except Models 1c and 4a where the criterion was relaxed and k was set equal to 10^{-3}. In this project the Monte Carlo observations were generated with 12 significant digits and a k value of 10^{-6} is appropriate. Using real world data with, say, 3 or 4 significant digits, 10^{-3} would be a more appropriate value for the convergence criterion.

No particular pattern can be discerned for the way FP estimates approach the final value in successive iterations. However, in all models

Table 5.1.2.
Quality of estimates and number of required iterations – Model 5f.

Item	NOIT [1]	FP estimates			$R^2(y_1; \text{sample})$			$R^2(y_1; \text{pred})$		
		β_{11}	γ_{11}	ω_{11}	TSLS	FP	URF	TSLS	FP	URF
1	6	0.81	0.66	0.34	0.85	0.84	0.76	0.79	0.82	0.81
2	6	0.92	0.81	0.55	0.82	0.84	0.75	0.78	0.79	0.82
3	6	1.75	1.21	0.48	0.77	0.70	0.69	0.54	0.69	0.48
4	7	0.83	1.11	0.60	0.88	0.82	0.85	0.72	0.56	0.83
24	9	0.90	0.51	0.33	0.83	0.82	0.74	0.75	0.71	0.75
25	9	1.81	0.79	0.13	0.92	0.76	0.88	0.59	0.51	0.57
26	9	0.66	1.16	0.85	0.88	0.84	0.87	0.45	0.35	0.57
27	9	0.93	0.98	0.55	0.89	0.81	0.88	0.58	0.60	0.49
49	11	0.52	0.64	0.41	0.75	0.68	0.77	0.67	0.62	0.75
50	11	0.74	0.73	0.49	0.82	0.82	0.71	0.84	0.83	0.83
51	11	0.90	1.29	0.69	0.82	0.88	0.80	0.45	0.64	0.63
52	11	1.46	1.44	0.45	0.91	0.93	0.88	0.84	0.68	0.68
74	16	1.33	0.85	0.26	0.89	0.89	0.82	0.69	0.63	0.68
75	16	1.16	1.01	0.55	0.88	0.92	0.89	0.50	0.64	−0.12
76	16	0.62	0.99	0.69	0.82	0.83	0.86	0.71	0.66	0.60
77	18	0.61	0.91	0.47	0.77	0.77	0.62	0.66	0.65	0.63
97	50	1.42	0.59	0.29	0.83	0.76	0.81	0.67	0.70	0.17
98	50	0.61	0.63	0.31	0.41	0.33	0.82	0.70	0.64	0.29
99	50	0.77	0.93	0.47	0.87	0.86	0.81	0.76	0.77	0.52
100	50	0.78	0.90	0.45	0.96	0.96	0.95	0.86	0.86	0.84
Mean	16	0.91	0.85	0.47	0.81	0.79	0.74	0.69	0.66	0.63
S.D.		0.38	0.32	0.18						

[1] Number of iterations in the sample.

except the ones in which convergence was a serious problem and the larger seven-equation system in Model 2d, the estimates changed very little after 10 iterations. In real world applications it will sometimes be necessary to start the iterations with $Y^* = 0$ instead of Y^* generated from the estimates of the unrestricted reduced-form equations. This will increase the number of iterations, and it is likely that in most cases the estimates would continue to change after 10 iterations, but probably not after 20 or 30. There is little that can be said on this point until further research on alternative starting points is carried out.

In all Monte Carlo runs reported in this monograph iterations were limited to 200. It is felt that the quality of estimates in samples that did not converge in 200 iterations would not have improved if the limit had been raised to, say, 500. Among the samples that did converge there is no theoretical reason to expect a correlation between number of iterations required and quality of estimates. The Monte Carlo results confirm this conjecture. This is illustrated in Table 2 and Chart 1.

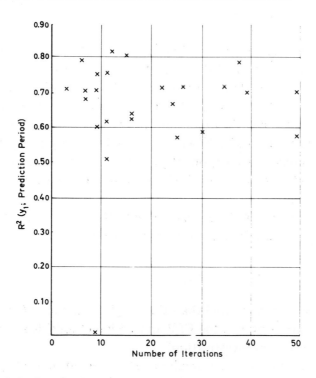

Chart 5.1.1. Quality of estimates and number of iterations. 25 samples from Model 5f.

Table 2 shows that the quality of estimates as measured by R^2 is not correlated with the number of required iterations among the 100 samples for Model 5f. Note, for example, that R^2 in the prediction period as obtained for FP is on the whole on par with the values obtained for the non-iterative TSLS Method. Likewise, Chart 1 shows no correlation between quality of estimates (measured by R^2) and the number of iterations. The predictive power (R^2) is the best single variable to use in measuring correlation between quality of estimates and number of iterations because any one of the six structural coefficients, or a combination, could cause the number of iterations to be large.

There are many ways in which convergence can sometimes be obtained when ordinary FP does not converge. We note the following three schemes for modifying the FP Method:

1. Modifying the change in estimates in the successive iterations by a scheme such as

$$a_i = a_{i-1} + d[a_i^{\mathrm{FP}} - a_{i-1}] \, , \tag{2}$$

where a_i is the final selection of the estimate in the ith iteration, d is less than 1, and a_i^{FP} is the FP proxy of the coefficient α_i in the ith iteration. This is the FFP Method reported by A.Ågren in Chapter 3.6.

2. Computing the proxy for Y^* in the ith step recursively by using components Y_k^*. The kth component proxy is computed by the use of (a) the component proxies Y_j^* ($j = 1, ..., k-1$) already computed, and (b) the remaining $n-k$ component proxies Y_j^* ($j = k+1, ..., n$) as computed in the $(i-1)$st step. This is the RFP Method reported by L.Bodin in Chapter 3.7.

3. Making a forecast of the final value of the estimate and using this as the final selection for the ith iteration, namely,

$$a_i = f(a_i^{\mathrm{FP}}, a_{i-1}, a_{i-2}, ...) \, , \tag{3}$$

where f is more complicated than the simple function in (2). This device, which carries over to the FFP and RFP methods, has not been explored in the present investigation.

In this project only a very small effort was spent on finding ways to speed up convergence (see publications by Ågren [1] and Bodin [1] for

Table 5.1.3
Number of iterations for convergence using the FFP Method
with a damping factor (d) in each iteration [1].

Model 1a			Model 1b			Model 1c	
d	Iterations		d	Iterations		d	Iterations
0.2	·14		0.1	85		0.1	110
0.8	9		0.3	29		0.2	63
1.0	7		0.5	16		0.3	47
1.2	10		0.7	10		0.4	41
1.6	16		0.8	8		0.5	41
1.8	29		0.9	6		0.6	46
2.0	[2]		1.0	5		0.7	60
			1.1	7		0.8	[2]
			1.2	8		0.9	[2]
			1.4	14		1.0	[2]
			1.6	[2]			
			1.8	[2]			
			2.0	[2]			

Model 3c			Model 3d			Model 3f	
d	Iterations		d	Iterations		d	Iterations
0.1	193		0.1	116		0.1	120
0.2	110		0.3	40		0.2	68
0.3	85		0.5	23		0.3	54
0.4	71		0.6	19		0.4	48
0.5	67		0.7	18		0.5	55
0.6	66		0.8	19		0.6	[2]
0.7	71		0.9	21		0.7	[2]
0.8	[2]		1.1	33		0.8	[2]
			1.3	[2]		0.9	[2]
			1.5	[2]		1.0	[2]

[1] See Chapter 3.6 for discussion of FFP.
All of the results for the 46 models in Chapter 10.2 were computed without a damping factor.
That is, the value of d was equal to 1. The results in this table are for one sample on each of
the models.
[2] There was no convergence within the 200 iteration limit.

more extensive research and analysis). Computing costs were not a serious problem and efforts were oriented toward evaluating the quality of
estimates among the four methods of estimation. According to the independent research by Ågren and Bodin the FFP and RFP techniques indi-

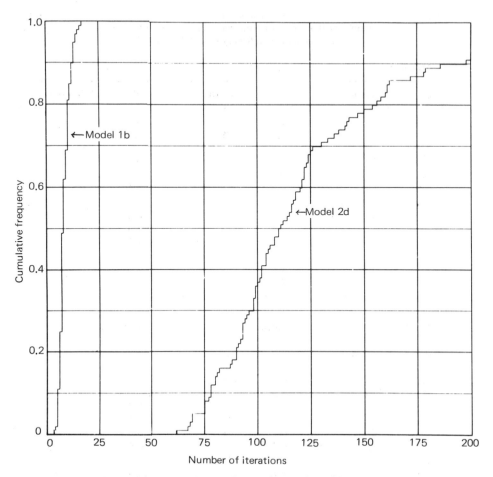

Chart 5.1.2. Cumulative distribution for number of iterations.

cate considerable promise for speeding up convergence. The results in Table 3 draw from the results obtained by Ågren.

The cumulative distribution for number of iterations for two different models is shown in Chart 2. Model 1b is an example where convergence was rapid and posed no problem at all. Model 2d is an example where convergence was somewhat of a problem, but most samples did converge within the 200 iteration limit.

The graphs are somewhat in line with what we would expect in the case of an asymmetric probability distribution. However, it is interesting that the slope of the cumulative distribution curve for Model 2d is fairly constant over the lower 70% of the curve.

Computational costs for FP do not appear to be a serious problem for most models. Except for the five models that had serious convergence problems, the average time required for 100 samples on each model was 10 minutes on the CDC 3600 computer. This included generating data, estimating parameters (OLS, TSLS, FP), and making predictions for the forecasting period. This makes a cost of approximately $1 per sample. If convergence is a serious problem, computing time must increase or an arbitrary limit must be imposed on the number of iterations. The effect of limiting the number of iterations is discussed in Chapter 5.3.

5.2. Size of Beta Coefficients

The size of beta coefficients in the model as specified affects convergence in two ways. First, the coefficients in the specified model obviously affect the size of beta coefficients in the FP estimates from the sample data in each step in the iteration technique. Second, they affect the degree of multicollinearity among the variables in the REID and GEID specifications.

It is difficult to analyze the first effect rigorously because the beta coefficients in the FP solution of a set of sample data are, in general, not the same as the values in the specified model. However, it is obviously the former rather than the latter that determines whether FP estimation will converge or diverge. Fortunately, Lyttkens (see 3.8) has worked out the exact solution for FP estimates in two-equation models, so the FP estimates can be computed in samples where the iteration method for FP does not give convergence. Ågren (see 3.6) has developed an expression in terms of the beta matrix in the FP solution of sample data that serves to explain when convergence will and will not be present.

There is a further complication in fully understanding convergence. In addition to the fact that the FP estimates of beta coefficients can differ from the values of beta coefficients in the specified model, the estimates in each iteration differ from the FP solution. That is, the beta coefficients in each iteration are different from the set of values that FP converges to in cases where it does indeed converge. Nevertheless, Ågren's results, which are briefly reported in 3.6, agree well with the results of the Monte Carlo investigation and the theoretical work of Lyttkens.

Although we do not have available the exact FP solution for the samples, and we do not have available the beta values in the successive iterations for the models that show slow convergence in Table 5.1.1, we can look for clues by analyzing the maximum α for the theoretical beta matrix. The following results are based on Ågren's theory as reported in 3.6: If $\beta_{12}\beta_{21} < 0$ we have the condition

$$\alpha_{max} = \frac{2}{1 + |\beta_{12}\beta_{21}|} \cdot \tag{1}$$

Only 40 of the 100 samples in Model 1c converged and we find

$$\alpha_{max}(\text{Model 1c}) = \frac{2}{1 + |3(-3)|} = 0.2 \,, \tag{2}$$

which is much less than $\alpha = 1$ which is used in FP. On the other hand, there was rapid convergence in Model 1b and we find

$$\alpha_{max}(\text{Model 1b}) = \frac{2}{1 + |1(-1)|} = 1 \,, \tag{3}$$

which is the α used in FP. Model 1e involved some problems in convergence, but much less than in the case of Model 1c, and we find

$$\alpha_{max}(\text{Model 1e}) = \frac{2}{1 + |0.5(-3)|} = 0.8 \,, \tag{4}$$

which is much closer to 1 than the value of 0.2 in (2).

Ågren's theory (see 3.6) does provide considerable insight into the problems in convergence. Although more research has yet to be carried out, we offer the following comments on how the size of specified beta coefficients affect convergence (see Chart 1 for illustration): As the spectral radius of matrix β (or, for the FFP method, of matrix K defined in 3.6.1) increases and approaches one we can expect (a) a higher percentage of the samples to have a spectral radius less than, but close to, one and, therefore, converge slowly and (b) a significant percentage of the samples to have a spectral radius greater than 1 and, therefore, not converge at all. This last conclusion has to be qualified to some extent owing to what we have called "apparent convergence"; see 3.7. As the spectral radius of the specified beta matrix increases and is greater than 1, we can expect (a) the average speed of convergence for samples with a spectral radius less than 1 will decrease because the distribution of the spectral radius will shift upwards, and (b) fewer samples will give true convergence because fewer samples will lead to FP estimates of β that have a spectral radius less than 1.

Our conjecture is that the eigenvalues of the following matrix K determine whether the iteration method will converge:

$$K = K(d) = d[\mathrm{B}] + (1-d)[\mathrm{I}] , \qquad (5)$$

where d is the damping factor used in the FFP Method; see 3.6.

Except for some ambiguity concerning the eigenvalues in (5) for the beta matrix in each iteration the effect of an increase in the largest eigenvalue is to increase the number of iterations required for convergence. The effect of a change in the specified model on the probability of a particular value for the spectral radius in a Monte Carlo sample is as illustrated in the sketches in Chart 1. The differences between Models A and B illustrate that changes in the beta matrix can have a large effect on convergence because of the difference in the distribution of values for the spectral radius in FP estimates of β in Monte Carlo samples. The

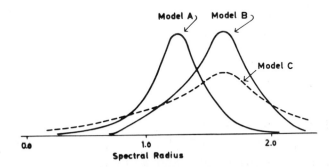

Chart 5.2.1. Sketches of distribution of spectral radius in Monte Carlo samples. (A) Reference model. (B) Model with a spectral radius greater than in A, but size of residuals and sample size the same. (C) Model with a spectral radius the same as in B, but larger residuals and/or smaller sample.

differences between Models B and C illustrate that there can be a difference in the frequency and speed of convergence in two models, even though the specified beta matrices are identical. If residuals are large and/or sample size is small, the beta coefficients in the FP solution are frequently quite different from the beta matrix specified in the design of the model.

In summarizing the conditions for FP convergence we can say that the spectral radius in (5) for the specified beta matrix gives a good clue as to whether convergence can be obtained. The spectral radius in (5) for the FP solution of the beta matrix for a set of sample data gives much more conclusive information, but this beta matrix will not be known unless the exact solution is obtained or the iteration method is used and converges. The only uncertainty about the convergence, once we know the spectral radius in (5), for the FP solution of sample data is the variation in the beta coefficients in the successive iterations. It might be possible for the spectral radius of the beta matrices in a set of successive iterations to be quite different from the spectral radius for the FP solution and, therefore, the conditions in the exact FP solution might not dictate the outcome of the iteration method.

In summarizing results on speed of convergence for models in which true convergence is possible Ågren's criterion (Chapter 3.6) suggests the conjecture that if the spectral radius in (5) is less than one and increasing, the expected number of iterations increases ($d = 1$ in (5) for the FP Method). It is easier to discuss this aspect in terms of the value chosen for d in (5) for the FFP Method. The optimum d (in Ågren's notation, α) is that value which minimizes the value of the spectral radius in (5). In Model 1e, for example, the optimum d

$$d_{opt}(\text{Model 1e}) = \frac{1}{1 + 3(0.5)} = 0.4 \tag{6}$$

compared to $d = 1$ which is used in FP. Here again, there is more need for research on FP as well as FFP, but the above summary is in line with the fairly extensive results obtained to date.

The second factor mentioned in the beginning of this section as being associated with size of beta coefficients and affecting speed of convergence is the degree of multicollinearity. It would seem that multicollinearity does not affect the conditions for convergence, but it is likely that it affects the speed of convergence when the necessary condition for true convergence are met. The size of beta coefficients affects the correlations between the η_i^* variables and the z_k variables on the right hand side of each equation in the REID/GEID specification. As pointed out in Chapter 7.6, it is possible to specify a beta matrix that also requires that there be correlations among the exogenous variables.

Table 5.2.1

Eigenvalues for the product moment matrix of explanatory variables [1] in the last iteration of FP estimation – Models 1a–1f.

	Equation 1				Equation 2			
	λ_0	λ_1	λ_2	λ_3	λ_0	λ_1	λ_2	λ_3
Model 1a	0.070	0.154	0.318	0.528	0.078	0.165	0.331	0.504
Model 1b	0.038	0.081	0.333	0.586	0.042	0.092	0.342	0.567
Model 1c	0.004	0.062	0.346	0.592	0.004	0.056	0.361	0.583
Model 1d	0.012	0.039	0.321	0.640	0.120	0.205	0.327	0.468
Model 1e	0.054	0.180	0.334	0.486	0.008	0.026	0.348	0.625
Model 1f	0.086	0.178	0.323	0.499	0.0004	0.007	0.345	0.648

[1] All eigenvalues are for the product moment matrix in the last iteration of FP estimates for each equation. λ_0 is the smallest eigenvalue among the 100 samples. λ_1 is the mean of the smallest eigenvalues in each of 100 samples. λ_2 and λ_3 are the means of the 2nd and 3rd smallest eigenvalues in each of the samples;

To obtain another view of the multicollinearity problem we can look at the eigenvalues for the product moment matrix used in computing the estimates of structural equations in the Monte Carlo samples. Table 1 gives summary statistics on the eigenvalues for the 100 Monte Carlo samples in each of the Models 1a–1f. Since these results represent Monte Carlo generated samples from the models they cannot be expected to agree perfectly with the eigenvalues for the product moment matrix of variables implied by the design of the respective models.

As we would expect, Model 1c has a very small eigenvalue in both equations and Model 1f has a very small eigenvalue in the second equation. Another interesting feature will be noted, namely that although the second equation in Model 1f has the smallest eigenvalue in both models the convergence problem in Model 1c was more severe. This is explained by the values for the spectral radius in (5). If Model 1f were changed so that β_{12} were closer to unity the convergence problem would become more severe than in Model 1c.

There is much evidence to support the theory that size of beta coefficients is very important. The effect of beta coefficients is not, however, unrelated to sample size, number of equations, and number of variables. These aspects are discussed in the remainder of the chapter.

5.3. Limiting the Number of Iterations

The number of iterations can be limited by setting a limit arbitrarily or by selecting an appropriate convergence criterion. The criterion of 10^{-6} and a limit of 200 iterations is considerably beyond what would be practical in applied work. Research to date suggests that both the convergence criterion and the iteration limit should be carefully selected in applied econometrics.

A limit on number of iterations could be imposed for one of two reasons. First, it is a practical consideration in the cost of computing estimates. Second, there is some evidence that in samples which pose a serious convergence problems the estimates become worse as the number of iterations increases.

An iteration limit of 200 was used for all but Model 5f among the 46 basic models described in Chapter 10.2 (see Table 5.1.1). However, in most cases the limit could have been 10 and the estimates would have been as good, if not better. To judge from investigations to date it is practical to work with a rather crude iteration limit, say, five times the number of equations to be estimated. It is not our intention to propose a general rule of thumb because more research should be carried out on that topic.

If a less stringent criterion is used such as 10^{-3} instead of 10^{-6} the limit on iterations is less important since convergence will be attained much sooner. The limit of 200 was selected for the Monte Carlo research reported in detail in this monograph mainly to determine if a stringent criterion and large number of iterations is important.

We shall consider two ways of studying the relation between quality of estimates and number of iterations. First, the convergence criterion or iteration limit can be changed and the mean and standard deviation

Table 5.3.1
Model 1c with different specifications for convergence

A. Model design

A.1. *Structural equations*

$$
\beta = \begin{bmatrix} 0 & 3 \\ -3 & 0 \end{bmatrix}
\qquad
\Gamma = \begin{bmatrix} 2 & 2 & & \\ & & 2 & 2 \end{bmatrix}
\qquad
\Omega = \begin{bmatrix} 0.2 & 0.2 & 0.6 & 0.6 \\ -0.6 & -0.6 & 0.2 & 0.2 \end{bmatrix}
$$

A.2. *Variance of endogenous and residual variables in the population and in the sample*

$$
\begin{array}{l}
\sigma^2(y_i) = 1 \\
\sigma^2(\delta_i) = 2 \quad i = 1, 2 \\
\sigma^2(\epsilon_i) = 0.2
\end{array}
\qquad
\begin{array}{l}
\text{Generated} \\
\text{in sample} \\
\text{period}
\end{array}
\left\{
\begin{array}{ll}
V(y_1) = 0.946 & V(y_2) = 1.023 \\
V(\delta_1) = 2.042 & V(\delta_2) = 1.936 \\
V(\epsilon_1) = 0.195 & V(\epsilon_2) = 0.203
\end{array}
\right.
$$

A.3. *Correlations among residuals and exogenous variables*

None

A.4. *Sample size and special design features*

1. 40 observations in both the sample and prediction periods.
2. FP estimates were computed with three different specifications on convergence.
   Specification a: iteration limit = 200; convergence criterion = 10^{-6}

	b:	10	10^{-6}
	c:	200	10^{-3}

B. Structural coefficients

B.1. *True coefficient vs average estimate from 100 samples*

	β_{12}	γ_{11}	γ_{12}	β_{21}	γ_{23}	γ_{24}
True	3	2	2	-3	2	2
OLS	0.8011	0.6777	0.6599	-0.8802	0.7216	0.7402
TSLS	2.9313	1.9585	1.9445	-3.2111	2.0858	2.1559
FP a	1.6500	0.9268	0.9131	-1.7610	0.9669	0.9329
b	2.9400	1.8375	1.8635	-3.2198	1.8742	2.0251
c	2.6181	1.6010	1.6337	-2.9855	1.7068	1.8412

Table 5.3.1 (continued)

B.2. *Observed standard deviation of 100 samples around observed mean*

	β_{12}	γ_{11}	γ_{12}	β_{21}	γ_{23}	γ_{24}
OLS	0.2466	0.2004	0.2088	0.3053	0.2548	0.2419
TSLS	0.8882	0.5606	0.6221	1.2679	0.7957	0.8102
FP a	0.9494	0.7663	0.7889	1.0405	0.8453	0.7475
b	0.9926	0.7049	0.8470	1.5436	0.7015	1.1419
c	0.9921	0.7466	0.7892	1.6674	0.9663	1.2334

B.3. *Average standard deviation from large sample formula*

	β_{12}	γ_{11}	γ_{12}	β_{21}	γ_{23}	γ_{24}
OLS	0.2622	0.2098	0.2104	0.2686	0.2109	0.2142
TSLS	0.9239	0.6075	0.6095	1.0952	0.6983	0.7132
FP a	0.5373	0.3239	0.3313	0.5941	0.3503	0.3300
b	1.0095	0.6197	0.6503	1.3494	0.7132	0.8454
c	0.8515	0.5178	0.5433	1.2792	0.6662	0.7941

B.4. *Observed standard deviation around true value of the coefficient*

	β_{12}	γ_{11}	γ_{12}	β_{21}	γ_{23}	γ_{24}
OLS	2.2127	1.3389	1.3563	2.1417	1.3035	1.2828
TSLS	0.8914	0.5621	0.6246	1.2854	0.8003	0.8251
FP a	1.6504	1.3187	1.3430	1.6179	1.3349	1.3029
b	0.9944	0.7234	0.8579	1.5592	0.9102	1.1422
c	1.0631	0.8456	0.8701	1.6675	1.0098	1.2436

B.5. *Number of iterations for FP*

Specification	Average	Smallest	Largest	Samples with no convergence
a	123.8	6	200	60
b	9.4	6	10	75
c	31.0	3	200	12

C. Reduced form coefficients

C.1. *True coefficient vs average estimate from 100 samples (4 out of 8 coefficients)*

	ω_{11}	ω_{13}	ω_{21}	ω_{23}
True	0.2	0.6	−0.6	0.2
OLS	0.4002	0.3273	−0.3359	0.4215
TSLS	0.2177	0.5821	−0.5994	0.2136
FP a	0.2172	0.3534	−0.3503	0.2241
b	0.1951	0.5306	−0.5592	0.1947
c	0.1952	0.4940	−0.5161	0.1972
URF	0.1929	0.5871	−0.6057	0.1937

Table 5.3.1 (continued)

C.2. Observed standard deviation of 100 samples around observed mean

	ω_{11}	ω_{13}	ω_{21}	ω_{23}
OLS	0.1131	0.1089	0.1121	0.1369
TSLS	0.0644	0.0701	0.0736	0.0601
FP a	0.1259	0.2187	0.2339	0.1170
b	0.0730	0.1874	0.1433	0.0902
c	0.0831	0.2034	0.1790	0.0863
URF	0.0720	0.0743	0.0782	0.0862

C.4. Observed standard deviation around true value of the coefficient

OLS	0.2299	0.2936	0.2869	0.2604
TSLS	0.0649	0.0723	0.0736	0.0616
FP a	0.1271	0.3296	0.3421	0.1193
b	0.0732	0.1998	0.1490	0.9094
c	0.0832	0.2294	0.1977	0.0863
URF	0.0723	0.0754	0.0784	0.0862

D. Eigenvalues for product moment matrix of explanatory variables (REID specification)

D.1. Equation 1

	Smallest in 100 samples	Average for 100 samples		
		λ_1	λ_2	λ_3
OLS	0.0233	0.0483	0.3064	0.6453
TSLS	0.0022	0.0169	0.2237	0.6595
FP a	0.0042	0.0619	0.3462	0.5918
b	0.0021	0.0185	0.3253	0.6562
c	0.0042	0.0270	0.3315	0.6414

D.2. Equation 2

OLS	0.0200	0.0492	0.3270	0.6237
TSLS	0.0014	0.0178	0.3456	0.6366
FP a	0.0035	0.0562	0.3608	0.5829
b	0.0009	0.0198	0.3489	0.6313
c	0.0009	0.0279	0.3521	0.6200
Unrestricted reduced form	0.1064	0.1511	0.2092	0.2780

Table 5.3.1 (continued)

E. Average R^2 from 100 samples

	E.1. *Sample period*			E.3. *Sample period* (adj. for D.F.)		
	y_1	y_2	y	y_1	y_2	y
True [1]	0.8	0.8	0.8			
Generated [1]	0.7853	0.7931	0.7892			
OLS	0.5650	0.5655	0.5653	0.5297	0.5303	0.5301
TSLS	0.8028	0.8055	0.8042	0.7868	0.7897	0.7883
FP a	0.5884	0.6016	0.5973	0.5550	0.5693	0.5622
b	0.7437	0.7692	0.7565	0.7229	0.7505	0.7368
c	0.7126	0.7401	0.7264	0.6893	0.7191	0.7043
URF	0.7868	0.7938	0.7903	0.7695	0.7771	0.7733

E.2. *Prediction period*

	y_1	y_2	y			
True	0.8	0.8	0.8			
Generated	0.7973	0.7921	0.7947			
OLS	0.5060	0.4990	0.5025			
TSLS	0.7748	0.7762	0.7755			
FP a	0.5506	0.5390	0.5448			
b	0.7100	0.7279	0.7190			
c	0.6772	0.7046	0.6909			
URF	0.7683	0.7696	0.7690			

[1] "True" refers to the population and "generated" refers to Monte Carlo data, see Part E of Table 10.1.1.

[2] The R^2 is adjusted for degrees of freedom; see Part E of Table 10.1.1.

for a set of samples can be compared. Second, for each sample the change in estimates with each new iteration can be studied. The latter is very laborious because of the great variation in the pattern among samples and the great variation among parameters within a sample.

Table 1 shows the results obtained in Model 1c for three different specifications on convergence, Specifications a–c. As discussed in Chapter 5.2, the convergence problem does not arise if the beta coefficients are small, i.e., if there is weak interdependence in the model. Hence, for the sake of illustration, we have chosen Model 1c which has strong interdependence and represents a case which on the whole is unfavorable to the FP method. Comparing Specifications a–c as defined in Part A.4 of the table, it is readily apparent that the estimates are better in Specifications b and c where the average numbers of iterations were less than in

Specification a. The estimates were generally better in Specification b where the limit was arbitrarily limited to 10 than in Specification c where iterations were limited by a relatively weak convergence criterion of 10^{-3}.

The results for the three different specifications on convergence for the model shown in Table 1 illustrate two points concerning apparent convergence. First, since the spectral radius of 3.0 for the theoretical β matrix is very large, it is likely that the condition for convergence in many of the samples that appeared to converge was not met and there were a considerable number of cases with apparent convergence, especially in Specification C. Second, since the estimates in Specification c are generally better than in Specification a, we can see that estimates obtained with apparent convergence are certainly acceptable. There is no reason to believe that apparent convergence leads to poor estimates. To repeat, the problem area is complex, and additional research has been initiated; see Chapters 3.6 and 3.7.

In models where convergence is not a serious problem the effect of restricting iterations by either of the two means is likely to have negligible effect on estimates. Model 1c described above was selected for special study because convergence was a serious problem. In spite of the improved results in Model 1c when iterations were limited the results for all but two of the 46 models in Chapter 10 were calculated with the original design of a 200 iteration limit and a convergence criterion of 10^{-6} in (5.1.1). It was felt that this was the best way to gain broad insight into the FP method.

5.4. Number of Variables per Equation and Number of Equations

In analyzing the effect of increasing size of model it is necessary to separate the effects from changes in the spectral radius from effects of changes in numbers of coefficients over which iterations must take place. Illustrations of these two effects can be obtained from Table 1. Within the C series in Table 1 the number of coefficients increase but the spectral radius of the specified beta matrix is constant because the theoretical beta matrix is identical in all three models. There is no difference in number of coefficients between Model 1i in the A series and Model 2d in the B series, but the spectral radius is much different. The

Table 5.4.1

Number of structural coefficients and speed of convergence

Model	Number of coefficients	Size of β coefficients	Variables per equation	Spectral radius [1]	Number of equations	Number of iterations			Samples with no convergence
						Average	Smallest	Largest	
A. Series on number of equations									
1g	6	±0.5	3	0.5	2	6	4	10	0
1h	15	±0.5	3	0.5	5	15	13	19	0
1i	21	±0.5	3	0.5	7	17	15	20	0
B. Series on number of equations									
2a	6	±1	3	1	2	8	4	17	0
2b	9	±1	3	1	3	25	15	50	0
2c	15	±1	3	1	5	67	32	200	3
2d	21	±1	3	1	7	120	61	200	9
C. Series on number of variables per equation									
2e	6	±1	3	1	2	8	4	17	0
2f	10	±1	5	1	2	15	9	35	0
2g	16	±1	8	1	2	28	14	200	1
D. Series on number of endogenous variables per equation									
3a	9	±0.5	3	0.5	3	12	9	20	0
3d	12	±0.5	4	0.87	3	51	11	200	12

[1] This is the spectral radius of the model as specified in the population. The spectral radius of the beta matrix in the FP solution of each sample will, in general, be different from the spectral radius of the specified beta matrix.

two models in the D series vary with respect to number of coefficients as well as size of the spectral radius.

The theoretical discussion on the effect of size of spectral radius was presented in Chapters 3.6, 3.7 and 5.2. The results in Table 1 are in agreement with the theory; namely, whenever one of two models had a larger spectral radius the speed of convergence was slower and frequency of convergence within the iteration limit was smaller. This can be seen by comparing the two models in the following pairs: Models 1g and 2a; Models 1h and 2c; Models 1i and 2d; Models 3a and 3d. In the last pair there was an increase in the number of coefficients as well as size of spectral radius, so it is not possible to attribute the cause to either of the two factors.

As the number of structural coefficients to be estimated increases we would naturally expect the number of iterations for convergence to increase. This is because the number of estimates that must meet the convergence criterion increases and because the number of ways that each estimate in a particular iteration can influence each estimate in the next iteration increases.

There is a difference between increasing the number of coefficients via more variables per equation and via more equations (e.g., compare Models 2c and 2g). There is also a difference between more endogenous variables per equation and more exogenous variables as seen by comparing results from Series 2 and 3 in Table 1. We note, however, that the spectral radius of Model 3d is larger than for Model 3a. Comparing Models 2g and 3d it appears quite clear that the number of endogenous variables per equation is an important factor. In Model 3d the spectral radius is smaller and there are fewer exogenous variables and structural coefficients, but convergence is much slower because of the full β matrix. It is conceivable (but not possible to test from available data) that the shape of the distribution of values for the spectral radius is quite different and this could explain many of the results in Table 1.

Models within both the A and B series in Table 1 show that the number of iterations increases quite rapidly as the number of equations increases. The rate of increase is more pronounced in the B series where the basic model has larger beta coefficients and a larger spectral radius.

The results for models within the C series show the speed of convergence is less as total number of variables in the model increases. In order to evaluate the rate of increase in number of iterations within the C series of Table 1 the increase should be compared with the rate in the B series where the beta coefficients and spectral radius of the specified model are the same. It is easily seen that increasing the number of coefficients by increasing the number of exogenous variables per equation has much less effect than increasing the number of exogenous variables by increasing the number of equations. Convergence was much slower in the case of 9 coefficients in Model 2b than for 10 coefficients in 2f. Likewise, convergence was slower for the 15 coefficients in Model 2c than for 16 coefficients in Model 2g. Here again, we wish to point out that although the spectral radius of the specified matrix is the same for all four models in the B series, the shape of the distribution of values for the spectral radius in Monte Carlo samples can be quite different.

The D series in Table 1 shows that convergence is more affected by number of endogenous variables than by either the number of exogenous variables or the number of equations. Convergence was much slower for the 12 coefficients in Model 3d than for the 16 coefficients in Model 2g. Convergence for the 3 equation Model 3d which has 6 coefficients on current endogenous variables was much slower than for the 7-equation Model 1i which has 7 coefficients on current endogenous variables.

The results in Table 1 and the above statements were selected as representing the overall results from studies on model size in the entire Monte Carlo study over the last two years. There are many other hypotheses concerning speed of convergence that could be developed but the general conclusions listed above are believed to be valid. Again, we must point out that there is an interaction among all the factors discussed in the Chapters 5.2–5.7.

All of these statements, of course, pertain to overidentified models. Just identified models converge in one iteration if TSLS estimates are used as start values since FP estimates are the same as TSLS estimates.

5.5. Size of Sample

The results from investigations of the effects of sample size and size of residuals must be analyzed carefully because of the ambiguity between apparent and true convergence and the difference in the starting values used in the FP Method. In classical models FP estimates approach TSLS estimates as sample size increases and/or size of residuals decrease. Consequently, even if true convergence is not possible it can be conjectured that apparent convergence will occur more frequently whenever TSLS estimates are used as a start and sample size increases and/or size of residuals decreases. In situations where true convergence for the specified model is possible, speed of convergence increases and frequency of true convergence in sample data increases as size of sample increases regardless of the start value used for FP.

The results from investigation of different sample sizes are in agreement with the theory presented in Chapters 3.6, 3.7 and 5.2. In all of the authors' Monte Carlo research there have been no exceptions to two general results. First, if the spectral radius of the specified matrix is less that one, convergence increases as the number of observations in the sample increases. Second, convergence is always attained when the theoretical population is used as sample data and TSLS estimates are used as starting values; however, in all models where the spectral radius is greater than one, it is apparent rather than true convergence that is attained. The results for Models 5f–5h in Table 5.1.1 are representative of the pattern of reduction in number of iterations as sample size is increased. The elasticity of the number of iterations with respect to sample size is greatest at small sample sizes. For most models the number of iterations decreases very slowly after sample size reaches a level of 5–10 times the number of coefficients to be estimated. The number of iterations required for apparent or true convergence approaches the lower limit very slowly. In Classic ID systems (see 1.2.6) and using TSLS estimates as a start the limiting number of iterations is only one. We are here touching upon the complex issue of the effect of different start values on the convergence properties of the FP procedure. This is a problem area that has been relatively little explored in our investigation. Speaking broadly, the choice of starting point is inconsequential if the beta coefficients are small (weak interdependence). When the model involves large values for beta coefficients the situation becomes considerably more complex, and more so in GEID systems than in Classic ID systems.

In pilot runs the sample size was made equal to the number of predetermined variables for several different models. Convergence was considerably slower than for a sample size of 40 that was used for all but

Table 5.5.1
Sample size and speed of convergence [1]

Model	Number of observations in sample	Number of iterations			No convergence in 50 iterations
		Average	Minimum	Maximum	
I [2]	4	34	6	50	1
	10	27	4	50	1
	40	6	3	9	0
	90	5	4	7	0
II [3]	10	25	20	34	0
	20	12	11	13	0
	90	9	8	10	0
III [4]	9	33	11	50	2
	15	28	6	50	1
	50	25	21	28	0

[1] These results are for models not included in Chapter 10.2.

[2] Model: $\beta = \begin{bmatrix} 0 & 3 \\ 0.5 & 0 \end{bmatrix}$ $\Gamma = \begin{bmatrix} 0.250 & 0.250 \\ & & 0.250 & 0.250 \end{bmatrix}$

10 samples: $\sigma^2(y_1) = 10$; $\sigma^2(y_2) = 1.25$; and $\sigma^2(x_j) = 1$; $R^2(y_j) = 0.5$.

[3] Model: $\beta = \begin{bmatrix} 0 & 0.5 & 0.5 \\ 0.5 & 0 & 0.5 \\ 0.5 & & 0 \end{bmatrix}$ $\Gamma = \begin{bmatrix} 0.153 & 0.153 & 0.153 \\ & & & 0.153 & 0.153 & 0.153 \\ & & & & & & 0.153 & 0.153 & 0.153 \end{bmatrix}$

10 samples: $\sigma^2(y_1) = 1.002$; $\sigma^2(y_2) = 0.932$, and $\sigma^2(y_3) = 0.483$; $\sigma^2(x_j) = 1$; $R^2(y_j) = 0.90$.

[4] Model: $\beta = \begin{bmatrix} 0 & 2 \\ & 0 & 2 \\ 2 & & 0 \end{bmatrix}$ $\Gamma = \begin{bmatrix} 0.837 & 0.837 & 0.837 \\ & & & 0.837 & 0.837 & 0.837 \\ & & & & & & 0.837 & 0.837 & 0.837 \end{bmatrix}$

10 samples: $\sigma^2(y_j) = 1.8$; $\sigma^2(x_j) = 1.0$; $R^2(y_j) = 0.5$.

three of the models presented in Chapter 10.2. The minimum number of observations in which the FP method can be used is the same as for OLS and is equal to the number of determining variables in the largest structural equation. Convergence is slow with very small sample sizes, but there is no evidence from any Monte Carlo results that it is not attainable if the maximum α in Ågrens' criterion (see 3.6) is not greater than the α used in the FP Method. Table 1 shows results when sample size approaches the number of predetermined variables. This is the point at which TSLS gives the same results as OLS. Four observations in Model I is the smallest sample size for which FP gives different results from OLS. Table 1 shows that the number of iterations is sensitive to sample size but does not increase without limit as sample size is decreased. [1]

Another effort to evaluate convergence was carried out by increasing the sample size in cases such as Models 3c and 3e where very few of the samples among the results in Chapter 10.2 converged. As samples were increased from 40 to 100 observations, the number of samples that did not converge decreased (note, we suspect that the higher percentage of convergence was due to apparent rather than true convergence; see Chapter 3.7). The computer program was not changed from the original design of 100 observations maximum, so no information is available to determine the sample size for which most samples from models such as 3c and 3e would converge within 200 iterations and a convergence criterion of 10^{-6}.

The effect of sample size on convergence can be summarized by saying that in situations where either apparent or true convergence is possible, convergence speeds up as sample size is increased, but it approaches the limit of only one required iteration very slowly. To repeat, in Classic ID systems and TSLS start the limiting number of iterations is only one. Although speed of convergence is more sensitive to changes in sample size at small sample sizes, the number of iterations does not increase indefinitely as sample size is reduced to the minimum. However, in earlier discussion we noted that even if the specified model will allow true convergence, the frequency of samples that will not allow true convergence will, in general, increase as sample size decreases.

5.6. Size of Residuals

How is the convergence of the FP procedure influenced by the size of the residuals? The question is interesting and important, but at the same time difficult and tricky. Speaking broadly, there are signs to indicate that larger residuals will speed up convergence, at least in the case of small beta coefficients (weak interdependence). For another thing, the size of the residuals affects the distribution of FP estimates of beta coefficients which in turn affects the frequency of apparent convergence (see 3.7).

Because of the ambiguity between apparent and true convergence a special and extensive study of Summers' model was carried out. The reason for choosing Summers' model is that the FP solution in each sam-

ple can be obtained in a non-iterative way by using the formulas given
by Lyttkens (1967); also, see in 3.8. Thus, even if the iterative technique for obtaining FP estimates does not converge for a particular sample it is possible to calculate the solution which fulfills the fix-point
properties. Likewise, for a sample that converges under apparent convergence it is possible to determine if the FP estimates from the iterative
technique are close to the values for the non-iterative FP solution of that
sample.

Four different specifications on Summers' model were designed especially to study the effects of the size of residuals on convergence of the
iterative technique for obtaining FP estimates. In the first round the
models were explored by the FP method in its original version (Chapter
3.5). Some of the ensuing results were puzzling and difficult to interpret.
The situation was then explored more in detail by the FFP and RFP
methods that were developed by A.Ågren and L.Bodin in the course of
our investigation (see 3.6–3.7). Reference is made to Example 2 in Chapter 3.6 for a brief report on an analysis of the four models by the FFP
method. The results are summed up in Tables 3.6.2 and 3.6.3. According
to the theorem in Chapter 3.6 the maximum α's for specifications 1 and
2 were 0.75, but the larger residuals in number 2 resulted in a maximum
α larger than one in 39 of the 100 samples. On the other hand, specifications 3 and 4 had a maximum α greater than 1 in the specified model,
but 3 of the samples in number 3 and 15 of the samples in number 4
had a maximum α less than one, and true convergence was thus possible.

Charts 3.6.1 and 3.6.2 show the distribution of maximum α for the
100 samples of each of the four specifications of Summers' model described in Table 3.6.2. The arrows in Charts 3.6.1 and 3.6.2 indicate the
value of maximum α in the model as specified while the histograms show
the frequency of specified values among the 100 Monte Carlo samples
on each specification. Charts 3.6.1 and 3.6.2 illustrate that the percentage of samples giving true convergence is affected by the size of the
residuals, and that the percentage will change in different directions
depending upon whether the value of α is below or above its "maximum"
value.

The results in Charts in 3.6.1 and 3.6.2 also provide useful information
on the selection of the optimum α for the FFP Method. For example,
an α of 0.2 would have led to convergence in all of the 100 samples for
each of the four specifications.

With the above insight into the effect of size of residuals on the distribution of maximum α in Monte Carlo samples we can turn to the results from the 46 models reported in Chapter 10.2. The size of residuals will be discussed in terms of the variances of the residuals in both the structural and reduced form equations. In Part A.2 in each of the tables in Chapter 10.2 the residuals in the structural equations appear as δ_i and the residuals in the reduced form appear as ϵ_i. When endogenous variables have been normalized to 1.0, the size of residuals can be discussed in terms of absolute size as opposed to a ratio of the variance of the residual to the variance of the dependent endogenous variable.

In the beginning of 5.6 we touched upon the problem of how speed of convergence is affected by size of residuals in the regression equations:

$$Y(\text{observed}) = BY^* + GZ + e , \qquad (1)$$

where the Y^* variables are calculated from the previous iteration (see eq. (3.5.4)), Z are predetermined variables, and e is an estimate of the residuals in the reduced form equations.

There is, however, a situation where δ must be considered along with ϵ as a measure for determining the effect of residuals on speed of convergence. If the $[I-\beta]$ matrix is very nearly singular, δ is very small compared to ϵ. This means that even if ϵ were 0.5, say, the value of each δ could be so small that a near perfect fit in direct least squares estimates of each structural equation is obtained. Several models with a nearly singular $[I-\beta]$ matrix were estimated and FP converged rapidly in all cases. None of these models are included in Chapter 10.2 since the results are too obvious in the light of the proximity theorem; see 3.3.3.

The speed of convergence in the series 5m−5s decreased as size of residuals increased. It is only in Model 5m where R^2 is only 0.2 that some of the samples did not converge. Since the spectral radius of the specified beta matrix in Models 5m−5s is one, it is likely that the spectral radius in several samples of each model was greater than one and that there was apparent rather than true convergence.

The average number of iterations in Model 5r was larger than in Model 5s. These results are in line with our theory. The spectral radius of the specified β matrix in Models 5r and 5s is only 0.67, so we would expect only a small percentage of samples to have a spectral radius greater than one; we find only two samples that did not converge in Model 5r.

Model 3e was one of two models for which convergence was not attained in any of the 100 samples with a limit of 200 iterations and a criterion of 10^{-6}. When the criterion was changed to 10^{-3} and the iteration limit was 50 the effect of increasing the size of residuals was as follows:

10 out of 10 samples did not converge with $\sigma^2(\epsilon) = 0.1$
6 out of 10 samples did not converge with $\sigma^2(\epsilon) = 0.9$
4 out of 10 samples did not converge with $\sigma^2(\epsilon) = 0.99$

Similar results were obtained when residuals were increased in other models where convergence was a serious problem. Since the spectral radius of the specified beta matrix was 2.0, we are led to the tentative conclusion that the results reflect a higher percentage of true convergence as size of residuals is increased; further, it would seem that a higher percentage of the convergent cases represent apparent convergence.

This study provides only limited results for studying convergence in cases such as Models 5m—5s because convergence in these cases is not a problem. For applied work it would be more meaningful to investigate convergence with a criterion considerably less stringent than the 10^{-6} used for most of the 46 models shown in Chapter 10.2. The less stringent the criterion, the greater the possibility of apparent convergence. As discussed in 3.7, this problem area is subject to research which will be reported in later publications.

5.7. GEID Models

The correlations among residuals and exogenous variables in GEID models seem to increase the required number of iterations a small amount. However, Part A of Table 1 shows negligible effect from correlations until the size of correlations reaches a value of 0.4.

The effect of increasing the size of correlation coefficients within the GEID specification can be explained by the larger difference between TSLS estimates as a starting point and the FP solution. Since the spectral radius of the specified beta matrix was one in Models 6f—6j, it is

Table 5.7.1
Speed of convergence in GEID models [1]

A. Increasing size of correlations among residuals and exogenous variables

Model	Size of correlations	Number of iterations			No convergence
		Average	Smallest	Largest	
6f	0.01	8.6	5	25	0
6g	0.05	8.9	4	27	0
6h	0.10	8.2	5	15	0
6i	0.20	9.3	6	20	0
6j	0.40	12.5	5	200	1

B. Comparison of GEID and classical models

Models		No. of equa-tions	Number of iterations						No convergence	
			Average		Smallest		Largest			
GEID	CLID		GEID	CLID	GEID	CLID	GEID	CLID	GEID	CLID
6a	2a	2	8.4	8.4	4	4	16	17	0	0
6b	2b	3	31	25	17	15	200	50	1	0
6c	2c	5	64	67	35	32	104	200	0	3

[1] GEID indicates General interdependent systems and CLID indicates Classic interdependent systems; see 1.2.6

likely that there was apparent rather than true convergence in many of the samples.

Part B of Table 1 shows no significant difference between Classic ID and GEID systems for three different sizes of models. The maximum size correlation in GEID models 6a–6c was 0.2, which supports the hypothesis that correlations must be fairly large before convergence is significantly affected.

The possibility of multiple (plural) solutions in GEID models, first discovered by E.Lyttkens (1967), is discussed in 3.8 and 3.9. When multiple solutions exist it is conceivable that convergence can be very slow because of possible oscillations among combinations of two or more sets of solutions; this situation was investigated quite thoroughly. However, both our theoretical work and the Monte Carlo results indicate that multiple solutions as a rule will not cause a problem in convergence. This means that the theories and hypotheses discussed in Chapter 5.2 are applicable to GEID as well as to classical models. Although more work has yet to be done on GEID models, it is reassuring to know that convergence is not a serious problem.

CHAPTER 6

Consistency of Estimates

Although it is rare to have a large number of observations available for estimating econometric models, the special quality of consistency of estimates receives much attention in econometrics. When a new method such as FP is developed, the consistency of the method is one of the first things that is verified.

Results from the large number of models analyzed in the research for this project give a fairly conclusive positive verdict on consistency for FP. There is a problem of plural solutions in some GEID specifications (see Chapter 3.8), but this is a basic issue in model building rather than a question of consistency of any particular method of estimation.

6.1. Results with Increasing Sample Size

The models for the results presented in Chapter 10.2 are either REID or GEID systems; see 1.4.4—5 and Chart 2.3.1. For the REID systems both TSLS and FP estimation are consistent, whereas TSLS is not consistent for GEID systems. Since comparison of FP with TSLS is a main purpose of our investigation, most of Chapters 4 to 8 will report about REID systems, and most of the results on GEID systems will be reported separately in Chapter 9.

A semantic point: Bias is a general term that covers the entire range from large-sample bias (inconsistency) to small-sample bias. In the context of this monograph both categories are in focus. For shortness in the phrasings and when there is no risk of misunderstanding, we shall take the term bias to refer to small-sample bias, and thus speak of bias vs inconsistency.

This chapter is mainly concerned with consistency vs inconsistency. To explore parameter estimates in this respect we shall consider results from samples with increasing size, namely 10, 40 and 80 observations.

The numerical results belonging under this subchapter are summed up in Table 1. The top of the table and the footnote reference specifies the theoretical model in accordance with formulas (1.4.75) and (1.4.87). The model is of Summers' type (1.4.83) and (1.4.97). The four variables x_i are exogenous and mutually independent. In the models shown in Table 1 the exogenous variables have unit variance,

$$\sigma^2(x_1) = \sigma^2(x_2) = \sigma^2(x_3) = \sigma^2(x_4) = 1 \, , \tag{1}$$

and the parameters and residual variances are specified so as to normalise the endogenous variables y_i to unit variance,

$$\sigma^2(y_1) = \sigma^2(y_2) = 1 \, . \tag{2}$$

The normalization process is explained in more detail in Appendix II. At this point we only mention that the magnitudes of coefficients and standard deviations are affected by the normalization but the ratio of any coefficients to its standard error is not affected.

The procedure for generating Monte Carlo data from the model has been described in Chapter 2. One hundred samples were generated for each of the three specified sample sizes in Table 1. The "10", "40" and "80" observation sample sizes were not taken from the same sequence of Monte Carlo data. The runs in each case were independent.

The results in Table 1 include only three of the six structural coefficients and only one of the eight reduced form coefficients. In this and the following tables in the monograph we have followed the practice of not showing all coefficients whenever the results for a few of the coefficients suffice to illustrate the essential features for all methods. Each

Table 6.1.1
Results from increasing sample size [1].

MODEL:

$$\beta = \begin{bmatrix} 0 & 1 \\ -1 & 0 \end{bmatrix} \quad \Gamma = \begin{bmatrix} k_1 & k_1 \\ & \\ & k_1 & k_1 \end{bmatrix} \quad \Omega = \begin{bmatrix} k_2 & k_2 & k_2 & k_2 \\ -k_2 & -k_2 & k_2 & k_2 \end{bmatrix}$$

where $k_1 = 0.894$ and $k_2 = 0.447$

$\sigma^2(y_i) = \sigma^2(x_k) = 1; \ \sigma^2(\delta_i) = 0.4; \ \sigma^2(\epsilon_i) = 0.2$

Results from 100 Monte Carlo samples:

	Mean of 100 estimates			S.D. around mean			S.D. around true value		
	Size of sample			Size of sample			Size of sample		
	10	40	80	10	40	80	10	40	80
β_{12}									
OLS	0.629	0.687	0.677	0.264	0.136	0.090	0.455	0.341	0.336
TSLS	0.909	1.028	1.011	0.387	0.190	0.128	0.397	0.192	0.129
FP	0.906	1.032	1.013	0.376	0.196	0.129	0.388	0.198	0.129
β_{21}									
OLS	−0.626	−0.666	−0.662	0.304	0.123	0.094	0.482	0.356	0.351
TSLS	−1.000	−1.018	−1.007	0.646	0.170	0.124	0.646	0.171	0.124
FP	−0.977	−1.022	−1.008	0.442	0.173	0.125	0.443	0.174	0.125
γ_{11}									
OLS	0.751	0.743	0.744	0.232	0.118	0.081	0.272	0.192	0.171
TSLS	0.867	0.904	0.892	0.275	0.145	0.095	0.276	0.145	0.095
FP	0.850	0.897	0.889	0.324	0.176	0.118	0.327	0.176	0.118
ω_{11}									
OLS	0.550	0.511	0.514	0.186	0.071	0.052	0.213	0.095	0.085
TSLS	0.476	0.443	0.444	0.151	0.061	0.049	0.153	0.061	0.049
FP	0.470	0.437	0.442	0.179	0.074	0.059	0.180	0.074	0.059
URF	0.477	0.438	0.442	0.199	0.072	0.059	0.201	0.072	0.059

[1] The complete design of the three models is given in the following tables: Model 5f (10 observations) − Table 10.2.32; Model 5g (which is Model 1b and has 40 observations) − Table 10.2.2; Model 5h (80 observations) − Table 10.2.33.

section of Table 1 summarizes the Monte Carlo results on selected statistics for each of three different sizes. The next four paragraphs provide helpful reminders for interpreting results such as those presented in Table 1.

OLS. Ordinary least squares regression has given the results shown in the table in the lines "OLS". The first section of the table reports the *means* of the estimates as obtained from the hundred sample series; the second and third sections show the *standard deviation* (S.D.) of the hundred estimates as calculated around the observed mean and theoretical mean respectively. The estimates of β_{ik}, γ_{ik} have been obtained by OLS as applied to the structural form. The OLS estimates of ω_{ik} have been generated from the OLS estimates of β_{ik}, γ_{ik} using formula (1.4.88).

TSLS. For two-stage least squares estimation the table arrangement is the same as for OLS. The estimates of β_{ik}, γ_{ik} have been obtained by the TSLS procedure, and using formula (1.4.88) these estimates have given the TSLS estimates of ω_{ik}.

FP. For fix-point estimation the arrangement of Table 1 is the same as for OLS and TSLS. Note that in FP estimation the iterative proxies $Y^{(s)}$ are obtained as the systematic parts of the iterative proxies of the reduced form (1.4.88a). In this sense the FP procedure yields a simultaneous estimation of all parameters of the model; not only the parameters β_{ik}, γ_{ik} of the structural form, but also the coefficients ω_{ik} of the reduced form. Otherwise expressed, and we are now referring to properties of FP estimates that are not shared by OLS and TSLS estimates, the FP estimates b_{ik}, g_{ik} of the parameters of the structural form match the FP estimates w_{ik} of the coefficients of the reduced form, and the observed residuals e_{it} as estimated by FP are the same in the structural form and the reduced form.

URF. These results are obtained only for the reduced form, URF being ordinary least squares regression as applied directly to the (unrestricted) reduced form.

In Table 1 and the present chapter the emphasis is on consistency vs inconsistency of the various estimation methods. At the same time Table 1 gives some information on bias in finite samples; comparisons with regard to such (small-sample) bias will be in focus in Chapter 7.

The bias in OLS estimates of structural coefficients and generated reduced form coefficients is in the nature of inconsistency, as we know from Chapter 3.3, and does not decrease with sample size. On the other hand, in REID systems there is no inconsistency in the URF estimates of

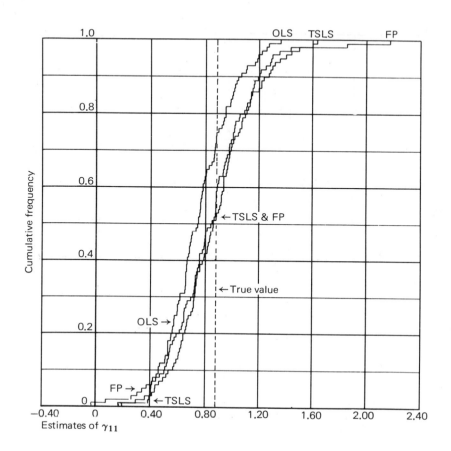

Chart 6.1.1. Cumulative distribution of estimates for γ_{11} in Model 5f – sample size 10.

coefficients in the reduced form equations regardless of sample size. It is, however, meaningful to ask how the bias in TSLS and FP estimates of both sets of equations reduces as sample size is increased.

The basic model used in the group on sample size (Models 5f–5h) shows relatively small bias for TSLS and FP even with small sample size. However, Table 1 does confirm that the average value of the estimate approaches the true value as sample size increases.

The cumulative distribution of selected estimates for Models 5f and 5g shown in Charts 1 and 2 also illustrate the property of consistency in TSLS and FP estimates. The distributions of estimates from TSLS

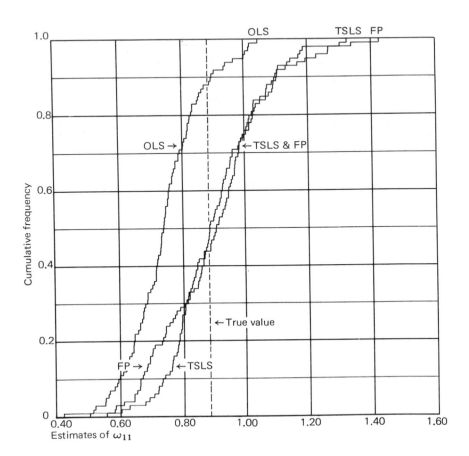

Chart 6.1.2. Cumulative distribution of estimates for γ_{11} in Model 5g — sample size 40.

and FP shift towards the true value of γ_{11} as the sample size is increased
from 10 observations in Model 5f to 40 observations in Model 5g. The
dispersion of estimates is, of course, reduced as sample size increases.

The model in Table 2 shows considerably more bias in estimates than
the model in Table 1 for each of the three sample sizes and, therefore,
provides a better illustration of the reduction in bias in FP as sample size
is increased. The greater bias arises because of the large difference in magnitude between the two beta coefficients and the larger variance of
residuals (ϵ_i).

The results in Table 2 are from pilot runs in which only part of the

Table 6.1.2
Special model to illustrate consistency [1].

MODEL:

$$\beta = \begin{bmatrix} 0 & 1.0607 \\ 1.4142 & 0 \end{bmatrix} \quad \Gamma = \begin{bmatrix} 0.07937 & 0.07937 \\ & & 0.2236 & 0.2236 \end{bmatrix}$$

$$\Omega = \begin{bmatrix} -0.1587 & -0.1587 & -0.4762 & -0.4762 \\ -0.2236 & -0.2236 & -0.4472 & -0.4472 \end{bmatrix}$$

$$\sigma^2(y_i) = 1; \quad \sigma^2(x_k) = 1; \quad \sigma^2(\delta_i) = \begin{matrix} 0.0125 \\ 0.1000 \end{matrix}; \quad \sigma^2(\epsilon_i) = 0.5$$

Results from 100 Monte Carlo samples:

	Mean of 100 estimates			S.D. around mean			S.D. around true value		
	Size of sample			Size of sample			Size of sample		
	10	40	90	10	40	90	10	40	90
β_{21}									
OLS	1.030	1.030	1.027	0.0707	0.0283	0.0215	0.3903	0.3846	0.3874
TSLS	1.015	1.307	1.456	0.7409	0.4044	0.4157	0.8427	0.4185	0.4185
FP	1.066	1.298	1.454	0.3478	0.4497	0.4072	0.4921	0.4638	0.4101
γ_{23}									
OLS	0.0443	0.0402	0.0396	0.0586	0.0271	0.0168	0.1887	0.1854	0.1847
TSLS	0.0291	0.1809	0.2415	0.5013	0.1820	0.1688	0.5378	0.1869	0.1697
FP	0.0557	0.1804	0.2379	0.1706	0.1872	0.1690	0.2395	0.1921	0.1697
ω_{11}									
OLS	1.0590	−0.6401	−0.1625	2.8353	49.5147	0.7647	2.9745	49.5170	0.7647
TSLS	0.5609	−0.1709	−0.1754	7.3730	0.2065	0.0597	7.3848	0.2068	0.0620
FP	−0.1321	−0.1595	−0.1662	0.2971	0.1183	0.0737	0.2983	0.1183	0.0740
URF	−0.1396	−0.1595	−0.1661	0.2962	0.1178	0.0733	0.2968	0.1178	0.0737

[1] This model is not one of the 46 models described in Chapter 10.2 and it will not be analyzed in detail in the monograph.

statistics were printed; therefore, the overall set of results for the models in Table 2 are not included in the summary tables in Chapter 10.2. Table 2 is included only to support the conclusions derived from the results in Table 1.

The models in Tables 1–2, as in most of our experiments, are generated so as to make current structural residuals uncorrelated, $r(\delta_{1t},\delta_{2t})=0$. For the model in Table 1 this property carries over to the reduced form, giving $r(\epsilon_{1t},\epsilon_{2t})=0$, while in Table 2 the current residuals of the reduced form are strongly intercorrelated.

Comparing the models in Tables 1-2 in the light of Ågren's criterion (see 3.6) $\beta_{12}\beta_{21}$ is < 1 in Table 1, and > 1 in Table 2. This makes for convergence of the FP iterations in Table 1, while Table 2 is a more difficult case, where the convergence in most samples is only apparent.

In Classic ID systems and REID systems where the interdependence is weak or moderate, all of the Monte Carlo runs show FP estimates as approaching the true value as sample size is increased. In models with strong interdependence the FP method often has failed to converge. These findings are in conformity with Ågren's theorem for the convergence of the FP and FFP procedures just referred to. The classical specification is defined as one where none of the residuals is correlated with the predetermined variables. The non-classical specification which we have labeled "general interdependent" (GEID) systems is more complex. As applied to GEID systems, TSLS and other classical estimation methods are inconsistent whereas the FP method can be extended to GEID systems and remains consistent under fairly general conditions. The present monograph is mainly devoted to a comparison between FP and other methods as applied to Classic ID systems, but limited results for GEID systems will be presented and discussed in Chapter 9.

6.2. Results Using Population Data

The consistency of TSLS estimates and the inconsistency of OLS estimates can be proved with relatively simple mathematics. FP estimates are consistent for a wider range of models but pose considerably more difficult problems when it comes to general analysis. Large-sample results for FP were studied by using the computer program to estimate a model from what we call *population data*; that is, the data series are such that the observed moments are exactly equal to the corresponding moments in the population. Population data for the special runs to test consistency was constructed from the variance—covariance matrix for exogenous and residual variables by factorization of the matrix and interpreting in terms of time series data. The finite time series thus constructed were read in as data, and the computer generated the observations on the endogenous variables. For example, the population data for verifying the consistency of FP estimates for Model 5f are shown in Table 1. The con-

Table 6.2.1
Population data for Model 5f [1]

t	y_{1t}	y_{2t}	x_{1t}	x_{2t}	x_{3t}	x_{4t}	δ_{1t}	δ_{2t}
1	λ	$-\lambda$	1					
2	λ	$-\lambda$		1				
3	λ	$+\lambda$			1			
4	λ	$+\lambda$				1		
5	$\tfrac{1}{2}\lambda\sqrt{2}$	$\tfrac{1}{2}\lambda\sqrt{2}$					$\lambda\sqrt{2}$	
6	$\tfrac{1}{2}\lambda\sqrt{2}$	$\tfrac{1}{2}\lambda\sqrt{2}$						$\lambda\sqrt{2}$

[1] $\lambda = 0.4472$; $\sigma^2(y_1) = \sigma^2(y_2) = 1.0$; $R^2(y_1) = R^2(y_2) = 0.8$.

structed sample is of size six; it is a general parallel that this set of data has the same features as the populations which are specified in the design of Model 5f. Any set of sample data that would yield variances and co-variances that are a scalar multiple of the specified variance–covariance matrix in the population could, of course, be used as population data.

In all cases using population data, the computer program reproduced all parameter values to the expected computational accuracy of 6 digits. This and other evidence obtained to date indicates that FP is consistent for both REID and GEID systems. [1]

6.3. Size of Beta Coefficients and Evidence on Consistency of FP

A theoretical analysis shows that the size of beta coefficients is of key relevance for the properties of FP and related procedures. In 6.3.1 we quote four points, with reference to Chapters 3.6–3.9 and other reports by Lyttkens, Ågren and Bodin (see the List of References) for the proofs and for further results.

6.3.1. (i) The REID specification is always well-defined in the popula-tion; that is, the set of parameters in a REID system exists and is unique. The only exception is when the matrix $[I-\beta]$ is singular; that is, when the determinant $[I-\beta]$ is zero.

(ii) For FP to converge when population data are used, it will as a rule suffice that all eigenvalues of matrix β be smaller than unity. The qualif-ication "as a rule" is necessary, for the argument is based on a fixed β

matrix, whereas the matrix varies in the course of the FP iterations.

If this condition is satisfied, it is probable that the FP will converge in a finite sample also. However, FP in general will not be convergent in a finite sample when the eigenvalues of β are larger than unity.

(iii) When the eigenvalue condition is satisfied in the population, the FP estimates, as a rule, will be consistent.

(iv) If the FP procedure does not converge, the procedure often will display *apparent convergence.*

6.3.2. Turning to the Monte Carlo experiments we shall as before present results for OLS, TSLS, and URF estimates in order to have reference material for judging FP estimates. In accordance with 6.3.1 (i)–(iv) we shall see that the size of beta coefficients has a large effect on the properties of all methods except URF. As also shows off in our Monte Carlo experiments, the size of beta coefficients has more effect on FP than on other methods because of the effect on speed of convergence (discussed in detail in Chapter 5).

It is well known that in the REID specification of models (see 1.4.4) the methods of TSLS and URF are consistent and OLS is not consistent regardless of the size of beta coefficients The small-sample bias of TSLS and the bias of OLS for all sample sizes does, however, depend on the size of beta coefficients. (GEID systems will be discussed in the next section and Chapter 9.)

The size of beta coefficients influences the degree of multicollinearity which in turn influences the dispersion of estimates for every method. The size of beta coefficients also influences the small-sample bias of OLS, TSLS, and FP as can be readily seen in the results presented in Chapter 7. Multicollinearity, in essence, reduces the variance of a determining variable that can be utilized in estimating a coefficient and, consequently, makes it more difficult to obtain a good estimate of the coefficient.

Table 1 shows the bias for a two-equation model with three sizes of the absolute value of beta coefficients. Table 6.1.1 shows how bias in Model 1b reduces as sample size is increased. This pattern of reduction in bias as sample size is increased is characteristic of all models with classical design. However, as the size of beta coefficients is increased, the sample sizes in a series such as in Table 6.1.1 must be larger in order to show that the average value of FP estimates approaches the true value

Table 6.3.1
Mean of estimates for three models with varying size of beta coefficients [1]

		Model 1a	Model 1b	Model 1c
β_{12}	True	0.5	1.0	3.0
	OLS	0.3772 (0.0092)	0.6874 (0.0136)	0.8011 (0.0247)
	TSLS	0.5026 (0.0110)	1.0284 (0.0190)	2.9313 (0.0889)
	FP	0.5028 (0.0109)	1.0322 (0.0196)	1.6500 (0.0949)
γ_{11}	True	0.7071	0.8944	2.0000
	OLS	0.6739 (0.0084)	0.7433 (0.0118)	0.6777 (0.0210)
	TSLS	0.7112 (0.0091)	0.9040 (0.0145)	1.9585 (0.0561)
	FP	0.7081 (0.0090)	0.8968 (0.0176)	0.9268 (0.0766)
ω_{11}	True	0.5657	0.4472	0.2000
	OLS	0.5876 (0.0074)	0.5111 (0.0071)	0.4002 (0.0113)
	TSLS	0.5668 (0.0075)	0.4433 (0.0061)	0.2077 (0.0064)
	FP	0.5644 (0.0074)	0.4372 (0.0074)	0.2172 (0.0126)
	URF	0.5647 (0.0077)	0.4384 (0.0072)	0.1929 (0.0072)

[1] The number in parentheses is the standard deviation of the mean.

as sample size increases. Furthermore, the averages from 100 samples presented in this monograph are difficult to interpret in cases where the majority of samples did not converge within the limit of 200 iterations. This points out the need for more research on the FFP and RFP methods since they hold promise of speeding up convergence.

A smaller number of Monte Carlo runs were made with different sample sizes for the larger models such as Model 2d which has 7 equations and Model 2g which has 8 determining variables per equation (see Tables 10.2.15 and 10.2.17 for complete specification of these models). In all cases the mean value of the estimates approached the true value as the sample size was increased. This was true even in cases like Model 3f (see Table 10.2.23) where a high percentage of the samples did not converge within the iteration limit specified for the Monte Carlo runs.

The types of models actually estimated and analyzed in this project by way of pilot studies were much larger than the 46 models shown in Chapter 10.2. Results from the Monte Carlo experiments not shown were also in accordance with the theoretical analysis briefly referred to in 6.3.1. It is possible to select beta coefficients for which small-sample bias is much greater than that shown for the three models in Table 1. In such cases a large sample is required to show that FP is consistent, but all evidence points to the fact that the method is indeed consistent. The special circumstance of plural solutions for some GEID models is discussed in the next section.

6.4. FP Gives Plural Solutions for Some GEID Systems

GEID models have correlations between the residual in one equation and the exogenous and η_i^* variables in other equations. Speaking broadly, GEID models are more complicated than corresponding REID models in regard to both the theoretical specification and the parameter estimation. The situation will be studied in some detail in Chapter 9. Right now we note that the passage from REID to GEID systems brings the following changes in the theoretical points (i)–(iv) in 6.3.1:

(i) In GEID models the parameters may or may not be uniquely determined by the second order moments of the population. When plural solutions of the parameters exist, these will as a rule have different residuals and different residual variances.

(ii) When plural solutions exist, it is a question whether the FP procedure converges, and whether it converges to the solution that has the smallest residual variances.

There are no plural solutions in the design of any of the GEID Models 6a–6c or 6f–6j. However, the Monte Carlo Sample data do not necessarily reflect the exact design of the specified model, and plural solutions could exist for some of the samples for each of these models. During the investigation of a large number of different models in pilot runs it was found that in some cases GEID models converged slower than corresponding classical models. This slower convergence would be expected if there were plural solutions for some samples.

FP appears to be consistent for the types of GEID Models 6a–6c and 6f–6j included in this monograph. Plural solutions have been found only in very special cases that were specifically designed to show that plural solutions can exist.

CHAPTER 7

Small-Sample Bias in Specific Parameters

7.1. Introduction

TSLS and FP estimates of interdependent systems are biased in small samples. OLS estimates are inconsistent, so the bias is not a function of sample size as far as the leading term is concerned. Although the degree of overfitting in URF depends on sample size, it does not produce inconsistency in the estimates of coefficients in the reduced form equations. However, it is because of overfitting in the unrestricted reduced form that TSLS estimates are biased in small samples. Increasing with the size of the system, this overfitting gave the incentive for the FP approach.

In many simple model designs of this study the bias in FP estimation of classical ID systems is in the direction of that in OLS, and in magnitude is between that of TSLS and OLS when the overidentification is strong. There are exceptions depending on the type of model and nature of the sample data. In some cases the bias in FP is smaller than that in TSLS, and in other cases it is greater than in OLS. The results in the following sections will reveal the importance of considering many models in developing general conclusions on the relative magnitude of bias in OLS, TSLS, and FP.

The degree of bias is different between estimates of structural and generated reduced form parameters. It is also different between beta

251

and gamma coefficients in the structural equations. The ranking of alternative methods of estimation with respect to degree of bias will depend on the particular parameter and situation that is selected for reference. In the remaining sections of this chapter we have attempted to give a summary of all of the different types and degrees of bias.

Our GEID models are very few and only part of the results are discussed in this chapter. The main difference between GEID and classical models is that in the GEID models the bias in TSLS is not confined to small samples; similarly, there is inconsistency in URF estimates of parameters in the reduced form equations.

In our Monte Carlo experiments the (small-sample) bias in TSLS and FP can conveniently be discussed in reference to the bias in OLS. Explicit formulas for OLS estimates in two classes of models within the classical design are given below. In the familiar two-equation model [1]

$$y_1 = \beta_1 y_2 + \gamma_1 x_1 + \gamma_2 x_2 + \delta_1 , \tag{1}$$

$$y_2 = \beta_2 y_1 + \gamma_3 x_3 + \gamma_4 x_4 + \delta_2 , \tag{2}$$

where $\sigma(x_i) = 1$; $r(x_i, \delta_j) = r(\delta_j, \delta_k) = r(x_h, x_i) = 0$ ($h, i = 1, 2, 3, 4; j, k = 1, 2$), the OLS estimates are inconsistent, as seen from their expected values:

$$E\{b_1\} = \beta_1 + \frac{\beta_2(1 - \beta_1 \beta_2)\,\sigma^2(\delta_1)}{\gamma_3^2 + \gamma_4^2 + \sigma^2(\delta_2) + \beta_2^2 \sigma^2(\delta_1)} , \tag{3}$$

$$E\{g_1\} = \gamma_1 \frac{\gamma_3^2 + \gamma_4^2 + \sigma^2(\delta_2)}{\gamma_3^2 + \gamma_4^2 + \sigma^2(\delta_2) + \beta_2^2 \sigma^2(\delta_1)} . \tag{4}$$

The estimates of $\beta_2, \gamma_2, \gamma_3$, and γ_4 can be easily determined by making appropriate substitutions in (3) and (4). If the positioning of exogenous variables is different from that shown in (1)–(2), the formulas (3)–(4) can be easily changed since their format is very simple.

In a second class of models where the number of equations is unspecified but there are only two current endogenous variables per equation (in what we have labeled a "one-loop" model with no lagged endogenous variables), the explicit expressions for OLS estimates are also simple:

Given the model

$$y_1 = \beta_1 y_2 + \gamma_1 x_1 + \delta_1, \tag{5}$$

$$y_2 = \beta_2 y_3 + \gamma_2 x_2 + \delta_2, \tag{6}$$

$$\vdots$$

$$y_m = \beta_m y_1 + \gamma_m x_m + \delta_m, \tag{7}$$

where $\sigma(x_i) = 1$; $r(x_i, \delta_j) = r(\delta_j, \delta_k) = r(x_h, x_i) = 0$ $(h, i, j, k = 1, 2, ..., m)$, the OLS estimates have the expected values

$$E\{b_1\} = \beta_1 + \frac{\beta_2\beta_3 \cdots \beta_m \ (1 - \beta_1\beta_2\beta_3 \cdots \beta_m) \ \sigma^2(\delta_1)}{K + (\beta_2\beta_3 \cdots \beta_m)^2 \sigma^2(\delta_1)}, \tag{8}$$

$$E\{g_1\} = \gamma_1 \frac{K}{K + (\beta_2\beta_3 \cdots \beta_m)^2 \sigma^2(\delta_1)}, \tag{9}$$

where

$$K = \gamma_2^2 + (\beta_2\gamma_3)^2 + (\beta_2\beta_3\gamma_4)^2 + \cdots + (\beta_2\beta_3 \cdots \beta_{m-1}\gamma_m)^2$$

$$+ [\sigma(\delta_2)]^2 + [\beta_2 \sigma(\delta_3)]^2 + [\beta_2\beta_3 \sigma(\delta_4)]^2$$

$$+ \cdots + [\beta_2\beta_3 \cdots \beta_{m-1} \sigma(\delta_m)]^2. \tag{10}$$

These formulas readily show the relative bias in estimates of beta and gamma coefficients. They also show how bias is affected by size of beta coefficients, size of residuals, and number of equations.

As mentioned earlier, these formulas will be helpful in evaluating the bias in FP and TSLS as well as OLS estimates. For example, if the total number of predetermined variables is less than the number of observations in the sample, a rough estimate of the bias in TSLS can be developed from the formula

$$\text{bias (TSLS)} = (L-1)N^{-1}\{\text{bias (OLS)}\}, \tag{11}$$

where L is the number of predetermined variables in excess of the number needed for identification of the equation and N is the number of observations in the sample.

We comment briefly on the bias in TSLS. First, if the number of predetermined variables entering the reduced form equation is equal to the number of observations in the sample, the bias in TSLS is the same as in OLS. Therefore, as models become large relative to sample size, the difference between OLS and TSLS vanishes. Second, we can gain further insight into bias in TSLS by considering the explicit expressions for bias of the order $1/N$. According to Nagar (1959) the bias in TSLS estimates of β_1 and γ_1 in (5) is as follows, for any specification of the other relations of the system,

$$
\begin{vmatrix} E(b_1 - \beta_1) \\ \\ E(g_1 - \gamma_1) \end{vmatrix} = \frac{(m-3)}{N} \begin{vmatrix} E(y_{2t}^{*2}) & E(x_{1t} y_{2t}^{*}) \\ \\ E(x_{1t} y_{2t}^{*}) & E(x_{1t}^{2}) \end{vmatrix}^{-1} \begin{vmatrix} E(\delta_{1t} \epsilon_{2t}) \\ \\ 0 \end{vmatrix} , \tag{12}
$$

where m is the total number of predetermined variables in the system and ϵ_{2t} is the residual in the reduced form equation for y_{2t}. Let us now suppose that all predetermined variables are uncorrelated and let y_{2t}^{**} denote the expression for y_{2t}^{*} (where $y_{2t}^{*} = y_{2t} - \epsilon_{2t}$) with the term containing x_{1t} excluded. Then

$$
E(b_1 - \beta_1) = \frac{(m-3)}{N E(y_{2t}^{**2})} E(\delta_{1t} \epsilon_{2t}) . \tag{13}
$$

In the special case of the one-loop system (5)–(7) we have

$$
E(y_{2t}^{**2}) = \frac{\gamma_2^2 + (\beta_2 \gamma_3)^2 + \cdots + (\beta_2 \beta_3 \cdots \beta_{m-1} \gamma_m)^2}{(1 - \beta_1 \beta_2 \cdots \beta_m)^2} \tag{14}
$$

and if $\delta_{1t}, \delta_{2t}, \ldots, \delta_{mt}$ are uncorrelated,

$$
E(\delta_{1t} \epsilon_{2t}) = \frac{\beta_2 \beta_3 \cdots \beta_m E(\delta_{1t}^2)}{1 - \beta_1 \beta_2 \cdots \beta_m} , \tag{15}
$$

whence

$$E(b_1-\beta_1) = \frac{(m-3)}{N} \; \frac{\beta_2\beta_3\cdots\beta_m(1-\beta_1\beta_2\cdots\beta_m)}{\gamma_2^2 + (\beta_2\gamma_3)^2 + \cdots + (\beta_2\beta_3\cdots\beta_{m-1}\gamma_m)^2} \; E(\delta_{1t}^2). \quad (16)$$

Furthermore it follows from formula (12) that

$$E(g_1-\gamma_1) = -\frac{E(x_{1t}y_{2t}^*)}{E(x_{1t}^2)} \; E(b_1-\beta_1), \qquad (17)$$

whence

$$E(g_1-\gamma_1) = -\frac{m-3}{N} \; \frac{\beta_2^2\beta_3^2\cdots\beta_m^2\gamma_1}{\gamma_2^2 + (\beta_2\gamma_3)^2 + \cdots + (\beta_2\beta_3\cdots\beta_{m-1}\gamma_m)^2} \; E(\delta_{1t}^2). \quad (18)$$

7.2. Small Bias in both FP and TSLS if Betas or Residuals are Small

When all beta coefficients are small, the model is near a situation where vector regression is appropriate and the troublesome problems resulting from simultaneous equations vanish. [1] This is easily seen in the explicit expressions for OLS estimates in the examples (3)–(4) and (8)–(9).

When residuals are small the proximity theorem holds (see Section 3.3.3). It is only necessary for the residuals in the reduced form equations to be small. If the beta coefficients are large, the residuals in the structural form of the model can be large even though the residuals in the reduced form are small. It is the difference between the variables y_i and their systematic parts η_i^* that causes bias in parameter estimates.

Among the 46 models in Chapter 10.2 there are 3 in which all beta coefficients are small and 2 in which the residuals in the structural equations are small. Because of the symmetrical nature of the models the four parameters listed in Table 1 show the degree of bias in the entire set of estimates of coefficients for these five models. [2]

From Table 1 it is easy to see that there is very little bias in either FP or TSLS in any of the estimates. This is true regardless of the number of

Table 7.2.1

Models with small bias in both FP and TSLS (mean and S.D. from 100 Monte Carlo samples) [1]

	β_{12}	γ_{11}	ω_{11}	ω_{21}
A. *Models in which all beta coefficients are small*				
Model 1a: Two-equation model with all betas equal to ± 0.5				
True	0.5	0.7071	0.5657	−0.2828
OLS	0.3772 (0.092)	0.6739 (0.084)	0.5876 (0.074)	−0.2296 (0.057)
TSLS	0.5026 (0.110)	0.7112 (0.091)	0.5668 (0.075)	−0.2864 (0.064)
FP	0.5028 (0.109)	0.7081 (0.090)	0.5644 (0.074)	−0.2854 (0.065)
URF			0.5647 (0.077)	−0.2919 (0.073)
Model 1i: Seven-equation one-loop model with all betas equal to ± 0.5				
True	0.5	0.5520	0.5476	−0.0086
OLS	0.4977 (0.067)	0.5550 (0.056)	0.5509 (0.055)	−0.0082 (0.003)
TSLS	0.5016 (0.069)	0.5550 (0.055)	0.5509 (0.055)	−0.0083 (0.003)
FP	0.5032 (0.068)	0.5535 (0.062)	0.5494 (0.061)	−0.0083 (0.003)
URF			0.5485 (0.080)	−0.0162 (0.083)
Model 3d: Three-equation full beta matrix with all betas equal to ± 0.5				
True	−0.5	0.5916	0.4226	0.2536
OLS	−0.1014 (0.136)	0.4812 (0.115)	0.4707 (0.107)	0.1431 (0.062)
TSLS	−0.4773 (0.288)	0.5778 (0.166)	0.4321 (0.107)	0.2366 (0.091)
FP	−0.4874 (0.286)	0.5705 (0.172)	0.4249 (0.111)	0.2415 (0.088)
URF			0.4246 (0.114)	0.2528 (0.122)
B. *Models in which the variances of residuals in structural equations are small*				
Model 5q: Two-equation model with $\sigma^2(\delta) = 0.1$				
True	1.0	0.9747	0.4873	−0.4873
OLS	0.9046 (0.074)	0.9323 (0.064)	0.5180 (0.039)	−0.4583 (0.031)
TSLS	0.9956 (0.077)	0.9767 (0.062)	0.4964 (0.037)	−0.4828 (0.030)
FP	0.9968 (0.078)	0.9801 (0.072)	0.4984 (0.043)	−0.4839 (0.035)
URF			0.4972 (0.044)	−0.4813 (0.039)
Model 2d: Seven-equation model with $\sigma^2(\delta) = 0.114$				
True	1.0	0.4781	0.2391	−0.2391
OLS	0.9411 (0.059)	0.4600 (0.054)	0.2816 (0.034)	−0.1894 (0.028)
TSLS	0.9878 (0.067)	0.4709 (0.056)	0.2528 (0.033)	−0.2206 (0.032)
FP	0.9919 (0.093)	0.4524 (0.128)	0.2410 (0.070)	−0.2120 (0.062)
URF			0.2417 (0.089)	−0.2313 (0.091)

[1] The first number is the mean, and the number in parentheses is the standard deviation of the estimates in 100 Monte Carlo samples.

current endogenous variables that appear in each structural equation (compare results for Models 3a and 3d in Chapter 10.2) and regardless of the number of equations (compare Models 1g and 1i as well as Models 2a and 2d in Chapter 10.2).

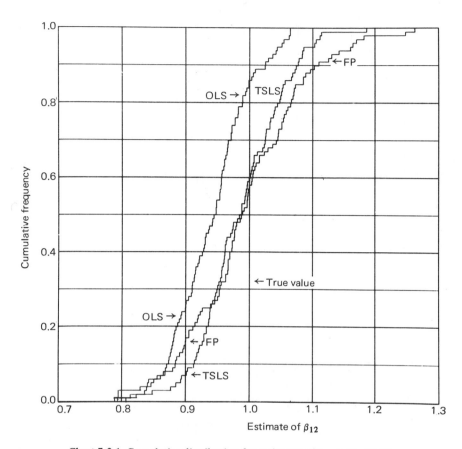

Chart 7.2.1. Cumulative distribution for estimates of β_{12} in Model 2d.

Graphs of the cumulative distributions for estimates of three parameters in Model 2d are shown in Charts 1−3. They show that FP and TSLS
are quite different with respect to dispersion of estimates, but they support the observation from Table 1 that there is practically no bias in
either FP or TSLS. Although bias in FP is small regardless of the number
of equations if all beta coefficients are small, the dispersion is affected
by the number of predetermined variables in the entire model. Dispersion of estimates will be discussed in detail in Chapter 8.

It is possible to construct Classic ID models in which neither the beta
coefficients nor the residuals in structural equations are small and FP

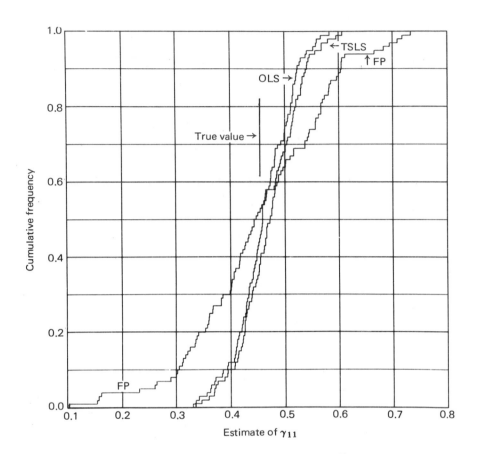

Fig. 7.2.2. Cumulative distribution for estimates of γ_{11} in Model 2d.

will have the same degree of bias as TSLS in small samples. However, these two classes of models (i.e. small betas and small residuals) are the main types for which the bias in FP and TSLS is the same, and they happen to be types for which the bias is small. The results in the next sections will show that bias in FP is considerably greater than that in TSLS in many situations where neither beta coefficients nor residuals are small.

In Classic ID systems, broadly speaking, both TSLS and FP are consistent, so the bias is in the nature of a small-sample bias. In the case of GEID systems FP will remain consistent, whereas TSLS in general will be inconsistent, giving a bias that does not tend to vanish with in-

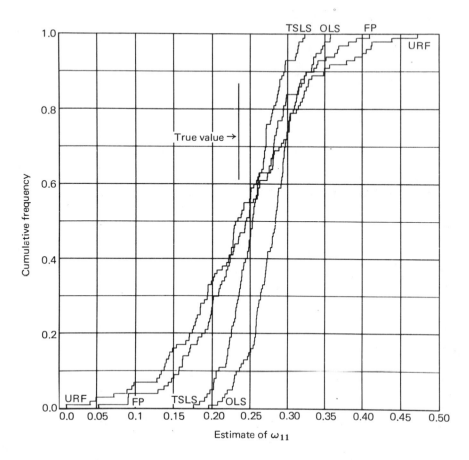

Fig. 7.2.3. Cumulative distribution for estimates of ω_{11} in Model 2d.

definitely large samples. Results in Table 9.2.1 show that bias in TSLS for the basic equation system in Model 1b becomes as great as that in FP when the correlation between residuals and exogenous variables is as small as ± 0.05. GEID models will be discussed in detail in Chapter 9.

7.3. Sample size

In applied econometrics we frequently review the trade-off between a longer (larger) sample period with more phenomena to explain and a

Table 7.3.1
Effect of increasing sample size on bias [1] (mean and S.D. from 100 Monte Carlo samples)

		Basic Model 1b			Basic Model 1d	
		Model 5f	Model 5g (= 1b)	Model 5h	Model 5i	Model 5j (= 1d)
Sample size		10	40	80	10	40
β_{12}	True	1.0	1.0	1.0	0.5	0.5
	OLS	0.6291 (0.264) [2]	0.6874 (0.136)	0.6766 (0.090)	−0.1485 (0.273)	−0.1523 (0.121)
	TSLS	0.9094 (0.387)	1.0284 (0.190)	1.0112 (0.128)	0.6124 (1.482)	0.4974 (0.252)
	FP	0.9059 (0.376)	1.0322 (0.196)	1.0127 (0.129)	0.5457 (0.747)	0.4986 (0.251)
γ_{11}	True	0.8944	0.8944	0.8944	0.8889	0.8889
	OLS	0.7514 (0.232)	0.7433 (0.118)	0.7435 (0.081)	0.5251 (0.259)	0.5276 (0.104)
	TSLS	0.8668 (0.275)	0.9040 (0.145)	0.8922 (0.095)	0.9291 (0.858)	0.8903 (0.173)
	FP	0.8502 (0.324)	0.8968 (0.176)	0.8894 (0.118)	0.8793 (0.403)	0.8887 (0.169)
ω_{11}	True	0.4472	0.4472	0.4472	0.6130	0.6130
	OLS	0.5504 (0.186)	0.5111 (0.071)	0.5141 (0.052)	0.5348 (0.725)	0.6079 (0.092)
	TSLS	0.4759 (0.151)	0.4433 (0.061)	0.4440 (0.049)	0.4891 (1.082)	0.6145 (0.076)
	FP	0.4700 (0.179)	0.4372 (0.074)	0.4418 (0.059)	0.5860 (0.168)	0.6135 (0.075)
	URF	0.4771 (0.199)	0.4384 (0.072)	0.4423 (0.059)	0.6075 (0.193)	0.6140 (0.078)
ω_{21}	True	−0.4472	−0.4472	−0.4472	−0.5517	−0.5517
	OLS	−0.3223 (0.182)	−0.3372 (0.063)	−0.3388 (0.051)	−0.4450 (0.849)	−0.5276 (0.078)
	TSLS	−0.4260 (0.155)	−0.4452 (0.062)	−0.4430 (0.045)	−0.3856 (1.541)	−0.5556 (0.071)
	FP	−0.4229 (0.199)	−0.4415 (0.078)	−0.4416 (0.056)	−0.5368 (0.174)	−0.5544 (0.073)
	URF	−0.4367 (0.197)	−0.4524 (0.067)	−0.4458 (0.048)	−0.5664 (0.202)	−0.5586 (0.077)

[1] There is considerably less bias in estimates of coefficients in the second than the first structural equation. The reason can be readily seen in the explicit expression for OLS estimates in (7.1.3)–(7.1.4).

[2] The number in parentheses is the observed standard deviation around the mean in 100 estimates. 0.1 of this number is a good estimate of the S.D. of the mean shown to the left of the parentheses.

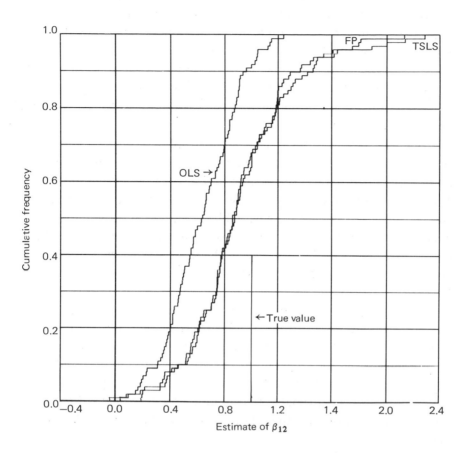

Chart 7.3.1. Cumulative distribution for estimates of β_{12} in Model 5f.

shorter sample period with less phenomena to explain. It would be helpful to know the advantages in terms of decreases in bias and dispersion
when sample size is increased, but the structure is known to remain constant. It would also be helpful to know if any one of the alternative
methods of estimation becomes clearly superior as sample size changes.

The five sets of Monte Carlo results on sample size in this study give
ample evidence that bias in FP, TSLS and OLS increases as sample size
reduces. Speaking broadly, the bias of the three methods will roughly be
of the same order of magnitude, but the relative size will vary from case
to case, largely depending upon the structure of the model. We have not
tried to press our analysis beyond this vague conclusion.

The results in Table 1, Chart 1 and Chart 6.1.1 support the above conclusions. As seen in Table 1, the dispersion of estimates is large enough that there is no discernible difference between TSLS and FP. This similarity between FP and TSLS would obviously change if sample size were less than the total number of predetermined variables since TSLS could not be used. This type of conclusion holds only when there is a fairly large difference in the degrees of freedom between the structural and reduced form equations.

Results in Table 1 show that bias in FP and TSLS is very small relative to dispersion when sample size is 10 or more times the number of predetermined variables. For example, the bias is not discernible in the 100 samples for Model 5g where there are 40 observations in the sample and a total of 4 predetermined variables in the model. It should be noted, however, that this result is based on Summers' model where the bias to the order $1/N$ vanishes for TSLS. The same holds true for FP estimates of beta coefficients because the predetermined variables are uncorrelated.

Unfortunately, it is not possible to generalize from the results in Table 1. The entire set of results indicates that the form of the model is very important in determining the effect on bias of a particular characteristic such as sample size. There are two different models in Table 1, but both of them are two-equation models with only four predetermined variables. It is probable that in models where bias in FP and TSLS are quite different, the relative bias would change with sample size.

7.4. Size of Residuals

The explicit expressions for OLS estimates in (7.1.3)–(7.1.4) and (7.1.8)–(7.1.9) show that (small-sample) bias depends on size of residuals. The bias in FP and TSLS also depend on the size of residuals.

The six models shown in Table 1 are the Monte Carlo results from models specifically designed to study the effect of size of residuals. The bias in TSLS and FP in the four models in Part A cannot be separated sharply from the dispersion around the means; this is outside the limited scope of our methods. The situation is illustrated in Charts 1 and 2. The

Table 7.4.1

Effect of increasing size of residuals on bias [1]

		A. Basic model 1b				B. Basic model 1d	
		Model 5m	Model 5n	Model 5p (= 1b)	Model 5q	Model 5r	Model 5s (= 1d)
$\sigma^2(\delta)$		1.6	1.0	0.4	0.1	1.58	0.395; 0.1
R^2		0.2	0.5	0.8	0.95	0.2	0.8
β_{12}	True	1.0	1.0	1.0	1.0	0.5	0.5
	OLS	0.0909 (0.175) [2]	0.3303 (0.168)	0.6874 (0.136)	0.9046 (0.074)	−0.6849 (0.115)	−0.1523 (0.121)
	TSLS	1.1077 (1.099)	0.9547 (0.392)	1.0284 (0.190)	0.9956 (0.077)	−0.1613 (1.486)	0.4974 (0.252)
	FP	1.0589 (1.086)	0.9614 (0.402)	1.0322 (0.196)	0.9968 (0.078)	0.0247 (0.975)	0.4986 (0.251)
γ_{11}	True	0.4472	0.7071	0.8944	0.9747	0.4443	0.8889
	OLS	0.2449 (0.142)	0.4777 (0.145)	0.7433 (0.118)	0.9323 (0.064)	0.1110 (0.120)	0.5276 (0.104)
	TSLS	0.4722 (0.390)	0.6926 (0.191)	0.9040 (0.145)	0.9767 (0.062)	0.2631 (0.419)	0.8903 (0.173)
	FP	0.4347 (0.362)	0.6950 (0.204)	0.8968 (0.176)	0.9801 (0.072)	0.3054 (0.305)	0.8887 (0.169)
ω_{13}	True	0.2236	0.3536	0.4472	0.4873	0.0773	0.1544
	OLS	0.2269 (0.052)	0.1437 (0.079)	0.3499 (0.069)	0.4602 (0.032)	−0.3028 (0.200)	−0.0839 (0.075)
	TSLS	0.2137 (0.132)	0.3424 (0.123)	0.4475 (0.071)	0.4855 (0.033)	0.0296 (0.206)	0.1425 (0.053)
	FP	0.2015 (0.128)	0.3332 (0.130)	0.4433 (0.079)	0.4879 (0.036)	0.0204 (0.144)	0.1372 (0.057)
	URF	0.2318 (0.155)	0.3589 (0.133)	0.4520 (0.087)	0.4835 (0.039)	0.0738 (0.166)	0.1526 (0.083)
ω_{23}	True	0.2236	0.3536	0.4472	0.4873	0.1545	0.3087
	OLS	0.2837 (0.159)	0.4362 (0.125)	0.5143 (0.073)	0.5104 (0.035)	0.4338 (0.252)	0.5068 (0.086)
	TSLS	0.2665 (0.161)	0.3742 (0.092)	0.4414 (0.064)	0.4890 (0.032)	0.1736 (0.225)	0.3095 (0.059)
	FP	0.2531 (0.145)	0.3577 (0.121)	0.4372 (0.078)	0.4908 (0.035)	0.1303 (0.198)	0.3000 (0.084)
	URF	0.2418 (0.146)	0.3562 (0.120)	0.4391 (0.079)	0.4920 (0.035)	0.1371 (0.171)	0.3000 (0.086)

[1] The bias in estimates of the second is less than in the first structural equation. Likewise, there is less bias in estimates of coefficients of variables x_1 and x_2 than variables x_3 and x_4 in the reduced form equations.

[2] The number in parentheses is the observed standard deviation around the mean of 100 Monte Carlo estimates shown just to the left of each parenthesis. 0.1 of this number is a good estimate of the S.D. of the mean.

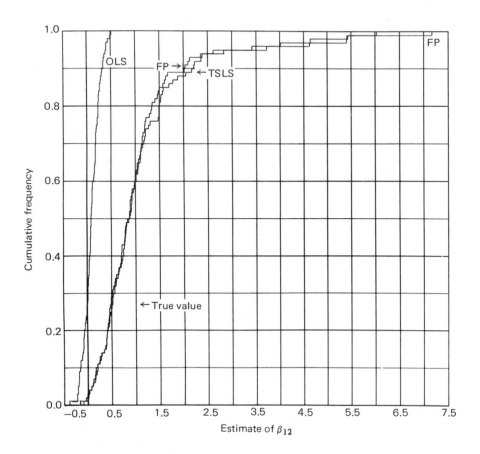

Chart 7.4.1. Cumulative distribution for estimates of β_{12} in Model 5m.

median and the mode of the distribution for TSLS and FP are to the
left of the true value of the coefficient, but there is a long upper tail.
As Basmann has pointed out, the moments for TSLS do not exist in
some cases; see Basmann [3]. This is one of the reasons why we place
much emphasis on the distributional properties of our sets of 100 replications of the Monte Carlo experiments using the distributions to check
and supplement the information gained from observed averages and
standard deviations. Results such as those presented in Table 1 and
Charts 1 and 2 are interesting and valuable even if the moments do not
exist.

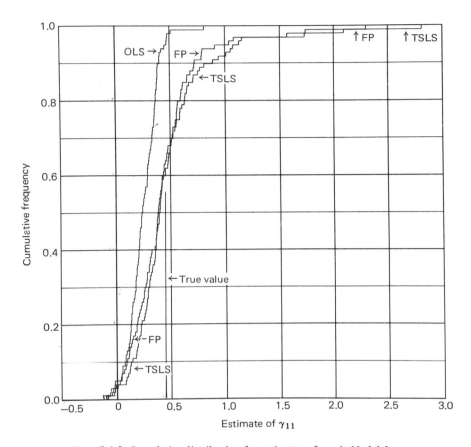

Chart 7.4.2. Cumulative distribution for estimates of γ_{11} in Model 5m.

Sketches and accompanying discussion of typical probability distributions are presented in Chapter 13. However, these sketches should not be considered sufficiently accurate to draw general conclusions with respect to degree of bias in FP and TSLS. The results in Part A of Table 1 show that bias for OLS is larger than the standard deviation around the mean but that the reverse is true for FP and TSLS. For a single set of estimates the error from the bias component in FP and TSLS is smaller than that from the dispersion around the mean.

When comparing Parts A and B in Table 1 we again see evidence of the effect of different sizes of beta coefficients. Two specific trends are

evident in Part B but not in Part A. First, bias in FP relative to the standard deviation around the mean increases as size of residuals increases.
Second, TSLS becomes more biased than FP as residuals become large.
In contrast, Charts 1 and 2 show no significant difference between FP
and TSLS. Graphs of the estimates for Model 5r are not available.

The individual parameters selected for Table 1 and Charts 1 and 2
were those for which bias in all methods was the largest. However, there
is no discernible difference in the relative bias among the methods between the parameters shown and the other parameters of the model
(see complete results in Chapter 10.2).

The results for Model 5r in Table 1 show that the bias in OLS, TSLS,
and FP estimates of structural parameters carries over into estimates of
reduced form coefficients. The relative bias among the methods is very
similar in all reduced form coefficients, but the absolute level is quite
different among the four different sets of reduced form coefficients. This
is easily seen since the parameters selected for presentation in Table 1
are those for which bias was the largest. Typical results for reduced form
coefficients are given in Part C of the tables in Chapter 10.2.

We know from the proximity theorem that bias in all methods is small
if the residuals are small (see Section 3.3.3). The results presented and
discussed in this chapter show that bias in all methods can become
severe as residuals become large. However, the size of beta coefficients
has a large effect on the relationship between bias and size of residuals.
This important aspect will be discussed in Chapter 7.6.

7.5. Number of Predetermined Variables

Although the results for the three Series 1g–1i, 2a–2d, and 2e–2g
show distinct trends in the predictive power for all methods (see 4.4.4
and 4.4.5) there are only slight discernable trends in the bias for any of
the methods in these three series of models. Table 1 gives the relevant
results for Series 2a–2d and 2e–2g. Results for the Series 1g–1i are not
shown because bias is not a serious problem in any of the models because all beta coefficients are small.

With one exception the results for Models 2g and 2d in Table 1 show
a difference in bias and dispersion even though the number of predeter-

Table 7.5.1

Effect of increasing number of predetermined variables on bias and dispersion [1]

	A. Greater number of variables per equation			B. Greater number of equations	
	Model 2e (= 1b)	Model 2f	Model 2g	Model 2a (= 1b)	Model 2d
Total number of predetermined variables	4	8	14	4	14
Number of equations	2	2	2	2	7
Number of variables per equation	4	6	9	4	4
$\sigma^2(\delta)$	0.4	0.4	0.4	0.4	0.1143
$\sigma^2(\epsilon)$	0.2	0.2	0.2	0.2	0.2
β_{12} True	1.0	1.0	1.0	1.0	1.0
OLS	0.6874 (0.136)	0.6487 (0.138)	0.6691 (0.138)	0.6874 (0.136)	0.9411 (0.059)
TSLS	1.0284 (0.190)	0.9640 (0.172)	0.9106 (0.162)	1.0284 (0.190)	0.9878 (0.067)
FP	1.0322 (0.196)	0.9647 (0.173)	0.9231 (0.165)	1.0322 (0.196)	0.9919 (0.093)
γ_{11} True	0.8944	0.6325	0.4781	0.8944	0.4781
OLS	0.7433 (0.118)	0.5212 (0.101)	0.4031 (0.111)	0.7433 (0.118)	0.4600 (0.054)
TSLS	0.9040 (0.145)	0.6171 (0.113)	0.4580 (0.124)	0.9040 (0.145)	0.4709 (0.056)
FP	0.8968 (0.176)	0.6248 (0.144)	0.4542 (0.137)	0.8968 (0.176)	0.4524 (0.128)
ω_{11} True	0.4472	0.3162	0.2390	0.4472	0.2390
OLS	0.5111 (0.071)	0.3620 (0.063)	0.2787 (0.070)	0.5111 (0.071)	0.2816 (0.034)
TSLS	0.4433 (0.061)	0.3168 (0.055)	0.2499 (0.064)	0.4433 (0.061)	0.2528 (0.033)
FP	0.4372 (0.074)	0.3179 (0.066)	0.2443 (0.069)	0.4372 (0.074)	0.2410 (0.070)
URF	0.4384 (0.072)	0.3197 (0.073)	0.2424 (0.092)	0.4384 (0.072)	0.2417 (0.089)
ω_{21} True	-0.4472	-0.3162	-0.2390	-0.4472	-0.2390
OLS	-0.3372 (0.063)	-0.2440 (0.057)	-0.1837 (0.055)	-0.3372 (0.063)	-0.1894 (0.028)
TSLS	-0.4452 (0.062)	-0.3102 (0.060)	-0.2278 (0.062)	-0.4452 (0.062)	-0.2206 (0.032)
FP	-0.4415 (0.078)	-0.3149 (0.074)	-0.2260 (0.067)	-0.4415 (0.078)	-0.2120 (0.062)
URF	-0.4524 (0.067)	-0.3124 (0.081)	-0.2355 (0.092)	-0.4524 (0.067)	-0.2313 (0.091)

[1] These results are the mean and standard deviation for the 100 Monte Carlo estimates. One-tenth of the standard deviation given in the parentheses is a good estimate of the standard deviation of the mean shown to the left of the parentheses.

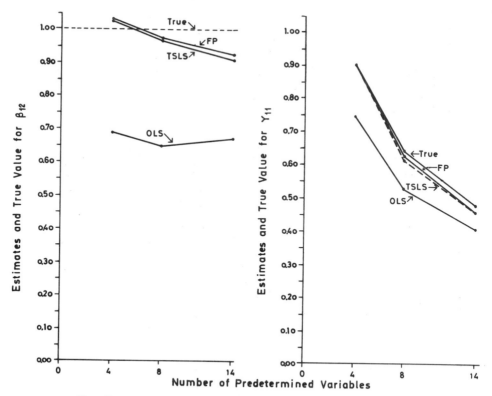

Chart 7.5.1. Bias and number of predetermined variables in the model
(data from Models 2e, 2f and 2g shown in Table 1).

mined variables is the same. This is because the variance of δ is only 0.1143 in Model 2d compared to 0.4000 in Model 2g. Both models were designed to have the same R^2 and therefore variance of δ had to be different. The FP estimates of gamma coefficients are an exception to the marked regularity of less bias in Model 2d than in 2g. Tables 10.2.15 and 10.2.17 show that the relative degree of bias and dispersion in FP estimates of all gamma coefficients in Models 2d and 2g is approximately the same as shown for γ_{11} in Table 1.

We know that bias in TSLS estimates increases as number of predetermined variables increase because of the greater amount of overfitting in the first stage. In Chart 1 the trend is clearly evident in the case of β_{12} but not evident for γ_{11}. In Table 1 we can see that dispersion around the mean is too large to allow us to detect any trend in the bias of gamma coefficients among Models 2e−2g.

Except for OLS there is very little bias in estimates of reduced form coefficients.

In summary we can say that bias increases as number of predetermined variables increases because of the greater amount of overfitting in the reduced form. Although the FP method does not depend on the reduced form and estimates do not have to start with URF, the bias in FP does increase as number of predetermined variables increases regardless of whether the greater number of variables arises because of greater number of equations or greater number of predetermined variables per equation. The bias is somewhat less pronounced for FP than for TSLS.

7.6. Specific Values of Beta Coefficients that Lead to Large Bias

We know from Chapters 5 and 6 that, in general, interdependent systems can be readily estimated by the TSLS or FP procedures if the beta coefficients are small or moderate (weak interdependence). When the betas are large the situation becomes more complex, and there are models where the estimation by FP and related methods becomes difficult or impossible.

Chart 1 was developed in an attempt to illustrate by way of some few two-equation models how bias in FP varies in relation to bias in TSLS and OLS. These graphs must be interpreted with caution because of the large sampling variation. Table 1 gives the standard deviation around the mean for the Monte Carlo results. The vertical tolerance intervals around the observed values for the FP estimates in Chart 1 were developed from the formula

$$\text{limits} = \frac{\text{mean } \alpha \pm 0.2 \text{ (S.D.)} - \text{true } \alpha}{\text{true } \alpha}, \tag{1}$$

where the middle term of the numerator is 2 times 0.1 of the standard deviation around the mean as measured in the 100 Monte Carlo samples. The distributions appear to be close enough to the normal that we can have a high confidence in statistical tests that show significant differences in the degree of bias relative to the true value of the coefficient among the models in part A of Table 1.

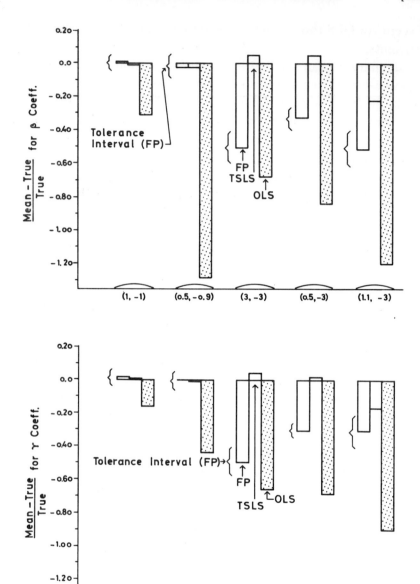

Chart 7.6.1. Bias in two-equation model as a function of size of beta coefficients
(data from Table 1, part A).

Table 7.6.1
Size of beta coefficients and magnitude of bias [1]

	β, selected [2]	γ, selected [2]	ω_{1i}	ω_{2i}
A. Two-equation models				
Model 1b	$\beta_{12} = 1$	$\gamma_{11} = 0.8944$	$\omega_{13} = 0.4472$	$\omega_{23} = 0.4472$
OLS	0.6874 (0.136)	0.7433 (0.118)	0.3499 (0.069)	0.5143 (0.073)
TSLS	1.0284 (0.190)	0.9040 (0.145)	0.4475 (0.071)	0.4414 (0.064)
FP	1.0322 (0.196)	0.8968 (0.176)	0.4433 (0.079)	0.4372 (0.078)
URF			0.4520 (0.087)	0.4391 (0.079)
Model 1d	$\beta_{12} = 0.5$	$\gamma_{11} = 0.8889$	$\omega_{13} = 0.1544$	$\omega_{23} = 0.3087$
OLS	−0.1523 (0.121)	0.5276 (0.104)	−0.0839 (0.075)	0.5068 (0.086)
TSLS	0.4974 (0.252)	0.8903 (0.173)	0.1425 (0.053)	0.3095 (0.059)
FP	0.4986 (0.251)	0.8887 (0.169)	0.1372 (0.057)	0.3000 (0.084)
URF			0.1526 (0.083)	0.3000 (0.086)
Model 1c	$\beta_{21} = -3.0$	$\gamma_{23} = 2.0$	$\omega_{11} = 0.2$	$\omega_{21} = -0.6$
OLS	−0.8802 (0.305)	0.7216 (0.255)	0.4002 (0.113)	−0.3359 (0.112)
TSLS	−3.2111 (1.268)	2.0858 (0.796)	0.2077 (0.064)	−0.5994 (0.074)
FP	−1.7610 (1.041)	0.9669 (0.845)	0.2172 (0.126)	−0.3503 (0.234)
URF			0.1929 (0.072)	−0.6057 (0.078)
Model 1e	$\beta_{21} = -3.0$	$\gamma_{23} = 2.0843$	$\omega_{11} = 0.2636$	$\omega_{21} = -0.7907$
OLS	0.6819 (0.313)	0.6806 (0.257)	0.5006 (0.076)	−0.3278 (0.137)
TSLS	−3.2261 (1.403)	2.1788 (0.886)	0.2678 (0.086)	−0.7642 (0.099)
FP	−2.0627 (0.462)	1.4067 (0.290)	0.3002 (0.066)	−0.6165 (0.170)
URF			0.2535 (0.102)	−0.8001 (0.108)
Model 1f	$\beta_{21} = -3.0$	$\gamma_{23} = 2.4460$	$\omega_{11} = 0.0922$	$\omega_{21} = -0.2765$
OLS	0.5276 (0.235)	0.2421 (0.180)	0.1510 (4.598)	−0.1744 (4.152)
TSLS	−2.3432 (3.508)	1.9527 (2.080)	0.1100 (0.095)	−0.2613 (0.090)
FP	−1.7233 (1.906)	1.6171 (1.182)	0.0619 (0.310)	−0.1818 (0.246)
URF			0.0842 (0.072)	−0.2855 (0.073)
B. Specially designed models: 3−5 equations				
Model 4a	$\beta_{12} = 0.157$	$\gamma_{11} = 0.339$	$\omega_{11} = -0.0096$	$\omega_{21} = -0.3843$
OLS	0.1167 (0.062)	0.3018 (0.056)	0.0435 (0.076)	−0.5328 (0.192)
TSLS	0.1523 (0.161)	0.3365 (0.076)	0.0053 (0.075)	−0.4402 (0.175)
FP	2.5085 (2.327)	−0.1212 (4.535)	0.0122 (0.075)	−0.4189 (0.150)
URF			0.0015 (0.074)	−0.4189 (0.150)
Model 4b	$\beta_{13} = 4.10$	$\gamma_{11} = -4.0$	$\omega_{11} = 0.556$	$\omega_{21} = 0.556$
OLS	4.0880 (0.047)	−3.9867 (0.049)	0.5746 (0.053)	0.5412 (0.039)
TSLS	4.1054 (0.049)	−4.0037 (0.050)	0.5446 (0.054)	0.5634 (0.040)
FP	0.2223 (1.735)	−0.2048 (1.676)	0.8230 (4.169)	0.2358 (1.344)
URF			0.5315 (0.089)	0.5717 (0.067)

Table 7.6.1
(continued)

Model 3c	$\beta_{12} = 2.0$	$\gamma_{11} = 0.982$	$\omega_{11} = 0.1091$	$\omega_{21} = -0.4364$
OLS	0.6016 (0.193)	0.3691 (0.148)	0.2984 (0.115)	−0.1150 (0.055)
TSLS	1.5760 (0.715)	0.7835 (0.347)	0.1657 (0.065)	−0.3950 (0.104)
FP	1.0240 (0.476)	0.2479 (0.223)	0.1208 (0.122)	−0.1308 (0.129)
URF			0.1057 (0.106)	−0.4382 (0.131)
Model 3b	$\beta_{12} = 1.0$	$\gamma_{11} = 0.5773$	$\omega_{11} = 0.2887$	$\omega_{21} = -0.2887$
OLS	0.5954 (0.145)	0.4551 (0.113)	0.3751 (0.092)	−0.1368 (0.049)
TSLS	0.9348 (0.248)	0.5515 (0.140)	0.3051 (0.080)	−0.2660 (0.084)
FP	0.9303 (0.282)	0.5228 (0.169)	0.2904 (0.097)	−0.2539 (0.095)
URF			0.2894 (0.096)	−0.2880 (0.131)

[1] Data in this table are the mean and standard deviation of 100 Monte Carlo estimates. One-tenth of the standard deviation shown in parentheses is a good estimate of the standard deviation of the mean shown just to the left of the parentheses.

[2] For Models 1b, 1d, 4a, 3c, and 3b the beta coefficient is β_{12} and the gamma coefficient is γ_{11}. For Models 1c, 1e and 1f the beta coefficient is β_{21} and the gamma coefficient is γ_{23}. For Model 4b the beta coefficient is β_{13} and the gamma coefficient is γ_{11}. Coefficients selected for Table 1 are those for which bias was largest. See tables in Chapter 10.2 for complete results on all models.

The explicit expressions for OLS estimates in (7.1.3)–(7.1.4) and (7.1.8)–(7.1.9) show how the values of beta coefficients affect bias in TSLS and OLS estimates. Chart 1 shows that the bias in FP in two-equation models is generally between that in OLS and TSLS. However, in the subsequent discussion of Part B of Table 1 we will see that this statement does not hold for all models. We recall from Table 5.3.1 that for Model 1c, at least, the bias in FP becomes greater as the convergence criterion is made more stringent. That is, in Model 1c the bias was considerably less when the criterion was 10^{-3} instead of 10^{-6} (see Table 5.3.1). We also recall from Chapter 5 that this feature is related to the phenomenon of apparent convergence.

For all these methods there are two sets of values for beta coefficients that lead to large bias. Bias on the whole is large when beta coefficients are large. From the sampling experiment it has also been found that bias is large when only part of the beta coefficients are close to one in absolute value. Model 1d leads to larger bias than Model 1b because only one of the coefficients is close to ±1. Models 1c and 1e lead to large bias because of one or more large beta coefficients. Model 1f has both features that lead to large bias since β_{12} is near unity and β_{21} is very large.

The relative bias in estimates of reduced form coefficients among OLS, TSLS and FP is approximately the same as in estimates of structural coefficients. Bias in the former is more difficult to analyze and summarize because each estimate is a function of the estimates of several structural coefficients. In Part A of Table 1 bias in relation to the true value is generally smaller in the reduced form than in the structural equations. [1] Also, the situation of bias in FP lying between that in OLS and TSLS does not hold for the reduced form coefficients.

The bias in the four models listed in Part B of Table 1 is more difficult to analyze because of the peculiar convergence problems that were encountered for FP. None of the 100 samples in Model 4b and only 36 of the samples in Model 3c converged with a convergence criterion of 10^{-6}. Only 50 of the samples in Model 4a converged with a criterion of 10^{-6}; all samples converged with a criterion of 10^{-3} which was used to obtain the results for Model 4a presented in this monograph. The analysis of apparent convergence and Ågren's criterion for the convergence of the FP and FFP methods in Chapters 5 and 6 explain many of the irregular features of Chart 1.

Although the variance of FP estimates in Models 4a and 4b is large, the results give clear indication of a large bias, larger than for OLS: In Model 3b with moderate size beta coefficients the bias in FP is significantly less than that for OLS estimates. In Model 3c the relationship between OLS and FP is not easy to summarize because it differs among the various structural coefficients.

In summary we can state that the size of beta coefficients has a large effect on the bias in all three methods for estimating structural coefficients. Since the values of beta coefficients are not known in applied econometrics it is difficult or impossible to make general statements about relative bias for any of the methods in applied work.

Statements are sometimes made to the effect that OLS estimates are biased toward zero. Even this generalization is true only in certain situations. For instance, in Summers' model it holds either if the two beta coefficients have different signs or if their product exceeds one. For the one-loop model in (7.1.5)–(7.1.7) similar conditions hold.

These results help point out the difficulty that can be expected in deriving mathematical expressions for small-sample distributions for any method of estimation. The specific values of most, if not all, the parameters in the model being estimated will have to be carried in the expressions for the distributions. [2]

These results also point out the fact that one can design a model such that any specified method will be better than other methods for any arbitrary criterion such as bias, dispersion, or predictive power. It was because of this observation that the authors designed the Monte Carlo research to include a wide range of models. The size of beta coefficients was one of the most important dimensions in the design of different models.

7.7. Lagged Endogenous Variables and Inter-Correlations among Exogenous Variables

The presence of lagged endogenous variables and correlations among exogenous variables leads to greater multicollinearity in both the reduced form and structural equations. The eigenvalue for the product moment matrix of predetermined variables shown at the bottom of Table 1 gives one measure of multicollinearity. Actually, the three models with lagged endogenous variables (5c—5e) do not show any higher degree of multicollinearity than comparable models having no lagged variables (1b and 5q). The rationale in designing Models 5c—5e involved obtaining different positioning of lagged variables within each structural equation.

Models 5c—5e with lagged endogenous variables are not strictly comparable to any of the models without lags because of different size residuals. Among the models without lagged variables Model 5q is the most similar to Models 5c—5e.

For all methods the degree of bias appears not to be significantly affected by the presence of lagged variables or correlations of the order ± 0.7 among exogenous variables. Charts 1—3 show the distributions for coefficients β_{12}, γ_{11} and γ_{12} in Model 5e. There is no apparent difference between the distribution for γ_{11} which has lagged variables (Chart 2) and the distribution of γ_{11} in Model 1b which has no lagged variables (Chart 6.1.2).

The effect of lagged endogenous variables is discussed in more detail

Table 7.7.1

Bias and presence of lagged endogenous variables and correlations among exogenous variables [1]

	With and without correlations among exogenous variables			With and without lagged endogenous variables			
	Model 1b	Model 5a	Model 5b	Model 5q	Model 5c	Model 5d	Model 5e
$\sigma^2(\delta)$	0.4	0.4	0.4	0.10	0.212	0.144	0.144
$\sigma^2(\epsilon)$	0.2	0.2	0.2	0.05	0.100	0.070	0.070
1st eq.				no lag	$y_{1,t-1}$ & $y_{2,t-1}$	$y_{2,t-1}$	$y_{1,t-1}$
2nd eq.				no lag	no lag	$y_{1,t-1}$	$y_{2,t-1}$
β_{12}	1.0	1.0	1.0	0.9747	1.0	1.0	1.0
OLS	0.6874 (0.136)	0.6572 (0.132)	0.6855 (0.128)	0.9046 (0.074)	0.8847 (0.077)	0.8619 (0.097)	0.8587 (0.095)
TSLS	1.0284 (0.190)	0.9709 (0.154)	0.9971 (0.173)	0.9956 (0.077)	0.9949 (0.082)	1.0068 (0.098)	1.0095 (0.107)
FP	1.0322 (0.196)	0.9677 (0.158)	0.9952 (0.181)	0.9968 (0.079)	0.9966 (0.084)	1.0095 (0.104)	1.0086 (0.108)
γ_{11}	0.8944	0.6845	1.65	0.9747	0.3	1.1314	1.1314
OLS	0.7433 (0.118)	0.5610 (0.135)	1.3913 (0.154)	0.9323 (0.064)	0.7344 (0.096)	1.0489 (0.096)	1.0502 (0.099)
TSLS	0.9040 (0.145)	0.6658 (0.136)	1.6474 (0.189)	0.9767 (0.062)	0.7744 (0.101)	1.1299 (0.093)	1.1348 (0.103)
FP	0.8968 (0.176)	0.6377 (0.204)	1.6357 (0.215)	0.9801 (0.072)	0.7660 (0.111)	1.1373 (0.101)	1.1318 (0.114)
ω_{11}	0.4472	0.3423	0.8750	0.4873	0.4	0.5657	0.5657
OLS	0.5111 (0.071)	0.3897 (0.089)	0.9651 (0.108)	0.5180 (0.039)	0.5454 (0.066)	0.6005 (0.050)	0.6052 (0.049)
TSLS	0.4433 (0.061)	0.3418 (0.068)	0.8344 (0.099)	0.4964 (0.037)	0.3938 (0.077)	0.5575 (0.044)	0.5632 (0.049)
FP	0.4372 (0.074)	0.3274 (0.105)	0.8312 (0.108)	0.4984 (0.043)	0.3891 (0.083)	0.5607 (0.046)	0.5624 (0.053)
URF	0.4384 (0.072)	0.3287 (0.111)	0.8321 (0.107)	0.4972 (0.044)	0.3856 (0.082)	0.5605 (0.046)	0.5602 (0.055)
ω_{21}	-0.4472	-0.3423	-0.8750	-0.4783	-0.4	-0.5657	-0.5657
OLS	-0.3372 (0.063)	-0.2599 (0.069)	-0.6258 (0.110)	-0.4583 (0.031)	-0.2154 (0.099)	-0.5189 (0.045)	-0.5172 (0.059)
TSLS	-0.4452 (0.062)	-0.3349 (0.075)	-0.8171 (0.102)	-0.4828 (0.030)	-0.3832 (0.082)	-0.5680 (0.042)	-0.5657 (0.049)
FP	-0.4415 (0.078)	-0.3225 (0.110)	-0.8135 (0.111)	-0.4839 (0.035)	-0.3787 (0.085)	-0.5705 (0.046)	-0.5638 (0.054)
URF	-0.4524 (0.067)	-0.3515 (0.094)	-0.8213 (0.103)	-0.4813 (0.039)	-0.3881 (0.084)	-0.5648 (0.048)	-0.5669 (0.050)

Mean of smallest eigenvalue for product moment matrix used in estimating coefficients in first structural equation

	Model 1b	Model 5a	Model 5b	Model 5q	Model 5c	Model 5d	Model 5e
OLS	0.1061	0.0869	0.0495	0.0973	0.0791	0.1013	0.0911
TSLS	0.0799	0.0809	0.0423	0.0910	0.0795	0.0919	0.0816
FP	0.0810	0.0818	0.0433	0.0910	0.0800	0.0927	0.0822

Mean of smallest eigenvalue for product moment matrix used in estimating coefficients in second structural equation

	Model 1b	Model 5a	Model 5b	Model 5q	Model 5c	Model 5d	Model 5e
OLS	0.1196	0.0915	0.0489	0.1035	0.0328	0.1059	0.0902
TSLS	0.0915	0.0842	0.0408	0.0977	0.0165	0.0972	0.0808
FP	0.0920	0.0948	0.0413	0.0983	0.0167	0.0977	0.0815

Mean of smallest eigenvalue for product moment matrix used in estimating coefficients in URF

	Model 1b	Model 5a	Model 5b	Model 5q	Model 5c	Model 5d	Model 5e
URF	0.1520	0.0544	0.0550	0.1472	0.0641	0.1432	0.1408

[1] The number in parentheses is the observed standard deviation around the mean in 100 estimates. 0.1 of this number is a good estimate of the S.D. of the mean shown to the left of the parentheses.

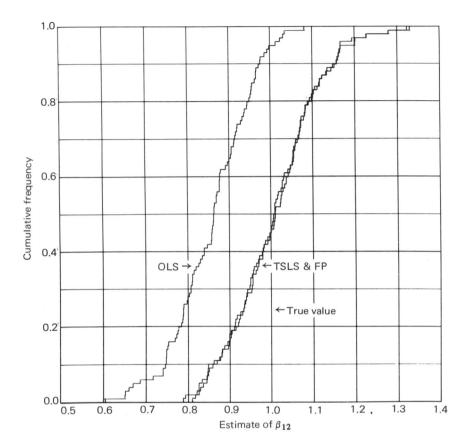

Chart 7.7.1. Cumulative distribution for estimates of β_{12} in Model 5e.

in Chapter 13 where the distribution of estimates for each method is compared with the normal distribution.

With respect to bias it appears that lagged endogenous variables can in most cases be treated like exogenous variables in interpreting empirical results. It also appears that multicollinearity of a degree present in Models 5a–5e does not have a significant effect on bias. This is no way should be construed to indicate that multicollinearity is not a serious problem in applied econometrics. It is indeed such a severe problem that in many empirical studies estimates are not even out of the vicinity of

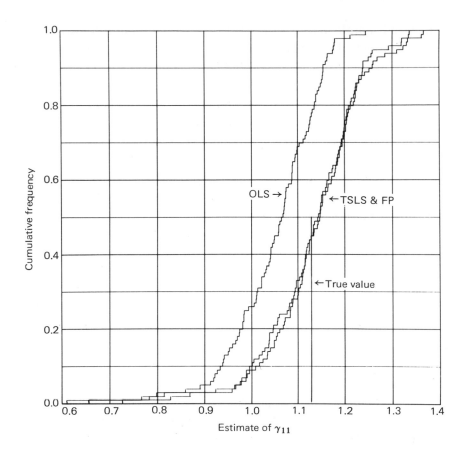

Chart 7.7.2. Cumulative distribution for estimates of γ_{11} in Model 5e.

rounding error, let alone a reliable measure of the effect of the so-called independent variable on the dependent variable. We point out that the degree of multicollinearity in Models 5a–5e is much less than we have observed in most applied econometric work. Unfortunately, the general topic of multicollinearity is much too complex to be adequately treated in this monograph. [1]

The theoretical results by A.L.Nagar and E.Lyttkens referred to in 3.9.2–3.9.4 shed light on some of the features discussed above. We spell out some implications of their formulas as applied to our 46 models. [2]

The small-sample bias of TSLS is on the whole small for slightly over-identified models. If a structural relation has one more parameter than needed for just identification, the small-sample bias of TSLS is of order c_2/N^2, the term c_1/N being absent, because $c_1 = 0$. This is in particular so for Summers' model with its six and eight coefficients in the structural and reduced forms, respectively. Thus for Summers' model the situation with regard to small-sample bias is to the advantage of TSLS relative to other methods, and in particular to FP estimates. Of the 46 models analysed in detail in this investigation, 18 are of Summers' type.

The general observation that TSLS is less biased than FP needs some qualification because most of our 46 models are designed so that the exogenous variables x_i are mutually uncorrelated. The small-sample bias of the FP estimates is then of order c/N^2 for the beta coefficients, and in general of order c/N for the gamma coefficients.

A related aspect is that in the cases of just identification and two variables in excess of the number needed for just identification, respectively, the small-sample bias of TSLS is numerically the same, but with different signs. For most of the Summers' models in our analysis, the bias in FP is the same as in TSLS for the betas, whereas the bias in general is larger for the gammas.

Another feature to the advantage of TSLS relative to FP for some of our models is that if the structural residuals are uncorrelated, the gamma estimates will have larger standard errors for FP than for TSLS.

As to the existence of moments of the FP estimates, the means but not the standard errors exist for Summers' model. For our one-loop models (Series 2a–d) the standard deviations exist for $n = 3$, but not for $n = 4$.

Finally, a comment on URF estimates: In GEID models URF in general is inconsistent for all parameters of the reduced form. In the special case of uncorrelated exonous variables, URF is inconsistent for the coefficient w_{ik} of a variable x_k that is correlated with the residual ϵ_i of the same relation, but for other coefficients it is consistent.

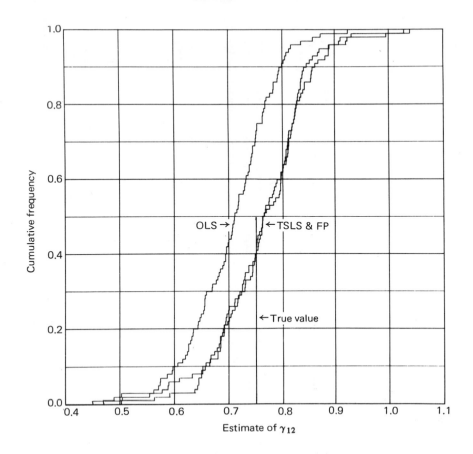

Chart 7.7.3. Cumulative distribution for estimates of γ_{12} in Model 5e.

7.8. GEID Specifications

For GEID (general interdependent) systems as defined in 1.4.5 FP is a consistent method, but there is a small-sample bias. The methods of OLS, TSLS, and URF are not consistent and there are both small-sample and large-sample bias. [1]

The inconsistency and small-sample bias vary from model to model. Hence, it is not possible to state that the bias in FP is less than that in

Table 7.8.1

Effect on bias of increasing size of correlations within the GEID specification [1]

Size corr.		Model 6e (= 5n) 0.0	Model 6f ± 0.01	Model 6g ± 0.05	Model 6h ± 0.10	Model 6i ± 0.20	Model 6j ± 0.40
β_{12}	True	1.0	1.0	1.0	1.0	1.0	1.0
	OLS	0.3303 (0.168)	0.3127 (0.166)	0.3230 (0.187)	0.3515 (0.150)	0.3673 (0.157)	0.5785 (0.227)
	TSLS	0.9547 (0.392)	0.9509 (0.354)	1.0272 (0.416)	0.9685 (0.340)	1.0158 (0.365)	1.0231 (0.363)
	FP	0.9614 (0.402)	0.9620 (0.351)	1.0262 (0.420)	0.9640 (0.337)	1.0247 (0.351)	1.0299 (0.456)
γ_{11}	True	0.7071	0.7071	0.7071	0.7071	0.7071	0.7071
	OLS	0.4777 (0.145)	0.4683 (0.142)	0.4772 (0.142)	0.4392 (0.134)	0.3898 (0.110)	0.3416 (0.129)
	TSLS	0.6926 (0.191)	0.6867 (0.208)	0.6869 (0.198)	0.6042 (0.168)	0.4782 (0.143)	0.3226 (0.155)
	FP	0.6950 (0.204)	0.6743 (0.225)	0.7335 (0.207)	0.6542 (0.203)	0.6712 (0.194)	0.6681 (0.235)
ω_{11}	True	0.3536	0.3536	0.3536	0.3536	0.3536	0.3536
	OLS	0.4304 (0.124)	0.4256 (0.125)	0.4348 (0.126)	0.3993 (0.123)	0.3466 (0.099)	0.2650 (0.108)
	TSLS	0.3659 (0.100)	0.3542 (0.098)	0.3554 (0.103)	0.3239 (0.103)	0.2529 (0.081)	0.1796 (0.099)
	FP	0.3662 (0.105)	0.3468 (0.116)	0.3790 (0.111)	0.3501 (0.117)	0.3496 (0.101)	0.3631 (0.116)
	URF	0.3668 (0.102)	0.3456 (0.120)	0.3778 (0.111)	0.3520 (0.116)	0.3515 (0.097)	0.3642 (0.075)
ω_{21}	True	-0.3536	-0.3536	-0.3536	-0.3536	-0.3536	-0.3536
	OLS	-0.1467 (0.073)	-0.1457 (0.072)	-0.1491 (0.083)	-0.1257 (0.061)	-0.1243 (0.064)	-0.1412 (0.068)
	TSLS	-0.3466 (0.105)	-0.3480 (0.090)	-0.3256 (0.095)	-0.2942 (0.082)	-0.2324 (0.087)	-0.1514 (0.079)
	FP	-0.3480 (0.112)	-0.3407 (0.104)	-0.3482 (0.098)	-0.3151 (0.089)	-0.3154 (0.092)	-0.2996 (0.106)
	URF	-0.3469 (0.125)	-0.3544 (0.112)	-0.3003 (0.121)	-0.2645 (0.110)	-0.1254 (0.101)	-0.0446 (0.072)

[1] The first number is the mean and the number in parentheses is the standard deviation of the estimates in 100 Monte Carlo samples. One-tenth of the number in parentheses is a good estimate of the standard error of the mean.

Table 7.8.2

Effect on bias of increasing model size within GEID and REID specifications [1]

		Two equations		Three equations		Five equations	
		Model 6a (GEID spec.)	Model 2a (REID spec.)	Model 6b (GEID spec.)	Model 2b (REID spec.)	Model 6c (GEID spec.)	Model 2c (REID spec.)
Size corr.		±0.1, ±0.2	0.0	±0.1, ±0.2	0.0	±0.1, ±0.2	0.0
β_{12}	True	1.0	1.0	1.0	1.0	−1.0	−1.0
	OLS	0.6872 (0.105)	0.6874 (0.136)	0.7910 (0.093)	0.8249 (0.087)	−0.9266 (0.073)	−0.9107 (0.070)
	TSLS	1.0075 (0.169)	1.0284 (0.190)	0.9173 (0.117)	0.9941 (0.104)	−0.9843 (0.086)	−0.9859 (0.072)
	FP	1.0065 (0.163)	1.0322 (0.196)	0.9968 (0.152)	1.0025 (0.119)	−0.9812 (0.100)	−1.0098 (0.111)
γ_{11}	True	0.8944	0.8944	0.7303	0.7303	0.5657	0.5657
	OLS	0.7083 (0.113)	0.7433 (0.118)	0.6099 (0.078)	0.6699 (0.085)	0.5768 (0.072)	0.5424 (0.067)
	TSLS	0.8338 (0.137)	0.9040 (0.145)	0.6502 (0.079)	0.7298 (0.090)	0.5947 (0.072)	0.5648 (0.067)
	FP	0.8925 (0.151)	0.8968 (0.176)	0.7144 (0.145)	0.7186 (0.123)	0.5426 (0.129)	0.5607 (0.139)
ω_{11}	True	0.4472	0.4472	0.3651	0.3651	0.2828	0.2828
	OLS	0.4866 (0.074)	0.5111 (0.071)	0.4041 (0.051)	0.4315 (0.047)	0.3525 (0.045)	0.3407 (0.045)
	TSLS	0.4199 (0.064)	0.4433 (0.061)	0.3663 (0.052)	0.3684 (0.045)	0.3165 (0.042)	0.3014 (0.042)
	FP	0.4480 (0.070)	0.4372 (0.074)	0.3592 (0.079)	0.3610 (0.064)	0.2787 (0.066)	0.2934 (0.076)
	URF	0.4501 (0.073)	0.4384 (0.072)	0.3609 (0.081)	0.3572 (0.068)	0.2789 (0.071)	0.2920 (0.087)
ω_{21}	True	−0.4472	−0.4472	−0.3651	−0.3651	0.2828	0.2828
	OLS	−0.3230 (0.062)	−0.3372 (0.063)	−0.2612 (0.040)	−0.2884 (0.050)	0.2415 (0.036)	0.2211 (0.035)
	TSLS	−0.4099 (0.059)	−0.4452 (0.062)	−0.3111 (0.042)	−0.3627 (0.052)	0.2822 (0.040)	0.2668 (0.041)
	FP	−0.4405 (0.069)	−0.4415 (0.078)	−0.3574 (0.072)	−0.3556 (0.064)	0.2699 (0.065)	0.2627 (0.066)
	URF	0.3803 (0.073)	−0.4524 (0.067)	0.3192 (0.074)	0.3706 (0.080)	0.3280 (0.077)	0.2786 (0.079)

[1] The first number is the mean and the number in parentheses is the standard deviation of the estimates in 100 Monte Carlo samples.

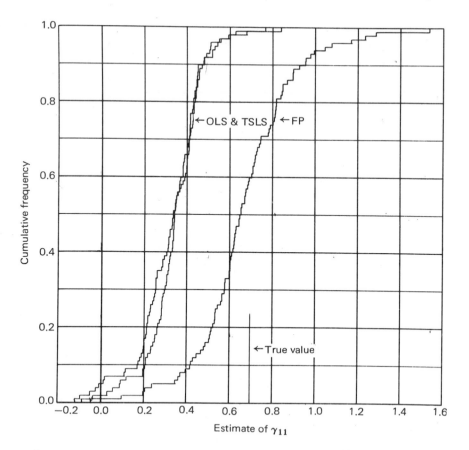

Chart 7.8.1. Cumulative distribution for estimates of γ_{11} in Model 6j.

the other methods for all sample sizes in GEID specifications. As the size of correlation in a GEID specification approaches zero, the total bias in FP relative to that in other methods will be similar to the various results shown for REID systems in the preceding subsections of this chapter. Within the scope of the present investigation most models with classical design have shown greater bias in FP than in TSLS, and in some instances greater than in OLS. URF estimates are, of course, unbiased in the classical design.[2]

The models in category six (see Chart 2.3.1) were designed in part to reveal conditions under which bias in FP becomes less than that in TSLS. The series of Models 6f–6j was designed to show the effect of an in-

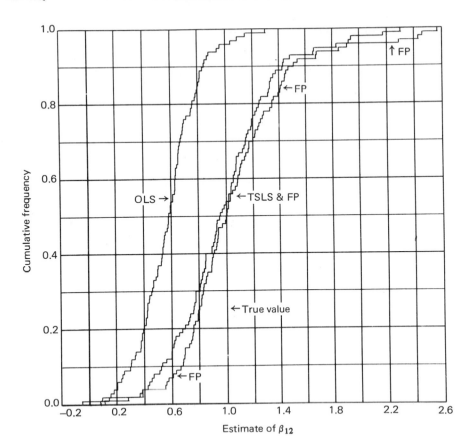

Chart 7.8.2. Cumulative distribution for estimates of β_{12} in Model 6j.

creasing size of GEID correlations (correlations between the residual in
one relation and exogenous variables in other relations; see 1.4.6).
Series 6a–6c has an increasing number of equations which in turn
allows more correlations to be specified within the GEID framework.
For example, the correlation between residuals ϵ_i and η_k^* variables shown
in Part A.3 (Tables 10.2.40–10.2.41) for Models 6b and 6c are not possible in a two-equation model such as Model 6a.

The bias among the coefficients within each of the Models 6a, 6b and
6c differ because of variation in the correlations that were built into the
design of the model. The complete results for these three models will
be discussed in Chapter 9.

Results in Tables 1 and 2 indicate that for a moderate sample size of

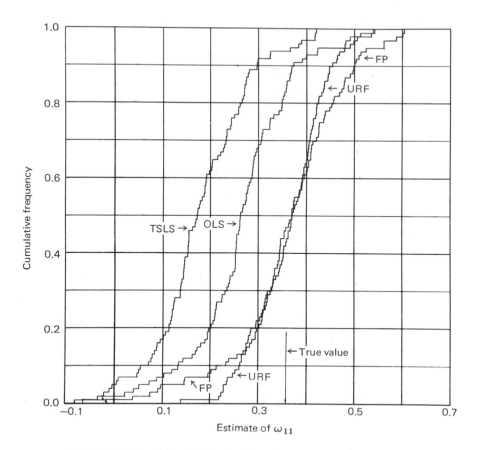

Chart 7.8.3. Cumulative distribution for estimates of ω_{11} in Model 6j.

40 used in estimating these models TSLS estimates become more biased than FP estimates with correlations as small as 0.10. The difference in the relative bias in FP and TSLS between estimates of beta and gamma coefficients can be readily seen in Charts 1 and 2. For example, in Model 6j the bias in TSLS estimates of γ_{11}, ω_{11} and ω_{21} is substantially greater than that in FP. Model 5n which is a comparable model except that it has the classical design shows no apparent difference between TSLS and FP in any of the estimates of coefficients.

In Table 2 we see that there is a substantial difference between the bias in TSLS and FP in each of the Models 6a–6c. On the other hand, in Model 2b, which is comparable to Model 6b except that it has the classical design, there is no apparent difference between TSLS and FP.

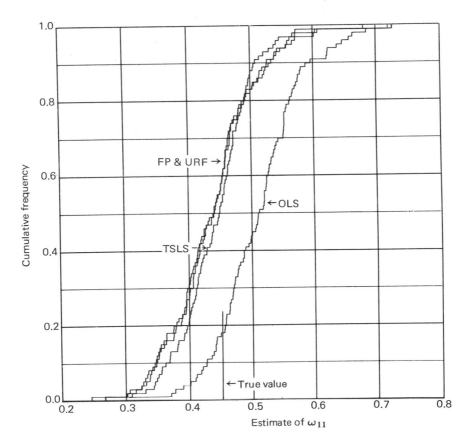

Chart 7.8.4. Cumulative distribution for estimates of ω_{11} in Model 1b.

For Model 6a and all models in Table 1 TSLS estimates of beta coefficients show no apparent bias. This is caused by the combined effect of the absence of correlations among the predetermined variables and the absence of prescribes zeros among the off-diagonal elements of the matrix B. In Model 6a, for example, the specification $r(\epsilon_1, x_1) = r(\epsilon_1, x_2)$ $= r(\epsilon_1, \eta_2^*) = 0$ also requires that the correlation $r(\epsilon_1, \eta_1^*)$ be zero. As shown in Part A.3 of Tables 10.2.40 and 41 this is not true for models with three or more equations. There is a significant bias in TSLS estimates of β_{12} in the three-equation model 6b, as shown in Table 2. Although the results indicate no apparent bias in TSLS estimates of β_{12} in the five-equation model 6c, there is significance bias in TSLS estimates of other beta coefficients in that model (see Part B.1 for Model 6c in

Table 10.2.41). The dispersion of FP estimates of β_{12} in Model 6b is somewhat greater than that for TSLS, but the bias is significantly less.

The difference in relative bias among OLS, TSLS, and FP estimates in GEID and classical specifications can be seen by comparing the distributions in Chart 1 with those in Chart 6.1.2. In the results for the classical design shown in Chart 6.1.2 the distributions for FP and TSLS are very similar and show little bias, but OLS estimates show large bias. In the results for the GEID design in Chart 1 the distributions for OLS and TSLS are very similar and show severe bias, but FP estimates show no apparent bias.

The relative bias among the different methods in estimates of reduced form coefficients depends on the particular coefficient selected for analysis. For example, URF estimates of ω_{11}, ω_{12}, ω_{23}, and ω_{24} are unbiased whereas URF estimates of the other coefficients are more biased than those given by any of the other methods. This is easily seen in results for Model 6j shown in Table 1. OLS estimates are biased for every coefficient, but are less biased in the set of coefficients for which URF has no bias. The difference in bias among the coefficients for any method is because of the difference in correlations within the GEID framework. In GEID specifications for Models 6a–6c and 6f–6j the correlations are as follows,

$$r(\epsilon_1, x_1) = r(\epsilon_1, x_2) = r(\epsilon_2, x_3) = r(\epsilon_2, x_4) = 0 \,, \qquad (1)$$

$$r(\epsilon_1, x_3) \,, \;\; r(\epsilon_1, x_4) \,, \;\; r(\epsilon_2, x_1) \,, \;\; r(\epsilon_2, x_2) \neq 0 \,. \qquad (2)$$

In words, the residual ϵ_i is uncorrelated with all exogenous variables that appear in the structural equation in which y_i is the dependent variable.

Charts 3 and 4 show the estimates of ω_{11} under GEID and classical specifications. OLS estimates show significantly less bias than TSLS estimates for ω_{11} in Model 6j, but the bias is the same for ω_{21} (see Table 1). Similarly, Chart 3 shows no apparent difference in the bias of FP and URF whereas the results in Table 2 show a large difference in estimates of ω_{21}.

There is no marked small-sample bias in FP estimates of ω_{12}, ω_{12}, ω_{23} and ω_{24} in any of the GEID models shown in Tables 1 and 2. There is, however, a significant small-sample bias in FP estimates of the other four reduced form coefficients when the size of correlation reaches a value of ± 0.1 in Series 6e—6j. The reason that there is no corresponding apparent bias among models in Series 6a—6c is that R^2 is 0.8 compared to 0.5 in Series 6e—6j (see Chapter 7.4 for discussion of size of residuals). The different bias properties of the two groups of reduced form coefficients is due partly to the absence of correlations between the predetermined variables.

The significant observation from the results for GEID specifications is that correlations as small as 0.1 will lead to greater total bias in TSLS than in FP estimates. This is true even when residuals are quite small. For example, in Model 6c variances of δ_i are 0.16 and variances of ϵ_i are 0.2. It is also significant to note that the larger the number of equations the greater the number of correlations that can exist between residuals and y_i^* or exogenous variables. A greater number of correlations usually leads to significant bias in a higher percentage of the coefficients in the model.

CHAPTER 8

Dispersion of Estimates

In this chapter we will discuss four measures of dispersion:

a) Observed standard deviation around the mean in the Monte Carlo results.

b) Extreme values in one or both tails of the observed distribution.

c) The relationship between the observed standard deviation and the mean of the estimated standard deviation from the large-sample formula. [1]

d) Observed standard deviation around the true value in the Monte Carlo results.

e) The relation between standard deviation of OLS, TSLS, and FP estimates of reduced form coefficients and the mean of the estimates of standard deviation from the large-sample formula for URF.

Small-sample bias, which was discussed in Chapter 7, influences the fourth measure, but it will not be discussed in detail again in this chapter.

As was true for predictive power and small-sample bias, we find that relative dispersion among the methods depends on the characteristics of the model being estimated. There are only a few general statements that can be made:

1. OLS has the smallest dispersion around the mean in the case of structural coefficients but not in the case of generated reduced form coefficients.

2. The observed standard deviation around the mean is approximately of the same magnitude as the mean of the estimated standard deviation from the large-sample formula in the 100 Monte Carlo samples for each of the methods, except in a small percentage of cases where extreme values occurred.

3. Extreme values are more common in FP and TSLS than in OLS or URF, but there is no apparent difference between FP and TSLS on the basis of our results.

There are several more general statements that can be made when specific characteristics of the model are known. These will be given in each of the sub-sections of this chapter.

If indeed the second moment in the distribution of estimates from small samples does not exist in some models, we have to be careful for the disturbing and large effect of extreme values on features explored. [2] We have endeavored to point out the extreme values among the results in the 46 models. It is possible to regenerate the data for any specific sample and reestimate the model with only a few minutes of computer time. This means that anyone has opportunity to study cases of extreme values if he so desires. [3]

8.1. In Models with Small Betas FP and TSLS are Approximately the Same

If all beta coefficients are small, the model is near a vector regression system and all methods which estimate structural coefficients give about the same results. Beta coefficients of ±0.5, as in the models displayed in Table 1, are not small enough that OLS is the same as other methods, but they are small enough that FP and TSLS are approximately the same.

In Table 1 we note two relationships among the three measures of dispersion in TSLS, FP, and URF. First, the observed standard deviation around the mean and the observed standard deviation around the true value are approximately the same. Second, the mean of the estimated standard deviation from the large sample formula is approximately the same as the observed standard deviation around the mean.

Extreme values are not shown in Table 1 because the smallest and

Table 8.1.1
Standard deviations of estimates of coefficients in models with small betas [1].

	β_{12}		γ_{11}		ω_{11}		ω_{21}	
	Mean	True	Mean	True	Mean	True	Mean	True

Model 1a: Two-equation model with all betas equal to ±0.5

	β_{12}		γ_{11}		ω_{11}		ω_{21}	
Coefficient value	0.5		0.7071		0.5657		−0.2828	
Standard deviation								
OLS	0.0916	0.1532	0.0837	0.0900	0.0741	0.0773	0.0571	0.0780
	(0.0903)		(0.0854)					
TSLS	0.1103	0.1103	0.0906	0.0907	0.0747	0.0747	0.0642	0.0643
	(0.1073)		(0.0897)					
FP	0.1093	0.1093	0.0902	0.0902	0.0739	0.0739	0.0651	0.0652
	(0.1076)		(0.0896)					
URF					0.0770	0.0770	0.0733	0.0739
					(0.0748)		(0.0736)	

Model 1i: Seven-equation model with all betas equal to ±0.5

	β_{12}		γ_{11}		ω_{11}		ω_{21}	
Coefficient value	0.5		0.5520		0.5476		−0.0086	
Standard deviation								
OLS	0.0672	0.0672	0.0556	0.0557	0.0553	0.0554	0.0029	0.0029
	(0.0618)		(0.0630)					
TSLS	0.0688	0.0688	0.0552	0.0553	0.0549	0.0550	0.0031	0.0031
	(0.0668)		(0.0633)					
FP	0.0682	0.0683	0.0617	0.0617	0.0613	0.0613	0.0034	0.0034
	(0.0693)		(0.0636)					
URF					0.0796	0.0796	0.0825	0.0828
					(0.0869)		(0.0868)	

Model 3d: Three-equation full beta matrix with all betas equal to ±0.5

	β_{12}		γ_{11}		ω_{11}		ω_{21}	
Coefficient value	−0.5		0.5916		0.4226		0.2536	
Standard deviation								
OLS	0.1358	0.4211	0.1152	0.1596	0.1067	0.1170	0.0617	0.1266
	(0.1364)		(0.1311)					
TSLS	0.2880	0.2889	0.1656	0.1662	0.1073	0.1077	0.0905	0.0921
	(0.2503)		(0.1643)					
FP	0.2861	0.2864	0.1715	0.1728	0.1107	0.1107	0.0880	0.0888
	(0.2613)		(0.1640)					
URF					0.1138	0.1138	0.1224	0.1224
					(0.1214)		(0.1221)	

[1] The standard deviations around the mean and around the true value are labeled "Mean" and "True" respectively. The number in parentheses is the mean of 100 estimates of the standard deviation from the unrevised large-sample formula; see Part B.3 of Table 10.1.1.

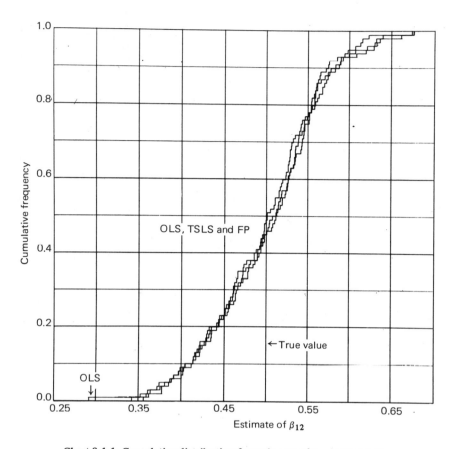

Chart 8.1.1. Cumulative distribution for estimates of β_{12} in Model 1i.

largest values were very similar for OLS, TSLS, and FP. The length of the tails of the distribution in Charts 1 and 2 are typical of all models with small betas. The graph for Model 3d would differ from graphs in Charts 1 and 2.in that OLS would be shifted because of bias but it would not show long tails. The distribution of URF estimates of ω_{21} in Model 1i has fairly long tails but does not show extreme values. The long tails are reflected in the much larger standard deviation around the mean (0.083 compared to 0.003 for other methods).

With betas of ±0.5 the bias in OLS estimates of structural coefficients is such that the standard deviation around the true value is usually larger

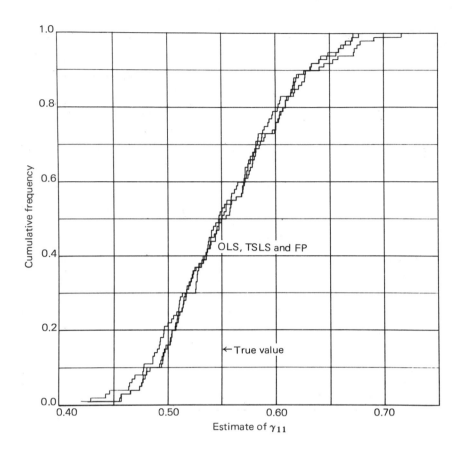

Chart 8.1.2. Cumulative distribution for estimates of γ_{11} in Model 1i.

than that for TSLS and FP. The standard deviation of OLS estimates around the mean is of course smaller than that for TSLS and FP.

8.2. Sample Size

From the large-sample formula we expect that the standard deviation around the mean should change with sample size according to the formula

$$\text{S.D. } (a_i-\bar{a}) = \left[\frac{N}{N-k} \text{ V(residual) } [XX']^{ii} \right]^{\frac{1}{2}}, \tag{1}$$

where N is sample size, k is the number of coefficients to be estimated in the equation and $[XX']^{ii}$ is the appropriate element in the inverse of the product moment matrix. V(residual) would be the variance of δ for OLS and the variance of ϵ in the case of TSLS, FP and URF. From this formula we would expect the standard deviation for sample size N relative to that for sample size 40 to be approximately $\sqrt{(40-k)/(N-k)}$.

In Table 1 we see that the results from all methods for Models 5f–5h are in line with our expectation, but results for OLS and TSLS in Models 5i and 5j are not.

There are no extreme values in Models 5f–5h. The absence of long tails in the distributions shown in Charts 6.1.1–2, 7.3.1 and 8.2.1 are typical of the distributions of all estimates in these three models. There are, however, extreme values in TSLS estimates of β_{12}, γ_{11}, ω_{11}, and ω_{21} and in OLS estimates of ω_{11} and ω_{21} in Model 5i. The smallest and largest values in the estimates for Model 5i are as follows:

	β_{12}		γ_{11}		ω_{11}		ω_{21}	
	Small	Large	Small	Large	Small	Large	Small	Large
OLS	−0.78	0.52	−0.44	1.18	−6.31	1.11	−1.04	7.72
TSLS	3.35	13.04	−0.46	8.33	−10.10	1.03	−0.96	14.78
FP	−2.59	3.15	−0.17	2.14	0.18	1.02	−0.96	−0.14
URF					0.20	1.45	−1.00	−0.08

The second smallest and second largest values were not extreme values, and the values were approximately the same for all methods. The large standard deviation for TSLS in the case of β_{12} and γ_{11} and the large standard deviation for OLS and TSLS in the case of ω_{11} and ω_{21} were caused by the single extreme value in each set of estimates. This can easily be seen by comparing one-tenth of each extreme value shown above with the corresponding standard deviation given in Table 1.

For TSLS the standard deviation of β_{12} and γ_{11} in Model 5i relative to the corresponding value in 5j is approximately 6 rather than 2.30 shown in line 2 of Table 1. For both TSLS and OLS the standard deviation of ω_{11} and ω_{21} in Model 5i relative to the corresponding value in Model 5j is 6 or larger rather than 2.45. These results are very likely

Table 8.2.1.
Dispersion of estimates and sample size [1].

A. Basic model 1b

	Model 5f		Model 5g (= 1b)		Model 5h	
	Mean	True	Mean	True	Mean	True
Sample size	10		40		80	
$\sqrt{(40-3)/(N-3)}$	2.30		1.0		0.652	
β_{12}	1.0		1.0		1.0	
Standard deviation:						
OLS	0.2640	0.4553	0.1363	0.3410	0.0899	0.3357
	(0.2832)		(0.1249)		(0.0849)	
TSLS	0.3869	0.3974	0.1901	0.1922	0.1280	0.1285
	(0.4132)		(0.1715)		(0.1150)	
FP	0.3763	0.3879	0.1955	0.1981	0.1288	0.1294
	(0.4502)		(0.1758)		(0.1161)	
γ_{11}	0.8944		0.8944		0.8944	
Standard deviation:						
OLS	0.2317	0.2723	0.1179	0.1917	0.0811	0.1713
	(0.2388)		(0.1109)		(0.0764)	
TSLS	0.2746	0.2760	0.1447	0.1450	0.0947	0.0947
	(0.2973)		(0.1318)		(0.0893)	
FP	0.3242	0.3272	0.1757	0.1757	0.1182	0.1183
	(0.3140)		(0.1338)		(0.0899)	
$\sqrt{(40-4)/(N-4)}$	2.45		1.0		0.647	
ω_{11}	0.4472		0.4472		0.4472	
Standard deviation:						
OLS	0.1864	0.2131	0.0709	0.0954	0.0520	0.0847
TSLS	0.1507	0.1534	0.0610	0.0611	0.0493	0.0494
FP	0.1786	0.1800	0.0737	0.0744	0.0587	0.0589
URF	0.1988	0.2010	0.0717	0.0722	0.0589	0.0591
	(0.1862)		(0.0748)		(0.0517)	
ω_{21}	−0.4472		−0.4472		−0.4472	
Standard deviation:						
OLS	0.1818	0.2206	0.0629	0.1267	0.0506	0.1196
TSLS	0.1549	0.1563	0.0620	0.0620	0.0445	0.0447
FP	0.1988	0.2003	0.0778	0.0780	0.0562	0.0565
URF	0.1974	0.1977	0.0665	0.0667	0.0482	0.0482
	(0.1842)		(0.0738)		(0.0518)	

[1] The standard deviations around the mean and around the true value are labeled "Mean" and "True" respectively. The number in parentheses is the mean of 100 estimates of the standard deviation from the unrevised large sample formula; see Part B.3 of Table 10.1.1.

Table 8.2.1
(continued)

B. Basic model 1d

	Model 5i		Model 5j (= 1d)	
	Mean	True	Mean	True
Sample size	10		40	
$\sqrt{(40-3)/(N-3)}$	2.30		1.0	
β_{12}	0.5		0.5	
Standard deviation:				
OLS	0.2733	0.7037	0.1209	0.6634
	(0.3167)		(0.1312)	
TSLS	1.4815	1.4863	0.2521	0.2521
	(1.8820)		(0.2550)	
FP	0.7468	0.7482	0.2512	0.2512
	(0.7885)		(0.2551)	
γ_{11}	0.8889		0.8889	
Standard deviation:				
OLS	0.2588	0.4465	0.1044	0.3761
	(0.2517)		(0.1091)	
TSLS	0.8581	0.8590	0.1726	0.1726
	(1.1077)		(0.1780)	
FP	0.4028	0.4029	0.1691	0.1691
	(0.4650)		(0.1771)	
$\sqrt{(40-4)/(N-4)}$	2.45		1.0	
ω_{11}	0.6130		0.6130	
Standard deviation:				
OLS	0.7249	0.7291	0.0915	0.0917
TSLS	1.0820	1.0891	0.0756	0.0756
FP	0.1681	0.1703	0.0746	0.0746
URF	0.1932	0.1933	0.0781	0.0781
	(0.1753)		(0.0750)	
ω_{21}	−0.5520		−0.5517	
Standard deviation:				
OLS	0.8486	0.8536	0.0779	0.0816
TSLS	1.5406	1.5496	0.0710	0.0711
FP	0.1735	0.1742	0.0725	0.0725
URF	0.2021	0.2026	0.0773	0.0776
	(0.1844)		(0.0746)	

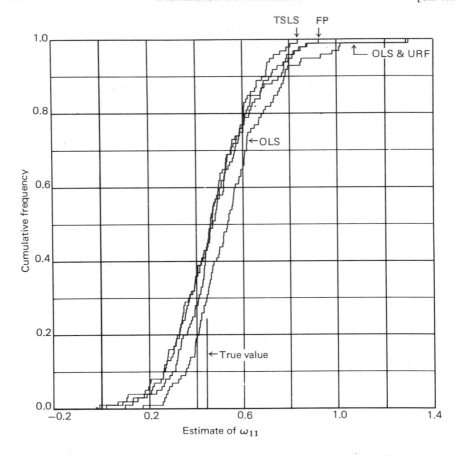

Chart 8.2.1. Cumulative distribution for estimates of ω_{11} in Model 5f.

caused by the presence of a small number of extreme values in OLS and TSLS estimates in Model 5i.

The mean of the estimated standard deviation from the large-sample formula in the 100 Monte Carlo samples is close to the observed standard deviation for each method in each of the models. This is true even in the situation where OLS and TSLS have extreme values in Models 5i.

The change in the standard deviation around the true value as sample size is increased is shown in Chart 2. As sample size increases the bias in OLS become the largest component in the deviation from the true value and the curve flattens out as shown. The small circles shown on the graph for each of the three coefficients are reference points derived from formula (1).

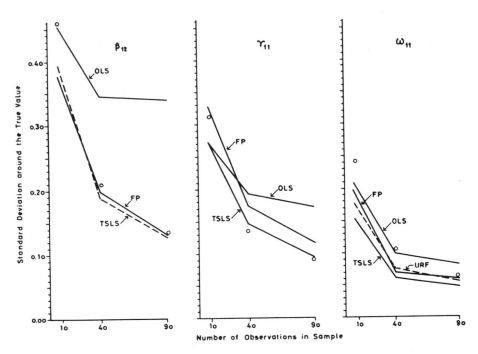

Chart 8.2.2. Standard deviation around the true value as function of sample size.

There is no significant change in the relative magnitude of standard deviation between FP and TSLS in Models 5f–5h (see Chart 2). The relationships shown are characteristic of all the coefficients in these models.

Graphs for the cumulative distribution of estimates in Model 5i are not available, but it is quite apparent that the standard deviation of OLS and TSLS estimates relative to FP becomes significantly larger as sample size is reduced. However, since the estimate in only one of the 100 samples contributed more than 75% of the observed standard deviation, these results could reflect mainly sampling variation. Since the same sample data were used for all methods we can at least say that the conditions which contributed to extreme values for OLS and TSLS in Model 5i did not produce extreme values for FP.

The mean of the estimated standard deviation for URF is similar to the observed standard deviation around the mean for FP estimates of reduced form coefficients in Model 5i, but it is much less than the observed standard deviation in the generated reduced form coefficients for

OLS and TSLS estimates. Whenever there is serious bias or extreme values in estimates of structural coefficients, we cannot expect that the estimated standard deviation for URF estimates will be a good estimate of the standard deviation of generated reduced form coefficients.

8.3. Size of Residuals

From the large-sample formula we know that the standard deviation around the mean should change with size of residuals according to formula (8.2.1). Although the residuals appropriate for assessing dispersion in OLS estimates (that is, δ_i) are different in the two structural equations

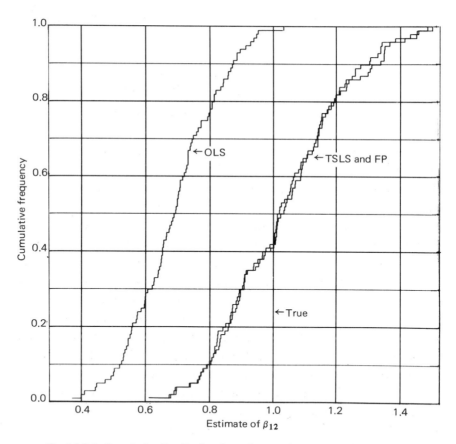

Chart 8.3.1. Cumulative distribution for estimates of β_{12} in Model 5p (= 1b).

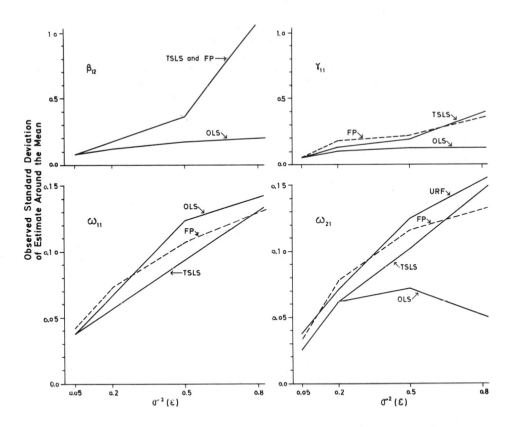

Chart 8.3.2. Size of residual in model specification and dispersion of parameter estimates.

for both Model 5r and Model 5s the relative size of the residuals is the same in both equations. In spite of the larger variance of δ_i in the first equation, the dispersion of OLS estimates around the mean is approximately the same in the first and second equations (see Table 10.2.38).

The results for Models 5m−5s follow the expectation from (8.2.1) except in the case of FP and TSLS estimates of β_{12}. Comparing the distributions of estimates for Models 5m and 5p we note that FP and TSLS have a thick upper tail in Model 5m. Since there are approximately 10 of the 100 samples that indicate a thick upper tail, it appears that the results reflect more than just sampling variation.

Because of the thick tail in TSLS and FP (see Charts 7.4.1 and 7.4.2) the dispersion in these methods relative to that in OLS becomes greater as size of residuals increases. This is shown in Chart 2 (note that the

Table 8.3.1
Effect of size of residuals on dispersion [1].

A. Basic model 1b

	Model 5m		Model 5n		Model 5p (= 1b)		Model 5q	
	Mean	True	Mean	True	Mean	True	Mean	True
$\sigma^2(\delta)$	1.6		1.0		0.4		0.1	
$\sigma^2(\epsilon)$	0.8		0.5		0.2		0.05	
β_{12}	1.0		1.0		1.0		1.0	
Standard dev.:								
OLS	0.1753	0.9258	0.1675	0.6903	0.1363	0.3410	0.0742	0.1209
	(0.1641)		(0.1534)		(0.1249)		(0.0687)	
TSLS	1.0994	1.1047	0.3920	0.3946	0.1901	0.1922	0.0774	0.0775
	(1.1719)		(0.3397)		(0.1715)		(0.0741)	
FP	1.0863	1.0879	0.4022	0.4040	0.1955	0.1981	0.0778	0.0779
	(1.1143)		(0.3480)		(0.1758)		(0.0753)	
γ_{11}	0.4472		0.7071		0.8944		0.9747	
Standard dev.:								
OLS	0.1424	0.2474	0.1448	0.2713	0.1179	0.1917	0.0638	0.0766
	(0.1607)		(0.1422)		(0.1109)		(0.0598)	
TSLS	0.3903	0.3911	0.1914	0.1919	0.1447	0.1450	0.0619	0.0619
	(0.3925)		(0.2033)		(0.1318)		(0.0624)	
FP	0.3624	0.3626	0.2041	0.2045	0.1757	0.1757	0.0715	0.0717
	(0.3681)		(0.2058)		(0.1338)		(0.0636)	
ω_{11}	0.2236		0.3536		0.4472		0.4873	
Standard dev.:								
OLS	0.1426	0.1444	0.1241	0.1459	0.0709	0.0954	0.0389	0.0496
TSLS	0.1314	0.1323	0.0998	0.1006	0.0610	0.0611	0.0367	0.0378
FP	0.1298	0.1300	0.1051	0.1059	0.0737	0.0744	0.0428	0.0442
URF	0.1364	0.1364	0.1020	0.1029	0.0717	0.0722	0.0439	0.0450
	(0.1504)		(0.1160)		(0.0748)		(0.0371)	
ω_{21}	−0.2236		−0.3536		−0.4472		−0.4873	
Standard dev.:								
OLS	0.0533	0.1955	0.0730	0.2194	0.0629	0.1267	0.0306	0.0422
TSLS	0.1487	0.1512	0.1047	0.1049	0.0620	0.0620	0.0302	0.0305
FP	0.1358	0.1400	0.1122	0.1123	0.0778	0.0780	0.0354	0.0356
URF	0.1632	0.1633	0.1246	0.1248	0.0665	0.0667	0.0394	0.0399
	(0.1488)		(0.1169)		(0.0738)		(0.0373)	

[1] The standard deviations around the mean and around the true value are labeled "Mean" and "True" respectively. The number in parentheses is the mean of 100 estimates of the standard deviation from the unrevised large-sample formula; see Part B.3 of Table 10.1.1.

Table 8.3.1
(continued)

B. Basic model 1d

	Model 5r		Model 5s (= 1d)	
	Mean	True	Mean	True
$\sigma^2(\delta)$	(1.58, 0.4)		(0.395, 0.1)	
$\sigma^2(\epsilon)$	0.8		0.2	
β_{12}	0.5		0.5	
Standard deviation:				
OLS	0.1148 (0.1174)	1.1904	0.1209 (0.1312)	0.6634
TSLS	1.4856 (1.4660)	1.6261	0.2521 (0.2550)	0.2521
FP	0.9750 (1.1390)	1.0850	0.2512 (0.2551)	0.2512
γ_{11}	0.4443		0.8889	
Standard deviation:				
OLS	0.1204 (0.1133)	0.3544	0.1044 (0.1091)	0.3761
TSLS	0.4190 (0.4461)	0.4565	0.1726 (0.1780)	0.1726
FP	0.3054 (0.3476)	0.3355	0.1691 (0.1771)	0.1691
ω_{11}	0.3066		0.6130	
Standard deviation:				
OLS	0.2487	0.2660	0.0915	0.0917
TSLS	0.1753	0.1754	0.0756	0.0756
FP	0.1576	0.1577	0.0746	0.0746
URF	0.1562 (0.1500)	0.1562	0.0781 (0.0750)	0.0781
ω_{21}	−0.2760		−0.5517	
Standard deviation:				
OLS	0.1984	0.2314	0.0779	0.0816
TSLS	0.1620	0.1621	0.0710	0.0711
FP	0.1570	0.1573	0.0725	0.0725
URF	0.1546 (0.1492)	0.1552	0.0773 (0.0746)	0.0776

scale of the horizontal axis is organized so as to emphasize the analogy to the trends in Chart 8.2.2). On the other hand, the bias in OLS estimates is large enough (see Chart 1) that the dispersion around the true value in all three methods stays about the same as size of residuals increases in Models 5m–5q (see Table 1).

The results for Model 5r are similar to those for Model 5m in that TSLS and FP have a thick tail. However, the results in Model 5r indicate that TSLS estimates have greater dispersion around the mean than FP for all coefficients.

The mean of the estimated standard deviation is close to the observed standard deviation for each coefficient in each method. This holds even in the cases where the distribution of FP and TSLS estimates have a thick tail.

Although results such as those in Charts 7.4.1–2 show a thick tail, there are not what we would call extreme values in any of the Models 5m–5s. Of course, definitions of an extreme value and thick tail are more or less arbitrary and the reader is free to use other classifications if he desires. The presentation of results in Charts 7.4.1–2 and 8.3.1 gives sound insight into the nature of the sampling distributions.

The estimated standard deviation of URF estimates of reduced form coefficients are quite close to the observed standard deviation of TSLS and FP generated estimates. As pointed out in Chapter 8.3, it is risky to assume that this condition holds in general.

8.4. Number of Predetermined Variables

On the basis of the large-sample formula we would expect the variance of estimates from all methods to vary inversely with the degrees of freedom (= sample size − number of determining variables) and directly with the size of residual. Holding $\sigma^2(\epsilon)$ constant there is a difference in $\sigma^2(\delta)$ between increasing the number of predetermined variables by increasing the number of equations (see the series in Models 2a–2d) and by increasing the number of variables per equation (see the series in Models 2e–2g). In the series of Models 2a–2d, for example, $\sigma^2(\delta)$ decreases as the number of predetermined variables increases.

For any given sample size URF estimates are affected by total number of predetermined variables regardless of where the predetermined variables appear in the structural equations. For a given number of predetermined variables, URF are unaffected by the difference between a large number of equations and a large number of variables per structural equation. On the other hand, estimates of beta and gamma coefficients by so-called limited information methods are affected one way by a large number of equations and in another way by a large number of variables per structural equation. There are three reasons for this. First, the degrees of freedom $(N-k)$ in estimating coefficients depend on number of variables in a structural equation (k_i) but do not depend on number of equations. Second, the magnitude of the appropriate element in the inverse of the matrix of determining variables (y_q^*, z_p) depends in part on the percentage of variables in the model that appears in each structural equation. Third, if R^2 and beta coefficients are held constant, the variance of δ_i remains constant as number of predetermined variables per equation increases, but decreases as number of equations increases. This last factor has a pronounced effect on OLS estimates.

The standard deviation of OLS and TSLS estimates is less in Model 2d than in Model 2a, in spite of the greater number of predetermined variables in the former. The reason in the case of OLS is easy to visualize because of the relative magnitude of $\sigma^2(\delta)$. In the case of TSLS it is explained by the fact that when the degrees of freedom in estimation of the reduced form become small TSLS estimates depend more on $\sigma^2(\delta)$ than on $\sigma^2(\epsilon)$.

Whereas standard deviation of TSLS estimates of gamma coefficients in Model 2d is less than in Model 2g, standard deviation of FP estimates is about the same in both models. Dispersion of FP estimates is more closely related to total numbers of predetermined variables than to the number of variables per structural equation.

The mean of the estimated standard deviation is close to the observed standard deviation for each method in each model. There are no extreme values in any of the models listed in Table 1.

Except for OLS estimates there is very little bias in Models 2a–2d and Models 2e–2g, and, therefore, the standard deviation of estimated around the true value and the mean are approximately the same.

In summary, we can state that dispersion of TSLS estimates are significantly less than for FP in Model 2d but in other models they are approx-

Table 8.4.1

Effect of increasing number of predetermined variables on dispersion [1].

	Model 2a (= 1b)		Model 2d		Model 2f		Model 2g	
	Mean	True	Mean	True	Mean	True	Mean	True
No. of equations	2		7		2		2	
No. var. per equation	4		4		6		9	
$\sigma^2(\delta)$	0.4		0.1143		0.4		0.4	
$\sigma^2(\epsilon)$	0.2		0.2		0.2		0.2	
No. predetermined var.	4		14		8		14	
β_{12}	1.0		1.0		1.0		1.0	
Standard dev.:								
OLS	0.1363	0.3410	0.0585	0.0830	0.1376	0.3773	0.1379	0.3584
	(0.1249)		(0.0591)		(0.1275)		(0.1281)	
TSLS	0.1901	0.1922	0.0666	0.0677	0.1724	0.1761	0.1617	0.1848
	(0.1715)		(0.0655)		(0.1703)		(0.1608)	
FP	0.1955	0.1981	0.0929	0.0933	0.1732	0.1768	0.1645	0.1816
	(0.1758)		(0.0769)		(0.1752)		(0.1728)	
γ_{11}	0.8944		0.4781		0.6325		0.4781	
Standard dev.:								
OLS	0.1179	0.1917	0.0536	0.0556	0.1008	0.1502	0.1112	0.1341
	(0.1109)		(0.0551)		(0.1068)		(0.1032)	
TSLS	0.1447	0.1450	0.0558	0.0563	0.1129	0.1139	0.1243	0.1259
	(0.1318)		(0.0562)		(0.1209)		(0.1113)	
FP	0.1757	0.1757	0.1280	0.1306	0.1435	0.1437	0.1368	0.1389
	(0.1338)		(0.0620)		(0.1250)		(0.1182)	
ω_{11}	0.4472		0.2390		0.3162		0.2390	
Standard dev.:								
OLS	0.0709	0.0954	0.0341	0.0545	0.0632	0.0781	0.0704	0.0808
TSLS	0.0610	0.0611	0.0326	0.0354	0.0553	0.0553	0.0638	0.0647
FP	0.0737	0.0744	0.0696	0.0696	0.0664	0.0664	0.0693	0.0695
URF	0.0717	0.0722	0.0891	0.0891	0.0727	0.0728	0.0915	0.0916
	(0.0748)		(0.0831)		(0.0799)		(0.0862)	
ω_{21}	−0.4472		−0.2390		−0.3162		−0.2390	
Standard dev.:								
OLS	0.0629	0.1267	0.0283	0.0572	0.0568	0.0919	0.0548	0.0779
TSLS	0.0620	0.0620	0.0319	0.0369	0.0600	0.0603	0.0616	0.0626
FP	0.0778	0.0780	0.0617	0.0674	0.0741	0.0741	0.0670	0.0682
URF	0.0665	0.0667	0.0913	0.0916	0.0812	0.0813	0.0922	0.0923
	(0.0738)		(0.0839)		(0.0802)		(0.0856)	

[1] The standard deviations around the mean and around the true values are labeled "Mean" and "True" respectively. The number in parentheses is the mean of 100 estimates of the standard deviation from the unrevised large-sample formula; see Part B.3 of Table 10.1.1.

imately the same. This again points out the major problem of methods that approach so-called full information. Models with many equations but only a few variables per equation make for large dispersion in full information methods but not in methods such as TSLS which operate on only one equation at a time.

Dispersion of estimates in Models 2a (= 1b) and 2d can also be studied by analyzing the cumulative distribution in Charts 6.1.2, 7.2.1, 7.2.2, 7.2.3, 7.8.4. and 8.3.1.

8.5. Specific Values of Beta Coefficients that Lead to Large Dispersion

The size of beta coefficients affects dispersion through the degree of multicollinearity among determining variables y_q^* are predetermined variables. In FP the size of beta coefficients also effect dispersion through the effect on convergence properties. Although econometric literature refers to the problem of identification as a zero or one proposition, it is actually a matter of degree as in the concept of multicollinearity. The concepts of identification and multicollinearity are useful when evaluating the relationship between size of beta coefficients and dispersion of estimates. When multicollinearity and identification problems become severe the term $[XX']^{ii}$ in (8.2.1) becomes large. Large betas produce a situation where it is hard to identify the effect of y_q^* as distinct from a linear combination of the predetermined variables in the same equation.

Models 1a and 3a are included in Table 1 as reference points. All beta coefficients in these two models are small and we find that dispersion is approximately the same for FP and TSLS. OLS estimates have smaller dispersion around the mean but because of bias the dispersion around the true value is about the same as for FP and TSLS. URF estimates of ω_{21} in Model 3a have significantly greater dispersion than FP and TSLS. Otherwise the results for URF are approximately the same as for FP and TSLS in both Models 1a and 3a.

All models other than 1a and 3a in Table 1 have a serious multi-collinearity situation: in Model 1d it is caused by the fact that only one of the beta coefficients is close to unity in absolute value; in Model 1c it is caused by large beta coefficients; and in Model 1f it is caused by both features. Some measure of severity of multicollinearity can be obtained

Table 8.5.1
Size of beta coefficients and dispersion of estimates [1].

A. Two-equation models

	Eigen-values[2]	β_{12}		γ_{11}		ω_{11}		ω_{21}	
		Mean	True	Mean	True	Mean	True	Mean	True
Model 1a		0.5		0.7071		0.5657		−0.2828	
OLS	0.174	0.0916	0.1532	0.0837	0.0900	0.0741	0.0773	0.0571	0.0780
	0.182	(0.0903)		(0.0854)					
TSLS	0.153	0.1103	0.1103	0.0906	0.0907	0.0747	0.0747	0.0642	0.0643
	0.162	(0.1073)		(0.0897)					
FP	0.154	0.1093	0.1093	0.0902	0.0902	0.0739	0.0739	0.0651	0.0652
	0.165	(0.1076)		(0.0896)					
URF	0.151					0.0770	0.0770	0.0733	0.0739
						(0.0748)		(0.0736)	
Model 1d		0.5		0.8889		0.6130		−0.5517	
OLS	0.069	0.1209	0.6634	0.1044	0.3761	0.0915	0.0917	0.0779	0.0816
	0.216	(0.1312)		(0.1091)					
TSLS	0.039	0.2521	0.2521	0.1726	0.1726	0.0756	0.0756	0.0710	0.0711
	0.201	(0.2550)		(0.1780)					
FP	0.039	0.2512	0.2512	0.1691	0.1691	0.0746	0.0746	0.0725	0.0725
	0.205	(0.2551)		(0.1771)					
URF	0.151					0.0781	0.0781	0.0773	0.0776
						(0.0750)		(0.0746)	
Model 1e		0.5		0.6591		0.2636		−0.7909	
OLS	0.197	0.0934	0.1190	0.0750	0.0791	0.0756	0.2488	0.1368	0.4827
	0.047	(0.0799)		(0.0786)					
TSLS	0.178	0.1093	0.1094	0.0812	0.0814	0.0855	0.0856	0.0990	0.1025
	0.016	(0.0923)		(0.0808)					
FP	0.180	0.1067	0.1076	0.1092	0.1305	0.0659	0.0754	0.1698	0.2433
	0.026	(0.1038)		(0.0817)					
URF	0.057					0.1015	0.1020	0.1081	0.1085
						(0.1038)		(0.1041)	
Model 1f		1.1		0.3963		0.0922		−0.2765	
OLS	0.177	0.0512	0.0841	0.0469	0.0501	4.5984	4.5988	4.1522	4.1535
	0.037	(0.0505)		(0.0478)					
TSLS	0.155	0.0615	0.0615	0.0506	0.0507	0.0952	0.0968	0.0896	0.0909
	0.005	(0.0598)		(0.0501)					
FP	0.178	0.0855	0.0868	0.1746	0.2196	0.3097	0.3112	0.2464	0.2640
	0.007	(0.0818)		(0.0659)					
URF	0.151					0.0715	0.0719	0.0732	0.0738
						(0.0734)		(0.0736)	
Model 1c		3.0		2.0		0.2		−0.6	
OLS	0.048	0.2466	2.2127	0.2104	1.3389	0.1131	0.2299	0.1121	0.2869
	0.049	(0.2622)		(0.2098)					
TSLS	0.017	0.8887	0.8914	0.5606	0.5621	0.0644	0.0649	0.0736	0.0736
	0.018	(0.9239)		(0.6075)					
FP	0.062	0.9494	1.6504	0.7663	1.3187	0.1259	0.1271	0.2339	0.3421
	0.056	(0.5373)		(0.3239)					
URF	0.151					0.0720	0.0723	0.0782	0.0784
						(0.0735)		(0.0749)	

Table 8.5.1
(continued)

B. Specially designed three- and five-equation models

	Eigen-values[2]	β_{12}		γ_{11}		ω_{11}		ω_{21}	
		Mean	True	Mean	True	Mean	True	Mean	True
Model 3a		0.5		0.491		0.4364		−0.1091	
OLS	0.221	0.1128	0.1605	0.1092	0.1107	0.1032	0.1038	0.0339	0.0521
	0.219	(0.1144)		(0.1130)					
TSLS	0.168	0.1633	0.1651	0.1145	0.1148	0.1052	0.1052	0.0529	0.0531
	0.163	(0.1635)		(0.1171)					
FP	0.168	0.1664	0.1682	0.1097	0.1098	0.1006	0.1006	0.0547	0.0548
	0.163	(0.1686)		(0.1171)					
URF						0.1015	0.1015	0.1212	0.1213
						(0.1211)		(0.1205)	
Model 3b		1.0		0.5773		0.2887		−0.2887	
OLS	0.176	0.1448	0.4297	0.1133	0.1666	0.0916	0.1259	0.0493	0.1597
	0.176	(0.1319)		(0.1250)					
TSLS	0.109	0.2484	0.2568	0.1401	0.1425	0.0801	0.0818	0.0840	0.0870
	0.111	(0.2251)		(0.1475)					
FP	0.111	0.2819	0.2904	0.1687	0.1773	0.0967	0.0967	0.0953	0.1015
	0.110	(0.2439)		(0.1503)					
URF						0.0957	0.0957	0.1308	0.1308
						(0.1204)		(0.1197)	
Model 4a		0.157		0.339		−0.0096		−0.3843	
OLS	0.118	0.0616	0.0736	0.0556	0.0669	0.0760	0.0832	0.1917	0.2425
	0.005	(0.0567)		(0.0494)					
TSLS	0.039	0.1613	0.1614	0.0763	0.0763	0.0753	0.0754	0.1747	0.1834
	0.001	(0.1840)		(0.0783)					
FP	0.029	2.3270	3.3080	4.5345	4.5397	0.0752	0.0762	0.1502	0.1541
	0.001	(2.6141)		(5.1035)					
URF						0.0738	0.0742	0.1502	0.1541
						(0.0667)		(0.1572)	

[1] The standard deviations around the mean and around the true value are labeled "Mean" and "True" respectively. The number in parentheses is the mean of 100 estimates of the standard deviation from the unrevised large-sample formula; see Part B.3 in Table 10.1.1.

[2] The values in this column are the means of the smallest eigenvalues in 100 samples for the first and second structural equations and for the reduced form (URF only).

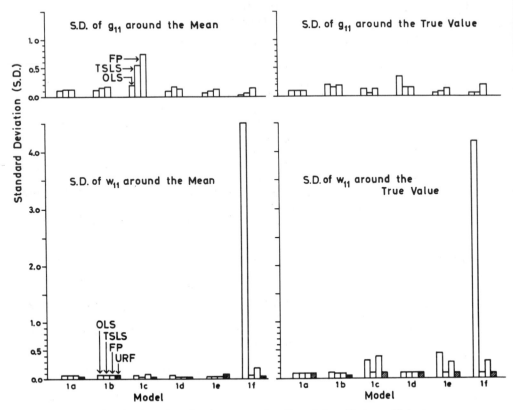

Chart 8.5.1. Dispersion of estimates as a function of size of beta coefficients.

from the eigenvalues given in the first column opposite each method. The smallest eigenvalues are found in TSLS and FP estimates of the second structural equation in Model 4a. In Model 1e it was necessary to specify correlations among exogenous variables in order to meet the condition that variances of all current endogenous variables be unity (see Chapter 2.3). Consequently, the eigenvalue for URF in Model 1e is less than in other models in Part A of Table 1.

The results for estimates of γ_{11} and ω_{11} among models in Part A of Table 1 show dramatic changes in relative dispersion as can be seen in Chart 1. Dispersion of estimates of structural coefficients is largest in the case of Model 1c, but for reduced form coefficients dispersion is largest in Model 1f. OLS and FP are affected more than TSLS. The most dramatic effect is in OLS estimates of ω_{11} in Model 1f. URF estimates are unaffected by size of beta coefficients except in Model 1e where the required design of correlations among exogenous variables increased dispersion slightly.

In Part B of Table 1 the dispersion of reduced form coefficients is approximately the same for all methods. However, in the case of structural coefficients, FP is very different from OLS and TSLS in Model 4a. The conditions for convergence (see Chapters 3.6 and 5.2) are not met in Model 4a.

The mean of the estimated standard deviation of FP estimates of structural coefficients in Models 1c and 1f are considerably less than the observed standard deviations. In all other cases in Table 1 the estimated and observed standard deviations are very similar.

The tails of several of the distributions of estimates shown in Table 1 are thick, but there are not what we could call extreme values in any of the distributions except FP estimates of ω_{11} in Model 1f. In this one case the smallest estimate in 100 samples (-2.9) was 10 standard deviations away from the mean and 20 times as far from the mean (0.06) as the next smallest value (-0.06).

The estimated standard deviation of URF estimates is, of course, a poor estimate of the standard deviation of OLS and FP estimates in Model 1f. This again points up the fact that the former cannot be used for estimating standard deviation of generated reduced form coefficients unless a considerable amount is known about the characteristics of the model being estimated.

The above discussion on the effects of beta coefficients on dispersion of estimates emphasizes the difference in relative performance among methods for different models. As stated in Chapter 2 we have endeavored to show results for a wide range of models in an attempt to give the reader a true insight into the differences among methods of estimation. Unfortunately, it is not possible to discuss all the results of all 46 different models in detail in a reasonable size monograph.

8.6. Lagged Endogenous Variables and Inter-Correlations among Exogenous Variables

Models 5a and 5b have the same design as Model 1b except for a correlation of ±0.7 between the two exogenous variables in each equation.

Table 8.6.1

Effect of correlation among exogenous variables on dispersion of estimates [1].

	Model 1b		Model 5b		Model 5a	
	Mean	True	Mean	True	Mean	True
β_{12}	1.0		1.0		1.0	
Standard deviation:						
OLS	0.1363	0.3410	0.1277	0.3394	0.1321	0.3674
	(0.1249)		(0.1221)		(0.1200)	
TSLS	0.1901	0.1922	0.1731	0.1731	0.1541	0.1568
	(0.1715)		(0.1620)		(0.1623)	
FP	0.1955	0.1981	0.1810	0.1811	0.1581	0.1614
	(0.1758)		(0.1632)		(0.1636)	
γ_{11}	0.8944		1.65		0.6845	
Standard deviation:						
OLS	0.1179	0.1917	0.1541	0.3011	0.1346	0.1827
	(0.1109)		(0.1680)		(0.1366)	
TSLS	0.1447	0.1450	0.1894	0.1894	0.1357	0.1370
	(0.1318)		(0.1983)		(0.1533)	
FP	0.1757	0.1757	0.2148	0.2150	0.2036	0.2089
	(0.1338)		(0.1996)		(0.1536)	
ω_{11}	0.4472		0.875		0.3423	
Standard deviation:						
OLS	0.0709	0.0954	0.1076	0.1403	0.0889	0.1007
TSLS	0.0610	0.0611	0.0992	0.1072	0.0679	0.0679
FP	0.0737	0.0744	0.1081	0.1166	0.1054	0.1064
URF	0.0717	0.0722	0.1071	0.1154	0.1111	0.1119
	(0.0748)		(0.1071)		(0.1041)	
ω_{21}	-0.4472		-0.875		-0.3423	
Standard deviation:						
OLS	0.0629	0.1267	0.1095	0.2722	0.0692	0.1076
TSLS	0.0620	0.0620	0.1024	0.1176	0.0752	0.0756
FP	0.0778	0.0780	0.1113	0.1272	0.1096	0.1114
URF	0.0665	0.0667	0.1032	0.1163	0.0943	0.0947
	(0.0738)		(0.1034)		(0.1034)	

[1] The standard deviations around the mean and around the true value are labeled "Mean" and "True" respectively. The number in parentheses is the mean of 100 estimates of the standard deviation from the unrevised large-sample formula; see Part B.3 of Table 10.1.1.

Table 8.6.2
Effect of presence of lagged endogenous variables on dispersion of estimates [1].

	Model 5q		Model 5c		Model 5d		Model 5e	
	Mean	True	Mean	True	Mean	True	Mean	True
$\sigma^2(\delta)$	0.10		0.212		0.144		0.144	
$\sigma^2(\epsilon)$	0.05		0.100		0.070		0.070	
1st eq.	no lag		$y_{1,t-1}$ & $y_{2,t-1}$		$y_{2,t-1}$		$y_{1,t-1}$	
2nd eq.	no lag		no lag		$y_{1,t-1}$		$y_{2,t-1}$	
β_{12}	1.0		1.0		1.0		1.0	
Standard deviation:								
OLS	0.0742	0.1209	0.0771	0.1387	0.0971	0.1688	0.0954	0.1705
	(0.0687)		(0.0759)		(0.0845)		(0.0857)	
TSLS	0.0774	0.0775	0.0816	0.0818	0.0978	0.0980	0.1066	0.1070
	(0.0741)		(0.0834)		(0.0958)		(0.0977)	
FP	0.0778	0.0779	0.0839	0.0840	0.1036	0.1040	0.1084	0.1087
	(0.0753)		(0.0845)		(0.0979)		(0.0988)	
γ_{11}	0.9747		0.8		1.1314		1.1314	
Standard deviation:								
OLS	0.0638	0.0766	0.0955	0.1159	0.0959	0.1265	0.0987	0.1278
	(0.0598)		(0.1098)		(0.0783)		(0.0789)	
TSLS	0.0619	0.0619	0.1007	0.1039	0.0928	0.0928	0.1027	0.1028
	(0.0624)		(0.1137)		(0.0846)		(0.0851)	
FP	0.0715	0.0717	0.1109	0.1160	0.1013	0.1015	0.1135	0.1135
	(0.0636)		(0.1149)		(0.0867)		(0.0859)	
ω_{11}	0.4873		0.4		0.5657		0.5657	
Standard deviation:								
OLS	0.0389	0.0496	0.0659	0.1596	0.0499	0.0608	0.0485	0.0625
TSLS	0.0367	0.0378	0.0774	0.0776	0.0436	0.0444	0.0492	0.0493
FP	0.0428	0.0442	0.0825	0.0832	0.0463	0.0466	0.0534	0.0535
URF	0.0439	0.0450	0.0818	0.0831	0.0464	0.0467	0.0549	0.0552
	(0.0371)		(0.0806)		(0.0459)		(0.0462)	
ω_{21}	−0.4873		−0.4		−0.5657		−0.5657	
Standard deviation:								
OLS	0.0306	0.0422	0.0989	0.2094	0.0453	0.0651	0.0592	0.0765
TSLS	0.0302	0.0305	0.0815	0.0832	0.0416	0.0417	0.0489	0.0489
FP	0.0354	0.0356	0.0845	0.0871	0.0463	0.0465	0.0540	0.0540
URF	0.0394	0.0399	0.0839	0.0847	0.0483	0.0483	0.0498	0.0498
	(0.0373)		(0.0783)		(0.0466)		(0.0464)	

[1] Model 5q is not strictly comparable to the other models because variance of ϵ is only 0.05 compared to 0.10, 0.07, and 0.07 in Models 5c−5e. The standard deviations around the mean and around the true value are labeled "Mean" and "True" respectively. The number in parentheses is the mean of 100 estimates of the standard deviation from the unrevised large-sample formula; see Part B.3 of Table 10.1.1.

The gamma coefficients were specified so that the condition of unit variance for all endogenous and exogenous variables was maintained. All results in Table 1 indicate no significant effect from correlations of ±0.7 among exogenous variables on dispersion of estimates of structural coefficients. There are no extreme values in any of the sets of estimates.

The dispersion in estimates of reduced form coefficients is larger in Models 5a and 5b than in Model 1b. The reason is evident in the relative size of eigenvalues shown in Part D.3 of Tables 10.2.2, 10.2.27 and 10.2.28. The smaller eigenvalues in Models 5a and 5b indicate that the correlations among exogenous variables created a multicollinearity problem. On the other hand, the eigenvalues for the structural equations show relatively little difference among Models 1b, 5a and 5b.

The correlation of ±0.7 in Models 5a and 5b is of moderate size. It is possible that correlations closer to one could have significant effect on dispersion in one or more of the methods of estimating structural coefficients. The results in this Monte Carlo research in no way indicate that the problem of multicollinearity in applied econometrics is unimportant.

Results in Table 2 indicate very little effect on dispersion from presence of lagged endogenous variables. When adjustment is made for differences in size of residuals (see $\sigma^2(\epsilon)$ in line 2 of Table 2) there is little difference among the observed standard deviations. OLS estimates in Models 5c–5e are biased as shown in Charts 7.7.1–7.7.3 but no more so than in models without lagged endogenous variables (e.g., see Charts 8.3.1 and 6.1.2)

In all models shown in Tables 1 and 2 the mean of the estimated standard deviation is close to the value of the observed standard deviation around the mean for each method. OLS estimates are, of course, biased and the estimated standard deviation is an underestimate of the standard deviation around the true value.

There were no extreme values in any of the distributions of estimates of parameters shown in Tables 1 and 2. If the multicollinearity problem had been made worse by specifying larger correlations among exogenous variables or specifying a lag structure that would lead to large correlations among determining variables there would, of course, be greater chances of obtaining extreme values.

8.7. GEID Specifications

The size of correlations in a GEID specification have a large effect on the bias of OLS and TSLS estimates, but they have little effect on dispersion around the mean. Chart 1 shows the change in dispers͏͏ as the size of correlations is increased in the series of Models 6f–6j.

Dispersion of TSLS estimates around the true value increases beca͏e

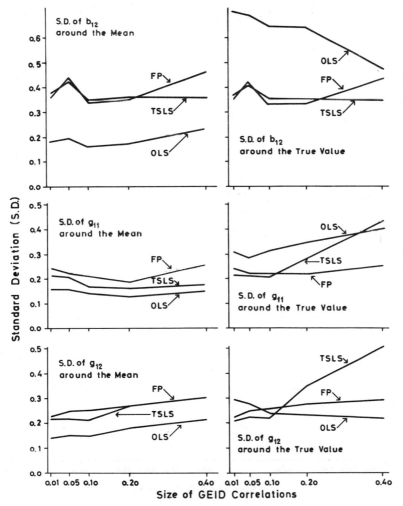

Chart 8.7.1. Dispersion of estimates of structural coefficients and increasing size of correlation within GEID specification; Models 6f–6j.

of the significant increase in bias. The increasing size of correlations has considerably more effect on TSLS than on OLS estimates. The bias in OLS estimates of β_{12} actually decrease, and, consequently, dispersion around the true value decreases.

The greater dispersion of FP estimates of β_{12} in Model 6j is caused by

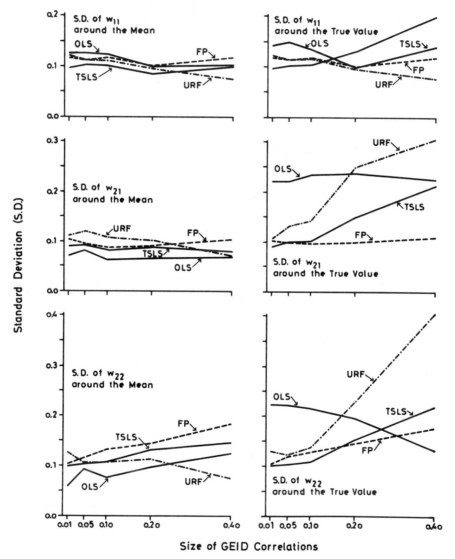

Chart 8.7.2. Dispersion of estimates of reduced form coefficients and increasing size of correlations within GEID specification; Models 6f–6j.

a thick upper tail (see Chart 7.8.2). We do not know if this is anything more than sampling variation. FP estimates of gamma coefficients and reduced form coefficients show very little change as size of correlations is increased in Series 6e–6j. The dispersion of estimates of reduced form coefficients is shown in Chart 2. The cumulative distribution of estimates of ω_{11} in Model 6j (Chart 7.8.3) gives good insight into the relative dispersion among the methods for coefficients of all variables which are not correlated with the residual ϵ. Within the GEID specification

$$r(x_1, \epsilon_1) = r(x_2, \epsilon_1) = r(x_3, \epsilon_2) = r(x_4, \epsilon_2) = 0 . \qquad (1)$$

However, as can be easily seen in Chart 2, the relative dispersion of estimates of ω_{21} and ω_{22} varies considerably within the Series 6f–6j. The URF estimates are affected because

$$r(x_1, \epsilon_2), r(x_2, \epsilon_2), r(x_3, \epsilon_1), r(x_4, \epsilon_1) \neq 0 . \qquad (2)$$

TSLS estimates are also affected by the conditions specified in (2).

There is no significant difference in dispersion around the mean and dispersion around the true value for any method in the Series 6a–6c. The correlations in this series are not large enough to have measurable effect on multicollinearity which in turn affects dispersion of estimates.

No extreme values occurred in any sets of estimates for Models 6a–6c and Models 6e–6j. The cumulative distributions for β_{12} and γ_{11} under a GEID specification in Model 6j (Charts 7.8.1 and 7.8.2) and under a classical specification in Model 1b (Charts 8.3.1 and 6.1.2) show that correlations of 0.4 or less do not lead to extreme values. Of course, if the correlations were increased to near unity the multicollinearity problem would become severe enough to produce extreme values.

The estimated standard deviations were a good estimate of the standard deviation of estimates around the mean in each method for each model. Several of the estimates from OLS, TSLS, and URF were significantly biased, and, consequently, the estimated standard deviation is an underestimate of the standard deviation around the true value.

CHAPTER 9

Some General ID (GEID) Models

9.1. Rationale of GEID Models

The limited scope of Chapter 9 must be emphasized. In line with the main orientation of the monograph, we shall mainly be concerned with estimation aspects. Chapter 9.2 links up with Chapters 4—8 in presenting and discussing our Monte Carlo results as regards Classic ID versus GEID systems. As before, our analysis deals with models that are of the special type where all structural relations are behavioral, and therefore are asymmetric in the sense of Chapter 3.2. One GEID model involves an identity or relation of instantaneous equilibrium; here the structural relations are brought into asymmetric form by a suitable normalization. As in the case of Classic ID systems, FP estimates of parameters of GEID systems discussed in Chapter 9.2 were obtained by an iterative procedure.

As will be shown in Chapter 9.3, the iterative FP estimates of Girshick-Haavelmo's model can be obtained in algebraic form. It is not easy to obtain algebraic solutions of FP estimates in models as large as five equations unless there are some special features that allow simplifications. Some of the simpler models in our GEID specifications allow algebraic solutions for the iterative FP estimates, as has been shown in Chapter 3.8.

Summarizing on the basis of Chapter 1.4, GEID systems differ from Classic ID systems in five fundamental respects:

(i) Classic ID systems allow interpretation in terms of apparent scatter; GEID systems in terms of genuine scatter.

A closely related feature is that GEID systems are designed for predictive inference in terms of conditional expectations (predictors).

(ii) Classic ID systems in general cannot be specified so that both the structural form and the reduced form allow inference in terms of predictors. This twofold inference in terms of predictors becomes possible after a slight reformulation of the structural relations of Classic ID systems. The reformulated systems are called REID (Reformulated ID) systems. GEID systems allow the same twofold inference in terms of predictors.

(iii) In overidentified ID systems (Classic or REID) the assumptions about zero intercorrelations between residuals and variables are more numerous than the free parameters of the model. In this respect Classic ID and REID systems differ radically from the mainstream of model building, not only in econometrics and other social sciences, but also in physics and other natural sciences. Most model designs are ruled by the "parity principle": the assumptions imposed on the model should be the same in number as the free parameters. The generalization from REID to GEID systems brings the model design in accordance with the parity principle.

(iv) The classical assumptions referred to in (iii) serve estimation purposes and have no other obvious rationale. The assumptions are needed for the direct estimation of the reduced form by OLS regression, for the TSLS and 3SLS estimation methods which use OLS in the first stage, and for LIML estimation.

The FP method tackles the estimation problem of REID and GEID systems by an iterative procedure that stays in the structural form and generates the reduced form only after having completed the parameter estimation.

(v) The classical assumptions referred to in (iii) permit a symmetric treatment of the current endogenous variables in the sense that they can be moved freely between the right and left members of the structural relations without this having any influence on the numerical values of the parameters. This symmetry in the design is alien to the predictor specification of the structural relations and is not present in GEID systems. Hence, the GEID systems bring the distinction between asymmetric and symmetric specification of the structural form to the foreground. Chapters 9.2 and 9.3 deal with asymmetric models. Problems concerning estimation of models under a symmetric approach are explored in Chapter 11, using a different kind of iterative approach.

9.2. Difference in Relative Performance of OLS, TSLS, and FP for Classic ID vs GEID models

9.2.1. Scope of Monte Carlo Experiments with GEID Models

Some of the differences in results between classical and GEID specifications have been taken up in the preceding discussions and tables on dispersion, bias, and predictive power. In this chapter we present a more detailed discussion on the relationship between relative performance among methods of estimation and type of GEID specification.

Our Monte Carlo experiments are designed to explore the problem are of GEID Models in two principal directions. One direction is exemplified in the Series 6a—6c where the number of correlations between residuals and exogenous variables is increased as the size of the model is increased. A second direction is exemplified in the Series 6e—6j where the absolute size of the correlations between residuals and exogenous variables is increased. Changes in both directions have a pronounced effect on relative performance among alternative methods of estimation.

9.2.2. A Specific Feature of Two-Relation GEID Models

The sharpest distinction in the first direction to be explored is between models with two equations and those with three or more equations. In a two-equation model both the GEID and classical specifications require:

$$r(\epsilon_1, y_2^*) = r(\epsilon_2, y_1^*) = 0 . \tag{1}$$

In systems with three or more relations, the conditions of type (1) are fulfilled by the classical but not always by the GEID specification. Consequently, methods such as TSLS, which give consistent estimates

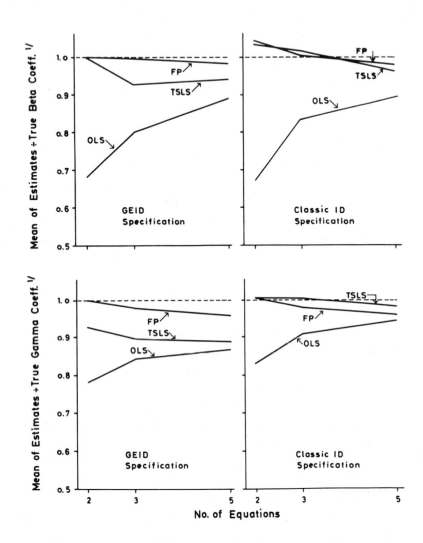

Chart 9.2.1. Changes in bias as size of model increases within GEID and classical specifications: (a) beta coefficient, (b) gamma coefficients.

[1] The models and coefficients are as follows: For the two-equation system the coefficients are β_{12} and γ_{11} from Models 6a and 2a for GEID and classical designs respectively; for the three-equation system the coefficients are β_{31} and γ_{35} from Models 6b and 2b; for the five-equation system the coefficients are β_{45} and γ_{47} from Models 6c and 2c. The particular coefficients shown for each equation system are those that appear to best indicate the differences among the three methods of estimation.

within the classical specification also give consistent estimates of beta coefficients within the GEID specification for all two-equation models. This is illustrated in the case of TSLS estimates of the beta coefficient for the two-equation model shown in Chart 1.

9.2.3. Relative Bias as Influenced by Correlations Between Residuals and Exogenous variables

Using bias as a general term for inconsistency and small-sample bias, we refer to three aspects in the quality of estimates of coefficients in a model; namely, bias in estimates of coefficients, dispersion of estimates of coefficients, and predictive power of an estimated model. The first aspect, bias, is highly interesting when comparing alternative methods. According to the general theory (see Chapter 3) the classical estimation methods as applied to GEID systems are inconsistent, whereas FP estimates are consistent.

Chart 1 clearly indicates that TSLS estimates become significantly more biased than FP estimates when there are correlations between residuals and exogenous variables. This is so even when correlations are as small as 0.10 in absolute value. Discussion in the latter part of this chapter will show that differences between TSLS and FP with respect to dispersion and predictive power are not as sensitive to the size and number of correlations as is the difference with respect to bias.

The results presented in Charts 1 and 2 show that FP estimates are not significantly affected by number and size of correlations even in small samples. TSLS estimates begin to show significant increase in inconsistency when the absolute value of correlations between residuals and exogenous variables reaches 0.10.

Likewise, OLS estimates begin to show a change in bias when the correlations are 0.10 or larger. Since OLS estimates are inconsistent even in the classical specification the inconsistency due to correlations within the GEID specification is an added component of bias. The results in Chart 2 and Table 1 show the added bias to be in the same direction as the bias under the classical specification, but this will not always be true because it depends upon the signs of the specified correlations.

TSLS estimates are affected more by the size of correlations between

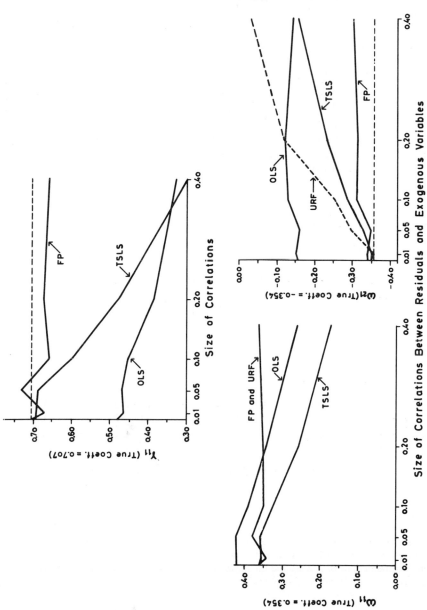

Chart 9.2.2. Consistency of FP vs inconsistency of OLS, TSLS and URF in GEID models; Models 6a–j.

Table 9.2.1

Increasing size of correlation in GEID models [1].

	β_{12}		γ_{11}		γ_{12}		ω_{11}	
True value	1.0		0.7071		0.7071		0.3536	
Model 6e (= 5n; correlations = 0.0)								
OLS	0.3303	(0.1675)	0.4777	(0.1448)	0.4581	(0.1566)	0.4304	(0.1241)
		(0.6903)		(0.2713)		(0.2942)		(0.1459)
TSLS	0.9547	(0.3920)	0.6926	(0.1914)	0.6899	(0.2351)	0.3659	(0.0998)
		(0.3946)		(0.1919)		(0.2357)		(0.1006)
FP	0.9614	(0.4022)	0.6950	(0.2041)	0.6586	(0.2558)	0.3662	(0.1051)
		(0.4040)		(0.2045)		(0.2604)		(0.1059)
URF							0.3668	(0.1020)
								(0.1029)
Model 6g (correlations = ±0.05)								
OLS	0.3230	(0.1868)	0.4772	(0.1420)	0.4800	(0.1477)	0.4348	(0.1256)
		(0.7023)		(0.2702)		(0.2709)		(0.1496)
TSLS	1.0272	(0.4161)	0.6869	(0.1978)	0.7675	(0.2284)	0.3554	(0.1034)
		(0.4170)		(0.1988)		(0.2363)		(0.1034)
FP	1.0262	(0.4204)	0.7335	(0.2066)	0.6870	(0.2545)	0.3790	(0.1110)
		(0.4212)		(0.2083)		(0.2553)		(0.1139)
URF							0.3778	(0.1114)
								(0.1140)
Model 6h (correlations = ±0.10)								
OLS	0.3515	(0.1498)	0.4392	(0.1341)	0.5206	(0.1481)	0.3993	(0.1234)
		(0.6656)		(0.2996)		(0.2382)		(0.1316)
TSLS	0.9685	(0.3403)	0.6042	(0.1682)	0.7885	(0.2106)	0.3239	(0.1029)
		(0.3418)		(0.1972)		(0.2258)		(0.1071)
FP	0.9640	(0.3370)	0.6542	(0.2028)	0.7021	(0.2453)	0.3501	(0.1166)
		(0.3389)		(0.2096)		(0.2454)		(0.1167)
URF							0.3520	(0.1157)
								(0.1157)

[1] The three numbers shown for each method for each coefficient are as follows: the first number is the mean of the estimates from 100 samples; the upper number in parentheses is the estimated standard deviation around the mean and the lower number in parentheses is the estimated standard deviation around the true value.

Table 9.2.1
(continued)

	β_{12}		γ_{11}		γ_{12}		ω_{11}	
Model 6i (correlations = ±0.20)								
OLS	0.3673	(0.1565)	0.3898	(0.1103)	0.5658	(0.1743)	0.3466	(0.0988)
		(0.6518)		(0.3359)		(0.2244)		(0.0990)
TSLS	1.0158	(0.3647)	0.4782	(0.1434)	0.9235	(0.2761)	0.2529	(0.0813)
		(0.3650)		(0.2701)		(0.3508)		(0.1294)
FP	1.0247	(0.3514)	0.6712	(0.1944)	0.7303	(0.2729)	0.3496	(0.1011)
		(0.3523)		(0.1977)		(0.2739)		(0.1012)
URF							0.3515	(0.0967)
								(0.0967)
Model 6j (correlations = ±0.40)								
OLS	0.5785	(0.2271)	0.3416	(0.1289)	0.7840	(0.2155)	0.2650	(0.1075)
		(0.4788)		(0.3876)		(0.2288)		(0.1393)
TSLS	1.0231	(0.3628)	0.3226	(0.1548)	1.1242	(0.2941)	0.1796	(0.0991)
		(0.3635)		(0.4145)		(0.5104)		(0.2002)
FP	1.0299	(0.4564)	0.6681	(0.2348)	0.7012	(0.2925)	0.3631	(0.1164)
		(0.4574)		(0.2380)		(0.2926)		(0.1168)
URF							0.3642	(0.0753)
								(0.0760)

residuals and exogenous variables than are OLS estimates. In Model 6j, where the correlations are ± 0.4, the bias in the TSLS estimates is greater than that in OLS estimates for all four gamma coefficients. As stated earlier, TSLS gives consistent estimates of beta coefficients in all the two-equation models under both classical and GEID specifications.

9.2.4. Relative Bias as Influenced by Number of Equations

The effect from increasing the number of equations, which in turn allows for more non-zero correlations to be specified, does not affect the degree of bias in estimates of gamma coefficients if the variance of the residuals remains constant. This point is well illustrated in the results for OLS and TSLS shown in Chart 1. The bias in TSLS is approximately the same for the models with 2, 3, and 5 equations, whereas the bias in OLS decreases as the number of equations increases. The models were designed so the variance of ϵ remains constant; consequently, the variance of δ must decrease as the number of equations increases. Since the bias in TSLS depends on ϵ and the bias in OLS depends on δ, the two methods show different effects as the number of equations is increased.

Although the bias in OLS under the classical design makes it difficult to judge the added bias from the correlations in a GEID model, the particular OLS estimates of gamma coefficients shown in Chart 1 indicate greater bias in GEID than in the classical specification. In both the classical and GEID specification OLS bias becomes less as the number of equations is increased, but in each of the models the bias under the GEID specification is larger than that under the classical specification. The direction of the bias depends on the signs of the GEID correlations; it need not be in the same direction as the bias under the classical specification.

9.2.5. Dispersion of Coefficient Estimates, Size of Correlations and Size of Model

Dispersion of estimates around the mean in GEID models is approximately the same as that in comparable REID models for each of the four methods. No extreme values occurred in any of the results from GEID models. This was to be expected since all of the models either had relatively small GEID correlations or had a type of interdependence that does not cause severe problems in estimation. GEID correlations which are less than 0.3 in absolute value should not be expected to have a large effect on dispersion. Summers' model with beta coefficients of ± 1 has been shown to be a type of interdependence that does not involve severe problems in estimation.

FP is consistent for all GEID models; small-sample bias is small when interdependence is of the type in Models 6a–c and 6e–j. Consequently, dispersion of FP estimates around the true value is similar to dispersion around the mean even with GEID correlations as large as ± 0.4.

OLS, TSLS and URF are inconsistent and we find that dispersion around the true value increases and in most cases exceeds that in FP estimates as GEID correlations exceed 0.1 in absolute value (see Chart

8.7.1). There is a slight qualification with respect to estimates of certain reduced form coefficients. The reduced form residual ϵ_i is uncorrelated with all exogenous variables that appear in the ith structural equation. Consequently, the estimates of reduced form coefficients on these variables are very little affected by the presence of GEID correlations.

As mentioned in the beginning of Chapter 8.7, dispersion of estimates does not reveal as many clear distinctions among methods of estimation as does bias. All results of our Monte Carlo experiments indicate that dispersion around the mean and the possibility for extreme estimates are approximately the same in GEID and Classic ID models.

9.2.6. GEID Specifications and Predictive Power of Alternative Methods

The relative performance of alternative methods as measured by predictive power [1] — the third criterion identified in section 9.2.3 — is difficult to judge. A basic decision in the evaluation is whether the correlations between residuals and exogenous variables in the sample period also hold in the prediction period. This assumption may or may not be true; hence the adoption of the assumption provides a piece of true or false information; if false, the situation interferes with the estimation procedures and the operative properties of the model. The FP procedure is not designed to exploit information to the effect that the sample and prediction periods have the same correlation structure. Hence if the information is true, this will in some respects be to the disadvantage of FP relative to methods which do exploit the information. This last point applies to comparisons with regard to predictive power. In fact, assuming that the correlations at issue have the same structure in the sample and prediction periods, the predictive power of a method that is known to give biased estimates of coefficients is likely to be greater than that for a method which gives unbiased estimates. That is, TSLS and URF estimates of a model are likely to have a higher predictive power than FP estimates. This is because the exogenous variables can act as proxy variables for the residuals when the correlation between the two remains constant in both the sample and prediction periods.

All of the Monte Carlo data for the eight GEID models studied in this monograph were generated under the same specification for both

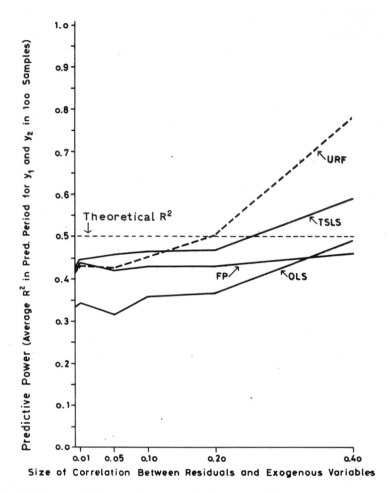

Chart 9.2.3. Effect of GEID correlations on predictive power. [Monte Carlo data were generated under the same specification for both the sample and prediction periods (see discussion in 9.2.6). Each model was designed to give $\sigma^2(y_i) = 1.0$ and $\sigma^2(\epsilon_i) = 0.5$.] Models 6e−j.

the sample and prediction periods. Consequently, the measures of predictive power do not reflect the main attribute of FP, namely, consistent estimates of structural coefficients. The authors' choice of having correlations remain constant in both periods was partly arbitrary and partly expediency in that computer programs were already available.

The change in predictive power for each method as the size of correlations between residuals and exogenous variables increases is shown in

Chart 3. FP is the only method for which the R^2 using the estimated model is less than the R^2 computed from the generated Monte Carlo data. Unless the estimates of parameters are biased so that the exogenous variables become proxies for the residuals, the R^2 from an estimated model will always be less than R^2 computed from the generated data.

The relative predictive power among the four methods when the correlations become large will vary, with trends like those shown at the right in Chart 3. FP estimates are less biased so the predictive power will be smaller than that for OLS, TSLS, and URF. The predictive power of OLS will be less than for TSLS and URF because of the inconsistency of OLS estimates of structural coefficients in an interdependent system.

Unless sample size is so small that URF is greatly affected by overfitting, the predictive power of URF will be larger than that for TSLS.

The conditions

$$r(\epsilon_1, x_3),\ r(\epsilon_1, x_4),\ r(\epsilon_2, x_1),\ r(\epsilon_2, x_2) \neq 0 \tag{2}$$

affect both URF and TSLS estimates. However, the effect of the non-zero correlations specified in (2) in the first stage of TSLS are diminished in the second stage where the only non-zero correlations between the residuals and determining variables are

$$r(\epsilon_1, \hat{y}_2^*),\ r(\epsilon_2, \hat{y}_1^*) \neq 0 \tag{3}$$

where $\hat{y}_i^*$ is the estimate of y_i^* from the first stage of TSLS. The correlations specified in (3) do not have the same effect on predictive power as those specified in (2).

Chart 4 shows the difference in predictive power between GEID and classical specifications. These models are comparable pairwise, except for the correlations between residuals and exogenous variables. Unfortunately, the sampling variation is so large that the small differences that might exist would not be noticeable in this set of results. It does, however, point out that when all GEID correlations are small (0.2 or less in the two series of GEID models under analysis) there is little

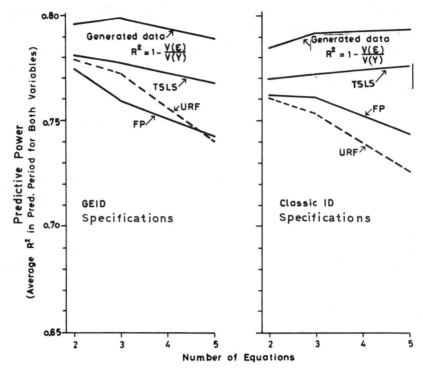

Chart 9.2.4. Predictive power in GEID and classic ID systems as size of model increases.
Models 6a–c and 2a–c.

effect on predictive power regardless of the number of non-zero correlations.

9.2.7. Summary Comments on Intercorrelations and Number of Relations

No precise statement can be made concerning the relative degree of bias among the methods until the model, including the number and size of correlations between residuals and exogenous variables, has been specified. We can, however, make two general statements that summarize the results from the Monte Carlo research with respect to bias.

First, in many models FP estimates are less biased than TSLS estimates even in small samples.

Second, when the size of correlations between residuals and exogenous variables is increased, bias in TSLS estimates increases more rapidly than bias in other methods. In some of the models TSLS estimates become more biased than FP estimates when correlations are as small as ± 0.2.

We would not expect the correlations between residuals and exogenous variables to have significant effect on dispersion of estimates around their expected value, and the Monte Carlo results bear this out. FP estimates might have a slightly larger dispersion in GEID than in comparable classical models, but our Monte Carlo results are not sufficient for proving this. The results presented in Table 1 show that it is only dispersion around the true value and not dispersion around the mean that is significantly affected by the size of correlations within the GEID specification. There were no extreme values for any method in any of the eight GEID models in our Monte Carlo work.

The choice of the best method with respect to predictive power, R^2, depends on whether the GEID correlations in the sample period remain constant in the prediction period. If they do, it is obvious that the inconsistent methods such as URF and TSLS will tend to have the highest predictive power; if they change, FP will tend to have the highest predictive power since it is the only consistent method among the four methods investigated.

The upshot of this is that the predictive power of an estimated model under the assumption that the correlations remain constant in the sample and prediction periods is not likely to provide a good judgment on alternative methods within situations where GEID models are appropriate. It is likely that many uses of an estimated GEID model would center on one or more specific coefficients in the structural equations.[2] That is, the coefficients would be used to predict the effect of one variable on another in the absence of any correlation that might be present in the sample period. In such cases the quality of estimates should be judged on how close the estimates are to the true value of the coefficient. The Monte Carlo results showing standard deviation around the true value (see Table 1) or bias in specific coefficients (see Charts 1—2) would be the most appropriate measures of quality of estimates in such situations. Since FP estimates are consistent and results to date indicate that small-sample bias is quite small, we can say that this method is generally superior to OLS, TSLS, and URF when GEID models are appropriate.

9.3. Algebraic FP (AFP) Estimation of Girshick-Haavelmo's Model [1]
by E.Lyttkens

Girshick and Haavelmo (1947) in one of the first applications of inter-dependent systems constructed a demand-supply model for food which is a standard reference in comparative studies of econometric method. Their pioneering model has five endogenous variables: food consumption per capita, y_{1t}; real retail prices of food product, y_{2t}; disposable real income per capita, y_{3t}; production of agricultural food products per capita, y_{4t}; real price received by the farmers for food production, y_{5t}. The lagged endogenous variables are $y_{5,t-1} = z_{1t}$ and $y_{3,t-1} = z_{4t}$. The exogenous variables are net investment per capita, z_{2t}; and time, with the year as time unit, $t = z_{3t}$. All variables except time (t) are expressed in index numbers (1935–39 = 100). The data are given in Table 1, reprinted from Girshick-Haavelmo (1947).

The five structural equations of the model are

$$y_{1t} = \beta_{12}y_{2t} + \beta_{13}y_{3t} + \gamma_{13}z_{3t} + \gamma_{14}z_{4t} + \gamma_{10} + \delta_{1t} \qquad (1a)$$

$$y_{1t} = \beta_{22}y_{2t} + \beta_{24}y_{4t} + \gamma_{23}z_{3t} + \gamma_{20} + \delta_{2t} \qquad (1b)$$

$$y_{3t} = \gamma_{32}z_{2t} + \beta_{34}z_{4t} + \gamma_{30} + \delta_{3t} \qquad (1c)$$

$$y_{4t} = \beta_{45}y_{5t} + \gamma_{41}z_{1t} + \gamma_{43}z_{3t} + \gamma_{40} + \delta_{4t} \qquad (1d)$$

$$y_{5t} = \beta_{52}y_{2t} + \gamma_{53}z_{3t} + \gamma_{50} + \delta_{5t} . \qquad (1e)$$

To apply asymmetric FP estimation it is required that each endogenous variable occurs on the left-hand side of just one equation. Therefore, we must put y_{2t} instead of y_{1t} on the left-hand side of one of the two first equations. With this choice we can obtain two versions of the respecified system and, thereby, two different FP estimates of the model.

9.3.1. First Version of the AFP (Algebraic FP) Estimation

In order to obtain the first version of the respecification we start by

Table 9.3.1
Original data used by Girshick-Haavelmo for estimating Model (1a–e) [1].

Calendar year	y_1 Food consumption per capita	y_2 Food prices ÷ by cost of living	y_3 Disposable income ÷ by cost of living	y_4 Food production per capita	y_5 Prices received by farmers for food ÷ by cost of living	z_1 $y_5(t-1)$	z_2 Investment per capita ÷ by cost of living	z_3 Time	z_4 $y_3(t-1)$
1922	98.6	100.2	87.4	108.5	99.1	98.0	92.9	1	77.4
1923	101.2	101.6	97.6	110.1	99.1	99.1	142.9	2	87.4
1924	102.4	100.5	96.7	110.4	98.9	99.1	100.0	3	97.6
1925	100.9	106.0	98.2	104.3	110.8	98.9	123.8	4	96.7
1926	102.3	108.7	99.8	107.2	108.2	110.8	111.9	5	98.2
1927	101.5	106.7	100.5	105.8	105.6	108.2	121.4	6	99.8
1928	101.6	106.7	103.2	107.8	109.8	105.6	107.1	7	100.5
1929	101.6	108.2	107.8	103.4	108.7	109.8	142.9	8	103.2
1930	99.8	105.5	96.6	102.7	100.6	108.7	92.9	9	107.8
1931	100.3	95.6	88.9	104.1	81.0	100.6	97.6	10	96.6
1932	97.6	88.6	75.1	99.2	68.6	81.0	52.4	11	88.9
1933	97.2	91.0	76.9	99.7	70.9	68.6	40.5	12	75.1
1934	97.3	97.9	84.6	102.0	81.4	70.9	64.3	13	76.9
1935	96.0	102.3	90.6	94.3	102.3	81.4	78.6	14	84.6
1936	99.2	102.2	103.1	97.7	105.0	102.3	114.3	15	90.6
1937	100.3	102.5	105.1	101.1	110.5	105.0	121.4	16	103.1
1938	100.3	97.0	96.4	102.3	92.5	110.5	78.6	17	105.1
1939	104.1	95.8	104.4	104.4	89.3	92.5	109.5	18	96.4
1940	105.3	96.4	110.7	108.5	93.0	89.3	128.6	19	104.4
1941	107.6	100.3	127.1	111.3	106.6	93.0	238.1	20	110.7
Sum	2015.1	2013.7	1950.7	2084.8	1941.9	1933.3	2159.7	210	1901.0
Mean	100.755	100.685	97.535	104.240	97.095	96.665	107.985	10.500	95.050

[1] The data are quoted from the source paper, Girshick-Haavelmo (1947).

rewriting the second structural equation as

$$y_{2t} = \beta'_{21}y_{1t} + \beta'_{24}y_{4t} + \gamma'_{23}z_{3t} + \gamma'_{20} + \delta'_{2t} . \qquad (2)$$

In order to compare FP estimates of this equation with those from other methods, we normalize again after estimation so that the coefficient of y_{1t} takes on unit value.

Since the third equation contains only one endogenous variable, it can be estimated directly by OLS, giving the systematic part of y_{3t},

$$y_{3t}^* = g_{32}z_{2t} + g_{34}z_{4t} + g_{30} \, . \tag{3}$$

The first equation is just identified, the number of endogenous variables y_i on the right-hand side of the equation being the same as the number of predetermined variables absent from the equation. Since the systematic parts y_{it}^* are linear expressions in the predetermined variables, it follows that y_{1t}^* can be obtained from the OLS regression of y_{1t} on all predetermined variables of the system. This gives

and

$$y_{1t} = w_{11}z_{1t} + w_{12}z_{2t} + w_{13}z_{3t} + w_{14}z_{4t} + w_{10} + e_{1t} \tag{4}$$

$$y_{1t}^* = w_{11}z_{1t} + w_{12}z_{2t} + w_{13}z_{3t} + w_{14}z_{4t} + w_{10} \, . \tag{5}$$

In other words, y_{1t}^* is obtained with the aid of the unrestricted reduced form.

We write the two last equations of (1a–e) and equation (2) in REID-GEID form (see 1.4.4),

$$y_{2t} = b'_{21}y_{1t}^* + b'_{24}y_{4t}^* + g'_{23}z_{3t} + g'_{20} + e'_{2t} \tag{6a}$$

$$y_{4t} = b_{45}y_{5t}^* + g_{41}z_{1t} + g_{43}z_{3t} + g_{40} + e_{4t} \tag{6b}$$

$$y_{5t} = b_{52}y_{2t}^* + g_{53}z_{3t} + g_{50} + e_{5t} \, . \tag{6c}$$

Here y_{1t}^* is already known according to formula (5) and can be treated as a predetermined variable. In the three-equation system (6a–c) we can then consider y_{1t}^*, z_{1t}, and z_{3t} as predetermined variables, with the result that the two first equations are just identified with respect to these predetermined variables. We denote by q'_{21}, p'_{21}, and p'_{23} the partial regression coefficients of y_{2t} on y_{1t}^*, z_{1t} and z_{3t} and by p'_{20} the corresponding constant term; for y_{4t} we use similar notations without primes. This gives

$$y_{2t}^* = q'_{21}y_{1t}^* + p'_{21}z_{1t} + p'_{23}z_{3t} + p'_{20} \, , \tag{7a}$$

$$y_{4t}^* = q_{45}y_{5t}^* + p_{41}z_{1t} + p_{43}z_{3t} + p_{40} \, . \tag{7b}$$

The reduction in the number of predetermined variables can be interpreted in the following way. When y_{1t}^* from expression (5) is inserted into (6) the variables z_{2t} and z_{4t} are explicitly introduced in the three-equation system considered. But the ratio between the coefficients of these two variables is already determined, and, therefore, $w_{12}z_{2t} + w_{14}z_{4t}$ acts as one predetermined variable.

Having obtained y_{2t}^* from equation (7a) we proceed to estimate the fifth equation of the system by means of OLS regression applied to equation (6c); y_{5t}^* is obtained as the systematic part of this regression. Now all five components y_{it}^* have been obtained. The remaining coefficients of the system are estimated by OLS applied to the respecified system, or rather by equating coefficients in the relations obtained.

9.3.2. Second Version of the AFP Estimation

A second version of the asymmetric respecification is obtained if we put y_{2t} on the left-hand side in the first equation, say

$$y_{2t} = \beta_{11}'' y_{1t} + \beta_{13}'' y_{3t} + \gamma_{13}'' z_{3t} + \gamma_{14}'' z_{4t} + \gamma_{10}'' + \delta_{1t}'', \qquad (8)$$

while y_{1t} is retained on the left-hand side of the second equation. Then, as before, y_{3t}^* is obtained directly from the third equation, while the first equation — which is now just identified — yields a value of y_{2t}^*, say

$$y_{2t}^* = w_{21}z_{1t} + w_{22}z_{2t} + w_{23}z_{3t} + w_{24}z_{4t} + w_{20}. \qquad (9)$$

Since we now know y_{2t}^*, the coefficients of the fifth equation as well as the value of y_{5t}^* can be estimated. Thereafter, the coefficients of the fourth equation as well as the value of y_{4t}^* is obtained. The next step is to estimate the coefficients of the second equation as well as y_{1t}^*, and, at last, the coefficients of the first equation written in the form (8) are obtained. For easy comparison, we have afterwards normalized so that the coefficient of y_{1t} takes on unit value in this equation.

The easy algebraic solution in this second version of the model can be explained in the following simple way: When y_{2t}^* is treated as a predetermined variable, the four last structural equations form a recursive system

Table 9.3.2

Parameter estimates in Girshick-Haavelmo's model as obtained by four asymmetric methods [1].

Abbreviations:

OLS	Ordinary least squares regression	(1a–e)
TSLS	Two stages least squares method	(1a–e)
AFP 1	Algebraic fix-point method, first version	(1a), (2), (1c–e)
AFP 2	Algebraic fix-point method, second version	(8), (1b–e)

Method	First equation					Second equation			
	b_{12}	b_{13}	g_{13}	g_{14}	g_{10}	b_{22}	b_{24}	g_{23}	g_{20}
OLS	−0.336	0.277	−0.234	0.064	103.967	0.139	0.559	0.308	25.292
TSLS	−0.486	0.290	−0.317	0.097	115.563	0.163	0.637	0.337	14.419
AFP 1	−0.342	0.236	−0.160	0.098	104.547	0.188	0.625	0.344	13.129
AFP 2	0.306	0.176	0.213	−0.109	60.96	0.215	0.543	0.333	18.976

Method	Third equation			Fourth equation				Fifth equation		
	g_{32}	g_{34}	g_{30}	b_{45}	g_{41}	g_{43}	g_{40}	b_{52}	g_{53}	g_{50}
OLS	0.203	0.367	40.720	0.037	0.066	−0.202	96.464	2.301	0.431	−139.145
TSLS	0.203	0.367	40.720	0.435	−0.215	−0.193	84.772	2.788	0.619	−190.097
AFP 1	0.203	0.367	40.720	0.907	−0.572	−0.199	73.594	2.710	0.589	−181.935
AFP 2	0.203	0.367	40.720	0.630	−0.383	−0.208	82.257	2.788	0.619	−190.095

[1] In AFP 1 the second relation is estimated as

$$y_{2t} = 5.331\, y_1^* - 3.331\, y_{4t}^* - 1.832\, z_{3t} - 69.988 + e'_{2t},$$

while in AFP 2 the first relation is estimated as

$$y_{2t} = 3.271\, y_{1t}^* - 0.576\, y_{3t}^* - 0.697\, z_{3t} + 0.358\, z_{4t} - 199.41 + e''_{1t}.$$

After substituting the systematic parts y_i^* by the observed variables y_i in the appropriate equation in each of the two versions, the tabulated coefficients have been obtained by solving for y_{1t}. This gives a unit value for the coefficient of y_{1t} in accordance with the original specification (1a–e).

in the sense that the remaining non-vanishing elements of the β matrix occur on the same side of the main diagonal. [2]

The results for the two asymmetric versions of Girshick-Haavelmo's model are given in the two last rows of Table 2.

9.3.3. Comparison with Other Asymmetric Methods

In Table 2 the two last rows give the values of the coefficients and constant terms as obtained from the two versions of the AFP method. [3] For comparison the solutions according to OLS regression and the TSLS method are given in the first two rows of Table 2.

The results of the two versions of the AFP method seem to fit rather well in the general picture outlined by the earlier methods. One striking exception occurs, however. In the second version of the AFP method the estimates of the first equation, which is just identified, differs greatly from the other estimates; note that b_{12}, g_{13} and g_{14} have the opposite sign when compared with the estimates obtained by the other methods. In spite of its theoretical disadvantages as regards the bias, the OLS method does not show spectacular deviations from the other methods, with exception for the fourth equation. For the third equation, which contains only one endogenous variable, all methods considered reduce to OLS. When the second version of the AFP method is used, y_{2t}^{*} is taken from the unrestricted reduced form, and therefore the estimates of the parameters of the fifth equation are the same as those obtained by the TSLS method.

CHAPTER 10

Monte Carlo Results for Each
of Forty-Six Models

10.1. Overall Features of the Experimental Design

Monte Carlo results for the 46 models are presented in Tables 10.2.1 through 10.2.46. Definitions of each statistic presented in these tables appear in Table 10.1.1. The results for the models appear in the same sequence as shown in Chart 2.3.1.

The tables in Chapter 10.2 give Monte Carlo results for the statistics of each model that are of most interest in applied econometrics. Not all of the statistics computed for each model are published here because some are of lesser interest and would take up more space than is warranted. The main text of the monograph includes some reference to statistics not provided in Chapter 10.2, but, for the most part, the tables and discussion in the main text are developed from the statistics shown in Tables 10.2.1 through 10.2.46.

A summary of the design for all of the models is given in Chart 2.3.1, whereas the complete specification of each model is given in Part A of each table. The following design features are the same for the Monte Carlo runs on each model and are not repeated in Part A of each table:

1. The exogenous and residual variables are normally distributed with mean zero and population variances shown in Part A.

2. The experiments on each model consisted of 100 samples (replica-

tions), with each sample being a simulated time-series generated from the model.

3. The exogenous and residual variables were regenerated for each sample and, therefore, are independent from sample to sample within the 100 replications for each model.

4. The variances of all exogenous variables are one. The coefficients on the exogenous variables in the structural equations were selected so as to obtain the desired variances for the endogenous variables, in most cases unity.

The notation in Part A.1 of each table is the same as that in the introduction, namely,

$$Y_t = \beta Y_t + \Gamma Z_t + \delta_t \tag{1}$$

$$Y_t = \beta H_t^* + \Gamma_t Z_t + \epsilon_t \tag{2}$$

$$Y_t = \Omega Z_t + \epsilon_t \quad \text{where} \quad \Omega = (I-\beta)^{-1}\Gamma \tag{3}$$

$$H_t^* = \Omega Z_t , \tag{4}$$

where Z_t is the set of predetermined variables made up of lagged endogenous and lagged or non-lagged exogenous variables as noted.

The structural form of all but three of the 46 models presented in this monograph has all behavioral relations in accordance with the notation in (1). Models 4a—4c were designed as symmetric models, and the notation

$$(I-\beta)Y_t = \Gamma Z_t + \delta_t \tag{5}$$

is preferable as the reader will appreciate. For further discussion of this point the reader is referred to Chapter 11.

Table 10.1.1
Definitions and formulas

A. *Model Design*

A.1. Coefficients in the Structural Form (SF) and Reduced Form (RF) Equations

SF: $Y_t = \beta Y_t + \Gamma Z_t + \delta_t$; $[I-\beta] Y_t = \Gamma Z_t + \delta_t$,

RF: $Y_t = \Omega Z_t + \epsilon_t$ with $\Omega = [I-\beta]^{-1} \Gamma$.

All predetermined variables are exogenous and all structural relations are behavioral, unless specific information given in Part A.1 indicates to the contrary.

A.2. Variance of Endogenous and Residual Variables in the Population and in the Sample

In most models the parameters were selected so the population variances of all endogenous variables (y_i) would be one. The variances of δ_i were selected so as to obtain the specified R^2 in each of the reduced form equations in the population. The observed variances in the sample period are also shown as a matter of general interest.

A.3. Correlation among Residuals and Exogenous Variables

To illustrate by a special case, we consider a loop model of the form

$$y_1 = \beta_{12} y_2 + \gamma_{11} x_1 + \gamma_{12} x_2 + \delta_1 \quad = \beta_{12} \eta_2^* + \gamma_{11} x_1 + \gamma_{12} x_2 + \epsilon_1$$

$$y_2 = \beta_{23} y_3 + \gamma_{23} x_3 + \gamma_{24} x_4 + \delta_2 \quad = \beta_{23} \eta_3^* + \gamma_{23} x_3 + \gamma_{24} x_4 + \epsilon_2$$

. . .   . . .

$$y_n = \beta_{n1} y_1 + \gamma_{n,2n-1} x_{2n-1} + \gamma_{n,2n} x_{2n} + \delta_n = \beta_{n1} \eta_1^* + \gamma_{n,2n-1} x_{2n-1} + \gamma_{n,2n} x_{2n} + \epsilon_n.$$

Here FP will give consistent estimates of coefficients even though ϵ_1, for example, may be correlated with η_k^*, ($k \neq 2$) or x_i ($i \neq 1,2$). This section in the specification of each model gives the correlations among residuals and exogenous and η_i^* variables whenever any correlations among these variables have been specified as non-zero in the model design.

A.4. Sample Size and Special Design Features

Besides the sample size this section gives brief comments on why this particular model design was selected. More complete information is available in Chart 2.3.1 and Chapter 2.3. For common features of the 46 models, see Chapter 10.1, points 1−4.

Table 10.1.1 (continued)

B. *Structural Coefficients*

B.1.   True Coefficient versus Average Estimate from 100 Estimates

True: This value comes from Table A.1, say α, being one of the coefficients β_{ik} or γ_{ik}.

$$\begin{array}{c|c} \text{OLS} \\ \text{TSLS} \\ \text{FP} \end{array} \quad a = \frac{1}{100} \sum_{s=1}^{100} a_s$$

where a_s is the estimate of α in the sth sample.

B.2.   Observed Standard Deviation around the Mean

$$\begin{array}{c|c} \text{OLS} \\ \text{TSLS} \\ \text{FP} \end{array} \quad d(a) = \left[\frac{1}{99} \sum_{s=1}^{100} [a_s - a]^2\right]^{1/2}.$$

B.3.   Average Standard Deviation from Large-Sample Formula

$$\begin{array}{c|c} \text{OLS} \\ \text{TSLS} \\ \text{FP} \end{array} \quad d^*(a) = \frac{1}{100} \sum_{s=1}^{100} d_s^*$$

as given by $(d_s^*)^2 = \{\text{est } V(\delta)\}[ZZ']^{kk}$ where est $V(\delta)$ is the estimate of the variance of the residual in the structural equation corrected for degrees of freedom and $[ZZ']^{kk}$ is the appropriate diagonal element in the inverse of the product moment matrix (exogenous and observed or computed endogenous variables) used for computing the estimate of the coefficient α.

B.4.   Observed Standard Deviation around the True Value of the Coefficient

$$\begin{array}{c|c} \text{OLS} \\ \text{TSLS} \\ \text{FP} \end{array} \quad D(a) = \left[[d(a)]^2 + [a - \text{True}]^2\right]^{1/2}.$$

B.5.   Number of Iterations for Fix-point (FP) Method

See Chapter 5.1 for criterion on successful convergence.

Table 10.1.1 (continued)

C. *Reduced Form Coefficients*

C.1.   True Coefficient versus Average Estimate from 100 Samples

True: This value is taken from Table A.1, say α, being one of the coefficients ω_{ik}.

$$\begin{array}{c|c} \text{OLS} \\ \text{TSLS} \\ \text{FP} \\ \text{URF} \end{array} \quad a = \frac{1}{100} \sum_{s=1}^{100} a_s$$

where a_s is the estimate of α in the sth sample. For OLS, TSLS and FP the estimate of α is generated from the corresponding estimates in B.1. URF is the unrestricted least squares estimates of the reduced form coefficient ω_{ik} at issue.

C.2.   Observed Standard Deviation of 100 Samples around the Observed Mean

$$\begin{array}{c|c} \text{OLS} \\ \text{TSLS} \\ \text{FP} \\ \text{URF} \end{array} \quad d(a) = \left[\frac{1}{99} \sum_{s=1}^{100} [a_s - a]^2 \right]^{\frac{1}{2}} .$$

C.3.   Average Standard Deviation from Large-Sample Formula

$$\text{URF} \qquad d^*(a) = \frac{1}{100} \sum_{s=1}^{100} d_s^*$$

as given by $(d_s^*)^2 = \{\text{est } V(\epsilon)\} [ZZ']^{kk}$ where est $V(\epsilon)$ is the estimate of the variance of the residual in the reduced-form equation corrected for degrees of freedom and $[ZZ']^{kk}$ is the appropriate diagonal element in the inverse of the product moment matrix of the exogenous variables.

C.4.   Observed Standard Deviation around the True Value of the Coefficient

$$\begin{array}{c|c} \text{OLS} \\ \text{TSLS} \\ \text{FP} \\ \text{URF} \end{array} \quad D(a) = \left[[d(a)]^2 + [a - \text{True}]^2 \right]^{\frac{1}{2}} .$$

D. *Eigenvalues for Product Moment Matrix of Explanatory Variables (REID or GEID Specification)*

$$\lambda_i = \frac{\lambda_i^*}{\sum_i \lambda_i^*}$$

where λ_i are eigenvalues arranged in ascending order and normalized to unit sum; the eigenval-

Table 10.1.1 (continued)

ues λ_i^* are calculated from the equations: $\text{Det}[ZZ'] - \lambda^*[I] = 0$ where $[ZZ']$ is the product moment matrix of the explanatory variables used in calculating the coefficients in the particular equation of interest.

The first column gives the smallest eigenvalue in 100 samples. In the last three columns, the first gives the average of the smallest eigenvalue λ_1 in each sample, the second and third give the average of the second and third smallest eigenvalues (λ_2 and λ_3) in each sample.

E. Average R^2 from 100 samples

The 6 numbers for the ith equation for both the sample and prediction periods are calculated from the following formulas:

The degrees of freedom (D.F.) for calculating variances are as follows:

		E.1 Sample period		E.2 Prediction period		E.3 Sample period (adj)	
		ϵ_i	y_i	ϵ_i	y_i	ϵ_i	y_i
True [a]	$R^2 = 1 - \dfrac{\sigma^2(\epsilon_i)}{\sigma^2(y_i)}$	--	--	--	--	--	--
Generated [a]	$R^2 = 1 - \dfrac{V(\epsilon_i)}{V(y_i)}$	N	N	P	P	N	N
OLS		N	N	P	P	N−m	N
TSLS	$R^2 = 1 - \dfrac{V(e_i)}{V(y_i)}$	N	N	P	P	N−m	N
FP		N	N	P	P	N−m	N
URF		N	N	P.	P	N−k	N

$\sigma^2(.)$ and $V(.)$ represent the variance of the relevant variable around zero. In calculating degrees of freedom, N is the number of observations in the sample period, P is the number of observations in the prediction period, k is the total number of predetermined variables, and m is the average number of explanatory variables among the behavioral equations. ϵ_i is the residual in the ith reduced form equation (see 1.3.3), and e_i its observed value. The residual (e_i) as observed at time "t" for each of the methods is calculated as follows:

$$e_{it} = [y_i - (w_{i1}x_1 + w_{i2}x_2 + \cdots + w_{ik}x_k)]_t$$

where x_i is the set of predetermined variables and w_{ik} is the set of estimated coefficients in the reduced from equation for the ith endogenous variable.

The statistics reported in Part E of the tables in this chapter represent the average of R^2 for 100 Monte Carlo samples. The value for each sample is calculated as shown above. The values given under capital Y refer to R^2 as an average for the component variables y_i ($i = 1,2,...,n$).

[a] Note that "true" refers to the population and therefore R^2 is calculated from the theoretical values $\sigma^2(\epsilon_i)$ and $\sigma^2(y_i)$. "Generated" refers to Monte-Carlo generated data and therefore R^2 is calculated using the observed variances $V(\epsilon_i)$ and $V(y_i)$ in either the sample or the prediction period.

10.2. Tables of Monte Carlo Results

Table 10.2.1. Model 1a

A. MODEL DESIGN

A.1. Structural equations

$$\beta = \begin{bmatrix} 0 & 0.5 \\ -0.5 & 0 \end{bmatrix} \qquad \Gamma = \begin{bmatrix} k & k & 0 & 0 \\ 0 & 0 & k & k \end{bmatrix} \qquad \Omega = \begin{bmatrix} 0.5657 & 0.5657 & 0.2828 & 0.2828 \\ -0.2828 & -0.2828 & 0.5657 & 0.5657 \end{bmatrix}$$

with $k = 0.7071$

A.2. Variance of endogenous and residual variables in the population and in the sample

$\sigma^2(y_i) = 1$

$\sigma^2(\delta_i) = 0.25 \qquad i = 1, 2$

$\sigma^2(\epsilon_i) = 0.2$

Generated in sample period:
$\begin{cases} V(y_1) = 0.984 & V(y_2) = 0.984 \\ V(\delta_1) = 0.255 & V(\delta_2) = 0.242 \\ V(\epsilon_1) = 0.203 & V(\epsilon_2) = 0.195 \end{cases}$

A.3. Correlation among residuals and exogenous variables

None

A.4. Sample size and special design features

1. 40 observations in both the sample and prediction periods.
2. This model is one in a series on size of beta coefficients in simple models (Models 1a-1f).

B. STRUCTURAL COEFFICIENTS

B.1. True coefficient versus average estimate from 100 samples

	β_{12}	γ_{11}	γ_{12}	β_{21}	γ_{23}	γ_{24}
True	0.5	0.7071	0.7071	−0.5	0.7071	0.7071
OLS	0.3772	0.6739	0.6646	−0.3947	0.6629	0.6865
TSLS	0.5026	0.7112	0.7014	−0.5130	0.6956	0.7190
FP	0.5028	0.7081	0.7014	−0.5126	0.6931	0.7170

B.2. Observerd standard deviation of 100 samples around observed mean

OLS	0.0916	0.0837	0.0925	0.1028	0.0861	0.0856
TSLS	0.1103	0.0906	0.0968	0.1274	0.0907	0.0905
FP	0.1093	0.0902	0.1010	0.1262	0.0987	0.0929

B.3. Average standard deviation from large-sample formula

OLS	0.0903	0.0854	0.0862	0.0862	0.0839	0.0825
TSLS	0.1073	0.0897	0.0905	0.1024	0.0879	0.0864
FP	0.1076	0.0896	0.0906	0.1028	0.0878	0.0867

B.4. Observed standard deviation around true value of the coefficient

OLS	0.1532	0.0900	0.1018	0.1472	0.0968	0.0880
TSLS	0.1103	0.0907	0.0970	0.1281	0.0914	0.0913
FP	0.1093	0.0902	0.1012	0.1268	0.0997	0.0934

B.5. Number of iterations for fix-point (FP) method

Average = 6.3;　　　Smallest = 4;　　　Largest = 10;　　　No convergence in 0 samples

C. REDUCED FORM COEFFICIENTS (4 out of 8 coefficients)

C.1. True coefficient versus average estimate from 100 samples

	ω_{11}	ω_{13}	ω_{21}	ω_{23}
True	0.5657	0.2828	−0.2828	0.5657
OLS	0.5876	0.2161	−0.2296	0.5776
TSLS	0.5668	0.2757	−0.2864	0.5537
FP	0.5644	0.2747	−0.2854	0.5522
URF	0.5647	0.2782	−0.2919	0.5521

C.2. Observed standard deviation of 100 samples around observed mean

OLS	0.0741	0.0532	0.0571	0.0735
TSLS	0.0747	0.0587	0.0642	0.0699
FP	0.0739	0.0591	0.0651	0.0786
URF	0.0770	0.0809	0.0733	0.0800

C.3. Average standard deviation from large-sample formula

URF	0.0748	0.0758	0.0736	0.0746

C.4. Observed standard deviation around true value of the coefficient

OLS	0.0773	0.0852	0.0780	0.0745
TSLS	0.0747	0.0591	0.0643	0.0709
FP	0.0739	0.0597	0.0652	0.0798
URF	0.0770	0.0810	0.0739	0.0811

D. EIGENVALUES FOR PRODUCT MOMENT MATRIX OF EXPLANATORY VARIABLES (REID SPECIFICATION)

	Smallest in 100 samples	Average for 100 samples λ_1	λ_2	λ_3
D.1. Equation 1				
OLS	0.0878	0.1743	0.3081	0.5176
TSLS	0.0687	0.1531	0.3196	0.5273
FP	0.0704	0.1542	0.3180	0.5277
D.2. Equation 2				
OLS	0.0768	0.1822	0.3225	0.4953
TSLS	0.0623	0.1624	0.3324	0.5052
FP	0.0776	0.1648	0.3310	0.5042
D.3. Unrestricted reduced form	0.1064	0.1511	0.2092	0.2780

E. AVERAGE R^2 FROM 100 SAMPLES

	E.1. Sample period y_1	y_2	Y	E.2. Prediction period y_1	y_2	Y
True	0.8	0.8	0.8	0.8	0.8	0.8
Generated (average)	0.7865	0.7944	0.7905	0.7872	0.7977	0.7925
OLS	0.7944	0.8021	0.7983	0.7550	0.7768	0.7659
TSLS	0.8041	0.8112	0.8077	0.7633	0.7822	0.7728
FP	0.8019	0.8110	0.8065	0.7630	0.7807	0.7719
URF	0.7885	0.7952	0.7919	0.7575	0.7762	0.7669

E.3. Sample period (adj. for D.F.)

	y_1	y_2	Y
OLS	0.7777	0.7861	0.7819
TSLS	0.7882	0.7959	0.7921
FP	0.7858	0.7957	0.7908

Table 10.2.2. Model 1b

A. MODEL DESIGN

A.1. Structural equations

$$\beta = \begin{bmatrix} 0 & 1 \\ -1 & 0 \end{bmatrix} \qquad \Gamma = \begin{bmatrix} k_1 & k_1 & 0 & 0 \\ 0 & 0 & k_1 & k_1 \end{bmatrix} \qquad \Omega = \begin{bmatrix} k_2 & k_2 & k_2 & k_2 \\ -k_2 & -k_2 & k_2 & k_2 \end{bmatrix}$$

with $k_1 = 0.8944$ and $k_2 = 0.4472$

A.2. Variance of endogenous and residual variables in the population and in the sample

$\sigma^2(y_i) = 1$

$\sigma^2(\delta_i) = 0.4 \qquad i = 1, 2$

$\sigma^2(\epsilon_i) = 0.2$

Generated in sample period:
$\begin{cases} V(y_1) = 0.950 & V(y_2) = 1.016 \\ V(\delta_1) = 0.388 & V(\delta_2) = 0.410 \\ V(\epsilon_1) = 0.203 & V(\epsilon_2) = 0.196 \end{cases}$

A.3. Correlation among residuals and exogenous variables

None

A.4. Sample size and special design features

1. 40 observations in both the sample and prediction periods.
2. This model is one in a series on size of beta coefficients in simple models (Models 1a-1f).

B. STRUCTURAL COEFFICIENTS

B.1. True coefficient versus average estimate from 100 samples

	β_{12}	γ_{11}	γ_{12}	β_{21}	γ_{23}	γ_{24}
True	1	0.8944	0.8944	−1	0.8944	0.8944
OLS	0.6874	0.7433	0.7390	−0.6660	0.7472	0.7307
TSLS	1.0284	0.9040	0.9021	−1.0177	0.8976	0.8849
FP	1.0322	0.8968	0.8928	−1.0220	0.8909	0.8841

B.2. Observed standard deviation of 100 samples around observed mean

OLS	0.1363	0.1179	0.1038	0.1232	0.1161	0.1025
TSLS	0.1901	0.1447	0.1248	0.1697	0.1318	0.1242
FP	0.1955	0.1757	0.1527	0.1728	0.1556	0.1445

B.3. Average standard deviation from large-sample formula

OLS	0.1249	0.1109	0.1098	0.1248	0.1104	0.1105
TSLS	0.1715	0.1318	0.1308	0.1716	0.1302	0.1307
FP	0.1758	0.1338	0.1327	0.1751	0.1314	0.1329

B.4. Observed standard deviation around true value of the coefficient

OLS	0.3410	0.1917	0.1869	0.3560	0.1875	0.1931
TSLS	0.1922	0.1450	0.1250	0.1706	0.1318	0.1246
FP	0.1981	0.1757	0.1527	0.1742	0.1556	0.1449

B.5. Number of iterations for fix-point (FP) method

Average = 8.37   Smallest = 4   Largest = 17   No convergence in 0 samples

C. REDUCED FORM COEFFICIENTS (4 out of 8 coefficients)

C.1. True coefficient versus average estimate from 100 samples

	ω_{11}	ω_{13}	ω_{21}	ω_{23}
True	0.4472	0.4472	$\div 0.4472$	0.4472
OLS	0.5111	0.3499	-0.3372	0.5143
TSLS	0.4433	0.4475	-0.4452	0.4414
FP	0.4372	0.4433	-0.4415	0.4372
URF	0.4384	0.4520	-0.4524	0.4391

C.2. Observed standard deviation of 100 samples around observed mean

OLS	0.0709	0.0694	0.0629	0.0725
TSLS	0.0610	0.0714	0.0620	0.0636
FP	0.0737	0.0794	0.0778	0.0784
URF	0.0717	0.0865	0.0665	0.0788

C.3. Average standard deviation from large-sample formula

URF	0.0748	0.0756	0.0738	0.0745

C.4. Observed standard deviation around true value of the coefficient

OLS	0.0954	0.1195	0.1267	0.0988
TSLS	0.0611	0.0714	0.0620	0.0639
FP	0.0744	0.0795	0.0780	0.0790
URF	0.0722	0.0866	0.0667	0.0792

D. EIGENVALUES FOR PRODUCT MOMENT MATRIX OF EXPLANATORY VARIABLES (REID SPECIFICATION)

	Smallest in 100 samples	Average for 100 samples		
		λ_1	λ_2	λ_3
D.1. Equation 1				
OLS	0.0561	0.1061	0.3179	0.5760
TSLS	0.0346	0.0799	0.3335	0.5866
FP	0.0383	0.0810	0.3334	0.5856
D.2. Equation 2				
OLS	0.0723	0.1196	0.3226	0.5578
TSLS	0.0486	0.0915	0.3396	0.5689
FP	0.0418	0.0920	0.3415	0.5665
D.3. Unrestricted reduced form	0.0894	0.1520	0.2087	0.2788

E. AVERAGE R^2 FROM 100 SAMPLES

E.1. Sample period / E.2. Prediction period

	y_1	y_2	Y	y_1	y_2	Y
True	0.8	0.8	0.8	0.8	0.8	0.8
Generated (average)	0.7806	0.7994	0.7900	0.7828	0.7895	0.7862
OLS	0.7624	0.7778	0.7701	0.7334	0.7422	0.7378
TSLS	0.7972	0.8137	0.8054	0.7658	0.7739	0.7699
FP	0.7925	0.8062	0.7994	0.7578	0.7674	0.7626
URF	0.7819	0.7997	0.7908	0.7570	0.7661	0.7616

E.3. Sample period (adj. for D.F.)

	y_1	y_2	Y
OLS	0.7431	0.7598	0.7515
TSLS	0.7808	0.7986	0.7896
FP	0.7757	0.7905	0.7831

Table 10.2.3. Model 1c

A. MODEL DESIGN

A.1. Structural equations

$$\beta = \begin{bmatrix} 0 & 3 \\ -3 & 0 \end{bmatrix} \qquad \Gamma = \begin{bmatrix} 2 & 2 & 0 & 0 \\ 0 & 0 & 2 & 2 \end{bmatrix} \qquad \Omega = \begin{bmatrix} 0.2 & 0.2 & 0.6 & 0.6 \\ -0.6 & -0.6 & 0.2 & 0.2 \end{bmatrix}$$

A.2. Variance of endogenous and residual variables in the population and in the sample

$\sigma^2(y_i) = 1.0$

$\sigma^2(\delta_i) = 2 \qquad i = 1, 2$

$\sigma^2(\epsilon_i) = 0.2$

Generated $\left(V(y_1) = 0.946 \quad V(y_2) = 1.023 \right.$
in sample $\left\{ V(\delta_1) = 2.042 \quad V(\delta_2) = 1.936 \right.$
period: $\left(V(\epsilon_1) = 0.195 \quad V(\epsilon_2) = 0.203 \right.$

A.3. Correlation among residuals and exogenous variables

None

A.4. Sample size and special design features

1. 40 observations in both the sample and prediction periods.
2. This model is one in a series on size of beta coefficients in simple models (Models 1a-1f).

B. STRUCTURAL COEFFICIENTS

B.1. True coefficient versus average estimate from 100 samples

	β_{12}	γ_{11}	γ_{12}	β_{21}	γ_{23}	γ_{24}
True	3	2	2	-3	2	2
OLS	0.8011	0.6777	0.6599	-0.8802	0.7216	0.7402
TSLS	2.9313	1.9585	1.9445	-3.2111	2.0858	2.1559
FP	1.6500	0.9268	0.9131	-1.7610	0.9669	0.9329

B.2. Observed standard deviation of 100 samples around observed mean

	β_{12}	γ_{11}	γ_{12}	β_{21}	γ_{23}	γ_{24}
OLS	0.2466	0.2104	0.2088	0.3053	0.2548	0.2419
TSLS	0.8887	0.5606	0.6221	1.2679	0.7957	0.8102
FP	0.9494	0.7663	0.7889	1.0405	0.8453	0.7475

B.3. Average standard deviation from large-sample formula

	β_{12}	γ_{11}	γ_{12}	β_{21}	γ_{23}	γ_{24}
OLS	0.2622	0.2098	0.2104	0.2686	0.2109	0.2142
TSLS	0.9239	0.6075	0.6095	1.0950	0.6983	0.7132
FP	0.5373	0.3239	0.3313	0.5941	0.3503	0.3300

B.4. Observed standard deviation around true value of the coefficient

	β_{12}	γ_{11}	γ_{12}	β_{21}	γ_{23}	γ_{24}
OLS	2.2127	1.3389	1.3563	2.1417	1.3035	1.2828
TSLS	0.8914	0.5621	0.6246	1.2854	0.8003	0.8251
FP	1.6504	1.3187	1.3430	1.6179	1.3349	1.3029

B.5. Number of iterations for fix-point (FP) method

Average = 123.81;   Smallest = 6;   Largest = 200   No convergence in 60 samples

C. REDUCED FORM COEFFICIENTS (4 out of 8 coefficients)

C.1. True coefficient versus average estimate from 100 samples

	ω_{11}	ω_{13}	ω_{21}	ω_{23}
True	0.2	0.6	−0.6	0.2
OLS	0.4002	0.3273	−0.3359	0.4215
TSLS	0.2077	0.5821	−0.5994	0.2136
FP	0.2172	0.3534	−0.3503	0.2241
URF	0.1929	0.5871	−0.6057	0.1937

C.2. Observed standard deviation of 100 samples around observed mean

OLS	0.1131	0.1089	0.1121	0.1369
TSLS	0.0644	0.0701	0.0736	0.0601
FP	0.1259	0.2187	0.2339	0.1170
URF	0.0720	0.0743	0.0782	0.0862

C.3. Average standard deviation from large-sample formula

URF	0.0735	0.0746	0.0749	0.0759

C.4. Observed standard deviation around true value of the coefficient

OLS	0.2299	0.2936	0.2869	0.2604
TSLS	0.0649	0.0723	0.0736	0.0616
FP	0.1271	0.3296	0.3421	0.1193
URF	0.0723	0.0754	0.0784	0.0862

D. EIGENVALUES FOR PRODUCT MOMENT MATRIX OF EXPLANATORY VARIABLES (REID SPECIFICATION)

	Smallest in 100 samples	Average for 100 samples		
		λ_1	λ_2	λ_3
D.1. Equation 1				
OLS	0.0233	0.0483	0.3064	0.6453
TSLS	0.0022	0.0169	0.3237	0.6595
FP	0.0042	0.0619	0.3462	0.5918
D.2. Equation 2				
OLS	0.0200	0.0492	0.3270	0.6237
TSLS	0.0014	0.0178	0.3456	0.6366
FP	0.0035	0.0562	0.3608	0.5829
D.3. Unrestricted reduced form	0.1064	0.1511	0.2092	0.2780

E. AVERAGE R^2 FROM 100 SAMPLES

E.1. Sample period   E.2. Prediction period

	y_1	y_2	Y	y_1	y_2	Y
True	0.8	0.8	0.8	0.8	0.8	0.8
Generated (average)	0.7853	0.7931	0.7892	0.7973	0.7921	0.7947
OLS	0.5650	0.5655	0.5653	0.5060	0.4990	0.5025
TSLS	0.8028	0.8055	0.8042	0.7748	0.7762	0.7755
FP	0.5884	0.6016	0.5950	0.5506	0.5390	0.5448
URF	0.7868	0.7938	0.7903	0.7683	0.7696	0.7690

E.3. Sample period (adj. for D.F.)

	y_1	y_2	Y
OLS	0.5297	0.5303	0.5301
TSLS	0.7868	0.7897	0.7883
FP	0.5550	0.5693	0.5622

Table 10.2.4. Model 1d

A. MODEL DESIGN

A.1. Structural equations

$$\beta = \begin{bmatrix} 0 & 0.5 \\ -0.9 & 0 \end{bmatrix} \quad \Gamma = \begin{bmatrix} 0.8889 & 0.8889 & 0 & 0 \\ 0 & 0 & 0.4474 & 0.4474 \end{bmatrix} \quad \Omega = \begin{bmatrix} 0.6130 & 0.6130 & 0.1544 & 0.1544 \\ -0.5517 & -0.5517 & 0.3087 & 0.3087 \end{bmatrix}$$

A.2. Variance of endogenous and residual variables in the population and in the sample

$\sigma^2(y_i) = 1.0, \quad 1.0$ 　　　　　　　　　　　　Generated $\begin{cases} V(y_1) = 0.999 & V(y_2) = 1.019 \\ \end{cases}$
$\sigma^2(\delta_i) = 0.395, 0.1$ 　　　　$i = 1,2$ 　　in sample $\begin{cases} V(\delta_1) = 0.403 & V(\delta_2) = 0.097 \end{cases}$
$\sigma^2(\epsilon_i) = 0.2, \quad 0.2$ 　　　　　　　　period: $\begin{cases} V(\epsilon_1) = 0.204 & V(\epsilon_2) = 0.201 \end{cases}$

A.3. Correlation among residuals and exogenous variables

　　None

A.4. Sample size and special design features

　　1. 40 observations in both the sample and prediction periods
　　2. The model is one in a series on size of beta coefficients in simple models (Models 1a-1f).

B. STRUCTURAL COEFFICIENTS

B.1. True coefficient versus average estimate from 100 samples

	β_{12}	γ_{11}	γ_{12}	β_{21}	γ_{23}	γ_{24}
True	0.5	0.8889	0.8889	−0.9	0.4474	0.4474
OLS	−0.1523	0.5276	0.5176	−0.8706	0.4333	0.4485
TSLS	0.4974	0.8903	0.8796	−0.9067	0.4388	0.4535
FP	0.4986	0.8887	0.8815	−0.9058	0.4240	0.4410

B.2. Observed standard deviation of 100 samples around observed mean

	β_{12}	γ_{11}	γ_{12}	β_{21}	γ_{23}	γ_{24}
OLS	0.1209	0.1044	0.1108	0.0622	0.0526	0.0521
TSLS	0.2521	0.1726	0.1899	0.0738	0.0536	0.0527
FP	0.2512	0.1691	0.1936	0.0748	0.0980	0.0851

B.3. Average standard deviation from large-sample formula

	β_{12}	γ_{11}	γ_{12}	β_{21}	γ_{23}	γ_{24}
OLS	0.1312	0.1091	0.1096	0.0519	0.0523	0.0513
TSLS	0.2550	0.1780	0.1781	0.0593	0.0533	0.0521
FP	0.2551	0.1771	0.1787	0.0623	0.0557	0.0547

B.4. Observed standard deviation around true value of the coefficient

	β_{12}	γ_{11}	γ_{12}	β_{21}	γ_{23}	γ_{24}
OLS	0.6634	0.3761	0.3875	0.0688	0.0545	0.0521
TSLS	0.2521	0.1726	0.1901	0.0741	0.0543	0.0531
FP	0.2512	0.1691	0.1937	0.0750	0.1008	0.0853

B.5. Number of iterations for fix-point (FP) method

　　Average = 7.11 　　Smallest = 4 　　Largest = 13 　　No convergence in 0 samples

C. REDUCED FORM COEFFICIENTS (4 out of 8 coefficients)

C.1. True coefficient versus average estimate from 100 samples

	ω_{11}	ω_{13}	ω_{21}	ω_{23}
True	0.6130	0.1544	−0.5517	0.3087
OLS	0.6079	−0.0839	−0.5276	0.5068
TSLS	0.6145	0.1425	−0.5556	0.3095
FP	0.6135	0.1372	−0.5544	0.3000
URF	0.6140	0.1526	−0.5586	0.3000

C.2. Observed standard deviation of 100 samples around observed mean

OLS	0.0915	0.0751	0.0779	0.0864
TSLS	0.0756	0.0531	0.0710	0.0593
FP	0.0746	0.0569	0.0725	0.0838
URF	0.0781	0.0832	0.0773	0.0856

C.3. Average standard deviation from large-sample formula

URF	0.0750	0.0760	0.0746	0.0756

C.4. Observed standard deviation around true value of the coefficient

OLS	0.0917	0.2499	0.0816	0.2161
TSLS	0.0756	0.0544	0.0711	0.0593
FP	0.0746	0.0594	0.0725	0.0843
URF	0.0781	0.0832	0.0776	0.0860

D. EIGENVALUES FOR PRODUCT MOMENT MATRIX OF EXPLANATORY VARIABLES (REID SPECIFICATION)

	Smallest in 100 samples	Average for 100 samples λ_1	λ_2	λ_3

D.1. Equation 1

	Smallest in 100 samples	λ_1	λ_2	λ_3
OLS	0.0312	0.0686	0.3056	0.6258
TSLS	0.0112	0.0387	0.3223	0.6390
FP	0.0116	0.0387	0.3214	0.6398

D.2. Equation 2

OLS	0.1010	0.2161	0.3233	0.4606
TSLS	0.0886	0.2007	0.3284	0.4709
FP	0.1204	0.2051	0.3271	0.4678

D.3. Unrestricted reduced form

Unrestricted reduced form	0.1064	0.1511	0.2092	0.2780

E. AVERAGE R^2 FROM 100 SAMPLES

E.1. Sample period / E.2. Prediction period

	y_1	y_2	Y	y_1	y_2	Y
True	0.8	0.8	0.8	0.8	0.8	0.8
Generated (average)	0.7889	0.7942	0.7916	0.7867	0.7943	0.7905
OLS	0.6964	0.7224	0.7094	0.6389	0.6871	0.6630
TSLS	0.8052	0.8093	0.8073	0.7657	0.7801	0.7729
FP	0.7992	0.8133	0.8063	0.7646	0.7752	0.7699
URF	0.7905	0.7948	0.7927	0.7586	0.7731	0.7659

E.3. Sample period (adj. for D.F.)

	y_1	y_2	Y
OLS	0.6718	0.6999	0.6858
TSLS	0.7894	0.7938	0.7917
FP	0.7829	0.7982	0.7906

Table 10.2.5. Model 1e

A. MODEL DESIGN

A.1. Structural equations

$$\beta = \begin{bmatrix} 0 & 0.5 \\ -3 & 0 \end{bmatrix} \quad \Gamma = \begin{bmatrix} 0.6591 & 0.6591 & 0 & 0 \\ 0 & 0 & 2.0843 & 2.0843 \end{bmatrix} \quad \Omega = \begin{bmatrix} 0.2636 & 0.2636 & 0.4169 & 0.4169 \\ -0.7909 & -0.7909 & 0.8337 & 0.8337 \end{bmatrix}$$

A.2. Variance of endogenous and residual variables in the population and in the sample

$$\sigma^2(y_i) = 1.0, \quad 1.0$$
$$\sigma^2(\delta_i) = 0.217, 2.17 \qquad i = 1, 2$$
$$\sigma^2(\epsilon_i) = 0.2, \quad 0.2$$

Generated $V(y_1) = 0.942 \quad V(y_2) = 0.991$
in sample $V(\delta_1) = 0.217 \quad V(\delta_2) = 2.103$
period $V(\epsilon_1) = 0.194 \quad V(\epsilon_2) = 0.193$

A.3. Correlation among residuals and exogenous variables

	x_1	x_2	x_3	x_4	δ_1	δ_2
x_1	1	0	0.707	0	0	0
x_2	0	1	0	0.707	0	0
x_3	0.707	0	1	0	0	0
x_4	0	0.707	0	1	0	0
δ_1	0	0	0	0	1	0.707
δ_2	0	0	0	0	0.707	1

Note: This is not a GEID specification since all $r(x_i, \delta_j) = 0$.

A.4. Sample size and special design features
1. 40 observations in both the sample and prediction periods.
2. This model is one in a series on size of beta coefficients in simple models (Models 1a-1f).

B. STRUCTURAL COEFFICIENTS

B.1. True coefficient versus average estimate from 100 samples

	β_{12}	γ_{11}	γ_{12}	β_{21}	γ_{23}	γ_{24}
True	0.5	0.6591	0.6591	-3	2.0843	2.0843
OLS	0.4263	0.6339	0.6440	-0.6819	0.6806	0.6974
TSLS	0.5053	0.6530	0.6615	-3.2261	2.1788	2.2528
FP	0.4859	0.5876	0.6092	-2.0627	1.4067	1.4559

B.2. Observed standard deviation of 100 samples around observed mean

OLS	0.0934	0.0750	0.0767	0.3126	0.2572	0.2472
TSLS	0.1093	0.0812	0.0780	1.4029	0.8863	0.9082
FP	0.1067	0.1092	0.1195	0.4618	0.2900	0.3103

B.3. Average standard deviation from large-sample formula

OLS	0.0799	0.0786	0.0786	0.2720.	0.2123	0.2157
TSLS	0.0923	0.0808	0.0807	1.2761	0.8087	0.8270
FP	0.1038	0.0817	0.0823	0.5546	0.3580	0.3656

B.4. Observed standard deviation around true value of the coefficient

OLS	0.1190	0.0791	0.0782	2.3391	1.4271	1.4088
TSLS	0.1094	0.0814	0.0780	1.4210	0.8913	0.9237
FP	0.1076	0.1305	0.1295	1.0449	0.7370	0.7008

B.5. Number of iterations for fix-point (FP) method.

Average = 134.25   Smallest = 11   Largest = 200   No convergence in 10 samples

C. REDUCED FORM COEFFICIENTS (4 out of 8 coefficients)

C.1. True coefficient versus average estimate from 100 samples

	ω_{11}	ω_{13}	ω_{21}	ω_{23}
True	0.2636	0.4169	−0.7907	0.8337
OLS	0.5006	0.2161	−0.3278	0.5230
TSLS	0.2678	0.4031	−0.7642	0.8029
FP	0.3002	0.3374	−0.6165	0.7122
URF	0.2535	0.4110	−0.8001	0.8322

C.2. Observed standard deviation of 100 samples around observed mean

OLS	0.0756	0.0816	0.1368	0.1740
TSLS	0.0855	0.0877	0.0990	0.1001
FP	0.0659	0.0606	0.1698	0.1340
URF	0.1015	0.1074	0.1081	0.1130

C.3. Average standard deviation from large-sample formula

URF	0.1038	0.1045	0.1041	0.1045

C.4. Observed standard deviation around true value of the coefficient

OLS	0.2488	0.2167	0.4827	0.3561
TSLS	0.0856	0.0888	0.1025	0.1047
FP	0.0754	0.1000	0.2433	0.1809
URF	0.1020	0.1076	0.1085	0.1130

D. EIGENVALUES FOR PRODUCT MOMENT MATRIX OF EXPLANATORY VARIABLES (REID SPECIFICATION)

	Smallest in 100 samples	Average for 100 samples		
		λ_1	λ_2	λ_3

D.1. Equation 1

OLS	0.0886	0.1966	0.3187	0.4848
TSLS	0.0612	0.1780	0.3285	0.4935
FP	0.0543	0.1796	0.3341	0.4863

D.2. Equation 2

OLS	0.0194	0.0472	0.3274	0.6254
TSLS	0.0010	0.0157	0.3459	0.6384
FP	0.0078	0.0263	0.3484	0.6253

D.3. Unrestricted reduced form	0.0288	0.0573	0.0872	0.3481

E. AVERAGE R^2 FROM 100 SAMPLES

E.1. Sample period				E.2. Prediction period		
	y_1	y_2	Y	y_1	y_2	Y
True	0.8	0.8	0.8	0.8	0.8	0.8
Generated (average)	0.7855	0.7940	0.7898	0.7975	0.7937	0.7956
OLS	0.7284	0.5886	0.6585	0.7101	0.5373	0.6237
TSLS	0.8039	0.8033	0.8036	0.7769	0.7753	0.7761
FP	0.7913	0.7559	0.7736	0.7733	0.7238	0.7486
URF	0.7871	0.7946	0.7909	0.7687	0.7723	0.7705

E.3. Sample period (adj. for D.F.)

	y_1	y_2	Y
OLS	0.7064	0.5552	0.6308
TSLS	0.7880	0.7874	0.7877
FP	0.7744	0.7361	0.7552

Table 10.2.6. Model 1f

A. MODEL DESIGN

A.1. Structural equations

$$\beta = \begin{bmatrix} 0 & 1.1 \\ -3 & 0 \end{bmatrix} \quad \Gamma = \begin{bmatrix} 0.3963 & 0.3963 & 0 & 0 \\ 0 & 0 & 2.4460 & 2.4460 \end{bmatrix} \quad \Omega = \begin{bmatrix} 0.0922 & 0.0922 & 0.6257 & 0.6257 \\ -0.2765 & -0.2765 & 0.5688 & 0.5688 \end{bmatrix}$$

A.2. Variance of endogenous and residual variables in the population and in the sample

$$\sigma^2(y_i) = 1.0 \qquad\qquad i = 1, 2$$
$$\sigma^2(\delta_1) = 0.0785 \qquad \sigma^2(\delta_2) = 2.9910$$
$$\sigma^2(\epsilon_i) = 0.2 \qquad\qquad i = 1, 2$$

Generated in sample period
$$\begin{cases} V(y_1) = 0.948 & V(y_2) = 0.983 \\ V(\delta_1) = 0.081 & V(\delta_2) = 2.896 \\ V(\epsilon_1) = 0.194 & V(\epsilon_2) = 0.195 \end{cases}$$

A.3. Correlation among residuals and exogenous variables

None

A.4. Sample size and special design features

1. 40 observations in both the sample and prediction periods.
2. This model is one in a series on size of beta coefficients in simple models (Model 1a-1f)

B. STRUCTURAL COEFFICIENTS

B.1. True coefficient versus average of estimate from 100 samples

	β_{12}	γ_{11}	γ_{12}	β_{21}	γ_{23}	γ_{24}
True	1.1	0.3963	0.3963	−3	2.4460	2.4460
OLS	1.0333	0.3787	0.3736	0.5276	0.2421	0.2443
TSLS	1.1015	0.3986	0.3931	−2.3432	1.9527	2.0612
FP	1.0849	0.2631	0.2857	−1.7233	1.6171	1.6647

B.2. Observed standard deviation of 100 samples around observed mean

OLS	0.0512	0.0469	0.0518	0.2352	0.1799	0.1841
TSLS	0.0615	0.0506	0.0540	3.5083	2.0804	2.2836
FP	0.0855	0.1746	0.1765	1.9060	1.1822	1.2023

B.3. Average standard deviation from large-sample formula

OLS	0.0505	0.0478	0.0483	0.1957	0.1500	0.1526
TSLS	0.0598	0.0501	0.0506	3.7585	2.2583	2.4265
FP	0.0818	0.0659	0.0676	1.7390	1.0922	1.1085

B.4. Observed standard deviation around true value of the coefficient

OLS	0.0841	0.0501	0.0566	3.5354	2.2112	2.2094
TSLS	0.0615	0.0507	0.0541	3.5693	2.1381	2.3158
FP	0.0868	0.2196	0.2083	2.2941	1.4438	1.4339

B.5. Number of iterations for fix-point (FP) method

Average = 51.94   Smallest = 5   Largest = 200   No convergence in 22 samples

C. REDUCED FORM COEFFICIENTS

C.1. True coefficient versus average estimate from 100 samples

	ω_{11}	ω_{12}	ω_{13}	ω_{14}	ω_{21}	ω_{22}	ω_{23}	ω_{24}
True	0.0922	0.0922	0.6257	0.6257	−0.2765	−0.2765	0.5688	0.5688
OLS	0.1510	0.0337	0.6610	0.5143	−0.1744	−0.2773	0.6338	0.4899
TSLS	0.1100	0.1078	0.6117	0.6310	−0.2613	−0.2583	0.5567	0.5744
FP	0.0619	0.1613	0.5846	0.5990	−0.1818	−0.1210	0.5431	0.5562
URF	0.0842	0.0879	0.6119	0.6329	−0.2855	−0.2765	0.5552	0.5743

C.2. Observed standard deviation of 100 samples around observed mean

	ω_{11}	ω_{12}	ω_{13}	ω_{14}	ω_{21}	ω_{22}	ω_{23}	ω_{24}
OLS	4.5984	5.4301	0.7109	1.4367	4.1522	4.9298	0.6368	1.3481
TSLS	0.0952	0.0883	0.0764	0.0713	0.0896	0.0880	0.0736	0.0705
FP	0.3097	0.6570	0.1589	0.1526	0.2464	0.5580	0.1482	0.1432
URF	0.0716	0.0841	0.0745	0.0707	0.0732	0.0825	0.0799	0.0719

C.3. Average standard deviation from large-sample formula

	ω_{11}	ω_{12}	ω_{13}	ω_{14}	ω_{21}	ω_{22}	ω_{23}	ω_{24}
URF	0.0734	0.0739	0.0745	0.0734	0.0736	0.0741	0.0746	0.0735

C.4. Observed standard deviation around true value of the coefficient

	ω_{11}	ω_{12}	ω_{13}	ω_{14}	ω_{21}	ω_{22}	ω_{23}	ω_{24}
OLS	4.5988	5.4304	0.7118	1.4410	4.1535	4.9298	0.6401	1.3504
TSLS	0.0968	0.0897	0.0777	0.0715	0.0909	0.0899	0.0745	0.0707
FP	0.3112	0.6606	0.1641	0.1549	0.2640	0.5793	0.1504	0.1438
URF	0.0719	0.0842	0.0758	0.0711	0.0738	0.0825	0.0810	0.0721

D. EIGENVALUES FOR PRODUCT MOMENT MATRIX OF EXPLANATORY VARIABLES (REID SPECIFICATION)

	Smallest in 100 samples	Average for 100 samples		
		λ_1	λ_2	λ_3
D.1. Equation 1				
OLS	0.0891	0.1765	0.3084	0.5152
TSLS	0.0702	0.1555	0.3197	0.5249
FP	0.0857	0.1784	0.3225	0.4991
D.2. Equation 2				
OLS	0.0199	0.0372	0.3268	0.6360
TSLS	0.00005	0.0052	0.3455	0.6492
FP	0.0004	0.0066	0.3451	0.6483
D.3. Unrestricted reduced form	0.1064	0.1511	0.2092	0.2780

E. AVERAGE R^2 FROM 100 SAMPLES

	E.1. Sample period			E.2. Prediction period		
	y_1	y_2	Y	y_1	y_2	Y
True	0.8	0.8	0.8	0.8	0.8	0.8
Generated (average)	0.7875	0.7943	0.7909	0.7984	0.7978	0.7981
OLS	−48.4951	−37.1061	−42.8006	−43.5358	−40.6280	−41.9819
TSLS	0.7969	0.8037	0.8003	0.7653	0.7732	0.7693
FP	0.2714	0.3180	0.2947	0.0243	0.1238	0.0741
URF	0.7888	0.7951	0.7920	0.7710	0.7762	0.7736

E.3. Sample period (adj. for D.F.)

	y_1	y_2	Y
OLS	−52.5082	−40.1958	−46.3520
TSLS	0.7804	0.7878	0.7841
FP	0.2123	0.2627	0.2375

Table 10.2.7. Model 1h

A. MODEL DESIGN

A.1. Structural equations

$$\beta = \begin{bmatrix} 0 & -0.5 & 0 & 0 & 0 \\ 0 & 0 & 0.5 & 0 & 0 \\ 0 & 0 & 0 & -0.5 & 0 \\ 0 & 0 & 0 & 0 & 0.5 \\ -0.5 & 0 & 0 & 0 & 0 \end{bmatrix} \quad \Gamma = \begin{bmatrix} k & k & 0 & 0 & 0 & 0 & 0 & 0 & 0 & 0 \\ 0 & 0 & k & k & 0 & 0 & 0 & 0 & 0 & 0 \\ 0 & 0 & 0 & 0 & k & k & 0 & 0 & 0 & 0 \\ 0 & 0 & 0 & 0 & 0 & 0 & k & k & 0 & 0 \\ 0 & 0 & 0 & 0 & 0 & 0 & 0 & 0 & k & k \end{bmatrix}$$

$$\Omega = \begin{bmatrix} k_1 & k_1 & -k_2 & -k_2 & -k_3 & -k_3 & k_4 & k_4 & k_5 & k_5 \\ k_5 & k_5 & k_1 & k_1 & k_2 & k_2 & -k_3 & -k_3 & -k_4 & -k_4 \\ k_4 & k_4 & -k_5 & -k_5 & k_1 & k_1 & -k_2 & -k_2 & -k_3 & -k_3 \\ -k_3 & -k_3 & k_4 & k_4 & k_5 & k_5 & k_1 & k_1 & k_2 & k_2 \\ -k_2 & -k_2 & k_3 & k_3 & k_4 & k_4 & -k_5 & -k_5 & k_1 & k_1 \end{bmatrix}$$

with $k = 0.5652$, $k_1 = 0.5481$, $k_2 = 0.2740$, $k_3 = 0.1370$, $k_4 = 0.0684$, $k_5 = 0.0342$.

A.2. Variance of endogenous and residual exogenous variables in the population and in the sample

$\sigma^2(y_i) = 1.0$

$\sigma^2(\delta_i) = 0.160$　　　$i = 1,2,...,5$

$\sigma^2(\epsilon_i) = 0.2$

Generated in sample period:

$V(y_1) = 0.990$　　$V(y_2) = 1.010$

$V(\delta_1) = 0.159$　　$V(\delta_2) = 0.158$

$V(\epsilon_1) = 0.200$　　$V(\epsilon_2) = 0.201$

A.3. Correlation among residuals and exogenous variables

None

A.4. Sample size and special design features

1. 40 observations in both the sample and prediction periods.
2. This model is one in a series on number of relations in a one-loop model (Model 1g (=1a), 1h, 1i).

B. STRUCTURAL COEFFICIENTS

B.1. True coefficient versus average estimate from 100 samples

	β_{12}	γ_{11}	γ_{12}	β_{23}	γ_{23}	γ_{24}	β_{34}	γ_{35}	γ_{36}	β_{45}	γ_{47}	γ_{48}	β_{51}	γ_{59}	$\gamma_{5,10}$
True	−.5	.5652	.5652	.5	.5652	.5652	−.5	.5652	.5652	.5	.5652	.5652	−.5	.5652	.5652
OLS	−.5039	.5668	.5595	.5031	.5558	.5720	−.4828	.5748	.5683	.4977	.5732	.5647	−.4897	.5623	.5727
TSLS	−.5142	.5670	.5596	.5096	.5556	.5718	−.4852	.5745	.5682	.5047	.5734	.5646	−.5000	.5625	.5731
FP	−.5144	.5697	.5571	.5111	.5649	.5683	−.4857	.5784	.5684	.5052	.5740	.5670	−.5001	.5653	.5747

B.2. Observed standard deviation of 100 samples around observed mean

OLS	.0675	.0569	.0669	.0752	.0755	.0681	.0660	.0635	.0635	.0589	.0712	.0674	.0645	.0653	.0640
TSLS	.0732	.0582	.0668	.0793	.0757	.0675	.0703	.0643	.0636	.0608	.0716	.0685	.0729	.0662	.0644
FP	.0735	.0607	.0796	.0808	.0876	.0745	.0705	.0690	.0744	.0630	.0754	.0755	.0776	.0801	.0778

B.3. Average standard deviation from large-sample formula

OLS	.0659	.0661	.0669	.0650	.0666	.0667	.0653	.0644	.0650	.0644	.0654	.0656	.0658	.0659	.0659
TSLS	.0726	.0666	.0673	.0714	.0670	.0671	.0718	.0647	.0654	.0709	.0657	.0660	.0726	.0663	.0663
FP	.0744	.0670	.0678	.0734	.0675	.0674	.0735	.0652	.0657	.0728	.0663	.0664	.0749	.0669	.0670

B.4. Observed standard deviation around true value of the coefficient

OLS	.0676	.0569	.0671	.0753	.0761	.0684	.0682	.0642	.0636	.0589	.0716	.0674	.0653	.0654	.0644
TSLS	.0746	.0582	.0670	.0799	.0763	.0678	.0718	.0650	.0637	.0610	.0721	.0685	.0729	.0663	.0649
FP	.0749	.0608	.0800	.0816	.0876	.0746	.0719	.0703	.0745	.0632	.0759	.0755	.0776	.0801	.0784

B.5. Number of iterations for fix-point (FP) method

Average = 15.35　　　Smallest = 13　　　Largest = 19　　　No convergence in 0 samples

C. REDUCED FORM COEFFICIENTS (13 out of 50 coefficients)

C.1. True coefficient versus average estimate from 100 samples

	ω_{11}	ω_{13}	ω_{15}	ω_{17}	ω_{19}	ω_{21}	ω_{23}	ω_{31}	ω_{33}	ω_{41}	ω_{43}	ω_{51}	ω_{53}
True	.5481	−.2740	−.1370	.0684	.0342	.0342	.5481	.0684	−.0342	−.1370	.0684	−.2740	.1370
OLS	.5506	−.2724	−.1410	.0680	.0330	.0322	.5398	.0642	−.0319	−.1338	.0662	−.2691	.1334
TSLS	.5497	−.2770	−.1454	.0706	.0347	.0338	.5385	.0667	−.0336	−.1384	.0697	−.2744	.1386
FP	.5522	−.2816	−.1470	.0711	.0351	.0341	.5475	.0671	−.0342	−.1391	.0709	−.2758	.1409
URF	.5570	−.2759	−.1579	.0822	.0283	.0309	.5390	.0644	−.0220	−.1406	.0669	−.2800	.1466

C.2. Observed standard deviation of 100 samples around observed mean

OLS	.0565	.0540	.0298	.0190	.0092	.0079	.0731	.0136	.0090	.0253	.0166	.0413	.0316
TSLS	.0577	.0550	.0318	.0208	.0100	.0090	.0734	.0149	.0095	.0283	.0183	.0462	.0353
FP	.0601	.0595	.0335	.0213	.0108	.0091	.0846	.0157	.0105	.0294	.0199	.0502	.0385
URF	.0724	.0886	.0824	.0840	.0970	.0800	.0930	.0806	.0719	.0753	.0778	.0767	.0878

C.3. Average standard deviation from large-sample formula

URF	.0816	.0841	.0808	.0830	.0819	.0818	.0840	.0817	.0842	.0815	.0842	.0811	.0839

C.4. Observed standard deviation around true value of the coefficient

OLS	.0566	.540	.0301	.0190	.0093	.0081	.0737	.0142	.0093	.0256	.0167	.0416	.0318
TSLS	.0577	.0551	.0330	.0209	.0100	.0090	.0740	.0150	.0095	.0283	.0183	.0462	.0354
FP	.0602	.0600	.0350	.0215	.0108	.0091	.0846	.0158	.0105	.0294	.0201	.0502	.0387
URF	.0729	.0886	.0851	.0851	.0972	.0881	.0934	.0807	.0729	.0754	.0778	.0769	.0884

D. Eigenvalues for product moment matrix of explanatory variables (REID SPECIFICATION)

| | Smallest in 100 samples | Average for 100 samples | | | Smallest in 100 samples | Average for 100 samples | |
		λ_1	λ_2			λ_1	λ_2
D.1. Equation 1					**D.4. Equation 4**			
OLS	0.1279	0.2235	0.3261		OLS	0.1592	0.2210	0.3274
TSLS	0.1196	0.2142	0.3270		TSLS	0.1223	0.2130	0.3280
FP	0.1166	0.2141	0.3292		FP	0.1401	0.2161	0.3249
D.2. Equation 2					**D.5. Equation 5**			
OLS	0.1414	0.2248	0.3244		OLS	0.1615	0.2286	0.3306
TSLS	0.1372	0.2174	0.3236		TSLS	0.1333	0.2182	0.3300
FP	0.1267	0.2199	0.3227		FP	0.1386	0.2196	0.3287
D.3. Equation 3					**D.6. Unrestricted reduced form**	N.a.		
OLS	0.1542	0.2315	0.3234					
TSLS	0.1387	0.2215	0.3255					
FP	0.1304	0.2227	0.3253					

E. AVERAGE R^2 FROM 100 SAMPLES

E.1. Sample period / E.2. Prediction period

	y_1	y_2	y_3	y_4	y_5	Y	y_1	y_2	y_3	y_4	y_5	Y
True	.8	.8	.8	.8	.8	.8	.8	.8	.8	.8	.8	.8
Generated (average)	.7894	.7926	.7963	.7970	.7911	.7933	.7894	.7907	.7806	.7916	.7924	.7889
OLS	.8029	.8090	.8101	.8101	.8061	.8076	.7733	.7737	.7653	.7745	.7771	.7728
TSLS	.8041	.8100	.8108	.8108	.8072	.8086	.7728	.7717	.7645	.7739	.7766	.7719
FP	.8054	.8112	.8123	.8129	.8098	.8103	.7705	.7682	.7612	.7708	.7704	.7682
URF	.7899	.7936	.7957	.7932	.7942	.7933	.7135	.7181	.7093	.7212	.7126	.7149

E.3. Sample period (adj. for D.F.)

	y_1	y_2	y_3	y_4	y_5	Y
OLS	.7869	.7935	.7947	.7947	.7904	.7920
TSLS	.7882	.7946	.7955	.7955	.7916	.7931
FP	.7896	.7959	.7971	.7977	.7944	.7949

Table 10.2.8. Model 1i

A. MODEL DESIGN:

A.1. Structural equations

$$\beta = \begin{bmatrix} 0 & 0.5 & 0 & 0 & 0 & 0 & 0 \\ 0 & 0 & -0.5 & 0 & 0 & 0 & 0 \\ 0 & 0 & 0 & 0.5 & 0 & 0 & 0 \\ 0 & 0 & 0 & 0 & -0.5 & 0 & 0 \\ 0 & 0 & 0 & 0 & 0 & 0.5 & 0 \\ 0 & 0 & 0 & 0 & 0 & 0 & -0.5 \\ 0.5 & 0 & 0 & 0 & 0 & 0 & 0 \end{bmatrix} \quad \Gamma = \begin{bmatrix} k & k & 0 & 0 & 0 & 0 & 0 & 0 & 0 & 0 & 0 & 0 & 0 & 0 \\ 0 & 0 & k & k & 0 & 0 & 0 & 0 & 0 & 0 & 0 & 0 & 0 & 0 \\ 0 & 0 & 0 & 0 & k & k & 0 & 0 & 0 & 0 & 0 & 0 & 0 & 0 \\ 0 & 0 & 0 & 0 & 0 & 0 & k & k & 0 & 0 & 0 & 0 & 0 & 0 \\ 0 & 0 & 0 & 0 & 0 & 0 & 0 & 0 & k & k & 0 & 0 & 0.0 \\ 0 & 0 & 0 & 0 & 0 & 0 & 0 & 0 & 0 & 0 & k & k & 0 & 0 \\ 0 & 0 & 0 & 0 & 0 & 0 & 0 & 0 & 0 & 0 & 0 & 0 & k & k \end{bmatrix}$$

$$\Omega = \begin{bmatrix} k_1 & k_1 & k_2 & k_2 & -k_3 & -k_3 & -k_4 & -k_4 & k_5 & k_5 & k_6 & k_6 & -k_7 & -k_7 \\ -k_7 & -k_7 & k_1 & k_1 & -k_2 & -k_2 & -k_3 & -k_3 & k_4 & k_4 & k_5 & k_5 & -k_6 & -k_6 \\ k_6 & k_6 & k_7 & k_7 & k_1 & k_1 & k_2 & k_2 & -k_3 & -k_3 & -k_4 & -k_4 & k_5 & k_5 \\ k_5 & k_5 & k_6 & k_6 & -k_7 & -k_7 & k_1 & k_1 & -k_2 & -k_2 & -k_3 & -k_3 & k_4 & k_4 \\ -k_4 & -k_4 & -k_5 & -k_5 & k_6 & k_6 & k_7 & k_7 & k_1 & k_1 & k_2 & k_2 & -k_3 & -k_3 \\ -k_3 & -k_3 & -k_4 & -k_4 & k_5 & k_5 & k_6 & k_6 & -k_7 & -k_7 & k_1 & k_1 & -k_2 & -k_2 \\ k_2 & k_2 & k_3 & k_3 & -k_4 & -k_4 & -k_5 & -k_5 & k_6 & k_6 & k_7 & k_7 & k_1 & k_1 \end{bmatrix}$$

with $k = 0.5520, k_1 = 0.5476, k_2 = 0.2738, k_3 = 0.1369, k_4 = 0.0684, k_5 = 0.0342, k_6 = 0.0171, k_7 = 0.0088$.

A.2. Variance of endogenous and residual variables in the population and in the sample

$\sigma^2(y_i) = 1$
$\sigma^2(\delta_i) = 0.1524 \quad i = 1, 2, \ldots, 7$
$\sigma^2(\epsilon_i) = 0.2$

Generated in sample period:
$\begin{cases} V(y_1) = 1.044 & V(y_2) = 1.054 \\ V(\delta_1) = \text{N.A.} & V(\delta_2) = \text{N.A.} \\ V(\epsilon_1) = \text{N.A.} & V(\epsilon_2) = \text{N.A.} \end{cases}$

A.3. Correlation among residuals and exogenous variables

None

A.4. Sample size and special design features

1. 40 observations in both the sample and prediction periods.
2. This model is one in a series on number of relations in a one-loop model (Models 1g (=1a), 1h, 1i).

B. STRUCTURAL COEFFICIENTS

B.1. True coefficient versus average estimate from 100 samples

	β_{12}	γ_{11}	γ_{12}	β_{23}	γ_{23}	γ_{24}	β_{34}	γ_{35}	γ_{36}	β_{45}	γ_{47}	γ_{48}
True	.5	.552	.552	−.5	.552	.552	.5	.552	.552	−.5	.552	.552
OLS	.4977	.5550	.5613	−.5021	.5525	.5519	.4950	.5672	.5479	−.4952	.5511	.5468
TSLS	.5016	.5550	.5616	−.5000	.5524	.5525	.4977	.5672	.5486	−.4968	.5510	.5469
FP	.5032	.5535	.5667	−.4972	.5552	.5515	.4993	.5612	.5477	−.4938	.5514	.5457

	β_{56}	γ_{59}	$\gamma_{5,10}$	β_{67}	$\gamma_{6,11}$	$\gamma_{6,12}$	β_{71}	$\gamma_{7,13}$	$\gamma_{7,14}$
True	.5	.552	.552	−.5	.552	.552	.5	.552	.552
OLS	.5033	.5504	.5534	−.4829	.5527	.5624	.4948	.5603	.5537
TSLS	.5007	.5503	.5535	−.4889	.5526	.5617	.4969	.5612	.5531
FP	.5017	.5506	.5547	−.4875	.5514	.5578	.4962	.5557	.5516

B.2. Observed standard deviation of 100 samples around observed mean

OLS	.0672	.0556	.0644	.0661	.0657	.0657	.0567	.0561	.0739	.0587	.0606	.0652
TSLS	.0688	.0552	.0638	.0722	.0667	.0654	.0652	.0572	.0741	.0629	.0606	.0651
FP	.0682	.0617	.0703	.0752	.0772	.0719	.0704	.0649	.0817	.0659	.0676	.0764

OLS	.0781	.0687	.0548	.0692	.0575	.0637	.0658	.0630	.0620
TSLS	.0828	.0686	.0549	.0751	.0582	.0644	.0724	.0626	.0620
FP	.0876	.0758	.0673	.0776	.0667	.0766	.0767	.0736	.0791

B.3. Average standard deviation from large-sample formula

OLS	.0618	.0630	.0642	.0630	.0639	.0635	.0631	.0630	.0627	.0632	.0635	.0641
TSLS	.0668	.0633	.0645	.0679	.0642	.0637	.0683	.0633	.0629	.0686	.0638	.0644
FP	.0693	.0636	.0651	.0706	.0645	.0641	.0712	.0637	.0634	.0713	.0644	.0650

OLS	.0653	.0653	.0635	.0653	.0653	.0643	.0627	.0658	.0649
TSLS	.0709	.0655	.0638	.0711	.0656	.0646	.0677	.0661	.0652
FP	.0738	.0660	.0642	.0738	.0660	.0650	.0701	.0666	.0656

B.4. Observed standard deviation around true value of the coefficient

OLS	.0672	.0557	.0651	.0661	.0657	.0657	.0569	.0581	.0740	.0589	.0606	0654
TSLS	.0688	.0553	.0645	.0722	.0667	.0654	.0652	.0592	.0742	.0630	.0606	.0653
FP	.0683	.0617	.0718	.0753	.0773	.0719	.0704	.0655	.0818	.0662	.0676	.0767

OLS	.0782	.0687	.0547	.0713	.0575	.0645	.0660	.0635	.0620
TSLS	.0828	.0686	.0549	.0759	.0582	.0651	.0725	.0633	.0620
FP	.0876	.0758	.0674	.0786	.0667	.0768	.0768	.0737	.0791

B.5. Number of iterations for fix-point (FP) method

Average = 16.76   Smallest = 15   Largest = 20   No convergence in 0 samples

C. REDUCED FORM COEFFICIENTS (10 out of 98 coefficients)

C.1. True coefficient versus average estimate from 100 samples

	ω_{11}	ω_{12}	ω_{13}	ω_{15}	ω_{21}	ω_{23}	ω_{25}	ω_{31}	ω_{33}	ω_{35}
True	.5476	.5476	.2738	−.1369	−.0086	.5476	−.2738	.0171	.0086	.5476
OLS	.5509	.5572	.2735	−.1409	−.0082	.5485	−.2832	.0162	.0081	.5630
TSLS	.5509	.5574	.2754	−.1413	−.0083	.5482	−.2819	.0165	.0082	.5629
FP	.5494	.5625	.2775	−.1398	−.0083	.5510	−.2774	.0165	.0083	.5570
URF	.5485	.5591	.2828	−.1355	−.0162	.5542	−.2752	.0337	−.0042	.5518

C.2. Observed standard deviation of 100 samples around observed mean

OLS	.0553	.0637	.0517	.0308	.0029	.0651	.0493	.0050	.0029	.0557
TSLS	.0549	.0632	.0526	.0320	.0031	.0661	.0518	.0053	.0031	.0568
FP	.0613	.0695	.0544	.0342	.0034	.0765	.0547	.0058	.0032	.0646
URF	.0796	.0925	.0939	.0969	.0825	.0889	.0926	.0935	.0852	.0843

C.3. Average standard deviation from large-sample formula

URF	.0869	.0890	.0868	.0867	.0868	.0872	.0870	.0841	.0840	.0838

C.4. Observed standard deviation around true value of the coefficient

OLS	.0554	.0644	.0517	.0311	.0029	.0651	.0502	.0051	.0029	.0578
TSLS	.0550	.0640	.0526	.0323	.0031	.0661	.0524	.0053	.0031	.0588
FP	.0613	.0711	.0545	.0343	.0034	.0766	.0548	.0058	.0032	.0653
URF	.0796	.0932	.0943	.0969	.0828	.0891	.0926	.0950	.0853	.0844

D. EIGENVALUES FOR PRODUCT MOMENT MATRIX OF EXPLANATORY VARIABLES (REID SPECIFICATION)

	Smallest in 100 samples	Average for 100 samples					Smallest in 100 samples	Average for 100 samples		
		λ_1	λ_2	λ_3				λ_1	λ_2	λ_3
D.1. Equation 1						D.3. Equation 3				
OLS	.1577	.2300	.3284	.4416		OLS	.1061	.2278	.3254	.4467
TSLS	.1291	.2240	.3288	.4472		TSLS	.1074	.2189	.3271	.4540
FP	.1263	.2224	.3306	.4470		FP	.1162	.2177	.3259	.4564
D.2. Equation 2						D.4. Equation 4				
						D.5. Equation 5				
OLS	.1430	.2288	.3198	.4515		D.6. Equation 6	N.a.			
TSLS	.1339	.2228	.3181	.4591		D.7. Equation 7				
FP	.1234	.2229	.3171	.4599		D.8. Unrestricted reduced form				

E. AVERAGE R^2 FROM 100 SAMPLES

E.1. Sample period

	y_1	y_2	y_3	y_4	y_5	y_6	y_7	Y
True	.8	.8	.8	.8	.8	.8	.8	.8
Generated (average)	.8066	.8030	.8023	.7966	.7900	.7900	.7872	.7965
OLS	.8191	.8175	.8161	.8102	.8051	.8050	.8022	.8107
TSLS	.8197	.8183	.8170	.8106	.8056	.8059	.8028	.8114
FP	.8221	.8205	.8198	.8138	.8086	.8088	.8057	.8142
URF	.8021	.8031	.8083	.7973	.7897	.7925	.7870	.7971

E.2. Prediction period

	y_1	y_2	y_3	y_4	y_5	y_6	y_7	Y
	.7928	.7876	.7935	.7877	.7863	.7867	.7796	.7877
OLS	.7773	.7718	.7766	.7731	.7693	.7721	.7621	.7718
TSLS	.7771	.7706	.7752	.7727	.7685	.7705	.7613	.7708
FP	.7726	.7683	.7723	.7694	.7647	.7669	.7555	.7671
URF	.6785	.6680	.6658	.6649	.6739	.6752	.6477	.6677

E.3. Sample period (adj. for D.F.)

OLS	.8044	.8027	.8012	.7948	.7893	.7892	.7862	.7954
TSLS	.8051	.8036	.8022	.7952	.7898	.7902	.7868	.7961
FP	.8077	.8059	.8052	.7987	.7931	.7933	.7899	.7991

Table 10.2.9. Model 1m

A. MODEL DESIGN

A.1. Structural equations

$$\beta = \begin{bmatrix} 0 & 0 \\ 0.5 & 0 \end{bmatrix} \quad \Gamma = \begin{bmatrix} 0.6325 & 0.6325 & 0 & 0 \\ 0 & 0 & 0.5244 & 0.5244 \end{bmatrix} \quad \Omega = \begin{bmatrix} 0.6325 & 0.6325 & 0 & 0 \\ 0.3162 & 0.3162 & 0.5244 & 0.5244 \end{bmatrix}$$

A.2. Variance of endogenous and residual variables in the population and in the sample

$\sigma^2(y_i) = 1$	$i = 1, 2$	Generated	$V(y_1) = 1.022 \quad V(y_2) = 0.965$
$\sigma^2(\delta_i) = 0.2$		in sample	$V(\delta_1) = 0.207 \quad V(\delta_2) = 0.192$
$\sigma^2(\epsilon_1) = 0.2 \quad \sigma^2(\epsilon_2) = 0.25$		period:	$V(\epsilon_1) = 0.207 \quad V(\epsilon_2) = 0.241$

A.3. Correlation among residuals and exogenous variables

None

A.4. Sample size and special design features

1. 40 observations in both the sample and prediction periods.
2. This model is one in a series of causal chain systems (Models 1m-1q).
3. TSLS and FP have been applied to the model as if it were an ID system, for comparison with OLS estimation, and to illustrate that the REID-GEID respecification can be applied to CC systems. [1]

B. STRUCTURAL COEFFICIENTS

B.1. True coefficient versus average estimate from 100 samples

	β_{12}	γ_{11}	γ_{12}	β_{21}	γ_{23}	γ_{24}
True	0	0.6325	0.6325	0.5	0.5244	0.5244
OLS	0	0.6277	0.6346	0.4967	0.5275	0.5180
TSLS	0	0.6277	0.6346	0.4965	0.5272	0.5181
FP	0	0.6277	0.6346	0.4965	0.5284	0.5146

B.2. Observed standard deviation of 100 samples around observed mean

OLS	0	0.0625	0.0799	0.0667	0.0692	0.0739
TSLS	0	0.0625	0.0799	0.0793	0.0703	0.0741
FP	0	0.0625	0.0799	0.0808	0.0774	0.0752

B.3. Average standard deviation from large-sample formula

OLS	0	0.0738	0.0730	0.0712	0.0719	0.0743
TSLS	0	0.0738	0.0730	0.0803	0.0724	0.0748
FP	0	0.0738	0.0730	0.0808	0.0727	0.0750

B.4. Observed standard deviation around true value of the coefficient

OLS	0	0.0627	0.0799	0.0668	0.0693	0.0742
TSLS	0	0.0627	0.0799	0.0794	0.0704	0.0744
FP	0	0.0627	0.0799	0.0809	0.0775	0.0758

B.5. Number of iterations for fix-point (FP) method

Average = 3   Smallest = 3   Largest = 3   No convergence in 0 samples

C. REDUCED FORM COEFFICIENTS

C.1. True coefficient versus average estimate from 100 samples

	ω_{11}	ω_{12}	ω_{13}	ω_{14}	ω_{21}	ω_{22}	ω_{23}	ω_{24}
True	0.6325	0.6325	0	0	0.3162	0.3162	0.5244	0.5244
OLS	0.6277	0.6346	0	0	0.3115	0.3155	0.5275	0.5180
TSLS	0.6277	0.6346	0	0	0.3115	0.3152	0.5272	0.5181
FP	0.6277	0.6346	0	0	0.3115	0.3151	0.5284	0.5146
URF	0.6260	0.6354	0.0027	−0.0078	0.3124	0.3231	0.5283	0.5156

C.2. Observed standard deviation of 100 samples around observed mean

OLS	0.0625	0.0799	0	0	0.0506	0.0589	0.0692	0.0739
TSLS	0.0625	0.0799	0	0	0.0576	0.0635	0.0703	0.0741
FP	0.0625	0.0799	0	0	0.0582	0.0638	0.0774	0.0752
URF	0.0639	0.0812	0.0684	0.0669	0.0859	0.0815	0.0786	0.0781

C.3. Average standard deviation from large-sample formula

URF	0.0765	0.0755	0.0764	0.0785	0.0823	0.0810	0.0821	0.0844

C.4. Observed standard deviation around true value of the coefficient

OLS	0.0627	0.0799	0	0	0.0508	0.0589	0.0693	0.0742
TSLS	0.0627	0.0799	0	0	0.0578	0.0635	0.0704	0.0744
FP	0.0627	0.0799	0	0	0.0584	0.0638	0.0775	0.0758
URF	0.0642	0.0813	0.0685	0.0674	0.0860	0.0818	0.0787	0.0786

D. EIGENVALUES FOR PRODUCT MOMENT MATRIX OF EXPLANATORY VARIABLES (REID SPECIFICATION)

	Smallest in 100 samples	Average for 100 samples		
		λ_1	λ_2	λ_3
D.1. Equation 1				
OLS	0.2216	0.4046	0.5954	0
TSLS	0.2216	0.4046	0.5954	0
FP	0.2216	0.4046	0.5954	0
D.2. Equation 2				
OLS	0.1578	0.2319	0.3225	0.4456
TSLS	0.1500	0.2198	0.3251	0.4551
FP	0.1437	0.2232	0.3261	0.4507
D.3. Unrestricted reduced form	0.0986	0.1499	0.2105	0.2771

E. AVERAGE R^2 FROM 100 SAMPLES

E.1. Sample period / E.2. Prediction period

	E.1. Sample period			E.2. Prediction period		
	y_1	y_2	Y	y_1	y_2	Y
True	0.8	0.75	0.775	0.8	0.75	0.775
Generated (average)	0.7899	0.7400	0.7650	0.7939	0.7352	0.7646
OLS	0.7993	0.7549	0.7771	0.7805	0.7182	0.7494
TSLS	0.7993	0.7560	0.7777	0.7805	0.7162	0.7484
FP	0.7993	0.7581	0.7787	0.7805	0.7145	0.7475
URF	0.7859	0.7390	0.7625	0.7726	0.7029	0.7378

E.3. Sample period (adj. for D.F.)

	y_1	y_2	Y
OLS	0.7887	0.7350	0.7619
TSLS	0.7887	0.7362	0.7625
FP	0.7887	0.7385	0.7636

A. MODEL DESIGN

A.1. Structural equations

$$\beta = \begin{bmatrix} 0 & 0 \\ 3 & 0 \end{bmatrix} \qquad \Gamma = \begin{bmatrix} 0.172 & 0.172 & 0.861 & 0 \\ 0 & 0 & -2.583 & 0.726 \end{bmatrix} \qquad \Omega = \begin{bmatrix} 0.172 & 0.172 & 0.861 & 0 \\ 0.516 & 0.516 & 0 & 0.726 \end{bmatrix}$$

A.2. Variance of endogenous and residual variables in the population and in the sample

$$\sigma^2(y_i) = 1.0, 1.11$$
$$\sigma^2(\delta_i) = 0.2, 0.2$$
$$\sigma^2(\epsilon_i) = 0.2, 2.0$$

Generated in sample period:
$$\begin{cases} V(y_1) = 0.9848 & V(y_2) = 1.1326 \\ V(\delta_1) = 0.197 & V(\delta_2) = 0.194 \\ V(\epsilon_1) = 0.197 & V(\epsilon_2) = 1.973 \end{cases}$$

A.3. Correlation among residuals and exogenous variables

$$(x_4, \delta_1) = -1.0$$

A.4. Sample size and special design features

1. 40 observations in both the sample and prediction periods.
2. This model is one in a series of causal chain systems (Models 1m-1q).
3. A correlation of −1 between x_4 and δ_1 was built into the design to emphasize the difference between CC systems and Classic ID systems.
4. TSLS and FP have been applied to the model as if it were an ID system, for comparison with OLS estimation, and to illustrate that the REID-GEID respecification can be applied to CC systems. [2]

B. STRUCTURAL COEFFICIENTS

B.1. True coefficient versus average estimate from 100 samples

	β_{12}	γ_{11}	γ_{12}	γ_{13}	β_{21}	γ_{23}	γ_{24}
True	0	0.172	0.172	0.861	3	−2.58	0.726
OLS	0	0.1841	0.1762		2.9911	−2.5740	0.7158
TSLS	0	0.1841	0.1762	N.a.	2.9911	−2.5740	0.7158
FP	0	0.1841	0.1762		3.0089	−2.5692	−0.5934

B.2. Observed standard deviation of 100 samples around observed mean

OLS	0	0.0732	0.0674		0.3296	0.2875	0.1719
TSLS	0	0.0732	0.0674	N.a.	0.3300	0.2878	0.1721
FP	0	0.0732	0.0674		2.2450	2.0953	0.0857

B.3. Average standard deviation from large-sample formula

OLS	0	0.0724	0.0734		0.2930	0.2647	0.1511
TSLS	0	0.0724	0.0734	N.a.	0.2931	0.2648	0.1511
FP	0	0.0724	0.0734		1.7211	1.5670	0.2307

B.4. Observed standard deviation around true value of the coefficient

OLS	0	0.0742	0.0675		0.3297	0.2876	0.1722
TSLS	0	0.0742	0.0675	N.a.	0.3300	0.2879	0.1722
FP	0	0.0742	0.0675		2.2450	2.0953	0.1579

B.5. Number of iterations for fix-point (FP) method

Average = 3   Smallest = 3   Largest = 3   No convergence in 0 samples

C. REDUCED FORM COEFFICIENTS

C.1. True coefficient versus average estimate from 100 samples

	ω_{11}	ω_{12}	ω_{13}	ω_{14}	ω_{21}	ω_{22}	ω_{23}	ω_{24}
True	0.172	0.172	0.861	0	0.516	0.516	0	0.726
OLS	0.1841	0.1762	0.8544	0	0.5468	0.5273	−0.0215	0.7158
TSLS	0.1841	0.1762	0.8544	0	0.5469	0.5273	−0.0215	0.7158
FP	0.1841	0.1762	0.8544	0	0.4883	0.4703	0.0080	−0.5934
URF	0.1721	0.1719	0.8606	−0.4472	0.5204	0.5066	−0.0027	−0.6250

C.2. Observed standard deviation of 100 samples around observed mean

OLS	0.0732	0.0674	0.0755	0	0.2145	0.2127	0.2442	0.1719
TSLS	0.0732	0.0674	0.0755	0	0.2148	0.2127	0.2443	0.1721
FP	0.0732	0.0674	0.0755	0	0.1413	0.1490	0.0961	0.0857
URF	0.0011	0.0013	0.0001	0.0001	0.0737	0.0934	0.0808	0.0800

C.3. Average standard deviation from large-sample formula

URF	0.0010	0.0011	0.0011	0.0011	0.0721	0.0726	0.0740	0.0732

C.4. Observed standard deviation around true value of the coefficient

OLS	0.0742	0.0675	0.0758	0	0.2167	0.2130	0.2451	0.1722
TSLS	0.0742	0.0675	0.0758	0	0.2170	0.2130	0.2451	0.1724
FP	0.0742	0.0675	0.0758	0	0.1440	0.1559	0.0964	1.3222
URF	0.0011	0.0013	0.0004	0.4472	0.0738	0.0939	0.0808	1.3534

D. EIGENVALUES FOR PRODUCT MOMENT MATRIX OF EXPLANATORY VARIABLES (REID SPECIFICATION)

	Smallest in 100 samples	Average for 100 samples		
		λ_1	λ_2	λ_3
D.1. Equation 1				
OLS	0.1337	0.2236	0.3278	0.4486
TSLS	0.1337	0.2236	0.3278	0.4486
FP	0.1337	0.2236	0.3278	0.4486
D.2. Equation 2				
OLS	0.0038	0.0101	0.3225	0.6674
TSLS	0.0038	0.0101	0.3225	0.6674
FP	0.0001	0.0143	0.3358	0.6499
D.3. Reduced form equations	0.0756	0.1488	0.2122	0.2804

E. AVERAGE R^2 FROM 100 SAMPLES

E.1. Sample period

	y_1	y_2	Y
True	0.8	0.82	0.81
Generated (average)	0.7909	−0.7827	0.0041
OLS	0.8047	−0.6508	0.0770
TSLS	0.8047	−0.6507	0.0770
FP	0.8047	0.8029	0.8038
URF	0.1000	0.8259	0.4630

E.2. Prediction period

	y_1	y_2	Y
True	0.8	0.82	0.81
Generated (average)	0.7937	−0.8523	−0.0293
OLS	0.7761	−1.0031	−0.1135
TSLS	0.7761	−1.0033	−0.1136
FP	0.7761	0.7577	0.7669
URF	0.1000	0.7919	0.4460

E.3. Sample period (adj. for D.F.)

	y_1	y_2	Y
OLS	0.7889	−0.7846	0.0021
TSLS	0.7889	−0.7845	0.0022
FP	0.7889	0.7869	0.7879

Table 10.2.11. Model 1p

A. MODEL DESIGN

A.1. Structural equations

$$\beta = \begin{bmatrix} 0 & 0 \\ 0.5 & 0 \end{bmatrix} \qquad \Gamma = \begin{bmatrix} k & k & 0 & 0 \\ 0 & 0 & k & k \end{bmatrix} \qquad \Omega = \begin{bmatrix} 0.6325 & 0.6325 & 0 & 0 \\ 0.3162 & 0.3162 & 0.6325 & 0.6325 \end{bmatrix}$$

with $k = 0.6325$

A.2. Variance of endogenous and residual variables in the population and in the sample

$\sigma^2(y_1) = 1.0 \qquad \sigma^2(y_2) = 1.3125$

$\sigma^2(\delta_1) = 0.2 \qquad \sigma^2(\delta_2) = 0.2625$

$\sigma^2(\epsilon_1) = 0.2 \qquad \sigma^2(\epsilon_2) = 0.3125$

Generated in sample period:
$\begin{cases} V(y_1) = 0.986 & V(y_2) = 1.278 \\ V(\delta_1) = 0.196 & V(\delta_2) = 0.261 \\ V(\epsilon_1) = 0.196 & V(\epsilon_2) = 0.311 \end{cases}$

A.3. Correlation among residuals and exogenous variables

None

A.4. Sample size and special design features

1. 40 observations in both the sample and prediction periods.
2. This model is one in a series of causal chain systems (Models 1m-1q).
3. TSLS and FP have been applied to the model as if it were an ID system, for comparison with OLS estimation, and to illustrate that the REID-GEID respecification can be applied to CC systems. [1]

B. STRUCTURAL COEFFICIENTS

B.1. True coefficient versus average estimate from 100 samples

	β_{12}	γ_{11}	γ_{12}	β_{21}	γ_{23}	γ_{24}
True	0	0.6325	0.6325	0.5	0.6325	0.6325
OLS	0	0.6366	0.6282	0.4910	0.6384	0.6194
TSLS	0	0.6366	0.6282	0.4873	0.6374	0.6202
FP	0	0.6366	0.6282	0.4892	0.6402	0.6225

B.2. Observed standard deviation of 100 samples around observed mean

OLS	0	0.0669	0.0726	0.0837	0.0830	0.0918
TSLS	0	0.0669	0.0726	0.0952	0.0823	0.0925
FP	0	0.0669	0.0726	0.0947	0.0883	0.1050

B.3. Average standard deviation from large-sample formula

OLS	0	0.0715	0.0716	0.0846	0.0832	0.0840
TSLS	0	0.0715	0.0716	0.0955	0.0838	0.0847
FP	0	0.0715	0.0716	0.0963	0.0840	0.0851

B.4. Observed standard deviation around true value of the coefficient

OLS	0	0.0670	0.0727	0.0842	0.0832	0.0927
TSLS	0	0.0670	0.0727	0.0960	0.0824	0.0933
FP	0	0.0670	0.0727	0.0953	0.0886	0.1055

B.5. Number of iterations for fix-point (FP) method

Average = 3   Smallest = 3   Largest = 3   No convergence in 0 samples

C. REDUCED FORM COEFFICIENTS

C.1. True coefficient versus average estimate from 100 samples

	ω_{11}	ω_{12}	ω_{13}	ω_{14}	ω_{21}	ω_{22}	ω_{23}	ω_{24}
True	0.6325	0.6325	0	0	0.3162	0.3162	0.6325	0.6325
OLS	0.6366	0.6282	0	0	0.3129	0.3086	0.6384	0.6194
TSLS	0.6366	0.6282	0	0	0.3101	0.3065	0.6374	0.6202
FP	0.6366	0.6282	0	0	0.3113	0.3077	0.6402	0.6225
URF	0.6360	0.6339	0.0023	0.0053	0.3148	0.3075	0.6415	0.6217

C.2. Observed standard deviation of 100 samples around observed mean

OLS	0.0669	0.0726	0	0	0.0664	0.0642	0.0830	0.0918
TSLS	0.0669	0.0726	0	0	0.0699	0.0704	0.0823	0.0925
FP	0.0669	0.0726	0	0	0.0696	0.0704	0.0883	0.1050
URF	0.0695	0.0753	0.0672	0.0812	0.0870	0.0942	0.0892	0.1047

C.3. Average standard deviation from large-sample formula

URF	0.0734	0.0739	0.0731	0.0744	0.0925	0.0930	0.0920	0.0937

C.4. Observed standard deviation around true value of the coefficient

OLS	0.0670	0.0727	0	0	0.0665	0.0646	0.0832	0.0927
TSLS	0.0670	0.0727	0	0	0.0702	0.0710	0.0824	0.0933
FP	0.0670	0.0727	0	0	0.0698	0.0709	0.0886	0.1055
URF	0.0696	0.0757	0.0672	0.0814	0.0870	0.0946	0.0897	0.1052

D. EIGENVALUES FOR PRODUCT MOMENT MATRIX OF EXPLANATORY VARIABLES (REID SPECIFICATION)

	Smallest in 100 samples	λ_1	λ_2	λ_3

	Smallest in 100 samples	λ_1	λ_2	λ_3
D.1. Equation 1				
OLS	0.2422	0.4083	0.5917	0
TSLS	0.2422	0.4083	0.5917	0
FP	0.2422	0.4083	0.5917	0
D.2. Equation 2				
OLS	0.1365	0.2234	0.3280	0.4485
TSLS	0.0986	0.2093	0.3298	0.4609
FP	0.0939	0.2109	0.3291	0.4599
D.3. Unrestricted reduced form	0.0974	0.1479	0.2112	0.2789

E. AVERAGE R^2 FROM 100 SAMPLES

E.1. Sample period

	y_1	y_2	Y
True	0.8	0.762	0.781
Generated (average)	0.7912	0.7487	0.7700
OLS	0.8015	0.7657	0.7836
TSLS	0.8015	0.7670	0.7843
FP	0.8015	0.7689	0.7852
URF	0.7905	0.7485	0.7695

E.2. Prediction period

	y_1	y_2	Y
True	0.8	0.762	0.781
Generated (average)	0.7928	0.7541	0.7735
OLS	0.7850	0.7370	0.7610
TSLS	0.7850	0.7357	0.7604
FP	0.7850	0.7329	0.7590
URF	0.7714	0.7276	0.7495

E.3. Sample period (adj. for D.F.)

	y_1	y_2	Y
OLS	0.7911	0.7467	0.7689
TSLS	0.7911	0.7481	0.7696
FP	0.7911	0.7502	0.7707

Table 10.2.12. Model 1q

A. MODEL DESIGN

A.1. Structural equations

$$\beta = \begin{bmatrix} 0 & 0 \\ 3 & 0 \end{bmatrix} \qquad \Gamma = \begin{bmatrix} k & k & 0 & 0 \\ 0 & 0 & k & k \end{bmatrix} \qquad \Omega = \begin{bmatrix} 0.6325 & 0.6325 & 0 & 0 \\ 1.8974 & 1.8974 & 0.6325 & 0.6325 \end{bmatrix}$$

with $k = 0.6325$

A.2. Variance of endogenous and residual variables in the population and in the sample

$$\sigma^2(y_1) = 1.0 \qquad \sigma^2(y_2) = 12.25$$
$$\sigma^2(\delta_1) = 0.2 \qquad \sigma^2(\delta_2) = 2.45$$
$$\sigma^2(\epsilon_1) = 0.2 \qquad \sigma^2(\epsilon_2) = 4.25$$

Generated in sample period:
$$\begin{cases} V(y_1) = 1.058 & V(y_2) = 12.899 \\ V(\delta_1) = 0.200 & V(\delta_2) = 2.479 \\ V(\epsilon_1) = 0.200 & V(\epsilon_2) = 4.352 \end{cases}$$

A.3. Correlation among residuals and exogenous variables

    None

A.4. Sample size and special design features

1. 40 observations in both the sample and prediction periods.
2. This model is one in a series of causal chain systems (Models 1m-1q).
3. TSLS and FP have been applied to the model as if it were an ID system, for comparison with OLS estimation, and to illustrate that the REID-GEID respecification can be applied to CC systems. [1]

B. STRUCTURAL COEFFICIENTS

B.1. True coefficient versus average estimate from 100 samples

	β_{12}	γ_{11}	γ_{12}	β_{21}	γ_{23}	γ_{24}
True	0	0.6325	0.6325	3	0.6325	0.6325
OLS	0	0.6448	0.6541	3.0044	0.6170	0.6111
TSLS	0	.6448	0.6541	2.9816	0.6172	0.6154
FP	0	0.6448	0.6541	2.9763	0.6326	0.6170

B.2. Observed standard deviation of 100 samples around observed mean

OLS	0	0.0812	0.0680	0.2408	0.2330	0.2193
TSLS	0	0.0812	0.0680	0.2415	0.2329	0.2171
FP	0	0.0812	0.0680	0.2458	0.3458	0.3332

B.3. Average standard deviation from large-sample formula

OLS	0	0.0715	0.0718	0.2553	0.2682	0.2605
TSLS	0	0.0715	0.0718	0.2857	0.2700	0.2621
FP	0	0.0715	0.0718	0.2913	0.2747	0.2666

B.4. Observed standard deviation around true value of the coefficient

OLS	0	0.0821	0.0713	0.2408	0.2335	0.2203
TSLS	0	0.0821	0.0713	0.2422	0.2334	0.2178
FP	0	0.0821	0.0713	0.2469	0.3458	0.3336

B.5. Number of iterations for fix-point (FP) method

    Average = 3   Smallest = 3   Largest = 3   No convergence in 0 samples

C. REDUCED FORM COEFFICIENTS

C.1. True coefficient versus average estimate from 100 samples

	ω_{11}	ω_{12}	ω_{13}	ω_{14}	ω_{21}	ω_{22}	ω_{23}	ω_{24}
True	0.6325	0.6325	0	0	1.8974	1.8974	0.6325	0.6325
OLS	0.6448	0.6541	0	0	1.9373	1.9648	0.6170	0.6111
TSLS	0.6448	0.6541	0	0	1.9224	1.9502	0.6172	0.6154
FP	0.6448	0.6541	0	0	1.9190	1.9460	0.6326	0.6170
URF	0.6429	0.6538	0.0051	0.0006	1.9163	1.9453	0.6394	0.6246

C.2. Observed standard deviation of 100 samples around observed mean

OLS	0.0812	0.0680	0	0	0.2907	0.2577	0.2330	0.2193
TSLS	0.0812	0.0680	0	0	0.2853	0.2589	0.2329	0.2171
FP	0.0812	0.0680	0	0	0.2866	0.2551	0.3458	0.3332
URF	0.0824	0.0676	0.0774	0.0852	0.3338	0.3330	0.3496	0.3421

C.3. Average standard deviation from large-sample formula

URF	0.0735	0.0738	0.0764	0.0742	0.3453	0.3467	0.3590	0.3490

C.4. Observed standard deviation around true value of the coefficient

OLS	0.0821	0.0713	0	0	0.2934	0.2664	0.2335	0.2203
TSLS	0.0821	0.0713	0	0	0.2864	0.2642	0.2334	0.2178
FP	0.0821	0.0713	0	0	0.2874	0.2597	0.3458	0.3336
URF	0.0831	0.0709	0.0776	0.0852	0.3348	0.3364	0.3497	0.3425

D. EIGENVALUES FOR PRODUCT MOMENT MATRIX OF EXPLANATORY VARIABLES (REID SPECIFICATION)

	Smallest in 100 samples	Average for 100 samples		
		λ_1	λ_2	λ_3

D.1. Equation 1

	Smallest in 100 samples	λ_1	λ_2	λ_3
OLS	0.2375	0.3903	0.6097	0
TSLS	0.2375	0.3903	0.6097	0
FP	0.2375	0.3903	0.6097	0

D.2. Equation 2

OLS	0.1528	0.2269	0.3238	0.4493
TSLS	0.1264	0.2173	0.3266	0.4561
FP	0.1307	0.2237	0.3230	0.4533

D.3. Unrestricted reduced form

	0.0897	0.1474	0.2093	0.2747

E. AVERAGE R^2 FROM 100 SAMPLES

	E.1. Sample period			E.2. Prediction period		
	y_1	y_2	Y	y_1	y_2	Y
True	0.8	0.653	0.727	0.8	0.653	0.727
Generated (average)	0.8033	0.6525	0.7279	0.7889	0.6387	0.7138
OLS	0.8132	0.6687	0.7410	0.7743	0.6185	0.6964
TSLS	0.8132	0.6697	0.7415	0.7743	0.6197	0.6970
FP	0.8132	0.6772	0.7452	0.7743	0.6197	0.6970
URF	0.8041	0.6482	0.7262	0.7583	0.5989	0.6786

E.3. Sample period (adj. for D.F.)

	y_1	y_2	Y
OLS	0.8033	0.6418	0.7226
TSLS	0.8023	0.6429	0.7231
FP	0.8033	0.6510	0.7271

Table 10.2.13. Model 2b

A. MODEL DESIGN

A.1. Structural equations

$$\beta = \begin{bmatrix} 0 & 1 & 0 \\ 0 & 0 & -1 \\ 1 & 0 & 0 \end{bmatrix} \qquad \Gamma = \begin{bmatrix} k_1 & k_1 & 0 & 0 & 0 & 0 \\ 0 & 0 & k_1 & k_1 & 0 & 0 \\ 0 & 0 & 0 & 0 & k_1 & k_1 \end{bmatrix} \qquad \Omega = \begin{bmatrix} k_2 & k_2 & k_2 & k_2 & -k_2 & -k_2 \\ -k_2 & -k_2 & k_2 & k_2 & -k_2 & -k_2 \\ k_2 & k_2 & k_2 & k_2 & k_2 & k_2 \end{bmatrix}$$

with $k_1 = 0.7303$ and $k_2 = 0.3651$

A.2. Variance of endogenous and residual variables in the population and in the sample

$$\sigma^2(y_i) = 1.0$$
$$\sigma^2(\delta_i) = 0.2667 \qquad i = 1, 2, 3$$
$$\sigma^2(\epsilon_i) = 0.2$$

Generated in sample period:

$\begin{cases} V(y_1) = 0.985 & V(y_2) = 0.972 \\ V(\delta_1) = 0.267 & V(\delta_2) = 0.266 \\ V(\epsilon_1) = 0.205 & V(\epsilon_2) = 0.193 \end{cases}$

A.3. Correlation among residuals and exogenous variables

None

A.4. Sample size and special design features

1. 40 observations in both the sample and prediction periods.
2. This model is one in a series on number of relations in one-loop models (Models 2a(=1b), 2b-2d).

B. STRUCTURAL COEFFICIENTS

B.1. True coefficient versus average estimate from 100 samples

	β_{12}	γ_{11}	γ_{12}	β_{23}	γ_{24}	γ_{25}	β_{31}	γ_{35}	γ_{36}
True	1	0.7303	0.7303	−1	0.7303	0.7303	1	0.7303	0.7303
OLS	0.8249	0.6699	0.6663	−0.8108	0.6686	0.6631	0.8291	0.6617	0.6778
TSLS	0.9941	0.7298	0.7278	−0.9858	0.7336	0.7281	1.0107	0.7314	0.7443
FP	1.0025	0.7186	0.7204	−0.9978	0.7295	0.7259	1.0064	0.7158	0.7302

B.2. Observed standard deviation of 100 estimates around observed mean

OLS	0.0871	0.0848	0.0859	0.1003	0.0965	0.0885	0.0996	0.0885	0.0841
TSLS	0.1042	0.0902	0.0950	0.1325	0.0985	0.0991	0.1169	0.0927	0.0905
FP	0.1191	0.1227	0.1358	0.1438	0.1530	0.1429	0.1478	0.1277	0.1285

B.3. Average standard deviation from large-sample formula

OLS	0.0978	0.0889	0.0903	0.0947	0.0886	0.0882	0.0958	0.0895	0.0877
TSLS	0.1195	0.0957	0.0974	0.1172	0.0963	0.0959	0.1192	0.0976	0.0953
FP	0.1255	0.0990	0.1005	0.1246	0.1001	0.1000	0.1225	0.0995	0.0972

B.4. Observed standard deviation around true value of the coefficient

OLS	0.1956	0.1041	0.1071	0.2141	0.1145	0.1111	0.1978	0.1120	0.0991
TSLS	0.1044	0.0902	0.0950	0.1333	0.0986	0.0991	0.1174	0.0927	0.0916
FP	0.1191	0.1233	0.1362	0.1438	0.1530	0.1430	0.1479	0.1285	0.1285

B.5. Number of iterations for fix-point (FP) method

Average = 24.93   Smallest = 15   Largest = 50   No convergence in 0 samples

C. REDUCED FORM COEFFICIENTS (8 out of 18 coefficients)

C.1. True coefficient versus average estimate from 100 samples

	ω_{11}	ω_{12}	ω_{13}	ω_{14}	ω_{15}	ω_{16}	ω_{21}	ω_{22}
True	0.3651	0.3651	0.3651	0.3651	−0.3651	−0.3651	−0.3651	−0.3651
OLS	0.4315	0.4300	0.3553	0.3518	−0.2834	−0.2911	−0.2884	−0.2863
TSLS	0.3684	0.3678	0.3672	0.3643	−0.3578	−0.3650	−0.3627	−0.3618
FP	0.3610	0.3614	0.3653	0.3643	−0.3536	−0.3605	−0.3556	−0.3568
URF	0.3572	0.3628	0.3612	0.3640	−0.3682	−0.3764	−0.3706	−0.3689

C.2. Observed standard deviation of 100 samples around observed mean

OLS	0.0473	0.0559	0.0608	0.0527	0.0482	0.0511	0.0501	0.0473
TSLS	0.0449	0.0499	0.0563	0.0545	0.0519	0.0576	0.0518	0.0555
FP	0.0635	0.0649	0.0810	0.0775	0.0633	0.0633	0.0635	0.0716
URF	0.0681	0.0702	0.0789	0.0795	0.0729	0.0873	0.0804	0.0769

C.3. Average standard deviation from large-sample formula

URF	0.0784	0.0786	0.0793	0.0791	0.0792	0.0771	0.0761	0.0762

C.4. Observed standard deviation around true value of the coefficient

OLS	0.0815	0.0857	0.0616	0.0544	0.0949	0.0899	0.0916	0.0919
TSLS	0.0450	0.0500	0.0563	0.0545	0.0524	0.0576	0.0519	0.0556
FP	0.0636	0.0650	0.0810	0.0775	0.0643	0.0635	0.0642	0.0721
URF	0.0686	0.0702	0.0790	0.0795	0.0730	0.0880	0.0806	0.0770

D. EIGENVALUES FOR PRODUCT MOMENT MATRIX OF EXPLANATORY VARIABLES (REID SPECIFICATION)

	Smallest in 100 samples	Average for 100 samples		
		λ_1	λ_2	λ_3
D.1. Equation 1				
OLS	0.0670	0.1447	0.3178	0.5375
TSLS	0.0540	0.1214	0.3300	0.5486
FP	0.0438	0.1231	0.3287	0.5481
D.2. Equation 2				
OLS	0.0761	0.1476	0.3101	0.5423
TSLS	0.0495	0.1244	0.3237	0.5519
FP	0.0491	0.1233	0.3273	0.5494
D.3. Equation 3				
OLS	0.0802	0.1444	0.3217	0.5339
TSLS	0.0418	0.1205	0.3363	0.5432
FP	0.0586	0.1241	0.3360	0.5399

D.4. Unrestricted reduced form   N.a.

E. AVERAGE R^2 FROM 100 SAMPLES

E.1. Sample period   E.2. Prediction period

	y_1	y_2	y_3	Y	y_1	y_2	y_3	Y
True	0.8	0.8	0.8	0.8	0.8	0.8	0.8	0.8
Generated (average)	0.7839	0.7896	0.7898	0.7878	0.7866	0.7924	0.7983	0.7924
OLS	0.7753	0.7829	0.7811	0.7798	0.7464	0.7538	0.7596	0.7533
TSLS	0.7993	0.8042	0.8043	0.8026	0.7647	0.7745	0.7812	0.7735
FP	0.7905	0.7953	0.7922	0.7927	0.7551	0.7638	0.7655	0.7615
URF	0.7803	0.7885	0.7886	0.7858	0.7458	0.7530	0.7603	0.7530

E.3. Sample period (adj. for D.F.)

	y_1	y_2	y_3	Y
OLS	0.7571	0.7653	0.7634	0.7619
TSLS	0.7830	0.7883	0.7884	0.7866
FP	0.7735	0.7787	0.7753	0.7758

Table 10.2.14. Model 2c

A. MODEL DESIGN

A.1. Structural equations

$$\beta = \begin{bmatrix} 0 & -1 & 0 & 0 & 0 \\ 0 & 0 & 1 & 0 & 0 \\ 0 & 0 & 0 & -1 & 0 \\ 0 & 0 & 0 & 0 & 1 \\ 1 & 0 & 0 & 0 & 0 \end{bmatrix} \quad \Gamma = \begin{bmatrix} k_1 & k_1 & 0 & 0 & 0 & 0 & 0 & 0 & 0 & 0 \\ 0 & 0 & k_1 & k_1 & 0 & 0 & 0 & 0 & 0 & 0 \\ 0 & 0 & 0 & 0 & k_1 & k_1 & 0 & 0 & 0 & 0 \\ 0 & 0 & 0 & 0 & 0 & 0 & k_1 & k_1 & 0 & 0 \\ 0 & 0 & 0 & 0 & 0 & 0 & 0 & 0 & k_1 & k_1 \end{bmatrix}$$

$$\Omega = \begin{bmatrix} k_2 & k_2 & -k_2 & -k_2 & -k_2 & -k_2 & k_2 & k_2 & k \\ k_2 & k_2 & k_2 & k_2 & k_2 & k_2 & -k_2 & -k_2 & -k \\ k_2 & k_2 & -k_2 & -k_2 & k_2 & k_2 & -k_2 & -k_2 & -k \\ -k_2 & -k_2 & k_2 & k_2 & k_2 & k_2 & k_2 & k_2 & k \\ -k_2 & -k_2 & k_2 & k_2 & k_2 & k_2 & -k_2 & -k_2 & k \end{bmatrix}$$

with $k_1 = 0.5657$ and $k_2 = 0.2828$

A.2. Variance of endogenous and residual variables in the population and in the sample

$$\sigma^2(y_i) = 1.0$$
$$\sigma^2(\delta_i) = 0.16 \qquad i = 1,2,\ldots,5$$
$$\sigma^2(\epsilon_i) = 0.2$$

Generated in sample period:
$$\begin{cases} V(y_1) = 1.010 & V(y_2) = 0.989 \\ V(\delta_1) = 0.156 & V(\delta_2) = 0.159 \\ V(\epsilon_1) = 0.200 & V(\epsilon_2) = 0.198 \end{cases}$$

A.3. Correlation among residuals and variables

None

A.4. Sample size and special design features

1. 40 observations in both the sample and prediction periods.
2. This model is one in a series on number of relations in one-loop models (Models 2a (=1b), 2b–2d).

B. STRUCTURAL COEFFICIENTS

B.1. True coefficient versus average estimate from 100 samples

	β_{12}	γ_{11}	γ_{12}	β_{23}	γ_{23}	γ_{24}	β_{34}	γ_{35}	γ_{36}	β_{45}	γ_{47}	γ_{48}	β_{51}	γ_{59}	$\gamma_{5,10}$
True	−1	.5657	.5657	1	.5657	.5657	−1	.5657	.5657	1	.5657	.5657	−1	.5657	.5657
OLS	−0.9107	.5424	.5374	.8908	.5342	.5327	−.9063	.5393	.5368	.8931	.5384	.5317	−.9070	.5506	.5312
TSLS	−0.9859	.5648	.5566	.9667	.5549	.5534	−.9820	.5603	.5569	.9636	.5583	.5541	−.9799	.5720	.5531
FP	−1.0098	.5607	.5624	.9677	.5195	.5350	−.9859	.5492	.5307	.9746	.5451	.5330	−.9855	.5478	.5480

B.2. Observed standard deviation of 100 samples around observed mean

OLS	.0705	.0668	.0651	.0652	.0683	.0714	.0754	.0707	.0713	.0704	.0702	.0708	.0696	.0617	.0582
TSLS	.0720	.0669	.0641	.0779	.0669	.0710	.0893	.0712	.0752	.0788	.0700	.0709	.0861	.0641	.0615
FP	.1107	.1391	.1506	.1033	.1351	.1396	.1026	.1215	.1251	.1031	.1288	.1451	.1056	.1301	.1074

B.3. Average standard deviation from large-sample formula

OLS	.0698	.0659	.0660	.0689	.0666	.0665	.0715	.0658	.0674	.0689	.0655	.0672	.0701	.0684	.0670
TSLS	.0795	.0681	.0679	.0790	.0689	.0688	.0822	.0680	.0695	.0788	.0675	.0695	.0800	.0705	.0692
FP	.0908	.0744	.0747	.0876	.0735	.0738	.0896	.0717	.0730	.0890	.0731	.0750	.0883	.0749	.0737

B.4. Observed standard deviation around true value of the coefficient

OLS	.1138	.0707	.0710	.1272	.0752	.0787	.1203	.0755	.0769	.1280	.0763	.0785	.1162	.0635	.0677
TSLS	.0734	.0669	.0647	.0847	.0678	.0721	.0911	.0714	.0757	.0868	.0704	.0718	.0884	.0644	.0628
FP	.1112	.1392	.1506	.1082	.1428	.1429	.1036	.1226	.1299	.1062	.1304	.1487	.1066	.1313	.1088

B.5. Number of iterations for fix-point (FP) method

Average = 67.07   Smallest = 32   Largest = 200   No convergence in 3 samples

C. REDUCED FORM COEFFICIENTS (10 out of 50 coefficients)

C.1. True coefficient versus average estimate from 100 samples

	ω_{11}	ω_{13}	ω_{15}	ω_{17}	ω_{19}	ω_{21}	ω_{23}	ω_{25}	ω_{27}	ω_{29}
True	.2828	−.2828	−.2828	.2828	.2828	.2828	.2828	.2828	−.2828	−.2828
OLS	.3407	−.3051	−.2742	.2476	.2254	.2211	.3356	.3013	−.2719	−.2475
TSLS	.3014	−.2912	−.2835	.2762	.2721	.2668	.2959	.2881	−.2805	−.2761
FP	.2934	−.2739	−.2782	.2705	.2640	.2627	.2722	.2765	−.2691	−.2620
URF	.2920	−.2808	−.2892	.2871	.2934	.2786	.2721	.2821	−.2909	−.2841

C.2. Observed standard deviation of 100 samples around observed mean

OLS	.0447	.0450	.0439	.0414	.0350	.0353	.0460	.0439	.0412	.0334
TSLS	.0424	.0426	.0435	.0406	.0393	.0408	.0408	.0424	.0387	.0356
FP	.0755	.0772	.0655	.0647	.0683	.0660	.0750	.0624	.0652	.0653
URF	.0868	.0842	.0758	.0695	.0803	.0786	.0824	.0746	.0813	.0838

C.3. Average standard deviation from large-sample formula

URF	.0793	.0823	.0790	.0809	.0832	.0794	.0822	.0792	.0810	.0832

C.4. Observed standard deviation around true value of the coefficient

OLS	.0731	.0502	.0447	.0543	.0672	.0711	.0700	.0476	.0426	.0486
TSLS	.0463	.0434	.0435	.0411	.0407	.0438	.0429	.0427	.0388	.0362
FP	.0762	.0777	.0657	.0659	.0708	.0690	.0757	.0627	.0666	.0685
URF	.0873	.0842	.0761	.0696	.0810	.0787	.0831	.0746	.0817	.0838

D. EIGENVALUES FOR PRODUCT MOMENT MATRIX OF EXPLANATORY VARIABLES (REID SPECIFICATION)

	Smallest in 100 samples	Average for 100 samples					Smallest in 100 samples	Average for 100 samples		
		λ_1	λ_2	λ_3				λ_1	λ_2	λ_3
D.1. Equation 1						**D.4. Equation 4**				
OLS	.1015	.1779	.3222	.4999		OLS	.0956	.0765	.3202	.5033
TSLS	.0788	.1606	.3304	.5090		TSLS	.0781	.1590	.3293	.5117
FP	.0838	.1552	.3320	.5128		FP	.0827	.1557	.3321	.5122
D.2. Equation 2						**D.5. Equation 5**				
OLS	.1085	.1807	.3165	.5028		OLS	.0889	.1804	.3141	.5055
TSLS	.1001	.1636	.3253	.5111		TSLS	.0689	.1638	.3229	.5133
FP	.0780	.1661	.3272	.5067		FP	.0656	.1631	.3243	.5126
D.3. Equation 3										
OLS	.1059	.1810	.3236	.4954		**D.6. Unrestricted reduced form**	N.a.			
TSLS	.0816	.1616	.3334	.5050						
FP	.0916	.1617	.3351	.5052						

E. AVERAGE R^2 FROM 100 SAMPLES

E.1. Sample period

E.2. Prediction period

	y_1	y_2	y_3	y_4	y_5	Y	y_1	y_2	y_3	y_4	y_5	Y
True	.8	.8	.8	.8	.8	.8	.8	.8	.8	.8	.8	.8
Generated (average)	.7929	.7927	.7868	.7790	.7858	.7874	.7891	.7875	.7966	.7943	.7953	.7926
OLS	.7961	.7938	.7866	.7796	.7882	.7889	.7528	.7541	.7650	.7625	.7602	.7589
TSLS	.8106	.8076	.8012	.7961	.8030	.8037	.7710	.7728	.7808	.7783	.7774	.7761
FP	.7931	.7874	.7790	.7777	.7797	.7834	.7375	.7421	.7501	.7437	.7441	.7435
URF	.7940	.7921	.7835	.7793	.7861	.7870	.7229	.7189	.7337	.7305	.7333	.7279

E.3. Sample period (adj. for D.F.)

	y_1	y_2	y_3	y_4	y_5	Y
OLS	.7796	.7771	.7693	.7617	.7710	.7718
TSLS	.7952	.7920	.7851	.7796	.7870	.7878
FP	.7763	.7702	.7611	.7597	.7618	.7658

Table 10.2.15. Model 2d

A. MODEL DESIGN

A.1. Structural equations

$$\beta = \begin{bmatrix} 0 & 1 & 0 & 0 & 0 & 0 & 0 \\ 0 & 0 & -1 & 0 & 0 & 0 & 0 \\ 0 & 0 & 0 & 1 & 0 & 0 & 0 \\ 0 & 0 & 0 & 0 & -1 & 0 & 0 \\ 0 & 0 & 0 & 0 & 0 & 1 & 0 \\ 0 & 0 & 0 & 0 & 0 & 0 & -1 \\ 1 & 0 & 0 & 0 & 0 & 0 & 0 \end{bmatrix} \quad \Gamma = \begin{bmatrix} k_1 & k_1 & 0 & 0 & 0 & 0 & 0 & 0 & 0 & 0 & 0 & 0 & 0 & 0 \\ 0 & 0 & k_1 & k_1 & 0 & 0 & 0 & 0 & 0 & 0 & 0 & 0 & 0 & 0 \\ 0 & 0 & 0 & 0 & k_1 & k_1 & 0 & 0 & 0 & 0 & 0 & 0 & 0 & 0 \\ 0 & 0 & 0 & 0 & 0 & 0 & k_1 & k_1 & 0 & 0 & 0 & 0 & 0 & 0 \\ 0 & 0 & 0 & 0 & 0 & 0 & 0 & 0 & k_1 & k_1 & 0 & 0 & 0 & 0 \\ 0 & 0 & 0 & 0 & 0 & 0 & 0 & 0 & 0 & 0 & k_1 & k_1 & 0 & 0 \\ 0 & 0 & 0 & 0 & 0 & 0 & 0 & 0 & 0 & 0 & 0 & 0 & k_1 & k_1 \end{bmatrix}$$

$$\Omega = \begin{bmatrix} k_2 & k_2 & k_2 & k_2 & -k_2 & -k_2 & -k_2 & -k_2 & k_2 & k_2 & k_2 & k_2 & -k_2 & -k_2 \\ -k_2 & -k_2 & k_2 & k_2 & -k_2 & -k_2 & -k_2 & -k_2 & k_2 & k_2 & k_2 & k_2 & -k_2 & -k_2 \\ k_2 & k_2 & k_2 & k_2 & k_2 & k_2 & k_2 & k_2 & -k_2 & -k_2 & -k_2 & -k_2 & k_2 & k_2 \\ k_2 & k_2 & k_2 & k_2 & -k_2 & -k_2 & k_2 & k_2 & k_2 & k_2 & -k_2 & -k_2 & -k_2 & -k_2 \\ -k_2 & -k_2 & -k_2 & -k_2 & k_2 & k_2 & k_2 & k_2 & k_2 & k_2 & -k_2 & -k_2 & k_2 & k_2 \\ -k_2 & -k_2 & -k_2 & -k_2 & k_2 & k_2 & k_2 & k_2 & -k_2 & -k_2 & k_2 & k_2 & -k_2 & -k_2 \\ k_2 & k_2 & k_2 & k_2 & -k_2 & -k_2 & -k_2 & -k_2 & k_2 & k_2 & k_2 & k_2 & k_2 & k_2 \end{bmatrix}$$

with $k_1 = 0.4781$ and $k_2 = 0.2390$

A.2. Variance of endogenous and residual variables in the population and in the sample

$\sigma^2(y_i) = 1.0$

$\sigma^2(\delta_i) = 0.1143 \qquad i = 1,2,...,7$

$\sigma^2(\epsilon_i) = 0.2$

Generated in sample period:
$\left\{ \begin{array}{ll} V(y_1) = 0.996 & V(y_2) = 0.961 \\ V(\delta_1) = \text{N.a.} & V(\delta_2) = \text{N.a.} \\ V(\epsilon_1) = \text{N.a.} & V(\epsilon_2) = \text{N.a.} \end{array} \right.$

A.3. Correlation among residuals and exogenous variables

None

A.4. Sample size and special design features

1. 40 observations in both the sample and prediction periods.
2. This model is one in a series on number of relations in one-loop models (Models 2a (=1b), 2b–2d).

B. STRUCTURAL COEFFICIENTS

B.1. True coefficient versus average estimate from 100 samples

	β_{12}	γ_{11}	γ_{12}	β_{23}	γ_{23}	γ_{24}	β_{34}	γ_{35}	γ_{36}	β_{45}	γ_{47}	γ_{48}
True	1	.4781	.4781	−1	.4781	.4781	1	.4781	.4781	−1	.4781	.4781
OLS	.9411	.4600	.4528	−.9268	.4635	.4675	.9299	.4677	.4639	−.9333	.4602	.4606
TSLS	.9878	.4709	.4624	−.9689	.4766	.4782	.9703	.4757	.4743	−.9746	.4711	.4706
FP	.9919	.4524	.4384	−.9633	.4329	.4537	.9686	.4602	.4392	−.9620	.4314	.4646

	β_{56}	γ_{59}	$\gamma_{5,10}$	β_{67}	$\gamma_{6,11}$	$\gamma_{6,12}$	β_{71}	$\gamma_{7,13}$	$\gamma_{7,14}$
True	1	.4781	.4781	−1	.4781	.4781	1	.4781	.4781
OLS	.9508	.4666	.4759	−.9416	.4650	.4573	.9406	.4713	.4611
TSLS	.9930	.4768	.4854	−.9870	.4762	.4679	.9815	.4810	.4713
FP	1.0025	.4658	.4906	−.9936	.4580	.4595	.9971	.4874	.4520

B.2. Observed standard deviation of 100 samples around observed mean

OLS	.0585	.0536	.0519	.0569	.0560	.0515	.0577	.0562	.0535	.0596	.0555	.0525
TSLS	.0666	.0558	.0521	.0603	.0571	.0536	.0585	.0551	.0549	.0646	.0574	.0527
FP	.0929	.1280	.1273	.0820	.1301	.1324	.0753	.1234	.1204	.0866	.1183	.1240

OLS	.0545	.0613	.0545	.0644	.0638	.0549	.0536	.0540	.0524
TSLS	.0651	.0629	.0547	.0706	.0634	.0562	.0564	.0547	.0544
FP	.0793	.1341	.1316	.0969	.1215	.1174	.0863	.1193	.1341

B.3. Average standard deviation from large-sample formula

OLS	.0591	.0551	.0557	.0581	.0565	.0577	.0579	.0566	.0569	.0566	.0567	.0562
TSLS	.0655	.0562	.0567	.0642	.0577	.0588	.0636	.0575	.0579	.0623	.0578	.0572
FP	.0769	.0620	.0628	.0746	.0632	.0649	.0731	.0626	.0629	.0724	.0621	.0621

OLS	.0572	.0554	.0562	.0580	.0568	.0555	.0582	.0560	.0570
TSLS	.0631	.0564	.0572	.0642	.0579	.0566	.0642	.0570	.0580
FP	.0740	.0626	.0634	.0743	.0632	.0619	.0759	.0637	.0641

B.4. Observed standard deviation around true value of the coefficient

OLS	.0830	.0566	.0577	.0927	.0579	.0526	.0908	.0572	.0554	.0894	.0583	.0553
TSLS	.0677	.0563	.0544	.0678	.0571	.0536	.0656	.0552	.0550	.0694	.0578	.0532
FP	.0933	.1306	.1333	.0898	.1377	.1346	.0816	.1247	.1265	.0920	.1272	.1247
OLS	.0734	.0624	.0545	.0869	.0651	.0587	.0800	.0544	.0551			
TSLS	.0655	.0629	.0552	.0718	.0634	.0571	.0594	.0548	.0548			
FP	.0793	.1347	.1322	.0971	.1232	.1189	.0863	.1197	.1366			

B.5. Number of iterations for fix-point (FP) method

Average = 120.07   Smallest = 61   Largest = 200   No convergence in 9 samples

C. REDUCED FORM COEFFICIENTS (9 out of 98 coefficients)

C.1. True coefficient versus average estimate from 100 samples

	ω_{11}	ω_{13}	ω_{15}	ω_{21}	ω_{23}	ω_{25}	ω_{31}	ω_{33}	ω_{35}
True	.2390	.2390	−.2390	−.2390	.2390	−.2390	.2390	.2390	.2390
OLS	.2816	.2667	−.2495	−.1894	.2837	−.2654	.2046	.1937	.2866
TSLS	.2528	.2524	−.2442	−.2206	.2558	−.2476	.2280	.2276	.2559
FP	.2410	.2274	−.2340	−.2120	.2304	−.2365	.2207	.2085	.2461
URF	.2417	.2381	−.2383	−.2313	.2257	−.2424	.2399	.2619	.2427

C.2. Observed standard deviation of 100 samples around observed mean

OLS	.0341	.0351	.0358	.0283	.0357	.0371	.0297	.0291	.0381
TSLS	.0326	.0350	.0362	.0319	.0331	.0357	.0323	.0329	.0359
FP	.0696	.0680	.0684	.0617	.0689	.0684	.0639	.0633	.0723
URF	.0891	.0899	.0868	.0913	.0907	.0903	.0876	.0827	.0866

C.3. Average standard deviation from large-sample formula

URF	.0831	.0844	.0857	.0839	.0850	.0866	.0850	.0862	.0873

C.4. Observed standard deviation around true value of the coefficient

OLS	.0545	.0447	.0373	.0572	.0571	.0455	.0455	.0539	.0609
TSLS	.0354	.0374	.0366	.0369	.0371	.0367	.0342	.0349	.0396
FP	.0696	.0690	.0686	.0674	.0694	.0684	.0665	.0703	.0726
URF	.0891	.0899	.0868	.0916	.0917	.0904	.0876	.0858	.0867

D. EIGENVALUES FOR PRODUCT MOMENT MATRIX OF EXPLANATORY VARIABLES (REID SPECIFICATION)

	Smallest in 100 samples	Average for 100 samples				Smallest in 100 samples	Average for 100 samples		
		λ_1	λ_2	λ_3			λ_1	λ_2	λ_3
D.1. Equation 1					D.3. Equation 3				
OLS	.1030	.1916	.3108	.4976	OLS	.1137	.1978	.3160	.4862
TSLS	.0921	.1772	.3164	.5064	TSLS	.0904	.1869	.3212	.4919
FP	.0789	.1750	.3185	.5064	FP	.0980	.1889	.3238	.4873
D.2. Equation 2					D.4. Equation 4				
					D.5. Equation 5				
OLS	.1084	.1804	.3208	.4988	D.6. Equation 6		N.a.		
TSLS	.0902	.1685	.3279	.5036	D.7. Equation 7				
FP	.0930	.1728	.3314	.4958	D.8. Unrestricted reduced form				

E. AVERAGE R^2 FROM 100 SAMPLES

E.1. Sample period   E.2. Prediction period

	y_1	y_2	y_3	y_4	y_5	y_6	y_7	Y	y_1	y_2	y_3	y_4	y_5	y_6	y_7	Y
True	.8	.8	.8	.8	.8	.8	.8	.8	.8	.8	.8	.8	.8	.8	.8	.8
Generated (average)	.7957	.7853	.7998	.8023	.8052	.7984	.7906	.7968	.7849	.7911	.7933	.7955	.7881	.7896	.7863	.7898
OLS	.7985	.7878	.8004	.8020	.8079	.8007	.7945	.7988	.7554	.7578	.7605	.7701	.7612	.7619	.7578	.7607
TSLS	.8099	.7998	.8136	.8151	.8195	.8120	.8058	.8108	.7662	.7709	.7729	.7810	.7726	.7726	.7686	.7721
FP	.7803	.7667	.7767	.7774	.7877	.7802	.7790	.7783	.7212	.7228	.7254	.7338	.7190	.7248	.7206	.7239
URF	.8012	.7909	.8016	.8016	.8057	.7974	.7921	.7987	.6686	.6704	.6684	.6872	.6592	.6700	.6627	.6695

E.3. Sample period (adj. for D.F.)

OLS	.7822	.7706	.7842	.7859	.7923	.7845	.7778	.7825
TSLS	.7945	.7836	.7985	.8001	.8049	.7968	.7901	.7955
FP	.7625	.7478	.7586	.7594	.7705	.7624	.7611	.7603

Table 10.2.16 Model 2f

A. MODEL DESIGN

A.1. Structural equations

$$B = \begin{bmatrix} 0 & 1 \\ -1 & 0 \end{bmatrix} \qquad \Gamma = \begin{bmatrix} k_1 & k_1 & 0 & 0 & k_1 & k_1 & 0 & 0 \\ 0 & 0 & k_1 & k_1 & 0 & 0 & k_1 & k_1 \end{bmatrix} \qquad \Omega = \begin{bmatrix} k_2 & k_2 & k_2 & k_2 & k_2 & k_2 & k_2 & k_2 \\ -k_2 & -k_2 & k_2 & k_2 & -k_2 & -k_2 & k_2 & k_2 \end{bmatrix}$$

with $k_1 = 0.6325$ and $k_2 = 0.3162$

A.2. Variance of endogenous and residual variables in the population and in the sample

$\sigma^2(y_i) = 1.0$

$\sigma^2(\delta_i) = 0.4 \qquad i = 1, 2$

$\sigma^2(\epsilon_i) = 0.2$

Generated in sample period:
$\begin{cases} V(y_1) = 0.959 & V(y_2) = 0.982 \\ V(\delta_1) = 0.403 & V(\delta_2) = 0.393 \\ V(\epsilon_1) = 0.198 & V(\epsilon_2) = 0.200 \end{cases}$

A.3. Correlation among residuals and exogenous variables

None

A.4. Sample size and special design features

1. 40 observations in both the sample and predictions periods.
2. This model is one in a series on number of exogenous variables in two-relation models (Models 2e(=1b), 2f,2g).

B. STRUCTURAL COEFFICIENTS

B.1. True coefficient versus average estimate from 100 samples

	β_{12}	γ_{11}	γ_{12}	β_{21}	γ_{23}	γ_{24}
True	1	0.6325	0.6325	−1	0.6325	0.6325
OLS	0.6487	0.5212	0.5192	−0.6779	0.5372	0.5116
TSLS	0.9640	0.6171	0.6193	−0.9889	0.6338	0.6076
FP	0.9647	0.6248	0.6121	−0.9998	0.6201	0.5962

B.2. Observed standard deviation of 100 samples around observed mean

OLS	0.1376	0.1008	0.1024	0.1291	0.1012	0.1146
TSLS	0.1724	0.1129	0.1168	0.1631	0.1130	0.1374
FP	0.1732	0.1435	0.1352	0.1747	0.1383	0.1587

B.3. Average standard deviation from large-sample formula

OLS	0.1275	0.1068	0.1057	0.1280	0.1050	0.1037
TSLS	0.1703	0.1209	0.1200	0.1710	0.1186	0.1175
FP	0.1752	0.1250	0.1231	0.1797	0.1228	0.1216

B.4. Observed standard deviation around true value of the coefficient

OLS	0.3773	0.1502	0.1527	0.3470	0.1390	0.1666
TSLS	0.1761	0.1139	0.1175	0.1635	0.1130	0.1396
FP	0.1768	0.1437	0.1367	0.1747	0.1389	0.1628

B.5. Number of iterations for fix-point (FP) method

Smallest = 14.81　　　　Smallest = 9　　　　Largest = 35　　　　No convergence in 0 samples

C. REDUCED FORM COEFFICIENTS (4 out of 16 coefficients)

C.1. True coefficient versus average estimate from 100 samples

	ω_{11}	ω_{13}	ω_{21}	ω_{23}
True	0.3162	0.3162	−0.3162	0.3162
OLS	0.3620	0.2405	−0.2440	0.3745
TSLS	0.3168	0.3103	−0.3102	0.3258
FP	0.3179	0.3024	−0.3149	0.3169
URF	0.3197	0.3203	−0.3124	0.3153

C.2. Observed standard deviation of 100 samples around observed mean

OLS	0.0632	0.0582	0.0568	0.0691
TSLS	0.0553	0.0588	0.0600	0.0558
FP	0.0664	0.0712	0.0741	0.0687
URF	0.0727	0.0750	0.0812	0.0710

C.3. Average standard deviation from large-sample formula

URF	0.0799	0.0790	0.0802	0.0792

C.4. Observed standard deviation around true value of the coefficient

OLS	0.0781	0.0955	0.0919	0.0904
TSLS	0.0553	0.0591	0.0603	0.0566
FP	0.0664	0.0725	0.0741	0.0687
URF	0.0728	0.0751	0.0813	0.0710

D. EIGENVALUES FOR PRODUCT MOMENT MATRIX OF EXPLANATORY VARIABLES (REID SPECIFICATION)

	Smallest in 100 samples	Average for 100 samples λ_1	λ_2	λ_3

D.1. Equation 1

	Smallest in 100 samples	λ_1	λ_2	λ_3
OLS	0.0346	0.0619	0.1333	0.1864
TSLS	0.0216	0.0474	0.1363	0.1906
FP	0.0239	0.0487	0.1367	0.1913

D.2. Equation 2

OLS	0.0268	0.0619	0.1343	0.1873
TSLS	0.0143	0.0468	0.1370	0.1915
FP	0.0129	0.0469	0.1375	0.1920

| D.3. Unrestricted reduced form | 0.0307 | 0.0511 | 0.0680 | 0.0865 |

E. AVERAGE R^2 FROM 100 SAMPLES

E.1. Sample period / E.2. Prediction period

	y_1	y_2	Y	y_1	y_2	Y
True	0.8	0.8	0.8	0.8	0.8	0.8
Generated (average)	0.7838	0.7886	0.7862	0.7889	0.7893	0.7891
OLS	0.7769	0.7809	0.7789	0.7240	0.7285	0.7263
TSLS	0.8088	0.8140	0.8114	0.7622	0.7631	0.7627
FP	0.7960	0.8015	0.7988	0.7479	0.7486	0.7488
URF	0.7809	0.7881	0.7845	0.7490	0.7390	0.7440

E.3. Sample period (adj. for D.F.)

	y_1	y_2	Y
OLS	0.7588	0.7631	0.7610
TSLS	0.7933	0.7989	0.7941
FP	0.7794	0.7859	0.7825

Table 10.2.17. Model 2g

A. MODEL DESIGN

A.1. Structural equations

$$\beta = \begin{bmatrix} 0 & 1 \\ -1 & 0 \end{bmatrix} \qquad \Gamma = \begin{bmatrix} k_1 & k_1 & 0 & 0 & 0 & 0 & 0 & 0 & 0 & k_1 & k_1 & k_1 & k_1 & k_1 \\ 0 & 0 & k_1 & k_1 & k_1 & k_1 & k_1 & k_1 & k_1 & 0 & 0 & 0 & 0 & 0 \end{bmatrix}$$

$$\Omega = \begin{bmatrix} k_2 & k_2 & k_2 & k_2 & k_2 & k_2 & k_2 & k_2 & k_2 & k_2 & k_2 & k_2 & k_2 & k_2 \\ -k_2 & -k_2 & k_2 & k_2 & k_2 & k_2 & k_2 & k_2 & k_2 & -k_2 & -k_2 & -k_2 & -k_2 & -k_2 \end{bmatrix}$$

with $k_1 = 0.4781$ and $k_2 = 0.2390$.

A.2. Variance of endogenous and residual variables in the population and in the sample

$\sigma^2(y_i) = 1$

$\sigma^2(\delta_i) = 0.4 \qquad i = 1, 2$

$\sigma^2(\epsilon_i) = 0.2$

Generated in sample period:
$\begin{cases} V(y_1) = 0.959 & V(y_2) = 0.981 \\ V(\delta_1) = 0.384 & V(\delta_2) = 0.392 \\ V(\epsilon_1) = 0.193 & V(\epsilon_2) = 0.195 \end{cases}$

A.3. Correlation among residuals and exogenous variables

None

A.4. Sample size and special design features

1. 40 observations in both the sample and prediction periods.
2. This model is one in a series on number of exogenous variables in two-relation models (Model 2e(=1b), 2f, 2g).

B. STRUCTURAL COEFFICIENTS (4 out of 14 gamma coefficients)

B.1. True coefficient versus average estimate from 100 samples

	β_{12}	γ_{11}	γ_{12}	β_{21}	γ_{23}	γ_{24}
True	1	0.4781	0.4781	−1	0.4781	0.4781
OLS	0.6691	0.4031	0.4021	−0.6632	0.4110	0.3798
TSLS	0.9106	0.4580	0.4524	−0.9189	0.4685	0.4464
FP	0.9231	0.4542	0.4335	−0.9341	0.4635	0.4244

B.2. Observed standard deviation of 100 samples around observed mean

	β_{12}	γ_{11}	γ_{12}	β_{21}	γ_{23}	γ_{24}
OLS	0.1379	0.1112	0.0985	0.1225	0.1112	0.1168
TSLS	0.1617	0.1243	0.1021	0.1475	0.1227	0.1232
FP	0.1645	0.1368	0.1384	0.1466	0.1475	0.1527

B.3. Average standard deviation from large-sample formula

	β_{12}	γ_{11}	γ_{12}	β_{21}	γ_{23}	γ_{24}
OLS	0.1281	0.1032	0.1011	0.1316	0.1048	0.1080
TSLS	0.1608	0.1113	0.1089	0.1652	0.1137	0.1176
FP	0.1728	0.1182	0.1146	0.1770	0.1208	0.1233

B.4. Observed standard deviation around true value of the coefficient

	β_{12}	γ_{11}	γ_{12}	β_{21}	γ_{23}	γ_{24}
OLS	0.3584	0.1341	0.1244	0.3584	0.1299	0.1527
TSLS	0.1848	0.1259	0.1053	0.1683	0.1231	0.1272
FP	0.1816	0.1389	0.1454	0.1607	0.1482	0.1619

B.5. Number of iterations for fix-point (FP) method

Average = 28.06;   Smallest = 14;   Largest = 200   No convergence in 1 sample

C. REDUCED FORM COEFFICIENTS (4 out of 28 coefficients)

C.1. True coefficient versus average estimate from 100 samples

	ω_{11}	ω_{13}	ω_{21}	ω_{23}
True	0.2390	0.2390	−0.2390	0.2390.
OLS	0.2787	0.1887	−0.1837	0.2852
TSLS	0.2499	0.2311	−0.2278	0.2563
FP	0.2443	0.2277	−0.2260	0.2505
URF	0.2424	0.2388	−0.2355	0.2466

C.2. Observed standard deviation of 100 samples around observed mean

OLS	0.0704	0.0573	0.0548	0.0755
TSLS	0.0638	0.0650	0.0616	0.0647
FP	0.0693	0.0746	0.0670	0.0802
URF	0.0915	0.0876	0.0922	0.0858

C.3. Average standard deviation from large-sample formula

URF	0.0862	0.0863	0.0856	0.0855

C.4. Observed standard deviation around true value of the coefficient

OLS	0.0808	0.0762	0.0779	0.0885
TSLS	0.0647	0.0655	0.0626	0.0670
FP	0.0695	0.0755	0.0682	0.0810
URF	0.0916	0.0876	0.0923	0.0861

D. EIGENVALUES FOR PRODUCT MOMENT MATRIX OF EXPLANATORY VARIABLES (REID SPECIFICATION)

	Smallest in 100 samples	Average for 100 samples		
		λ_1	λ_2	λ_3
D.1. Equation 1				
OLS	0.0197	0.0337	0.0603	0.0796
TSLS	0.0112	0.0270	0.0604	0.0803
FP	0.0092	0.0274	0.0606	0.0807
D.2. Equation 2				
OLS	0.0208	0.0333	0.0596	0.0809
TSLS	0.0132	0.0268	0.0594	0.0815
FP	0.0135	0.0279	0.0596	0.0817
D.3. Unrestricted reduced form	0.0073	0.0158	0.0225	0.0285

E. AVERAGE R^2 FROM 100 SAMPLES

	E.1. Sample period			E.2. Prediction period		
	y_1	y_2	Y	y_1	y_2	Y
True	0.8	0.8	0.8	0.8	0.8	0.8
Generated (average)	0.7944	0.7920	0.7932	0.7956	0.7955	0.7956
OLS	0.8072	0.8096	0.8084	0.7067	0.6945	0.7006
TSLS	0.8328	0.8345	0.8336	0.7413	0.7352	0.7383
FP	0.8130	0.8167	0.8148	0.7143	0.7089	0.7116
URF.	0.7922	0.7936	0.7929	0.6877	0.6819	0.6848

E.3. Sample period (adj. for D.F.)

	y_1	y_2	Y
OLS	0.7590	0.7620	0.7605
TSLS	0.7910	0.7930	0.7920
FP	0.7663	0.7709	0.7685

Table 10.2.18. Model 3a

A. MODEL DESIGN

A.1. Structural equations

$$\beta = \begin{bmatrix} 0 & 0.5 & 0 \\ 0 & 0 & -0.5 \\ 0.5 & 0 & 0 \end{bmatrix} \qquad \Gamma = \begin{bmatrix} k & k & 0 & 0 & 0 & 0 \\ 0 & 0 & k & k & 0 & 0 \\ 0 & 0 & 0 & 0 & k & k \end{bmatrix}$$

$$\Omega = \begin{bmatrix} .4364 & .4364 & .2182 & .2182 & -.1091 & -.1091 \\ -.1091 & -.1091 & .4364 & .4364 & -.2182 & -.2182 \\ .2182 & .2182 & .1091 & .1091 & .4364 & .4364 \end{bmatrix} \text{ with } k = 0.491$$

A.2. Variance of endogenous and residual variables in the population and in the sample

$\sigma^2(y_i) = 1.0$

$\sigma^2(\delta_i) = 0.4821 \qquad i = 1,2,3$

$\sigma^2(\epsilon_i) = 0.5$

Generated in sample period:
$\begin{cases} V(y_1) = 0.994 & V(y_2) = 0.971 \\ V(\delta_1) = 0.472 & V(\delta_2) = 0.472 \\ V(\epsilon_1) = 0.488 & V(\epsilon_2) = 0.487 \end{cases}$

A.3. Correlation among residuals and exogenous variables

None

A.4. Sample size and special design features

1. 40 observations in both the sample and prediction periods.
2. This model is one in a series on size of beta coefficients in three-equation models with one loop (Models 3a–3c).

B. STRUCTURAL COEFFICIENTS

B.1. True coefficient versus average estimate from 100 samples

	β_{12}	γ_{11}	γ_{12}	β_{23}	γ_{23}	γ_{24}	β_{31}	γ_{35}	γ_{36}
True	.5	.491	.491	−.5	.491	.491	.5	.491	.491
OLS	.3858	.4728	.4827	−.3802	.4713	.4782	.4057	.4688	.4610
TSLS	.4760	.4826	.4924	−.4714	.4814	.4892	.5135	.4830	.4715
FP	.4758	.4860	.4920	−.4764	.4783	.4910	.5111	.4708	.4694

B.2. Observed standard deviation of 100 samples around observed mean

	β_{12}	γ_{11}	γ_{12}	β_{23}	γ_{23}	γ_{24}	β_{31}	γ_{35}	γ_{36}
OLS	.1128	.1092	.1141	.1287	.1202	.1220	.1067	.1190	.1255
TSLS	.1633	.1145	.1180	.1426	.1205	.1237	.1723	.1220	.1296
FP	.1664	.1097	.1266	.1489	.1294	.1407	.1697	.1296	.1461

B.3. Average standard deviation from large-sample formula

	β_{12}	γ_{11}	γ_{12}	β_{23}	γ_{23}	γ_{24}	β_{31}	γ_{35}	γ_{36}
OLS	.1144	.1130	.1123	.1142	.1109	.1115	.1105	.1093	.1099
TSLS	.1635	.1171	.1167	.1620	.1151	.1159	.1573	.1143	.1148
FP	.1686	.1171	.1160	.1669	.1155	.1151	.1620	.1142	.1142

B.4. Observed standard deviation around true value of the coefficient

	β_{12}	γ_{11}	γ_{12}	β_{23}	γ_{23}	γ_{24}	β_{31}	γ_{35}	γ_{36}
OLS	.1605	.1107	.1141	.1758	.1218	.1227	.1424	.1211	.1290
TSLS	.1651	.1148	.1180	.1454	.1209	.1237	.1728	.1223	.1311
FP	.1682	.1098	.1266	.1508	.1300	.1407	.1701	.1312	.1477

B.5. Number of iterations for fix-point (FP) method

Average = 11.7   Smallest = 9   Largest = 20   No convergence in 0 samples

C. REDUCED FORM COEFFICIENTS (12 out of 18 coefficients)

C.1. True coefficient versus average estimate from 100 samples

	ω_{11}	ω_{12}	ω_{13}	ω_{14}	ω_{15}	ω_{16}	ω_{21}	ω_{23}	ω_{25}	ω_{31}	ω_{33}	ω_{35}
True	.4364	.4364	.2182	.2182	−.1091	−.1091	−.1091	.4364	−.2182	.2182	.1091	.4364
OLS	.4473	.4564	.1736	.1736	−.0627	−.0624	−.0696	.4461	−.1666	.1815	.0688	.4435
TSLS	.4348	.4426	.2073	.2059	−.0946	−.0925	−.1040	.4333	−.2015	.2211	.1030	.4339
FP	.4372	.4421	.2065	.2054	.0937	.0923	.1059	.4299	.1989	.2214	.1014	.4232
URF	.4390	.4421	.2205	.2072	−.1030	−.0999	−.1042	.4296	−.2162	.2283	.1086	.4298

C.2. Observed standard deviation of 100 samples around observed mean

OLS	.1032	.1067	.0755	.0695	.0300	.0300	.0339	.1137	.0675	.0639	.0324	.1121
TSLS	.1052	.1056	.0964	.0794	.0476	.0441	.0529	.1102	.0730	.0860	.0574	.1087
FP	.1006	.1140	.1015	.0823	.0507	.0464	.0547	.1164	.0788	.0848	.0594	.1172
URF	.1015	.1129	.1263	.1127	.1174	.1323	.1212	.1202	.1118	.1222	.1124	.1237

C.3. Average standard deviation from large-sample formula

URF	.1211	.1205	.1192	.1204	.1202	.1194	.1205	.1188	.1197	.1177	.1161	.1170

C.4. Observed standard deviation around true value of the coefficient

OLS	.1038	.1086	.0877	.0826	.0553	.0555	.0521	.1141	.0850	.0737	.0517	.1123
TSLS	.1052	.1058	.0970	.0803	.0498	.0471	.0531	.1102	.0749	.0860	.0577	.1087
FP	.1006	.1141	.1022	.0832	.0530	.0493	.0548	.1166	.0811	.0849	.0599	.1179
URF	.1015	.1130	.1263	.1132	.1176	.1326	.1213	.1204	.1118	.1226	.1124	.1239

D. EIGENVALUES FOR PRODUCT MOMENT MATRIX OF EXPLANATORY VARIABLES (REID SPECIFICATION)

	Smallest in 100 samples	Average for 100 samples				Smallest in 100 samples	Average for 100 samples		
		λ_1	λ_2	λ_3			λ_1	λ_2	λ_3
D.1. Equation 1						**D.3. Equation 3**			
OLS	.1380	.2212	.3234	.4554		OLS	.1361	.2220	.3241	.4539
TSLS	.0701	.1680	.3336	.4984		TSLS	.0786	.1683	.3378	.4939
FP	.0739	.1680	.3346	.4974		FP	.0598	.1719	.3344	.4937
D.2. Equation 2						**D.4. Unrestricted reduced form**	N.a.		
OLS	.1182	.2185	.3183	.4632						
TSLS	.0444	.1630	.3332	.5038						
FP	.0549	.1627	.3350	.5023						

E. AVERAGE R^2 FROM 100 SAMPLES

E.1. Sample period

	y_1	y_2	y_3	$Y.$
True	.5	.5	.5	.5
Generated (average)	.4993	.4856	.4996	.4948
OLS	.5224	.5156	.5286	.5222
TSLS	.5341	.5267	.5408	.5339
FP	.5327	.5253	.5420	.5333
URF	.4957	.4867	.5078	.4967

E.2. Prediction period

	y_1	y_2	y_3	Y
True	.5	.5	.5	.5
Generated (average)	.4861	.4747	.5036	.4881
OLS	.4437	.4223	.4566	.4409
TSLS	.4448	.4308	.4518	.4425
FP	.4406	.4191	.4475	.4357
URF	.3998	.3866	.3968	.3944

E.3. Sample period (adj. for D.F.)

	y_1	y_2	y_3	$Y.$
OLS	.4837	.4763	.4904	.4835
TSLS	.4963	.4883	.5036	.4961
FP	.4948	.4868	.5049	.4955

Table 10.2.19. Model 3b

A. MODEL DESIGN

A.1. Structural equations

$$\beta = \begin{bmatrix} 0 & 1 & 0 \\ 0 & 0 & -1 \\ 1 & 0 & 0 \end{bmatrix} \qquad \Gamma = \begin{bmatrix} k_1 & k_1 & 0 & 0 & 0 & 0 \\ 0 & 0 & k_1 & k_1 & 0 & 0 \\ 0 & 0 & 0 & 0 & k_1 & k_1 \end{bmatrix} \qquad \Omega = \begin{bmatrix} k_2 & k_2 & k_2 & k_2 & -k_2 & -k_2 \\ -k_2 & -k_2 & k_2 & k_2 & -k_2 & -k_2 \\ k_2 & k_2 & k_2 & k_2 & k_2 & k_2 \end{bmatrix}$$

with $k_1 = 0.5774$ and $k_2 = 0.2887$.

A.2. Variance of endogenous and residual variables in the population and in the sample

$\sigma^2(y_i) = 1$
$\sigma^2(\delta_i) = 0.6667 \qquad i = 1,2,3$
$\sigma^2(\epsilon_i) = 0.5$

Generated
in sample
period:
$\begin{cases} V(y_1) = 0.972 & V(y_2) = 0.974 \\ V(\delta_1) = 0.653 & V(\delta_2) = 0.653 \\ V(\epsilon_1) = 0.485 & V(\epsilon_2) = 0.484 \end{cases}$

A.3. Correlation among residuals and exogenous variables

None

A.4. Sample size and special design features

1. 40 observations in both the sample and prediction periods.
2. This model is one in a series on size of beta coefficients in three-relation models with one loop (Models 3a–3c).

B. STRUCTURAL COEFFICIENTS

B.1. True coefficient versus average estimate from 100 samples

	β_{12}	γ_{11}	γ_{12}	β_{23}	γ_{23}	γ_{24}	β_{31}	γ_{35}	γ_{36}
True	1	.5773	.5773	−1	.5773	.5773	1	.5773	.5773
OLS	.5954	.4551	.4677	−.5969	.4480	.4616	.6234	.4553	.4534
TSLS	.9348	.5515	.5640	−.9182	.5440	.5548	.9849	.5628	.5501
FP	.9303	.5228	.5277	−.9363	.5133	.5433	.9756	.5022	.5169

B.2. Observed standard deviation of 100 samples around observed mean

OLS	.1448	.1133	.1288	.1616	.1254	.1372	.1261	.1332	.1341
TSLS	.2484	.1401	.1536	.1987	.1424	.1513	.2469	.1617	.1602
FP	.2819	.1687	.2157	.2333	.2000	.2353	.2463	.1931	.2382

B.3. Average standard deviation from large-sample formula

OLS	.1319	.1250	.1247	.1290	.1228	.1230	.1299	.1226	.1220
TSLS	.2251	.1475	.1488	.2115	.1439	.1437	.2265	.1490	.1458
FP	.2439	.1503	.1493	.2330	.1488	.1477	.2415	.1480	.1484

B.4. Observed standard deviation around true value of the coefficient

OLS	.4297	.1666	.1691	.4343	.1801	.1795	.3972	.1806	.1826
TSLS	.2568	.1425	.1542	.2149	.1462	.1530	.2474	.1623	.1625
FP	.2904	.1773	.2213	.2419	.2100	.2377	.2475	.2072	.2457

B.5. Number of iterations for fix-point (FP) method

Average = 29.68   Smallest = 12   Largest = 200   No convergence in 3 samples

C. REDUCED FORM COEFFICIENTS (12 out of 18 coefficients)

C.1. True coefficient versus average estimate from 100 samples

	ω_{11}	ω_{12}	ω_{13}	ω_{14}	ω_{15}	ω_{16}	ω_{21}	ω_{23}	ω_{25}	ω_{31}	ω_{33}	ω_{35}
True	.2887	.2887	.2887	.2887	−.2887	−.2887	−.2887	.2887	−.2887	.2887	.2887	.2887
OLS	.3751	.3857	.2182	.2259	−.1285	−.1300	−.1368	.3698	−.2204	.2325	.1343	.3750
TSLS	.3051	.3103	.2776	.2801	−.2532	−.2491	−.2660	.3015	−.2778	.2928	.2640	.3102
FP	.2904	.2932	.2589	.2672	−.2304	−.2336	−.2539	.2833	−.2554	.2768	.2432	.2790
URF	.2894	.2924	.2888	.2837	−.2808	−.2703	−.2880	.2821	−.2867	.2997	.2869	.2852

C.2. Observed standard deviation of 100 samples around observed mean

OLS	.0916	.1050	.0775	.0899	.0523	.0539	.0493	.1027	.0852	.0704	.0519	.1066
TSLS	.0801	.0804	.0970	.0876	.0810	.0780	.0840	.0857	.0840	.0821	.0885	.0898
FP	.0967	.1206	.1146	.1172	.1007	.1105	.0953	.1075	.1062	.1008	.1121	.1106
URF	.0957	.1212	.1286	.1142	.1169	.1333	.1308	.1106	.1164	.1159	.1202	.1179

C.3. Average standard deviation from large-sample formula

URF	.1204	.1199	.1185	.1197	.1197	.1189	.1197	.1179	.1188	.1193	.1177	.1183

C.4. Observed standard deviation around true value of the coefficient

OLS	.1259	.1429	.1048	.1097	.1685	.1676	.1597	.1309	.1092	.0901	.1629	.1372
TSLS	.0818	.0833	.0976	.0880	.0884	.0875	.0870	.0867	.0847	.0822	.0919	.0923
FP	.0967	.1207	.1184	.1192	.1164	.1235	.1015	.1076	.1113	.1015	.1210	.1110
URF	.0957	.1213	.1286	.1143	.1172	.1346	.1308	.1108	.1164	.1164	.1202	.1180

D. EIGENVALUES FOR PRODUCT MOMENT MATRIX OF EXPLANATORY VARIABLES (REID SPECIFICATION)

	Smallest in 100 samples	Average for 100 samples		
		λ_1	λ_2	λ_3
D.1. Equation 1				
OLS	.0975	.1757	.3107	.5136
TSLS	.0319	.1094	.3407	.5499
FP	.0183	.1113	.3480	.5407
D.2. Equation 2				
OLS	.0800	.1755	.3112	.5132
TSLS	.0301	.1113	.3409	.5478
FP	.0309	.1104	.3484	.5412

	Smallest in 100 samples	Average for 100 samples		
		λ_1	λ_2	λ_3
D.3. Equation 3				
OLS	.0879	.1773	.3176	.5051
TSLS	.0288	.1114	.3464	.5421
FP	.0331	.1128	.3470	.5402
D.4. Unrestricted reduced form	N.a.			

E. AVERAGE R^2 FROM 100 SAMPLES

E.1. Sample period

	y_1	y_2	y_3	Y
True	.5	.5	.5	.5
Generated (average)	.4892	.4888	.5087	.4956
OLS	.4538	.4603	.4707	.4616
TSLS	.5260	.5319	.5384	.5321
FP	.4993	.5103	.5170	.5089
URF	.4873	.4952	.5090	.4972

E.2. Prediction period

	y_1	y_2	y_3	Y
True	.5	.5	.5	.5
Generated (average)	.4754	.4837	.5078	.4890
OLS	.3539	.3578	.4001	.3706
TSLS	.4250	.4349	.4608	.4402
FP	.3862	.3958	.4340	.4053
URF	.3860	.3872	.4123	.3952

E.3. Sample period (adj. for D.F.)

	y_1	y_2	y_3	Y
OLS	.4095	.4165	.4278	.4179
TSLS	.4876	.4939	.5010	.4942
FP	.4587	.4706	.4778	.4691

Table 10.2.20 Model 3c

A. MODEL DESIGN

A.1. Structural equations

$$\beta = \begin{bmatrix} 0 & 2 & 0 \\ 0 & 0 & -2 \\ 2 & 0 & 0 \end{bmatrix} \qquad \Gamma = \begin{bmatrix} k & k & 0 & 0 & 0 & 0 \\ 0 & 0 & k & k & 0 & 0 \\ 0 & 0 & 0 & 0 & k & k \end{bmatrix}$$

$$\Omega = \begin{bmatrix} 0.1091 & 0.1091 & 0.2182 & 0.2182 & -0.4364 & -0.4364 \\ -0.4364 & -0.4364 & 0.1091 & 0.1091 & -0.2182 & -0.2182 \\ 0.2182 & 0.2182 & 0.4364 & 0.4364 & 0.1091 & 0.1091 \end{bmatrix}$$

with $k = 0.9820$

A.2. Variance of endogenous and residual variables in the population and in the sample

$\sigma^2(y_i) = 1.0$

$\sigma^2(\delta_i) = 1.9286 \qquad i = 1, 2, 3$

$\sigma^2(\epsilon_i) = 0.5$

Generated in sample period:
$\begin{cases} V(y_1) = 0.954 & V(y_2) = 0.991 \\ V(\delta_1) = 1.888 & V(\delta_2) = 1.889 \\ V(\epsilon_1) = 0.478 & V(\epsilon_2) = 0.484 \end{cases}$

A.3. Correlation among residuals and exogenous variables

None

A.4. Sample size and special design features

1. 40 observations in both the sample and prediction periods.
2. This model is one in a series on size of beta coefficients in three-relation models with one loop (Models 3a-3c).

B. STRUCTURAL COEFFICIENTS

B.1. True coefficient versus average estimate from 100 samples

	β_{12}	γ_{11}	γ_{12}	β_{23}	γ_{23}	γ_{24}	β_{31}	γ_{35}	γ_{36}
True	2	0.9820	0.9820	-2	0.9820	0.9820	2	0.9820	0.9820
OLS	0.6016	0.3692	0.3783	-0.6369	0.3657	0.3906	0.6436	0.3744	0.3844
TSLS	1.5759	0.7835	0.8041	-1.6419	0.8027	0.8226	1.6611	0.8138	0.8048
FP	1.0239	0.2479	0.2648	-0.9539	0.2222	0.2718	0.9715	0.2382	0.2827

B.2. Observed standard deviation of 100 samples around observed mean

OLS	0.1934	0.1478	0.1579	0.1749	0.1478	0.1690	0.2099	0.1834	0.1574
TSLS	0.7152	0.3469	0.3994	0.5057	0.2775	0.2911	0.5326	0.3324	0.3098
FP	0.4759	0.2229	0.2628	0.8038	0.2761	0.2974	0.6122	0.2865	0.2939

B.3. Average standard deviation from large-sample formula

OLS	0.1801	0.1598	0.1611	0.1790	0.1595	0.1592	0.1807	0.1589	0.1572
TSLS	0.5573	0.3161	0.3201	0.5083	0.2967	0.2951	0.5837	0.3312	0.3174
FP	0.5016	0.1986	0.2054	0.5786	0.2091	0.2204	0.5355	0.2001	0.2100

B.4. Observed standard deviation around true value of the coefficient

OLS	1.4117	0.6305	0.6240	1.3743	0.6338	0.6151	1.3725	0.6347	0.6180
TSLS	0.8314	0.3997	0.4372	0.6196	0.3304	0.3319	0.6313	0.3725	0.3569
FP	1.0858	0.7672	0.7638	1.3192	0.8084	0.7700	1.1969	0.7971	0.7585

B.5. Number of iterations for fix-point (FP) method

Average = 142.03   Smallest = 18   Largest = .200   No convergence in 64 samples

C. REDUCED FORM COEFFICIENTS (9 out of 18 coefficients)

	ω_{11}	ω_{13}	ω_{15}	ω_{21}	ω_{23}	ω_{25}	ω_{31}	ω_{33}	ω_{35}
True	0.1091	0.2182	−0.4364	−0.4364	0.1091	−0.2182	0.2182	0.4364	0.1091
OLS	0.2985	0.1737	−0.1086	−0.1150	0.2982	−0.1882	0.1889	0.1061	0.3026
TSLS	0.1657	0.2544	−0.3809	−0.3950	0.1642	−0.2491	0.2556	0.3900	0.1645
FP	0.1208	0.1060	−0.1383	−0.1308	0.1176	−0.1303	0.1190	0.1168	0.1100
URF	0.1057	0.2178	−0.4273	−0.4382	0.1032	−0.2187	0.2290	0.4323	0.1080

C.2. Observed standard deviation of 100 samples around observed mean

OLS	0.1145	0.0848	0.0646	0.0552	0.1199	0.1019	0.0914	0.0570	0.1444
TSLS	0.0653	0.1034	0.1192	0.1038	0.0828	0.1068	0.0839	0.1172	0.0830
FP	0.1224	0.1352	0.1984	0.1287	0.1508	0.1717	0.1437	0.1398	0.1857
URF	0.1056	0.1214	0.1216	0.1307	0.1091	0.1193	0.1081	0.1281	0.1121

C.3. Average standard deviation from large-sample formula

URF	0.1188	0.1170	0.1183	0.1200	0.1181	0.1189	0.1207	0.1192	0.1197

C.4. Observed standard deviation around true value of the coefficient

OLS	0.2212	0.0958	0.3341	0.3261	0.2239	0.1062	0.0960	0.3352	0.2414
TSLS	0.0865	0.1096	0.1315	0.1118	0.0995	0.1112	0.0919	0.1261	0.0998
FP	0.1230	0.1757	0.3581	0.3316	0.1510	0.1929	0.1746	0.3488	0.1857
URF	0.1057	0.1214	0.1219	0.1307	0.1093	0.1193	0.1086	0.1282	0.1121

D. EIGENVALUES FOR PRODUCT MOMENT MATRIX OF EXPLANATORY VARIABLES (REID SPECIFICATION)

	Smallest in 100 samples	Average for 100 samples		
		λ_1	λ_2	λ_3

D.1. Equation 1

	Smallest in 100 samples	λ_1	λ_2	λ_3
OLS	0.0672	0.1174	0.3098	0.5728
TSLS	0.0045	0.0427	0.3488	0.6085
FP	0.0129	0.0657	0.3723	0.5619

D.2. Equation 2

	Smallest in 100 samples	λ_1	λ_2	λ_3
OLS	0.0570	0.1187	0.3146	0.5667
TSLS	0.0113	0.0453	0.3523	0.6024
FP	0.0042	0.0637	0.3730	0.5633

D.3. Equation 3

	Smallest in 100 samples	λ_1	λ_2	λ_3
OLS	0.0643	0.1209	0.3164	0.5627
TSLS	0.0016	0.0452	0.3549	0.5999
FP	0.0055	0.0616	0.3748	0.5636

D.4. Unrestricted reduced form   N.a.

E. AVERAGE R^2 FROM 100 SAMPLES

E.1. Sample period

	y_1	y_2	y_3	Y
True	0.5	0.5	0.5	0.5
Generated (average)	0.4830	0.4957	0.4972	0.4920
OLS	0.2414	0.2468	0.2474	0.2452
TSLS	0.4976	0.5147	0.5137	0.5087
FP	0.2527	0.2743	0.2309	0.2526
URF	0.4875	0.4998	0.4940	0.4938

E.2. Prediction period

	y_1	y_2	y_3	Y
	0.5	0.5	0.5	0.5
	0.4755	0.4957	0.4943	0.4885
	0.1200	0.1420	0.1456	0.1359
	0.3924	0.4242	0.4268	0.4145
	0.1101	0.1708	0.1106	0.1305
	0.3769	0.3995	0.4116	0.3960

E.3. Sample period (adj. for D.F.)

	y_1	y_2	y_3	Y
OLS	0.1799	0.1857	0.1864	0.1840
TSLS	0.4569	0.4754	0.4743	0.4689
FP	0.1921	0.2155	0.1685	0.1920

Table 10.2.21. Model 3a

A. MODEL DESIGN

A.1. Structural equations

$$\beta = \begin{bmatrix} 0 & -0.5 & 0.5 \\ 0.5 & 0 & -0.5 \\ -0.5 & 0.5 & 0 \end{bmatrix} \quad \Gamma = \begin{bmatrix} k & k & 0 & 0 & 0 & 0 \\ 0 & 0 & k & k & 0 & 0 \\ 0 & 0 & 0 & 0 & k & k \end{bmatrix} \quad \Omega = \begin{bmatrix} .4226 & .4226 & -.0845 & -.0845 & .2536 & .2536 \\ .2536 & .2536 & .4226 & .4226 & -.0845 & -.0845 \\ -.0845 & -.0845 & .2536 & .2536 & .4226 & .4226 \end{bmatrix}$$

with $k = 0.5916$

A.2. Variance of endogenous and residual variables in the population and in the sample

$$\sigma^2(y_i) = 1.0$$
$$\sigma^2(\delta_i) = 0.7 \qquad i = 1,2,3$$
$$\sigma^2(\epsilon_i) = 0.5$$

Generated in sample period:
$\begin{cases} V(y_1) = 0.981 & V(y_2) = 1.004 \\ V(\delta_1) = 0.699 & V(\delta_2) = 0.696 \\ V(\epsilon_1) = 0.493 & V(\epsilon_2) = 0.501 \end{cases}$

A.3. Correlation among residuals and exogenous variables

None

A.4. Sample size and special design features

1. 40 observations in both the sample and prediction periods.
2. This model is one in a series on size of beta coefficients in three-relation models with a full beta matrix (Models 3d–3f).

B. STRUCTURAL COEFFICIENTS

B.1. True coefficient versus average estimate from 100 samples

	β_{12}	β_{13}	γ_{11}	γ_{12}	β_{21}	β_{23}	γ_{23}	γ_{24}	β_{31}	β_{32}	γ_{35}	γ_{36}
True	−.5	.5	.5916	.5916	.5	−.5	.5916	.5916	−.5	.5	.5916	.5916
OLS	−.1014	.2938	.4812	.4670	.2993	−.1056	.4843	.4794	−.1028	.3098	.4546	.4886
TSLS	−.4773	.4591	.5778	.5688	.4713	−.4826	.6014	.6002	−.4685	.4906	.5614	.5985
FP	−.4874	.4865	.5705	.5578	.5064	−.5026	.5913	.5990	−.4682	.5075	.5360	.5924

B.2. Observed standard deviation of 100 samples around observed mean

	β_{12}	β_{13}	γ_{11}	γ_{12}	β_{21}	β_{23}	γ_{23}	γ_{24}	β_{31}	β_{32}	γ_{35}	γ_{36}
OLS	.1358	.1252	.1152	.1291	.1125	.1359	.1402	.1445	.1546	.1291	.1581	.1401
TSLS	.2880	.2488	.1656	.1555	.2320	.2508	.1673	.1913	.2776	.2353	.1839	.1779
FP	.2861	.2585	.1715	.1692	.2346	.2688	.1831	.1993	.2864	.2308	.1997	.1871

B.3. Average standard deviation from large-sample formula

	β_{12}	β_{13}	γ_{11}	γ_{12}	β_{21}	β_{23}	γ_{23}	γ_{24}	β_{31}	β_{32}	γ_{35}	γ_{36}
OLS	.1364	.1288	.1311	.1292	.1325	.1369	.1308	.1323	.1405	.1324	.1330	.1328
TSLS	.2503	.2292	.1643	.1610	.2296	.2662	.1703	.1723	.2490	.2221	.1627	.1651
FP	.2613	.2452	.1640	.1600	.2402	.2772	.1688	.1719	.2575	.2306	.1609	.1670

B.4. Observed standard deviation around true value of the coefficient

	β_{12}	β_{13}	γ_{11}	γ_{12}	β_{21}	β_{23}	γ_{23}	γ_{24}	β_{31}	β_{32}	γ_{35}	γ_{36}
OLS	.4211	.2412	.1596	.1794	.2301	.4172	.1765	.1829	.4262	.2299	.2092	.1739
TSLS	.2889	.2521	.1662	.1572	.2338	.2514	.1676	.1915	.2794	.2355	.1864	.1780
FP	.2864	.2589	.1728	.1725	.2347	.2688	.1831	.1994	.2882	.2309	.2073	.1871

B.5. Number of iterations for fix-point (FP) method

Average = 50.84   Smallest = 11   Largest = 200   No convergence in 12 samples

C. REDUCED FORM COEFFICIENTS (12 out of 18 coefficients

C.1. True coefficient versus average estimate from 100 samples

	ω_{11}	ω_{12}	ω_{13}	ω_{14}	ω_{15}	ω_{16}	ω_{21}	ω_{23}	ω_{25}	ω_{31}	ω_{33}	ω_{35}
True	.4226	.4226	−.0845	−.0845	.2536	.2536	.2536	.4226	−.0845	−.0845	.2536	.4226
OLS	.4707	.4563	−.0059	−.0012	.1312	.1423	.1431	.4712	−.0134	−.0038	.1476	.4416
TSLS	.4321	.4273	−.0839	−.0748	.2232	.2388	.2366	.4415	−.0906	−.0756	.2502	.4110
FP	.4249	.4165	−.0769	−.0686	.2199	.2460	.2415	.4292	−.0826	−.0679	.2474	.3920
URF	.4246	.4209	−.0942	−.0600	.2440	.2526	.2528	.4295	−.0998	−.0721	.2668	.3881

C.2. Observed standard deviation of 100 samples around observed mean

OLS	.1067	.1209	.0635	.0600	.0705	.0723	.0617	.1299	.0586	.0697	.0682	.1442
TSLS	.1073	.1152	.1048	.0953	.0924	.0997	.0905	.1145	.0887	.1004	.0909	.1182
FP	.1107	.1228	.1047	.1005	.0960	.1016	.0880	.1252	.0858	.1068	.0854	.1347
URF	.1138	.1257	.1388	.1412	.1240	.1131	.1224	.1278	.1176	.1280	.1199	.1466

C.3. Average standard deviation from large-sample formula

URF	.1214	.1187	.1200	.1207	.1214	.1203	.1221	.1211	.1221	.1230	.1214	.1233

C.4. Observed standard deviation around true value of the coefficient

OLS	.1170	.1255	.1010	.1027	.1413	.1327	.1266	.1387	.0921	.1066	.1260	.1454
TSLS	.1077	.1153	.1048	.0958	.0973	.1008	.0921	.1160	.0889	.1007	.0910	.1188
FP	.1107	.1230	.1050	.1017	.1017	.1019	.0888	.1254	.0858	.1081	.0856	.1381
URF	.1138	.1257	.1391	.1433	.1244	.1131	.1224	.1280	.1186	.1286	.1206	.1506

D. EIGENVALUES FOR PRODUCT MOMENT MATRIX OF EXPLANATORY VARIABLES (REID SPECIFICATION)

	Smallest in 100 samples	Average for 100 samples				Smallest in 100 samples	Average for 100 samples		
		λ_1	λ_2	λ_3			λ_1	λ_2	λ_3
D.1. Equation 1						D.3. Equation 3			
OLS	.0553	.1172	.2040	.2824		OLS	.0666	.1131	.2050	.2817
TSLS	.0108	.0704	.1743	.3061		TSLS	.0223	.0676	.1782	.3017
FP	.0071	.0692	.1758	.3051		FP	.0139	.0682	.1730	.3038
D.2. Equation 2						D.4. Unrestricted reduced form	N.a.		
OLS	.0646	.1113	.2011	.2876					
TSLS	.0062	.0644	.1721	.3097					
FP	.0075	.0629	.1739	.3044					

E. AVERAGE R^2 FROM 100 SAMPLES

E.1. Sample period

	y_1	y_2	y_3	Y
True	.5	.5	.5	.5
Generated (average)	.4885	.4863	.4793	.4847
OLS	.4859	.4892	.4803	.4851
TSLS	.5409	.5398	.5339	.5382
FP	.5386	.5391	.5328	.5368
URF	.4919	.4897	.4860	.4892

E.2. Prediction period

	y_1	y_2	y_3	Y
True	.5	.5	.5	.5
Generated (average)	.4871	.4940	.4848	.4886
OLS	.4048	.4052	.3856	.3985
TSLS	.4206	.4311	.4196	.4238
FP	.4127	.4298	.4104	.4176
URF	.3817	.3983	.3713	.3838

E.3. Sample period (adj. for D.F.)

OLS	.4288	.4324	.4226	.4279
TSLS	.4899	.4887	.4821	.4869
FP	.4873	.4879	.4809	.4853

Table 10.2.22. Model 3e

A. MODEL DESIGN

A.1. Structural equations

$$\beta = \begin{bmatrix} 0 & 1 & 1 \\ 1 & 0 & 1 \\ 1 & 1 & 0 \end{bmatrix} \qquad \Gamma = \begin{bmatrix} k & k & 0 & 0 & 0 & 0 \\ 0 & 0 & k & k & 0 & 0 \\ 0 & 0 & 0 & 0 & k & k \end{bmatrix} \qquad \Omega = \begin{bmatrix} 0 & 0 & -k_2 & -k_2 & -k_2 & -k_2 \\ -k_2 & -k_2 & 0 & 0 & -k_2 & -k_2 \\ -k_2 & -k_2 & -k_2 & -k_2 & 0 & 0 \end{bmatrix}$$

with $k = 0.7071$ and $k_2 = 0.3536$

A.2. Variance of endogenous and residual variables in the population

$\sigma^2(y_i) = 1.0$
$\sigma^2(\delta_i) = 1.0 \qquad i = 1,2,3$
$\sigma^2(\epsilon_i) = 0.5$

Generated in sample period:
$\begin{cases} V(y_1) = 0.987 & V(y_2) = 1.019 \\ V(\delta_1) = 0.980 & V(\delta_2) = 0.998 \\ V(\epsilon_1) = 0.500 & V(\epsilon_2) = 0.499 \end{cases}$

A.3. Correlation among residuals and exogenous variables

None

A.4. Sample size and special design features

1. 40 observations in both the sample and prediction periods.
2. This model is one in a series on size of beta coefficients in three-relation models with a full beta matrix (Models 3d–3f).

B. STRUCTURAL COEFFICIENTS

B.1. True coefficient versus average estimate from 100 samples

	β_{12}	β_{13}	γ_{11}	γ_{12}	β_{21}	β_{23}	γ_{23}	γ_{24}	β_{31}	β_{32}	γ_{35}	γ_{36}
True	1	1	.7071	.7071	1	1	.7071	.7071	1	1	.7071	.7071
OLS	.5005	.5018	.3517	.3426	.5268	.4801	.3405	.3807	.4995	.4798	.3377	.3578
TSLS	.8712	.9546	.6436	.6321	.9477	.8771	.6316	.6585	.9335	.9319	.6652	.6670
FP	.4026	.4078	.6785	.1227	.3012	.5542	.1493	.1383	.5969	.2091	.1183	.1556

B.2. Observed standard deviation of 100 samples around observed mean

	β_{12}	β_{13}	γ_{11}	γ_{12}	β_{21}	β_{23}	γ_{23}	γ_{24}	β_{31}	β_{32}	γ_{35}	γ_{36}
OLS	.1257	.1383	.1280	.1425	.1582	.1567	.1327	.1332	.1379	.1568	.1433	.1223
TSLS	.2881	.3223	.2227	.2171	.2819	.3339	.2074	.2039	.3131	.3137	.2111	.2243
FP	1.1296	1.0317	.3538	.3911	1.9765	1.9565	.4512	.4574	1.3821	1.9689	.3815	.3692

B.3. Average standard deviation from large-sample formula

	β_{12}	β_{13}	γ_{11}	γ_{12}	β_{21}	β_{23}	γ_{23}	γ_{24}	β_{31}	β_{32}	γ_{35}	γ_{36}
OLS	.1388	.1424	.1295	.1312	.1444	.1442	.1303	.1295	.1476	.1482	.1348	.1337
TSLS	.3101	.3344	.2315	.2306	.3286	.3310	.2308	.2261	.3396	.3560	.2512	.2454
FP	1.0187	.9087	.3196	.3423	1.9327	1.9031	.4641	.4767	1.5192	1.9695	.4366	.4163

B.4. Observed standard deviation around true value of the coefficient

	β_{12}	β_{13}	γ_{11}	γ_{12}	β_{21}	β_{23}	γ_{23}	γ_{24}	β_{31}	β_{32}	γ_{35}	γ_{36}
OLS	.5151	.5170	.3777	.3914	.4989	.5430	.3899	.3525	.5191	.5433	.3962	.3701
TSLS	.3156	.3255	.2316	.2297	.2867	.3558	.2207	.2096	.3201	.3210	.2152	.2279
FP	1.2778	1.1896	.3550	.7032	2.0964	2.0066	.7174	.7299	1.4397	2.1218	.7016	.6637

B.5. Number of iterations for fix-point (FP) method

Average = 200　　　Smallest = 200　　　Largest = 200　　　No convergence in 100 samples

C. REDUCED FORM COEFFICIENTS (9 out of 18 coefficients)

C.1. True coefficient versus average estimate from 100 samples

	ω_{11}	ω_{13}	ω_{15}	ω_{21}	ω_{23}	ω_{25}	ω_{31}	ω_{33}	ω_{35}
True	0	−0.3536	−0.3536	−0.3536	0	−0.3536	−0.3536	−0.3536	0
OLS	−1.5366	−4.1615	−4.1174	−1.8596	−3.9253	−4.0681	−1.7325	−4.0849	−3.7218
TSLS	−0.0495	−0.3634	−0.3822	−0.3708	−0.0390	−0.3929	−0.3845	−0.3656	−0.0528
FP	.0673	.0523	−0.1053	.0269	.2259	−0.0445	−0.0466	.0642	−0.1536
URF	−0.0037	−0.3476	−0.3534	−0.3390	−0.0015	−0.3632	−0.3524	−0.3357	−0.0083

C.2. Observed standard deviation of 100 samples around observed mean

OLS	14.2909	26.2609	30.2776	13.6258	24.9149	28.5065	14.3527	25.3079	28.8841
TSLS	.0889	.0958	.0955	.1226	.0949	.0820	.1112	.1013	.0903
FP	4.0562	1.0757	.6274	1.3432	1.5074	.5270	3.4736	.9227	1.8120
URF	.1239	.1191	.1203	.1244	.1308	.1181	.1192	.1166	.1351

C.3. Average standard deviation from large-sample formula

URF	.1219	.1214	.1219	.1214	.1211	.1215	.1209	.1203	.1207

C.4. Observed standard deviation around true value of the coefficient

OLS	14.3733	26.5355	30.5106	13.7088	25.2222	28.7445	14.4188	25.5815	29.1229
TSLS	.1018	.0963	.0997	.1238	.1026	.0909	.1154	.1020	.1046
FP	4.0568	1.1497	.6747	1.3961	1.5242	.6110	3.4871	1.0129	1.8185
URF	.1240	.1193	.1203	.1253	.1308	.1184	.1192	.1180	.1354

D. EIGENVALUES FOR PRODUCT MOMENT MATRIX OF EXPLANATORY VARIABLES (REID SPECIFICATION)

	Smallest in 100 samples	Average for 100 samples				Smallest in 100 samples	Average for 100 samples		
		λ_1	λ_2	λ_3			λ_1	λ_2	λ_3
D.1. Equation 1						**D.3. Equation 3**			
OLS	.0481	.0939	.1395	.2511		OLS	.0495	.0894	.1346	.2505
TSLS	.0092	.0433	.1017	.3016		TSLS	.0070	.0394	.0953	.3034
FP	.0005	.0242	.1015	.3444		FP	.0007	.0216	.0996	.3358
D.2. Equation 2						**D.4. Unrestricted reduced form**	N.a.		
OLS	.0450	.0924	.1410	.2538					
TSLS	.0073	.0425	.1011	.3086					
FP	.0001	.0227	.1004	.3486					

E. AVERAGE R^2 FROM 100 SAMPLES

E.1. Sample period

	y_1	y_2	y_3	Y
True	.5	.5	.5	.5
Generated (average)	.4843	.4939	.4818	.4867
OLS	−2538.47	−2590.56	−3089.84	−2739.62
TSLS	.5086	.5232	.5158	.5159
FP	−36.2605	−10.5297	−25.5596	−24.1166
URF	.4819	.4929	.4891	.4880

E.2. Prediction period

	y_1	y_2	y_3	Y
True	.5	.5	.5	.5
Generated (average)	.4790	.4768	.4713	.4757
OLS	−5124.30	−4182.61	−3909.29	−4405.40
TSLS	.3975	.3841	.4018	.3945
FP	−48.3502	−11.1925	−29.4942	−29.6790
URF	.3720	.3644	.3773	.3712

E.3. Sample period (adj. for D.F.)

	y_1	y_2	y_3	Y
OLS	−2820.6333	−2878.5111	−2849.5722	−3042.1300
TSLS	.4540	.4702	.4620	.4621
FP	−40.4005	−11.8108	−28.5110	−27.9074

Table 10.2.23. Model 3.

A. MODEL DESIGN

A.1. Structural equations

$$\beta = \begin{bmatrix} 0 & -1 & 1 \\ 1 & 0 & -1 \\ -1 & 1 & 0 \end{bmatrix} \quad \Gamma = \begin{bmatrix} k_1 & k_1 & 0 & 0 & 0 & 0 \\ 0 & 0 & k_1 & k_1 & 0 & 0 \\ 0 & 0 & 0 & 0 & k_1 & k_1 \end{bmatrix} \quad \Omega = \begin{bmatrix} k_2 & k_2 & 0 & 0 & k_2 & k_2 \\ k_2 & k_2 & k_2 & k_2 & 0 & 0 \\ 0 & 0 & k_2 & k_2 & k_2 & k_2 \end{bmatrix}$$

with $k_1 = 0.7071$ and $k_2 = 0.3536$

A.2. Variance of endogenous and residual variables in the population and in the sample

$\sigma^2(y_i) = 1.0$ Generated $V(y_1) = 0.980$ $V(y_2) = 1.007$

$\sigma^2(\delta_i) = 1.0$ $i = 1,2,3$ in sample $V(\delta_1) = 1.019$ $V(\delta_2) = 1.017$

$\sigma^2(\epsilon_i) = 0.5$ period: $V(\epsilon_1) = 0.506$ $V(\epsilon_2) = 0.509$

A.3. Correlation among residuals and exogenous variables

None

A.4. Sample size and special design features

1. 40 observations in both the sample and prediction periods.
2. This model is one in a series on size of beta coefficients in three-relation models with a full beta matrix (Models 3d–3f).

B. STRUCTURAL COEFFICIENTS

B.1. True coefficient versus average estimate from 100 samples

	β_{12}	β_{13}	γ_{11}	γ_{12}	β_{21}	β_{23}	γ_{23}	γ_{24}	β_{31}	β_{32}	γ_{35}	γ_{36}
True	−1	1	.7071	.7071	1	−1	.7071	.7071	−1	1	.7071	.7071
OLS	.0116	.4783	.3445	.3396	.5040	.0064	.3378	.3767	−.0063	.5242	.3528	.3851
TSLS	−.8205	.8733	.6424	.6398	.9088	−.8120	.6342	.6825	−.8714	.9623	.6582	.6699
FP	−.4038	.7620	.3880	.4023	.8034	−.4154	.3929	.4437	−.4560	.8454	.4131	.4402

B.2. Observed standard deviation of 100 samples around observed mean

	β_{12}	β_{13}	γ_{11}	γ_{12}	β_{21}	β_{23}	γ_{23}	γ_{24}	β_{31}	β_{32}	γ_{35}	γ_{36}
OLS	.1541	.1483	.1270	.1488	.1444	.1566	.1301	.1352	.1523	.1129	.1417	.1433
TSLS	.4073	.3004	.2184	.2378	.3303	.4072	.1991	.2408	.4920	.3115	.2672	.2531
FP	.3177	.2582	.1560	.1648	.3110	.3832	.1827	.2056	.4128	.2836	.1891	.2120

B.3. Average standard deviation from large-sample formula

	β_{12}	β_{13}	γ_{11}	γ_{12}	β_{21}	β_{23}	γ_{23}	γ_{24}	β_{31}	β_{32}	γ_{35}	γ_{36}
OLS	.1634	.1408	.1302	.1310	.1447	.1639	.1326	.1324	.1675	.1437	.1307	.1290
TSLS	.4675	.3217	.2377	.2395	.3341	.4533	.2356	.2378	.4779	.3256	.2405	.2280
FP	.3352	.2709	.1605	.1618	.3015	.3552	.1710	.1736	.3719	.2892	.1669	.1677

B.4. Observed standard deviation around true value of the coefficient

	β_{12}	β_{13}	γ_{11}	γ_{12}	β_{21}	β_{23}	γ_{23}	γ_{24}	β_{31}	β_{32}	γ_{35}	γ_{36}
OLS	1.0233	.5424	.3842	.3965	.5166	1.0185	.3915	.3570	1.0053	.4890	.3816	.3524
TSLS	.4451	.3260	.2278	.2471	.3427	.4485	.2120	.2421	.5085	.3138	.2716	.2558
FP	.6756	.3512	.3552	.3465	.3679	.6990	.3635	.3341	.6829	.3230	.3495	.3409

B.5. Number of iterations for fix-point (FP) method

Average = 186.5   Smallest = 36   Largest = 200   No convergence in 91 samples

C. REDUCED FORM COEFFICIENTS (12 out of 18 coefficients)

C.1. True coefficient versus average estimate from 100 samples

	ω_{11}	ω_{12}	ω_{13}	ω_{14}	ω_{15}	ω_{16}	ω_{21}	ω_{23}	ω_{25}	ω_{31}	ω_{33}	ω_{35}
True	.3536	.3536	0	0	.3536	.3536	.3536	.3536	0	0	.3536	.3536
OLS	.4031	.3919	.1037	.1150	.1940	.2093	.2059	.3951	.0966	.1034	.2042	.4058
TSLS	.3794	.3733	.0068	.0111	.3131	.3240	.3277	.3662	−.0046	.0108	.3328	.3745
FP	.3497	.3648	.0602	.0699	.2447	.2624	.2608	.3424	.0601	.0630	.2560	.3644
URF	.3458	.3548	−.0018	.0192	.3417	.3279	.3395	.3412	−.0069	−.0091	.3522	.3449

C.2. Observed standard deviation of 100 samples around observed mean

	ω_{11}	ω_{12}	ω_{13}	ω_{14}	ω_{15}	ω_{16}	ω_{21}	ω_{23}	ω_{25}	ω_{31}	ω_{33}	ω_{35}
OLS	.1433	.1652	.0682	.0726	.0915	.0871	.0949	.1431	.0728	.0616	.0797	.1530
TSLS	.1259	.1205	.0799	.0901	.0969	.1071	.1077	.1012	.0741	.1221	.0948	.1037
FP	.1333	.1503	.0888	.1050	.1103	.1197	.1342	.1239	.0925	.1033	.1140	.1433
URF	.1334	.1358	.1204	.1284	.1218	.1211	.1259	.1250	.1217	.1228	.1192	.1249

C.3. Average standard deviation from large-sample formula

	ω_{11}	ω_{12}	ω_{13}	ω_{14}	ω_{15}	ω_{16}	ω_{21}	ω_{23}	ω_{25}	ω_{31}	ω_{33}	ω_{35}
URF	.1226	.1204	.1222	.1215	.1206	.1203	.1232	.1230	.1213	.1231	.1230	.1213

C.4. Observed standard deviation around true value of the coefficient

	ω_{11}	ω_{12}	ω_{13}	ω_{14}	ω_{15}	ω_{16}	ω_{21}	ω_{23}	ω_{25}	ω_{31}	ω_{33}	ω_{35}
OLS	.1516	.1696	.1241	.1360	.1840	.1685	.1756	.1490	.1210	.1204	.1693	.1617
TSLS	.1285	.1221	.0802	.0908	.1050	.1111	.1108	.1020	.0742	.1226	.0971	.1058
FP	.1334	.1507	.1073	.1261	.1550	.1505	.1632	.1242	.1103	.1210	.1501	.1437
URF	.1336	.1358	.1204	.1298	.1224	.1238	.1267	.1256	.1219	.1231	.1192	.1252

D. EIGENVALUES FOR PRODUCT MOMENT MATRIX OF EXPLANATORY VARIABLES (REID SPECIFICATION)

D.1. Equation 1

	Smallest in 100 samples	Average for 100 samples λ_1	λ_2	λ_3
OLS	.0308	.0665	.1901	.2817
TSLS	.0025	.0278	.1739	.3086
FP	.0089	.0402	.1679	.3049

D.2. Equation 2

	Smallest in 100 samples	Average for 100 samples λ_1	λ_2	λ_3
OLS	.0336	.0680	.1907	.2740
TSLS	.0034	.0291	.1658	.3092
FP	.0025	.0410	.1593	.3102

D.3. Equation 3

	Smallest in 100 samples	Average for 100 samples λ_1	λ_2	λ_3
OLS	.0358	.0665	.2001	.2815
TSLS	.0044	.0271	.1767	.3175
FP	.0080	.0373	.1689	.3194

D.4. Unrestricted reduced form

N.a.

E. AVERAGE R^2 FROM 100 SAMPLES

E.1. Sample period

	y_1	y_2	y_3	Y
True	.5	.5	.5	.5
Generated (average)	.4686	.4870	.4971	.4842
OLS	.4287	.4314	.4522	.4374
TSLS	.5145	.5332	.5332	.5270
FP	.4932	.5033	.5069	.5011
URF	.4752	.4891	.4973	.4872

E.2. Prediction period

	y_1	y_2	y_3	Y
True	.5	.5	.5	.5
Generated (average)	.4828	.4965	.4961	.4918
OLS	.3445	.3352	.3732	.3510
TSLS	.4147	.4377	.4235	.4253
FP	.3785	.3772	.3788	.3782
URF	.3797	.3969	.3926	.3897

E.3. Sample period (adj. for D.F.)

	y_1	y_2	y_3	Y
OLS	.3652	.3682	.3913	.3749
TSLS	.4606	.4813	.4813	.4744
FP	.4369	.4481	.4521	.4457

Table 10.2.24. Model 4a: Girshick-Haavelmo's Model

A. MODEL DESIGN

A.1. Structural equations

$$\begin{array}{ccc} & t \quad x_{1t} \quad y_{3,t-1} \quad y_{5,t-1} \\ \beta = \begin{bmatrix} 0 & 0.157 & 0 & 0.653 & 0 \\ -4.07 & 0 & 1.01 & 0 & 0 \\ 0 & 0 & 0 & 0 & 0 \\ 0 & 0 & 0 & 0 & 0.556 \\ 0 & 2.88 & 0 & 0 & 0 \end{bmatrix} & \Gamma = \begin{bmatrix} .339 & 0 & 0 & 0 \\ -.424 & 0 & .208 & 0 \\ 0 & .203 & .367 & 0 \\ -.190 & 0 & 0 & -.300 \\ .656 & 0 & 0 & 0 \end{bmatrix} & \Omega = \begin{bmatrix} -.0096 & .0418 & .1180 & -.0333 \\ -.3843 & .3471 & .0981 & .1353 \\ 0 & .2030 & .3670 & 0 \\ -.4434 & .0556 & .1571 & -.0834 \\ -.4526 & .1002 & .2830 & .0390 \end{bmatrix} \end{array}$$

A.2. Variance of endogeneous and residual variables in the population and in the sample

$\sigma^2(y_i) = 7.55$, 27.76 , 133.02, 17.50 , 182.41   Generated $V(y_i) = 6.767$, 27.193, 110.477, 18.151, 165.702

$\sigma^2(\delta_i) = 1.15$, 16.2 , 15.5 , 38.2 , 31.3   in sample $V(\delta_i) = 1.145$, 17.051, 15.767, 37.307, 29.859

$\sigma^2(\epsilon_i) = 1.954$, 11.195, 15.5 , 7.474, 79.187   period: $V(\epsilon_i) = 1.997$, 11.073, 15.767, 7.193, 79.729

A.3. Correlation among residuals and exogenous variables

None

A.4. Sample size and special design features

1. There were 20 observations in the sample period and 40 observations in the prediction period.
2. This model is one in a series of familiar models (Models 4a–4c).
3. This particular model is that of Girshick-Haavelmo (1947), except the variables are measured around their means and the first equation is solved for y_2 instead of y_1.

B. STRUCTURAL COEFFICIENTS

B.1. True coefficient versus average estimate from 100 samples

	β_{12}	β_{14}	γ_{11}	β_{21}	β_{23}	γ_{21}	γ_{23}	γ_{32}	γ_{33}	β_{45}	γ_{41}	γ_{44}	β_{52}	γ_{51}
True	.157	.653	.339	−4.07	1.01	−.424	.208	.203	.367	.556	−.190	−.300	2.88	.656
OLS	.1167	.5830	.3018	−1.5514	.4846	−.4658	.1690	.2038	.3413	.1000	−.2510	−.0259	2.4922	.4390
TSLS	.1523	.6382	.3365	− .0506	.1827	−.5604	.2626	.2038	.3413	.4876	−.1580	−.2115	2.7833	.5829
FP	2.5085	−5.5974	−.1212	.6818	−.3752	−.6709	.6135	.2038	.3413	.5449	−.1486	−.2381	2.7833	.5829

B.2. Observed standard deviation of 100 samples around observed mean

OLS	.0616	.0661	.0556	.5711	.1502	.1415	.0844	.0242	.0902	.0809	.1457	.1011	.2996	.2534
TSLS	.1613	.1595	.0763	44.4272	8.9234	3.4963	1.5739	.0242	.0902	.2751	.1011	.1756	.4647	.3212
FP	2.3270	61.7247	4.5345	47.2339	6.5881	4.1252	7.3586	.0242	.0902	.4637	.2655	.2488	.4647	.3212

B.3. Average standard deviation from large-sample formula

OLS	.0567	.0494	.1454	.0872	.0878
TSLS	.1840	.0783	8.080	1.3498	.2842
FP	2.6141	5.1035	1.239	1.8381	.4386

B.4. Observed standard deviation around true value of the coefficient

OLS	.0736	.0963	.0669	2.5825	.5464	.1475	.0930	.0242	.0937	.4631	.1580	.2921	.4900	.3336
TSLS	.1614	.1602	.0763	44.6087	8.9617	3.4990	1.5748	.0242	.0937	.2835	.1060	.1966	.4747	.3294
FP	3.3080	61.9224	4.5397	47.3553	6.7321	4.1326	7.3698	.0242	.0937	.4638	.2687	.2564	.4747	.3294

B.5. Number of iterations for fix-point (FP) method

Average = 5   Smallest = 5   Largest = 5   No convergence in 0 samples

C. REDUCED FORM COEFFICIENTS (10 out of 18 coefficients)

C.1. True coefficient versus average estimate from 100 samples

	ω_{11}	ω_{13}	ω_{21}	ω_{23}	ω_{32} [a]	ω_{33} [a]	ω_{41}	ω_{43}	ω_{51}	ω_{53}
True	−.0096	.1180	−.3843	.0981	.2030	.3670	−.4434	.1571	−.4526	.2830
OLS	.0435	.0603	−.5328	.2443	.2038	.3413	−.3349	.0567	−.8868	.6093
TSLS	.0053	.1080	−.4402	.1321	.2038	.3413	−.4156	.1367	−.6437	.3617
FP	.0122	.1229	−.4189	.1387	.2038	.3413	−.4104	.1633	−.5874	.3816
URF	.0015	.1024	−.4189	.1387	.2038	.3315	−.4221	.1286	−.6139	.3947

C.2. Observed standard deviation of 100 samples around observed mean

OLS	.0760	.0277	.1917	.0735	.0242	.0902	.1360	.0483	.5150	.1992
TSLS	.0753	.0728	.1747	.1459	.0242	.0902	.1418	.1040	.4921	.4347
FP	.0752	.0724	.1502	.0982	.0242	.0902	.1260	.1047	.4187	.2797
URF	.0738	.0477	.1502	.0982	.0242	.1153	.1323	.0955	.4466	.2584

C.3. Average standard deviation from large-sample formula

URF	.0667	.0445	.1572	.1053	.0242	.1243	.1274	.0853	.4150	.2782

C.4. Observed standard deviation around true value of the coefficient

OLS	.0832	.0640	.2425	.1636	.0242	.0938	.1740	.1114	.6736	.3823
TSLS	.0754	.0735	.1834	.1498	.0242	.0938	.1445	.1060	.5279	.4418
FP	.0762	.0726	.1541	.1063	.0242	.0938	.1302	.1049	.4399	.2966
URF	.0742	.0502	.1541	.1063	.0242	.1206	.1340	.0997	.4748	.2815

[a] These estimates are the same as γ_{23} and γ_{24} because the third structural equation is in reduced form.

D. EIGENVALUES FOR PRODUCT MOMENT MATRIX OF EXPLANATORY VARIABLES (REID SPECIFICATION)

	Smallest in 100 samples	Average for 100 samples				Smallest in 100 samples	Average for 100 samples		
		λ_1	λ_2	λ_3			λ_1	λ_2	λ_3
D.1. Equation 1					D.4. Equation 4				
OLS	.0565	.1181	.2059	.6760	OLS	.0179	.0770	.1971	.7259
TSLS	.0006	.0392	.1682	.7926	TSLS	.0058	.0627	.1331	.8042
FP	.00000007	.0285	.1590	.8125	FP	.0039	.0584	.1332	.8004
D.2. Equation 2					D.5. Equation 5				
OLS	.0013	.0050	.1284	.8666	OLS	.0768	.2098	.7902	
TSLS	.00000004	.0006	.1272	.8722	TSLS	.0149	.1263	.8737	
FP	.00000003	.0011	.1262	.8728	FP	.0149	.1263	.8737	
D.3. Equation 3					D.6. Unrestricted reduced form	N.a.			
OLS	.0258	.0444	.9556						
TSLS	.0258	.0444	.9556						
FP	.0258	.0444	.9556						

E. AVERAGE R^2 FROM 100 SAMPLES

E.1. Sample period   E.2. Prediction period

	y_1	y_2	y_3	y_4	y_5	Y	y_1	y_2	y_3	y_4	y_5	Y
True												
Generated (average)	.6906	.5502	.8534	.5830	.4694	.6293	.6074	.7892	.8000	.8372	.5491	.7166
OLS	.5328	.4099	.8681	.4369	.3811	.5258	−.0015	.4520	.7748	.6537	−.3703	.3017
TSLS	.6379	.3138	.8681	.5623	.1381	.5040	.0176	.5835	.7748	.6866	.0387	.4204
FP	.6360	.6425	.8681	.5725	.5608	.6560	−.0094	.6296	.7748	.6990	.1557	.4499
URF	.6939	.5531	.8548	.5821	.4775	.6323	.2635	.6296	.6454	.7240	.1259	.4777

E.3. Sample period (adj. for D.F.)

	y_1	y_2	y_3	y_4	y_5	Y
OLS	.4567	.3138	.8466	.3452	.2803	.4485
TSLS	.5790	.2021	.8466	.4910	−.0022	.4242
FP	.5767	.5843	.8466	.5029	.4893	.6000

Table 10.2.25. Model 4b: simple Keynesian model, A

A. MODEL DESIGN

A.1. Structural equations

$$
\beta = \begin{bmatrix} 0 & 0 & 4.1 \\ 0 & 0 & 0.5 \\ 1 & 1 & 0 \end{bmatrix} \quad
\Gamma = \begin{matrix} \overset{y_{3,t-1}\ \ x_{1t}\ \ y_{2,t-1}}{\begin{bmatrix} -4 & 0 & 0 \\ 0 & 0 & 0.444 \\ 0 & 1 & 0 \end{bmatrix}} \end{matrix} \quad
\Omega = \begin{bmatrix} 0.5556 & -1.1389 & -0.5057 \\ 0.5556 & -0.1389 & 0.3823 \\ 1.1111 & -0.2778 & -0.1233 \end{bmatrix}
$$

Equation 3 is the identity: $y_{3t} - y_{1t} - y_{2t} - x_{1t} = 0$

A.2. Variance of endogenous and residual variables in the population and in the sample

$\sigma^2(y_i) = 1.363, 3.038, \ 3.868$ Generated $\Big\{$ $V(y_i) = 1.336, \ 3.057, \ 3.8783$

$\sigma^2(\delta_i) = 0.005, 0.010, \ 0.0$ in sample $V(\delta_i) = 0.005, \ 0.010, \ 0$

$\sigma^2(\epsilon_i) = 0.013, 0.0075, 0.0012$ periods: $V(\epsilon_i) = 0.0129, 0.0074, 0.0011$

A.3. Correlation among residuals and exogenous variables

None

A.4. Sample size and special design features

1. 40 observations in both the sample and prediction period.
2. This model is one in a series of familiar models (Models 4a-4c).
3. Models 4b and 4c were designed as two typical small-size Keynesian systems.
4. One of the characteristic roots of the underlying difference equation is unity, and therefore the stochastic process defined by the model is not stationary [3]. The population variances of the endogenous variables are subject to a slight increase with time. The lack of stationarity has only a moderate effect on the Monte Carlo results because the generated series in the sample period has only 40 observations. The FP, TSLS and URF methods are applicable for consistent estimation of the parameters of the model even though the population variances of the endogenous variables are not constant.

B. STRUCTURAL COEFFICIENTS

B.1. True coefficient versus average estimate from 100 samples

	β_{13}	γ_{11}	β_{23}	γ_{23}	β_{31}	β_{32}	γ_{32}
True	4.10	−4	0.5	0.444	1	1	1
OLS	4.0880	−3.9867	0.4855	0.4606			
TSLS	4.1054	−4.0037	0.5090	0.4350	Third relation is an identity		
FP	0.2223	−0.2048	0.0421	0.9505			

B.2. Observed standard deviation in 100 samples around observed mean

OLS	0.0471	0.0485	0.0413	0.0494
TSLS	0.0485	0.0498	0.0426	0.0514
FP	1.7346	1.6761	0.2686	0.3003

B.3. Average standard deviation from large-sample formula

OLS	0.0401	0.0405	0.0467	0.0536
TSLS	0.0405	0.0410	0.0471	0.0540
FP	0.2637	0.3071	0.0553	0.0708

B.4. Observed standard deviation around true value of the coefficient

OLS	0.0486	0.0503	0.0438	0.0521
TSLS	0.0488	0.0500	0.0435	0.0522
FP	4.2480	4.1488	0.5309	0.5888

B.5. Number of iterations for fix-point (FP) method

Average = 200   Smallest = 200   Largest = 200   No convergence in 100 samples

C. REDUCED FORM COEFFICIENTS

C.1. True coefficient versus average estimate from 100 samples

	ω_{11}	ω_{12}	ω_{13}	ω_{21}	ω_{22}	ω_{23}	ω_{31}	ω_{32}	ω_{33}
True	0.5556	−1.1389	−0.5057	0.5556	−0.1389	0.3823	1.1111	−0.2778	−0.1233
OLS	0.5746	−1.1442	−0.5276	0.5412	−0.1358	0.3985	1.1158	−0.2800	−0.1291
TSLS	0.5446	−1.1361	−0.4948	0.5634	−0.1407	0.3742	1.1079	−0.2768	−0.1206
FP	0.8230	−1.1845	−0.8921	0.2358	−0.2851	0.7273	1.0588	−0.4696	−0.1648
URF	0.5315	−1.1385	−0.4803	0.5717	−0.1389	0.3651	1.1032	−0.2774	−0.1151

C.2. Observed standard deviation of 100 samples around observed mean

OLS	0.0527	0.0135	0.0619	0.0394	0.0098	0.0467	0.0138	0.0052	0.0154
TSLS	0.0535	0.0136	0.0636	0.0401	0.0099	0.0480	0.0139	0.0052	0.0157
FP	4.1688	6.0266	4.5045	1.3441	1.9177	1.4609	5.4743	7.9186	5.9226
URF	0.0889	0.0184	0.1017	0.0673	0.0135	0.0774	0.0282	0.0062	0.0314

C.3. Average standard deviation from large-sample formula

URF	0.0960	0.0189	0.1090	0.0725	0.0143	0.0824	0.0286	0.0056	0.0325

C.4. Observed standard deviation around true value of the coefficient

OLS	0.0559	0.0141	0.0656	0.0421	0.0103	3.4218	0.0145	0.0056	0.0165
TSLS	0.0547	0.0142	0.0641	0.0408	0.0100	3.4461	0.0143	0.0053	0.0159
FP	4.1773	6.0268	4.5210	1.3817	1.9233	3.4204	5.4746	7.9209	5.9228
URF	0.0922	0.0185	0.1049	0.0691	0.0135	3.4558	0.0293	0.0062	0.0324

D. EIGENVALUES FOR PRODUCT MOMENT MATRIX OF EXPLANATORY VARIABLES (REID SPECIFICATION)

	Smallest in 100 samples	Average for 100 samples λ_1	λ_2
D.1. Equation 1			
OLS	0.000752	0.0159	0.9841
TSLS	0.000732	0.0157	0.9843
FP	0.001797	0.0592	0.9408
D.2. Equation 2			
OLS	0.000963	0.0242	0.9758
TSLS	0.000944	0.0240	0.9760
FP	0.000629	0.0590	0.9410

D.3. Unrestricted reduced form   N.a.

E. AVERAGE R^2 FROM 100 SAMPLES

E.1. Sample period / E.2. Prediction period

	y_1	y_2	y_3	Y	y_1	y_2	y_3	Y
True								
Generated (average)	0.9898	0.9919	0.9990	0.9936	0.9901	0.9942	0.9993	0.9945
OLS	0.9901	0.9922	0.9991	0.9938	0.9892	0.9938	0.9993	0.9941
TSLS	0.9902	0.9922	0.9991	0.9938	0.9892	0.9938	0.9993	0.9941
FP	−2.6585	−1.7343	−36.2673	−2.6732	−27.1496	−0.5077	−20.5283	−1.7585
URF	0.9897	0.9918	0.9990	0.9935	0.9889	0.9936	0.9992	0.9939

E.3. Sample period (adj. for D.F.)

	y_1	y_2	y_3	Y
OLS	0.9896	0.9918	0.9990	0.9935
TSLS	0.9897	0.9918	0.9990	0.9935
FP	−2.8509	−1.8782	−42.5463	−2.8663

Table 10.2.26. Model 4c: simple Keynesian model, B

A. MODEL DESIGN

A.1. Structural equations

$$\beta = \begin{bmatrix} 0 & 0 & 3.2 \\ 0 & 0 & 0.8 \\ 1 & 1 & 0 \end{bmatrix} \qquad \Gamma = \begin{bmatrix} y_{3,t-1} & y_{3,t-2} & x_{1t} \\ -2 & -1 & 0 \\ 0 & 0 & 0 \\ 0 & 0 & 1 \end{bmatrix} \qquad \Omega = \begin{bmatrix} 0.1333 & 0.0667 & -1.0667 \\ 0.5333 & 0.2667 & -0.2667 \\ 0.6667 & 0.3333 & -0.3333 \end{bmatrix}$$

Equation 3 is the identity: $y_{3t} - y_{1t} - y_{2t} - x_{1t} = 0$

A.2. Variance of endogenous and residual variables in the population [4] and in the sample

$\sigma^2(y_i) = 0.020$, 0.044 , 0.067 Generated $V(y_i) = 0.019$, 0.047 , 0.070
$\sigma^2(\delta_i) = 0.01$, 0.005 , 0 in sample $V(\delta_i) = 0.0098, 0.0051, 0$
$\sigma^2(\epsilon_i) = 0.0057, 0.0034, 0.0017$ period: $V(\epsilon_i) = 0.0058, 0.0035, 0.0016$

A.3. Correlation among residuals and exogenous variables

    None

A.4. Sample size and special design features

1. 40 observations in both the sample and prediction periods.
2. This model is one in a series of familiar models (Models 4a-4c)
3. Model 4b and 4c were designed as two typical small-size Keynesian systems.
4. One of the characteristic roots of the underlying difference equation is unity, and therefore the stochastic process defined by the model is not stationary [3]. The population variances of the endogenous variables are subject to a slight increase with time. The lack of stationarity has only a moderate effect on the Monte Carlo results because the generated series in the sample period has only 40 observations. The FP, TSLS and URF methods are applicable for consistent estimation of the parameters of the model even though the population variances of the endogenous variables are not constant.

B. STRUCTURAL COEFFICIENTS

B.1. True coefficient versus average estimate from 100 samples

	β_{13}	γ_{11}	γ_{12}	β_{23}	β_{31}	β_{32}	γ_{33}
True	3.2	−2	−1	0.8	1	1	1
OLS	2.0130	−1.2084	−0.5969	0.7331			
TSLS	3.3883	−2.0666	−1.0061	0.8240	Third relation is an identity		
FP	1.1424	−0.5253	−0.5479	0.5932			

B.2. Observed standard deviation of 100 samples around observed mean

OLS	0.2687	0.2887	0.2590	0.0972
TSLS	0.9673	0.6115	0.3818	0.1078
FP	1.2147	1.5712	1.4724	0.3806

B.3. Average standard deviation from large-sample formula

OLS	0.2461	0.2795	0.2474	0.0714
TSLS	0.6578	0.5216	0.3830	0.0818
FP	0.6681	0.8144	0.8316	0.1223

B.4. Observed standard deviation around true value of the coefficient

OLS	1.2170	0.8426	0.4790	0.1179
TSLS	0.9854	0.6151	0.3818	0.1104
FP	4.5091	2.9742	2.1363	0.4332

B.5. Number of iterations for fix-point (FP) method

——   Average = 189.31   Smallest = 29   Largest = 200   No convergence in 93 samples

C. REDUCED FORM COEFFICIENTS (6 out of 9 coefficients)

C.1. True coefficient versus average estimate from 100 samples

	ω_{11}	ω_{12}	ω_{13}	ω_{21}	ω_{22}	ω_{23}
True	0.1334	0.0667	−1.0667	0.5393	0.2667	−0.2667
OLS	0.1965	0.0948	−1.1637	0.5052	0.2514	−0.4282
TSLS	0.1158	0.0593	−1.0611	0.5331	0.2607	−0.2670
FP	0.0755	0.0653	−0.8520	0.2629	0.2023	0.2239
URF	0.0839	0.0873	−1.0442	0.5564	0.2403	−0.2787

C.2. Observed standard deviation of 100 samples around observed mean

OLS	0.1495	0.0792	0.1077	0.1018	0.1062	0.0781
TSLS	0.0667	0.0352	0.0309	0.0952	0.0878	0.0457
FP	0.2449	0.2504	0.3771	0.5830	0.5548	0.4006
URF	0.2243	0.2284	0.1376	0.1844	0.1889	0.1039

C.3. Average standard deviation from large-sample formula

URF	0.2296	0.2319	0.1244	0.1784	0.1801	0.0964

C.4. Observed standard deviation around the true value of the coefficient

OLS	0.1623	0.0840	0.1430	0.1058	0.1073	0.1791
TSLS	0.0690	0.0360	0.0322	0.0952	0.0880	0.0457
FP	0.2517	0.2504	0.4356	0.6429	0.5586	0.6336
URF	0.2297	0.2293	0.1400	0.1858	0.1908	0.1046

D. EIGENVALUES FOR PRODUCT MOMENT MATRIX OF EXPLANATORY VARIABLES (REID SPECIFICATION)

	Smallest in 100 samples	Average for 100 samples		
		λ_1	λ_2	λ_3
D.1. Equation 1				
OLS	0.000711	0.0239	0.0362	0.9400
TSLS	0.000229	0.0113	0.0324	0.9564
FP	0.000162	0.0220	0.0809	0.8971
D.2. Equation 2				
OLS	1	1		
TSLS	1	1		
FP	1	1		

D.3. Unrestricted reduced form   N.a.

E. AVERAGE R^2 FROM 100 SAMPLES

E.1. Sample period					E.2. Prediction period			
	y_1	y_2	y_3	Y	y_1	y_2	y_3	Y
True	−	−	−	−	−	−	−	−
Generated (average)	0.6811	0.8029	0.9058	0.7966	0.7126	0.8740	0.9440	0.8435
OLS	0.6546	0.7970	0.7815	0.7444	0.6220	0.8552	0.8822	0.7865
TSLS	0.6881	0.8088	0.9156	0.8042	0.6919	0.8668	0.9395	0.8327
FP	0.6131	0.4564	0.2830	0.4508	0.5365	0.4691	0.3743	0.4600
URF	0.6822	0.8034	0.9104	0.7987	0.6737	0.8629	0.9384	0.8250

E.3. Sample period (adj. for D.F.)

	y_1	y_2	y_3	Y
OLS	0.6364	0.7863	0.7700	0.7310
TS	0.6716	0.7987	0.9112	0.7939
FP	0.5927	0.4278	0.2453	0.4219

Table 10.2.27. Model 5a

A. MODEL DESIGN

A.1. Structural equations

$$\beta = \begin{bmatrix} 0 & 1 \\ -1 & 0 \end{bmatrix} \qquad \Gamma = \begin{bmatrix} k_1 & k_1 & 0 & 0 \\ 0 & 0 & k_1 & k_1 \end{bmatrix} \qquad \Omega = \begin{bmatrix} k_2 & k_2 & k_2 & k_2 \\ -k_2 & -k_2 & k_2 & k_2 \end{bmatrix}$$

with $k_1 = 0.6845$ and $k_2 = 0.3423$

A.2. Variance of endogenous and residual variables in the population and in the sample

$\sigma^2(y_i) = 1.0$

$\sigma^2(\delta_i) = 0.4$ $i = 1, 2$

$\sigma^2(\epsilon_i) = 0.2$

Generated in sample period:

$\begin{cases} V(y_1) = 0.975 & V(y_2) = 0.996 \\ V(\delta_1) = 0.377 & V(\delta_2) = 0.389 \\ V(\epsilon_1) = 0.193 & V(\epsilon_2) = 0.190 \end{cases}$

A.3. Correlation among residuals and exogenous variables

$r(x_1, x_2) = r(x_3, x_4) = 0.707$

A.4. Sample size and special design features

1. 40 observations in both the sample and prediction periods.
2. This model is one in a series on intercorrelation between exogenous variables in two-relation models (Models 5a-5b).

B. STRUCTURAL COEFFICIENTS

B.1. True coefficient versus average estimate from 100 samples

	β_{12}	γ_{11}	γ_{12}	β_{21}	γ_{23}	γ_{24}
True	1	0.6845	0.6845	−1	0.6845	0.6845
OLS	0.6572	0.5610	0.5704	−0.6695	0.5659	0.5718
TSLS	0.9709	0.6658	0.6783	−0.9850	0.6698	0.6750
FP	0.9677	0.6377	0.6945	−0.9896	0.6465	0.6927

B.2. Observed standard deviation of 100 samples around observed mean

OLS	0.1321	0.1346	0.1455	0.1119	0.1467	0.1480
TSLS	0.1541	0.1357	0.1509	0.1466	0.1699	0.1637
FP	0.1581	0.2036	0.2254	0.1564	0.2177	0.1977

B.3. Average standard deviation from large-sample formula

OLS	0.1200	0.1366	0.1388	0.1205	0.1381	0.1380
TSLS	0.1623	0.1533	0.1564	0.1616	0.1548	0.1545
FP	0.1636	0.1536	0.1589	0.1649	0.1562	0.1577

B.4. Observed standard deviation around true value of the coefficient

OLS	0.3674	0.1827	0.1849	0.3489	0.1886	0.1860
TSLS	0.1568	0.1370	0.1510	0.1474	0.1705	0.1640
FP	0.1614	0.2089	0.2256	0.1567	0.2210	0.1979

B.5. Number of iterations for fix-point (FP) method

Average = 9.06 ;   Smallest = 5 ;   Largest = 32   No convergence in 0 samples

C. REDUCED FORM COEFFICIENTS

C.1. True coefficient versus average estimate from 100 samples

	ω_{11}	ω_{12}	ω_{13}	ω_{14}	ω_{21}	ω_{22}	ω_{23}	ω_{24}
True	0.3423	0.3423	0.3423	0.3423	−0.3423	−0.3423	0.3423	0.3423
OLS	0.3897	0.3976	0.2563	0.2605	−0.2599	−0.2639	0.3940	0.3968
TSLS	0.3418	0.3491	0.3301	0.3333	−0.3349	−0.3379	0.3438	0.3469
FP	0.3274	0.3570	0.3167	0.3411	−0.3225	−0.3465	0.3314	0.3562
URF	0.3287	0.3562	0.3448	0.3223	−0.3515	−0.3287	0.3287	0.3554

C.2. Observed standard deviation of 100 samples around observed mean

OLS	0.0889	0.1045	0.0747	0.0785	0.0692	0.0740	0.0997	0.0942
TSLS	0.0679	0.0809	0.0815	0.0823	0.0752	0.0679	0.0859	0.0831
FP	0.1054	0.1191	0.1061	0.1028	0.1096	0.1075	0.1106	0.1027
URF	0.1111	0.1222	0.1061	0.1111	0.0943	0.0906	0.1107	0.1072

C.3. Average standard deviation from large-sample formula

URF	0.1041	0.1060	0.1033	0.1038	0.0134	0.1056	0.1031	0.1039

C.4. Observed standard deviation around true value of the coefficient

OLS	0.1007	0.1182	0.1139	0.1134	0.1076	0.1078	0.1123	0.1087
TSLS	0.0679	0.0812	0.0824	0.0828	0.0756	0.0680	0.0859	0.0832
FP	0.1064	0.1200	0.1091	0.1028	0.1114	0.1076	0.1111	0.1036
URF	0.1119	0.1230	0.1061	0.1128	0.0947	0.0916	0.1115	0.1080

D. EIGENVALUES FOR PRODUCT MOMENT MATRIX OF EXPLANATORY VARIABLES (REID SPECIFICATION)

	Smallest in 100 samples	Average for 100 samples		
		λ_1	λ_2	λ_3

D.1. Equation 1

	Smallest in 100 samples	λ_1	λ_2	λ_3
OLS	0.0430	0.0868	0.1550	0.7582
TSLS	0.0213	0.0809	0.1319	0.7873
FP	0.0220	0.0818	0.1326	0.7856

D.2. Equation 2

	Smallest in 100 samples	λ_1	λ_2	λ_3
OLS	0.0436	0.0915	0.1580	0.7505
TSLS	0.0360	0.0842	0.1360	0.7798
FP	0.0332	0.0848	0.1366	0.7786

D.3. Unrestricted reduced form

	Smallest in 100 samples	λ_1	λ_2	λ_3
D.3. Unrestricted reduced form	0.0278	0.0544	0.0833	0.3423

E. AVERAGE R^2 FROM 100 SAMPLES

E.1. Sample period   E.2. Prediction period

	y_1	y_2	Y	y_1	y_2	Y
True	0.8	0.8	0.8	0.8	0.8	0.8
Generated (average)	0.7939	0.8009	0.7974	0.7915	0.7900	0.7908
OLS	0.7801	0.7825	0.7813	0.7376	0.7449	0.7413
TSLS	0.8097	0.8137	0.8117	0.7759	0.7761	0.7760
FP	0.8052	0.8085	0.8069	0.7697	0.7676	0.7687
URF	0.7950	0.7994	0.7972	0.7684	0.7696	0.7690

E.3. Sample period (adj. for D.F.)

	y_1	y_2	Y
OLS	0.7623	0.7649	0.7636
TSLS	0.7943	0.7986	0.7964
FP	0.7894	0.7930	0.7912

Table 10.2.28. Model 5b

A. MODEL DESIGN

A.1. Structural equations

$$\beta = \begin{bmatrix} 0 & 1 \\ -1 & 0 \end{bmatrix} \qquad \Gamma = \begin{bmatrix} k_1 & k_1 & 0 & 0 \\ 0 & 0 & k_1 & k_1 \end{bmatrix} \qquad \Omega = \begin{bmatrix} k_2 & k_2 & k_2 & k_2 \\ -k_2 & -k_2 & k_2 & k_2 \end{bmatrix}$$

with $k_1 = 1.65$ and $k_2 = 0.875$

A.2. Variance of endogenous and residual variables in the population and in the sample

$\sigma^2(y_i) = 1.0$
$\sigma^2(\delta_i) = 0.4 \qquad\qquad i = 1, 2$
$\sigma^2(\epsilon_i) = 0.2$

Generated in sample period:
$\begin{cases} V(y_1) = 1.011 & V(y_2) = 0.978 \\ V(\delta_1) = 0.388 & V(\delta_2) = 0.397 \\ V(\epsilon_1) = 0.203 & V(\epsilon_2) = 0.190 \end{cases}$

A.3. Correlation among residuals and exogenous variables

$r(x_1, x_2) = r(x_3, x_4) = -0.707$

A.4. Sample size and special design features

1. 40 observations in both the sample and prediction periods
2. This model is one in a series on intercorrelation between exogenous variables in two-relation models (Models 5a-5b).

B. STRUCTURAL COEFFICIENTS

B.1. True coefficient versus average estimate from 100 samples

	β_{12}	γ_{11}	γ_{12}	β_{21}	γ_{23}	γ_{24}
True	1.0	1.65	1.65	−1.0	1.65	1.65
OLS	0.6855	1.3913	1.4068	−0.6550	1.3554	1.3682
TSLS	0.9971	1.6474	1.6649	−0.9928	1.6360	1.6523
FP	0.9952	1.6397	1.6387	−0.9924	1.6263	1.6408

B.2. Observed standard deviation of 100 samples around observed mean

	β_{12}	γ_{11}	γ_{12}	β_{21}	γ_{23}	γ_{24}
OLS	0.1277	0.1541	0.1474	0.1258	0.1953	0.1737
TSLS	0.1730	0.1894	0.1917	0.1698	0.2193	0.2036
FP	0.1810	0.2148	0.2057	0.1703	0.2339	0.2011

B.3. Average standard deviation from large-sample formula

	β_{12}	γ_{11}	γ_{12}	β_{21}	γ_{23}	γ_{24}
OLS	0.1221	0.1680	0.1688	0.1208	0.1641	0.1651
TSLS	0.1620	0.1983	0.1996	0.1661	0.1996	0.2011
FP	0.1632	0.1996	0.1986	0.1680	0.2008	0.2020

B.4. Observed standard deviation around true value of the coefficient

	β_{12}	γ_{11}	γ_{12}	β_{21}	γ_{23}	γ_{24}
OLS	0.3394	0.3011	0.2844	0.3672	0.3535	0.3310
TSLS	0.1731	0.1894	0.1923	0.1700	0.2197	0.2036
FP	0.1811	0.2150	0.2060	0.1705	0.2351	0.2013

B.5. Number of iterations for fix-point (FP) method

Average = 7.9   Smallest = 4   Largest = 200   No convergence in 14 samples

C. REDUCED FORM COEFFICIENTS

C.1. True coefficient versus average estimate from 100 samples

	ω_{11}	ω_{12}	ω_{13}	ω_{14}	ω_{21}	ω_{22}	ω_{23}	ω_{24}
True	0.875	0.875	0.875	0.875	−0.875	−0.875	0.875	0.875
OLS	0.9651	0.9758	0.6379	0.6440	−0.6258	−0.6326	0.9374	0.9472
TSLS	0.8344	0.8431	0.8149	0.8227	−0.8172	−0.8256	0.8271	0.8361
FP	0.8312	0.8312	0.8088	0.8160	−0.8135	−0.8136	0.8233	0.8323
URF	0.8321	0.8314	0.8203	0.8264	−0.8213	−0.8376	0.8194	0.8270

C.2. Observed standard deviation of 100 samples around observed mean

OLS	0.1076	0.1024	0.1218	0.1136	0.1095	0.1040	0.1169	0.1065
TSLS	0.0992	0.0985	0.1157	0.1059	0.1024	0.1027	0.1016	0.0985
FP	0.1081	0.1062	0.1233	0.1080	0.1113	0.1112	0.1076	0.1045
URF	0.1071	0.1052	0.1212	0.1137	0.1032	0.1045	0.1080	0.1018

C.3. Average standard deviation from large-sample formula

URF	0.1071	0.1075	0.1048	0.1049	0.1034	0.1039	0.1014	0.1014

C.4. Observed standard deviation around true value of the coefficient

OLS	0.1403	0.1437	0.2666	0.2574	0.2722	0.2638	0.1325	0.1248
TSLS	0.1072	0.9856	0.1304	0.1181	0.1176	0.1140	0.1123	0.1059
FP	0.1166	0.1149	0.1399	0.1231	0.1272	0.1270	0.1194	0.1129
URF	0.1154	0.1139	0.1330	0.1237	0.1163	0.1109	0.1215	0.1125

D. EIGENVALUES FOR PRODUCT MOMENT MATRIX OF EXPLANATORY VARIABLES (REID SPECIFICATION)

	Smallest in 100 samples	Average for 100 samples		
		λ_1	λ_2	λ_3

D.1. Equation 1

	Smallest in 100 samples	λ_1	λ_2	λ_3
OLS	0.0284	0.0495	0.3517	0.5987
TSLS	0.0210	0.0423	0.3284	0.6293
FP	0.0215	0.0433	0.3243	0.6324

D.2. Equation 2

	Smallest in 100 samples	λ_1	λ_2	λ_3
OLS	0.0217	0.0489	0.3503	0.6008
TSLS	0.0165	0.0408	0.3295	0.6297
FP	0.0163	0.0413	0.3270	0.6317

D.3. Unrestricted reduced form

	Smallest	λ_1	λ_2	λ_3
	0.0295	0.0550	0.0846	0.3386

E. AVERAGE R^2 FROM 100 SAMPLES

E.1. Sample period

	y_1	y_2	Y
True	0.8	0.8	0.8
Generated (average)	0.7930	0.7977	0.7954
OLS	0.7796	0.7829	0.7813
TSLS	0.8092	0.8139	0.8116
FP	0.8056	0.8103	0.8080
URF	0.7930	0.7985	0.7958

E.2. Prediction period

	y_1	y_2	Y
True	0.8	0.8	0.8
Generated (average)	0.7924	0.8033	0.7979
OLS	0.7372	0.7529	0.7451
TSLS	0.7740	0.7837	0.7789
FP	0.7695	0.7797	0.7746
URF	0.7676	0.7768	0.7722

E.3. Sample period (adj. for D.F.)

	y_1	y_2	Y
OLS	0.7617	0.7653	0.7636
TSLS	0.7937	0.7988	0.7963
FP	0.7898	0.7949	0.7924

Table 10.2.29. Model 5c

A. MODEL DESIGN

A.1. Structural equations

$$y_{1,t-1} \quad y_{2,t-1} \quad x_{3t} \quad x_{4t}$$

$$\beta = \begin{bmatrix} 0 & 1 \\ -1 & 0 \end{bmatrix} \qquad \Gamma = \begin{bmatrix} 0.8 & -0.8 & 0 & 0 \\ 0 & 0 & 1.2649 & 1.2649 \end{bmatrix} \qquad \Omega = \begin{bmatrix} 0.4 & -0.4 & 0.6325 & 0.6325 \\ -0.4 & 0.4 & 0.6325 & 0.6325 \end{bmatrix}$$

A.2. Variance of endogenous and residual variables in the population and in the sample

$\sigma^2(y_i) = 1.0$ Generated $\begin{cases} V(y_1) = 1.028 & V(y_2) = 0.997 \\ V(\delta_1) = 0.209 & V(\delta_2) = 0.218 \\ V(\epsilon_1) = 0.109 & V(\epsilon_2) = 0.104 \end{cases}$

$\sigma^2(\delta_i) = 0.2119$ $i = 1, 2$ in sample

$\sigma^2(\epsilon_i) = 0.106$ period:

A.3. Correlation among residuals and exogenous variables

  None

A.4. Sample size and special design features

1. 40 observations in both the sample and prediction periods.
2. This model is one in a series on lagged endogenous variables in two-relation models (Models 5c-5e).
3. The γ coefficients were chosen so that (a) the characteristic roots of the underlying difference equation would be 0.8 and 0; (b) the specifications in A.2. would be met; and (c) the variances of the exogenous variables would be identically one.

B. STRUCTURAL COEFFICIENTS

B.1. True coefficient versus average estimate from 100 samples

	β_{12}	γ_{11}	γ_{12}	β_{21}	γ_{23}	γ_{24}
True	1	0.8	−0.8	−1	1.2649	1.2649
OLS	0.8847	0.7344	−0.7339	−0.4059	0.8831	0.8952
TSLS	0.9949	0.7744	−0.7729	−1.0363	1.2839	1.3014
FP	0.9966	0.7660	−0.7583	−1.0409	1.2813	1.3007

B.2. Observed standard deviation of 100 samples around observed mean

OLS	0.0771	0.0955	0.1075	0.1928	0.1346	0.1461
TSLS	0.0816	0.1007	0.1094	0.4237	0.2897	0.2895
FP	0.0839	0.1109	0.1250	0.4394	0.3019	0.3062

B.3. Average standard deviation from large-sample formula

OLS	0.0759	0.1098	0.1113	0.1457	0.1126	0.1136
TSLS	0.0834	0.1137	0.1152	0.3178	0.2190	0.2215
FP	0.0845	0.1149	0.1164	0.3255	0.2219	0.2262

B.4. Observed standard deviation around true value of the coefficient

OLS	0.1387	0.1159	0.1262	0.6246	0.4048	0.3975
TSLS	0.0818	0.1039	0.1127	0.4253	0.2903	0.2918
FP	0.0840	0.1160	0.1318	0.4413	0.3023	0.3083

B.5. Number of iterations for fix-point (FP) method

  Average = 8.23   Smallest = 5   Largest = 21   No convergence in 0 samples

C. REDUCED FORM COEFFICIENTS

C.1. True coefficient versus average estimate from 100 samples

	ω_{11}	ω_{12}	ω_{13}	ω_{14}	ω_{21}	ω_{22}	ω_{23}	ω_{24}
True	0.4	−0.4	0.6325	0.6325	−0.4	0.4	0.6325	0.6325
OLS	0.5454	−0.5452	0.5740	0.5815	−0.2154	0.2144	0.6512	0.6585
TSLS	0.3938	−0.3929	0.6274	0.6361	−0.3832	0.3813	0.6330	0.6410
FP	0.3891	−0.3847	0.6253	0.6351	−0.3787	0.3740	0.6305	0.6384
URF	0.3856	−0.3839	0.6300	0.6397	−0.3881	0.3900	0.6300	0.6401

C.2. Observed standard deviation of 100 samples around observed mean

OLS	0.0659	0.0774	0.0467	0.0577	0.0989	0.0986	0.0516	0.0508
TSLS	0.0774	0.0778	0.0425	0.0510	0.0815	0.0796	0.0459	0.0449
FP	0.0825	0.0823	0.0475	0.0642	0.0845	0.0860	0.0570	0.0522
URF	0.0818	0.0784	0.0589	0.0530	0.0839	0.0811	0.0571	0.0522

C.3. Average standard deviation from large-sample formula

URF	0.0806	0.0819	0.0545	0.0549	0.0783	0.0795	0.0531	0.0535

C.4. Observed standard deviation around true value of the coefficient

OLS	0.1596	0.1645	0.0749	0.0770	0.2094	0.2102	0.0549	0.0571
TSLS	0.0776	0.0781	0.0428	0.0512	0.0832	0.0818	0.0459	0.0457
FP	0.0832	0.0837	0.0480	0.0643	0.0871	0.0898	0.0570	0.0525
URF	0.0831	0.0800	0.0590	0.0535	0.0847	0.0817	0.0572	0.5709

D. EIGENVALUES FOR PRODUCT MOMENT MATRIX OF EXPLANATORY VARIABLES (REID SPECIFICATION)

	Smallest in 100 samples	Average for 100 samples		
		λ_1	λ_2	λ_3
D.1. Equation 1				
OLS	0.0297	0.0791	0.3305	0.5904
TSLS	0.0302	0.0795	0.3121	0.6084
FP	0.0302	0.0800	0.3101	0.6099
D.2. Equation 2				
OLS	0.0139	0.0328	0.3162	0.6510
TSLS	0.0017	0.0165	0.3257	0.6578
FP	0.0016	0.0167	0.3249	0.6584
D.3. Unrestricted reduced form	0.0221	0.0641	0.1932	0.2834

E. AVERAGE R^2 FROM 100 SAMPLES

E.1. Sample period

	y_1	y_2	Y
True	0.9	0.8940	0.8970
Generated (average)	0.8872	0.8905	0.8889
OLS	0.8748	0.8815	0.8782
TSLS	0.8953	0.8981	0.8967
FP	0.8920	0.8964	0.8942
URF	0.8872	0.8902	0.8887

E.2. Prediction period

	y_1	y_2	Y
True	0.9	0.8940	0.8970
Generated (average)	0.8842	0.8920	0.8881
OLS	0.8506	0.8614	0.8560
TSLS	0.8750	0.8811	0.8781
FP	0.8716	0.8778	0.8747
URF	0.8709	0.8776	0.8743

E.3. Sample period (adj. for D.F.)

	y_1	y_2	Y
OLS	0.8646	0.8719	0.8683
TSLS	0.8868	0.8898	0.8883
FP	0.8832	0.8880	0.8856

Table 10.2.30. Model 5d

A. MODEL DESIGN

A.1. Structural equations

$$y_{2,t-1} \quad x_{3t} \quad y_{1,t-1} \quad x_{4t}$$

$$\beta = \begin{bmatrix} 0 & 1 \\ -1 & 0 \end{bmatrix} \qquad \Gamma = \begin{bmatrix} 1.1314 & 0.7589 & 0 & 0 \\ 0 & 0 & 1.1314 & 0.7589 \end{bmatrix} \qquad \Omega = \begin{bmatrix} 0.5657 & 0.3795 & 0.5657 & 0.3795 \\ -0.5657 & -0.3795 & 0.5657 & 0.3795 \end{bmatrix}$$

A.2. Variance of endogenous and residual variables in the population and in the sample

$$\sigma^2(y_i) = 1.0$$
$$\sigma^2(\delta_i) = 0.1440 \qquad i = 1, 2$$
$$\sigma^2(\epsilon_i) = 0.07$$

Generated in sample period:
$$\begin{cases} V(y_1) = 0.984 & V(y_2) = 1.035 \\ V(\delta_1) = 0.139 & V(\delta_2) = 0.146 \\ V(\epsilon_1) = 0.070 & V(\epsilon_1) = 0.072 \end{cases}$$

A.3. Correlation among residuals and exogenous variables

None

A.4. Sample size and special design features

1. 40 observations in both the sample and prediction periods.
2. This model is one in a series on lagged endogenous variables in two-relation models (Models 5c-5e)
3. The γ's were chosen such that (a) the characteristic roots of the underlying difference equation would be 0.8 and -0.8; (b) the specifications in A.2. would be met; and (c) the variances of the exogenous variables would be identically one.

B. STRUCTURAL COEFFICIENTS

B.1. True coefficient versus average estimate from 100 samples

	β_{12}	γ_{11}	γ_{12}	β_{21}	γ_{23}	γ_{24}
True	1	1.1314	0.7589	-1	1.1314	0.7589
OLS	0.8619	1.0489	0.7101	-0.8690	1.0578	0.7208
TSLS	1.0068	1.1299	0.7662	-1.0235	1.1451	0.7788
FP	1.0095	1.1373	0.7517	-1.0220	1.1366	0.7799

B.2. Observed standard deviation of 100 samples around observed mean

OLS	0.0971	0.0959	0.0676	0.0940	0.0948	0.0817
TSLS	0.0978	0.0928	0.0741	0.0958	0.0852	0.0787
FP	0.1036	0.1013	0.0980	0.0969	0.0993	0.0909

B.3. Average standard deviation from large-sample formula

OLS	0.0845	0.0783	0.0678	0.0878	0.0814	0.0701
TSLS	0.0958	0.0846	0.0723	0.1000	0.0884	0.0748
FP	0.0979	0.0867	0.0731	0.1008	0.0887	0.0756

B.4. Observed standard deviation around true value of the coefficient

OLS	0.1688	0.1265	0.0834	0.1612	0.1200	0.0901
TSLS	0.0980	0.0928	0.0745	0.0986	0.0863	0.0812
FP	0.1040	0.1015	0.0983	0.0994	0.0994	0.0933

B.5. Number of iterations for fix-point (FP) method

Average = 8.19   Smallest = 5   Largest = 17   No convergence in 0 samples

C. REDUCED FORM COEFFICIENTS

C.1. True coefficient versus average estimate from 100 samples

	ω_{11}	ω_{12}	ω_{13}	ω_{14}	ω_{21}	ω_{22}	ω_{23}	ω_{24}
True	0.5657	0.3795	0.5657	0.3795	−0.5657	−0.3795	0.5657	0.3795
OLS	0.6005	0.4069	0.5191	0.3539	−0.5189	−0.3522	0.6058	0.4129
TSLS	0.5575	0.3784	0.5664	0.3854	−0.5680	−0.3853	0.5653	0.3847
FP	0.5607	0.3711	0.5631	0.3866	−0.5705	−0.3770	0.5608	0.3850
URF	0.5605	0.3700	0.5707	0.3852	−0.5648	−0.3927	0.5606	0.3869

C.2. Observed standard deviation of 100 samples around observed mean

OLS	0.0499	0.0376	0.0473	0.0427	0.0453	0.0391	0.0515	0.0466
TSLS	0.0436	0.0387	0.0415	0.0408	0.0416	0.0349	0.0422	0.0420
FP	0.0463	0.0499	0.0493	0.0473	0.0463	0.0461	0.0506	0.0465
URF	0.0464	0.0506	0.0433	0.0468	0.0483	0.0459	0.0505	0.0463

C.3. Average standard deviation from large-sample formula

URF	0.0459	0.0407	0.0465	0.0446	0.0466	0.0449	0.0441	0.0450

C.4. Observed standard deviation around true value of the coefficient

OLS	0.0608	0.0467	0.0664	0.0498	0.0651	0.0478	0.0653	0.0573
TSLS	0.0444	0.0385	0.0415	0.0412	0.0417	0.0354	0.0422	0.0423
FP	0.0466	0.0500	0.0494	0.0478	0.0465	0.0462	0.0508	0.0468
URF	0.0467	0.0515	0.0436	0.0470	0.0483	0.0478	0.0508	0.0469

D. EIGENVALUES FOR PRODUCT MOMENT MATRIX OF EXPLANATORY VARIABLES (REID SPECIFICATION)

	Smallest in 100 samples	Average for 100 samples		
		λ_1	λ_2	λ_3
D.1. Equation 1				
OLS	0.0286	0.1013	0.3139	0.5848
TSLS	0.0201	0.0919	0.3189	0.5892
FP	0.0206	0.0927	0.3191	0.5882
D.2. Equation 2				
OLS	0.0292	0.1059	0.3199	0.5742
TSLS	0.0216	0.0972	0.3242	0.5787
FP	0.0223	0.0977	0.3227	0.5797
D.3. Unrestricted reduced form	0.0539	0.1432	0.2019	0.2694

E. AVERAGE R^2 FROM 100 SAMPLES

E.1. Sample period / E.2. Prediction period

	E.1. Sample period			E.2. Prediction period		
	y_1	y_2	Y	y_1	y_2	Y
True	0.9	0.9	0.9	0.9	0.9	0.9
Generated (average)	0.9193	0.9186	0.9190	0.9174	0.9151	0.9163
OLS	0.9190	0.9189	0.9190	0.9037	0.8997	0.9017
TSLS	0.9252	0.9251	0.9252	0.9097	0.9077	0.9087
FP	0.9239	0.9224	0.9232	0.9066	0.9054	0.9060
URF	0.9191	0.9192	0.9192	0.9073	0.9045	0.9059

E.3. Sample period (adj. for D.F.)

	y_1	y_2	Y
OLS	0.9124	0.9123	0.9124
TSLS	0.9191	0.9190	0.9191
FP	0.9177	0.9161	0.9170

Table 10.2.31. Model 5e

A. MODEL DESIGN

A.1. Structural equations

$$y_{1,t-1} \quad x_{3t} \quad y_{2,t-1} \quad x_{4t}$$

$$\beta = \begin{bmatrix} 0 & 1 \\ -1 & 0 \end{bmatrix} \quad \Gamma = \begin{bmatrix} 1.1314 & 0.7589 & 0 & 0 \\ 0 & 0 & -1.1314 & 0.7589 \end{bmatrix} \quad \Omega = \begin{bmatrix} 0.5657 & 0.3795 & -0.5657 & 0.3795 \\ -0.5657 & -0.3795 & -0.5657 & 0.3795 \end{bmatrix}$$

A.2. Variance of endogenous and residual variables in the population and in the sample

$\sigma^2(y_i) = 1.0$ Generated $\begin{cases} V(y_1) = 1.066 & V(y_2) = 1.039 \\ V(\delta_1) = 0.148 & V(\delta_2) = 0.146 \\ V(\epsilon_2) = 0.0729 & V(\epsilon_2) = 0.0741 \end{cases}$

$\sigma^2(\delta_i) = 0.1440 \quad i = 1, 2$ in sample

$\sigma^2(\epsilon_i) = 0.07$ period:

A.3. Correlation among residuals and exogenous variables

None

A.4. Sample size and special design features

1. 40 observations in both the sample and prediction periods.
2. This model is one in a series on lagged endogenous variables in two-relation models (Models 5c-5e).
3. The γ's were chosen such that (a) the characteristic roots of the underlying difference equation would be 0.8 and -0.8; (b) the specifications in A.2 would be met; and (c) the variances of the exogenous variables would be identically one.

B. STRUCTURAL COEFFICIENTS

B.1. True coefficient versus average estimate from 100 samples

	β_{12}	γ_{11}	γ_{12}	β_{21}	γ_{23}	γ_{24}
True	1	1.1314	0.7589	-1	-1.1314	0.7589
OLS	0.8587	1.0502	0.7055	-0.8568	-1.0615	0.7095
TSLS	1.0095	1.1348	0.7636	-1.0096	-1.1476	0.7649
FP	1.0086	1.1318	0.7618	-1.0078	-1.1488	0.7564

B.2. Observed standard deviation of 100 samples around observed mean

OLS	0.0954	0.0987	0.0794	0.0993	0.0753	0.0735
TSLS	0.1066	0.1027	0.0812	0.1054	0.0816	0.0755
FP	0.1084	0.1135	0.0950	0.1059	0.0939	0.0964

B.3. Average standard deviation from large-sample formula

OLS	0.0857	0.0789	0.0699	0.0851	0.0790	0.0687
TSLS	0.0977	0.0851	0.0745	0.0982	0.0856	0.0734
FP	0.0988	0.0859	0.0754	0.0995	0.0871	0.0739

B.4. Observed standard deviation around true value of the coefficient

OLS	0.1705	0.1278	0.0957	0.1743	0.1027	0.0886
TSLS	0.1070	0.1028	0.0813	0.1058	0.0832	0.0757
FP	0.1087	0.1135	0.0950	0.1062	0.0955	0.0964

B.5. Number of iterations for fix-point (FP) method

Average = 7.98;   Smallest = 4;   Largest = 14   No convergence in 0 samples

C. REDUCED FORM COEFFICIENTS

C.1. True coefficient versus average estimate from 100 samples

	ω_{11}	ω_{12}	ω_{13}	ω_{14}	ω_{21}	ω_{22}	ω_{23}	ω_{24}
True	0.5657	0.3795	−0.5657	0.3795	−0.5657	−0.3795	−0.5657	0.3795
OLS	0.6052	0.4067	−0.5238	0.3500	−0.5172	−0.3478	−0.6128	0.4092
TSLS	0.5632	0.3797	−0.5724	0.3817	−0.5657	−0.3804	−0.5699	0.3798
FP	0.5624	0.3794	−0.5732	0.3775	−0.5638	−0.3792	−0.5712	0.3764
URF	0.5602	0.3789	−0.5714	0.3851	−0.5669	−0.3805	−0.5710	0.3756

C.2. Observed standard deviation of 100 samples around observed mean

OLS	0.0485	0.0411	0.0484	0.0408	0.0592	0.0488	0.0444	0.0392
TSLS	0.0492	0.0438	0.0446	0.0410	0.0489	0.0364	0.0406	0.0376
FP	0.0534	0.0512	0.0514	0.0493	0.0540	0.0430	0.0452	0.0501
URF	0.0549	0.0524	0.0473	0.0512	0.0498	0.0473	0.0446	0.0493

C.3. Average standard deviation from large-sample formula

URF	0.0462	0.0454	0.0462	0.0450	0.0464	0.0459	0.0467	0.0457

C.4. Observed standard deviation around true value of the coefficient

OLS	0.0625	0.0493	0.0640	0.0503	0.0765	0.0582	0.0647	0.0492
TSLS	0.0493	0.0438	0.0451	0.0411	0.0489	0.0364	0.0408	0.0376
FP	0.0535	0.0512	0.0519	0.0493	0.0540	0.0430	0.0455	0.0502
URF	0.0552	0.0524	0.0476	0.0513	0.0498	0.0473	0.0449	0.0495

D. EIGENVALUES FOR PRODUCT MOMENT MATRIX OF EXPLANATORY VARIABLES (REID SPECIFICATION)

	Smallest in 100 samples	Average for 100 samples		
		λ_1	λ_2	λ_3

D.1. Equation 1

	Smallest	λ_1	λ_2	λ_3
OLS	0.0291	0.0911	0.3068	0.6021
TSLS	0.0268	0.0816	0.3126	0.6058
FP	0.0270	0.0822	0.3122	0.6056

D.2. Equation 2

	Smallest	λ_1	λ_2	λ_3
OLS	0.0460	0.0902	0.3134	0.5963
TSLS	0.0312	0.0808	0.3191	0.6001
FP	0.0317	0.0815	0.3204	0.5981

D.3. Unrestricted reduced form

	Smallest	λ_1	λ_2	λ_3
D.3. Unrestricted reduced form	0.0489	0.1408	0.2027	0.2703

E. AVERAGE R^2 FROM 100 SAMPLES

E.1. Sample period

	y_1	y_2	Y
True	0.9	0.9	0.9
Generated (average)	0.9180	0.9196	0.9188
OLS	0.9187	0.9192	0.9190
TSLS	0.9252	0.9256	0.9254
FP	0.9229	0.9242	0.9236
URF	0.9192	0.9196	0.9194

E.2. Prediction period

	y_1	y_2	Y
True	0.9	0.9	0.9
Generated (average)	0.9195	0.9120	0.9158
OLS	0.9064	0.8953	0.9009
TSLS	0.9114	0.9057	0.9086
FP	0.9090	0.9029	0.9060
URF	0.9091	0.9025	0.9058

E.3. Sample period (adj. for D.F.)

	y_1	y_2	Y
OLS	0.9121	0.9126	0.9124
TSLS	0.9191	0.9196	0.9194
FP	0.9166	0.9181	0.9174

Table 10.2.32. Model 5f

A. MODEL DESIGN

A.1. Structural equations

$$\beta = \begin{bmatrix} 0 & 1 \\ -1 & 0 \end{bmatrix} \qquad \Gamma = \begin{bmatrix} k_1 & k_1 & 0 & 0 \\ 0 & 0 & k_1 & k_1 \end{bmatrix} \qquad \Omega = \begin{bmatrix} k_2 & k_2 & k_2 & k_2 \\ -k_2 & -k_2 & k_2 & k_2 \end{bmatrix}$$

with $k_1 = 0.8944$ and $k_2 = 0.4472$

A.2. Variance of endogenous and residual variables in the population and in the sample

$\sigma^2(y_i) = 1.0$

$\sigma^2(\delta_i) = 0.4 \qquad i = 1, 2$

$\sigma^2(\epsilon_i) = 0.2$

Generated in sample period:
$\begin{cases} V(y_1) = 0.981 & V(y_2) = 0.956 \\ V(\delta_1) = 0.393 & V(\delta_2) = 0.440 \\ V(\epsilon_1) = 0.212 & V(\epsilon_2) = 0.205 \end{cases}$

A.3. Correlation among residuals and exogenous variables

None

A.4. Sample size and special design features

1. 10 and 40 observations respectively in the sample and prediction periods.
2. This model is one in a series on varying sample size in two-relation models (Models 5f, 5g(=1b), 5h, 5i, 5j(=1d)).

B. STRUCTURAL COEFFICIENTS

B.1. True coefficient versus average estimate from 100 samples

	β_{12}	γ_{11}	γ_{12}	β_{21}	γ_{23}	γ_{24}
True	1	0.8944	0.8944	−1	0.8944	0.8944
OLS	0.6291	0.7514	0.7346	−0.6261	0.7438	0.6902
TSLS	0.9094	0.8668	0.8516	−1.0002	0.9165	0.8648
FP	0.9059	0.8502	0.8315	−0.9774	0.8485	0.8352

B.2. Observed standard deviation of 100 samples around observed mean

OLS	0.2640	0.2317	0.2487	0.3043	0.2730	0.2739
TSLS	0.3869	0.2746	0.3167	0.6457	0.4581	0.4444
FP	0.3763	0.3242	0.3760	0.4423	0.3582	0.3896

B.3. Average standard deviation from large-sample formula

OLS	0.2832	0.2388	0.2477	0.2898	0.2584	0.2681
TSLS	0.4132	0.2973	0.3055	0.4781	0.3572	0.3636
FP	0.4502	0.3140	0.3267	0.4657	0.3344	0.3585

B.4. Observed standard deviation around true value of the coefficient

OLS	0.4553	0.2723	0.2956	0.4821	0.3118	0.3416
TSLS	0.3974	0.2760	0.3196	0.6457	0.4586	0.4454
FP	0.3879	0.3272	0.3812	0.4429	0.3611	0.3941

B.5. Number of iterations for fix-point (FP) method

Average = 16.05　　　Smallest = 6　　　Largest = 50　　　No convergence in 7 samples (Iteration limit of 50)

C. REDUCED FORM COEFFICIENTS

C.1. True coefficient versus average estimate from 100 samples

	ω_{11}	ω_{12}	ω_{13}	ω_{14}	ω_{21}	ω_{22}	ω_{23}	ω_{24}
True	0.4472	0.4472	0.4472	0.4472	−0.4472	−0.4472	0.4472	0.4472
OLS	0.5504	0.5329	0.3301	0.3070	−0.3223	−0.3133	0.5354	0.4901
TSLS	0.4759	0.4626	0.4149	0.3923	−0.4260	−0.4166	0.4813	0.4501
FP	0.4700	0.4524	0.3917	0.3803	−0.4229	−0.4034	0.4617	0.4497
URF	0.4771	0.4387	0.4433	0.4026	−0.4367	−0.4478	0.4561	0.4314

C.2. Observed standard deviation of 100 samples around observed mean

OLS	0.1864	0.1771	0.1728	0.1602	0.1818	0.1761	0.1951	0.1740
TSLS	0.1507	0.1528	0.1620	0.1610	0.1549	0.1580	0.1571	0.1345
FP	0.1786	0.1806	0.1713	0.1783	0.1988	0.1818	0.1926	0.1969
URF	0.1988	0.1994	0.1970	0.2251	0.1974	0.1911	0.2194	0.1710

C.3. Average standard deviation from large-sample formula

URF	0.1862	0.1898	0.1914	0.1897	0.1842	0.1890	0.1881	0.1868

C.4. Observed standard deviation around true value of the coefficient

OLS	0.2131	0.1967	0.2087	0.2129	0.2206	0.2212	0.2141	0.1792
TSLS	0.1534	0.1536	0.1652	0.1701	0.1563	0.1609	0.1608	0.1345
FP	0.1800	0.1807	0.1801	0.1904	0.2003	0.1870	0.1931	0.1969
URF	0.2010	0.1996	0.1970	0.2295	0.1977	0.1911	0.2196	0.1717

D. EIGENVALUE FOR PRODUCT MOMENT MATRIX OF EXPLANATORY VARIABLES (REID SPECIFICATION)

	Smallest in 100 samples	Average for 100 samples		
		λ_1	λ_2	λ_3
D.1. Equation 1				
OLS	0.0171	0.0907	0.2688	0.6405
TSLS	0.0028	0.0728	0.2720	0.6552
FP	0.0025	0.0750	0.2745	0.6505
D.2. Equation 2				
OLS	0.0181	0.0932	0.2878	0.6189
TSLS	0.0018	0.0761	0.2904	0.6334
FP	0.0063	0.0777	0.2917	0.6306
D.3. Unrestricted reduced form	0.0095	0.0758	0.1587	0.2861

E. AVERAGE R^2 FROM 100 SAMPLES

	E.1. Sample period			E.2. Prediction period		
	y_1	y_2	Y	y_1	y_2	Y
True	0.8	0.8	0.8	0.8	0.8	0.8
Generated (average)	0.7362	0.7518	0.7440	0.8018	0.7888	0.7953
OLS	0.7706	0.7773	0.7740	0.6246	0.6057	0.6152
TSLS	0.8082	0.8183	0.8133	0.6918	0.6932	0.6925
FP	0.7947	0.8038	0.7993	0.6593	0.6291	0.6442
URF	0.7402	0.7480	0.7441	0.6267	0.6353	0.6310

E.3. Sample period (adj. for D.F.)

	y_1	y_2	Y
OLS	0.6723	0.6819	0.6771
TSLS	0.7260	0.7404	0.7332
FP	0.7067	0.7197	0.7132

Table 10.2.33. Model 5h

A. MODEL DESIGN

A.1. Structural equations

$$B = \begin{bmatrix} 0 & 1 \\ -1 & 0 \end{bmatrix} \qquad \Gamma = \begin{bmatrix} k_1 & k_1 & 0 & 0 \\ 0 & 0 & k_1 & k_1 \end{bmatrix} \qquad \Omega = \begin{bmatrix} k_2 & k_2 & k_2 & k_2 \\ -k_2 & -k_2 & k_2 & k_2 \end{bmatrix}$$

with $k_1 = 0.8944$ and $k_2 = 0.4472$

A.2. Variance of endogenous and residual variables in the population and in the sample

$$\sigma^2(y_i) = 1.0$$
$$\sigma^2(\delta_i) = 0.4 \qquad i = 1, 2$$
$$\sigma^2(\epsilon_i) = 0.2$$

Generated in sample period:
$$\begin{cases} V(y_1) = 0.9975 & V(y_2) = 0.9903 \\ V(\delta_1) = 0.3981 & V(\delta_2) = 0.3994 \\ V(\epsilon_1) = 0.1989 & V(\epsilon_2) = 0.1998 \end{cases}$$

A.3. Correlation among residuals and exogenous variables

None

A.4. Sample size and special design features

1. 80 observations in the sample and 20 observations in the prediction period.
2. This model is one in a series on varying sample size in two-relation models (Models 5f, 5g(=1b), 5h, 5i, 5j(=1d)).

B. STRUCTURAL COEFFICIENTS

B.1. True coefficient versus average estimate from 100 samples

	β_{12}	γ_{11}	γ_{12}	β_{21}	γ_{23}	γ_{24}
True	1	0.8944	0.8944	−1	0.8944	0.8944
OLS	0.6766	0.7435	0.7501	−0.6618	0.7557	0.7450
TSLS	1.0112	0.8922	0.9010	−1.0065	0.9056	0.9059
FP	1.0127	0.8894	0.8975	−1.0082	0.9098	0.8993

B.2. Observed standard deviation of 100 samples around observed mean

OLS	0.0899	0.0811	0.0788	0.0939	0.0817	0.0753
TSLS	0.1280	0.0947	0.0997	0.1238	0.0870	0.0889
FP	0.1288	0.1182	0.1032	0.1247	0.0966	0.1072

B.3. Average standard deviation from large-sample formula

OLS	0.0849	0.0764	0.0766	0.0860	0.0759	0.0764
TSLS	0.1150	0.0893	0.0896	0.1177	0.0891	0.0904
FP	0.1161	0.0899	0.0900	0.1188	0.0900	0.0907

B.4. Observed standard deviation around true value of the coefficient

OLS	0.3357	0.1713	0.1644	0.3510	0.1610	0.1673
TSLS	0.1285	0.0947	0.0999	0.1240	0.0877	0.0896
FP	0.1294	0.1183	0.1032	0.1250	0.0978	0.1073

B.5. Number of iterations for fix-point (FP) method

Average = 7.38   Smallest = 4   Largest = 14   No convergence in 0 samples

C. REDUCED FORM COEFFICIENTS (4 out of 8 coefficients)

C.1. True coefficient versus average estimate from 100 samples

	ω_{11}	ω_{13}	ω_{21}	ω_{23}
True	0.4472	0.4472	−0.4472	0.4472
OLS	0.5141	0.3516	−0.3388	0.5222
TSLS	0.4440	0.4520	−0.4430	0.4507
FP	0.4418	0.4538	−0.4416	0.4524
URF	0.4423	0.4502	−0.4458	0.4528

C.2. Observed standard deviation of 100 samples around observed mean

OLS	0.0520	0.0452	0.0506	0.0486
TSLS	0.0493	0.0444	0.0445	0.0451
FP	0.0587	0.0474	0.0562	0.0525
URF	0.0589	0.0550	0.0482	0.0527

C.3. Average standard deviation from large-sample formula

URF	0.0517	0.0513	0.0518	0.0514

C.4. Observed standard deviation around true value of the coefficient

OLS	0.0847	0.1057	0.1196	0.0894
TSLS	0.0494	0.0447	0.0447	0.0452
FP	0.0589	0.0479	0.0565	0.0528
URF	0.0591	0.0551	0.0482	0.0530

D. EIGENVALUES FOR PRODUCT MOMENT MATRIX OF EXPLANATORY VARIABLES (REID SPECIFICATION)

	Smallest in 100 samples	Average for 100 samples		
		λ_1	λ_2	λ_3
D.1. Equation 1				
OLS	0.0818	0.1208	0.3284	0.5508
TSLS	0.0529	0.0926	0.3486	0.5588
FP	0.0564	0.0932	0.3479	0.5590
D.2. Equation 2				
OLS	0.0751	0.1149	0.3276	0.5574
TSLS	0.0397	0.0868	0.3455	0.5676
FP	0.0396	0.0869	0.3473	0.5658
D.3. Unrestricted reduced form	0.1352	0.1777	0.2218	0.2667

E. AVERAGE R^2 FROM 100 SAMPLES

	E.1. Sample period			E.2. Prediction period		
	y_1	y_2	Y	y_1	y_2	Y
True	0.8	0.8	0.8	0.8	0.8	0.8
Generated (average)	0.7954	0.7936	0.7945	0.7845	0.7970	0.7908
OLS	0.7710	0.7684	0.7697	0.7455	0.7535	0.7495
TSLS	0.8035	0.8013	0.8024	0.7736	0.7886	0.7811
FP	0.8011	0.7987	0.7999	0.7715	0.7861	0.7788
URF	0.7960	0.7936	0.7948	0.7700	0.7861	0.7781

E.3. Sample period (adj. for D.F.)

	y_1	y_2	Y
OLS	0.7621	0.7594	0.7608
TSLS	0.7958	0.7936	0.7947
FP	0.7934	0.7909	0.7924

Table 10.2.34. Model 5i

A. MODEL DESIGN

A.1. Structural equations

$$\beta = \begin{bmatrix} 0 & 0.5 \\ -0.9 & 0 \end{bmatrix} \quad \Gamma = \begin{bmatrix} 0.8889 & 0.8889 & 0 & 0 \\ 0 & 0 & 0.4474 & 0.4474 \end{bmatrix} \quad \Omega = \begin{bmatrix} 0.6133 & 0.6133 & 0.1543 & 0.1543 \\ -0.5520 & -0.5520 & 0.3087 & 0.3087 \end{bmatrix}$$

A.2. Variance of endogenous variables and residuals in the population and in the sample

$\sigma^2(y_i) = 1.0$ $i = 1, 2$ Generated $\{$ $V(y_1) = 0.982$ $V(y_2) = 0.946$

$\sigma^2(\delta_i) = 0.395, 0.100$ in sample $V(\delta_1) = 0.400$ $V(\delta_2) = 0.098$

$\sigma^2(\epsilon_i) = 0.2$ $i = 1, 2$ period: $V(\epsilon_1) = 0.197$ $V(\epsilon_2) = 0.209$

A.3. Correlation among residuals and exogenous variables

     None

A.4. Sample size and special design features

     1. 10 and 40 observations respectively in the sample and prediction period.
     2. This model is one in a series on varying sample size in two-relation models (Models 5f, 5g(=1b), 5h, 5i, 5j(=1d)).

B. STRUCTURAL COEFFICIENTS

B.1. True coefficient versus average estimate from 100 samples

	β_{12}	γ_{11}	γ_{12}	β_{21}	γ_{23}	γ_{24}
True	0.5	0.8889	0.8889	-0.9	0.4474	0.4474
OLS	-0.1485	0.5251	0.5405	-0.8843	0.4444	0.4280
TSLS	0.6124	0.9291	0.9913	-0.9156	0.4577	0.4382
FP	0.5457	0.8793	0.9333	-0.9266	0.4144	0.3943

B.2. Observed standard deviation of 100 samples around observed mean

OLS	0.2733	0.2588	0.2337	0.1494	0.1242	0.1338
TSLS	1.4815	0.8581	1.0764	0.1844	0.1470	0.1418
FP	0.7468	0.4028	0.5004	0.2226	0.2248	0.2140

B.3. Average standard deviation from large-sample formula

OLS	0.3167	0.2517	0.2607	0.1271	0.1226	0.1205
TSLS	1.8820	1.1077	1.3530	0.1555	0.1327	0.1273
FP	0.7885	0.4650	0.5337	0.1908	0.1571	0.1522

B.4. Observed standard deviation around true value of the coefficient

OLS	0.7037	0.4465	0.4195	0.1502	0.1242	0.1352
TSLS	1.4863	0.8590	1.0814	0.1851	0.1474	0.1421
FP	0.7482	0.4029	0.5024	0.2242	0.2272	0.2205

B.5. Number of iterations for fix-point (FP) method

     Average = 158   Smallest = 5   Largest = 200   No convergence in 2 samples

C. REDUCED FORM COEFFICIENTS (4 out of 8 coefficients)

C.1. True coefficient versus average estimate from 100 samples

	ω_{11}	ω_{13}	ω_{21}	ω_{23}
True	0.6133	0.1543	−0.5520	0.3087
OLS	0.5348	−0.1437	−0.4450	0.5862
TSLS	0.4891	0.0666	−0.3856	0.4292
FP	0.5860	0.1283	−0.5368	0.2947
URF	0.6075	0.1852	−0.5664	0.2877

C.2. Observed standard deviation of 100 samples around observed mean

OLS	0.7249	0.4402	0.8486	0.5201
TSLS	1.0820	0.6445	1.5406	0.9039
FP	0.1681	0.1447	0.1735	0.1799
URF	0.1932	0.1841	0.2021	0.1854

C.3. Average standard deviation from large-sample formula

URF	0.1753	0.1805	0.1844	0.1900

C.4. Observed standard deviation around true value of the coefficient

OLS	0.7291	0.5316	0.8553	0.5895
TSLS	1.0891	0.6504	1.5496	0.9119
FP	0.1703	0.1470	0.1742	0.1804
URF	0.1933	0.1867	0.2026	0.1866

D. EIGENVALUES FOR PRODUCT MOMENT MATRIX OF EXPLANATORY VARIABLES (REID SPECIFICATION)

	Smallest in 100 samples	Average for 100 samples		
		λ_1	λ_2	λ_3
D.1. Equation 1				
OLS	0.01275	0.0581	0.2729	0.6690
TSLS	0.000064	0.0364	0.2772	0.6864
FP	0.00294	0.0363	0.2756	0.6881
D.2. Equation 2				
OLS	0.01608	0.1287	0.2913	0.5800
TSLS	0.00773	0.1172	0.2913	0.5915
FP	0.00640	0.1178	0.2928	0.5894
D.3. Unrestricted reduced form	0.008799	0.0713	0.1550	0.2764

E. AVERAGE R^2 FROM 100 SAMPLES

E.1. Sample period

	y_1	y_2	Y
True	0.8	0.8	0.8
Generated (aver.)	0.7595	0.7280	0.7438
OLS	−0.0072	0.3583	0.1756
TSLS	−1.4564	−0.5059	−0.9812
FP	0.8144	0.8261	0.8203
URF	0.7646	0.7292	0.7469

E.2. Prediction period

	y_1	y_2	Y
	0.8	0.8	0.8
	0.7887	0.7936	0.7912
	−0.1698	−0.4968	−0.3333
	−1.0915	−3.2371	−2.1643
	0.6941	0.6655	0.6798
	0.6480	0.6413	0.6447

E.3. Sample period (adj. for D.F.)

OLS	−0.4389	0.0833	−0.1777
TSLS	−2.5091	−1.1513	−1.8302
FP	0.7349	0.7516	0.7433

Table 10.2.35. Model 5m

A. MODEL DESIGN

A.1. Structural equations

$$\beta = \begin{bmatrix} 0 & 1 \\ -1 & 0 \end{bmatrix} \qquad \Gamma = \begin{bmatrix} k_1 & k_1 & 0 & 0 \\ 0 & 0 & k_1 & k_1 \end{bmatrix} \qquad \Omega = \begin{bmatrix} k_2 & k_2 & k_2 & k_2 \\ -k_2 & -k_2 & k_2 & k_2 \end{bmatrix}$$

with $k_1 = 0.4472$ and $k_2 = 0.2236$

A.2. Variance of endogenous and residual variables in the population and in the sample

$\sigma^2(y_i) = 1.0$

$\sigma^2(\delta_i) = 1.6 \qquad i = 1, 2$

$\sigma^2(\epsilon_i) = 0.8$

Generated in sample period:

$\begin{cases} V(y_1) = 1.006 & V(y_2) = 1.004 \\ V(\delta_1) = 1.647 & V(\delta_2) = 1.545 \\ V(\epsilon_1) = 0.8034 & V(\epsilon_2) = 0.7928 \end{cases}$

A.3. Correlation among residuals and exogenous variables

None

A.4. Sample size and special design features

1. 40 observations in both the sample and prediction periods.
2. This model is one in a series on varying size of residuals in two-relation models (Models 5m, 5n, 5p(=1b), 5q, 5r, 5s(=1d)).

B. STRUCTURAL COEFFICIENTS

B.1. True coefficient versus average estimate from 100 samples

	β_{12}	γ_{11}	γ_{12}	β_{21}	γ_{23}	γ_{24}
True	1	0.4472	0.4472	−1	0.4472	0.4472
OLS	0.0909	0.2449	0.2384	−0.1441	0.2811	0.2603
TSLS	1.1077	0.4722	0.4927	−0.9627	0.4889	0.4446
FP	1.0589	0.4347	0.4216	−0.9439	0.4499	0.4018

B.2. Observed standard deviation of 100 samples around observed mean

OLS	0.1753	0.1424	0.1564	0.1750	0.1591	0.1720
TSLS	1.0994	0.3903	0.4037	0.7454	0.3341	0.3191
FP	1.0863	0.3624	0.3209	0.7145	0.2916	0.3138

B.3. Average standard deviation from large-sample formula

OLS	0.1641	0.1607	0.1622	0.1612	0.1573	0.1584
TSLS	1.1719	0.3925	0.4322	0.8164	0.3238	0.3109
FP	1.1143	0.3681	0.3413	0.7988	0.2948	0.2818

B.4. Observed standard deviation around true value of the coefficient

OLS	0.9258	0.2474	0.2609	0.8736	0.2300	0.2540
TSLS	1.1047	0.3911	0.4063	0.7463	0.3367	0.3191
FP	1.0879	0.3626	0.3219	0.7167	0.2916	0.3171

B.5. Number of iterations for fix-point (FP) method

Average = 18.14;   Smallest = 5;   Largest = 200;   No convergence in 5 samples

C. REDUCED FORM COEFFICIENTS (4 out of 8 coefficients)

C.1. True coefficient versus average estimate from 100 samples

	ω_{11}	ω_{13}	ω_{21}	ω_{23}
True	0.2236	0.2236	−0.2236	0.2236
OLS	0.2466	0.2269	−0.0355	0.2837
TSLS	0.2390	0.2137	−0.1964	0.2665
FP	0.2306	0.2015	−0.1896	0.2531
URF	0.2252	0.2318	−0.2190	0.2418

C.2. Observed standard deviation of 100 samples around observed mean

	ω_{11}	ω_{13}	ω_{21}	ω_{23}
OLS	0.1426	0.0522	0.0533	0.1586
TSLS	0.1314	0.1324	0.1487	0.1612
FP	0.1298	0.1278	0.1358	0.1448
URF	0.1364	0.1550	0.1632	0.1461

C.3. Average standard deviation from large-sample formula

	ω_{11}	ω_{13}	ω_{21}	ω_{23}
URF	0.1504	0.1495	0.1488	0.1481

C.4. Observed standard deviation around true value of the coefficient

	ω_{11}	ω_{13}	ω_{21}	ω_{23}
OLS	0.1444	0.0523	0.1955	0.1696
TSLS	0.1323	0.1328	0.1512	0.1668
FP	0.1300	0.1297	0.1400	0.1478
URF	0.1364	0.1552	0.1633	0.1472

D. EIGENVALUES FOR PRODUCT MOMENT MATRIX OF EXPLANATORY VARIABLES (REID SPECIFICATION)

	Smallest in 100 samples	Average for 100 samples		
		λ_1	λ_2	λ_3

D.1. Equation 1

	Smallest in 100 samples	λ_1	λ_2	λ_3
OLS	0.1265	0.1972	0.3145	0.4882
TSLS	0.0008	0.0538	0.3711	0.5752
FP	0.0009	0.0582	0.3723	0.5696

D.2. Equation 2

	Smallest in 100 samples	λ_1	λ_2	λ_3
OLS	0.1110	0.1959	0.3226	0.4815
TSLS	0.0023	0.0492	0.3867	0.5641
FP	0.0033	0.0521	0.3855	0.5624

D.3. Unrestricted reduced form

	Smallest in 100 samples	λ_1	λ_2	λ_3
	0.0884	0.1497	0.2090	0.2737

E. AVERAGE R^2 FROM 100 SAMPLES

E.1. Sample period

	y_1	y_2	Y
True	0.2	0.2	0.2
Generated (average)	0.1943	0.2018	0.1981
OLS	0.1518	0.1726	0.1622
TSLS	0.2362	0.2528	0.2445
FP	0.2369	0.2500	0.2435
URF	0.1915	0.2051	0.1983

E.2. Prediction period

	y_1	y_2	Y
True	0.2	0.2	0.2
Generated (average)	0.2094	0.1669	0.1882
OLS	0.0883	0.0202	0.0543
TSLS	0.1336	0.0674	0.1005
FP	0.1321	0.0805	0.1063
URF	0.1154	0.0681	0.0918

E.3. Sample period (adj. for D.F.)

	y_1	y_2	Y
OLS	0.0830	0.1055	0.0943
TSLS	0.1743	0.1922	0.1832
FP	0.1750	0.1892	0.1822

Table 10.2.36. Model 5n

A. MODEL DESIGN

A.1. Structural equations

$$\beta = \begin{bmatrix} 0 & 1 \\ -1 & 0 \end{bmatrix} \qquad \Gamma = \begin{bmatrix} k_1 & k_1 & 0 & 0 \\ 0 & 0 & k_1 & k_1 \end{bmatrix} \qquad \Omega = \begin{bmatrix} k_2 & k_2 & k_2 & k_2 \\ -k_2 & -k_2 & k_2 & k_2 \end{bmatrix}$$

with $k_1 = 0.7071$ and $k_2 = 0.3536$

A.2. Variance of endogenous and residual variables in the population and in the sample

$\sigma^2(y_i) = 1.0$

$\sigma^2(\delta_i) = 1.0 \qquad i = 1, 2$

$\sigma^2(\epsilon_i) = 0.5$

Generated in sample period:

$\begin{cases} V(y_1) = 1.001 & V(y_2) = 1.025 \\ V(\delta_1) = 0.9984 & V(\delta_2) = 1.014 \\ V(\epsilon_1) = 0.4961 & V(\epsilon_2) = 0.5101 \end{cases}$

A.3. Correlation among residuals and exogenous variables

None

A.4. Sample size and special design features

1. 40 observations in both the sample and prediction periods.
2. This model is one in a series on varying size of residuals in two-relation models (Models 5m, 5n, 5p(=1b), 5q, 5r, 5s(=1d)).

B. STRUCTURAL COEFFICIENTS

B.1. True coefficient versus average estimate from 100 samples

	β_{12}	γ_{11}	γ_{12}	β_{21}	γ_{23}	γ_{24}
True	1	0.7071	0.7071	−1	0.7071	0.7071
OLS	0.3303	0.4777	0.4581	−0.3452	0.4832	0.4749
TSLS	0.9547	0.6926	0.6899	−1.0014	0.7171	0.6883
FP	0.9614	0.6950	0.6586	−1.0090	0.6902	0.6688

B.2. Observed standard deviation of 100 samples around observed mean

OLS	0.1675	0.1448	0.1566	0.1431	0.1441	0.1507
TSLS	0.3920	0.1914	0.2351	0.3550	0.2223	0.2054
FP	0.4022	0.2041	0.2558	0.3628	0.2536	0.2371

B.3. Average standard deviation from large-sample formula

OLS	0.1534	0.1422	0.1445	0.1567	0.1493	0.1458
TSLS	0.3397	0.2033	0.2106	0.3481	0.2161	0.2069
FP	0.3480	0.2058	0.2065	0.3584	0.2148	0.2080

B.4. Observed standard deviation around true value of the coefficient

OLS	0.6903	0.2713	0.2942	0.6703	0.2663	0.2768
TSLS	0.3946	0.1919	0.2357	0.3550	0.2225	0.2063
FP	0.4040	0.2045	0.2604	0.3629	0.2542	0.2402

B.5. Number of iterations for fix-point (FP) method

Average = 8.37;   Smallest = 5;   Largest = 19;   No convergence in 0 samples

C. REDUCED FORM COEFFICIENTS (4 out 0f 8 coefficients)

C.1. True coefficient versus average estimate from 100 samples

	ω_{11}	ω_{13}	ω_{21}	ω_{23}
True	0.3536	0.3536	−0.3536	0.3536
OLS	0.4304	0.1437	−0.1467	0.4362
TSLS	0.3659	0.3424	−0.3466	0.3742
FP	0.3662	0.3332	−0.3480	0.3577
URF	0.3668	0.3589	−0.3469	0.3562

C.2. Observed standard deviation of 100 samples around observed mean

OLS	0.1241	0.0790	0.0730	0.1250
TSLS	0.0998	0.1233	0.1047	0.0923
FP	0.1051	0.1296	0.1122	0.1208
URF	0.1020	0.1328	0.1246	0.1204

C.3. Average standard deviation from large-sample formula

URF	0.1160	0.1193	0.1169	0.1206

C.4. Observed standard deviation around true value of the coefficient

OLS	0.1459	0.2243	0.2194	0.1498
TSLS	0.1006	0.1238	0.1049	0.0946
FP	0.1059	0.1312	0.1123	0.1209
URF	0.1029	0.1329	0.1248	0.1204

D. EIGENVALUES FOR PRODUCT MOMENT MATRIX OF EXPLANATORY VARIABLES (REID SPECIFICATION)

	Smallest in 100 samples	Average for 100 samples		
		λ_1	λ_2	λ_3
D.1. Equation 1				
OLS	0.0861	0.1508	0.3127	0.5365
TSLS	0.0209	0.0747	0.3524	0.5729
FP	0.0231	0.0772	0.3549	0.5678
D.2. Equation 2				
OLS	0.0739	0.1556	0.3096	0.5348
TSLS	0.0161	0.0777	0.3474	0.5750
FP	0.0168	0.0794	0.3468	0.5738
D.3. Unrestricted reduced form	0.0972	0.1491	0.2095	0.2759

E. AVERAGE R^2 FROM 100 SAMPLES

E.1. Sample period   E.2. Prediction period

	y_1	y_2	Y	y_1	y_2	Y
True	0.5	0.5	0.5	0.5	0.5	0.5
Generated (average)	0.4859	0.4918	0.4889	0.4898	0.4689	0.4794
OLS	0.4249	0.4243	0.4246	0.3519	0.3283	0.3401
TSLS	0.5261	0.5289	0.5275	0.4386	0.4157	0.4272
FP	0.5173	0.5191	0.5182	0.4273	0.4055	0.4164
URF	0.4892	0.4954	0.4923	0.4273	0.4042	0.4158

E.3. Sample period (adj. for D.F.)

	y_1	y_2	Y
OLS	0.3783	0.3776	0.3779
TSLS	0.4877	0.4907	0.4892
FP	0.4782	0.4801	0.4791

Table 10.2.37. Model 5q

A. MODEL DESIGN

A.1. Structural equations

$$\beta = \begin{bmatrix} 0 & 1 \\ -1 & 0 \end{bmatrix} \qquad \Gamma = \begin{bmatrix} k_1 & k_1 & 0 & 0 \\ 0 & 0 & k_1 & k_1 \end{bmatrix} \qquad \Omega = \begin{bmatrix} k_2 & k_2 & k_2 & k_2 \\ -k_2 & -k_2 & k_2 & k_2 \end{bmatrix}$$

with $k_1 = 0.9747$ and $k_2 = 0.4873$

A.2. Variance of endogenous and residual variables in the population and in the sample

$\sigma^2(y_i) = 1.0$

$\sigma^2(\delta_i) = 0.1 \qquad i = 1, 2$

$\sigma^2(\epsilon_i) = 0.05$

Generated in sample period:

$\begin{cases} V(y_1) = 1.025 & V(y_2) = 1.023 \\ V(\delta_1) = 0.096 & V(\delta_2) = 0.102 \\ V(\epsilon_1) = 0.050 & V(\epsilon_2) = 0.049 \end{cases}$

A.3. Correlation among residuals and exogenous variables

None

A.4. Sample size and special design features

1. 40 observations in both the sample and prediction periods.
2. This model is one in a series on varying size of residuals in two-relation models (Models 5m, 5n, 5p(=1b), 5q, 5r, 5s(=1d)).

B. STRUCTURAL COEFFICIENTS

B.1. True coefficient versus average estimate from 100 samples

	β_{12}	γ_{11}	γ_{12}	β_{21}	γ_{23}	γ_{24}
True	1	0.9747	0.9747	−1	0.9747	0.9747
OLS	0.9046	0.9323	0.9250	−0.8887	0.9190	0.9255
TSLS	0.9956	0.9767	0.9684	−0.9765	0.9629	0.9671
FP	0.9968	0.9801	0.9634	−0.9751	0.9666	0.9580

B.2. Observed standard deviation of 100 samples around observed mean

	β_{12}	γ_{11}	γ_{12}	β_{21}	γ_{23}	γ_{24}
OLS	0.0742	0.0638	0.0537	0.0766	0.0619	0.0625
TSLS	0.0774	0.0619	0.0554	0.0789	0.0631	0.0647
FP	0.0778	0.0715	0.0702	0.0794	0.0725	0.0711

B.3. Average standard deviation from large-sample formula

	β_{12}	γ_{11}	γ_{12}	β_{21}	γ_{23}	γ_{24}
OLS	0.0687	0.0598	0.0591	0.0677	0.0602	0.0612
TSLS	0.0741	0.0624	0.0616	0.0727	0.0626	0.0635
FP	0.0753	0.0636·	0.0622	0.0736	0.0636	0.0640

B.4. Observed standard deviation around true value of the coefficient

	β_{12}	γ_{11}	γ_{12}	β_{21}	γ_{23}	γ_{24}
OLS	0.1209	0.0766	0.0732	0.1351	0.0833	0.0795
TSLS	0.0775	0.0619	0.0558	0.0823	0.0642	0.0651
FP	0.0779	0.0717	0.0711	0.0832	0.0730	0.0730

B.5. Number of iterations for fix-point (FP) method

Average = 7.89;   Smallest = 5;   Largest = 14;   No convergence in 0 samples

C. REDUCED FORM COEFFICIENTS (4 out of 8 coefficients)

C.1. True coefficient versus average estimate from 100 sa.nples

	ω_{11}	ω_{13}	ω_{21}	ω_{23}
True	0.4873	0.4873	−0.4873	0.4873
OLS	0.5180	0.4602	−0.4583	0.5104
TSLS	0.4964	0.4855	−0.4828	0.4890
FP	0.4984	0.4879	−0.4839	0.4908
URF	0.4972	0.4835	−0.4813	0.4920

C.2. Observed standard deviation of 100 samples around observed mean

OLS	0.0389	0.0323	0.0306	0.0352
TSLS	0.0367	0.0331	0.0302	0.0315
FP	0.0428	0.0364	0.0354	0.0349
URF	0.0439	0.0392	0.0394	0.0354

C.3. Average standard deviation from large-sample formula

URF	0.0371	0.0365	0.0373	0.0368

C.4. Observed standard deviation around true value of the coefficient

OLS	0.0496	0.0422	0.0422	0.0421
TSLS	0.0378	0.0331	.0.0305	0.0315
FP	0.0442	0.0364	0.0356	0.0351
URF	0.0450	0.0394	0.0399	0.0357

D. EIGENVALUES FOR PRODUCT MOMENT MATRIX OF EXPLANATORY VARIABLES (REID SPECIFICATION)

	Smallest in 100 samples	Average for 100 samples		
		λ_1	λ_2	λ_3

D.1. Equation 1

	Smallest in 100 samples	λ_1	λ_2	λ_3
OLS	0.0498	0.0973	0.3057	0.5970
TSLS	0.0440	0.0910	0.3096	0.5994
FP	0.0447	0.0910	0.3104	0.5986

D.2. Equation 2

OLS	0.0350	0.1035	0.3127	0.5838
TSLS	0.0277	0.0977	0.3163	0.5860
FP	0.0278	0.0983	0.3154	0.5863

D.3. Unrestricted reduced form

D.3. Unrestricted reduced form	0.0907	0.1472	0.2092	0.2766

E. AVERAGE R^2 FROM 100 SAMPLES

E.1. Sample period　　　　　　　　　　　　　　　E.2. Prediction period

	y_1	y_2	Y	y_1	y_2	Y
True	0.95	0.95	0.95	0.95	0.95	0.95
Generated (average)	0.9496	0.9493	0.9495	0.9470	0.9428	0.9449
OLS	0.9513	0.9506	0.9510	0.9388	0.9352	0.9370
TSLS	0.9536	0.9529	0.9533	0.9419	0.9392	0.9406
FP	0.9523	0.9514	0.9519	0.9401	0.9373	0.9387
URF	0.9501	0.9493	0.9497	0.9407	0.9374	0.9391

E.3. Sample period (adj. for D.F.)

	y_1	y_2	Y
OLS	0.9474	0.9466	0.9470
TSLS	0.9498	0.9491	0.9495
FP	0.9484	0.9475	0.9480

Table 10.2.38. Model 5r

A. MODEL DESIGN

A.1. Structural equations

$$\beta = \begin{bmatrix} 0 & 0.5 \\ -0.9 & 0 \end{bmatrix} \quad \Gamma = \begin{bmatrix} 0.4443 & 0.4443 & 0 & 0 \\ 0 & 0 & 0.2222 & 0.2222 \end{bmatrix} \quad \Omega = \begin{bmatrix} 0.3066 & 0.3066 & 0.0773 & 0.0773 \\ -0.2760 & -0.2760 & 0.1545 & 0.1545 \end{bmatrix}$$

A.2. Variance of endogenous variables and residuals in the population and in the sample

$\sigma^2(y_i) = 1.0, i = 1, 2$
$\sigma^2(\delta_i) = 1.58, 0.40$
$\sigma^2(\epsilon_i) = 0.80, i = 1, 2$

Generated in sample period:
$V(y_1) = 1.008 \quad V(y_2) = 1.007$
$V(\delta_1) = 1.613 \quad V(\delta_2) = 0.3873$
$V(\epsilon_1) = 0.8148 \quad V(\epsilon_2) = 0.8025$

A.3. Correlation among residuals and exogenous variables

None

A.4. Sample size and special design features

1. 40 observations in both the sample and prediction periods.
2. This model is one in a series on varying size of residuals in two-relation models (Models 5m, 5n, 5p(=1b), 5q, 5r, 5s(=1d)).
3. This model was designed to be compared with model 5m to see if the relative performance of FP and TSLS as R^2 decreases depends on β.

B. STRUCTURAL COEFFICIENTS

B.1. True coefficient versus average estimate from 100 samples

	β_{12}	γ_{11}	γ_{12}	β_{21}	γ_{23}	γ_{24}
True	0.5	0.4443	0.4443	−0.9	0.2222	0.2222
OLS	−0.6849	0.1110	0.1033	−0.7709	0.1950	0.2248
TSLS	−0.1613	0.2631	0.2380	−0.9296	0.2144	0.2403
FP	0.0247	0.3054	0.2970	−0.9220	0.1515	0.1698

B.2. Observed standard deviation in 100 samples around observed mean

OLS	0.1148	0.1204	0.1259	0.1023	0.1044	0.0992
TSLS	1.4856	0.4190	0.4812	0.3136	0.1255	0.1171
FP	0.9750	0.3054	0.3633	0.3047	0.1454	0.1329

B.3. Average standard deviation from large-sample formula

OLS	0.1174	0.1133	0.1139	0.1003	0.1024	0.1005
TSLS	1.4657	0.4461	0.4808	0.2863	0.1254	0.1208
FP	1.1387	0.3476	0.3992	0.2982	0.1220	0.1183

B.4. Observed standard deviation around true value of the coefficient

OLS	1.1904	0.3544	0.3635	0.1647	0.1079	0.0992
TSLS	1.6261	0.4565	0.5236	0.3150	0.1257	0.1185
FP	1.0847	0.3355	0.3920	0.3055	0.1617	0.1429

B.5. Number of iterations for fix-point (FP) method

Average = 12.31;   Smallest = 5;   Largest = 200;   No convergence in 2 samples

C. REDUCED FORM (4 out of 8 coefficients)

C.1. True coefficient versus average estimate from 100 samples

	ω_{11}	ω_{13}	ω_{21}	ω_{23}
True	0.3066	0.0773	−0.2760	0.1545
OLS	0.2123	−0.3028	−0.1570	0.4338
TSLS	0.3127	0.0296	−0.2807	0.1736
FP	0.3008	0.0204	−0.2659	0.1303
URF	0.3084	0.0738	−0.2897	0.1371

C.2. Observed standard deviation of 100 samples around the observed mean

OLS	0.2487	0.1995	0.1984	0.2523
TSLS	0.1753	0.2064	0.1620	0.2246
FP	0.1576	0.1435	0.1570	0.1975
URF	0.1562	0.1664	0.1546	0.1712

C.3. Average standard deviation from large-sample formula

URF	0.1500	0.1519	0.1492	0.1511

C.4. Observed standard deviation around true value of the coefficient

OLS	0.2660	0.4293	0.2314	0.3764
TSLS	0.1754	0.2118	0.1621	0.2254
FP	0.1577	0.1544	0.1573	0.1990
URF	0.1562	0.1664	0.1552	0.1721

D. EIGENVALUES FOR PRODUCT MOMENT MATRIX OF EXPLANATORY VARIABLES (REID SPECIFICATION)

	Smallest in 100 samples	Average for 100 samples		
		λ_1	λ_2	λ_3

D.1. Equation 1

OLS	0.1064	0.1781	0.3117	0.5101
TSLS	0.00038	0.0302	0.3771	0.5927
FP	0.00052	0.0307	0.3759	0.5934

D.2. Equation 2

OLS	0.0157	0.2274	0.3233	0.4493
TSLS	0.0047	0.0875	0.3737	0.5388
FP	0.0031	0.0898	0.3727	0.5375

D.3. Unrestricted reduced form   0.1064

	0.1511	0.2092	0.2780

E. AVERAGE R^2 FROM 100 SAMPLES

E.1. Sample period

	y_1	y_2	Y
True	0.2	0.2	0.2
Generated (average)	0.1842	0.1947	0.1895
OLS	−0.1900	−0.0986	−0.1443
TSLS	−4.4010	−4.0153	−4.2075
FP	0.1364	0.1365	0.1365
URF	0.1909	0.1979	0.1944

E.2. Prediction period

	y_1	y_2	Y
True	0.2	0.2	0.2
Generated (average)	0.1772	0.1901	0.1837
OLS	−0.3808	−0.2250	−0.3029
TSLS	−0.3731	−2.9374	−1.6553
FP	0.0306	0.0410	0.0358
URF	0.0693	0.1061	0.0877

E.3. Sample period (adj. for D.F.)

	y_1	y_2	Y
OLS	−0.2865	−0.1877	−0.2371
TSLS	−4.8390	−4.4223	−4.6306
FP	0.0664	0.0665	0.0665

Table 10.2.39. Model 6a

A. MODEL DESIGN

A.1. Structural equations

$$B = \begin{bmatrix} 0 & 1 \\ -1 & 0 \end{bmatrix} \qquad \Gamma = \begin{bmatrix} k_1 & k_1 & 0 & 0 \\ 0 & 0 & k_1 & k_1 \end{bmatrix} \qquad \Omega = \begin{bmatrix} k_2 & k_2 & k_2 & k_2 \\ -k_2 & -k_2 & k_2 & k_2 \end{bmatrix}$$

with $k_1 = 0.8944$ and $k_2 = 0.4472$

A.2. Variance of endogenous and residual variables in the population and in the sample

$$\sigma^2(y_i) = 1.0$$
$$\sigma^2(\delta_i) = 0.4 \qquad i = 1, 2$$
$$\sigma^2(\epsilon_i) = 0.2$$

Generated $\begin{cases} V(y_1) = 0.998 & V(y_2) = 1.005 \\ V(\delta_1) = 0.391 & V(\delta_2) = 0.390 \\ V(\epsilon_1) = 0.193 & V(\epsilon_2) = 0.197 \end{cases}$
in sample
period:

A.3. Correlation among residuals and exogenous variables

	x_1	x_2	x_3	x_4		x_1	x_2	x_3	x_4
ϵ_1	0	0	0.141	−0.141	δ_1	−0.1	0.1	0.1	−0.1
ϵ_2	0.141	−0.141	0	0	δ_2	0.1	−0.1	0.1	−0.1

A.4. Sample size and special design features

1. 40 observations in both the sample and prediction periods.
2. This model is one in a series on number of relations in a GEID specification with relatively small correlations (Models 6a-6c).

B. STRUCTURAL COEFFICIENTS

B.1. True coefficient versus average estimate from 100 samples

	β_{12}	γ_{11}	γ_{12}	β_{21}	γ_{23}	γ_{24}
True	1	0.8944	0.8944	−1	0.8944	0.8944
OLS	0.6872	0.7083	0.8009	−0.6674	0.7851	0.7186
TSLS	1.0075	0.8338	0.9647	−0.9875	0.9464	0.8440
FP	1.0065	0.8925	0.9000	−0.9939	0.8841	0.8996

B.2. Observed standard deviation of 100 samples around observed mean

	β_{12}	γ_{11}	γ_{12}	β_{21}	γ_{23}	γ_{24}
OLS	0.1045	0.1127	0.0971	0.1044	0.1061	0.0989
TSLS	0.1686	0.1372	0.1366	0.1409	0.1304	0.1137
FP	0.1629	0.1511	0.1421	0.1500	0.1470	0.1418

B.3. Average standard deviation from large-sample formula

	β_{12}	γ_{11}	γ_{12}	β_{21}	γ_{23}	γ_{24}
OLS	0.1218	0.1056	0.1129	0.1231	0.1115	0.1064
TSLS	0.1634	0.1216	0.1333	0.1651	0.1315	0.1229
FP	0.1671	0.1303	0.1292	0.1704	0.1281	0.1321

B.4. Observed standard deviation around true value of the coefficient

	β_{12}	γ_{11}	γ_{12}	β_{21}	γ_{23}	γ_{24}
OLS	0.3298	0.2176	0.1348	0.3486	0.1523	0.2017
TSLS	0.1688	0.1500	0.1536	0.1415	0.1404	0.1244
FP	0.1630	0.1511	0.1422	0.1501	0.1474	0.1419

B.5. Number of iterations for fix-point (FP) method

Average = 8.39;   Smallest = 4;   Largest = 16;   No convergence in 0 samples

C. REDUCED FORM COEFFICIENTS

C.1. True coefficient versus average estimate from 100 samples

	ω_{11}	ω_{12}	ω_{13}	ω_{14}	ω_{21}	ω_{22}	ω_{23}	ω_{24}
True	0.4472	0.4472	0.4472	0.4472	−0.4472	−0.4472	0.4472	0.4472
OLS	0.4866	0.5502	0.3688	0.3367	−0.3230	−0.3659	0.5392	0.4940
TSLS	0.4199	0.4854	0.4749	0.4231	−0.4099	−0.4754	0.4769	0.4265
FP	0.4480	0.4522	0.4428	0.4486	−0.4405	−0.4449	0.4445	0.4527
URF	0.4501	0.4509	0.5091	0.3949	−0.3803	−0.5111	0.4477	0.4515

C.2. Observed standard deviation of 100 samples around observed mean

OLS	0.0738	0.0618	0.0633	0.0535	0.0623	0.0635	0.0662	0.0675
TSLS	0.0643	0.0582	0.0679	0.0563	0.0589	0.0648	0.0625	0.0643
FP	0.0698	0.0682	0.0782	0.0627	0.0689	0.0710	0.0717	0.0728
URF	0.0728	0.0713	0.0771	0.0716	0.0734	0.0801	0.0759	0.0740

C.3. Average standard deviation from large-sample formula

URF	0.0726	0.0725	0.0718	0.0737	0.0730	0.0728	0.0716	0.0737

C.4. Observed standard deviation around true value of the coefficient

OLS	0.0837	0.1201	0.1008	0.1228	0.1389	0.1032	0.1133	0.0822
TSLS	0.0699	0.0696	0.0733	0.0612	0.0697	0.0707	0.0692	0.0675
FP	0.0698	0.0684	0.0783	0.0627	0.0692	0.0710	0.0718	0.0730
URF	0.0729	0.0714	0.0989	0.0887	0.0993	0.1025	0.0759	0.0741

D. EIGENVALUES FOR PRODUCT MOMENT MATRIX OF EXPLANATORY VARIABLES (GEID SPECIFICATION)

	Smallest in 100 samples	Average for 100 samples		
		λ_1	λ_2	λ_3
D.1. Equation 1				
OLS	0.0501	0.1141	0.3172	0.5687
TSLS	0.0282	0.0899	0.3309	0.5791
FP	0.0297	0.0911	0.3339	0.5751
D.2. Equation 2				
OLS	0.0593	0.1112	0.3042	0.5847
TSLS	0.0360	0.0862	0.3176	0.5962
FP	0.0340	0.0875	0.3186	0.5939
D.3. Unrestricted reduced form	0.0849	0.1469	0.2055	0.2762

E. AVERAGE R^2 FROM 100 SAMPLES

	E.1. Sample period			E.2. Prediction period		
	y_1	y_2	Y	y_1	y_2	Y
True	0.8	0.8	0.8	0.8	0.8	0.8
Generated (average)	0.7990	0.7948	0.7969	0.7914	0.7975	0.7945
OLS	0.7842	0.7836	0.7839	0.7433	0.7593	0.7513
TSLS	0.8149	0.8151	0.8150	0.7762	0.7873	0.7818
FP	0.8075	0.8066	0.8071	0.7689	0.7815	0.7752
URF	0.8047	0.8040	0.8044	0.7760	0.7835	0.7798

E.3. Sample period (adj. for D.F.)

	y_1	y_2	Y
OLS	0.7667	0.7661	0.7664
TSLS	0.7999	0.8001	0.8000
FP	0.7919	0.7909	0.7914

Table 10.2.40. Model 6b

A. MODEL DESIGN

A.1. Structural equations

$$\beta = \begin{bmatrix} 0 & +1 & 0 \\ 0 & 0 & -1 \\ +1 & 0 & 0 \end{bmatrix} \quad \Gamma = \begin{bmatrix} k_1 & k_1 & 0 & 0 & 0 & 0 \\ 0 & 0 & k_1 & k_1 & 0 & 0 \\ 0 & 0 & 0 & 0 & k_1 & k_1 \end{bmatrix} \quad \Omega = \begin{bmatrix} k_2 & k_2 & k_2 & k_2 & -k_2 & -k_2 \\ -k_2 & -k_2 & k_2 & k_2 & -k_2 & -k_2 \\ k_2 & k_2 & k_2 & k_2 & k_2 & k_2 \end{bmatrix}$$

with $k_1 = 0.7303$ and $k_2 = 0.3651$

A.2. Variance of endogenous and residual variables in the population and in the sample

$\sigma^2(y_i) = 1.0$

$\sigma^2(\delta_i) = 0.267 \qquad i = 1, 2, 3$

$\sigma^2(\epsilon_i) = 0.2$

Generated in sample period:
$\begin{cases} V(y_1) = 0.986 & V(y_2) = 1.004 \\ V(\delta_1) = 0.275 & V(\delta_2) = 0.262 \\ V(\epsilon_1) = 0.196 & V(\epsilon_2) = 0.204 \end{cases}$

A.3. Correlation among residuals and exogenous variables

	x_1,x_2	x_3,x_4	x_5,x_6	y_1^*	y_2^*	y_3^*
ϵ_1	0	0.116	0.116	0	0	0.189
ϵ_2	0.116	0	−0.116	0.189	0	0
ϵ_3	0.116	−0.116	0	0	−0.189	0

	x_1,x_2	x_3,x_4	x_5,x_6
δ_1	−0.1	0.1	0.2
δ_2	0.2	−0.1	−0.1
δ_3	0.1	−0.2	−0.1

A.4. Sample size and special design features

1. 40 observations in both the sample and prediction periods.
2. This model is one in a series on number of relations in a GEID specification with relatively small correlations (Models 6a-6c).

B. STRUCTURAL COEFFICIENTS

B.1. True coefficient versus average estimate from 100 samples

	β_{12}	γ_{11}	γ_{12}	β_{23}	γ_{23}	γ_{24}	β_{31}	γ_{35}	γ_{36}
True	1	0.7303	0.7303	−1	0.7303	0.7303	1	0.7303	0.7303
OLS	0.7910	0.6099	0.6115	−0.8091	0.6117	0.6155	0.8042	0.6159	0.6217
TSLS	0.9173	0.6502	0.6533	−0.9294	0.6514	0.6539	0.9254	0.6535	0.6579
FP	0.9968	0.7144	0.7136	−1.0159	0.7181	0.7143	0.9996	0.7103	0.7309

B.2. Observed standard deviation of 100 samples around observed mean

OLS	0.0930	0.0778	0.0962	0.0830	0.0917	0.0724	0.0802	0.0806	0.0842
TSLS	0.1174	0.0792	0.0969	0.1002	0.0985	0.0716	0.0982	0.0918	0.0908
FP	0.1521	0.1449	0.1658	0.1379	0.1593	0.1562	0.1244	0.1308	0.1381

B.3. Average standard deviation from large-sample formula

OLS	0.0889	0.0833	0.0857	0.0875	0.0833	0.0836	0.0891	0.0842	0.0823
TSLS	0.1050	0.0875	0.0904	0.1029	0.0876	0.0878	0.1049	0.0883	0.0863
FP	0.1245	0.0990	0.1017	0.1246	0.1006	0.1001	0.1236	0.0984	0.0964

B.4. Observed standard deviation around true value of the coefficient

OLS	0.2288	0.1434	0.1528	0.2082	0.1499	0.1357	0.2116	0.1400	0.1374
TSLS	0.1436	0.1126	0.1238	0.1226	0.1262	0.1047	0.1233	0.1197	0.1161
FP	0.1521	0.1458	0.1666	0.1388	0.1598	0.1570	0.1244	0.1323	0.1381

B.5. Number of iterations for fix-point (FP) method

Average = 31.35;   Smallest = 17;   Largest = 200;   No convergence in 1 sample

C. REDUCED FORM COEFFICIENTS (8 out of 18 coefficients)

C.1. True coefficient versus average estimate from 100 samples

	ω_{11}	ω_{12}	ω_{13}	ω_{14}	ω_{15}	ω_{16}	ω_{21}	ω_{22}
True	0.3651	0.3651	0.3651	0.3651	−0.3651	−0.3651	−0.3651	−0.3651
OLS	0.4041	0.4046	0.3204	0.3220	−0.2588	−0.2614	−0.2612	−0.2620
TSLS	0.3663	0.3671	0.3347	0.3361	−0.3087	−0.3114	−0.3111	−0.3127
FP	0.3592	0.3569	0.3569	0.3539	−0.3533	−0.3630	−0.3574	−0.3562
URF	0.3609	0.3529	0.4211	0.4119	−0.3245	−0.3178	−0.3192	−0.3231

C.2. Observed standard deviation of 100 samples around observed mean

OLS	0.0513	0.0610	0.0579	0.0503	0.0400	0.0418	0.0403	0.0481
TSLS	0.0521	0.0557	0.0595	0.0521	0.0456	0.0477	0.0420	0.0511
FP	0.0793	0.0801	0.0870	0.0814	0.0686	0.0687	0.0719	0.0832
URF	0.0810	0.0837	0.0780	0.0754	0.0719	0.0654	0.0739	0.0745

C.3. Average standard deviation from large-sample formula

URF	0.0734	0.0746	0.0741	0.0736	0.0737	0.0721	0.0745	0.0758

C.4. Observed standard deviation around true value of the coefficient

OLS	0.0644	0.0727	0.0731	0.0662	0.1136	0.1118	0.1114	0.1138
TSLS	0.0521	0.0557	0.0668	0.0596	0.0725	0.0718	0.0684	0.0732
FP	0.0795	0.0805	0.0874	0.0822	0.0696	0.0687	0.0723	0.0837
URF	0.0811	0.0846	0.0960	0.0887	0.0826	0.0807	0.0870	0.0855

D. EIGENVALUES FOR PRODUCT MOMENT MATRIX OF EXPLANATORY VARIABLES (GEID SPECIFICATION)

	Smallest in 100 samples	Average for 100 samples λ_1	λ_2	λ_3
D.1. Equation 1				
OLS	0.0764	0.1692	0.3135	0.5173
TSLS	0.0389	0.1497	0.3250	0.5253
FP	0.0611	0.1283	0.3309	0.5408
D.2. Equation 2				
OLS	0.0899	0.1657	0.3098	0.5245
TSLS	0.0618	0.1455	0.3217	0.5328
FP	0.0294	0.1261	0.3247	0.5492
D.3. Equation 3				
OLS	0.0913	0.1654	0.3241	0.5105
TSLS	0.0691	0.1460	0.3340	0.5199
FP	0.0559	0.1253	0.3410	0.5337

D.4. Unrestricted reduced form   N.a.

E. AVERAGE R^2 FROM 100 SAMPLES

E.1. Sample period	y_1	y_2	y_3	Y	E.2. Prediction period y_1	y_2	y_3	Y
True	0.8	0.8	0.8	0.8	0.8	0.8	0.8	0.8
Generated (average)	0.7878	0.7881	0.7923	0.7894	0.7962	0.7898	0.8084	0.7981
OLS	0.7853	0.7868	0.7874	0.7865	0.7608	0.7590	0.7732	0.7643
TSLS	0.8017	0.8023	0.8036	0.8025	0.7730	0.7726	0.7904	0.7787
FP	0.7920	0.7954	0.7908	0.7927	0.7527	0.7543	0.7732	0.7601
URF	0.8004	0.8013	0.8017	0.8011	0.7684	0.7698	0.7802	0.7728

E.3. Sample period (adj. for D.F.)

	y_1	y_2	y_3	Y
OLS	0.7679	0.7695	0.7702	0.7692
TSLS	0.7856	0.7863	0.7877	0.7865
FP	0.7751	0.7788	0.7738	0.7759

Table 10.2.41 Model 6c

A. MODEL DESIGN

A.1. Structural equations

$$B = \begin{bmatrix} 0 & -1 & 0 & 0 & 0 \\ 0 & 0 & 1 & 0 & 0 \\ 0 & 0 & 0 & -1 & 0 \\ 0 & 0 & 0 & 0 & 1 \\ -1 & 0 & 0 & 0 & 0 \end{bmatrix} \quad \Gamma = \begin{bmatrix} k_1 & k_1 & 0 & 0 & 0 & 0 & 0 & 0 & 0 & 0 \\ 0 & 0 & k_1 & k_1 & 0 & 0 & 0 & 0 & 0 & 0 \\ 0 & 0 & 0 & 0 & k_1 & k_1 & 0 & 0 & 0 & 0 \\ 0 & 0 & 0 & 0 & 0 & 0 & k_1 & k_1 & 0 & 0 \\ 0 & 0 & 0 & 0 & 0 & 0 & 0 & 0 & k_1 & k_1 \end{bmatrix}$$

$$\Omega = \begin{bmatrix} k_2 & k_2 & -k_2 & -k_2 & -k_2 & -k_2 & k_2 & k_2 & k_2 & k_2 \\ k_2 & k_2 & k_2 & k_2 & k_2 & k_2 & -k_2 & -k_2 & -k_2 & -k_2 \\ k_2 & k_2 & -k_2 & -k_2 & k_2 & k_2 & -k_2 & -k_2 & -k_2 & -k_2 \\ -k_2 & -k_2 & k_2 & k_2 & k_2 & k_2 & k_2 & k_2 & k_2 & k_2 \\ -k_2 & -k_2 & k_2 & k_2 & k_2 & k_2 & -k_2 & -k_2 & k_2 & k_2 \end{bmatrix}$$

with $k_1 = 0.5657$ and $k_2 = 0.2828$

A.2. Variance of endogenous and residual variables in the population and in the sample

$\sigma^2(y_i) = 1$

$\sigma^2(\delta_i) = 0.16 \qquad i = 1,2,...,5$

$\sigma^2(\epsilon_i) = 0.2$

Generated in sample period:

$V(y_1) = 1.023 \qquad V(y_2) = 0.999$

$V(\delta_1) = 0.162 \qquad V(\delta_2) = 0.163$

$V(\epsilon_1) = 0.200 \qquad V(\epsilon_2) = 0.200$

A.3. Correlation among residuals and exogenous variables

	x_1	x_2	x_3	x_4	x_5	x_6	x_7	x_8	x_9	x_{10}
ϵ_1	0	0	0.1	0.1	0.1	0.1	0.1	0.1	0.1	0.1
ϵ_2	0.1	0.1	0	0.	0.1	0.1	0.1	0.1	0.1	0.1
ϵ_3	0.1	0.1	−0.1	−0.1	0	0	0.1	0.1	0.1	0.1
ϵ_4	0.1	0.1	0.1	0.1	−0.1	−0.1	0	0	0.1	0.1
ϵ_5	0.1	0.1	0.1	0.1	0.1	0.1	0.1	0.1	0	0

	x_1	x_2	x_3	x_4	x_5	x_6	x_7	x_8	x_9	x_{10}
δ_1	0.1	0.1	0.1	0.1	0.2	0.2	0.2	0.2	0.2	0.2
δ_2	0	0	0.1	0.1	0.1	0.1	0	0	0	0
δ_3	0.2	0.2	0	0	−0.1	−0.1	0.1	0.1	0.2	0.2
δ_4	0	0	0	0	−0.2	−0.2	−0.1	−0.1	0.1	0.1
δ_5	0.1	0.1	0.2	0.2	0.2	0.2	0.2	0.2	0.1	0.1

A.4. Sample size and special design features

1. 40 observations in both the sample and prediction periods.
2. This model is one in a series on number of relations in a GEID specification with relatively small correlations (Models 6a–6c).

B. STRUCTURAL COEFFICIENTS

B.1. True coefficient versus average estimate from 100 samples

	β_{12}	γ_{11}	γ_{12}	β_{23}	γ_{23}	γ_{24}	β_{34}	γ_{35}	γ_{36}	β_{45}	γ_{47}	γ_{48}	β_{51}	γ_{59}	$\gamma_{5,10}$
True	−1	.5657	.5647	1	.5657	.5657	−1	.5657	.5657	1	.5657	.5657	−1	.5657	.5657
OLS	−.9266	.5768	.5774	.9368	.5893	.5854	−.8898	.4978	.4991	.8840	.4921	.4865	−.9378	.5820	.5805
TSLS	−.9843	.5947	.5950	1.0208	.6159	.6126	−.9454	.5115	.5123	.9415	.5060	.5017	−.9921	.5988	.5984
FP	−.9812	.5426	.5572	.9992	.5640	.5548	−.9954	.5417	.5455	.9865	.5421	.5204	−.9935	.5570	.5175

B.2. Observed standard deviation of 100 samples around observed mean

	β_{12}	γ_{11}	γ_{12}	β_{23}	γ_{23}	γ_{24}	β_{34}	γ_{35}	γ_{36}	β_{45}	γ_{47}	γ_{48}	β_{51}	γ_{59}	$\gamma_{5,10}$
OLS	.0728	0.717	.0636	.0751	.0682	.0688	.0596	.0581	.0643	.0682	.0553	.0653	.0741	.0706	.0701
TSLS	.0858	.0721	.0670	.0811	.0732	.0719	.0709	.0594	.0666	.0749	.0584	.0666	.0795	.0710	.0714
FP	.0996	.1293	.1166	.0980	.1407	.1268	.1084	.1307	.1303	.1117	.1294	.1262	.1006	.1290	.1356

B.3. Average standard deviation from large-sample formula

	β_{12}	γ_{11}	γ_{12}	β_{23}	γ_{23}	γ_{24}	β_{34}	γ_{35}	γ_{36}	β_{45}	γ_{47}	γ_{48}	β_{51}	γ_{59}	$\gamma_{5,10}$
OLS	.0721	.0673	.0689	.0737	.0680	.0691	.0674	.0655	.0644	.0666	.0657	.0642	.0714	.0681	.0691
TSLS	.0814	.0691	.0707	.0841	.0706	.0717	.0758	.0670	.0658	.0746	.0671	.0657	.0805	.0700	.0711
FP	.0881	.0726	.0747	.0907	.0743	.0752	.0892	.0746	.0731	.0890	.0754	.0737	.0885	.0755	.0753

B.4. Observed standard deviation around true value of the coefficient

	β_{12}	γ_{11}	γ_{12}	β_{23}	γ_{23}	γ_{24}	β_{34}	γ_{35}	γ_{36}	β_{45}	γ_{47}	γ_{48}	β_{51}	γ_{59}	$\gamma_{5,10}$
OLS	.1034	.0726	.0649	.0982	.0722	.0716	.1253	.0894	.0926	.1346	.0921	.1026	.0967	.0725	.0716
TSLS	.0872	.0777	.0735	.0837	.0888	.0858	.0895	.0804	.0854	.0950	.0835	.0924	.0799	.0783	.0785
FP	.1014	.1313	.1169	.0980	.1407	.1273	.1085	.1329	.1319	.1125	.1315	.1341	.1008	.1293	.1439

B.5. Number of iterations for fix-point (FP) method

Average = 65.39   Smallest = 35   Largest = 104   No convergence in 0 samples

C. REDUCED FORM COEFFICIENTS (10 out of 50 coefficients)

C.1. True coefficient versus average estimate from 100 samples

	ω_{11}	ω_{13}	ω_{15}	ω_{17}	ω_{19}	ω_{21}	ω_{23}	ω_{25}	ω_{27}	ω_{29}
True	.2828	−.2828	−.2828	.2828	.2828	.2828	.2828	.2828	−.2828	−.2828
OLS	.3525	−.3326	−.2628	.2316	.2409	.2415	.3598	.2849	−.2509	−.2602
TSLS	.3165	−.3211	−.2719	.2544	.2819	.2822	.3275	.2775	−.2596	−.2870
FP	.2787	−.2831	−.2706	.2689	.2699	.2669	.2901	.2779	−.2757	−.2761
URF	.2789	−.2362	−.2549	.3130	.3116	.3280	.2828	.3263	−.2429	−.2410

C.2. Observed standard deviation of 100 samples around observed mean

OLS	.0453	.0384	.0352	.0366	.0358	.0360	.0405	.0415	.0402	.0350
TSLS	.0417	.0376	.0366	.0392	.0394	.0398	.0389	.0394	.0415	.0372
FP	.0658	.0703	.0656	.0658	.0617	.0645	.0745	.0704	.0690	.0617
URF	.0711	.0824	.0740	.0805	.0818	.0765	.0799	.0716	.0834	.0757

C.3. Average standard deviation from large-sample formula

URF	.0784	.0780	.0798	.0795	.0786	.0783	.0783	.0799	.0799	.0787

C.4. Observed standard deviation around true value of the coefficient

OLS	.0831	.0629	.0405	.0629	.0551	.0548	.0870	.0416	.0514	.0417
TSLS	.0536	.0537	.0382	.0482	.0394	.0398	.0593	.0398	.0475	.0374
FP	.0659	.0703	.0667	.0673	.0631	.0661	.0749	.0706	.0694	.0621
URF	.0712	.0947	.0791	.0860	.0867	.0889	.0799	.0838	.0911	.0865

D. EIGENVALUES FOR PRODUCT MOMENT MATRIX OF EXPLANATORY VARIABLES (GEID SPECIFICATION)

	Smallest in 100 samples	Average for 100 samples λ_1	λ_2	λ_3		Smallest in 100 samples	Average for 100 samples λ_1	λ_2	λ_3
D.1. Equation 1					**D.4. Equation 4**				
OLS	.0837	.1721	.3102	.5177	OLS	.1021	.1915	.3201	.4884
TSLS	.0603	.1559	.3180	.5261	TSLS	.0838	.1769	.3266	.4963
FP	.0792	.1656	.3224	.5120	FP	.0676	.1620	.3292	.5088
D.2. Equation 2					**D.5. Equation 5**				
OLS	.0958	.1645	.3153	.5202	OLS	.0982	.1654	.3171	.5176
TSLS	.0740	.1479	.3241	.5280	TSLS	.0826	.1501	.3259	.5240
FP	.0710	.1586	.3259	.5155	FP	.0657	.1651	.3238	.5111
D.3. Equation 3					**D.6. Unrestricted reduced form**		N.a.		
OLS	.1155	.1921	.3173	.4906					
TSLS	.0848	.1764	.3264	.4972					
FP	.0789	.1597	.3351	.5052					

E. AVERAGE R^2 FROM 100 SAMPLES

E.1. Sample period

	y_1	y_2	y_3	y_4	y_5	Y
True	.8	.8	.8	.8	.8	.8
Generated (average)	.7984	.7933	.7941	.7900	.7918	.7935
OLS	.7695	.7932	.7961	.8020	.7770	.7875
TSLS	.7957	.8056	.8117	.8076	.7979	.8037
FP	.7846	.7867	.7879	.7861	.7842	.7859
URF	.8093	.8035	.8070	.8012	.8043	.8051

E.2. Prediction period

	y_1	y_2	y_3	y_4	y_5	Y
	.8	.8	.8	.8	.8	.8
	.7799	.7911	.7942	.7932	.7904	.7898
	.7087	.7581	.7685	.7782	.7395	.7506
	.7401	.7727	.7831	.7814	.7616	.7678
	.7216	.7512	.7554	.7450	.7418	.7430
	.7256	.7475	.7489	.7475	.7378	.7415

E.3. Sample period (adj. for D.F.)

	y_1	y_2	y_3	y_4	y_5	Y
OLS	.7508	.7764	.7796	.7859	.7589	.7703
TSLS	.7791	.7898	.7964	.7920	.7815	.7878
FP	.7671	.7694	.7707	.7688	.7667	.7685

Table 10.2.42. Model 6f

A. MODEL DESIGN

A.1. Structural equations

$$\beta = \begin{bmatrix} 0 & 1 \\ -1 & 0 \end{bmatrix} \qquad \Gamma = \begin{bmatrix} k_1 & k_1 & 0 & 0 \\ 0 & 0 & k_1 & k_1 \end{bmatrix} \qquad \Omega = \begin{bmatrix} k_2 & k_2 & k_2 & k_2 \\ -k_2 & -k_2 & k_2 & k_2 \end{bmatrix}$$

with $k_1 = 0.7071$ and $k_2 = 0.3536$

A.2. Variance of endogenous and residual variables in the population and in the sample

$\sigma^2(y_i) = 1.0$

$\sigma^2(\delta_i) = 1.0 \qquad i = 1, 2$

$\sigma^2(\epsilon_i) = 0.5$

Generated in sample period:
$\begin{cases} V(y_1) = 0.974 & V(y_2) = 0.994 \\ V(\delta_1) = 0.999 & V(\delta_2) = 0.991 \\ V(\epsilon_1) = 0.495 & V(\epsilon_2) = 0.499 \end{cases}$

A.3. Correlation among residuals and exogenous variables

	x_1	x_2	x_3	x_4
ϵ_1	0	0	0.01	−0.01
ϵ_2	0.01	−0.01	0	0

	x_1	x_2	x_3	x_4
δ_1	−0.01	0.01	0.01	−0.01
δ_2	0.01	−0.01	0.01	−0.01

A.4. Sample size and special design features

1. 40 observations in both the sample and prediction periods.
2. This model is one in a series on size of correlation between residuals and predetermined variables in GEID models (Models 6e(=5n), 6f-6j).

B. STRUCTURAL COEFFICIENTS

B.1. True coefficient versus average estimate from 100 samples

	β_{12}	γ_{11}	γ_{12}	β_{21}	γ_{23}	γ_{24}
True	1	0.7071	0.7071	−1	0.7071	0.7071
OLS	0.3127	0.4683	0.4678	−0.3429	0.4605	0.4786
TSLS	0.9509	0.6867	0.7102	−1.0390	0.7130	0.7082
FP	0.9620	0.6743	0.7049	−1.0469	0.6671	0.7147

B.2. Observed standard deviation of 100 samples around observed mean

OLS	0.1658	0.1424	0.1453	0.1422	0.1400	0.1462
TSLS	0.3536	0.2084	0.2124	0.3413	0.2013	0.2111
FP	0.3506	0.2247	0.2288	0.3556	0.2370	0.2470

B.3. Average standard deviation from large-sample formula

OLS	0.1553	0.1422	0.1451	0.1567	0.1466	0.1453
TSLS	0.3587	0.2101	0.2183	0.3638	0.2182	0.2115
FP	0.3645	0.2100	0.2190	0.3732	0.2129	0.2177

B.4. Observed standard deviation around true value of the coefficient

OLS	0.7070	0.2780	0.2800	0.6723	0.2836	0.2713
TSLS	0.3570	0.2094	0.2124	0.3435	0.2014	0.2111
FP	0.3527	0.2271	0.2288	0.3587	0.2404	0.2471

B.5. Number of iterations for fix-point (FP) method

Average = 8.58;   Smallest = 5;   Largest = 25;   No convergence in 0 samples

C. REDUCED FORM COEFFICIENTS

C.1. True coefficient versus average estimate from 100 samples

	ω_{11}	ω_{12}	ω_{13}	ω_{14}	ω_{21}	ω_{22}	ω_{23}	ω_{24}
True	0.3536	0.3536	0.3536	0.3536	−0.3536	−0.3536	0.3536	0.3536
OLS	0.4256	0.4241	0.1271	0.1333	−0.1457	−0.1407	0.4195	0.4371
TSLS	0.3542	0.3631	0.3304	0.3296	−0.3480	−0.3598	0.3654	0.3249
FP	0.3468	0.3566	0.3122	0.3306	−0.3407	−0.3569	0.3396	0.3645
URF	0.3456	0.3584	0.3566	0.3343	−0.3544	−0.3703	0.3390	0.3632

C.2. Observed standard deviation of 100 samples around observed mean

OLS	0.1252	0.1236	0.0728	0.0795	0.0721	0.0596	0.1243	0.1337
TSLS	0.0977	0.0945	0.0944	0.1082	0.0896	0.0998	0.0891	0.1059
FP	0.1164	0.1003	0.1189	0.1132	0.1043	0.1092	0.1127	0.1216
URF	0.1202	0.0963	0.0964	0.1270	0.1117	0.1264	0.1197	0.1235

C.3. Average standard deviation from large-sample formula

URF	0.1173	0.1178	0.1186	0.1189	0.1166	0.1171	0.1179	0.1183

C.4. Observed standard deviation around true value of the coefficient

OLS	0.1444	0.1423	0.2379	0.2342	0.2200	0.2211	0.1407	0.1576
TSLS	0.0977	0.0950	0.0972	0.1108	0.0898	0.1000	0.0899	0.1067
FP	0.1166	0.1003	0.1259	0.1155	0.1051	0.1092	0.1136	0.1221
URF	0.1205	0.0927	0.0964	0.1285	0.1117	0.1276	0.1206	0.1239

D. EIGENVALUES FOR PRODUCT MOMENT MATRIX EXPLANATORY VARIABLES (GEID SPECIFICATION)

	Smallest in 100 samples	Average for 100 samples		
		λ_1	λ_2	λ_3
D.1. Equation 1				
OLS	0.0834	0.1474	0.3142	0.5384
TSLS	0.0071	0.0712	0.3513	0.5775
FP	0.0074	0.0735	0.3521	0.5745
D.2. Equation 2				
OLS	0.0820	0.1545	0.3200	0.5255
TSLS	0.0199	0.0757	0.3571	0.5672
FP	0.0198	0.0782	0.3574	0.5644
D.3. Unrestricted reduced form	0.0956	0.1496	0.2109	0.2779

E. AVERAGE R^2 FROM 100 SAMPLES

E.1. Sample period

	y_1	y_2	Y
True	0.5	0.5	0.5
Generated (average)	0.4783	0.4874	0.4829
OLS	0.4073	0.4151	0.4112
TSLS	0.5092	0.5247	0.5169
FP	0.4974	0.5146	0.5060
URF	0.4719	0.4897	0.4808

E.2. Prediction period

	y_1	y_2	Y
True	0.5	0.5	0.5
Generated (average)	0.4926	0.4744	0.4835
OLS	0.3467	0.3472	0.3470
TSLS	0.4491	0.4437	0.4464
FP	0.4401	0.4296	0.4349
URF	0.4404	0.4187	0.4296

E.3. Sample period (adj. for D.F.)

	y_1	y_2	Y
OLS	0.3592	0.3677	0.3635
TSLS	0.4694	0.4861	0.4777
FP	0.4566	0.4752	0.4659

Table 10.2.43. Model 6g

A. MODEL DESIGN

A.1. Structural equations

$$\beta = \begin{bmatrix} 0 & 1 \\ -1 & 0 \end{bmatrix} \qquad \Gamma = \begin{bmatrix} k_1 & k_1 & 0 & 0 \\ 0 & 0 & k_1 & k_1 \end{bmatrix} \qquad \Omega = \begin{bmatrix} k_2 & k_2 & k_2 & k_2 \\ -k_2 & -k_2 & k_2 & k_2 \end{bmatrix}$$

with $k_1 = 0.7071$ and $k_2 = 0.3536$

A.2. Variance of endogenous and residual variables in the population and in the sample

$$\sigma^2(y_i) = 1.0$$
$$\sigma^2(\delta_i) = 1.0 \qquad i = 1, 2$$
$$\sigma^2(\epsilon_i) = 0.5$$

Generated in sample period:
$$V(y_1) = 1.047 \quad V(y_2) = 1.001$$
$$V(\delta_1) = 1.046 \quad V(\delta_2) = 1.007$$
$$V(\epsilon_1) = 0.520 \quad V(\epsilon_2) = 0.506$$

A.3. Correlation among residuals and exogenous variables

$$\begin{array}{c} \\ \epsilon_1 \\ \epsilon_2 \end{array} \begin{array}{cccc} x_1 & x_2 & x_3 & x_4 \\ \begin{bmatrix} 0 & 0 & 0.071 & -0.071 \\ 0.071 & -0.071 & 0 & 0 \end{bmatrix} \end{array} \qquad \begin{array}{c} \\ \delta_1 \\ \delta_2 \end{array} \begin{array}{cccc} x_1 & x_2 & x_3 & x_4 \\ \begin{bmatrix} -0.05 & 0.05 & 0.05 & -0.05 \\ 0.05 & -0.05 & 0.05 & -0.05 \end{bmatrix} \end{array}$$

A.4. Sample size and special design features

1. 40 observations in both the sample and prediction periods.
2. This model is one in a series on size of correlation between residuals and predetermined variables in GEID models (Models 6e(=5n), 6f-6j).

B. STRUCTURAL COEFFICIENTS

B.1. True coefficient versus average estimate from 100 samples

	β_{12}	γ_{11}	γ_{12}	β_{21}	γ_{23}	γ_{24}
True	1	0.7071	0.7071	−1	0.7071	0.7071
OLS	0.3230	0.4772	0.4800	−0.3476	0.4831	0.4434
TSLS	1.0272	0.6869	0.7675	−0.9618	0.7413	0.6305
FP	1.0262	0.7335	0.6870	−0.9740	0.6845	0.6606

B.2. Observed standard deviation of 100 samples around observed mean

OLS	0.1868	0.1420	0.1477	0.1642	0.1550	0.1458
TSLS	0.4161	0.1978	0.2284	0.2965	0.2079	0.1978
FP	0.4204	0.2066	0.2545	0.3138	0.2358	0.2699

B.3. Average standard deviation from large-sample formula

OLS	0.1588	0.1452	0.1509	0.1518	0.1444	0.1417
TSLS	0.3939	0.2129	0.2399	0.3348	0.2155	0.1982
FP	0.3990	0.2235	0.2257	0.3441	0.2067	0.2097

B.4. Observed standard deviation around true value of the coefficient

OLS	0.7023	0.2702	0.2709	0.6727	0.2724	0.3013
TSLS	0.4170	0.1988	0.2363	0.2990	0.2107	0.2121
FP	0.4212	0.2083	0.2553	0.3149	0.2369	0.2739

B.5. Number of iterations for fix-point (FP) method

Average = 8.91;   Smallest = 4;   Largest = 27   No convergence in 0 samples

C. REDUCED FORM COEFFICIENTS

C.1. True coefficient versus average estimate from 100 samples

	ω_{11}	ω_{12}	ω_{13}	ω_{14}	ω_{21}	ω_{22}	ω_{23}	ω_{24}
True	0.3536	0.3536	0.3536	0.3536	−0.3536	−0.3536	0.3536	0.3536
OLS	0.4348	0.4368	0.1398	0.1327	−0.1491	−0.1526	0.4398	0.4029
TSLS	0.3554	0.3922	0.3691	0.3150	−0.3256	−0.3639	0.3821	0.3251
FP	0.3790	0.3488	0.3410	0.3243	−0.3482	−0.3280	0.3527	0.3379
URF	0.3778	0.3437	0.4000	0.3016	−0.3003	−0.4112	0.3574	0.3314

C.2. Observed standard deviation of 100 samples around observed mean

OLS	0.1256	0.1299	0.0905	0.0867	0.0833	0.0908	0.1370	0.1276
TSLS	0.1034	0.0983	0.1182	0.1088	0.0952	0.1037	0.0961	0.1001
FP	0.1110	0.1149	0.1335	0.1314	0.0979	0.1196	0.1103	0.1268
URF	0.1114	0.1158	0.1247	0.1271	0.1206	0.1100	0.1129	0.1294

C.3. Average standard deviation from large-sample formula

URF	0.1196	0.1197	0.1163	0.1200	0.1187	0.1182	0.1155	0.1184

C.4. Observed standard deviation around true value of the coefficient

OLS	0.1496	0.1543	0.2322	0.2373	0.2208	0.2206	0.1619	0.1368
TSLS	0.1034	0.1056	0.1192	0.1154	0.0992	0.1042	0.1002	0.1039
FP	0.1139	0.1150	0.1341	0.1346	0.0980	0.1223	0.1103	0.1278
URF	0.1140	0.1162	0.1331	0.1373	0.1319	0.1242	0.1130	0.1313

D. EIGENVALUES FOR PRODUCT MOMENT MATRIX OF EXPLANATORY VARIABLES (GEID SPECIFICATION)

	Smallest in 100 samples	Average for 100 samples		
		λ_1	λ_2	λ_3
D.1. Equation 1				
OLS	0.0648	0.1509	0.3146	0.5345
TSLS	0.0086	0.0744	0.3519	0.5737
FP	0.0085	0.0777	0.3527	0.5696
D.2. Equation 2				
OLS	0.0817	0.1523	0.3132	0.5345
TSLS	0.0119	0.0763	0.3537	0.5699
FP	0.0143	0.0793	0.3603	0.5604
D.3. Unrestricted reduced form	0.0811	0.1489	0.2100	0.2782

E. AVERAGE R^2 FROM 100 SAMPLES

E.1. Sample period				E.2. Prediction period		
	y_1	y_2	Y	y_1	y_2	Y
True	0.5	0.5	0.5	0.5	0.5	0.5
Generated (average)	0.4894	0.4815	0.4855	0.4977	0.4979	0.4978
OLS	0.4257	0.4174	0.4216	0.3428	0.3188	0.3308
TSLS	0.5303	0.5217	0.5260	0.4530	0.4533	0.4532
FP	0.5185	0.5099	0.5142	0.4375	0.4268	0.4322
URF	0.4963	0.4861	0.4912	0.4436	0.4331	0.4384

E.3. Sample period (adj. for D.F.)

	y_1	y_2	Y
OLS	0.3791	0.3702	0.3747
TSLS	0.4922	0.4829	0.4876
FP	0.4795	0.4702	0.4748

Table 10.2.44. Model 6h

A. MODEL DESIGN

A.1. Structural equations

$$\beta = \begin{bmatrix} 0 & 1 \\ -1 & 0 \end{bmatrix} \qquad \Gamma = \begin{bmatrix} k_1 & k_1 & 0 & 0 \\ 0 & 0 & k_1 & k_1 \end{bmatrix} \qquad \Omega = \begin{bmatrix} k_2 & k_2 & k_2 & k_2 \\ -k_2 & -k_2 & k_2 & k_2 \end{bmatrix}$$

with $k_1 = 0.7071$ and $k_2 = 0.3536$

A.2. Variance of endogenous and residual variables in the population and in the sample

$\sigma^2(y_i) = 1.0$

$\sigma^2(\delta_i) = 1.0 \qquad i = 1, 2$

$\sigma^2(\epsilon_i) = 0.5$

Generated in sample period:

$V(y_1) = 1.014 \quad V(y_2) = 0.988$

$V(\delta_1) = 1.000 \quad V(\delta_2) = 0.997$

$V(\epsilon_1) = 0.502 \quad V(\epsilon_2) = 0.496$

A.3. Correlation among residuals and exogenous variables

	x_1	x_2	x_3	x_4		x_1	x_2	x_3	x_4
ϵ_1	0	0	0.141	−0.141	δ_1	−0.1	0.1	0.1	−0.1
ϵ_2	0.141	−0.141	0	0	δ_2	0.1	−0.1	0.1	−0.1

A.4. Sample size and special design features

1. 40 observations in both the sample and prediction periods.
2. This model is one in a series on size of correlation between residuals and predetermined variables in GEID models (Models 6e(=5n), 6f-6j).

B. STRUCTURAL COEFFICIENTS

B.1. True coefficient versus average estimate from 100 samples

	β_{12}	γ_{11}	γ_{12}	β_{21}	γ_{23}	γ_{24}
True	1	0.7071	0.7071	−1	0.7071	0.7071
OLS	0.3515	0.4392	0.5206	−0.3286	0.4961	0.4505
TSLS	0.9685	0.6042	0.7885	−0.9703	0.7968	0.6128
FP	0.9640	0.6542	0.7021	−0.9716	0.6847	0.6834

B.2. Observed standard deviation of 100 samples around observed mean

OLS	0.1498	0.1341	0.1481	0.1436	0.1493	0.1350
TSLS	0.3403	0.1682	0.2106	0.3305	0.2314	0.1758
FP	0.3370	0.2028	0.2453	0.3450	0.2693	0.2156

B.3. Average standard deviation from large-sample formula

OLS	0.1546	0.1419	0.1518	0.1558	0.1515	0.1362
TSLS	0.3326	0.1919	0.2236	0.3423	0.2323	0.1855
FP	0.3358	0.2015	0.2108	0.3516	0.2132	0.2038

B.4. Observed standard deviation around true value of the coefficient

OLS	0.6656	0.2996	0.2382	0.6866	0.2585	0.2899
TSLS	0.3418	0.1972	0.2258	0.3318	0.2482	0.1995
FP	0.3389	0.2096	0.2454	0.3462	0.2702	0.2169

B.5. Number of iterations for fix-point (FP) method

Average = 8.2;   Smallest = 5;   Largest = 15;   No convergence in 0 samples

C. REDUCED FORM COEFFICIENTS

C.1. True coefficient versus average estimate from 100 samples

	ω_{11}	ω_{12}	ω_{13}	ω_{14}	ω_{21}	ω_{22}	ω_{23}	ω_{24}
True	0.3536	0.3536	0.3536	0.3536	−0.3536	−0.3536	0.3536	0.3536
OLS	0.3993	0.4713	0.1563	0.1405	−0.1257	−0.1536	0.4490	0.4087
TSLS	0.3239	0.4152	0.3865	0.2978	−0.2942	−0.3849	0.4177	0.3282
FP	0.3501	0.3689	0.3341	0.3290	−0.3151	−0.3466	0.3580	0.3648
URF	0.3520	0.3629	0.4514	0.2571	−0.2645	−0.4371	0.3552	0.3644

C.2. Observed standard deviation of 100 samples around observed mean

OLS	0.1234	0.1281	0.0805	0.0739	0.0609	0.0769	0.1296	0.1201
TSLS	0.1029	0.1018	0.1155	0.0924	0.0819	0.1066	0.1041	0.1030
FP	0.1166	0.1223	0.1335	0.1073	0.0894	0.1290	0.1282	0.1189
URF	0.1157	0.1165	0.1098	0.1111	0.1105	0.1085	0.1281	0.1200

C.3. Average standard deviation from large-sample formula

URF	0.1171	0.1181	0.1164	0.1139	0.1165	0.1178	0.1157	0.1137

C.4. Observed standard deviation around true value of the coefficient

OLS	0.1316	0.1740	0.2131	0.2256	0.2359	0.2143	0.1609	0.1321
TSLS	0.1071	0.1190	0.1201	0.1079	0.1012	0.1111	0.1223	0.1061
FP	0.1167	0.1233	0.1349	0.1101	0.0973	0.1292	0.1283	0.1194
URF	0.1157	0.1169	0.1470	0.1472	0.1419	0.1369	0.1281	0.1205

D. EIGENVALUES FOR PRODUCT MOMENT MATRIX OF EXPLANATORY VARIABLES (GEID SPECIFICATION)

	Smallest in 100 samples	Average for 100 samples λ_1	λ_2	λ_3

D.1. Equation 1

	Smallest in 100 samples	λ_1	λ_2	λ_3
OLS	0.0894	0.1536	0.3166	0.5299
TSLS	0.0213	0.0815	0.3538	0.5647
FP	0.0209	0.0874	0.3540	0.5586

D.2. Equation 2

	Smallest in 100 samples	λ_1	λ_2	λ_3
OLS	0.0712	0.1450	0.3148	0.5402
TSLS	0.0122	0.0714	0.3549	0.5737
FP	0.0144	0.0781	0.3548	0.5672
D.3. Unrestricted reduced form	0.1008	0.1548	0.2090	0.2765

E. AVERAGE R^2 FROM 100 SAMPLES

	E.1. Sample period y_1	y_2	Y	E.2. Prediction period y_1	y_2	Y
True	0.5	0.5	0.5	0.5	0.5	0.5
Generated (average)	0.4950	0.4878	0.4914	0.5078	0.4921	0.5000
OLS	0.4298	0.4286	0.4292	0.3664	0.3475	0.3570
TSLS	0.5358	0.5284	0.5321	0.4672	0.4545	0.4609
FP	0.5179	0.5183	0.5181	0.4410	0.4293	0.4352
URF	0.5104	0.5023	0.5064	0.4678	0.4402	0.4540

E.3. Sample period (adj. for D.F.)

	y_1	y_2	Y
OLS	0.3836	0.3823	0.3829
TSLS	0.4982	0.4902	0.4942
FP	0.4788	0.4792	0.4790

Table 10.2.45. Model 6i

A. MODEL DESIGN

A.1. Structural equations

$$\beta = \begin{bmatrix} 0 & 1 \\ -1 & 0 \end{bmatrix} \qquad \Gamma = \begin{bmatrix} k_1 & k_1 & 0 & 0 \\ 0 & 0 & k_1 & k_1 \end{bmatrix} \qquad \Omega = \begin{bmatrix} k_2 & k_2 & k_2 & k_2 \\ -k_2 & -k_2 & k_2 & k_2 \end{bmatrix}$$

with $k_1 = 0.7071$ and $k_2 = 0.3536$

A.2. Variance of endogenous and residual variables in the population and in the sample

$$\sigma^2(y_i) = 1.0$$
$$\sigma^2(\delta_i) = 1.0 \qquad\qquad i = 1, 2$$
$$\sigma^2(\epsilon_i) = 0.5$$

Generated in sample period:
$$\begin{cases} V(y_1) = 0.982 & V(y_2) = 0.999 \\ V(\delta_1) = 1.003 & V(\delta_2) = 1.023 \\ V(\epsilon_1) = 0.487 & V(\epsilon_2) = 0.527 \end{cases}$$

A.3. Correlation among residuals and exogenous variables

$$\begin{array}{c} \\ \epsilon_1 \\ \epsilon_2 \end{array} \begin{array}{cccc} x_1 & x_2 & x_3 & x_4 \\ \begin{bmatrix} 0 & 0 & 0.283 & -0.283 \\ 0.283 & -0.283 & 0 & 0 \end{bmatrix} \end{array} \qquad \begin{array}{c} \\ \delta_1 \\ \delta_2 \end{array} \begin{array}{cccc} x_1 & x_2 & x_3 & x_4 \\ \begin{bmatrix} -0.2 & 0.2 & 0.2 & -0.2 \\ 0.2 & -0.2 & 0.2 & -0.2 \end{bmatrix} \end{array}$$

A.4. Sample size and special design features

1. 40 observations in both the sample and prediction periods.
2. This model is one in a series on size of correlation between residuals and predetermined variables in GEID models (Models 6e(=5n), 6f-6j).

B. STRUCTURAL COEFFICIENTS

B.1. True coefficient versus average estimate from 100 samples

	β_{12}	γ_{11}	γ_{12}	β_{21}	γ_{23}	γ_{24}
True	1	0.7071	0.7071	−1	0.7071	0.7071
OLS	0.3673	0.3898	0.5658	−0.3726	0.5480	0.4159
TSLS	1.0158	0.4782	0.9235	−0.9703	0.8796	0.5090
FP	1.0247	0.6712	0.7303	−0.9724	0.6830	0.6620

B.2. Observed standard deviation of 100 samples around observed mean

OLS	0.1565	0.1103	0.1743	0.1708	0.1602	0.1452
TSLS	0.3647	0.1434	0.2761	0.3623	0.2443	0.1893
FP	0.3514	0.1944	0.2729	0.3603	0.2467	0.2260

B.3. Average standard deviation from large-sample formula

OLS	0.1626	0.1334	0.1588	0.1649	0.1649	0.1403
TSLS	0.3516	0.1713	0.2548	0.3232	0.2439	0.1747
FP	0.3718	0.2106	0.2176	0.3418	0.2118	0.2047

B.4. Observed standard deviation around true value of the coefficient

OLS	0.6518	0.3359	0.2244	0.6502	0.2258	0.3254
TSLS	0.3650	0.2701	0.3508	0.3635	0.2991	0.2740
FP	0.3523	0.1977	0.2739	0.3614	0.2479	0.2305

B.5. Number of iterations for fix-point (FP) method

Average = 9.26;   Smallest = 6;   Largest = 20;   **No convergence in 0 samples**

C. REDUCED FORM COEFFICIENTS

C.1. True coefficient versus average estimate from 100 samples

	ω_{11}	ω_{12}	ω_{13}	ω_{14}	ω_{21}	ω_{22}	ω_{23}	ω_{24}
True	0.3536	0.3536	0.3536	0.3536	−0.3536	−0.3536	0.3536	0.3536
OLS	0.3466	0.4993	0.1758	0.1331	−0.1243	−0.1839	0.4838	0.3688
TSLS	0.2529	0.4745	0.4369	0.2560	−0.2324	−0.4368	0.4561	0.2691
FP	0.3496	0.3684	0.3519	0.3278	−0.3154	−0.3491	0.3483	0.3436
URF	0.3515	0.3625	0.5544	0.1676	−0.1254	−0.5523	0.3463	0.3476

C.2. Observed standard deviation of 100 samples around observed mean

OLS	0.0988	0.1445	0.0857	0.0776	0.0635	0.0970	0.1301	0.1241
TSLS	0.0813	0.1167	0.1175	0.1023	0.0874	0.1291	0.1178	0.1051
FP	0.1011	0.1160	0.1472	0.1086	0.0920	0.1417	0.1125	0.1181
URF	0.0967	0.1084	0.1110	0.1184	0.1011	0.1119	0.1185	0.1110

C.3. Average standard deviation from large-sample formula

URF	0.1062	0.1063	0.1087	0.1093	0.1093	0.1093	0.1118	0.1123

C.4. Observed standard deviation around true value of the coefficient

OLS	0.0990	0.2052	0.1974	0.2338	0.2379	0.1955	0.1841	0.1251
TSLS	0.1294	0.1680	0.1440	0.1414	0.1494	0.1536	0.1562	0.1349
FP	0.1012	0.1169	0.1472	0.1116	0.0996	0.1419	0.1126	0.1185
URF	0.0967	0.1088	0.2294	0.2205	0.2496	0.2280	0.1187	0.1112

D. EIGENVALUES FOR PRODUCT MOMENT MATRIX OF EXPLANATORY VARIABLES (GEID SPECIFICATION)

	Smallest in 100 samples	Average for 100 samples λ_1	λ_2	λ_3
D.1. Equation 1				
OLS	0.0660	0.1323	0.3122	0.5555
TSLS	0.0108	0.0645	0.3489	0.5866
FP	0.0157	0.0716	0.3585	0.5699
D.2. Equation 2				
OLS	0.0605	0.1346	0.3151	0.5503
TSLS	0.0178	0.0718	0.3469	0.5813
FP	0.0208	0.0821	0.3485	0.5695
D.3. Unrestricted reduced form	0.1027	0.1507	0.2056	0.2742

E. AVERAGE R^2 FROM 100 SAMPLES

E.1. Sample period	y_1	y_2	Y	E.2. Prediction period y_1	y_2	Y
True	0.5	0.5	0.5	0.5	0.5	0.5
Generated (average)	0.4948	0.4604	0.4776	0.4686	0.4911	0.4799
OLS	0.4380	0.4243	0.4312	0.3352	0.3824	0.3588
TSLS	0.5484	0.5341	0.5413	0.4386	0.4871	0.4629
FP	0.5194	0.5034	0.5114	0.4015	0.4517	0.4266
URF	0.5680	0.5519	0.5600	0.4811	0.5296	0.5054

E.3. Sample period (adj. for D.F.)

	y_1	y_2	Y
OLS	0.3924	0.3776	0.3851
TSLS	0.5118	0.4963	0.5041
FP	0.4804	0.4631	0.4718

Table 10.2.46. Model 6j

A. MODEL DESIGN

A.1. Structural equations

$$\beta = \begin{bmatrix} 0 & 1 \\ -1 & 0 \end{bmatrix} \qquad \Gamma = \begin{bmatrix} k_1 & k_1 & 0 & 0 \\ 0 & 0 & k_1 & k_1 \end{bmatrix} \qquad \Omega = \begin{bmatrix} k_2 & k_2 & k_2 & k_2 \\ -k_2 & -k_2 & k_2 & k_2 \end{bmatrix}$$

with $k_1 = 0.7071$ and $k_2 = 0.3536$

A.2. Variance of endogenous and residual variables in the population and in the sample

$$\sigma^2(y_i) = 1.0$$
$$\sigma^2(\delta_i) = 1.0 \qquad i = 1, 2$$
$$\sigma^2(\epsilon_i) = 0.5$$

Generated in sample period:
$$\begin{cases} V(y_1) = 1.026 & V(y_2) = 0.980 \\ V(\delta_1) = 1.002 & V(\delta_2) = 0.997 \\ V(\epsilon_1) = 0.507 & V(\epsilon_2) = 0.492 \end{cases}$$

A.3. Correlation among residuals and exogenous variables

$$
\begin{array}{c}
\begin{array}{cccc} x_1 & x_2 & x_3 & x_4 \end{array} \\
\begin{array}{c} \epsilon_1 \\ \epsilon_2 \end{array}
\begin{bmatrix} 0 & 0 & 0.566 & -0.566 \\ 0.566 & -0.566 & 0 & 0 \end{bmatrix}
\end{array}
\qquad
\begin{array}{c}
\begin{array}{cccc} x_1 & x_2 & x_3 & x_4 \end{array} \\
\begin{array}{c} \delta_1 \\ \delta_2 \end{array}
\begin{bmatrix} -0.4 & 0.4 & 0.4 & -0.4 \\ 0.4 & -0.4 & 0.4 & -0.4 \end{bmatrix}
\end{array}
$$

A.4. Sample size and special design features

1. 40 observations in both the sample and prediction periods.
2. This model is one in a series on size of correlation between residuals and predetermined variables in GEID models (Models 6e(=5n), 6f-6j).

B. STRUCTURAL COEFFICIENTS

B.1. True coefficient versus average estimate from 100 samples

	β_{12}	γ_{11}	γ_{12}	β_{21}	γ_{23}	γ_{24}
True	1	0.7071	0.7071	−1	0.7071	0.7071
OLS	0.5785	0.3416	0.7840	−0.5602	0.7732	0.3397
TSLS	1.0231	0.3226	1.1242	−0.9431	1.0651	0.3189
FP	1.0299	0.6681	0.7012	−0.9406	0.6774	0.6530

B.2. Observed standard deviation of 100 samples around observed mean

	β_{12}	γ_{11}	γ_{12}	β_{21}	γ_{23}	γ_{24}
OLS	0.2271	0.1289	0.2155	0.2013	0.1842	0.1171
TSLS	0.3628	0.1548	0.2941	0.3830	0.2978	0.1346
FP	0.4564	0.2348	0.2925	0.4752	0.2421	0.2202

B.3. Average standard deviation from large-sample formula

	β_{12}	γ_{11}	γ_{12}	β_{21}	γ_{23}	γ_{24}
OLS	0.2018	0.1282	0.2031	0.1908	0.1931	0.1265
TSLS	0.2905	0.1395	0.2642	0.2726	0.2487	0.1363
FP	0.3678	0.2059	0.2196	0.3418	0.2082	0.1975

B.4. Observed standard deviation around true value of the coefficient

	β_{12}	γ_{11}	γ_{12}	β_{21}	γ_{23}	γ_{24}
OLS	0.4788	0.3876	0.2288	0.4837	0.1957	0.3856
TSLS	0.3635	0.4145	0.5104	0.3872	0.4657	0.4109
FP	0.4574	0.2380	0.2926	0.4789	0.2439	0.2267

B.5. Number of iterations for fix-point (FP) method

Average = 12.5;   Smallest = 5;   Largest = 200;   No convergence in 1 sample.

C. REDUCED FORM COEFFICIENTS

C.1. True coefficient versus average estimate from 100 samples

	ω_{11}	ω_{12}	ω_{13}	ω_{14}	ω_{21}	ω_{22}	ω_{23}	ω_{24}
True	0.3536	0.3536	0.3536	0.3536	−0.3536	−0.3536	0.3536	0.3536
OLS	0.2650	0.5909	0.3299	0.1449	0.1412	−0.3225	0.5858	0.2619
TSLS	0.1796	0.5857	0.5393	0.1679	−0.1514	−0.5181	0.5478	0.1746
FP	0.3631	0.3632	0.3656	0.3270	−0.2996	−0.3444	0.3576	0.3488
URF	0.3642	0.3502	0.7606	0.0400	0.0446	−0.7539	0.3436	0.3520

C.2. Observed standard deviation of 100 samples around observed mean

OLS	0.1075	0.1331	0.1181	0.0641	0.0679	0.1243	0.1189	0.0958
TSLS	0.0991	0.1325	0.1356	0.0817	0.0792	0.1445	0.0948	0.0847
FP	0.1164	0.1119	0.1660	0.0946	0.1061	0.1794	0.1113	0.1093
URF	0.0753	0.0664	0.0681	0.0642	0.0720	0.0738	0.0648	0.0731

C.3. Average standard deviation from large-sample formula

URF	0.0694	0.0719	0.0707	0.0706	0.0691	0.0714	0.0702	0.0699

C.4. Observed standard deviation around true value of the coefficient

OLS	0.1393	0.2721	0.1205	0.2183	0.2230	0.1281	0.2609	0.1326
TSLS	0.2002	0.2673	0.2299	0.2051	0.2172	0.2190	0.2161	0.1980
FP	0.1168	0.1123	0.1664	0.0983	0.1191	0.1751	0.1114	0.1094
URF	0.0760	0.0665	0.4128	0.3201	0.3173	0.4070	0.0659	0.0731

D. EIGENVALUES FOR PRODUCT MOMENT MATRIX OF EXPLANATORY VARIABLES (GEID SPECIFICATION)

	Smallest in 100 samples	Average for 100 samples		
		λ_1	λ_2	λ_3
D.1. Equation 1				
OLS	0.0345	0.0750	0.3212	0.6038
TSLS	0.0132	0.0493	0.3357	0.6150
FP	0.0114	0.0760	0.3477	0.5763
D.2. Equation 2				
OLS	0.0302	0.0785	0.3126	0.6089
TSLS	0.0129	0.0532	0.3276	0.6191
FP	0.0161	0.0825	0.3507	0.5668
D.3. Unrestricted reduced form	0.0993	0.1508	0.2071	0.2720

E. AVERAGE R^2 from 100 SAMPLES

	E.1. Sample period			E.2. Prediction period		
	y_1	y_2	Y	y_1	y_2	Y
True	0.5	0.5	0.5	0.5	0.5	0.5
Generated (average)	0.4934	0.4827	0.4881	0.5070	0.4738	0.4904
OLS	0.5473	0.5377	0.5424	0.5059	0.4765	0.4912
TSLS	0.6365	0.6432	0.6399	0.5925	0.6022	0.5974
FP	0.5381	0.5280	0.5331	0.4786	0.4402	0.4594
URF	0.8160	0.8115	0.8138	0.8001	0.7901	0.7951

E.3. Sample period (adj. for D.F.)

	y_1	y_2	Y
OLS	0.5106	0.5002	0.5054
TSLS	0.6070	0.6143	0.6107
FP	0.5006	0.4897	0.4952

Symmetric and Asymmetric Estimation Methods

by Ejnar Lyttkens

11.1. Asymmetry of the TSLS Method

The TSLS method has the asymmetric feature that in each structural relation it carries just one current endogenous variable to the left-hand member. With reference to the review in Chapter 3.3 of the two-stage least squares (TSLS) method, the first stage of TSLS forms the estimate Y_t^* as the systematic part of the unrestricted reduced form according to formula (3.4.1). In the second stage the least squares method is applied to each equation of the relation

$$Y_t = B Y_t^* + G Z_t + e_t \; ; \tag{1}$$

that is, in the ith equation we form the least squares regression of y_{it} on those components y_{pt}^* and z_{qt} which occur on the right-hand side of the ith equation. Equivalently, Theil (1958, p. 336) pointed out the possibility of subtracting the estimated residuals of the unrestricted reduced form from Y_t before the application of the least squares method in the second stage. Hence it is seen that the second stage of TSLS can also be described as the application of the least squares method to each equation of the system

$$Y_t^* = B Y_t^* + G Z_t + v_t \; . \tag{2}$$

For the symmetric specification of ID systems it is typical that any endogenous variable in a structural relation may be placed in the left-hand member; this casts the relation in the form (1) when dividing through with the coefficient of the left-hand variable. This gives as many versions of the structural relation as the number of current endogenous variables that occur in the relation. As a consequence, each equation gives as many different sets of estimates B, G according to the TSLS method as there are endogenous variables in the equation. In this respect the situation is the same as in ordinary least squares regression, namely that it is not a trivial matter to prescribe unit value to one of the coefficients.

We shall use a notation system that does not specify which variable is actually placed in the left-hand member. Hence we write

$$B_1 = K[I-B] , \qquad G_1 = KG , \qquad (3a-b)$$

where K is a diagonal matrix with diagonal elements k_{ii} that are subject to further specification, depending upon the normalization procedure adopted. The ith row vectors of B_1 and G_1 will be denoted b_i, g_i.

Following an earlier paper (Lyttkens (1964b)), we shall consider a compromise between the various TSLS estimates of a structural relation. The device is to use orthogonal regression if no predetermined variables are present in the equation; otherwise, the corresponding procedure is applied to the residuals of the least squares regression of Y_t^* on the predetermined variables present in the equation. This means that the following ratio is minimized,

$$\frac{\sum_{t=1}^{T} (b_i Y_t^* - g_i Z_t)^2}{b_i b_i'} , \qquad (4)$$

where the coefficient vectors b_i, g_i are not subject to any specified normalization. By the minimization we take account of the restrictions that some coefficients are prescribed zeros.

The drawback of the orthogonal regression is its sensitiveness to scale factors of the variables. In the present context we can get rid of this difficulty by dividing each endogenous variable by its estimated standard deviation, or rather by the estimated residual standard deviation as obtained from the unrestricted form, since the asymptotic standard errors of the components of Y_t^* are closely related to these standard deviations. The previous analysis is applied to the new variables obtained in one of these two ways, and then we return to the original scaling of the variables. This way of proceeding does not change the estimates according to the TSLS method, but in the intermediate solution the function to be minimized is

$$\frac{\sum_{t=1}^{T} (b_i Y_t^* - g_i Z_t)^2}{b_i \hat{\Psi} b_i'}. \tag{5}$$

Here $\hat{\Psi}$ is the diagonal matrix of the estimated variances of endogenous variables or estimated residual variances of the unrestricted reduced form, as the case may be, and the elements of $\hat{\Psi}$ are treated as constants during the minimization. It should be noted that the ordinary least variance ratio estimate (see section 11.3) is obtained if $\hat{\Psi}$ is replaced by the estimated covariance matrix of the residual variable of the unrestricted reduced form. In the present context we shall restrict ourselves to the choice of a diagonal matrix $\hat{\Psi}$, because we are interested in solutions which are a compromise between those obtained with the aid of the TSLS method. For a diagonal matrix $\hat{\Psi}$ this property follows under certain conditions from Frisch's theorem (Frisch, 1934). As pointed out by Malinvaud (1964 p. 51) the restriction to diagonal matrices is essential.

To study the effect of the asymmetry we shall consider several special types of equations that can occur in a GEID system. We shall first deal with an overidentified equation containing only two endogenous variables and no predetermined variables. Let us compare the scatter diagram of y_{1t}^* and y_{2t}^* for a small sample with that for a larger sample. In Chart 1 we see the two regression lines and the orthogonal regression line for a small sample and in Chart 2 those for a larger sample.

For Classic ID systems, y_{1t}^* and y_{2t}^* are consistent estimates of the conditional expected values of y_{1t} and y_{2t} for given values of the pre-

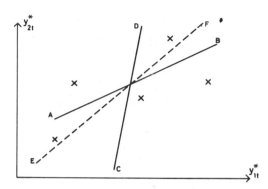

Chart 11.1.1. Scatter diagram of y_{1t}^* and y_{2t}^* for a small sample.
The different least squares regression lines
AB = regression line of y_{2t}^* on y_{1t}^*
CD = regression line of y_{1t}^* on y_{2t}^*
EF = orthogonal regression line.

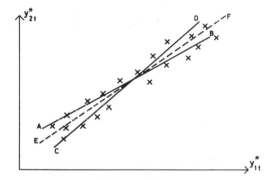

Chart 11.1.2. Scatter diagram of y_{1t}^* and y_{2t}^* for a larger sample.
The same regression lines as in Chart 1. (When sample size tends
to infinity, the three regression lines will coincide.)

determined variables. Therefore the values of y_{1t}^* and y_{2t}^* will approach stochastically to a linear configuration when the sample size increases. This means that the two regression lines, as well as the line obtained by minimizing the function (5), will tend to coincide. In other words, the two solutions according to the TSLS method will tend stochastically to the same line when sample size increases, as will also the intermediate solutions considered in this section.

For GEID systems, y_{1t}^* and y_{2t}^* are not consistent estimates of the corresponding quantities defined by the generated reduced form. In this

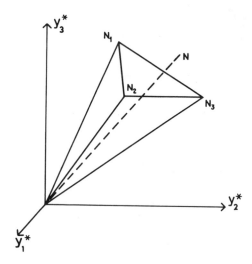

Chart 11.1.3. The normals of the three regression planes, N_1, N_2 and N_3, and the normal of the orthogonal regression plane, N, in the y_1^*, y_2^*, y_3^*-space for a small sample.

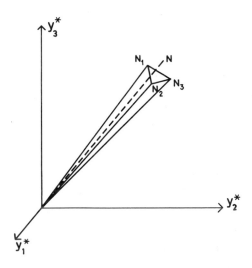

Chart 11.1.4. The normals of the regression planes in the y_1^*, y_2^*, y_3^*-space for a larger sample. (When the sample size tends to infinity, all regression lines tend stoachstically to the true relation.)

case y_{1t}^* and y_{2t}^* in general do not tend to a linear configuration when sample size increases, and the two solutions according to the TSLS method will tend to different lines. But in this case the very definition of the model points out which one to choose, although none of them will give a consistent estimate of the line corresponding to the GEID specification.

Next we shall consider an overidentified equation that contains three endogenous variables, but no predetermined variables. Let N_1, N_2 and N_3 denote the normals of three regression planes, namely that of y_{1t}^* on y_{2t}^* and y_{3t}^*, that of y_{2t}^* on y_{1t}^* and y_{3t}^*, and that of y_{3t}^* on y_{1t}^* and y_{2t}^*. These planes represent the three possible estimates according to the TSLS method. We assume that it is possible to choose the direction of the normals in such a way that the angle between any two of them will be smaller than $\frac{1}{2}\pi$. Then according to Frisch's theorem, the normal N of the orthogonal regression plane (Chart 3) as well as the normal of the plane defined by minimizing the function (5) is situated within the solid angle defined by the three normals N_1, N_2, and N_3. Again, when the sample size tends to infinity, the planes considered will tend stochastically to their common theoretical counterpart in the case of a Classic ID system (Chart 4), but they will remain systematically different in the case of a GEID system.

As a third illustration we shall deal with an equation with two endogenous variables y_{1t} and y_{2t} and one predetermined variable z_{1t}. Let us consider the planes obtained in the three-dimensional space of y_{1t}, y_{2t} and z_{1t}. It is a common feature of the least variance ratio estimate and the TSLS estimate that $g_i Z_t$ can be obtained as the systematic part of the linear least squares regression of $b_i Y_t$ on the predetermined variables present in the equation. Let p_{11}^* and p_{21}^* be the regression coefficients of y_{1t} and y_{2t} on z_{1t}. Then it follows that the plane defined by the least variance ratio estimate as well as the one defined by the TSLS estimate will pass through the line

$$\frac{y_{1t}}{p_{11}^*} = \frac{y_{2t}}{p_{21}^*} = z_{1t} \,. \tag{6}$$

If the equation is underidentified, which in the present case means that z_{1t} is the only predetermined variable of the whole system, every plane through the line will represent an estimate; that is, the solution is un-determined. If the equation is just identified (that is, two predetermined variables are present in the system) the planes considered will coincide, the resulting plane thus being the same for the least variance ratio esti-mate and the TSLS estimates. Lastly, if the equation is overidentified, two planes through the line (6) are obtained from the TSLS solutions. The planes which minimize the functions (4) and (5), respectively, are situated between them. This follows from Frisch's theorem applied to the residuals of the regressions of y^*_{1t} and y^*_{2t} on z_{1t}. As to the plane defined by the least variance ratio estimate, however, it cannot even in the present simple case be ascertained to be situated between the planes obtained from the TSLS estimates.

11.2. Asymmetry of the 3SLS Method

The 3SLS method takes account of the correlations between the residuals in the structural form. Since these correlations are unknown, the TSLS estimate of the covariance matrix of the structural form is used. Let V be this estimate of the residual product moment matrix. The 3SLS method can be described as finding the values of B and G which minimize the function

$$\sum_{t=1}^{T} (Y_t - BY^*_t - GZ_t)'\, V^{-1}(Y_t - BY^*_t - GZ_t) \qquad (1)$$

with respect to the elements of B and G that are not prescribed zeros. It is easily seen that the rather lengthy expressions for the 3SLS estima-tor (Zellner and Theil, 1962) are obtained from this condition.

Since Y^*_t is the systematic part of the unrestricted reduced form we can, as in the previous section, replace Y_t by Y^*_t. If this replacement is made in formula (1) we can describe the 3SLS estimator as that which minimizes the function

$$\sum_{t=1}^{T} (Y^*_t - BY^*_t - GZ_t)'\, V^{-1}(Y^*_t - BY^*_t - GZ_t). \qquad (2)$$

From this formula we conclude that the asymmetry of the TSLS method carries over to the 3SLS method.

11.3. Symmetry of the Classic Maximum Likelihood Method

Adopting a symmetric notation we write the structural form as

$$\beta_1 Y_t = \Gamma Z_t + \delta_t ,\tag{1}$$

with the reduced form

$$Y_t = \Omega Z_t + \epsilon_t ,\tag{2}$$

where Ω fulfills the condition

$$\beta_1 \Omega = \Gamma \tag{3}$$

and the residuals are connected by the relation

$$\beta_1 \epsilon_t = \delta_t .\tag{4}$$

Formally, the system (1.4.64) can be regarded as a special case of (1), namely where

$$\beta_1 = I - \beta .$$

Note that matrix β_1 in (1) in general will not have mere units in the main diagonal. The ith row vector of β_1 and Γ will be denoted by β_i, y_i, in analogy to Chapter 11.1.

The residual vector δ_t is assumed to have zero mean and to be independent of all Z_τ for $\tau \leqslant t$, and, for those components of Z_τ which are exogenous variables, also for $\tau > t$. Furthermore we suppose that residuals referring to different time points are uncorrelated, and that the covariance matrix of the simultaneous residuals is the same for all time points. The distribution of the residuals is supposed to be simultaneously normal. Because of the relation (4) the same properties are valid for the residuals of the reduced form. Let θ be the product moment matrix of the residuals of the reduced form. Then the logarithm of the likelihood function can be written (cf. Malinvaud (1964 p. 578))

$$\log L = -\tfrac{1}{2} nT \log 2\pi - \tfrac{1}{2} T \log \theta - \tfrac{1}{2} \sum_{t=1}^{T} (Y_t - \Omega Z_t)' \theta^{-1} (Y_t - \Omega Z_t) . \quad (5)$$

Here the coefficients of the structural form only appear in the relation $B_1 \Omega = \Gamma$. This relation is evidently fulfilled even if the coefficients of the first equation are multiplied by a constant, the second equation with another constant, and so on. Again, these constants can be chosen so that one of the non-zero coefficients of each equation takes on unit value, but this special case does not have any influence on the ratios between the structural coefficients within one equation. Let $\hat{\theta}$ be the maximum likelihood estimate of θ. Then

$$\hat{\theta} = \frac{1}{T} \sum_{t=1}^{T} (Y_t - WZ_t)(Y_t - WZ_t)' , \quad (6)$$

with

$$W = B_1 G . \quad (7)$$

The maximum likelihood estimate of the coefficients is then obtained by minimizing the determinant of $\hat{\theta}$ with due regard to the condition $W = B_1 G$. This is the customary exposition for the procedure of estimating the coefficients β, Γ according to the full information maximum likelihood (FIML) method (cf. Malinvaud (1964) p. 578).

11.3.1. The LIML (Limited Information Maximum Likelihood) or Least Variance Ratio Estimate

When the ith equation is estimated, the restrictions imposed on this equation are more important than the other restrictions. This has led to the limited information maximum likelihood (LIML) method (Anderson and Rubin, 1949). In LIML estimation, $\hat{\theta}$ is minimized subject only to the condition

$$b_i W = g_i ,$$
(8)

where b_i and g_i denote the row vectors of the elements of the ith rows of B_1 and G. It is immediately seen that this estimate is symmetric in the same sense as the FIML method.

Reference is made to the fact that the Limited Information estimate is equivalent to the least variance ratio estimate (cf. Johnston (1963) p. 255). Let M be the matrix of the product sums of the residuals of the unrestricted reduced form estimate. Then the least variance ratio estimate is that which minimizes

$$\frac{\sum_{t=1}^{T} (b_i Y_t - g_i Z_t)^2}{b_i M b_i'}$$
(9)

with respect to the coefficients that are not prescribed zeros. Equivalently, we can minimize the ratio

$$\frac{\sum_{t=1}^{T} (b_i Y_t^* - g_i Z_t)^2}{b_i M b_i'}$$
(10)

since the difference between these two functions has unit value for each set of values of b_i and g_i. The latter ratio is written down to show the connection with the ratio (11.1.5); the diagonal elements of M can be used as the elements of the diagonal matrix $\hat{\Psi}$.

11.3.2. The Special Case Where the Residuals of the Structural Form are Independent

As defined in Chapter 2, most of the models for the Monte Carlo runs explored in this volume belong to this type. In this case the likelihood function is conveniently taken from the structural form, and its logarithm turns out to be (cf. Klein, 1953)

$$\log L = -\tfrac{1}{2} Tn \log 2\pi + T \log(\det B_1) - \sum_{i=1}^{n} \log \sigma(\delta_i) -$$

$$\sum_{i=1}^{n} \frac{1}{2\sigma^2(\delta_i)} \sum_{t=1}^{T} (\beta_i Y_t - \gamma_i Z_t)^2 , \tag{11}$$

and if $s(\delta_i)$ denotes the estimate of $\sigma(\delta_i)$ we have

$$s^2(\delta_i) = \frac{1}{T} \sum_{t=1}^{T} (b_i Y_t - g_i Z_t)^2 . \tag{12}$$

The FIML estimate — again considering the special case where the residuals of the structural form are independent — is then obtained by minimizing

$$\frac{s^2(\delta_1)\, s^2(\delta_2) \cdots s^2(\delta_n)}{(\det B_1)^2} . \tag{13}$$

The value of this function depends only on the ratios of the coefficients within each equation. This holds true even in the special case where β is triangular — the case of a causal chain model. The point of this comment is that the situation is similiar to unirelational regression. [1] The FIML estimate is the same as for OLS, when the left-hand variable is specified by the model; hence there arises no choice between different regressions, as e.g. in the TSLS method.

11.4. Iterative Instrumental Variables (IIV) Estimation [1]

The FP method as well as the TSLS and 3SLS methods are asymmetric in the sense that to place different variables on the left-hand side gives different regressions and different estimates of the ratios between the coefficients within each equation. On the other hand, the FIML method as well as the LIML method are symmetric in the sense that the estimates of the ratios between the coefficients within each equation are independent of the normalization rule for the coefficients. In this section we shall present a symmetric counterpart to the FP method designed for the Classic ID specification.

As in the previous section we write the structural form in the following way,

$$\beta_1 Y_t = \Gamma Z_t + \delta_t .$$

(1)

For the systematic part of the right-hand member we introduce the notation Φ_t,

$$\Phi_t = \Gamma Z_t .$$

(2)

For the systematic part of the reduced form we use, as before, the notation H_t^*, giving

$$H_t^* = \beta_1^{-1} \Gamma Z_t .$$

(3)

The estimated equation, as obtained in iteration number s, is written as

$$B_1^{(s)} Y_t = G^{(s)} Z_t + d_t^{(s)} .$$

(4)

The systematic part of the right-hand member of this equation is denoted by $\Phi_t^{(s)}$,

$$\Phi_t^{(s)} = G^{(s)} Z_t .$$

(5)

The corresponding estimate of H_t^* is denoted by $Y_t^{(s)}$, and is taken as the systematic part of the estimated reduced form as generated from (4). Thus the following relation is fulfilled:

$$B_1^{(s)} Y_t^{(s)} = G^{(s)} Z_t .$$

(6)

The main difference between (6) and relation (1.3.5) of the FP method is that (6) does not include $Y_t^{(s-1)}$ explicitly. Solving for $Y_t^{(s)}$ we obtain

$$Y_t^{(s)} = (B_1^{(s)})^{-1} G^{(s)} Z_t . \qquad (7)$$

In the special case where all endogenous variables of the system occur in each equation, the author's first approach was a NIPALS procedure applied to the structural form and the reduced form alternatively:[2] when $B_1^{(s)}$ is known, $G^{(s)}$ is obtained by applying the least squares method to each equation of the structural form (4). Thereafter we form the OLS regression (without explicit constant terms) of the components of Y_t on the components of $\Phi_t^{(s)}$ as given by (5). Apart from normalization constants, $B^{(s+1)}$ is obtained as the inverse of the matrix of the partial regression coefficients of Y_t on the components of $\Phi_t^{(s)}$. For a brief account of this method applied to Summers' model, we again refer to Wold (1966c). Apart from the separate iteration of $B_1^{(s)}$ and $G^{(s)}$ this NIPALS method is equivalent to the iterative instrumental variables (IIV) method, which we shall now present. The shift to instrumental variables has the advantage that it admits a natural extension to systems where endogenous variables are specified as absent in one or more equations.

The iterative instrumental variables method (Lyttkens, 1967b) will now be specified in terms of the start, the passage from the $(s-1)$th to the sth iteration, and the normalization of the coefficients.

The start. For each equation a set of initial instrumental variables is chosen from the predetermined variables or from some convenient linear combinations of them, for instance those given by (3.5.3a) or (3.5.3b). In accordance with Note 1 in Chapter 3.5, (3.5.3a) may again serve as an initial choice of the coefficients of the endogenous variables, and in accordance with Note 1 of Chapter 3.5 the start should then specify $b_{ij}^{(1)} = 0$ for $i \neq j$ for all structural relations that are not identities. As regards (3.5.3b) we note that the second stage of the TSLS method can be considered as an instrumental variables method as well as a regression procedure. This follows from the relations $\sum_t z_{lt} y_{kt}^* = \sum_t z_{lt} y_{kt}$ and $\sum_t y_{jt}^* y_{kt}^* = \sum_t y_{jt}^* y_{kt}$, $(j, k = 1, 2, ..., n; l = 1, 2, ..., m)$. Similarly, and more immediately, OLS regression can be interpreted as an instrumental variables approach; in fact, (3.5.3c) is obtained if the regressors are treated as instrumental variables.

It is more in line with the symmetry of the method now considered to use either the LIML estimates, or the estimates obtained by minimizing one of the functions (11.1.4) or (11.1.5), as the first proxies of the coefficients. Such a more sophisticated starting procedure is of course more laborious than the ones mentioned before.

The step from the $(s-1)$st to the sth iteration in the special case where all endogenous variables occur in each equation. The coefficients of the ith equation are calculated from two sets of conditions, namely $\sum_t z_{lt} d_{it}^{(s)} = 0$ if z_{lt} occurs in the ith equation, and $\sum_t \Phi_{jt}^{(s-1)} d_{it}^{(s)} = 0$ where the relation for $j = i$ is excluded because it follows from the previous conditions. Here we make use of the expression for $d_{it}^{(s)}$ obtained from formula (4). Having performed this procedure for all equations of the system, we immediately obtain $\Phi_t^{(s)}$ from relation (5), and the step is completed. In this case the whole procedure (with possible exception for the start) stays within the structural form. It follows, however, from formulas (5) and (6) that the components of $y_t^{(s)}$ are linear combinations of the components of $\Phi_t^{(s)}$, and they too can therefore be used as instrumental variables. As we shall now see, this fact gives us a natural generalization to more general econometric systems.

The step from the $(s-1)$st to the sth iteration in the general case. The coefficients of the ith equation in iteration number s are obtained from the conditions $\sum_t y_{kt}^{(s-1)} d_{it}^{(s)} = 0$ when y_{kt} occurs in the ith equation, and from $\sum_t z_{lt} d_{it}^{(s)} = 0$ when z_{lt} occurs in the ith equation. The expressions for $d_{it}^{(s)}$ are obtained from the ith component of (4). In other words, those components $y_{kt}^{(s-1)}$, which pertain to the endogenous variables present in the ith equation, are used as instrumental variables of the ith equation. Even in this case we get one more relation than is needed, but it follows from the ith component of (6) that the relations are in agreement, with a possible exception for the first iteration. Having obtained all coefficients of the system, the value of $Y_t^{(s)}$ is obtained from formula (7), and this completes the step from the $(s-1)$st to the sth iteration.

If identities occur among the structural equations, the given values of their coefficients are employed throughout, so that these given values are included in the matrices $G^{(s)}$ and $B_1^{(s)}$ when $y_t^{(s)}$ is calculated from formula (7).

The normalization of the coefficients. The relations given above determine only the ratio between the coefficients within each equation. Therefore we have to add a normalization condition, for instance that the sum of squares of the coefficients of the endogenous variables should have unit value for each equation, and that the sign of one coefficient of each equation should be prescribed in advance. In practice, however, it is usually preferable to prescribe unit value to one coefficient in each structural equation. The normalization can in principle be made after the iteration procedure, but for control purposes it is usually more convenient to normalize the coefficients in each iteration step.

A symmetric counterpart to the GEID specification can be constructed by assuming that the residual δ_{it} is uncorrelated with those components of z_t, which occur in the ith equation as well as all components of the vector Φ_t. This condition also implies that δ_{it} is uncorrelated with all component variables η_{it}^*. Since $\epsilon_t = \beta_1^{-1} \delta_t$ it follows that ϵ_t is also uncorrelated with all components η_{it}^*. At first it might seem natural to restrict the non-correlation assumptions between δ_{it} and H_t^* to those components η_{it}^* for which the corresponding components of Y_t occur in the ith structural equation. Such a condition would, of course, correspond to the iterative procedure, but it is not sufficient even for obtaining non-correlation between η_{it}^* and ϵ_{it}. Hence we are forced to retain the conditions $E(\Phi_{it}\delta_{kt}) = 0$ $(i, k = 1, ..., n)$ if we want a model suitable for prediction purposes.

11.5. Algebraic Instrumental Variables (AIV) Estimation of Summers' Model

The instrumental variables which are used in the previous section are not known in advance, and therefore they are estimated together with the coefficients with the aid of an iterative method. For simple systems, however, it is possible to avoid the iteration and treat the problem algebraically (Lyttkens, 1967a). We shall now apply this procedure to the same simple two-relation system, Summers' model, for which the asymmetric AFP estimation was utilized in Chapter 3.8. Again, in the instrumental variables approach of this section, a non-linear problem is met with. In general two different sets of estimates are obtained.

In the symmetric specification, applied to the sample, we write Summers' model (1.4.69) as

$$b_{11} y_{1t} + b_{12} y_{2t} = g_{11} z_{1t} + g_{12} z_{2t} + d_{1t} , \tag{1a}$$

$$b_{21} y_{1t} + b_{22} y_{2t} = g_{23} z_{3t} + g_{24} z_{4t} + d_{2t} . \tag{1b}$$

In accordance with the notations of the previous section we denote the systematic part of the right-hand members by $\hat{\varphi}_{1t}$ and $\hat{\varphi}_{2t}$,

$$\hat{\varphi}_{1t} = g_{11} z_{1t} + g_{12} z_{2t} , \tag{2a}$$

$$\hat{\varphi}_{2t} = g_{23} z_{3t} + g_{24} z_{4t} . \tag{2b}$$

Since the endogenous variables y_{1t} and y_{2t} occur in both equations, we can use $\hat{\varphi}_{2t}$ as instrumental variable for the first equation and $\hat{\varphi}_{1t}$ as instrumental variable for the second equation. Therefore the coefficients of the first structural equation obey the following relations

$$b_{11} \sum \hat{\varphi}_{2t} y_{1t} + b_{12} \sum \hat{\varphi}_{2t} y_{2t} = g_{11} \sum \hat{\varphi}_{2t} z_{1t} + g_{12} \sum \hat{\varphi}_{2t} z_{2t} , \tag{3a}$$

$$b_{11} \sum z_{1t} y_{1t} + b_{12} \sum z_{1t} y_{2t} = g_{11} \sum z_{1t}^2 + g_{12} \sum z_{1t} z_{2t} , \tag{3b}$$

$$b_{11} \sum z_{2t} y_{1t} + b_{22} \sum z_{2t} y_{2t} = g_{11} \sum z_{1t} z_{2t} + g_{12} \sum z_{2t}^2 . \tag{3c}$$

Let A denote the fourth order determinant in which the ith row is

$$\sum z_{it} z_{1t} , \quad \sum z_{it} z_{2t} , \quad \sum z_{it} y_{1t} , \quad \sum z_{it} y_{2t} \quad (i = 1, 2, 3, 4) ,$$

and let A_{jk} be the minors of this determinant. Solving the system (3) for the coefficients of the first structural equation, we obtain the following relations by a procedure similar to the one used in Chapter 3.8,

$$\lambda_1 b_{11} = A_{43}g_{23} + A_{33}g_{24},\tag{4a}$$

$$\lambda_1 b_{12} = -A_{44}g_{23} - A_{34}g_{24},\tag{4b}$$

$$\lambda_1 g_{11} = -A_{41}g_{23} - A_{31}g_{24},\tag{4c}$$

$$\lambda_1 g_{12} = A_{42}g_{23} + A_{32}g_{24},\tag{4d}$$

where λ_1 is an auxiliary parameter. From these equations the ratios between the coefficients of the first structural equation are obtained in terms of the ratio between g_{23} and g_{24}.

Denoting by C the fourth order determinant in which the ith row is

$$\sum z_{it}y_{1t}, \sum z_{it}y_{2t}, \sum z_{it}z_{3t}, \sum z_{it}z_{4t} \quad (i = 1, 2, 3, 4),$$

and by C_{jk} the minors of this determinant, we obtain with the aid of a similar treatment of the second structural equation:

$$\lambda_2 b_{21} = -C_{21}g_{11} - C_{11}g_{12},\tag{5a}$$

$$\lambda_2 b_{22} = C_{22}g_{11} + C_{12}g_{12},\tag{5b}$$

$$\lambda_2 g_{23} = C_{23}g_{11} + C_{13}g_{12},\tag{5c}$$

$$\lambda_2 g_{24} = -C_{24}g_{11} - C_{14}g_{12}.\tag{5d}$$

By introducing these expressions for g_{23} and g_{24} into the system (4) the following reations are obtained for the coefficients in the first structural relation,

$$\lambda b_{11} = (A_{43}C_{23} - A_{33}C_{24})g_{11} + (A_{43}C_{13} - A_{33}C_{14})g_{12},\tag{6a}$$

$$\lambda b_{12} = -(A_{44}C_{23} - A_{34}C_{24})g_{11} - (A_{44}C_{13} - A_{34}C_{14})g_{12},\tag{6b}$$

$$\lambda g_{11} = -(A_{41}C_{23} - A_{31}C_{24})g_{11} - (A_{41}C_{13} - A_{31}C_{14})g_{12},\tag{6c}$$

$$\lambda g_{12} = (A_{42}C_{23} - A_{32}C_{24})g_{11} + (A_{42}C_{13} - A_{32}C_{14})g_{12},\tag{6d}$$

where $\lambda = \lambda_1 \lambda_2$. On the other hand, substituting the expressions for g_{11} and g_{12} according to (4c–d) into the system (5), the following relations for the coefficients of the second structural equation are obtained,

$$\lambda b_{21} = (A_{41}C_{21} - A_{42}C_{11})g_{23} + (A_{31}C_{21} - A_{32}C_{11})g_{24} , \tag{7a}$$

$$\lambda b_{22} = -(A_{41}C_{22} - A_{42}C_{12})g_{23} - (A_{31}C_{22} - A_{32}C_{12})g_{24} , \tag{7b}$$

$$\lambda g_{23} = -(A_{41}C_{23} - A_{42}C_{13})g_{23} - (A_{31}C_{23} - A_{32}C_{13})g_{24} , \tag{7c}$$

$$\lambda g_{24} = (A_{41}C_{24} - A_{42}C_{14})g_{23} + (A_{31}C_{24} - A_{32}C_{14})g_{24} . \tag{7d}$$

From the last two equations of this system, or from the last two equations of system (6), the following equation for λ is obtained:

$$\lambda^2 + (A_{41}C_{23} - A_{42}C_{13} - A_{31}C_{24} + A_{32}C_{14})\lambda +$$

$$+ (A_{41}A_{32} - A_{42}A_{31})(C_{14}C_{23} - C_{13}C_{24}) = 0 , \tag{8}$$

which is a "secular equation" in the sense of the classic theory of least squares. The form of the constant term is easily inferred from the fact that the determinant of the right-hand side of the last two equations of each of the systems (6) and (7) is the product of the determinants of the last two equations of systems (4) and (5).

For each of the two roots of the equation for λ we obtain the ratios of the coefficients of the first structural equation from (6), and those of the second structural equation from (7). The computations will be easier by first calculating the ratio between g_{11} and g_{12} from the last two equations of (6), then the ratios between the coefficients in the second structural equation from (5), and finally the remaining ratios of the coefficients of the first structural equation from (4). In order to determine the coefficients themselves and not only their ratios, we have to add a normalization condition, for instance $b_{11} = b_{22} = 1$. If a symmetric condition is desired we may alternatively prescribe $b_{11}^2 + b_{12}^2 = b_{21}^2 + b_{22}^2 = 1$, and positive signs for b_{11} and b_{22}.

In the classical case where the residuals are uncorrelated with all predetermined variables, the occurrence of two solutions need some clarification. In the first place, we note that if z_{3t} is used as instrumental variable of the first structural equation, the ratio γ_{11}/γ_{12} is estimated as $-A_{41}/A_{42}$, while the estimate is $-A_{31}/A_{32}$ if z_{4t} is used as instrumental variable. Due to the classical assumptions the corresponding ratios in the theoretical distribution are equal (with exception of singular cases), which shows that one of the roots of the secular equation (8) vanishes for the theoretical distribution. The vanishing root leads to another value for γ_{11}/γ_{12}, namely the theoretical counterpart to $-C_{1j}/C_{2j}$ which is the same for all j ($j = 1,2,3,4$), and for γ_{23}/γ_{24} the theoretical counterpart of A_{3j}/A_{4j} ($j = 1,2,3,4$). If this ratio between γ_{23} and γ_{24} is used for constructing the theoretical counterpart to the system (3), the matrix of the theoretical moments corresponding to the product sums contains only vanishing third order determinants. This implies that the instrumental variable is of no use for determining the ratio between the coefficients. Thus the solution which is obtained from the vanishing eigenvalue is singular. This result gives the hint that for a sample from populations subject to the classical specification, the solution should be chosen that corresponds to the root of (8) with the largest absolute value.

When the roots of the secular equation (8) have unequal absolute values, the iterative instrumental variables (IIV) method (see 11.4) leads to that set of estimated coefficients which corresponds to the eigenvalue which has the largest absolute value. This last statement is subject to the proviso that none of the start values of g_{11}/g_{12} and g_{23}/g_{24} are chosen to correspond exactly to the set of estimated coefficients obtained from the smallest eigenvalue. Now if we carry $\hat{\varphi}_{2t}^{(s)}$ instead of $\hat{\varphi}_{2t}$ into (3a), we find that system (4) and, by analogy, also system (5) provides the IIV estimates in the $(s+1)$st iteration. After one more iteration it is found that the systems (6) and (7) can be used for passing directly from the sth to the $(s+2)$nd IIV iteration. But the iterations obtained from (6c–d) and (7c–d), respectively, converge to the estimates corresponding to the absolutely largest eigenvalue (see e.g. Bodewig, 1959, p. 270). This result extends to the whole systems (6) and (7) and, moreover, to the original IIV method.

The case where the roots of the secular equation (8) are imaginary is not excluded. However, in the Classic ID specification the theoretical counterpart to the secular equation (8) has a vanishing constant term, and therefore a sample with imaginary roots usually represents an extreme deviation from the population.

When constant terms occur in the two structural equations, the procedure of this section can be applied to the deviations from the sample means. Alternatively, the fourth order determinants A and C can be bordered by a fifth row and a fifth column in the way described at the end of Chapter 3.8.

11.6. An Iterative Method for Partly Respecified Systems

In the FP method a respecified form (3.2.5b) of the interdependent system is used, whereas the IIV method employs the original form (3.2.4) of the interdependent system. Sometimes it may happen that the respecification is made only for the behavioral equations, while other types of equations, including equilibrium equations and identities, are kept in their original form. Specifically, if a system consists only of behavioral relations and identities, it is natural to respecify the behavioral relations but not the identities. Sometimes equations occur which are treated symmetrically with respect to some but not all endogenous variables occurring in the equation. An example of such a partial respecification is given in Chapter 11.7.

The partly respecified interdependent system will be written as

$$\beta_1 Y_t = \beta H_t^* + \Gamma Z_t + \epsilon_t^* , \tag{1}$$

where the diagonal elements of β and at least one element of each pair of corresponding elements of β_1 and β are prescribed zeros, and where β_1 as well as $\beta_1 - \beta$ are non-singular matrices. The vector H_t^* is given by

$$H_t^* = (\beta_1 - \beta)^{-1} \Gamma Z_t , \tag{2}$$

while the residual vector ϵ_t^* fulfils the condition

$$\epsilon_t^* = \beta_1 \epsilon_t , \tag{3}$$

where ϵ_t is the residual vector of the reduced form.

If the ith equation is asymmetrically specified, which implies that the only non-vanishing element of the ith row of $\mathbf{B}_1$ is β_{ii} ($= 1$, say), then we have $\epsilon_{it}^* = \epsilon_{it}$. On the other hand, if the ith equation is symmetrically specified, so that all elements of the ith row of $\mathbf{B}_1$ vanishes, then we have $\epsilon_{it}^* = \delta_{it}$, where δ_{it} is the residual of the original structural form. The identities, if any, are considered as symmetrically specified equations without residuals.

For the estimation of a partly respecified system, we suggest the following iterative method. This reduces to the FP method if the system is completely respecified, so that $\mathbf{B}_1 = I$, and to the IIV method if the system is in its original form, so that $\mathbf{B} = 0$.

The start. As shown in Chapter 11.4 the alternative initial values $y_t^{(0)}$ given by (3.5.3a–c) can be used not only for the FP method but also for the IIV method, the first approximation of the coefficients being the same for both of these methods. Therefore these starting values can also be used for the present iterative method.

The step from the $(s-1)$st to the sth iteration. Suppose that we have arrived at the proxy $Y_t^{(s-1)}$. In approximation number s the estimated system is written as[1]

$$B_1^{(s)} Y_t = B^{(s)} Y_t^{(s-1)} + G^{(s)} Z_t + e_t^{(s)} . \tag{4}$$

The coefficients of the ith equation are obtained with the aid of the conditions $\sum_t y_{kt}^{(s-1)} e_{it}^{(s)} = 0$ for $k \neq i$ if y_{kt} occurs in the ith equation in its original form, and $\sum_t z_{lt} e_{it}^{(s)} = 0$ if z_{lt} occurs in the ith equation. This procedure means that the estimation of the coefficients for given $Y_t^{(s-1)}$ is performed by the FP method in the case of a completely respecified equation, and by the IIV method if an equation is in original form. In the latter case the relation obtained by using $y_{it}^{(s-1)}$ itself as instrumental variable is in accordance with the other relations, with possible exception for the start. Identities do not enter into consideration in this part of the procedure.

Having obtained the values of the coefficients $B_1^{(s)}$, $B^{(s)}$, $G^{(s)}$ we proceed to estimate $y_t^{(s)}$. A natural compromise between relation (3.5.5) for the FP method and relation (11.4.6) for the IIV method is to stipulate

$$B_1^{(s)} Y_t^{(s)} = B^{(s)} Y_t^{(s-1)} + G^{(s)} Z_t \,. \qquad (5)$$

Thus, for each completely respecified equation we obtain one component of $Y_t^{(s)}$ in the same way as in the FP method; that is, by the systematic part of the OLS regression of the left-hand endogenous variable of the equation on the components of $Y_t^{(s-1)}$ and Z_t which occur on the right-hand side of the equation. In order to obtain the whole vector $Y_t^{(s)}$ we solve for this vector and get the following iteration formula:

$$Y_r^{(s)} = (B_1^{(s)})^{-1} [B^{(s)} Y_t^{(s-1)} + G^{(s)} Z_t] \,. \qquad (6)$$

Here the known value of the coefficients in the identities are included in $B_1^{(s)}$ and $G^{(s)}$. In the special case where all relations of the structural form are either completely respecified equations (behavioral relations, typically), or identities, all elements of the matrix $B_1^{(s)}$ are known or prescribed; hence the matrix $(B_1^{(s)})^{-1}$ that occurs in formula (6) can be calculated once and for all in advance of the iterative process.

The normalization of the coefficients. As before, we presume that the diagonal elements of β_1 are non-vanishing. We prescribe unit value for one non-vanishing element of each row of B_1, or unit value for the sum of squares of the elements of each row of B_1. In the latter case, a positive value is assigned to one non-vanishing element in each row. Both these procedures result in the same normalization for the completely respecified equations as the one used when the FP method is applied.

In the systems considered here, the classical specification can be generalized in a way analogous to the one used in Chapter 11.4. The residual ϵ_{it}^* is assumed to be uncorrelated with the components of Z_t, which occur in the equation, and with all components of the vector $\Phi_t = \Gamma Z_t$. It follows that the components of ϵ_t^* are uncorrelated with the components of H_t^*, and relation (2) then implies that the components of ϵ_t are also uncorrelated with the components of H_t^*.

In the special case where the system consists only of completely respecified equations and identities, we can as an alternative use the original GEID specification where only as many non-correlation assumptions are made as are needed for the estimation procedure. It follows from the GEID specification that the residual ϵ_{it} of the reduced form and the corresponding systematic part η_{it}^* are uncorrelated if the ith structural equation is completely respecified. Thus, the comparison shows that the GEID specification makes use of the smallest number of non-correlation assumptions, whereas the specification mentioned above implies that the residuals are uncorrelated with the systematic part in each relation of the reduced form. In general this last specification involves a larger number of zero correlation assumptions. The parity principle (see 3.2) is honored in the first design but not in the second.

11.7. Algebraic Estimation of Girshick-Haavelmo's Model in a Partly Respecified Version

The AFP estimation of Girshick-Haavelmo's model in Chapter 9.3 was performed in two ways, subject to two different specifications. In model (9.3.1) y_{1t} occurs on the left-hand side of the two first structural equations, and the two alternative specifications arise when one of these equations is rewritten so that y_{2t} instead of y_{1t} occurs on the left-hand side of the equation.

In this section we shall use a partial respecification of the two first equations, so that both y_{1t} and y_{2t} in these equations will occur with their observed values. For easy comparison with the previous results we retain the original normalization of the coefficients as well as their signs as indicated by (9.3.1). In this way the partly respecified version of the first two equations of (9.3.1), when spelled out for the sample, are written as

$$y_{1t} = b_{12}y_{2t} + b_{13}y_{3t}^* + g_{13}z_{3t} + g_{14}z_{4t} + g_{10} + e_{1t}^* \qquad (1\,\text{a})$$

$$y_{1t} = b_{22}y_{2t} + b_{24}y_{4t}^* + g_{23}z_{3t} + g_{20} + e_{2t}^* . \qquad (1\,\text{b})$$

For the other structural equations the earlier version is retained, a respecification which is complete in the sense of Chapter 9.3.

As in Chapter 9.3, the coefficients of the third structural equation of (9.3.1) are estimated by means of OLS regression, and the systematic part of the regression again gives the estimate (9.3.3) of y_{3t}^*. After introducing this value of y_{3t}^* into the first structural equation (1a), which is just identified, we proceed by estimating the five coefficients of the first structural equation from the five linear conditions

$$\sum z_{1t} e_{1t}^* = \sum z_{2t} e_{1t}^* = \sum z_{3t} e_{1t}^* = \sum z_{4t} e_{1t}^* = \sum e_{1t}^* = 0 . \tag{2}$$

In this way we get the estimates of these coefficients as originally obtained by Girshick-Haavelmo (1947, p. 102); who, however, made use of the method of indirect least squares, with the modification that the expression for y_{3t}^* as obtained from the third structural equation was used instead of the one obtained from the unrestricted reduced form.

Next the expression for y_{3t}^*, as obtained from the third equation, is introduced into the first equation of the system. The first, second, fourth and fifth structural equations will then form a system of four equations where z_{2t} and z_{4t} occur only in the first equation, namely, as the linear expression z_{2t}^* (say) given by

$$z_{2t}^* = b_{12} g_{32} z_{2t} + (b_{13} g_{34} + g_{14}) z_{4t} . \tag{3}$$

Having thus reduced the four predetermined variables to three, we find that the second and fourth equations are just identified. Since the fourth equation is asymmetrically specified, this implies that y_{4t}^* is obtained as the systematic part of OLS regression of y_{4t} on z_{1t}, z_{2t}^*, and z_{3t}, say

$$y_{4t}^* = p_{41}^* z_{1t} + p_{42}^* z_{2t}^* + p_{43}^* z_{3t} + p_{40}^* , \tag{4}$$

where p_{41}^*, p_{42}^*, and p_{43}^* are the partial regression coefficients of y_{4t} on z_{1t}, z_{2t}^*, and z_{3t}, and p_{40}^* is the corresponding constant term. This expression for y_{4t}^* is introduced into the second equation as given in (1b). We then obtain the coefficients of this second equation from the four conditions

$$\sum z_{1t} e_{2t}^* = \sum z_{2t}^* e_{2t}^* = \sum z_{3t} e_{2t}^* = \sum e_{2t}^* = 0 . \tag{5}$$

Equation (1b) is subtracted from equation (1a), and the equation thus obtained is solved for y_{2t}. The systematic part of the expression for y_{2t}

that results gives the value of y_{2t}^*, since y_{3t}^* and y_{4t}^* are already known. Thereafter, the fifth equation is estimated by means of OLS regression of y_{5t} on y_{2t}^* and z_{3t}. The systematic part of this regression gives y_{5t}^*. Finally the coefficients of the fourth equation can be estimated from the regression of y_{4t} on y_{5t}^*, z_{1t}, z_{3t}, or equivalently by equating coefficients, after having replaced y_{4t} by the expression for y_{4t}^* obtained earlier.

Let us now compare the method of estimation used in this section with the first version of the algebraic FP method as given in Chapter 9.2. As to 9.2 we note that since the first equation is just identified, we can calculate y_{1t}^* from the unrestricted reduced form, while in the present specification the coefficients of the first structural equation are obtained, separately, the expression for y_{3t}^* being calculated in advance. Concerning the estimation of the other equations we note that the predetermined variables z_{2t} and z_{4t} can be effectively replaced by one variable, namely y_{1t}^* (or, equivalently, $p_{12}z_{2t}+p_{14}z_{4t}$) in the algebraic FP estimation, and by z_{2t}^* as given by (3) in the case now considered. Numerically, the ratio between the coefficients of z_{2t} and z_{4t} in the combined predetermined variable is $p_{12}/p_{14}=0.259$ in the former case and $(b_{13}g_{34}+g_{14})/(b_{13}g_{32})=0.354$ in the present case. The numerical difference between these ratios is the clue to the differences between the two methods under comparison, in the sense that if the ratios were equal, the estimates obtained by the two methods would coincide.

The calculations have, to a large extent, utilized Girshick-Haavelmo's own results, especially their matrices $P**N$. These can be described as formed by the product sums of (1) the endogenous variables present in the equation and (2) the residuals of the OLS regressions of the predetermined variables absent from the equations on those present in the equation.

The resulting estimates are shown in Table 1, where Girshick-Haavelmo's own results are quoted for comparison. To repeat, Girshick-Haavelmo's parameter estimates for the first equation are the same as those obtained by the method considered in this section. For the other equations Girshick-Haavelmo's estimates are, in fact, LIML estimates. For the third structural equation these reduce to ordinary regression coefficients. Since the first equation is just identified, the LIML estimate of this equation coincides with the TSLS estimate (see the second row of Table

Table 11.7.1

Parameter estimates in Girshick-Haavelmo's model with the aid of different methods *

Method	First equation					Second equation			
	b_{12}	b_{13}	g_{13}	g_{14}	g_{10}	b_{22}	b_{24}	g_{23}	g_{20}
GH	−0.246	0.247	−0.104	0.051	97.677	0.157	0.653	0.339	13.240
LIML	−0.486	0.290	−0.317	0.097	115.563				
FIML	−0.794	0.379	−0.573	0.118	138.489	0.223	0.565	0.372	15.478
APR	−0.246	0.247	−0.104	0.051	97.677	0.191	0.614	0.345	13.851

Method	Third equation			Fourth equation				Fifth equation		
	g_{32}	g_{34}	g_{30}	b_{45}	g_{41}	g_{43}	g_{40}	b_{52}	g_{53}	g_{50}
GH	0.203	0.367	40.720	0.556	−0.300	−0.190	81.224	2.883	0.656	−200.067
FIML	0.193	0.408	37.899	0.524	−0.257	−0.002	78.196	2.778	0.654	−189.462
APR	0.203	0.367	40.720	0.857	−0.539	−0.201	75.281	2.725	0.595	−183.545

* Abbreviations: GH　　= Girshick-Haavelmo's estimates

　　　　　　　　LIML = limited information maximum likelihood method

　　　　　　　　FIML = full information maximum likelihood method

　　　　　　　　APR　= algebraically calculated estimates of the partially respecified system.

The FIML estimates are quoted from Eisenpress (1962, p. 346).

GII coincides with LIML for the four last equations.

Also, see other estimates of the same models in Table 9.3.2, and results on 100 Monte Carlo samples from Girshick-Haavelmo's model in Table 10.2.24.

9.3.2). A comparison between the estimates of the first version of the AFP method in Table 9.3.2 and the parameter estimates of the partly respecified version confirms the close relation between these two sets of estimates.

CHAPTER 12

Special Features Brought to Light

The econometrician should be familiar with many methods of estimation. Similarly, he should be prepared to carry out extensive and penetrating mathematical analysis of each specified model in order to understand its special properties prior to proceeding with estimation. Knowledge of alternative methods of estimation plus the insight from extensive mathematical analysis will reveal many potential improvements in his initial specification of the model and selection of a method. These improvements will be invaluable in overcoming the problems in obtaining good estimates of parameters.

Results from research efforts similar to the one reported in this monograph add to our general knowledge about developing and using models. They should provide help to the econometrician since the focus is on specific problems of model building. The main thrust in our monograph is the FP method and its possibilities for avoiding the difficulties that arise when using the reduced form as a starting point in the estimation procedure. A second thrust is the review of operative procedures of the estimated structural relations (Chapter 1.4).

The conclusions and insights presented in this and the next chapter are, admittedly, only a part of the understanding an analyst needs for developing reliable and useful models. Nevertheless, they are important and should be given explicit attention at the onset of each modeling effort.

Research on methods of estimation quickly reveals that the class of equation systems called interdependent models is too large to be treated as one type of system. Likewise, the number of possible methods for estimating parameters of interdependent models is too large to be classed as one type.

The summary comments offered in Chapter 13 are in line with the original objectives of our overall research effort, whereas the summary comments in the present chapter represent insights and conclusions that have evolved somewhat as side issues throughout the research. This, of course, does not imply that either set of comments is of lesser importance.

12.1. Degree and Type of Interdependence is Important

Although there is no unambiguous way to measure either degree or type of interdependence, both concepts are important in analysis of so-called simultaneous equation models. We suggest that the degree of interdependence be defined in terms of the size of beta coefficients and that the type of interdependence be defined in terms of both the position matrix for beta coefficients and the difference equation that evolves from the specified lag structure among endogenous variables. These are not formal definitions but merely guides to the reader as to what aspects are referred to under each topic.

At the onset it is necessary to distinguish between stochastic and exact relations. In fact, the topic of degree and type of interdependence would be very straightforward if all relations in a system were exact. The larger the residuals the more important the concept of degree and type of interdependence becomes. This will be highlighted in the next section.

The degree of interdependence as measured by size of beta coefficients is discussed in terms of models where endogenous and exogenous variables have been normalized to a common variance. Without this normalization differences in size of coefficients could reflect nothing more than scaling of variables which has no significance beyond accuracy in computations.

Since there is no interdependence when all beta coefficients are zero (off-diagonal betas in the symmetric specification), it is intuitively obvious that interdependence increases as size of beta coefficients increases. However, as shown in Section 4.4.1 and Chapters 5.2 and 7.6, there is a special type of interdependence that emerges when the absolute values of some of the beta coefficients are less than one and some are greater than one. This condition can occur only when there are correlations among the exogenous variables; these correlations add to the difficulty in estimating the parameters of the model.

The suggested measure of degree of interdependence (size of beta coefficients) can be related to quality of estimates from various methods of estimation. First, the bias in OLS increases as size of the absolute value of beta coefficients increase. Second, the multicollinearity among the y_i^* and predetermined variables in the second and subsequent stages of multistage methods increases as size of the absolute value of beta coefficients increases. Third, the difficulties in convergence of the iterative procedure in FP increase as size of beta coefficients increases.

As suggested earlier, the type of interdependence can best be related to the non-zero positions in the beta matrix. Econometric literature contains many references to "block-recursive" systems, a particularly interesting case in the design of the position matrices. For estimation purposes each block is really a separable model because within the beta matrix there are zeros in every position that relates endogenous variables from two different blocks. Consequently, the block-recursive model will not be discussed further in this chapter.

The number of beta coefficients in each equation is an important feature in the type of interdependence. The results presented in Chapter 5 show that difficulties in convergence increase as number of current endogenous variables per equation increase.[1] In general, the degree of multicollinearity in the second stage of TSLS increases as the number of current endogenous variables in an equation increases.

Least squares as applied to the unrestricted reduced form equations is the only method of estimation that is not affected by the degree of interdependence measured in terms of the size of beta coefficients. It can be said to be affected by the type of interdependence, however. The non-zero positions of the beta matrix determine the number of predetermined variables that enter each of the reduced form equations and this, in turn, has a direct bearing on the problems of estimating the unrestricted reduced form. A most difficult problem in the method of TSLS is the large degree of overfitting in the first stage. In many situations the model specification and the available data make it impossible to obtain meaningful estimates of the unrestricted reduced form in the first stage of TSLS.

It is quite obvious that the simple dichotomy between multi- and unirelational models is not very discriminating. There is need to recognize differences in both degree and type of interdependence within the former category. In each specific modeling effort the amount of mathematical analysis that the econometrician should do will, of course, carry him much beyond that offered by the above concepts on degree and type of interdependence. The concepts are given specific attention at this point only because they seem to have been neglected in econometric literature. The extensive investigation of many different models in this research project brought the aspects of degree and type of interdependence to the forefront.

12.2. **Overidentification De-emphasized with Emergence of LIML and TSLS Estimation**

In overidentified models the unrestricted estimates of reduced form coefficients provide alternative and, in general, conflicting estimates of structural coefficients. The alternative sets of estimates of structural coefficients raise the same question as in instrumental variables: Which set should be accepted? Although the number of alternatives provided by the unrestricted reduced form is usually not as great as in the case of instrumental variables, the selection is difficult because there is no clear means of making a choice.

The emergence of LIML and TSLS took the spotlight off the problem of overidentification. Unrestricted estimates of reduced form coefficients are obtained in the first stage of TSLS, and these are used in the second stage to estimate the structural relations, a procedure which avoids inconsistency in OLS estimates of the structural form. Under the classic assumptions TSLS estimates are consistent, and the situation can be explained in terms of the REID specification. In the first stage, the residual sums of squares in the unrestricted reduced form are minimized,

$$y_i = \sum_{j=1}^{m} w_{ij} z_j + e_i' , \qquad (1)$$

In the second stage, the residual sums of squares in the REID specification of the structural form are minimized,

$$y_i = \sum_{j=1}^{p} b_{ij} y_j^* + \sum_{n=1}^{q} g_{in} z_n + e_i'' , \qquad (2)$$

In (2), y_j^* as given by the systematic part of (1) is used as a proxy for η_j^*. The FP method resembles TSLS, but it is an iterative method whereby the y_j^* as computed from the least squares estimates of (2) in each iteration are used in the subsequent least squares estimates of (2). In the population under the classic assumptions, the residuals in (1) and (2) are the same in the case of both TSLS and FP. In other words, estimates of the unrestricted reduced form using population data do not give rise to alternative estimates of structural coefficients, and on the classic assumptions the resulting estimates are consistent.

Basmann (1965, 1966) has placed emphasis on an identifiability test statistic which is an aspect of the overidentification problem. However, the focus in his use of the identifiability test statistic is on detecting possible misspecifications of the system of structural relations. In a misspecified model the residuals in (1) and (2) above will not be the same even in the population. Bias in estimates of structural coefficients will appear in finite samples even when the system of relations is correctly specified. The interpretation of the identifiability test statistic centers on the separation of differences in the residuals in (1) and (2) above that result from the sampling variation or small-sample bias from differences that stem from misspecification of the model.

12.3. Relationship between URF and Generated Reduced Form in FP Estimation

When a structural equation is just identified the estimates of coefficients in that equation can be obtained by algebraic solution of the un-

restricted reduced form coefficients. If a model has only behavioral relations, there is a one-to-one correspondence between structural and reduced form equations via the dependent variables. That is, each endogenous variable appears as a dependent variable once and only once in
the structural equations, just as in the reduced form equations. In the
case of FP the generated reduced form yields the same coefficients as
URF for each equation that corresponds to a just identified structural
equation. This is not the case for TSLS or limited information maximum
likelihood estimates.

The iterative technique in FP explains how agreement between the
URF and generated reduced form for each equation corresponding to
the just identified equations in the structural form is brought about.[1]
TSLS stops after what can be called the first iteration, and agreement
between the URF and generated reduced form does not occur.

In the example

$$y_1 = b_{12}y_2^* + g_{11}x_1 + g_{12}x_2 + e_1 \, , \tag{1}$$

$$y_2 = b_{21}y_1^* + g_{23}x_3 + e_2 \, , \tag{2}$$

or in reduced form

$$y_1^* = w_{11}x_1 + w_{12}x_2 + w_{13}x_3 + e_1' \, , \tag{3}$$

$$y_2^* = w_{21}x_1 + w_{22}x_2 + w_{23}x_3 + e_2' \, , \tag{4}$$

the first structural equation is just identified and FP estimates of the
structural equations gives rise to e_1 in (1) that is identical to the e_1' in
(3) when the latter equation is estimated by the method of unrestricted
reduced form. Likewise, the estimates of w_{11}, w_{12} and w_{13} in (3) generated from the FP estimates of the structural equations (1)−(2) will be
identical to the URF estimates.

This is one illustration of how FP squeezes more information out of
the data via successive iterations.

12.4. Predictive Power as a Test for Comparing Alternative Methods

There are two strong incentives for using predictive power, as measured by the familiar R^2 statistic, in regression analysis for comparing alternative methods of estimation. First, there is need for a single measure on quality of estimates of coefficients in the entire model. Second, the R^2 statistic is in line with information content as measured in information theory.

The estimate of predictive power should be developed from data not used in deriving estimates of coefficients. In this monograph predictive power was estimated as:

$$R^2 = 1 - \frac{\sum_{i=N+1}^{N+P} (y_i - \hat{y}_i)^2}{\sum_{i=N+1}^{N+P} y_i^2} \tag{1}$$

where $\hat{y}_i$ is the prediction of y_i from the estimated model, observations $1, 2, ..., N$ were used in developing estimates of parameters, and the remaining observations $N+1, N+2, ..., N+P$ were used for developing a measure of predictive power. The estimate of R^2 using sample data is acceptable only if other data are not available. In Monte Carlo experiments it is easy and cheap to generate data beyond the so-called sample period to be used only for developing an unbiased estimate of predictive power. This, then, becomes a true simulation of applied econometrics where the model builder estimates a model from data on past periods $(1, 2, ..., N)$ and uses the estimated model to make predictions for future time periods $(N+1, N+2, ..., N+P)$.

The need for a summary statistic on quality of the overall estimated model is evident from the number of arbitrary choices if one or a small number of individual parameters are to be used in judging quality. Even the small models analyzed in this monograph had up to 16 coefficients with no way of specifying any one coefficient as more important than another. Even if one or a small set of coefficients is selected there is no clear choice as to which of the properties such as bias and variance is the more important quality. The predictive power test usually involves

every estimated coefficient and involves each of the commonly recognized qualities such as bias and variance of each estimated coefficient in
the model.

The agreement between R^2 and information content as measured in
information theory is described in Section 8 of Chapter 1.4. The R^2
measure of predictive power is the amount of information about the
dependent variable that can be extracted from the predetermined variables via the estimated coefficients. This relationship between predictive
power and amount of information makes the former appealing as a
measure of the overall quality of an estimated model.

With a single measure of quality of estimates it is easy to compare the
quality of two different methods of estimating coefficients. Considerable emphasis has been placed on predictive power throughout this
monograph enabling the authors to compare alternative methods of
estimation relatively easily.

Virtually no emphasis has been placed on predictive power in earlier
Monte Carlo studies reported in the literature. There has, however, been
some discussion concerning prediction as the major role of econometric
models.[1] The authors share the view that prediction is the major role of
econometric models, but detailed discussion of this topic is beyond the
context of this monograph.

12.5. Full Information Methods Questionable for Large Models

So-called full information methods must estimate coefficients in all
equations simultaneously. The limited information methods estimate
only one equation at a time. The latter approach has been viewed by
many as less efficient because *a priori* information about other parts of
the model is ignored when estimating each equation.

Until recently the so-called full information methods have seldom
been used because of the large computational problem. With the rapidly
expanding capacity and speed of computers it is now time to assess if
full information methods really hold promise for providing better estimates than methods like TSLS and FP.[1] Specifically, we are thinking of
full information methods as including the residual variances to be estimated simultaneously with the coefficients.

Because of its iterative nature FP can be viewed as closer to full information methods than TSLS. We have seen that in the classical design of models there were only a few instances where FP gave as good or better estimates than TSLS. On the other hand, in the GEID specification FP generally gave better results than TSLS. This suggests that there is a price to be paid for bringing in larger amounts of *a priori* information, and this price can be greater or less than the gain depending on the nature of the model.

The incentive for full information methods also has implications within the philosophy of building and testing models. In most cases the parts of a model should be viewed as hypotheses to be tested. If the entire specification is honored in estimation of parameters, it is not possible to test any part of the specification.[2] For example, the limited information methods allow the model builder to test the hypothesis that all zero positions in each row of the β and Γ matrices are correct. The entire specification is not treated as "*a priori* information" but as a combination of *a priori* information and hypotheses to be tested.

The authors' conclusion on the use of full information methods is that the incentive for these methods must be qualified. Even if the model is correctly specified, there are certain situations in which "imposing the *a priori* information" contained in the model specification is well worth the price, but there are other situations in which it is not. The specification of possible non-zero correlations in GEID models is an example of *a priori* information that is honored in the FP method of estimation. It is important to note that it was not necessary to employ a true full information method to make use of this *a priori* information in many situations. The FP has worked well in these situations.

The final verdict on full information over limited information methods must be based on (a) the net value of full information methods if the specification is true, (b) the need to test rather than accept hypotheses concerning the specification of a model to be estimated, and (c) the consequences of imposing an incorrect specification. The main feature of this research was a Monte Carlo experiment where the correct specification of the model was always used and no information was generated on items (b) and (c). We know that it is only in item (a) that full information methods can have a net positive contribution.

This research has raised three major considerations concerning the net value of full information methods when the specification of the method is known to be correct. First, the nature of *a priori* information varies from model to model and the advantage of using all rather than part of the *a priori* information varies. Second, as in the case of GEID models there is often a special type of estimation procedure (such as FP) which is short of a full information method but which can exploit the special *a priori* information in the model specification. Third, there are probably many situations in which a full information method will yield poorer estimates than a limited information method because the *a priori* information has small value relative to the price that must be paid for the added complexity of estimating all parameters of the model simultaneously. The poorer performance of FP relative to TSLS in most of the 46 models in Chapter 10.2 which have the classical design illustrates this point.

12.6. Accuracy in Computations

Accuracy in computations of econometric models has become an issue for two reasons. First, in cases where two different computers were used on the same data the estimated coefficients have turned out to be quite different.[1] Second, some researchers have discarded part of the Monte Carlo samples in an experiment because of indications that estimates were heavily influenced by rounding errors in calculations.[2] This is a dangerous practice because these samples are likely to have generated estimates of coefficients quite different from those in other samples.

The computer and computational routines used in this study have generated useful information on computational accuracy. There was no problem with accuracy in any of the 100 samples for any of the 46 different models. The 12 digit capacity in the CDC 3600 single precision is sufficiently greater than the 8 digit capacity in many other computers that the familiar problem of rounding errors turns out to be of no concern in most economic models. It appears that the nature of many economic models and the number of digits carried in most economic data are such that 8 digit capacity is on the fringe of the accuracy required if rounding errors are not to be a problem.

Most problems in computer accuracy arise either in inverting a matrix or in calculation of eigenvalues. It is a good policy to develop and print a check on accuracy for both of these operations. The check used in this study was to compute the product of a matrix and its inverse each time an inverse was calculated. The product was printed and analyzed to determine the accuracy involved. The errors in this inverse check were usually of the order 10^{-8} or less.

Another check on accuracy is provided by the eigenvalues which were calculated for every matrix that was inverted (see part D of Table 10.1.1 for definition). The eigenvalues were computed for the purpose of analyzing the degree of multicollinearity in each equation to be estimated. This means that one set of eigenvalues was calculated for the product moment matrix of determining variables in each structural relation and one set was calculated for the product moment matrix of all predetermined variables used in estimating the reduced form coefficients. The smallest eigenvalue among the 100 samples for each product moment matrix was printed.

As noted from the first column of numbers in Part D of the tables in Chapter 10.2, none of the computed values were negative. In fact, none were less than 0.00001. All eigenvalues are supposed to be positive, but if the calculated values reflect only rounding errors the computed value is equally likely to be positive or negative. Negative eigenvalues have been identified and pointed out in previous Monte Carlo work.[3]

Another important factor in computational accuracy in this project was the handling of sample data. For the 100 samples on each model the generating of data and estimation of parameters were both done in the same computer program. All numbers were left in binary form until the printout of estimated parameters. This eliminated any errors that might arise in truncating numbers for printing and any errors that might arise in handling of data tapes or punched cards.

In summary the authors can state that accuracy in computations was not a problem in this investigation. Furthermore, the results provide evidence that normal computer machinery has sufficient accuracy for estimating small- and moderate-size econometric models. There is no connotation about the accuracy of estimates in applied econometrics because this involves accuracy of the sample data. Observations on most economic variables are reported in 2 or 3 digits whereas the Monte Carlo data in this study were expressed in 12 digits.

CHAPTER 13

Any Verdict yet?

The chapter title quotes the question posed and discussed in the
Econometrica Symposium in 1960.[1] Referring to the new vistas
opened up by the approach of interdependent systems as initiated in
1943 by Trygve Haavelmo, the question branches into two lines of inquiry. One line refers to interdependent systems as a new type of econometric model design, and is adressed specifically to the performance
of these models in applied use. A key aspect of the question is that the
structural form of interdependent systems does not allow the same type
of cause-effect inference and/or predictive inference as unirelational
models and causal chain systems; hence the question is whether this
loss of operative inference is outweighed by the gains that arise by the
inference from the reduced form being potentially more general than
in causal chain systems. The other line of inquiry refers to the problems
of statistical technique posed by an interdependent system, in particular the problem of consistent estimation of their parameters.

The loss of operative inference from the structural form is particularly glaring in the special case where all structure relations are behavioral. Therefore, this case has been placed in the center of our study.
The approach of ID systems is given a new twist by a partial reorientation in that the models are designed as Reformulated ID (REID) or
General ID (GEID) systems, and the parameters are estimated by the
fix-point (FP) method and related approaches.

471

The results of our study indicate that because of this partial reorientation the positions of interdependent systems can be moved forward in both of the lines of inquiry in which we would like a verdict. The REID and GEID specifications restore the structural relations as instruments of operative inference by replacing each current endogenous variable which appears as explanatory variable by its expected value. This substitution is optional; without change in the numerical values of parameters a REID or GEID system can be reformulated to make an ordinary interdependent system.

Regarding the inquiry on the statistical techniques for ID systems, we point out that the new FP method of estimation restores the parity principle of numbers of residual correlation assumptions and parameters to be estimated, and still provides consistent parameter estimates. This is a drastic change in relation to the classic estimation methods which in large ID systems require correlation assumptions that outnumber by a large factor the parameters to be estimated. Our study shows that the FP method can handle the parameter estimation even in small samples if the interdependence is weak or moderate or if the residuals are not too large.

The research reported in this monograph was designed to cover a wide range in types of models in order to develop a basis for judging the four methods under consideration. The authors know of no other study (Monte Carlo investigations or mathematical analysis of small-sample distributions) that has covered as many types of models and as wide a range in the size of such parameters as beta coefficients and residual variances.[2]

Do the results in this study give a final verdict on the best method of estimation or, at least, a clear indication of what line of research would lead to the same? If not, do the results provide any hints on one or both parts of the question? Do the results suggest that the intensity of research on the question of a best method be increased so that the issues can be resolved?

This report does not provide a final verdict on alternative methods of estimation and it provides only qualified answers to the questions on proper direction and intensity of future work. More importantly, these results show that relative performance of methods will depend on (a) the specific nature of the model (i.e., the model from which the sample data were generated), (b) the specific operative use of the estimated model, and (c) the amount of available data for use in estimating parameters of the model. Econometrics and applied economics are too complex and encompass too much variety to assume that there is a single best method for estimating all economic models.[3] For example, the new vistas opened up with the new REID and GEID formulations reveal the robustness but also the complexity of interdependent models.

Sketches of several small-sample distributions are presented in Chapter 13.1. Each of the sketches appears to indicate a clear choice among methods. However, each sketch represents an accurate comparison among the methods for only a *small* range in type of models.

The reader is reminded that the sketches in Chapter 13.1 pertain only to estimates of structural coefficients. This limitation was for convenience in exposition and carries no connotation with respect to the relative importance among the three major sets of statistics — estimates of structural coefficients, estimates of reduced form coefficients, and predictive power. Also, the Monte Carlo work to date is insufficient for drawing firm conclusions about small-sample distributions; the sketches should be accepted as representing early insight. The authors are confident that there are at least some models for which each set of sketches is representative, but they are not clear as to the exact range in types of models each sketch represents or to the frequency with which each type of model will be encountered in applied work.

13.1. Sketches of Distributions for Parameter Estimates

13.1.1. GEID Models

The sketches shown in the Charts in Chapter 13.1 provide a general feel for differences among methods of estimation but are not a complete summary of the many statistics presented in Chapters 4–9. Each sketch presents a general perspective for estimates of all coefficients in specific models. For example, the upper part of Chart 1 is a general perspective for estimates of all beta and gamma coefficients in a range of GEID models that have GEID correlations (i.e. correlations between residuals and excluded variables; see 1.4.5) that are small.

As shown in Chart 1 the relationship among alternative methods de-

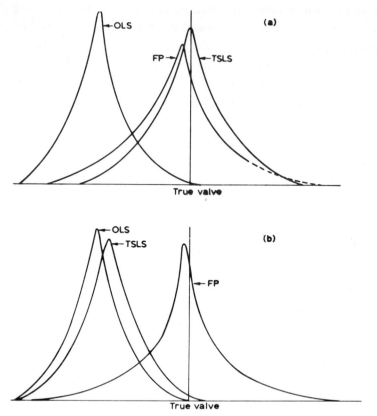

Chart 13.1.1. Sketches of distributions of parameter estimates for GEID specifications. See 1.4.5 for definition of GEID correlations.

pends on the size of GEID correlations. If these are small, TSLS estimates have less bias than FP, but in most models this relationship will be reversed when the correlations exceed 0.05 in absolute value. From the discussions in earlier chapters the reader should be well aware that the effect from a particular size of correlation depends on the size of the model, the size of residuals, and the size of beta coefficients. This is one of the reasons why Chart 1 should be regarded as providing only a general perspective.

    Chart 1 also shows the bias of OLS as unchanged as the size of correlations increases in a GEID specification. Actually, the bias in OLS estimates of a specified coefficient increases or decreases depending on the signs of the GEID correlations. Furthermore, the bias of OLS can be greater or less than for TSLS and can be in the same or opposite direction. Likewise, the bias for both OLS and TSLS can be in the same or opposite direction to that in FP.

Increasing size of GEID correlations has little effect on bias in FP, but it does increase the variance by causing thicker and longer tails in the distribution. Larger GEID correlations make for greater bias in TSLS unless there is severe overfitting in the first stage — a case where TSLS estimates have the same characteristics as OLS estimates. The variances of TSLS estimates tend to decrease as the correlations become larger.

The sketches in Chart 1 are more representative of estimates of gamma coefficients than they are of beta coefficients or reduced form coefficients. For example, in two-equation models bias of OLS and TSLS estimates of beta coefficients are not affected by GEID correlations. In the case of estimates of reduced form coefficients the range of possible relationships among alternative methods is greater than in the case of structural coefficients because the estimate of each reduced form coefficient is a function of several coefficients in the structural relations. Biases in each of several structural coefficients can either cancel each other and produce slight bias in the estimate of a reduced form coefficient or augment one another and produce greater bias in reduced form coefficients than in structural coefficients.

Although relatively little work has been done on GEID models thus far, it appears that the contrast between Parts (a) and (b) of Chart 1 arises from differences in the size of GEID correlations and differences in the size of the model. The bias in OLS and TSLS for given size of GEID correlations increases little as the size of model increases, but there is a tendency for FP to squeeze more information out of the data relative to TSLS as the size of model increases. In some cases this feature makes for lesser small-sample bias in FP than in TSLS.

13.1.2. Size of Beta Coefficients in REID Specification

A major finding from our Monte Carlo experiments is that whenever all beta coefficients are small, the distributions for TSLS and FP are similar and the distribution for OLS has only slight bias. In Model 1a the largest absolute value for beta coefficients was 0.5 and the distributions are similar to those shown in Part (a) of Chart 2. The large bias and variance in Part (b) in relation to Part (a) occurs in either of the following situations: (1) all beta coefficients are large as in Model 1c with values of ± 3.0 or (2) some but not all betas are close to unity as in Model 1f with $\beta_{12} = 1.1$ and $\beta_{21} = -3.0$.

Sketches in Chart 2 were developed only to illustrate how the relationship among the small-sample distributions of the three methods changes as size of beta coefficients changes. The degree of bias and sampling variation will, of course, depend on size of the model, size of residuals, and sample size, as well as size of beta coefficients. Note that the horizontal scales in Parts (a) and (b) of Chart 2 are the same whereas the vertical scales are not. Frequency distributions always have unit area; consequently, the OLS curve in (a) is 3 times higher than in (b).

Unless sample size is small, the bias in TSLS estimates is only slightly affected by size of beta coefficients. But bias in OLS is very much affected by size of beta coefficients. Unless sample size is very large, say 20 times the number of coefficients to be estimated, the bias in FP estimates is also very much affected by size of beta coefficients.

The dispersion in all three methods increases as beta coefficients become large. As shown in Chart 2 the increase in dispersion is greater in FP and TSLS than in OLS. If all beta coefficients are large, the dispersion of FP estimates is greater than that for TSLS estimates. However, in models where some but not all beta coefficients are near unity in absolute value, the dispersion in TSLS can be larger or smaller than that in FP.

It is interesting to note from our experiments that bias and dispersion of direct estimates of reduced form coefficients change relatively little as size of beta coefficients changes. If there is no special reason to estimate structural coefficients and if sample size is so large as to eliminate the pitfall of overfitting, there is an advantage in the method of unrestricted estimates of reduced form coefficients because these estimates are not affected by size of beta coefficients.

The possible effects from different size beta coefficients are more extensive than shown in Chart 2. As models become large, some combination of values for beta coefficients will produce almost any specified set of relationships among small sample distributions for different meth-

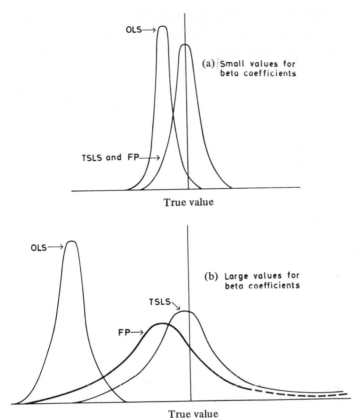

Chart 13.1.2. Sketches of distributions of parameter estimates for different sizes of beta coefficients.

ods of estimation. The sketches in Chart 2 are only meant to illustrate the change in bias and variance that can result from change in values of beta coefficients.

13.1.3. Larger Models under REID Specification

The quality of estimates of coefficients in a model depends on the size of the model. There are, however, several ways in which size of a model can be measured. These include number of equations, number of structural (reduced form) coefficients, number of predetermined variables, and number of variables per structural equation. The various methods are affected differently by increases in model size as measured by each of the various measures.

For most economic models it is typical that all of the predetermined variables in the entire model appear in each reduced form equation; therefore, the effect of model size on unrestricted reduced form estimates is best measured by total number of predetermined variables in the entire model. Unless degrees of freedom in the first stage of TSLS are few, this method as well as OLS are mainly affected by number of variables per structural equation. This would be true for all methods that operate on one structural equation at a time. The effect of model size on FP estimates is best measured in terms of total number of coefficients in the structural equations. This is likely to be true of all methods which are in the direction of so-called full information since they operate on all structural equations simultaneously.

As shown in Chart 3 the distribution of FP estimates is similar to that for TSLS in the case of large number of variables per equation but quite different in the case of large number of equations. The sketches are drawn to represent situations where the total number of predetermined variables in the models represented by graphs (a) and (b) is the same. If sample size were held constant but the model changed so that total number of predetermined variables increases, the distribution of TSLS estimates would approach that for OLS. In such situations the variance of FP estimates would exceed that for OLS and TSLS, but the bias could be smaller or larger depending upon the structure of the beta matrix.

The bias of OLS is less in the situation portrayed in the upper part of Chart 3 because the variance of residuals in the structural equations is smaller. As the number of equations in a model increases but the R^2 in the reduced form equations is held constant, the variance of the residuals in the structural equations usually decrease (see part A.2 in the tables for various models in Chapter 10.2). This tendency will depend on the size of beta coefficients, but where the absolute size of beta coefficients is held constant (e.g., the models in Series 2a−2d), the statement is certainly true.

The sketches in Chart 3 were developed from Monte Carlo results where the largest number of equations in any model was 7 and the largest number of variables in each structural equation was 8. It is precari-

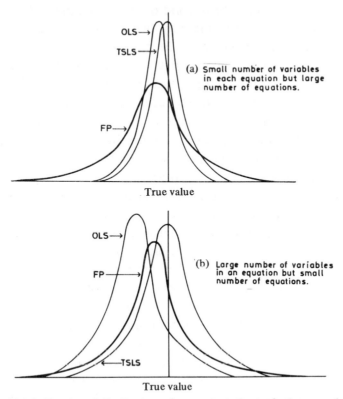

Chart 13.1.3. Sketches of distributions of parameter estimates for larger models.

ous to apply the conclusions from these results to huge models, say, 100 or more equations. If the "symmetrical nature" of the models in the Series 2a–2d always held, the sketches in Chart 3 might well represent the actual relationships among the sample distributions for the various methods for all size models. By "symmetrical nature" we mean equal variances of exogenous variables, equal absolute values for beta coefficients, and zero correlations among residuals and among exogenous variables. The more information the model incorporates in specified hypotheses, the more possibilities it opens for the iterative procedure of the FP method to squeeze the data for this information. However, as size of model increases, the variety of forms the model can have increases rapidly and, therefore, no specific statement can be made about the relationships among the small-sample distributions for alternative estimates of structural coefficients in all large models.

Very large models — more than 30 equations or more than 60 predetermined variables — seem to be beyond the present state-of-the-art in economic model building. There are only two general conclusions the authors are willing to make concerning the properties of alternative methods for estimating very large models. First, because economic data are usually limited, the overfitting in the first stage of TSLS will become severe as model size increases, and TSLS estimates will be equivalent to OLS. Since OLS is relatively little affected by increasing number of equations in a model we have fairly good insight into the limiting nature of TSLS estimates in large models. Second, since FP and other methods which are in the direction of so-called full information methods increase in complexity in proportion to the total number of coefficients to be estimated in the entire model, there are few opportunities for general conclusions concerning properties of these estimators in very large models. It is always possible to construct a model that is block-recursive, and the complexity should be measured by the size of the models within each block. Sometimes the block-recursive property can be obtained only by employing untenable assumptions. If the block-recursiveness of a model is incorrectly specified, this will in general make the parameter estimates biased.

It is conceivable that the overall quality of estimates of a model would be better if some selected beta coefficients were arbitrarily assumed to be zero in order to obtain a block-recursive model. The reader can easily envision for himself the impossibility of making general statements about estimates of models which have been arbitrarily redesigned into block-recursive models. For example, if the coefficient that was assigned a zero value were the coefficient of greatest interest in the entire model this practice would be self defeating. In Monte Carlo work we know the values of beta coefficients and can calculate the importance of each coefficient for any stated purpose. In applied econometrics we do not know the value of beta coefficients and the practice of arbitrarily setting some coefficients to zero to obtain a block-recursive model can be very dangerous.

13.1.4. Sample Size under REID Specification

The variance of estimates from all methods reduces as sample size increases. The bias of FP and TSLS reduces to zero as sample size increases under the classical assumptions. However, the relationship between the distributions for FP and TSLS changes as sample size varies.

The sketches in the upper part of Chart 4 were designed to represent a situation where sample size is small but not so small that there are no degrees of freedom in the first stage of TSLS. If there are no degrees of freedom in the first stage, TSLS either breaks down or becomes the same as OLS which, in general, has a larger small sample bias than FP. There are numerous situations in econometric models presented in the literature where there were in fact no degrees of freedom for estimating the unrestricted reduced form.[1] These situations raise very fundamental questions in model building and estimation but have not been addressed in the research being reported on in this monograph.

As is shown in the bottom half of Chart 4 there is a sample size for which the distributions of FP and TSLS estimates will be essentially the same for any given model. The required sample size depends on the beta matrix, but in most cases it is less than 20 times the number of coefficients to be estimated. As the sample is reduced below the required size, the bias in FP estimates is significantly larger than for TSLS as shown in Part (a) of Chart 4. It is quite likely that in most situations in applied econometrics the sample size will be short of the size for which the two distributions would be similar.

In models where convergence of FP is a severe problem, the variance of FP estimates from small samples will be much larger. The sketches in Chart 4 are representative only of those models for which FP does not have severe problems in convergence. In situations where convergence is slow the estimates can be recalculated with an arbitrary but low iteration limit, giving FP estimates that are similar to TSLS estimates.[2]

The sketches in Chart 4 portray only a general pattern of change when going from large to small sample size. Other characteristics such as size of beta coefficients, size of model, and size of residuals play an important part in determining the properties of small-sample distributions for all three methods. The sketches were drawn to represent what the au-

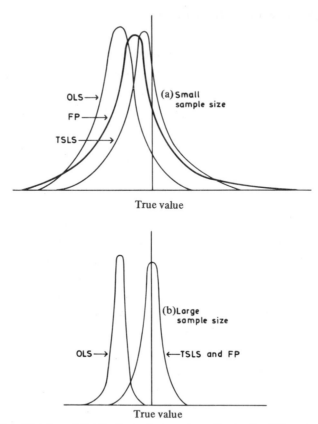

Chart 13.1.4. Sketches of distributions of parameter estimates for different sample sizes.

thors feel would be typical situations in applied econometrics. Small sample size would be where the number of observations is 2 or 3 times the number of structural coefficients, and large sample size would be where the number of observations exceeds 15 or 20 times the number of structural coefficients. The former situation is encountered frequently when fitting small models from annual time series data. The latter situation is encountered often when using cross-section data or time-series data with monthly or quarterly observation periods.

13.1.5. Size of Residuals Under REID Specification

Both bias and variance are affected by the size of residuals. The effect on OLS estimates is best measured in terms of the residuals in the structural form of the model (see $\sigma^2(\delta)$ in Part A.2. of the tables in Chapter 10.2). The effect of size of residuals on FP, TSLS and other consistent estimators is best measured in terms of the residuals in the reduced form of the model (see $\sigma^2(\epsilon)$ in part A.2 of the tables in Chapter 10.2). The sketches in Chart 5 are referenced to the size of residuals in the reduced form.

The size of residuals at which the small-sample distribution of FP estimates is essentially the same as that for TSLS depends on sample size, size of model, and structure of the beta matrix. For most models there will be very little difference when R^2 exceeds 0.95. If beta coefficients are relatively small, the two distributions will be similar for R^2 as low as 0.85 or 0.9. On the other hand, if convergence in FP estimates is slow, R^2 might have to approach 0.99 before the two distributions are similar.

The relative degree of bias between FP and TSLS is not as easily summarized as indicated in Chart 5. For all models under the classical assumptions there appears to be some size of residuals where bias in FP is greater than that in TSLS. However, as variance of residuals increases and R^2 approaches zero the bias in TSLS often exceeds the bias in FP as shown in the upper part of Chart 5. Sample size and structure of the beta matrix appear to be the most important factors in determining whether bias in FP exceeds that in TSLS as R^2 approaches zero.

The authors believe that the situation portrayed in the upper part of Chart 5 will be encountered fairly frequently in applied econometrics. The high R^2 values (i.e., 0.80 to 0.99) which are frequently computed for macro-economic models fitted from time-series data are not likely to be typical of the bulk of econometric work in the future. These large R^2 statistics arise because of generally high collinearity among time-series data, especially when several lagged endogenous variables are included in the model. They do not prove that the model has been well specified and that true residual variances are small.

In econometric models other than macro models of the national

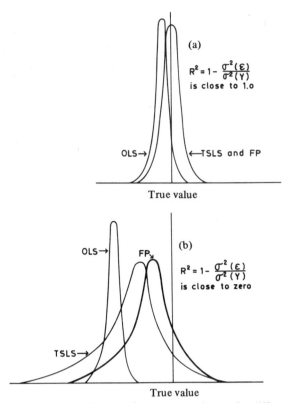

Chart 13.1.5. Sketches of distributions of parameter estimates for different sizes of residuals.

economy and models estimated from cross-section data, R^2 values between 0.20 and 0.50 are fairly common. The sets of estimates in the
trial-and-error exploratory stage of a research project can be expected
to yield R^2 values of 0.10 or less. These are a few of the reasons why
the low R^2 situation portrayed in the bottom part of Chart 5 is likely
to be quite relevant in applied work.

The models investigated in the Monte Carlo work to date suggest that
the advantages of FP over TSLS increases as the true R^2 decreases and
is below 0.50. We wish to point out, however, that it is risky to generalize because the structure of the beta matrix is very important and there
is no way of determining in advance the types of beta matrices that will
be encountered in applied work.

13.2. Methods and Types of Models not Considered

The main incentive for the large Monte Carlo study that is reported on in this monograph was the development of a new method, fix-point (FP). Each of the three alternative methods considered in this study were selected for a special reason. OLS is very simple to apply and can be used with smaller sample sizes than TSLS and other methods which operate on the unrestricted reduced form equations in the process of computing estimates of structural coefficients. TSLS is probably the most commonly used of the consistent estimators in interdependent models and appears to be one of the best methods presently available. Unrestricted least squares estimates of the reduced form equations, at least under the classical assumptions, avoids the many problems in obtaining unbiased estimates and is relatively easy to analyze since the theory of least squares is well known.

The four methods described in this report cover a wide range in types of methods, but the results cannot be used to pass verdict on all possible methods. Some additional methods plus summary comments on how results from them might compare with one or more of the methods considered in this report are described below.

The approach of Bayesian statistics, which has seen a strong revival in the 1960's, has two main features.[1] First, if *a priori* information on values of parameters is specific and well founded, the advantages of this approach over TSLS is similar to the advantages of TSLS over URF. Second, the uncertainty concerning the validity of so-called *a priori* information makes it very difficult to specify the properties of Bayesian methods. It should be pointed out that the "Bayesian" approach is really much more familiar than is realized. The arbitrary limitation on the size of model that many of us impose on ourselves can be viewed as a form of *a priori* specification of parameter values. Also, special assumptions that will lead to block-recursive models are in the category of *a priori* information. The concept of building upon previous "knowledge" is so well founded in scientfic pursuits that some form of Bayesian approach must be recognized. However, it is still an open question as to how formal the introduction of *a priori* information into the process of estimating parameters of a specific model should be.

The so-called full information maximum likelihood method has been

discussed only briefly in this report (see Chapter 11.3).[2] The concept of
a full information method extends beyond the methods currently proposed. For example, stability conditions for the overall model could be
imposed. There is, in fact, a very wide range of possible restrictions
pertaining to predictions from the overall model of which stability of
the estimated model is only one type. These conditions might be very
hard to impose in the estimation procedure, but are a direction in development of methods that has not been explored in this project. If
methods along this line require procedures that operate on all equations
simultaneously as opposed to TSLS which operates on one equation at a
time, the authors predict that except for rare situations where large
samples are available, the quality of estimates will be less than that for
TSLS. The often poorer performance of FP in relation to TSLS under
the classical assumptions in our Monte Carlo experiments is an indication of a possible poorer performance of methods which operate on all
equations simultaneously. This difference would be even greater in applied work when specification errors in any part of the model can exert
an influence on estimates of all parameters in the entire model. It is important to point out that some preliminary results on models with 10–20
relations indicate that beyond a certain size FP might gain in relation
to TSLS because the iterative technique squeezes more information out
of the data.

   The use of instrumental variables is another line of estimation methods that has not been explored extensively in this project (see Chapters
11.4 and 11.5). One would also have to consider the practice proposed
by some econometricians of arbitrarily selecting a subset of predetermined variables to use in obtaining direct estimates of reduced form coefficients. Since the choice of instrumental variables is so arbitrary and
so large, there is little that can be said about the quality of estimates
that can be expected from this line of development. In a moderate size
model, say ten equations, the choice of instrumental variables can involve thousands of alternatives.[3] A large part of the arbitrariness at
issue is removed in the symmetric design of ID models and estimation
methods presented by E.Lyttkens in Chapter 11.4–11.5. His approach
is symmetric in the same sense as other classic ID methods, namely that
it is invariant to a move of the current endogenous variables between
the left and right members of the structural form relations. Lyttkens'

approach is similar to Classic ID systems (but different from REID and GEID systems) in that the structural relations do not allow a predictor specification; see 1.4.4–1.4.5.

When estimating models from time series data the multicollinearity problem is usually so severe that estimates using different sets of instrumental variables are often quite similar. This, however, is not proof that use of instrumental variables is a promising direction in developing better methods of estimation. If as F.M.Fisher (1966) points out, we know how to select as instrumental variables those predetermined variables which are causally related to current endogenous variables but are not highly correlated with other variables chosen as instrumental variables, the method holds promise.[4] Unfortunately, this information is not known in the early stages of trial and error in designing the model. Therefore, it is probable that the approach of instrumental variables will lead the model builder in erroneous directions from which he cannot easily recover. It is conceivable that as more and more is learned about appropriate models for economic phenomena, the method of instrumental variables will be more useful. In the present state of econometric model building the method appears to be dangerous.

In addition to TSLS there are numerous other so-called limited information estimators. These have been quite extensively discussed in the literature and have been studied in various other Monte Carlo studies; see the brief review of alternative methods in Chapter 11 (e.g. Duesenberry et al. [1], Ch. 15). The concensus of most people appears to be that is 1) TSLS considerably easier to apply and is 2) probably as good if not better than other limited information methods for most all models likely to be encountered in applied econometrics. It is conceivable that some of the other methods might be simpler with respect to developing exact small-sample distributions but this remains to be seen. For use in evaluating FP, TSLS seemed to be the best member of the limited-information class to use for comparison.

While FP is designed for models with arbitrary GEID correlations, TSLS is designed for the special case when all GEID correlations are zero. Just as FP is appropriate for the special condition in GEID models, many other methods can be designed for other types of conditions, for example models that involve logarithmic variables, ratios or other nonlinear features. This is an open ended class of estimators and few generalizations can be drawn about performance of alternative methods. The comparison of general methods with a more specialized method such as TSLS will very likely be similar to comparisons between FP and TSLS in the estimation of GEID models. If the violation of the special conditions is quite severe (e.g., GEID correlations as high as 0.4 as in Model 6j), the general method will be considerably superior. The special conditions in GEID specifications are among the most important conditions in economic model building, and in these cases FP is likely to be better than other specially designed methods.

The above paragraphs are not meant to be a complete summary or even a complete list of other methods. They are intended to provide more prespective in evaluating the results of the four methods that were studied extensively in this project. Other valuable vistas in estimation methods can be obtained by outlining different types of models than those included in this Monte Carlo study. For purposes of this discussion models not included in this study can be grouped into three classes, namely, nonlinear models, recursive models, and very large models.

The term nonlinear models is used to refer to models that are non-linear in the current endogenous variables. FP holds considerable promise for obtaining consistent estimates of parameters in these models. The iterative approach which is the basis of FP estimation lends itself to handling a wide range of nonlinear forms (e.g. logarithms, squares, and ratios. Nonlinear models were not included in this study for two reasons. First, the properties of FP turned out to be more difficult to study than originally anticipated so all resources were oriented towards studying the simpler linear models. Second, the range of possible non-linear models is so great that there is little hope of deriving definitive results from Monte Carlo work. The exclusion of nonlinear models in the results presented in this monograph might well present a bias against FP relative to TSLS. However, the authors can do no more at this stage than point out this possibility.

Four recursive models were included in this study mainly for illustrative purposes. No block-recursive models were included because each block can be considered as a separate interdependent model. Each of the methods considered in this report is unaffected by the presence of other sets of interdependent relations in a block-recursive model as long as the predetermined variables which enter each set of reduced form equations are properly specified.

The important property of so-called recursive models is the zero correlation between each residual and the determining variables in the same
equation. The triangular beta matrix is only of interest in that it helps
support the hypothesis about the above zero order correlations. If the
"true" model is indeed recursive, there is every reason to specify it as
such and to use OLS for estimating the parameters. This can be seen in
the results for Models 1m - 1q (see, for example, the variance of estimates of structural coefficients in Part B.1 and predictive power in Part
E of Tables 10.2.9—10.2.12). If, on the other hand, the model is almost
recursive and the question is whether it should be considered as recursive in order to use OLS, the answer can be selected from anyone of the
sets of OLS estimates among the many Monte Carlo results presented in
this monograph. The true model and the characteristics of the sample
data do not change because of a misspecification of the model to be estimated. It is possible to design a model in which a deliberate misspecification of the model will lead to a more useful estimated model for a
specific purpose such as forecasting. However, such situations are not
likely to be encountered frequently in applied work, and it is very doubt-
ful if recursive models obtained by deliberate misspecification of a
model will produce better results.

A special note must be added to the discussion of block-recursive
models. Virtually all models of real world phenomena are in some way
arbitrarily limited in size. Therefore, each model can be viewed as one
block in an overall block-recursive model. This realization is a warning
against severe criticism of the block-recursive concept. In the current
state-of-the art and with the usual limitations of data the concept might
well be necessary. Perhaps the only option is whether the model builder
acknowledges the inevitable block-recursive specification or assumes
that the model is independent of variables not included in the model.
Since all of the Monte Carlo results presented in this volume were derived
from data generated by the same model that was being estimated, the
block-recursive feature did not enter the analysis.

Large models were not studied explicitly in this project. There is so
much yet to learn about properties of different methods in small models
that all resources in this project were oriented towards small models.[5]
Although Series 2a—2d and Series 2e—2g were designed to permit inferences about various characteristics of small sample distributions in

the case of large models, there are two important phenomena in a large model that suggest caution in making such inferences. First, it is very easy to specify an economic model such that the number of predetermined variables exceeds the number of observations in the available sample data. This creates problems that were not analyzed in this study. Second, large models allow a great range in the form of the beta matrix. Although the authors endeavored to investigate and present results for a wide range in structure of beta matrices they cannot claim to have covered anywhere near the many structures that can occur in large models.

The reader is reminded that with only a few exceptions the models presented in this monograph were normalized so that the population variances of all endogenous and exogenous variables in a model were unity. When the Monte Carlo results are used to obtain insight into the properties of estimates in situations where real world data are used, it will be necessary to make suitable transformations. It was important to normalize variables in this project so that the true differences in the structure of coefficient matrices, especially the beta matrices, could be easily visualized. However, the economist is used to thinking in terms of the magnitude of coefficients he obtains when calculating estimates from real world data where the variables are not normalized. The transformation of estimates of coefficients derived from real world data can be done by using the variances of variables in the sample data (see Appendix II for details).

The three methods used in making comparisons with the FP method and the 46 different models analyzed in this study were chosen with the aim of providing broad and relevant insight into applied work in econometrics. The authors' reflection now that this phase of research is over is that the choices of methods and models were, on the whole, good ones. If the additional methods and models discussed in the above paragraphs could have been included, there would be many more useful results; but the cost and time for the project would have had to have been many times larger.

The authors wish to point out what could be an important qualification on the results and conclusions presented. The decision to analyze small models with relatively small "kernels" (see discussion and chart in Chapter 1.2) has led to considerable insight into the tricky problems in estimation, but has also possibly introduced a subtle bias in the set of results for judging alternative methods. First, if larger models tend to have small residuals and therefore a large "kernel" OLS will come to the foreground as a desirable method because of the proximity theorem (see Chapter 3.3). Second, some preliminary results indicate that the iterative procedure in FP tends to squeeze more information out of the data in relation to other methods as the model becomes large (say, 20 relations). If this preliminary finding holds in general for large models, it is possible that the best way to improve upon the simple and straightforward method of OLS is through applications of the iterative techniques of FP, FFP and RFP.

13.3. Criteria For Judging Estimation Methods

Evidence for judging methods of estimation can come from three general sources, namely, Monte Carlo investigations, mathematical expressions for exact sample distributions, and observed usefulness of models which are estimated from real world data and used in decision making. The latter is the ultimate and most desired measure, but it provides little information in the early stages of developing methods. Mathematical expressions can usually be developed only under a set of assumptions that are unrealistic in real world applications of econometrics. If mathematical expressions could be developed for all types of models without restrictive assumptions, they would provide complete information; but this is beyond reasonable expectation in the near future. Monte Carlo investigations provide great flexibility, but they are expensive if used extensively and can be quite dangerous if used only sparingly before developing firm conclusions. The authors suggest that Monte Carlo investigations, such as those presented in this monograph, be used for developing tentative conclusions on the relative merits of alternative methods. The results should, of course, be integrated with any mathematical expressions that are developed for exact sampling distributions in specialized cases. Observations on usefulness of alternative methods in applied work should be given more attention that is seen in current econometric literature.

Monte Carlo analyses are weak in that they provide little information about the extreme tails of the distributions. If, as Basmann[1] points out, the first and second moments of the distributions for TSLS do not exist in some types of models, the results of Monte Carlo samples are possibly misleading. There is a special consideration on this point. If in some models the mean and variance of distributions of estimates of certain parameters do not exist, we know that there is possibility of very extreme values of estimates in a small percentage of applications. It is likely that the model builder will be able to detect these special situations based on general knowledge of the subject area and can disregard the results. The method must be recognized as being less robust, because of the need for this practice, but the method is more useful than is indicated by the non-existence of the mean and variance in small-sample distributions.

If a specified operative use of an estimated model is to be the basis for judging alternative methods, the choice of the parameter(s) and the choice of characteristics of the estimates of the parameter(s) can be deduced from the operative use. It is much easier to select a criterion in a specific application of methods than in a general appraisal. For example, the model builder will have experience about the approximate structure of the model; furthermore, he will know the sample size, and the relative importance of the properties of bias and variance. For these reasons the authors suggest that selection of the "best method" be made relative to a specific application wherever possible.

If the selection of a criterion for judging methods is, as the authors suggest, best made in line with circumstances in a specific purpose in model building, it is important to outline the important types of circumstances. This is what the authors have tried to do in the design of Chapters 6—9. Considerable evidence was presented to show that on each of several criteria the relative performance of alternative methods varies significantly as size of sample or the structure of the model changes.

In Monte Carlo experiments where models are arbitrarily specified there are many choices concerning parameters and characteristics of estimates of these parameters when judging alternative methods. The authors' strategy in organizing this monograph was to include many types of results for each model. These included measures of predictive power and the mean and standard deviation of estimates of both structural coefficients and reduced form coefficients. In the absence of knowledge about which parameter of a model will be of most interest, the predictive power of the estimated model as described in Chapter 4 is probably the best single criterion. However, by presenting many results for each model the authors hope that this monograph can be used as a reference book for applied econometrics. If the model builder is interested in the estimate of some particular parameter(s) of a model, he will be able to review the results for the corresponding parameter in the same or similar model presented here and thus gain a feel for the properties of estimates from different methods.

There is an incentive to use a single and relatively simple criterion for judging alternative methods of estimation in special investigations such as those reported on in this monograph. The authors' suggestion for such a criterion is the predictive power of the estimated model as measured by the familiar R^2 statistic. Extensive results on the predictive power as measured both within and outside the sample period are presented in Chapter 4. For any given class of models and for operative uses that are in line with the R^2 statistics, the results in Chapter 4 give fairly definitive conclusions on the preferred method of estimation.

13.4. Comments on Methods of Estimation and Model Specification

Our research included analysis of alternative methods of estimation and alternative specifications of a model (Classic, REID and GEID). The authors feel that selection of a preferred method should not be separated from decisions on type of model specification. In applied work, the decision on both the type of specification and the method of estimation should be made after careful review of the sample data and the contemplated operative uses of the estimated model.[1]

URF can be ruled out for two situations. First, if the total number of predetermined variables is large in relation to the average number of determining variables per equation in the structural form, the overfitting problem in URF is likely to make it inferior to methods such as TSLS and FP which operate on the structural form. Second, if there is a need to have an estimate of one or more structural coefficients, URF is definitely out. The authors have indicated elsewhere that they feel estimates of structural equations provide opportunity for a much

greater range of operative uses of an econometric model.[2] The only
situation where URF appears to be best is when overfitting is only a
minor problem, the model builder has confidence in the specification
of the model, and forecasting of endogenous variables for specified values of predetermined variables under a *ceteris paribus* clause is the only
contemplated operative use of the estimated model.

Unless there is reason to believe that all residuals (see δ_i in Part A of
Table 10.1.1) are small or all beta coefficients are small, it appears to
the authors that OLS has to be ruled out as a technique in estimating
interdependent models. The bias of OLS under conditions other than
those described above can be so large that it is questionable if the estimates of parameters would be of much value. We make no statement,
however, about how likely a model where all "true" residuals (δ_i) or
beta coefficients are small is likely to be encountered.

The selection between TSLS and FP depends very much on whether
a REID or GEID specification is a better representation of the pheno-
menum being modeled. In the REID specification there is a certain dualism in the comparison between TSLS and FP. TSLS is based on less
general assumptions than FP and thereby exploits more of the information that is embodied in data where the classical assumptions in the
REID specification are satisfied. In the first stage of TSLS the conditions
that each residual (δ) is uncorrelated with determining variables in the
corresponding relation is exploited. At the same time, the iterative procedure of FP squeezes the data for more information than TSLS. Which of
the two tendencies dominates depends on the model. In the models explored in the present monograph the tendency toward TSLS dominates
the performance of the two approaches. In large models with small residuals the situation is rather in favor of FP and related methods.

The condition that enables the TSLS method to exploit more information in the REID specification leads to inconsistency in TSLS under
the GEID specification. Consequently, FP is a preferred method for
GEID specifications. In making a choice between TSLS and FP it is
necessary to judge the attractiveness of the GEID approach in model
building.

Only a partial answer can be given to the question on whether the
GEID approach circumvents major problems in model building. Both
the GEID and Classic ID approaches have obvious advantages and disad-

vantages. It seems that a compromise between strict reliance on one or the other approach is the best. Starting with the classic ID specification, the model builder might proceed in the following sequence: Drop the assumption that each residual is uncorrelated with every predetermined variable in the model; use some FP technique for parameter estimation; accept each structural relation as a predictor relation subject to ancillary information about both the predetermined and current endogenous variables that appear on the right-hand side of the relation; disregard the fact that the ensuing prediction is biased because the ancillary information is in terms of observed variables (y_i) instead of the systematic component (y_i^*) and accept the prediction as an approximation; and disregard the conceptual contradiction that the variable on the left and the current endogenous variables on the right interchange as cause and effect variables in different structural relations. The contradiction can be accepted as resulting from the approximation that ignores short lags between cause and effect.

The choice between GEID systems with fix-point estimation and Classic ID systems with TSLS or another classic estimation method is new and manyfaceted. The present investigation is of limited scope, focussing on small and simple ID systems where all structural relations are behavioral. These models were specified with only small or moderate amounts of over-identification; sample sizes were large enough to provide only slight overfitting in the reduced form. In most models there was only slight deviation from the parity principle of equal numbers of (a) parameters to be estimated and (b) zero correlations between residuals and explanatory variables. Our investigation shows that under these conditions TSLS is often better than FP estimation. However, recent research indicates that the relative performance is reversed for larger and more general systems. Research is in rapid progress but commenting upon forthcoming results would carry us outside the scope of this monograph.

Symbols, Abbreviations, and Formats for References

Parts A–E are a list of the most frequently used symbols and abbreviations in the main text.

A. Models

		See
CC	– Causal chain systems	1.4.2
CLID	– Classic ID systems	1.4.3
GEID	– General ID systems	1.4.5
ID	– Interdependent systems	1.4.3
REID	– Reformulated ID systems	1.4.4
VR	– Vector regression systems	1.4.1

B. Methods of Estimation

		See
AFP	– Algebraic fix-point method	3.8
AIV	– Algebraic instrumental variables method	11.5
APR	– Algebraic estimation method for partially respecified systems	11.7
FP	– Fix-point method	3.5

FFP	—	Fractional fix-point method	3.6
FIML	—	Full information maximum likelihood method	11.3
IIV	—	Iterative instrumental variables method	11.4
LIML	—	Limited information maximum likelihood method	11.3.1
OLS	—	Ordinary least squares regression	3.3
R_1 FP	—	Recursive fix-point estimation, single sequence	3.7.1
RFP	—	Recursive fix-point estimation, double sequence	3.7.2
TSLS	—	Two-stage least squares method	3.4
3SLS	—	Three-stage least squares method	11.2
URF	—	Unrestricted least squares estimates of coefficients in reduced form relations	3.3.2

C. Variables and Parameters in Models

1. Variables with the same notations for theoretical and observed items.

		See
y_i	— ith endogenous variable, or	1.4
	row vector of observations on y_i	(1.3.35b)
y_{it}	— Variable y_i at time period t	(1.4.1)
Y	— Column vector of the endogenous variables,	(1.4.2a)
	or matrix of observations on the endogenous	
	variables	(1.3.34)
Y_t	— Vector variable Y at time period t	(1.4.2b)
$y_{i,t-s}$	— Variable y_i at time period $t-s$	(1.4.5b)
x_j	— jth exogenous variable, or	1.4
	row vector of observations on x_j	(1.3.35b)
x_{jt}	— Variable x_j at time period t	(1.4.3)
X	— Column vector of the exogenous variables,	(1.4.2a)
	or matrix of observations on the exogenous	
	variables	(1.3.34)
X_t	— Vector variable X at time period t	(1.3.35a)
z_k	— kth predetermined variable; this can be an	1.4
	exogenous variable or a lagged endogenous	
	variable	(1.4.5)

z_{kt}	—	Variable z_k at time period t	(1.4.4)
Z	—	Column vector of predetermined variables,	(1.4.2a)
		or matrix of observations of predetermined	
		variables	(1.3.34)
Z_t	—	Vector variable at time period t	(1.4.2b)

2. Variables and parameters with different notations for theoretical (T) and empirical (E) concepts

T	E			See
α	a	—	General notation for the parameters in the model under consideration	10.2
α_{max}	a_{max}	—	Maximum fraction in FFP method to make the iterations converge	3.6.1
β_{ik}	b_{ik}	—	Coefficient for the kth endogenous variable in the ith structural relation	(1.4.22a)
β	B	—	Matrices of coefficients β_{ik} and b_{ik}, respectively	(1.4.22a)
γ_{ik}	g_{ik}	—	Coefficient for the kth predetermined variable in the ith structural relation	(1.4.7a)
Γ	G	—	Matrices of coefficients γ_{ik} and g_{ik}, respectively	(1.4.7a)
δ_i	d_i	—	residual in the ith structural relation, or (for d_i) row vector of observations on d_i.	(1.4.33) (1.3.35b)
δ_{it}	d_{it}	—	residuals δ_i and d_i at time period t	(1.3.35b)
δ	d	—	Column vectors of residuals δ_i and d_i	(1.4.33)
δ_t	d_t	—	Vectors δ and d at time period t	(1.3.35a)
ϵ_i	e_i	—	residual in the ith relation of the reduced form, or (for e_i) row vector of observations on e_i	(1.4.34a) (1.3.35b)
ϵ_{it}	e_{it}	—	residuals ϵ_i and e_i at time period t	(1.3.35b)
ϵ	e	—	Column vectors of residuals ϵ_i and e_i	(1.4.34a)
ϵ_t	e_t	—	Vectors ϵ and e at time period t	(1.3.35a)

T	E		See
ω_{ik}	w_{ik}	— Coefficient for the kth variable in the ith relation of generated reduced form	(1.4.24)
Ω	W	— Matrices of coefficients ω_{ik} and w_{ik}	(1.4.24)
π_{ik}	p_{ik}	— Coefficient for the kth variable in the ith relation of unrestricted reduced form	(1.4.30)
Π	P	— Matrices of coefficients π_{ik} and p_{ik}	(1.4.30)
η_i^*	y_i^*	— Systematic part of endogenous variable y_i; or	(1.4.49b)
		(for y_i^*) row vector of observations on y_i^*	(1.3.35b)
η_{it}^*	y_{it}^*	— Variables η_i^* and y_i^* at time period t	(1.4.49b)
H^*	Y^*	— Column vectors of variables η_i^* and y_i	(1.4.78)
H_t^*	Y_t^*	— Vectors H^* and Y^* at time period t	(1.4.2b)
$\sigma(.)$	$s(.)$	— Standard deviation (S.D.) of variable (.)	(1.3.7)
$\sigma^2(.)$	$V(.)$	— Variance of variable (.)	(1.3.7)
$(.)$	$(\hat{.})$	— Theoretical item (.) and corresponding estimated item $(\hat{.})$	

D. Miscellaneous Symbols and Abbreviations

$(\bar{.})$	— Average over a set of observations on the variable (.)	(1.3.3a)
$E(.)$	— Expected value of the variable (.)	1.3
$E(*|**)$	— Conditional expectation (= predictor) of the variable (*) for given item or items (**)	(1.2.2)
est $(.)$	— estimated value of item (.)	(1.3.3)
Φ_{it}	— Predetermined part of ith structural relation at time period t	(11.4.2)
Φ_t	— Column vector of the predetermined parts at time period t	(11.4.2)
Φ	— Covariance matrix of GEID residuals ϵ	3.10
Ψ_i	— Auxiliary linear expression in the predetermined variables for representation of the ith relation of the unrestricted reduced form	(3.10.5)

			See
Ψ_{it}	—	The auxiliary variable Ψ_i at time period t	(3.10.5)
Ψ	—	Diagonal matrix of variances of endogenous variables or of unrestricted reduced form residuals	(11.1.5)
I	—	Identity matrix	(1.4.24b)
M	—	Number of auxiliary observations, later discarded, before the sample period	2.2
N	—	Number of observations in the sample period	2.2
N.a.	—	Item not available	
P	—	Number of observations in the prediction period	2.2
O_i	—	ith mode of inference or operative procedure	$\begin{cases} 1.2.3 \\ 1.4.2 \end{cases}$
O_1^*	—	Mode O_1 qualified by the REID reformulation	1.4.4
O_π	—	Mode O_2 qualified by dropping restrictions on the reduced form	1.4.2
pred (.)	—	predicted value of the variable (.)	$\begin{cases} (1.4.11) \\ (1.4.42) \end{cases}$
$p_i(a)$	—	ath position in ith row of matrix Γ	(1.4.7b)
$q_i(b)$	—	bth position in ith row of matrix β	(1.4.23a)
R^2	—	Ratio of variance of systematic part of a variable to the variance of the variable;	1.2.10

$$\text{True } R^2 = 1 - \frac{\sigma^2(\epsilon_i)}{\sigma^2(y_i)} \qquad \text{Table 10.1.1}$$
$$\text{Part E}$$

which is also referred to as Population R^2

$$\text{Generated } R^2 = 1 - \frac{s^2(\epsilon_i)}{s^2(y_i)} \qquad \text{Table 10.1.1}$$
$$\text{Part E}$$

where $s^2(\epsilon_i)$ and $s^2(y_i)$ are calculated from the generated Monte Carlo data.

See

$$\text{Method (.) } R^2 = 1 - \frac{s^2(y_i - \text{pred } y_i)}{s^2(y_i)}$$

Table 10.1.1

Part E

where $s^2(y_i)$ is defined above, and pred y_i are the predicted values of y_i using the estimation Method (.)

$Y_t^{(s)}$ — Proxy for Y_t^* in FP, FFP and RFP estimation (3.5.2)

$\mathsf{Y}_t^{(s)}$ — Auxiliary proxy for η^* in FFP estimation (3.6.2)

E. Format of References Within the Monograph

Chapter 3	— Refers to all of Chapter 3
Chapter 3.2 or briefly 3.2	— Refers to Subchapter 2 of Chapter 3
3.2.4	— Refers to Section 4 in Subchapter 2 of Chapter 3
(1)	— Refers to the first equation in the same subchapter in which the reference is made
Chart 2	— Refers to the second chart in the same subchapter in which the reference is made
Table 2	— Same as for chart
(2.5.1)	— Refers to the first equation appearing in Chapter 2.5. This format is used for referencing an equation in a different subchapter or chapter
Chart 4.3.2	— Refers to the second chart within Chapter 4.3. This format is used when referencing a chart in a different subchapter or chapter
Table 4.3.2	— Same as for chart
Malinvaud (1964)	— Refers to a 1964 publication by Malinvaud. A complete reference appears in the alphabetical and chronological list of references at the end of the monograph
[2]	— Refers to publication number 2 of an author or group of authors in the list of references.

Normalizing Variables

The differences in quality of estimates among various methods of estimation depends quite heavily on size of beta coefficients and on variances of both endogenous and exogenous variables. It is difficult, however, to visualize the size of coefficients unless the variances of the variables have been normalized. Consequently, we chose to specify the population variances of endogenous and exogenous variables as unity in the Monte Carlo generation of data for most of the 46 models presented in this monograph. In a few of the models where we felt it was desirable to recognize the model as it usually appears, the variances of the endogenous variables were not normalized (see Models 1m—1q and 4a—4c).

The complete specification of an interdependent model involves five of the following six parts:

1. Position matrices B and Γ;
2. Product moment matrix of residuals;
3. Correlations between residuals and exogenous variables;
4. Product moment matrix of exogenous variables;
5. Numerical values of coefficients in β and Γ; and
6. Product moment matrix of endogenous variables (current and lagged endogenous that appear in the model).

Normally, number 1 is specified first so we need not be concerned with the problem that there is not necessarily a unique specification of item 1 for a given specification of items 2—6.

The research upon which this monograph is based has revealed a more interesting non-uniqueness, namely, that in GEID models the numerical values of coefficients are not always uniquely determined by 1–4 and 6 above. This is discussed in Chapter 3. Another aspect that has been stressed in this monograph is the "parity principle" between unknown coefficients and the number of zero correlation assumptions on the residuals (see 1.2.6). OLS is ruled by this parity principle and it is a key incentive in the GEID approach to honor this principle. Classic ID and REID systems do not honor this principle (see 1.4.5).

The normalizing of variables is directly associated with the fourth and sixth specification above. The diagonal elements in the product moment matrices of both endogenous and exogenous variables all equal unity.

Some of the 46 models presented in this monograph were first formulated in terms of parameter values and variances observed in empirical models. These specifications were then changed as shown in the following example of a two-equation model:
Original specification:

$$y_1' = \beta_{12}' y_2' + \gamma_{11}' x_1' + \gamma_{12}' x_2' + \delta_1' \tag{1}$$

$$y_2' = \beta_{21}' y_1' + \gamma_{23}' x_3' + \gamma_{24}' x_4' + \delta_2' . \tag{2}$$

Specification with normalization:

$$y_1 = \beta_{12}' \left[\frac{\sigma(y_2')}{\sigma(y_1')} \right] y_2 + \gamma_{11}' \left[\frac{\sigma(x_1')}{\sigma(y_1')} \right] x_1 + \gamma_{12}' \left[\frac{\sigma(x_2')}{\sigma(y_1')} \right] x_2 + \frac{\delta_1'}{\sigma(y_1')}$$

$$= \beta_{12} y_2 + \gamma_{11} x_1 + \gamma_{12} x_2 + \delta_1 \tag{3}$$

$$y_2 = \beta_{21}' \left[\frac{\sigma(y_1')}{\sigma(y_2')} \right] y_1 + \gamma_{23}' \left[\frac{\sigma(x_3')}{\sigma(y_2')} \right] x_3 + \gamma_{24}' \left[\frac{\sigma(x_4')}{\sigma(y_2')} \right] x_4 + \frac{\delta_2'}{\sigma(y_2')}$$

$$= \beta_{21} y_1 + \gamma_{23} x_3 + \gamma_{24} x_4 + \delta_2 , \tag{4}$$

where variances of y_1, y_2, x_1, x_2, x_3, and x_4 all equal 1.

The normalization was used in order to facilitate interpretation of results among the forty-six models. However, the reader who would like to use these results to help interpret data or results in applied work should be aware of the following important features of normalization:

1. The ratio of an estimated coefficient to its estimated standard deviation does not change as a result of normalizing. For example, in the above equations

$$\frac{b_{12}}{s(b_{12})} = \frac{b'_{12}}{\sigma(y'_2)} \frac{\sigma(y'_1)}{s(b'_{12})} \frac{\sigma(y'_2)}{\sigma(y'_1)} = \frac{b'_{12}}{s(b'_{12})} \tag{5}$$

2. The measure of goodness of fit (R^2) does not change with normalization.

3. The *relative* magnitudes of the variances of estimated coefficients change with normalization. Therefore, in comparing the quality of estimates of various coefficients the evaluation should be made in terms of the ratio of estimated variances to the estimate of the respective coefficient rather than in terms of the absolute value of estimated variances.

4. The computational accuracy in manipulation of the product moment matrices is increased as a result of normalization.

5. The relative size of beta coefficients and the effects of different size beta coefficients on quality of estimates is more easily studied if the variables have been normalized.

We emphasize that normalization was used in order to standardize the Monte Carlo experiment to the maximum extent possible. The greater the amount of standardization the greater the amount of insight that can be gained from a given number of Monte Carlo runs.

One particularly interesting observation resulted from the normalization in models developed to study the effect of multi-collinearity. If all endogenous and exogenous variables have a constant variance the specifications of either the beta coefficients or the correlation matrix for exogenous and residual variables imposes certain restrictions on the other. For example, in the model (3)–(4) the absolute values for β_{12} and β_{21} must both be unity, less than unity, or greater than unity if all correlations among exogenous and residual variables are zero.

The relationship between size of beta coefficients and degree of multicollinearity can easily be illustrated in the case of Model (3)–(4). For example, if the absolute value of β_{12} but not of β_{21} approaches unity, and correlations among exogenous and residual variables are zero, multicollinearity is large because the product moment matrix of η_1^*, x_3, and x_4 becomes nearly singular. If the absolute value of one of the betas is less than one and the other greater than one, there must be non-zero correlations among the set of exogenous and residual variables, and the severity of multicollinearity will depend on the nature of these correlations.

The research leading to this monograph has revealed that even linear interdependent models are complex to understand. The technique of normalizing endogenous and exogenous variables before analyzing the model reduces the complexity slightly. In this project, normalization made comparison among different methods of estimation considerably easier. It is very likely that normalization in models developed from real world data might well provide greater insight into the structure of the true model as well as into the difficulties in obtaining reliable estimates of parameters.

Notes

Preface

[1] See Mosbaek-Wold [1] in conjunction with Chapter 1.4 of this volume.

[2] Duesenberry *et al.* (1965).

Chapter 1.2

[1] The reader is assumed to have a working knowledge of the current literature on interdependent systems, e.g., Goldberger (1964), Johnston (1963), Malinvaud (1964) and Theil (1958).

[2] The two-equation ID model (5)–(6) is referred to extensively in this monograph. It is simple, yet instructive to use in illustrations. The model is called Summers' Model because Robert Summers (1965) has done extensive research and published Monte Carlo results on such a model.

[3] Reference is made to a forthcoming progress report; Wold-Lyttkens, (1969).

[4] Mosbaek-Wold [1].

⁵ *"Eo ipso* predictor, or briefly "predictor" is a synonym for a stochastic relationship specified by a conditional expectation, linear or nonlinear; see Wold [9]. For the general arguments about predictors see Wold [7]–[8], [10].

⁶ Cf. Wold [14]. To link up with the pre-Muth discussion, see Wold-Juréen (1952/53), Chapter 7.7.

⁷ R.A.Fisher [1], p. 69. For comparison with nonexperimental situations, see Wold [5].

⁸ Pioneering work on the theory and application of predictive testing was done by Stone (1965), Suits (1967), Theil (1958). Also cf. the test known as the *Janus quotient*; Gadd-Wold (1965).

⁹ This is evident from Klein's view (1968, p. 79f) that useful models might have to contain as many as 1000 relations.

Chapter 1.3

¹ Since the 1920s and 1930s "errors in variables" and "errors in relations" have been used in the terminology of econometrics; see Frisch [1] and [3], Koopmans [1], Tintner [1]. Based on the notions of apparent and genuine scatter, the present review draws from earlier work of the authors; see Wold-Juréen [1], and Wold [22]–[23]. While the terms apparent and genuine scatter are rather new, the underlying notions are of old standing; see Eisenhart [1]. The distinction between "errors" and "shocks" belongs to the same order of ideas; see Frisch [2] and Ladd [1].

For the theorems on predictors used in the exposition, see Wold [7]–[10],[12],[14]. A key feature is that the predictor specification covers both experimental data (nonstochastic explanatory variables) and nonexperimental data (stochastic explanatory variables). For the customary treatment of this last dualism, see the exposition given by Cramér (1945/46), Chapters 21, 23 and 37, based on the works of R.A. Fisher and M.S. Bartlett.

² The early references in Note 1 are repeated as background for this introductory passage.

³ For a recent review see Wold [24].

⁴ Tinbergen (1940).

Chapter 1.4

[1] For general background references, see Note 1 in Chapter 1.2. Regarding the use of VR systems as a basis for comparisons between CC and ID systems, see Wold-Juréen (1952/53), and Wold [12],[14],[19]. For further treatment of the aspects discussed, see Mosbaek-Wold [1] and subsequent references.

[2] Reference is made to the pioneering works on forecasting according to the chain principle; see Yule (1927); Frisch (1933); Tinbergen (1937, 1940). For a review of forecasting techniques from the present points of view, see Wold [2],[6],[12],[19]−[20].

[3] See Wold [9].

[4] The approach was introduced by Tinbergen [1]−[2], and is also known as "recursive systems"; see Wold-Juréen [1] and Wold [3]−[4]. The terms "causal chains" and "interdependent systems" were coined later; an early reference is Bentzel-Hansen (1954). Schoenman (1966) presents a conceptual causal chain model and tests it by application to Swedish data.

Causal flows is a general term for multirelational models such that some or all of the relations are specified in terms of cause and effect. Causal chains and interdependent systems are special cases of causal flows. Another broad class of causal flows are S.Wright's models (1934) designed in terms of "path coefficients"; see Wold [9].

[5] See Note 5 in Chapter 1.2. Also see Chapter 3.3.

[6] For a more complete argument and for further references, see Wold-Juréen (1952/1953), Chapter 12.7, Theorems 1 and 2. The argument carries over to models specified in terms of predictors; see Wold [12].

[7] The approach was introduced by Haavelmo (1943), but the distinction between ID and CC systems was not emphasized at once; see Bentzel-Wold (1946).

[8] For the proof of this statement and a partial discussion of its implications, see Wold [7]−[9].

[9] This is a key topic in the Symposium debate "Any verdict yet?" in Econometrica, 28; see Christ *et al.* (1960). The debate reflects an array of different attitudes toward the relevance of the structural form. An extreme position is taken by T.-Ch.Liu who maintains that the structural form has no other purpose than to serve as an auxiliary device for constructing the reduced form.

[10] See Wold [12],[14] −[15]. Also cf. the references in Note 8 of Chapter 1.4.

[11] The designing of REID systems and the generalisation from REID to GEID systems was a logical progress but did involve several steps; see Wold [9],[15],[18].

[12] For a prepublication of this section, see Ågren-Wold (1969), Section 1.

[13] See Mosbaek-Wold [1] and Wold [3], [5], [6], [17], [22], [25], [27]. These papers include extensive bibliographies and focus on causal concepts from the general point of view of scientific method. The list of References in the present volume includes the noted works by Marschak-Andrews (1944) and Blalock (1964).

[14] See Note 9 in Chapter 1.4. For a recent reference, see Brown *et al.*, (1967).

[15] This fundamental point has been strongly emphasized by E.A. Robinson [1] −[2].

[16] For reviews from the present points of view, see Wold [12], [20]. Also see Chapter 2.6.

[17] See Yule (1927). For a recent review see Wold [21]; also cf. Wold [1].

[18] Reference is made to Wold [9], where the situation is considered from the point of view of using purely statistical methods to assess the causal order between a set of interrelated variables.

[19] Reference is made to Kullback (1959), Theil (1968) and Tintner-Rama Sastry (1969).

Chapter 2

[1] Different conclusions on relative performance of alternative methods from Monte Carlo studies can be accounted for by differences in the structure of the specified model. For results on other Monte Carlo studies see Basmann (1958), Brown (1959), Cragg (1967), Foote (1958), Ladd (1956), Nagar (1960), Neiswanger and Yancey (1959), Quandt (1965), Summers (1965), and Wagner (1958). Also cf. Chow (1964).

[2] Cragg (1967) reports results on 26 experiments (models). The 46 models studied in the present report cover a greater range in size of beta

coefficients and size of residuals. Also, the 46 models include GEID systems and include models of different size (number of variables per equation and number of equations); the experimental data for each of the 46 models included a sample period and a prediction period with the latter being used for obtaining a measure of predictive power. For more references on Monte Carlo studies, see preceding note.

Chapter 2.1

[1] For a broad review of model building from the point of view of experimental versus nonexperimental data, see Wold [5], [16], [20],[22], [23], [27].

[2] For a discussion of this point, see Christ (1966).

Chapter 2.2

[1] Johnston (1963, p. 293) among others has pointed out how very little forecasting efficiency has been used as a means of measuring quality of parameter estimates in Monte Carlo studies.

Chapter 2.3

[1] It should be pointed out that the models in most other Monte Carlo studies have been either a two-relation demand-supply model or a four-equation model with three behavioral equations and an identity; see the list of references in Note 1, Chapter 2.

Chapter 2.4

[1] The FP method has not been included in the published results of any other Monte Carlo study, but the other three methods have been included in several studies. Additional methods such as Three-stage Least Squares, Limited Information Maximum Likelihood, Full Information Maximum Likelihood, and various members of the k-class esti-

mators have been included in some experiments; see Note 1 of Chapter 2 for references.

[2] See Wold [15], [18].

[3] This feature of the FP method is brought in further relief in Chapter 3.10.

[4] See the progress report, Wold-Lyttkens, eds. (1969), which includes further references.

Chapter 3.2

[1] This point has been subject to much discussion; for a brief review, see Wold-Juréen [1], Chapter 3.2.

Chapter 3.3

[1] The exposition draws from Bentzel-Wold (1946). Regarding the transition to predictor specification, see Wold [7]−[10].

[2] See Haavelmo (1943).

[3] The proximity theorem states that if the residual of an ordinary regression (1a) is small, say $\sigma(\epsilon) \leqslant \Delta_1$, and has small intercorrelations with the regressors z_k, say $r(\epsilon, z_k) \leqslant \Delta_2$, then the large-sample bias of OLS is small of the second order of magnitude, giving $E(|b_i - \beta_i|) \leqslant c \Delta_1 \Delta_2$; see Wold-Juréen (1952/1953, p. 37) and Wold-Faxér (1957).

Chapter 3.4

[1] Assumption B of the theorem in 1.3.5 and the ensuing proof of consistency is known as the "ergodicity" argument. An early reference, covering autoregressive processes and related stationary models, is Wold (1938).

Chapter 3.5

[1] For most computer programs the specification (3a) will suffice; for programs that work with very high accuracy the matrix inversion involved has to be specified by making $B^{(1)} = 0$.

Chapter 3.6

[1] The exposition is based on Ågren (1967); also see Ågren-Wold (1969). For a brief review of the theory and applications of the FFP method, see Wold-Lyttkens, eds (1969). Further results will be reported in the author's forthcoming doctorial thesis, Ågren [2].
[2] Ågren (1967), essentially an adaptation of general methods by Bellman (1960) and Varga (1962).

Chapter 3.7

[1] The exposition is based on Bodin (1968 a,c). In Wold-Lyttkens, eds. (1969) the author gives a brief review of the theory and application of Recursive FP methods. Further results will be reported in the author's forthcoming doctorial thesis, Bodin [5].

Chapter 3.8

[1] The exposition is mainly based on Lyttkens (1967).

Chapter 3.9

[1] In the case where $Z_1 Z_2' = 0$ holds for the observed values themselves, FP and TSLS estimates of b_{12} and b_{21} are the same; also, FP and URF estimates of w_1 and w_2 coincide. Apart from the GEID-terms the formulas for the standard errors and the leading term in the small sample bias when $E(Z_1 Z_2') = 0$ are most easily obtained by considering the case $Z_1 Z_2' = 0$.

Chapter 4.1

[1] Foote (1958) and Summers (1965) used a form of predictive power in judging alternative estimates, but in most other Monte Carlo studies the judgment of best method was based on bias, variance and mean square error of estimates; see Note 1 of Chapter 2 for list of references.

[2] Quandt (1965, p. 96) used seven different criteria for judging the quality of an estimate. The results, as we would expect, were quite ambiguous with respect to the goal of selecting a best method.

[3] Stekler (1968) and Theil (1958,1966) among others have suggested various alternatives to R^2 as a measure of predictive power. The authors selected R^2 over alternatives because (1) its relation to information content, (2) so-called "turning points" are not of major concern in this study, and (3) a large number of forecasting periods could be generated and used for measuring predictive power.

Chapter 4.2

[1] See, e.g., discussion by the authors in Mosbaek-Wold [1].

Chapter 5.5

[1] A related aspect of the FP method is that it can sometimes work even when applied to underidentified models. For a case in point, see Wold [26].

Chapter 6.2

[1] Note that none of the 46 models was specified to give plural solutions such as described in Chapter 3.8. It was only after the construction of the 46 models that models with plural solutions were discovered; see Lyttkens (1967) and the brief exposition in 3.8.

Chapter 7.1

[1] E.Lyttkens assisted with derivation and checking of the formulas in Chapter 7.1.

Chapter 7.2

[1] Quandt (1965) points out that his Monte Carlo results show that TSLS and OLS estimates improve as the size of off-diagonal beta coefficients decrease in absolute value.

[2] The proximity argument states that OLS is nearly consistent if the residuals ϵ_i are small. The argument leads us to expect that the small-sample bias of TSLS and FP is negligible since these methods are consistent for the models under analysis.

Residual variances of 0.20 (giving residual standard deviations of 0.45) can hardly be said to be "small", so it is a question whether the proximity theorem applies. The results of Table 1 indicate that the biasing influence of the residuals shows off more in the OLS than in the TSLS and FP estimates. Similarly, if the beta coefficients are ± 0.5 there is still a considerable interdependence in the system, and the results in Table 1 indicate that the biasing effect of the interdependence is more marked for OLS than for TSLS and FP.

Chapter 7.6

[1] This could be expected, for the passage from the structural form to the reduced form is a transformation. Transformation of data involves loss of information, and loss of information is associated with larger bias.

[2] Large-sample formulas of this nature have been derived by E.Lyttkens; see Chapter 3.9 and Wold-Lyttkens, eds (1969).

Chapter 7.7

[1] We spell out some observations on results in Table 7.7.1. Correlations among exogenous variables increased multicollinearity more in the reduced form than in structural equations. In the former the smallest eigenvalue in Models 5a and 5b was only one-third as large as in the case of Model 1b. The smaller effect in the case of structural equations is explained by the fact that there are correlations between η_i^* and each x_j appearing in the structural equation, and the introduction of correlations among the x_j variables does not contribute much additional multicollinearity.

Table 1 also shows that the smallest eigenvalue in the reduced form equations is about the same size in Models 5a and 5b, but the size is quite different in the case of the structural equations. This is also explained by the correlation between η_i^* and x_j variables appearing in the same structural relation. The absolute value of the correlation that was introduced was the same in both models; namely, $r(x_1, x_2) = r(x_3, x_4) = +0.7$ in Model 5a and $r(x_1, x_2) = r(x_3, x_4) = -0.7$ in Model 5b. However, since η_2^* is correlated with x_1 and x_2 because of the interdependence in the model, the sign of the correlation that is introduced between x_1 and x_2 does affect the amount of increase in multicollinearity in the set of explanatory variables (η_2^*, x_1, x_2).

The above observations indicate the importance of the "interdependence in a model" in determining the quality of parameter estimates. The reader should carefully note that results in Table 1 and Charts 1–3 provide only rough guides on interpreting the effects from lagged endogenous variables and correlation among exogenous variables in applied work. For example, the presence of lagged variables in models estimated from time-series data usually increases multicollinearity a great deal more than shown in Table 1 simply because of high autocorrelation in most economic series.

[2] We are indebted to Professor E. Lyttkens for a discussion of these implications.

Chapter 7.8

[1] Owing to special features of our GEID models, URF provides consistent estimates for some of their reduced form coefficients; see the last remark in Chapter 7.7 and the comments in connection with formulas (1)–(2) on p. 286.

[2] To a large extent, this can be explained by the fact that most of our models are only slightly overidentified; recent results by E.Lyttkens (see Chapter 3.9 and comments on pages 276–278) show that such models favour the TSLS method.

Chapter 8

[1] Since the Monte Carlo results were computed, E.Lyttkens has found that the large-sample formula used in the program is not correct (see 3.9). However, the error is small in most models and the results shown in the following sections confirm this.

[2] Comparison of estimates in Monte Carlo experiments with finite samples provides useful information even though the moments of one or more estimates might not exist; see Basmann (1963), Johnston (1963).

[3] The authors do not share Christ's view (1966, p. 476) that "outliers" in Monte Carlo results should be discarded and an *a priori* limiting value "M" be used instead of the actual estimate in these cases. We do agree with Christ that the samples should not be discarded as suggested by Summers (1965) and others. Extreme values are one of the characteristics that help in differentiating among alternative methods.

Chapter 9.2

[1] The reader is reminded that predictive power as used here means the prediction of endogeous variables from estimated parameters of the model and known values of exogenous variables. There are, of course, other types of useful and valid predictions using one or more of the estimated parameters of the model.

[2] See Mosbaek-Wold [1] for a discussion from the points of view of the present report.

Chapter 9.3

[1] The exposition is largely based on Lyttkens (1967).

[2] For this remark the author wants to thank Professor F.M. Fisher, who pointed out the similarity to a recursive system during the discussion of his paper at the first Blaricum meeting of the Econometric Society.

[3] The calculations were performed by Mr. H.Michalsen, Computing Centre, Technical University of Norway. The computer programs were a modification of his earlier programs for the FP method.

Chapter 10.2

[1] For the sake of uniformity in the computer output, Part D of Tables 10.2.9–10.2.12 give R^2 for the CC systems when interpreted as ID systems,

$$R^2 = 1 - \frac{\sigma^2(\epsilon_i)}{\sigma^2(y_i)}, \quad \text{whereas } R^2 = 1 - \frac{\sigma^2(\delta_i)}{\sigma^2(y_i)}$$

where R^2 is defined in accordance with the theory of CC systems. The difference shows off for y_2, where the CC specification gives $R^2 = 0.8$, and OLS gives about the same value in large samples.

[2] The correlation between δ_1 and x_4 invalidates the relation (1.4.66) between residuals δ_i and ϵ_i, and thereby the formulas for R^2 as given in Note 1 of this chapter.

[3] See Robinson [1]; for the unirelational case, see Wold [1].

Chapter 11.3

[1] In its dual definition, $\hat{\psi}$ then should be formed by the estimated residual variances of the unrestricted reduced form.

[2] Bentzel-Wold (1946).

Chapter 11.4

[1] The exposition in 11.4–11.5 leans heavily on Lyttkens (1967).
[2] Quoted by Wold [18], Section 5.1.3, in his first presentation of NIPALS procedures.

Chapter 11.6

[1] We drop the star (∗) of the estimate e_t^* in the notation for its proxies, just as for Y_t^* and $Y_t^{(s)}$.

Chapter 12.1

[1] One of the conclusions that Cragg (1967) and Quandt (1965) draw from their results is that the difficulties of estimation decrease as the β matrix becomes more sparce and $I-\beta$ approaches the diagonal matrix of vector regression.

Chapter 12.3

[1] This property of the reduced form relation that corresponds to a just identified structural relation is exploited by Lyttkens in his algebraic solution of Girshick-Haavelmo's model (see Chapter 9.3).

Chapter 12.4

[1] Klein (1968, p. 12) states that estimation of models, theory testing and prediction are all parts of the same problem but also cites prediction *per se* as an important use of estimated models.

Chapter 12.5

[1] See Klein [3] –[4].

[2] Basmann [6] among others has stressed this aspect.

Chapter 12.6

[1] See Summers (1965) for referring to a case in point.

[2] Cf. Wagner (1958) and Cragg (1967).

[3] Wagner (1958), Summers (1965).

Chapter 13

[1] Christ *et al.* (1960).

[2] See Notes 1–2 in Chapter 2 for discussion on range of models in other Monte Carlo studies.

[3] The mixed results from other Monte Carlo studies also support these observations; see the list in Note 1 of Chapter 2. In Monte Carlo studies which covered only a small range in types of models, it has appeared that there are some clear choices among methods; but these results cannot be used for general inferences.

Chapter 13.1

[1] See, for example, the special techniques that had to be employed in the Klein, Ball *et al.* (1961) model of the United Kingdom and the Duesenberry *et al.* (1965) model for the United States.

[2] The following should be remembered in nonconvergent or slowly converging cases: An iteration limit of 2 will give the TSLS estimates. If the limit is increased but kept small the estimates will differ from TSLS, but they will not tend to diverge from the true value as is the case with unlimited iterations. Results indicate that there can be apparent convergence during the first iterations and this can produce estimates with small or no bias.

Chapter 13.2

[1] See Bartlett (1965), de Finetti (1955) and, for a fresh broad exposition, Zellner (1970).

[2] L.R.Klein [1]–[6] is the leading protagonist of full information maximum likelihood estimation of ID systems; also cf. Chow [1]–[2] and Eisenpress [1].

[3] For an elaboration of this point, see Ågren-Wold (1969), p. 548.

[4] Also see Duesenberry *et al.* (1965), Chapter 15.

[5] Although the seven behavioral equation system included in our study cannot be considered a large model, it is much larger than the two- and three-behavioral equation models used in other Monte Carlo studies; see references to other studies in Note 1 in Chapter 2. On the other hand, the models are nowhere near the 1000-equation systems that Klein (1968, p. 79–80) suggests should be constructed for actual forecasting.

Chapter 13.3

[1] Basmann (1957). Also cf. the discussion in Section 3.9.4 of this volume.

Chapter 13.4

[1] For a summary of results from several other Monte Carlo studies and the models used in the same, see Christ (1966) and Johnston (1963).

[2] Mosbaek-Wold (1965); Klein (1968).

References

Andersson, T.W. and H.Rubin: Estimation of the parameters of a single equation in a complete system of stochastic equations. *Annals of Mathematical Statistics, 20,* 46–53 (1949).

Ågren, A. [1]: *The fractional fix-point method.* FL Thesis, University Institute of Statistics, Uppsala, Sweden (1967).

Ågren, A. [2]: *Extensions of the fix-point method. Theory and applications.* Forthcoming FD Thesis, University of Uppsala, Sweden (1970).

Ågren, A. and H.Wold: On the structure and estimation of general interdependent systems. Pages 543–565 in *Krishnaiah* (1969).

Barger, H. and L.R.Klein: A quarterly model of the United States economy. *Journal of the American Statistical Association, 49,* 413–437 (1954).

Bartlett, M.S.: R.A.Fisher and the last fifty years of statistical methodology. *Journal of the American Statistical Association, 60,* 395–409 (1965).

Basmann, R.L. [1]: A generalized classical method of linear estimation of coefficients in a structural equation. *Econometrica, 25,* 77–83 (1957).

Basmann, R.L. [2]: An experimental investigation of some small sample properties of (GCL) estimators of structural equations: Some preliminary results. *Econometric Society, Chicago meeting, Dec. 1958.*

Basmann, R.L. [3] : A note on the exact finite sample frequency functions of generalized classical linear estimators in two leading overidentified cases. *Journal of the American Statistical Association, 56,*
619–636 (1961).

Basmann, R.L. [4] : Letter to the Editor. *Econometrica, 30,* 824–826
(1962).

Basmann, R.L. [5] : A note on the exact finite sampling frequency functions of generalized classical linear estimators in a leading three equation case. *Journal of the American Statistical Association, 58,* 161–
171 (1963).

Basmann, R.L. [6] : On the application of the identifiability test statistic in the predictive testing of explanatory economic models, I–II.
Indian Economic Journal, 13, 387–423 (1965) and *14,* 233–252
(1966).

Bellman, R.: *Introduction to Matrix Analysis.* McGraw-Hill, New York
1960.

Bentzel, R. and B.Hansen: On recursiveness and interdependency in
economic models. *Review of Economic Studies, 22,* 153–168 (1954).

Bentzel, R. and H.Wold: On statistical demand analysis from the view-
point of simultaneous equations. *Skandinavisk Aktuarietidskrift, 29,*
95–114 (1946).

Blalock, H.M. Jr.: *Causal Inferences in Nonexperimental Research.*
Univ. of North Carolina Press, Chapel Hill, N.C. 1964.

Bodin, L. [1] : Studies of explicit and fractional fix-point estimation of
interdependent systems. *FL Thesis, University Institute of Statistics,
Uppsala,* Sweden (1968a).

Bodin, L. [2] : Fix-point estimation of Pavlopoulos' model of the Greek
economy 1949–59. *Seminar Paper, University Institute of Statistics,
Uppsala,* Sweden (1968b).

Bodin, L. [3] : Short notes on fix-point estimation of interdependent
systems. *Seminar paper, University Institute of Statistics, Uppsala,*
Sweden (1968c).

Bodin, L. [4] : One-loop models estimated by recursive fix-point methods and other fix-point techniques. *Seminar paper, University Institute of Statistics, Uppsala,* Sweden (1968d).

Bodin, L. [5] : *Recursive Fix-point Estimation.* Forthcoming FD Thesis,
University of Uppsala, Sweden (1970).

Brown, T.M.: Simplified full maximum likelihood and comparative structural estimates. *Econometrica, 27,* 638–653 (1959).

Brown, T.M., B.Oury and R.Rodrigues, eds.: Summary of the discussions. Pages 393–399 in *Wold, Orcutt et al.* (1967).

Chernoff, H. and N.Divinsky: The computation of maximum-likelihood estimates of linear structural equations. Pages 236–302 in *Hood and Koopmans* (1953).

Chow, G.C. [1]: A comparison of alternative estimators for simultaneous equations. *Econometrica, 32,* 532–553 (1964).

Chow, G.C. [2]: Two methods of computing full-information maximum-likelihood estimates in simultaneous stochastic equations. *International Economic Review, 9,* 100–112 (1968).

Christ, C.F.: *Econometric Models and Methods.* Wiley, New York 1966.

Christ, C.F., C.Hildreth and T.-Ch.Liu: A symposium on simultaneous equation estimation. *Econometrica, 28,* 835–865 (1960).

Cragg, J.G.: On the relative small-sample properties of several structural-equation estimators. *Econometrica, 35,* 89–110 (1967).

Cramér, H.: *Mathematical Methods of Statistics.* Almqvist and Wiksell, Uppsala 1945; Univ. Press, Princeton, N.J. 1946.

de Finetti, B.: La notion de "horizon bayesien". Pages 57–71 in *Colloque sur l'Analyse Statistique, Bruxelles 1954.* Masson, Paris 1955.

Duesenberry, J.S., G.Fromm, L.R.Klein and E.Kuh: *The Brookings Quarterly Econometric Model of the United States.* Rand McNally, Chicago 1965.

Dutta, M. and V.Su: An econometric model of Puerto Rico. *Review of Economic Studies, 36,* 319–333 (1969).

Eisenhart, C.: The interpretation of certain regression methods and their use in biological and industrial research. *Annals of Mathematical Statistics, 10,* 162–186 (1939).

Eisenpress, H.: Note on the computation of full-information maximum-likelihood estimates of coefficients of a simultaneous system. *Econometrica, 30,* 343–347 (1962).

Fisher, F.M.: *The Identification Problem in Econometrics.* McGraw-Hill, New York 1966.

Fisher, R.A.: *The Design of Experiments.* Oliver and Boyd, Edinburgh 1935.

Foote, R.J.: Analytical tools for studying demand and price structures.

Pages 128–142 in *Agriculture Handbook 146*, U.S. Dept. of Agriculture, Washington D.C. 1958.

Frisch, R. [1]: Correlation and scatter in statistical variables. *Nordisk Statistisk Tidskrift, 8*, 36–102 (1928).

Frisch, R. [2]: Propagation problems and impulse problems in dynamic economics. Pages 171–205 in *Economic Essays in Honour of Gustav Cassel*. Allen and Unwin, London 1933.

Frisch, R. [3]: *Statistical Confluence Analysis by Means of Complete Regression Systems*. Publication No. 5, University Institute of Economics, Oslo, 1934.

Gadd, A. and H.Wold: The Janus coefficient: A measure for the accuracy of prediction. Pages 229–235 in *Wold* (1964).

Gel'fand, I.M. and A.M.Yaglom: Calculation of the amount of information about a random function contained in another such function. Pages 199–246 in *American Mathematical Society Translations, Ser. 2, Vol. 12*, translated from *Uspehi Mat. Nauk, 12, No. 1* (1957).

Gini, C.: Sull'interpolazione di una retta quando i valori della variabile indipendente sono affetti da errori accidentali. *Metron, 1, No. 3*, 63–82 (1921).

Girshick, M.A. and T.Haavelmo: Statistical analysis of the demand for food: Examples of simultaneous estimation of structural equations. *Econometrica, 15*, 79–110 (1947).

Goldberger, A.S.: *Econometric Theory*. Wiley, New York 1964.

Haavelmo, T.: The statistical implications of a system of simultaneous equations. *Econometrica, 11*, 1–12 (1943).

Hood, W.C. and T.C.Koopmans, eds.: *Studies in Econometric Method*. Wiley, New York 1953.

Johnston, J.: *Econometric Methods*. McGraw-Hill, New York 1963.

Klein, L.R. [1]: *Economic Fluctuations in the United States, 1921–1941*. Wiley, New York 1950.

Klein, L.R. [2]: *A Textbook of Econometrics*. Row and Peterson, Evanston, Ill. 1953.

Klein, L.R. [3]: The efficiency of estimation in econometric models. Pages 216–232 in *Essays in Economics and Econometrics in Honor of Harold Hotelling*, ed. R.W.Pfouts. Univ. of North Carolina Press, Chapel Hill 1960.

Klein, L.R. [4] : Single equation vs. equation system methods of estimation in econometrics. *Econometrica, 28*, 866–871 (1960).

Klein, L.R. [5] : Problems in the estimation of interdependent systems. Pages 51–87 in *Peltier and Wold* (1966).

Klein, L.R. [6] : *An Essay on the Theory of Economic Prediction.* The Academic Bookstore, Helsinki 1968.

Klein, L.R., R.J.Ball, A.Hazlewood and P.Vandome: *An Econometric Model of the United Kingdom.* Blackwell, Oxford 1961.

Klein, L.R. and A.S.Goldberger: *An Econometric Model of the United States, 1929–52.* North-Holland Publ. Co., Amsterdam 1955.

Kolmogorov, A.: Theorie der Überführung von Information. Pages 91–116 in *Arbeiten zur Informationstheorie I*, VEB Deutscher Verlag der Wissenschaften, Berlin, translated from *Izdat. Akad, Nauk SSSR, Moscow*, 1957.

Koopmans, T.C. [1] : *Linear Regression Analysis of Economic Time Series.* Bohn, Haarlem 1936.

Koopmans, T.C., ed. [2] : *Statistical Inference in Dynamic Economic Models.* Wiley, New York 1950.

Krishnaiah, P.R., ed.: *Multivariate Analysis, II.* Academic Press, New York 1969.

Kullback, S.: *Information Theory and Statistics.* Wiley, New York 1959.

Ladd, G.W.: Effects of shocks and errors in estimation: An empirical comparison. *Journal of Farm Economics, 38*, 485–495 (1956).

Liu, T.-Ch.: See *Christ et al.* (1960).

Lyttkens, E. [1] : On a class of multidimensional conditional characteristic functions and semi-invariants. *Arkiv för Astronomi, 1*, 27–45 (1949).

Lyttkens, E. [2] : Standard errors of regression coefficients by autocorrelated residuals. Pages 169–228 in *Wold* (1964).

Lyttkens, E. [3] : Some notes on econometric models. Pages 322–340 in *Wold* (1964).

Lyttkens, E. [4] : Über die bedingte Verteilung der zufälligen Fehler für gegebene beobachtete Werte mehrerer Veränderlichen. *Tagung über Mathematische Statistik und Wahrscheinlichkeit, Oberwolfach April 1966.*

Lyttkens, E. [5] : On the fix-point method and related problems; including an explicit treatment of the estimation problem of Girshick-Haavelmo's model. *Econometric Society, Blaricum meeting, Jan. 1967.*

Mackeprang, E.P.: *Theories of Price*. (Danish.) Bugge, Copenhagen 1906.

Malinvaud, E.: *Méthodes Statistiques de l'Econométrie*. Dunod, Paris 1964.

Marschak, J. and W.H.Andrews Jr.: Random simultaneous equations and the theory of production. *Econometrica, 12*, 143–205 (1944).

Mosbaek, E.J.: Book review of Duesenberry *et al*. (1965), The Brookings Quarterly Econometric Model. *Econometrica, 36,* 194–196 (1968).

Mosbaek, E.J. and H.Wold: Estimation versuś operative use of parameters in models for non-experimental situations. *First World Congress of Econometrics, Rome, September 1965.* French translation in *Economies et Sociétés, 4,* 531–555 (1970).

Muth, J.F.: Rational expectations and the theory of price movements. *Econometrica, 29*, 315–335 (1961).

Nagar, A.L. [1]: The bias and moment matrix of the general k-class estimators of the parameters in simultaneous equations. *Econometrica, 27,* 575–595 (1959).

Nagar, A.L. [2]: A Monte Carlo study of alternative simultaneous equation estimators. *Econometrica, 28,* 573–590 (1960).

Neiswanger, W.A. and T.A.Yancey: Parameter estimates and autonomous growth. *Journal of the American Statistical Association, 54,* 389–402 (1959).

Pavlopoulos, P.: *A Statistical Model for the Greek Economy 1949–1959.* North-Holland Publ. Co., Amsterdam 1966.

Peltier, R. and H.Wold, eds.: *La Technique des Modèles dans les Sciences Humaines*. Entretiens de Monaco en Sciences Humaines, Session 1964. Union Européenne d'Editions, Monaco (1966).

Quandt, R.E.: On certain small-sample properties of k-class estimators. *International Economic Review, 6,* 92–104 (1965).

Robinson, E.A. [1]: Wavelet composition of time-series. Pages 37–106 in *Wold* (1964).

Robinson, E.A. [2]: Realizability and minimum-delay aspects of multi-channel models. Pages 129–230 in *Wold, Orcutt et al.* (1967).

Robinson, E.A. and H.Wold: Minimum-delay structure of least-squares and eo-ipso predicting systems for stationary stochastic processes. Pages 192–196 in *Rosenblatt* (1963).

Rosenblatt, M., ed.: *Time Series Analysis*. Wiley, New York 1963.

Salviucci, P., ed.: Semaine d'étude sur le rôle de l'analyse économétrique dans la formulation de plans de développement. *Scripta Varia, 28*. Pontifical Academy of Sciences, Vatican City 1965.

Schoenman, J.-C.: *An Analog of Short-Period Economic Change*. Almqvist and Wiksell, Stockholm 1966.

Stekler, H.O.: Forecasting with econometric models: An evaluation. *Econometrica, 36*, 437–463 (1968).

Stone, R.: The analysis of economic systems. Pages 3–113 in *Salviucci* (1965).

Suits, D.B.: Applied econometric forecasting and policy analysis. Pages 231–289 in *Wold, Orcutt et al.* (1967).

Summers, R.: A capital intensive approach to the small sample properties of various simultaneous equation estimators. *Econometrica, 33*, 1–41 (1965).

Theil, H. [1]: Estimation of parameters of econometric models. *Bulletin de l'Institut International de Statistique, 34, No. 2*, 122–129 (1954).

Theil, H. [2]: Economic Forecasts and Policy. North-Holland Publ. Co., Amsterdam 1958.

Theil, H. [3]: *Applied Economic Forecasting*. Rand McNally, Chicago 1966.

Theil, H. [4]: *Economics and Information Theory*. North-Holland Publ. Co., Amsterdam 1968.

Tinbergen, J. [1]: *An Econometric Approach to Business Cycle Problems*. Hermann, Paris 1937.

Tinbergen, J. [2]: Econometric business cycle research. *Review of Economic Studies, 7*, 73–90 (1940).

Tinbergen, J. [3]: *On the Theory of Economic Policy*. North-Holland Publ.Co., Amsterdam 1952.

Tinbergen, J. [4]: *Economic Policy: Principles and Design*. North-Holland Publ. Co., Amsterdam 1956.

Tintner, G.: *Handbuch der Ökonometrie*. Springer, Berlin 1960.

Tintner, G. and V.M.Rama Sastry: Information theory and the statistical estimation of econometric relations. Pages 687–696 in *Krishnaiah* (1969).

van der Waerden, B.L.: *Mathematische Statistik*. Springer, Berlin 1957.

Varga, R.S.: *Matrix Iterative Analysis*. Prentice-Hall, Englewood Cliffs, N.J. 1962.

Wagner, H.M.: A Monte Carlo study of estimates of simultaneous linear structual equations. *Econometrica, 26*, 117−133 (1958).

Wold, H. [1]: *A Study in the Analysis of Stationary Time Series*. Almqvist and Wiksell, Uppsala 1938.

Wold, H. [2]: On prediction in stationary time-series. *Annals of Mathematical Statistics, 19*, 558−567 (1948).

Wold, H. [2a]: On least square regression with autocorrelated variables and residuals. *Bulletin of the International Statistical Institute, 32, Part 2*, 277−289 (1950).

Wold, H. [3]: Causality and econometrics. *Econometrica, 22*, 62−174 (1954).

Wold, H. [4]: Possibilités et limitations des systèmes a chaîne causale. *Cahiers du Séminaire d'Econométrie de R.Roy, 3*, 81−101. Centre National de la Recherche Scientifique, Paris (1955).

Wold, H. [5]: Causal inference from observational data. A review of ends and means. *Journal of the Royal Statistical Society, Ser. A, 119*, 28−60 (1956).

Wold, H. [6]: A case study of interdependent versus causal chain systems. *Review of the International Statistical Institute, 5*, 5−25 (1958).

Wold, H. [7]: Ends and means in econometric model building. Basic considerations reviewed. Pages 355−434 in *Probability and Statistics. The Harald Cramér Volume*. Almqvist and Wiksell, Stockholm (1959); Wiley, New York (1960).

Wold, H. [8]: Construction principles of simultaneous equations models in econometrics. *Bulletin of the International Statistical Institute, 38, No. 4*, 111−138 (1961).

Wold, H. [9]: Unbiased predictors. *Proceedings of the Fourth Berkeley Symposium of Mathematical Statistics and Probability, 1*, 719−761 (1961).

Wold, H. [10]: On the consistency of least squares regression. *Sankyā, A, 25, No. 2*, 211−215 (1963).

Wold, H., ed. [11]: *Econometric Model Building. Essays on the Causal Chain Approach*. North-Holland Publ. Co., Amsterdam 1964.

Wold, H. [12]: Forecasting by the chain principle. Pages 471−497 in *Rosenblatt (1963)*; also pages 5−36 in *Wold (1964)*.

Wold, H., ed. [13]: A graphic introduction to stochastic processes.
    Pages 7–76 in *Bibliography on Time Series and Stochastic Processes*,
    ed. H.Wold. Oliver and Boyd, Edinburgh 1965.

Wold, H. [14]: Toward a verdict on macroeconomic simultaneous
    equations. Pages 115–166 in *Salviucci* (1965).

Wold, H. [15]: A fix-point theorem with econometric background.
    I–II. *Arkiv för Matematik, 6*, 209–240 (1965).

Wold, H. [16]: The approach of model building. Crossroads of proba-
    bility theory, statistics and theory of knowledge. Pages 1–38 in *Pel-
    tier and Wold* (1966).

Wold, H. [17]: On the definition and meaning of causal concepts. Pages
    265–295 in *Peltier and Wold* (1966).

Wold, H. [18]: Nonlinear estimation by iterative least squares proce-
    dures. Pages 411–444 in *Research Papers in Statistics. Festschrift for
    J.Neyman*. Wiley, New York (1966).

Wold, H. [19]: Time as the realm of forecasting. Pages 525–560 in *In-
    terdisciplinary Perspectives of Time*. The New York Academy of
    Sciences, New York 1967.

Wold, H. [20]: Forecasting and scientific method. Pages 1–65 in *Wold,
    Orcutt et al.* (1967).

Wold, H. [21]: Cycles. Pages 70–80 in *International Encyclopedia of
    the Social Sciences*, 16. Macmillan, New York 1968.

Wold, H. [22]: Ends and means of scientific method, with special re-
    gard to the social sciences. *Acta Universitatis Upsaliensis, 17*, 96–140
    (1968).

Wold, H. [23]: Nonexperimental statistical analysis from the general
    point of view of scientific method. *Bulletin of the International Sta-
    tistical Institute, 52, No. 1*, 391–424 (1969).

Wold, H. [24]: E.P.Mackeprang's question concerning the choice of re-
    gression. A key problem in the evolution of econometrics. Pages 325–
    341 in *Economic Models, Estimation and Risk Programming. Essays
    in Honor of Gerhard Tintner*, ed. K.A.Fox, J.K.Sengupta and G.V.L.
    Narasimham. Springer, Berlin 1969.

Wold, H. [25]: Econometrics as pioneering in nonexperimental model
    building. *Econometrica, 37*, 369–381 (1969).

Wold, H. [26]: Review of Franklin M.Fisher: The Identification Prob-
    lem in Econometrics. *Econometrica, 37*, 547–549 (1969).

Wold, H. [27] : Mergers of economics and philosophy of science. A cruise in deep seas and shallow waters. *Synthese, 20*, 427–482 (1969).

Wold, H. and P.Faxér: On the specification error in regression analysis. *Annals of Mathematical Statistics, 28*, 265–267 (1957).

Wold, H. and L.Juréen: *Demand Analysis. A Study in Econometrics.* Geber, Stockholm 1952; Wiley, New York 1953.

Wold, H. and E.Lyttkens, eds.: Nonlinear Iterative Partial Least Squares (NIPALS) Estimation Procedures. Forthcoming in *Bulletin of the International Statistical Institute, 53* (1969).

Wold, H., G.H.Orcutt, E.A.Robinson, D.B.Suits and P.de Wolff: *Forecasting on a Scientific Basis.* Gulbenkian Institute of Science, Centre of Economics and Finance, Lisbon 1967.

Wright, S.: The method of path coefficients. *Annals of Mathematical Statistics, 5*, 161–215 (1934).

Yule, G.U.: On a method of investigating periodicities in disturbed series, with special reference to Wolfer's sunspot numbers. *Philosophical Transactions of the Royal Society, 226*, 267–298 (1927).

Zellner, A.: *Bayesian Inference in Econometrics.* Wiley, New York (In press, 1970).

Zellner, A. and H.Theil: Three-stage least squares: Simultaneous estimation of simultaneous equations. *Econometrica, 30,* 54–78 (1962).

Subject Index

Author Index

541